COGNITIVE-BEHAVIORAL STRATEGIES IN CRISIS INTERVENTION

COGNITIVE-BEHAVIORAL STRATEGIES IN CRISIS INTERVENTION

Second Edition

Edited by
FRANK M. DATTILIO
ARTHUR FREEMAN

Foreword by **AARON T. BECK**

The Guilford Press
New York   London

Library of Congress Cataloging-in-Publication Data

Cognitive-behavioral strategies in crisis intervention / edited by Frank M. Dattilio and Arthur Freeman ; foreword by Aaron T. Beck.–2nd ed.
    p. cm.
Includes bibliographical references and index.
ISBN 1-57230-579-7
    1. Crisis intervention (Mental health services) 2. Cognitive therapy. I. Dattilio, Frank M. II. Freeman, Arthur M.
RC480.6.C63 2000
616.89'142–dc21

00-024985

About the Editors

Frank M. Dattilio, PhD, ABPP, is Clinical Associate in Psychiatry at the Center for Cognitive Therapy, University of Pennsylvania School of Medicine, and Clinical Director of the Center for Integrative Psychotherapy in Allentown, Pennsylvania. A clinical psychologist, he is listed in the National Register of Health Service Providers in Psychology. He is also a diplomate in behavioral and clinical psychology of the American Board of Professional Psychology and is a visiting professor at several major universities throughout the world. He remains a guest lecturer at the Harvard Medical School.

Dr. Dattilio trained in behavior therapy in the Department of Psychiatry at Temple University School of Medicine under the direct supervision of the late Joseph Wolpe, and completed a postdoctoral fellowship at the Center for Cognitive Therapy, University of Pennsylvania School of Medicine, under Aaron T. Beck. He has more than 100 professional publications to his credit in the areas of anxiety disorders, behavioral problems, and marital and family discord, and has also presented extensively on cognitive-behavioral therapy throughout the United States, Canada, Africa, Europe, South America, Australia, Cuba, and Mexico. Dr. Dattilio's works have been translated into more than a dozen languages and are used as required reading worldwide. Among his many publications are *Cognitive Therapy with Couples* (1990), *Comprehensive Casebook of Cognitive Therapy* (1992), *Cognitive Therapy with Children and Adolescents: A Casebook for Clinical Practice* (1995), *Case Studies in Couple and Family Therapy: Systemic and Cognitive Perspectives* (1998), *The Family Psychotherapy Treatment Planner* (2000), *Comparative Treatments of Couples Dysfunction* (2000), and *Panic Disorder: Assessment and Treatment through a Wide-Angle Lens* (2000). He has also filmed several professional videotapes and audiotapes, including the popular series *Five Approaches to Linda* with M. Goldfried, A. A. Lazarus, W. Glasser, and J. F. Masterson (Lehigh University Media, 1996). He is on the board of several professional journals and has received a number of professional awards for outstanding achievement in the field of psychology.

Arthur Freeman, EdD, ABPP, is Professor and Chair of the Department of Psychology and director of the doctoral program in clinical psychology at the Philadelphia College of Osteopathic Medicine. Dr. Freeman completed a postdoctoral fellowship at the Center for Cognitive Therapy at the University of Pennsylvania under Aaron T. Beck, and also studied with Albert Ellis in New York.

In addition to over 40 book chapters, reviews, and journal articles, he has published 20 professional books, including *Cognitive Therapy of Personality Disorders* (with Aaron T. Beck), *Clinical Applications of Cognitive Therapy* (with J. Pretzer, B. Fleming, and K. M. Simon), and *The Comprehensive Casebook of Cognitive Therapy* (with Frank M. Dattilio), and two popular books, *Woulda, Coulda, Shoulda: Overcoming Mistakes and Missed Opportunities* and *The Ten Dumbest Mistakes Smart People Make, and How to Overcome Them* (both with Rose DeWolf). His work has been translated into almost a dozen languages. Dr. Freeman serves on the editorial boards of several U.S. and international journals. He is a diplomate in behavioral and clinical psychology of the American Board of Professional Psychology and a fellow of the American Psychological Association, the American Psychological Society, the Academy of Clinical Psychology, and the Pennsylvania Psychological Association. He is past president of the Association for Advancement of Behavior Therapy. Dr. Freeman has been a visiting professor of Psychiatry and Psychology at the Universities of Umeå and Göteborg (Sweden), the University of Catania (Italy), and the Shanghai Second Medical University (China). He has lectured in more than 22 countries.

Contributors

Francis R. Abueg, PhD, director and founder of Trauma Resource Consulting (TresCon) of Los Altos, California, is a clinical psychologist and researcher who has been active in the study and treatment of trauma survivors for more than 15 years. He formerly held the post of associate director for research at the Menlo Park, California, division of the National Center for Posttraumatic Stress Disorder (PTSD). He is coeditor of a comprehensive treatment volume on trauma for The Guilford Press entitled *Cognitive-Behavioral Therapies for Trauma* (1998). He continues to teach in the Department of Psychiatry at Stanford University School of Medicine.

David Castro-Blanco, PhD, ABPP, received his PhD in clinical psychology from St. John's University in New York in 1990. Following receipt of the degree, he was awarded an NIMH-supported Minority Professional Development Fellowship. His postdoctoral clinical research training, specializing in adolescent suicide prevention, was conducted at Columbia–Presbyterian Medical Center/New York State Psychiatric Institute, where he received a faculty appointment to the Columbia University College of Physicians and Surgeons. Dr. Castro-Blanco served as staff psychologist in the Adolescent Day Hospital of Long Island Jewish Medical Center before joining the faculty of the Department of Psychology at the Philadelphia College of Osteopathic Medicine in 1996, where he directs the training clinic. Dr. Castro-Blanco is board certified in Clinical Psychology by the American Board of Professional Psychology.

Esther Deblinger, PhD, is the clinical director of the Center for Children's Support and an associate professor of psychiatry at the University of Medicine and Dentistry of New Jersey (UMDNJ) School of Osteopathic Medicine. Dr. Deblinger has extensive research, teaching, and clinical experience in the field of child sexual abuse. Her research, examining the impact of child sexual abuse and the treatment of the resulting sequelae, has been supported by the Foundation of UMDNJ, the National Center on Child Abuse and Neglect, and the

National Institute of Mental Health. She coauthored the book *Treating Sexually Abused Children and Their Nonoffending Parents: A Cognitive Behavioral Approach* (1996) and frequently speaks on this topic. Currently, Dr. Deblinger is a section editor for the journal *Child Maltreatment* and serves as a board member for the American Professional Society on the Abuse of Children and the Friends of the Children.

Helen M. DeVries, PhD, is an associate professor of psychology at Wheaton College, Wheaton, Illinois, where she teaches and conducts research in the doctoral program in clinical psychology. She completed postdoctoral training in geropsychology at Stanford University School of Medicine and the Department of Veterans Affairs Medical Center, Palo Alto, California, and in neuropsychology at the Medical College of Virginia.

Raymond DiGiuseppe, PhD, ABPP, is an associate professor of psychology and director of the graduate program in school psychology at St. John's University, New York. He is also director of training and research at the Institute for Rational-Emotive Therapy. He has coauthored *The Practitioner's Guide to Rational-Emotive Therapy, Rational-Emotive Therapy for Alcoholics and Substance Abusers, Rational-Emotive Couples Counseling,* and *Inside RET.*

Robert A. DiTomasso, PhD, ABPP, is professor, vice-chair, and director of clinical research at the Department of Psychology at the Philadelphia College of Osteopathic Medicine. He earned his doctoral degree in professional–scientific psychology at the University of Pennsylvania, where he received the William E. Arnold Award in recognition of outstanding leadership and scholarship. He completed a clinical psychology internship under the direction of the late Joseph Wolpe, MD, at the Behavior Therapy Unit of Eastern Pennsylvania Psychiatric Institute, Temple University School of Medicine, Department of Psychiatry. He has had extensive teaching experience, having served as adjunct associate professor at the West Jersey Health System Family Medicine Residency. His specialty is the cognitive-behavioral treatment of anxiety and anxiety-related medical disorders. He has been an active contributor to the professional literature and has published over 32 chapters, articles, and reviews.

Norman B. Epstein, PhD, is professor in the Department of Family Studies at the University of Maryland, College Park, and maintains a part-time private practice in Rockville, Maryland. He is a fellow of the American Psychological Association and a clinical member and approved supervisor of the American Association for Marriage and Family Therapy. He has published three books, including *Cognitive-Behavioral Marital Therapy,* as well as numerous book chapters and journal articles, with an emphasis on couple and family assessment and treatment.

Craig D. Fisher, MA, is a graduate student in the clinical psychology doctoral program at the American School of Professional Psychology, Virginia Campus.

Gina Fusco, MA, received her master's degree in counseling psychology at Chestnut Hill College and is currently a PsyD candidate in clinical psychology at the Philadelphia College of Osteopathic Medicine. Over the past 7 years, she has been a supervisor of two crisis and emergency services departments for large managed care organizations within the Philadelphia region, and for a short time worked in a crisis setting in Belfast, Northern Ireland. Currently, she is employed at Friends Hospital in Philadelphia, Pennsylvania, as the evaluation, assessment, and intervention coordinator, where her responsibilities entail creating and managing an outpatient program designed to evaluate high-risk patients presenting with crisis and to provide crisis intervention and brief cognitive-behavioral treatment.

Dolores Gallagher-Thompson, PhD, is a clinical psychologist at the Veterans Affairs Palo Alto Health Care System and the Stanford Geriatric Education Center. In these roles, she is responsible for training interns and postdoctoral fellows in clinical geropsychology, with a particular emphasis on depression and family caregiving. Most recently, she has been investigating cultural differences in caregiving distress in Hispanic American and European American caregivers. She is a fellow of the Gerontological Society of America.

Wayne A. Gordon, PhD, ABPP, is a professor of rehabilitation medicine, associate director of the Department of Rehabilitation Medicine at Mount Sinai School of Medicine, New York, and the chief of the rehabilitation psychology and neuropsychology service at that facility. Dr. Gordon holds a diplomate in clinical neuropsychology and is a fellow of the Academy of Behavioral Medicine Research. He has published more than 100 articles and book chapters and was active in clinical research in the fields of stroke and traumatic brain injury (TBI). He is currently the project director of an NIDRR-funded grant focused on issues of community integration of individuals with TBI, the Technical Assistance Program for School Age Children with TBI (TBI-TAP), and a certificate program for training school personnel on educational needs of children with TBI.

Donald K. Granvold, PhD, is professor and director of the master's program, School of Social Work, the University of Texas at Arlington, and maintains a part-time private practice. He is a clinical member and approved supervisor of the American Association for Marriage and Family Therapy. Dr. Granvold is a founding fellow of the Academy of Cognitive Therapy and is a van Amerigen Foundation Fellowship Scholar of the Beck Institute. He has published extensively in the areas of cognitive-behavioral and constructivist treatment in couple and family therapy. Among his publications is the edited volume *Cognitive and Behavioral Treatment: Methods and Applications*.

L. Kevin Hamberger, PhD, is a professor of family and community medicine in the Department of Family and Community Medicine at the Medical College of Wisconsin, Milwaukee. He conducts a program of treatment and research for domestically violent men, and a training program for health care professionals to identify and help partner violence victims. He has published 65 articles and chapters and five books. Dr. Hamberger is a member of the Wisconsin Governor's Council on Domestic Abuse and is on the editorial boards of *Journal of Family Violence, Journal of Interpersonal Violence,* and *Journal of Aggression, Maltreatment, and Trauma.*

Kenneth R. Harbert, PhD, CHES, PA-C, is an associate professor in the Department of Physician Assistant Studies at the Philadelphia College of Osteopathic Medicine and University of the Sciences in Philadelphia. He has 20 years of experience in dealing with traumatic stress as a clinician in psychiatry and occupational medicine and as a clinical educator. He was cofounder and coleader of the "Back in The World" program, a closed-group systematic approach to treatment for posttraumatic stress disorders. He was the codirector and team leader for the Geisinger Medical Center critical incident stress management (CISM) team. He has acted as the clinical director for CISM regional and state EMS teams and is a nationally certified physician assistant and nationally certified health specialist. He has completed a variety of standardized training in CISM and has been trained as a trainer through the International Critical Incident Stress Foundation.

Anne Hope Heflin, PhD, is an associate professor of psychology at the American School of Professional Psychology, Virginia Campus. She was previously on the faculty at the University of Medicine and Dentistry of New Jersey School of Osteopathic Medicine, where her clinical work focused on the evaluation and treatment of children who have been sexually abused. Her primary interests include child sexual abuse and children's responses to harm.

Mary R. Hibbard, PhD, is an associate professor of rehabilitation medicine, Mount Sinai School of Medicine, New York, New York. She holds a diplomate in rehabilitation psychology and is a current member of the board of Rehabilitation Psychology. Dr. Hibbard has been an active researcher in the fields of stroke and traumatic brain injury over the past two decades. She is currently the director of research for an NIDRR-funded grant focused on issues of community integration for individuals with traumatic brain injury. In addition, she is the training director of a Rehabilitation Services Administration-funded training program for the predoctoral interns and postdoctoral fellows in rehabilitation psychology and neuropsychology. She maintains an active private practice focused on clinical neuropsychology and cognitive remediation and is widely published in the field of clinical neuropsychology, rehabilitation psychology, traumatic brain injury, and stroke.

Amy Holtzworth-Munroe, PhD, is a full professor in the Psychology Department at Indiana University. For 15 years, she has conducted research on the problem of violent husbands, including studies comparing the social skills of violent and nonviolent husbands and examining the marital interaction behaviors of violent couples. Her recent research focuses on the identification of subtypes of male batterers. She has led batterer treatment groups and, working with her local domestic violence taskforce, has set up a new batterers' treatment program. Through writings and workshops, she is involved in educating marital/family therapists about violent husbands. She serves on a variety of journal editorial boards, is a past associate editor of *Cognitive Therapy and Research,* and is a member of an NIH grant review panel in the area of family violence.

Philip C. Kendall, PhD, ABPP, is head of the Division of Clinical Psychology and professor of psychology at Temple University, where he directs the Child and Adolescent Anxiety Disorders Clinic. Dr. Kendall is the editor of the *Journal of Consulting and Clinical Psychology,* author of numerous research articles and books, and recipient of several research grant awards from the NIMH. His published works include *Clinical Psychology, Cognitive-Behavioral Therapy for Impulsive Children,* Volumes 8 through 12 of the *Annual Review of Behavior Therapy, Cognitive-Behavioral Interventions, Anxiety and Depression,* and *Anxiety Disorders in Youth.* He is a fellow of the American Psychological Association (APA) and the American Association for the Advancement of Science, a past president of the Association for Advancement of Behavior Therapy and Section III of the Division of Clinical Psychology of the APA, and a diplomate of the American Board of Professional Psychology. Dr. Kendall was recently awarded Temple University's "Great Teacher" award and elected president of APA's Division 52 (Clinical Child Psychology).

Samuel Knapp, EdD, is the professional affairs officer with the Pennsylvania Psychological Association. He is a licensed psychologist in Pennsylvania and has written several books and more than 70 book chapters and articles on ethics and other professional issues in psychology.

Lynne M. Kothera, PhD, is a senior psychologist in the Department of Rehabilitation Medicine, Mount Sinai Medical Center. She is the codirector of a training program for a Rehabilitation Services Administration-funded training program for predoctoral interns and postdoctoral fellows in rehabilitation psychology and clinical neuropsychology. Dr. Kothera completed a 2-year postdoctoral fellowship in clinical neuropsychology at the Institute of Living in Hartford, Connecticut, and is a postdoctoral candidate in psychoanalysis and psychotherapy at New York University.

Karel D. Kovnat, PhD, is a diplomate in counseling psychology of the American Board of Professional Psychology. Dr. Kovnat received her PhD from the University of Pennsylvania. She completed her postdoctoral fellowship in anxiety disorders and phobias at Case Western Reserve University, Cleveland, where she subsequently served as a faculty member for 10 years. Currently, she is an assistant professor in the Division of Neuropsychology at the school of Medicine at Wake Forest University. She works with patients on the inpatient rehabilitation service at Wake Forest University Baptist Medical Center.

Donna M. Martin, MA, has a master's degree in counseling psychology from Kutztown University, in Kutztown, Pennsylvania. She is presently a doctoral candidate in the PsyD program in clinical psychology at the Philadelphia College of Osteopathic Medicine (PCOM). She is the coordinator of distance learning, continuing education, and recruitment for the Department of Psychology at PCOM. In this capacity, Ms. Martin works closely with PCOM PsyD students at distance learning sites, who attend videoconferenced and on-site classes in Harrisburg and East Stroudsburg, Pennsylvania. During the current academic year, she is working on her dissertation and is an intern at the Center for Brief Therapy in Philadelphia.

Laurence Miller, PhD, is a psychologist in private practice, specializing in clinical and forensic neuropsychology, crisis intervention and trauma therapy, psychotherapy and rehabilitation, law enforcement behavioral science, and corporate consulting and management training. Dr. Miller is the police psychologist for the West Palm Beach Police Department and the clinical director of the Palm Beach County Critical Incident Stress Debriefing Team. He is board certified in forensic traumatology by the American Academy of Experts in Traumatic Stress, and is a certified trainer by the International Critical Incident Stress Foundation. Dr. Miller is on the adjunct faculty of Florida Atlantic University, regularly conducts educational workshops and training seminars, and is the author of numerous publications pertaining to the brain, behavior, health, law, and society.

Elizabeth Muran, PhD, completed a postgraduate fellowship at the Institute for Rational-Emotive Therapy. She is a senior partner and independent practitioner of the Cognitive-Interpersonal Therapy Group in New York City and an adjunct assistant professor at Columbia University. She has authored and presented professional papers on posttraumatic stress disorder.

Cory F. Newman, PhD, ABPP, is director of the Center for Cognitive Therapy in the Department of Psychiatry at the University of Pennsylvania School of Medicine. Dr. Newman is a diplomate in behavioral psychology of the American Board of Professional Psychology. He specializes in the treatment of substance abuse, bipolar disorder, couples in distress, and borderline personality disorder. Dr. Newman is an international lecturer on these topics, and is chair of the first APA-approved continuing education course on cognitive-behavioral therapy on the Internet. In addition to publishing dozens of articles and chapters, Dr. Newman is coauthor of three books, *Cognitive Therapy of Substance Abuse, Cognitive Therapy of Borderline Personality Disorder,* and *Choosing to Live: How to Defeat Suicide through Cognitive Therapy.*

J. Russell Ramsay, PhD, completed a 2-year postdoctoral fellowship in cognitive therapy at the Center for Cognitive Therapy. He is currently the clinical director of the Center for Cognitive Therapy's Bucks County Office as well as an instructor of psychology in the Department of Psychiatry at the University of Pennsylvania School of Medicine. In addition, Dr. Ramsay is involved in direct patient care, the supervision of trainees, and research on the treatment of borderline personality disorder. He has lectured and published professional papers on numerous topics related to cognitive therapy.

Mark A. Reinecke, PhD, ABPP, is associate professor of clinical psychiatry and director of the Center for Cognitive Therapy at the University of Chicago School of Medicine. He is also on the faculty of the School of Social Service Administration and directs the Program in Mental Health Research at the University of Chicago. He has lectured internationally on cognitive therapy and has authored a number of articles and chapters on cognitive therapy and clinical child psychology. Among his works are *Cognitive Therapy of Suicidal Behavior* and *Cognitive Therapy with Children and Adolescents*. He is a fellow of the Academy of Cognitive Therapy and a diplomate of the American Board of Professional Psychology.

Stephen E. Schlesinger, PhD, received his degree from the State University of New York at Buffalo. He maintains a private practice in clinical psychology, with offices in Chicago and Oak Park, Illinois. He is cofounder of The Couples' Workshop in Chicago and an assistant professor in the Department of Psychiatry and Behavioral Sciences of Northwestern University Medical School. His research and publications are in the areas of addictions, and marital and family therapy.

Leon VandeCreek, PhD, ABPP, is dean of the School of Professional Psychology at Wright State University. He is a diplomate in clinical psychology of the American Board of Professional Psychology and a fellow of Divisions 12 (clinical), 29 (psychotherapy), and 42 (independent practice) of the American Psychological Association. He is the author or coauthor of more than 60 articles, chapters, and books. His most recent book, coauthored with Dr. Samuel Knapp, is entitled *Treating Patients with Memories of Abuse: Legal Risk Management.* He served for 8 years as a member of the APA Insurance Trust, a corporation that makes available to APA members a broad range of insurance products. Within APA he has served on the Ethics Committee, the Board of Educational Affairs (chair in 1999), and the Council of Representatives.

Dale S. Watson, PhD, is a clinical neuropsychologist who, in addition to maintaining a neuropsychology practice, is an expert witness and court consultant with respect to traumatic brain injury and the brain–behavior link in psychological trauma and disability. He serves on the faculty of the Wright Institute in Berkeley, California.

George W. Woods, MD, is a forensic psychiatrist in private practice in the San Francisco Bay Area. He is highly regarded for his work in both criminal and civil litigation, usually in cases involving psychological trauma. He also serves on the clinical faculty in psychiatry at the University of California at Davis School of Medicine. Since 1998, he has been active in providing direct services to and consultation on behalf of Project Kenya, a nonprofit organization of Kenyan professionals responding to the aftermath of the U.S. Embassy Bombing in Nairobi.

Foreword

Since the first edition of this book appeared in 1994, cognitive therapy has continued to grow exponentially throughout the world. Its broad range of applications has caused it to become one of the fastest growing modalities of psychotherapy in existence.

Crises and natural disasters occur throughout the world on a daily basis. The need for effective strategies in crisis intervention has become more essential than ever, especially in light of the rapid growth of our world's population and the increasing conflicts between nations. It is fitting that the second edition of this book is published on the cusp of the new millennium.

The editors, both former students of mine, have become leaders in the world of cognitive therapy. Frank Dattilio and Art Freeman have once again compiled a powerful text, applied to a comprehensive range of crisis situations and prepared by some of the finest contributors in the field of cognitive therapy.

This second edition is superior to the first in several ways. Although it covers many of the topics presented in the former edition, these chapters have been updated with the most recent research on assessment and treatment interventions on each topic.

The introductory chapter provides a similar overview of crisis intervention and the need for short-term effective treatments. The remaining chapters highlight the clinical syndromes that are commonly encountered in outpatient settings, such as panic disorder, cluster B disorders, suicide/depression, substance abuse, rape trauma, child sexual abuse, divorce, and problems with couples, families, and older adults.

A comprehensive chapter on neurological problems and medical patients as well as one on ethical and legal issues address areas that are of particular concern to today's mental health practitioners. There are also several new additions to the book that cover timely topics. Special chapters on critical incident stress debriefing and youth crisis in the schools have been added along with a revised section on large-scale disasters and an innovative chapter on traumatized psychotherapists.

   The text's quality is the result of an excellent selection of authors with a background rich in clinical experience and empirical research. In addition, each chapter has been strategically organized to provide the reader with a thorough overview of the application of cognitive therapy to a broad variety of settings. Drs. Dattilio and Freeman are highly respected worldwide as authors and educators of cognitive therapy. Combined, their works have been translated into more than 20 languages and are utilized as primary teaching references nationally as well as internationally.

   This second edition of *Cognitive-Behavioral Strategies in Crisis Intervention* provides the most up-to-date information on cutting-edge interventions. These will prove invaluable to clinicians who wish to sharpen their skills in this area. This text is a necessity for the frontline practitioner and will clearly serve as a resource for continued research in the field.

AARON T. BECK, MD
University Professor of Psychiatry
University of Pennsylvania School of Medicine

Preface

During the compilation of the initial edition of this text, we had no idea that its popularity would soar as it did. As a result of its uniqueness and versatility with various populations, *Cognitive-Behavioral Strategies in Crisis Intervention* has become one of the more widely used texts in graduate institutions and training programs in more than 25 countries throughout the world. As a result, we are honored to provide a second edition, which, in our opinion, is superior to the first edition in several ways.

Crisis intervention continues to be an important and crucial area of the mental health delivery system. Despite the increased need for improved strategies with crisis intervention, the literature in cognitive-behavioral therapy remains surprisingly lean. It is our hope that this second edition will help bridge the gap in the professional literature on the application of cognitive-behavioral interventions that have proven effective in short-term situations.

As with the first edition, this edition of the book has been designed for both the active crisis worker, who comes in contact daily with crisis situations in outpatient and outreach programs, as well as the private practitioner, who may confront crisis situations on a more infrequent basis. Regardless of the setting, the techniques and strategies discussed in each chapter are short term and time effective.

The chapters selected for this text were carefully designed to address the spectrum of situations found among crisis settings. Although it is impossible to include every type of crisis imaginable, we have attempted to assemble chapters that provide a representative sampling of the most common themes encountered.

Cognitive-behavioral techniques are becoming increasingly popular among mental health professionals. In fact, there has been a 600% increase in professional interest in cognitive therapy since 1970 (Freeman & Dattilio, 1992). Reports of 113 self-designated eclectic psychotherapists indicate that the three most common theoretical combinations employed in practice all used cognitive-behavioral therapy to some degree (Alford & Norcross, 1991). This is most likely due to a number of factors. For one, cognitive-behavioral techniques as they stand are practical to use with many of the disorders found in crisis settings. In addition, they are well adapted to short-term or brief therapy, and they are compatible with many other modalities of treatment. Cognitive-behavioral therapy articulates well with contemporary developments in cognitive psychology and social psychology as well as other concepts of developmental psychology (Beck, 1976). In addition, cognitive-behavioral therapy combines techniques from a number of schools of thought and is regarded as one of the most versatile modalities of treatment (Dattilio, 1998).

The use of cognitive-behavioral strategies is in its infancy with regard to the field of crisis intervention. It is hoped that the second edition of this book will serve, as the first has, as an impetus for future research to test which techniques are most effective in a crisis environment.

REFERENCES

Alford, B., & Norcross, J. C. (1991). Cognitive therapy as integrative therapy. *Journal of Psychotherapy Integration, 1*(1), 175–190.

Beck, A. T. (1976). *Cognitive therapy and the emotional disorders.* New York: International Universities Press.

Dattilio, F. M. (1998). Preface. In F. M. Dattilio (Ed.), *Case studies in couple and family therapy: Systemic and cognitive perspectives* (pp. xix–xxiii). New York: Guilford Press.

Freeman, A., & Dattilio, F. M. (1992). Cognitive therapy in the year 2000. In A. Freeman & F. M. Dattilio (Eds.), *Comprehensive casebook of cognitive therapy* (pp. 375–379). New York: Plenum.

Acknowledgments

As much as we are reluctant to admit it, the assembly of the second edition of this text was even more fun the first. This is because of the top-quality contributors with whom we had the pleasure of working. It goes without saying that without them, the text would not exist. Hence, we consider ourselves fortunate to have a group of contributors who are not only seasoned writers but excellent clinicians as well. Many are colleagues with whom we have worked on previous texts or in actual clinical practice. So, to them we extend our hearty thanks.

We also say thank you to Professor Ian Birkey at Lehigh University for his comments on the early draft of the table of contents and suggestions for revisions for this edition.

Our information and our inspiration as editors and writers are also attributed to our teacher and mentor, Aaron T. Beck, to whom we owe much of what we know on the topic of cognitive therapy. His research and literary work sparked our own resolve to put into writing what we know and to gather the expertise of our colleagues/contributors.

Such a work is not produced without an excellent secretarial staff. We thank Ms. Carol Jaskolka for her superb word processing and organizational skills. We are also grateful to the fine editorial and production staff at The Guilford Press, in particular, Seymour Weingarten, editor-in-chief, with whom it is a pleasure to work. He is a compassionate, successful, and well-respected editor and publisher in the field, and it is our honor and privilege to work with him.

Finally, we thank our spouses, significant others, and family members for their patience and forbearance while we were engrossed in this project.

FRANK M. DATTILIO
ARTHUR FREEMAN

Contents

PART II
SPECIAL TOPICS

COGNITIVE–BEHAVIORAL STRATEGIES IN CRISIS INTERVENTION

1

Introduction

Arthur Freeman
Frank M. Dattilio

In the 6 years that have passed since the release of the first edition of this text, the world has continued to endure crises. There have been numerous wars and atrocities across the globe and catastrophes sparked by weather conditions and other natural upheavals. The crime rate has gone up and then come back down.

As previously predicted, the need for crisis intervention has only increased (Dattilio & Freeman, 1994). Because of the high number of crisis situations, our world has been more in need of crisis intervention than ever before.

The term *crisis* generally evokes an image of any one of a number of very negative life events. Floods, fires, earthquakes, tornadoes, and rapes, by their very nature, may involve situations of life-threatening proportions. The pictures and experiences of the victims of these disasters strike a chord within all of us. A crisis may, however, also relate to circumstances or experiences that threaten one's home, family, property, or sense of well-being. A psychological crisis may involve a loss or threat of a loss or a radical change in one's relationship with oneself or with some significant other (Goldenberg, 1983). For an adolescent preparing for a social event, the development of a pimple may be a crisis. The issue of what produces or fuels a crisis is not simply defined by a particular situation or set of circumstances but rather by the individual's perception of the event and his/her ability (or inability) to effectively cope with that circumstance. In the same situation, different individuals deal with the potential crisis with varying degrees of competence or success. Simply stated, crisis results when stress and tension in an individual's life mounts to unusual proportions (Greenstone & Leviton, 1993).

Crisis theory (Burgess & Holstrom, 1974) posits that crisis results when homeostasis is disrupted. That is, when the individual's balance—however precarious or firm it might be—is thrown off and the individual is no longer able to cope with the situation effectively. The result would be that the individual would then manifest a number of symptoms that become the clinical markers for the crisis response, often necessitating some crisis intervention. In general, *crisis intervention* is aimed at a psychological resolution of an immediate crisis in

1

an individual's life and restoring him/her to at least the level of functioning that existed before the crisis period (Aguilera, 1990). Rosenbaum and Calhoun (1977) regard a crisis as involving some precipitating event that is time limited and disrupts the individual's usual coping and problem-solving capabilities. Slaiku (1990) offers a definition that synthesizes the definitions of crisis as "a temporary state of upset and disorganization, characterized chiefly by an individual's inability to cope with a particular situation using customary methods of problem-solving, and by the potential for a radically positive or negative outcome" (p. 15). This definition focuses on several specific areas. The first part of the definition addresses the "temporary" nature of crisis situations. For most individuals, crises are immediate, transient, and temporary. For other individuals, however, the temporary nature of crisis may lead to years of upset. Their life crises may become part of a posttraumatic stress that would be more long term and chronic and, in fact, would become a way of life. Other individuals have a predisposition to view certain stimuli as dangerous and thereby damaging. They may see many circumstances as crisis laden. For these individuals, there is no one crisis but a series of "brushfires" that continue to strain the individual's coping ability throughout life.

The second part of the definition addresses the individual's response of being upset. The term *upset* can be broadened to include the most common responses to crisis, those of anxiety and depression. In more severe reactions, there may also be disorganization. This disorganization may involve confusion and decreased problem-solving ability. In its severest form, it might include brief reactive psychoses. The disorganization may be cognitive (e.g., mental confusion), behavioral (e.g., acting in random or uncharacteristic ways), or emotional (e.g., being emotionally labile). The individual's *inability to cope,* the focus of the next part of the definition, revolves more specifically around the issue of problem-solving ability. If an individual's balance is disrupted and some form of anxiety results, the individual's cognitive flexibility decreases, problem solving will suffer, and avoidance or denial may be used as coping strategies. By using the common or traditional techniques for personal coping, many individuals find themselves overwhelmed. Their customary methods of problem solving are not adequate to the present task requirements.

The final part of the definition involves the potential for rather weighty consequences. Loss of health, property, or loved ones and death are well within the definition of weighty consequences that could lead to a radically positive or negative outcomes. Negative outcomes would include loss of self-esteem, loss of esteem of others, or, in cultural contexts, the loss of "face." Slaiku (1990) presents the possibility that the crisis situation could also lead to powerful positive outcomes, including the opportunity for new experiences, starting over, or gaining new skills, behaviors, and even insights, including the appreciation of our human vulnerability to life's perils. During the interim between the first and second editions of this volume, while I (F. M. D.) was thinking about the personal effects of crisis, I was reminded of how frightening an actual crisis can be. While visiting a University Medical School in Cairo, Egypt, in the mid-1990s, my wife and I were invited by one of the department members to a picnic at their summer home in Fayiûm. This summer home was essentially an oasis in the Sahara desert, which consisted of a plantation-style home surrounded by palm trees and greenery. After a delightful day of fun and 140°F temperatures, we hitched a ride back to our hotel with one of the psychiatrists in the department who was also heading back to Cairo. Even though we were provided with clear directions, the lack of road signs and landmarks caused us some confusion—with the result that we got lost in the desert! It was late in the day and still scorchingly hot. There was no other traffic on the lonely sand-covered roads and, to make matters worse, I also happened to notice that we were frighteningly low on fuel. Now, as much as I hate to admit it, my wife has always been the more emotionally tranquil one in the marriage—so, it was no surprise that she slept through the entire ordeal. I, on the other hand, proceeded to experience all of the diagnostic criteria constituting a panic attack in record-breaking speed until I was able to engage in some cognitive self-talk. These symptoms were accompanied by catastrophic images of being found months later in skeleton form, sitting upright in a sand-covered Mercedes-Benz. The entire crisis lasted about 20 minutes, albeit a hair-raising 20 minutes. We finally located the famous step pyramid in the distance and were able to navigate our way to a long road leading to one of the main entrances of the Sahara. I was never so happy to see a sign in Arabic announcing the exit way from the desert along with the friendly familiar logo at the bottom that read, "Drink Coca Cola!" I'll never forget that brief crisis. Although this event had a happy ending, it is an example of how vulnerable and helpless any of us can become at a moment's notice. This clearly helped me to appreciate the true sense of crisis and our need to respect our human vulnerabilities.

Usually, when individuals are in a crisis situation and their present resources are not adequate to the task, they call on little-used reserves of personal fortitude and spirit to carry them through. They may also call on little-used or infrequently practiced skills to help them prevail. Or, if they have the added advantage of a family or social network on which they might call for assistance, support, or encouragement, they use that network as a further and significant resource.

In addition, they may search for or create temporary systems of support to assist them through the crisis. If one has an extensive repertoire of coping strategies and the techniques to implement the strategies, a supportive family system, good friends, or a therapist on whom to call, potential life crises can be more easily weathered. What becomes a crisis or why a particular situation is a crisis at one time and not another is a central issue underlying the treatment of the patient who ends up in crisis. The strategies and techniques for intervening in crisis situations are the focus of this volume. Our goal in this introductory chapter is to present a theoretical and conceptual basis and rationale for a cognitive-behavioral format for the delivery of crisis intervention services.

DISCUSSION

Erikson's (1951) psychosocial theory of development was formulated as a "crisis theory" based on the idea that crises are not necessarily negative life occurrences that injure or destroy the individual but rather points of growth. This growth can add to individuals' strength, provide them with a coping repertoire and helping them to succeed in every area of life. Or, the lack of resolution of these crises can lead to a poor coping style. Erikson's model states that throughout life, the individual encounters a number of predictable life crises (he identified eight). By the nature and degree of resolution or nonresolution of these crises, the individual grows and develops in a particular direction. This growth and development leads to the development of an idiosyncratic life view and its attendant behaviors, cognitions, and emotions. Individually, and in combination, the eight crises subsume virtually every possible life schema. Overall, the resolution or nonresolution of the life crises determines the development of the individual's personal, family, cultural, gender, and age-related schema (Freeman, 1993). This schema will then be the template for that individual's behavior.

Erikson views the initial resolution of these crises as amenable to change throughout life, inasmuch as all eight crises are concurrent rather than sequential (aging, death, illness, etc.). A particular crisis may be more prevalent at a particular point in life, the crises do not start and end during a particular developmental period. This fact then presents a much more optimistic view for ongoing crisis resolution. If an individual has not managed to successfully cope with a particular crisis or resolve it in a positive direction, there are other opportunities to resolve it throughout life.

By understanding the particular types of behaviors that emerge from the resolution or nonresolution of these life crises, the therapist can understand the individual's coping style and strategies. This understanding of the individual's schema sets the stage for tailoring interventions more effectively to help individuals and families resolve or cope with present life crises. The first major therapeutic task is discerning and manifesting a particular schema that will then allow therapists to work with their patients to examine the schema, the advantages and disadvantages of maintaining it, and ways of disputing and/or altering it. This schematic focus is central to the cognitive-behavioral approach to crisis intervention.

SCHEMATA

Schemata are hypothesized structures that guide and organize the processing of information and the understanding of life experience. Beck (1967, 1976) has suggested that schemata are the cognitive substrate that generate the various cognitive distortions seen in patients. These schemata serve to increase or decrease the individual's vulnerability to various situations. These schemata or basic rules of life begin to be formed as a force in cognition and behavior from the earliest points in life and are well fixed by the middle childhood years. They are the accumulation of the individual's learning and experience within the family group; religious group; ethnic, gender, or regional subgroup; and broader society. The particular extent or effect that a given schema has on an individual's life depends on (1) how strongly that schema is held; (2) how essential the individual sees that schema to his/her safety, well-being, or existence; (3) the individual's previous learning vis-à-vis the importance and essential nature of a particular schema; (4) how early a particular schema was internalized; and (5) how powerfully, and by whom, the schema was reinforced.

Schemata can be active or dormant, with the more active schemata being the rules that govern day-to-day behavior. The dormant schemata are called into play to control behavior in times of stress. The schemata may be either compelling or noncompelling. The more compelling the schemata, the more likely it is that the individual or family will respond to the schemata.

Schemata are in a constant state of change and evolution. Environmental data and experience are only taken in by individuals as they can utilize them in terms of their own subjective experience. The self-schemata then become selective as the individual may ignore environmental stimuli. There is an active and evolutionary process by which all perceptions and cognitive structures are applied to new functions (*assimilation*) while new cognitive structures are developed to serve old functions in new situations (*accommodation*). Some individuals persist in utilizing old structures without fitting them to the new circumstances in which they are involved—they use them in toto without measuring fit or appropriateness. They may further fail to accommodate or build new structures.

Schemata are cognitive structures that can be described in great detail. We can also deduce them from behavior or automatic thoughts. The behavioral component involves the manner in which the belief system governs the individual's responses to a particular stimulus or set of stimuli. In seeking to alter a particular schema that has endured for a long time, the professional must help the individual deal with the belief from as many different perspectives as possible. A pure cognitive strategy would leave the behavioral and affective untouched. The pure affective strategy is similarly limited, and, of course, the strict behavioral approach is limited by its disregard for cognitive-affective elements. In many cases we find that an individual's particular schemata are consensually validated.

The cognitive-behavioral approach first involves an intrapsychic focus on the individual's automatic thoughts and schemata. This part of the therapeutic work deals with the individual's belief systems, assumptions about self, world, experience, and the future, and general perceptions. A second focus of the therapy is interpersonal and deals with the individual's style of relating to others. The third focus of the therapy is external, on changing behaviors to effect better coping. This external focus involves learning new behaviors/responses, trying the new behaviors, evaluating the result of the new behaviors, and developing and using available resources.

The particular attributes of cognitive therapy make it ideal for crisis intervention work. The specific attributes involve the *activity* of the model. This part of the model invites the patient to be an active part of the therapy, helping to restore a sense of control over his/her life.

Second, the *directiveness* of the model is important because it encourages the therapist to be active and direct in guiding the therapy. The therapist's job is more than restatement and reformulation. The therapist will share hypotheses; utilize guided discovery; encourage the patient; serve as a resource person; and be a case manager and, in certain cases, an advocate for the patient.

Third, the *structure of the therapy* calls for the establishment of a discrete problem list that helps both patient and therapist clarify where the therapy is going and evaluate how the therapy is progressing. This structure is essential for the patient in crisis and commensurate with most models of crisis intervention (Greenstone & Leviton, 1993).

The content and the direction of the therapy are established early in the collaboration. Having established and agreed on a problem list and focus for therapy, the therapist and patient structure the individual sessions through agenda setting and homework.

Agenda setting is used to provide for maximum success in the minimal time often available to the therapy. Rather than having the therapy session wander and meander, the therapist can work with the patient to set an agenda for the session, help to focus the therapy work, and make better use of time, energy, and available skills. Agenda setting at the beginning of the session allows both patient and therapist to put issues of concern on the agenda for the day. By setting an agenda, the therapist models a problem-solving focus. Accomplishing the items on the agenda requires that the therapist be skilled at setting priorities and pacing the session, taking into account the needs of the patient. This is a skill that is refined through practice and experience. However, even seasoned therapists may feel tense and anxious and exhibit a loss of effectiveness when they are first learning how to pace a session that is built around a collaborative agenda.

The *short-term nature of the therapy* is a fourth requirement for crisis intervention. Research protocols for testing the efficacy of cognitive therapy generally involve 12 to 20 sessions over a period of no more than 20 weeks, whereas the treatment of a crisis situation may need to be more rapid, but not necessarily limited to 20 weeks. For certain patients the length of therapy may be 6 sessions; for other patients, 50 sessions. The length of the therapy and the frequency and length of the sessions are all negotiable. The problems being worked on, the skills of the patient and the therapist, the time available for therapy, and financial resources all have the potential to dictate the parameters of treatment. As noted earlier, adherence to a treatment protocol has a positive effect for both patient and therapist in that it helps to maintain a focus in the therapy.

A fifth issue is the development of *collaboration*. The therapist and patient must work together as a team. The collaboration is not always 50:50 but may, with the crisis patient be 70:30 or 90:10, with the therapist providing most of the energy or work within the session or in the therapy more generally. The more dysfunctional the patient, the less energy the patient may have available to use in the therapy. The therapeutic focus would be to help such patients make maximum use of their energy and build greater energy.

A sixth issue is that the cognitive therapy model is a *dynamic* model of therapy. The dynamic cognitive approach to therapy promotes rapid self-disclosure of individual cognitions in order to increase understanding through enhanced knowledge and an understanding of thoughts, beliefs, and attitudes. Early schemata develop and are modified within the family group. Cognitive therapy with families can provide a context for observing these schemata in operation (see Dattilio, 1993, 1998, and Chapter 13, this volume; Teichman, 1992).

Seventh, cognitive therapy is a *psychoeducational* model of therapy. It is a skill building or coping model of therapy as opposed to a cure model. Patients in cognitive therapy ideally gain skills to cope more effectively with their own thoughts and behaviors that may be dysfunctional. Rather than cure, the cognitive therapist helps the patient to acquire a range of coping strategies for present and future exigencies of life.

Finally, the cognitive therapy model is a *social/interpersonal* model. We do not exist in social vacuums. The relationships of the individual to his/her significant others, friends, and work colleagues are all schematically based and are essential foci for the therapy. If the individual is isolated, there may be great gaps in his/her resource network.

Obviously, if one does not have external resources and few internal resources on which to call, a crisis will result. In some cases individuals have what objectively appears to be a wealth of support, but the support is not accepted by the individual or is perceived by the hopeless individual as not sufficient or available. In Edward Arlington Robinson's poem *Richard Cory*, Cory was seen to have everything. He was wealthy, handsome, well dressed, and sophisticated. Despite all these apparent resources however, "one calm summer night, [Richard Cory] went home and put a bullet through his head."

Highlighting the importance of understanding the individual's schemata, available resources, and belief in those resources, we can look at the Social Readjustment Scale (Holmes & Rahe, 1967). In this scale, the death of a spouse is rated number one. It is seen as the most powerful stressor and the standard against which all other life stressors are measured. The death of a close family member is rated as 5 on the scale, and the death of a friend as 7. If the spouse was much loved, it is easily understandable as to why it is perceived as a situation of the highest stress. In the case of an embittered and estranged couple, the death of a spouse may be a solution to long-term stress, bringing with it relief and even financial security. Or, in the case of a loved spouse with a terminal illness and intractable pain, the eventual death of that spouse, family member, or friend may be prayed for out of love and caring. The eventual death may be a great relief because of the peace and surcease the death will bring to the terminally ill individual. In such cases, then, the rating level on the Social Readjustment Scale would be lower.

Slaiku (1990) states, "Short-term, time-limited therapy is the treatment of choice in crisis situations" (p. 98). In this respect, the active, directive, goal-oriented, structured, collaborative, and problem-solving nature of cognitive therapy make it the ideal crisis intervention treatment model. The immediate goals of cognitive-behavioral strategies in crisis intervention are threefold: (1) The evaluation and assessment of the immediacy of the crisis situation, (2) an assessment of the individual's coping repertoire to deal with the crisis, and (3) the generation of options of thought, perception, and behavior. Some individuals have a skill deficit in problem solving. This requires the direct teaching of better problem-solving skills. Other individuals have the problem-solving strategies and techniques available but see their ability as far less than it is. A more behavioral approach is necessary in the former situation, whereas a more cognitive approach is called for in the latter situation.

Using Slaiku's (1990) definition described earlier, there are several possible points of intervention. The initial point of intervention is the recognition that the situation that brings on the upset and disorganization is *temporary*. This implies that by seeing the situation with a long-term focus it may be possible to "wait it out." For example, the panic patient has difficulty seeing the long view. The idea of waiting out the bodily response and not responding by running is somehow seen by the panic patient as impossible. Working with the patient to develop the long-term view may help to decrease the crisis perception. The perception of immediate danger and the need to avoid it cause panic patients to act in self-defeating ways in the ideal interest of saving their life.

A second point of intervention involves *upset*. Clearly, if the situation were not as upsetting, there would be no crisis. The upset is caused by a perception that can be questioned or challenged. For example, a businessman reported being in crisis over the economic downturn and the possible loss of his business. He reported that every time he thought of losing his business he would then extend the thought to losing everything. He would picture losing his home, his car, his wife, his children, his self-respect, and the respect of others. He would, in his view, be living on a hot-air vent in the street, housed in a large cardboard carton. His upset came not simply from the reality of his business difficulties but rather from his catastrophic style of thinking.

The third point of intervention relates to *disorganization*. If the individual's thoughts, actions, and emotions are confused and disorganized, the clear therapeutic strategy is to offer some structure and a format for problem solving. The therapist must recognize that confusion and disorganization are common themes for virtually all psychological problems. Patients' complaints that they "need to get their life/head/marriage together" are quite common. For patients seeing themselves in crisis, this collection of parts or pieces may be more emergent.

The cognitive therapy model is especially helpful with the disorganized patient. For example, a woman who was date-raped saw her only avenue of action being to flee her job and school program. She was overwhelmed by the thoughts, images, and feelings related to the rape. She was further confused by the contradictory advice and information offered by others, which was compounded by legal issues and threats. She described her reaction as running off in 10 directions simultaneously. No direction gave her answers or peace.

Each of us uses a fairly limited repertoire of techniques for coping with life. Our day-to-day life is rather familiar and comfortable. We can expect certain consequences when we act in particular ways. If, for example, an individual begins her morning commute at 6:30 A.M., she will likely experience little traffic. If, however, she leaves at 8:00 A.M., she may be in the middle of the heaviest commuter traffic. She then knows that she has to leave earlier to avoid the "crisis" of the morning rush. If she lives in an area that experiences heavy winter snow, she considers driving in snow to be part of the risk or price to pay for living in that area. Ideally, she has coped by having snow tires, sand in the trunk, a shovel, cold-weather gear, a blanket, and flares. If there is snow in an area that is not prepared for it, even a coating of snow becomes a crisis of major proportions.

A final point of intervention is to help the individual *reduce the potential for a radical outcome*. If the outcome were uncomfortable rather than catastrophic, the crisis potential would be significantly reduced.

Historically, the concept of crisis intervention dates back to the Lemberger Freiwilligern Rettungsgesellschaft (Lemberg Rescue Society) organized in Vienna in the latter part of the 19th century (1883–1906). In 1906, the Anti-Suicide Department of the Salvation Army was organized in London, and the National Save-a-Life League was set up in New York City (Farberow & Schneidman, 1961). Crisis counseling was developed during World War II, when psychologists and psychiatrists who were working near the battlefield saw cases of extreme "battle fatigue" ("shell shock" in World War I; posttraumatic stress disorder in Vietnam). They found that dealing with the crisis close to the front line rather than being sent back to a rear area hospital was very helpful for the patient. The counseling took a focused approach. The goal was to return the soldier to active duty as quickly as possible.

With the opening of the Suicide Prevention Center in Los Angeles in the early 1950s, a basic model for the modern crisis center was established, and soon similar suicide prevention centers and general crisis intervention hotlines began to spring up around the country. In large part, they emerged in answer to the general climate of social concern and awareness of the late 1950s and 1960s. This became particularly pronounced with the enactment of the Community Mental Health Centers Act of 1963, in which crisis units played a major role (Dattilio, 1984). With the innovation of the suicide prevention hotline, crisis intervention hotlines began to diversify and specify their focus. This came about because suicide intervention centers were asked to help people deal with all types of crisis. Out of this developed teen hotlines, drug abuse hotlines, rape hotlines, and hotlines for the elderly. The telephone began to be used as a means of keeping in contact and following up with patients discharged from psychiatric facilities. Poison control hotlines were developed, community rumor control hotlines, homework hotlines, and general community service hotlines appeared to help callers with problems such as garbage removal or pest control, low standard of housing, voter registration, pollution, and many others.

Currently there are more than 1,400 grass roots crisis centers and crisis units affiliated with the American Association of Suicidology or local community mental health centers. There are also more than 900 victim assistance, rape crisis, and child sexual abuse intervention programs as well as 1,250 battered women's shelters and hotlines. This does not include the thousands of crisis services available through community hospital emergency rooms or psychiatric emergency service centers (Roberts, 1990).

ASSESSMENT

As in any other circumstance, assessment is crucial during crisis situations, particularly because the given situation may be critical at the time and require an almost immediate response. What makes assessment difficult is that it must be conducted almost three times as quickly as in the normal course of treatment and, in some cases, under difficult circumstances. When a crisis situation presents itself with little or no opportunity to implement formal assessment inventories or questionnaires, a paradigm is recommended for quick structured interviewing. Greenstone and Leviton (1993) recommend adhering to the following steps:

1. *Immediacy.* Intervention usually begins at the moment that the intervener encounters the individual in crisis. The intervener must immediately attempt to size up the situation, alleviate anxiety, prevent further disorientation, and ensure that sufferers do not harm themselves or cause harm to others.

2. *Taking control.* Here it is important for the intervener to be clear about what and whom they are attempting to control. The purpose of assuming control is not to conquer or overwhelm the victim, but to help reorder the chaos that exists in the sufferer's world at the moment of the crisis. The one conducting the crisis intervention provides the needed structure until the victim(s) is able to regain control. Consequently, it is important to enter the crisis scene cautiously. Approaching the crisis situation slowly and carefully can prevent unnecessary grief and give the professional time to mentally absorb what he/she is encountering.

It is important for the professional intervening to make every attempt to remain stable, supportive and able to establish a structured environment. This may involve using personal presence, including strength control and making every effort to have a calming effect on the crisis situation and exercising some emotional control over the victim. Research usually indicates that victims respond to structure and those who represent it, if they sense genuineness and sincerity by the professional doing the interview.

3. *Assessment.* Intervening usually involves making a quick evaluation on the spot. This means attempting to understand how and why the individual got into a crisis situation at this particular time and which specific problem among the ones that may be present are of immediate concern. Assessment also involves the use of management and identifying any variables that would hinder the problem management process.

The bottom line consists in how the intervener can implement the most effective help in the least amount of time. Consequently, lengthy histories are forfeited in favor of focusing on the assessment of the present crisis and the events that occurred within the immediate hours surrounding the crisis—more specifically, pinpointing the precipitating events.

If time permits, there are a number of inventories that have been designed to utilize in crisis situations. One is the modified version of the Structured Clinical Interview Schedule for DSM-IV, which is known as the Upjohn version (SCID-UP-R). This is an abridged version of the Structured Clinical Interview Schedule that allows the intervener to provide a more expedient method of assessment in crisis situations (Spitzer & Williams, 1986). In addition, there are other scales such as the American Academy of Crisis Interveners Lethality Scale (Greenstone & Leviton, 1993, pp. 19–20). This scale allows an individual to quickly assess criteria in a crisis situation by summing up the scores and matching the total with the criteria.

4. *Decide how to handle the situation after the assessment.* This essentially involves using the material that was gained during the assessment stage and deciding on an avenue for intervention. This may also involve exploring the possible options available to the individual in crisis and either handling the situation at the moment or referring it out as needed.

The reader is referred to the individual chapters of this book for more detail on various assessment tools for the respective crisis situations.

TREATMENT

Obviously, models of brief psychotherapy have been the treatment of choice in crisis settings. There are several models of brief psychotherapy; however, they all maintain the common goal of removing and alleviating specific symptoms in a timely fashion. The intervention may lead to some personality reconstruction, but this is not considered a primary goal (Aguilera, 1990).

The focused cognitive therapy approach to crisis intervention has five stages: The first stage is the development of a relationship with the patient and a building of rapport. If the therapist expects to aid the individual in crisis, he/she must earn some basic trust of this individual. The patient must feel comfortable enough to allow a free flow of information about the crisis in which he/she is currently involved. The therapist's behavior is instrumental in developing this rapport. The therapist has to be able to convey a nonjudgmental attitude to the patient and a feeling of interest and concern in the patient's problem. In a more serious crisis, levels of trust tend to develop more easily, thus the patient may have already assumed a certain level of trust in meeting with the therapist. Therefore, to some degree the rapport will not be as difficult to develop. However, in a less serious crisis, rapport is an especially important aspect of the counseling relationship because it may be more difficult to develop.

The second stage is the initial evaluation of the severity of the crisis situation. Such an evaluation allows the therapist to get some idea of the immediate physical danger to the patient. It might also offer some idea as to the type of schemata held by the person with whom the therapist is dealing. The therapist must determine which course of action to take. Finally, the therapist must assist the patient in identifying the specific problem he/she is experiencing. Oftentimes patients' confusion and disorganization render them unable to define their problem. The therapist must make every effort to help individuals focus on the specific areas creating problems as opposed to attempting to deal with the vagaries of "depression," "anxiety," or "communication problems." It is important, however, not to focus on one specific problem too early in the contact because there is a chance the therapist could be overlooking other significant problems. Developing a problem list ensures a more specific focus within the broader context.

Once the problem is established, the third stage involves helping the patient assess and mobilize his/her strengths and resources. This may be in the form of identifying friends in the immediate vicinity who could help as well as various internal strengths and resources the person in crisis is likely to overlook. It is extremely useful to have the cognitive and behavioral resources menu handy and available.

In the fourth stage the therapist and patient must work jointly to develop a positive plan of action (collaboration and problem solving). An essential aspect of this collaboration includes eliciting the patient's commitment to the plan of action. At this point, the technique of problem solving is especially applicable. If the nature of the crisis is such that problem solving is not an appropriate mechanism, the last stage becomes necessary. A resource that may be called into play at this point is the therapist as advocate for the patient. In such cases, the therapist may need to become more demonstrative in aiding the patient in making a decision. Stage five involves testing ideas and new behaviors. How well the new coping techniques work can be evaluated and the strategies revised accordingly.

CRISIS PATIENTS

The therapist dealing with patients in crisis is under a special pressure. Burnout occurs rather frequently. There is often no place for therapists to vent their own frustrations and upset. This may create a perception of crisis for the therapist. The notion of "therapist heal thyself" is easier said than done. Crisis workers may need peer supervision or some outlet for the pressure of working with patients in crisis. The reader is referred to Chapter 18 of this volume on traumatized psychotherapists for a more elaborate discussion of this topic.

The crisis intervention work often represents the only link that individuals in crisis believe that they have. Even when there is not a life-or-death outcome, the patient's perception is often that in some vague way his/her very existence is being threatened. When the individual is experiencing a peak in his/her emotional distress, the therapeutic environment can be seen as the only tie, however tenuous, to survival. For the patient accustomed to the idea of receiving help, the decision to seek professional help is less frightening. Too often, patients do not seek help until the problems have reached crisis proportions. For more dependent patients, help seeking may in fact be overdeveloped as a coping strategy (Beck, Freeman, & Associates, 1990). Such patients see every problem as a potential crisis; therefore, frequently seek help and need support. Conversely, the more autonomous patient may avoid seeking help, fearing ridicule or criticism on the part of the therapist.

Given the need for rather rapid conceptualization and intervention, we divide crisis patients into the following five general categories.

1. *The adolescent style.* This type of patient may or may not be chronologically adolescent. These patients are generally experiencing some major life changes having to do with self-image. They are extremely reluctant to show any signs that might suggest dependency, vulnerability, weakness, or lack of self-confidence. For this reason, any request for help may be perceived by these patients as very threatening to their self-image. Typical schemata for these individuals revolve around issues of loss, dependence, and fear.

2. *The isolate.* Such individuals are typically distressed to the point of lacking all motivation to make social contact. Their crises revolve around social interactions or the lack of social involvement. The main problems with such patients include their frequent lack of social skills, fear of rejection, passivity, and apathy. Their schemata often dictate that unless they receive absolute guarantees of recognition or support, they will refuse to become socially involved.

3. *The desperate individual.* This type of patient exemplifies for many what crisis intervention is all about. He/she experiences some sudden psychological shock and is in desperate need of some type of immediate help. This shock may come from an environmental disaster or a psychological loss. As a result of this shock, the individual has most likely lost contact with reality or this contact is extremely shaky. The therapist may represent the final link to reality. Of-

tentimes, the mere sound of a caring, concerned voice is enough to begin to bring this patient back from a state of despair. For example, a therapist reported meeting with a woman patient who was in crisis. He extended the session to double its time to help her move away from her determination of suicide. At some point in the session the patient asked for a cigarette. The therapist's office partner smoked and kept a pack of cigarettes in the desk drawer. He offered one to the patient and he smoked one also even though he had not smoked cigarettes in many years. When he believed that the patient was able to weather the crisis, he ended the session and set another appointment time for the following day. When the patient came in the next day, she was calmer and less confused. When the therapist asked her about her reaction to the previous day's session, she replied, "I don't remember anything that we talked about. All I remember is that you gave me a cigarette."

4. *The one-shot crisis contact.* This person is typically a relatively normal, emotionally stable individual. Although the crises experienced by such people vary, there are specific reasons they call for therapy. They will come in to therapy to get help to deal with the specific crisis situation. They perceive themselves as mainly seeking someone to help them through some current situation. For this reason, a brief cognitive approach is especially well suited. This individual is simply looking for some immediate advice or someone to act as a sounding board to advise him/her on alternative plans of action, which the individual may have already developed.

5. *The chronic patient.* Such patients seek therapy for another in the long history of brushfires. Therapy means that they will be able to call at any time and that whenever they call they will be able to find someone to listen to them and help them through the crisis of the day. We are reminded of the Confucian idea that if we give a person a fish he can eat for a day, but if we teach him to fish, he can feed himself. For this type of patient, long histories of therapeutic contact have taught them that they do not need to learn to cope. They can come to therapy and have the therapist do their coping for them. The utilization of cognitive therapy techniques in crisis intervention offers advantages both to patients in their ability to receive help and to therapists in their ability to offer help.

The patient often feels powerless to change his/her circumstances or unmotivated to problem-solve and reason a solution. By working collaboratively and actively to identify cognitive distortions and automatic thoughts and to suggest alternatives, the therapist can provide patients with some hope for resolving their seemingly insoluble difficulties.

Cognitive-behavioral therapy is attractive "because most of the concepts of cognitive and behavior therapy are consistent with commonly shared notions of human nature, the neophyte therapist can readily assimilate them" (Beck, 1976, p. 318). The theories of cognitive-behavioral therapy are easily delineated, and, most important, the link between theory and practice is clear. By virtue of its ease of learning, cognitive and behavior therapy techniques also make crisis intervention work much more satisfying for the therapist.

ISSUES IN CRISIS INTERVENTION

Confidentiality

The issue of confidentiality is a sensitive one; knowing when to maintain confidentiality and when it is essential to break confidentiality is a very important issue (see VandeCreek & Knapp, Chapter 19, this volume, for an expanded discussion). Although confidentiality relies in large part on therapist judgment and accurate assessment of the severity of the situation, there is a general set of ethical standards. A life-threatening situation is one in which the patient is in danger of bodily injury or death. Once the therapist has established that there is a life-threatening situation, the therapist is no longer ethically bound to confidentiality and may have to exercise certain options. For example, if there is a crisis or emergency (e.g., homicide or suicide) the therapist may need to involve the police or insist that the patient offer the name of the spouse, friend, roommate, parent, or significant other who can be an available resource if assistance is necessary. The individual in crisis can enlist the support of these resources throughout the treatment process.

Cognitive Functioning

We use the term *cognitive functioning* to include intelligence, ability to comprehend and process information, and ability to understand both practical and abstract concepts of crisis, illness, injury, and health. The disorganization of the patient at the point of crisis may thus alter the therapeutic approach.

If, for example, patients or family members do not have a sufficient fund of knowledge to understand the nature of the present trauma, care must be taken to ensure that explanations are made in the simplest terms. Jargon, complex medical explanations, shorthand descriptions, or abstract concepts may be acknowledged as understood but really leave the patient and family puzzled by the events, treatment, and sequelae of the trauma (or treatment).

If the family is not English speaking, it is essential that explanations be offered in their primary language and within the context of their cultural values. Trauma service interpreters must be trained in addressing the practical and emotional needs of the patients and families and be able to translate the psychological concepts of the therapist into clear and digestible understanding (Dattilio, 1999).

Case Example

Ramon, age 6, was struck by a car while playing in the street. He was rushed to the hospital and was in treatment in the trauma unit. He was conscious but had several lacerations causing a great deal of bleeding. His mother, who had accompanied him in the ambulance, was distraught. She spoke Spanish and was demanding explanations of what was happening to her son. Would he live? Would he be able to walk again? While her questions were understood, it was difficult to explain the nature of the treatment and the necessary periods of observation and care. In addition to being upset, this woman was uneducated and unsophisticated. A Spanish-speaking nurse was unable to communicate to her the problems and the treatment, but a Spanish-speaking 8-year-old girl in the waiting room offered her services to the interpreter. This option worked well. The girl understood both Spanish and English, and when the treatment was explained to her she could both frame and phrase it in terms that the mother could understand and thus the crisis diminished.

Mourning

Any loss has the effect of reducing one's ability to cope. The sequelae of an emergency may be the permanent loss of a family member through death or the temporary loss of a family member who is hospitalized. In addition, the result of the crisis might be the loss of a cognitive faculty, physical skill or ability, body parts, or intellectual or physical prowess.

The therapist must recognize and deal directly with losses, both real and imagined. In some cases family members may refuse to recognize the loss. The therapist must walk the line between maintaining hope and facing reality, encouraging the search for treatment options while evaluating the potential for success, and preparing for the worst while hoping for the best.

The mourning process must be identified for the patient. Patients must be helped to accept that any loss must be mourned, and that the mourning process is normal, natural, and necessary. Often, follow-up treatment is especially important because the initial loss and mourning will be followed by another mourning process that might begin long after the immediate crisis. There is, in many cases, a "sleeper effect" in which the full effect of the loss does not become clear until the patient or significant other is gone.

Case Example

Alexander, age 62, was brought into the trauma unit by ambulance because he had suffered a stroke at home. Sara, his wife of 41 years, had called 911, and she stayed with him in the trauma unit. At first it was not clear whether Alexander would survive. When he was examined and stabilized, the doctors discovered that he had suffered a massive stroke that had affected both motor and language areas.

Alexander had been physically active since his retirement; he and Sara played golf, weather permitting, throughout the year. Alexander also jogged daily. Sara kept repeating, "He'll be running again soon. You'll see. He's never been sick." When the doctors pointed out that Alexander would need a long recuperative period, physical therapy, and probably speech and language therapy, Sara continued to repeat her mantra about his rapid recovery.

The goal of the crisis intervention was to help Sara to build a positive outlook while taking into account the reality of the damage to her husband. If she were to maintain unrealistic expectations, refuse to mourn the loss of the man she had known for 43 years, or make demands of Alexander that he could not meet, serious interpersonal and intrapsychic conflicts would ensue.

Premorbid Personality, Lifestyle, and Interests

The particular interpersonal style, life choices, or intrapsychic conflicts can often provide a context for understanding the patient's or spouse's reaction to the crisis. In many cases the dependent individual reacts to the trauma by seeking help, reassurance, or comfort. The more autonomous individual may be resistant to help, refuse treatment, and generally avoid therapy with statements such as "I'll be OK," "Just leave me (us) alone," "I (we) can do it myself (ourselves)." In other cases, the premorbid personality style may not be a good predictor of the emotional reaction to the trauma. For example, under stress the "strong, silent type" becomes helpless and dependent whereas the weak and helpless individual shows an internal strength and fortitude that may carry an entire family throughout the crisis. This can be explained by the existence of dormant schemata (Freeman, 1993; Freeman & Leaf, 1989) that become active under the stress of the trauma. When the stress of the trauma is removed, however, the individual may return to his/her previous style of functioning.

Case Example

Sal was a 51-year-old male. He was driving on a rain-slick highway when he was hit by a tractor trailer from behind. He suffered severe head injuries and whether he would survive was questionable. The family was concerned for his wife, Alice; they felt she would be unable to survive his death. "She needs him. She cannot take care of herself. She has serious health problems." Sal did eventually die as a result of the accident, but it was Alice who was clearly the support of the rest of the family. In the wake of Sal's death she seemed to rise to the occasion, supporting the children and other relatives. The weakness and deference that she had displayed throughout her entire life was put aside so that she could care for others. On follow-up she maintained her strength for several weeks. However, she soon suffered a "nervous breakdown" and was seen for inpatient psychiatric treatment. She became depressed, helpless, and dependent, requesting the help of the nursing staff with almost all of her activities of daily living.

Discrepancy between Actual and Perceived Difficulty in Coping

As much as possible, it is important to make clear the discrepancy between actual and predicted problems for effective coping. It is essential for the patient to be realistic in terms of expectations for coping, recovery, and survival.

Case Example

Al, a 39-year-old construction worker, was injured in the collapse of a structure while working on a home construction site. He was rushed to the hospital by a community ambulance team after having his back, neck, and head stabilized and supported. He reported no feeling in the lower extremities on admission. After receiving a phone call with the news, his wife rushed to the trauma unit along with her mother and three children (ages 2, 3, and 5). Despite assurances that tests and radiological studies showed no damage and a good prognosis for complete recovery, Al, his wife, and his mother-in-law were negative and pessimistic about his ever walking again. The family perceived Al as being a quadriplegic—unable to work, confined to a wheelchair, unable to care for or feed himself, and ultimately dying. Even though some sensation returned to Al's legs rather quickly, their view was that the crisis was only beginning.

Reinforce Even Small Therapeutic Gains

A frequent concomitant of crisis is depression. The negative view of self (I am unable to cope), the world, and experience (It's unfair; why has this happened to me?) and the negative view of the future (I will always be this way; I will die) are the progenitors of depressive affect (Beck, Rush, Shaw, & Emery, 1979; Freeman, Pretzer, Fleming, & Simon, 1990). The patient's awareness of depressive symptomatology moderates the therapeutic strategy to identify the areas of greatest difficulty and focus rather quickly on these issues. Any small gain or improvement in dealing with the crisis must be identified and reinforced. Such reinforcement can lift the patient's mood. It is necessary to socialize patients to the cognitive model and help them to begin identifying automatic thoughts and schemata.

Case Example

Marla came for therapy as a result of her loss of a relationship. When Marla's fiancé told her that he no longer wanted to marry her, Marla reacted by trying to kill herself. She was in the hospital for several days as a result of a drug overdose. She had ingested a lethal amount of medication but was found when the police broke into her apartment after receiving a call from Marla's mother. Prior to the overdose, Marla had not been going to work and voiced hopelessness regarding a recovery. She saw only dark, bleak, and empty days ahead of her. The only solution was death.

As Marla became better equipped to view the crisis of the break-up in perspective, she was helped to challenge some of her depressogenic thoughts (e.g., "I will never find anyone who will love me this much," "My love will never be returned," "I will never have children," "I have no worth"). As she challenged these thoughts, Marla's level of depression decreased and she was less suicidal.

The next step was to go beyond the immediate crisis and help "inoculate" Marla from responding in the same way to future losses.

Emphasize the Collaborative Therapeutic Relationship

The therapist must be seen as a warm, supportive, competent, reasonable individual and must work toward building and maintaining the working alliance. Given the nature of crises the relationship must be built immediately. Empathy is the most important element, because, with a patient in crisis, sympathy will likely have a negative effect on the overall therapeutic work. There are likely many other people in the patient's world who offer sympathy. What the patient needs from the therapist is someone who can enter the patient's internal reality and then offer support and strategies for effective coping.

Case Example

Mary had lost her family in a house fire. She felt profound guilt for not having died along with her children and her husband. Neighbors offered their condolences; her minister made several visits to the hospital to express his sorrow and sympathy; and she received sympathy cards from her children's schoolmates. Nothing seemed to help her. After Mary expressed her anger over yet another sympathy card, her sister asked, "What do you want from these people? They are trying their best to let you know how they feel." Mary's response was that everyone was expressing how they felt and no one seemed to try to understand how she felt.

Barriers to Patient Empowerment

Empowerment is an essential in treating patients in crisis. Patients must be helped to recognize their right and ability to be empowered. The goal of empowerment may be limited by the manner in which it is presented, by its implementation, or by misunderstanding the idea or model.

By definition, empowerment implies that one person or agency gives, offers, provides, or allows another person or agency to have or assume power. This definition assumes that the power giver has it within his/her purview to give or allow power. It further implies that the receiver is willing to assume the proffered power. The power may be related to work, taking charge of one's life, or one's surroundings. Given the admirable goal, demonstrated potential, and egalitarian focus, empowerment may be doomed to fail for a variety of reasons. The ability to facilitate change in oneself and/or one's family group is critical to the development of empowerment. Too often self-change is impeded by repetitive, stylistic errors in personal information processing. Simply put, we can make errors in judgment, computation, reasoning, or perception. There are many examples of individuals who are smart, educated, talented, perceptive, and competent but who continue to repeat the same mistakes and find themselves in sequential crises. Their mistake-making style becomes idiosyncratic and may cause them difficulties at work, at home, in relationships, or within themselves.

It is important to help individuals to identify their particular schematic style and then to develop strategies to overcome impediments to change. Impediments to change include lack of practice in new behavior, environmental stressors interfering with change, personal ideas about ability to change oneself or family, personal ideas about consequence of change to self or group, group or family ideas about need to avoid change, secondary gain from maintaining status quo in spite of cost, lack of motivation, rigidity, and vague or unrealistic goals. In therapy, if the goals are not agreed on, patient frustration will result.

Threshold and Vulnerability

The ability to cope with a stressor and whether the same stressors precipitate a crisis depends on the individual's threshold for response. In different situations, the individual's threshold will be very different. A surgeon working in a critical care setting is able to deal with medical emergencies with competence and skill. Once past the doors of the operating room, he/she may be unable to cope with the normal exigencies of life.

If we picture coping ability on a scale of 0 to 100, we can literally map an individual's normal threshold for coping. If, for example, the normal stress of life is 60 and one's threshold is 75, there is a cushion of 15 to accommodate extraordinary stress. If, due to higher than normal stress, the stress of life increases to 80, the individual would be overwhelmed and in difficulty. If, however, the stressors of life remain the same but one's threshold decreases, the individual will likewise be overwhelmed.

The factors that lower threshold are called *vulnerability factors*. These are circumstances, situations, or deficits that have the effect of decreasing the patient's ability to cope effectively with life stressors or to see available options. The following list gives examples of such factors:

1. *Acute illness*. This may span the range from a severe and debilitating illness to more transient illnesses such as headaches, viral infections, and so on.

2. *Chronic illness.* When the health problem is chronic, there can be an acute exacerbation of suicidal thinking.
3. *Deterioration of health.* There may be a loss of activity due to aging.
4. *Hunger.* During times of food deprivation, the individual is often more vulnerable to a variety of stimuli. There have been recent studies linking a depressive diagnosis to those with an eating disorder.
5. *Anger.* When individuals are angry, they can lose appropriate problem-solving ability. They may also lose impulse control or overrespond to stimuli that they are usually able to ignore.
6. *Fatigue.* In a similar fashion, fatigue decreases both problem-solving strategies and impulse control.
7. *Loneliness.* When individuals see themselves as isolated, leaving this unhappy world may seem to be a reasonable option.
8. *Major life loss.* Following the loss of a significant other through death, divorce, or separation, individuals often see themselves as having reduced options. They lose interest in what happens to them.
9. *Poor problem-solving ability.* Certain individuals may have impaired problem-solving ability. This deficit may not be obvious until the individual is placed in situations of great stress. The ability to deal with minor problems is a poor indicator of the individual's ability to deal with a crisis.
10. *Substance abuse.* The abuse of many substances can cause two types of problems: acute, in which the patient's judgment is compromised during periods of intoxication, and more chronic, in which judgment may be impaired more generally. Such problems increase suicidality.
11. *Chronic pain.* Chronic pain may cause the individual to view suicide as a method for ending the pain.
12. *Poor impulse control.* Certain patients have poor impulse control because of organic (hyperactivity) or functional problems. Patients with bipolar illness, borderline, antisocial, or histrionic personality disorders may all have impulse control deficits.
13. *New life circumstances.* Changing jobs, marital status, homes, or family status are all stressors that are vulnerability factors.

These factors can, alone or in combination, increase the patient's suicidal thinking or actions, lower threshold for anxiety stimuli, or increase the patient's vulnerability to depressogenic thoughts and situations (Freeman & Simon, 1989). The vulnerability factors can have a summation effect. That is, when several vulnerability factors operate at the same time, they may continue to lower the threshold. For example, if an individual who has a history of effective coping (threshold = 90; life stress = 60) suddenly loses the ability to cope and ends up in crisis, the family is often surprised. They may disregard the fact that the individual has had a stroke (–10), his wife has a broken leg (–7), his son is getting divorced (–6), his daughter has lost her job (–5), his oldest grandchild is having difficulty in school (–5), and his pet dog has been hit by a car (–4). His threshold is now 54, low enough to have him respond to normal life stress as if it were a crisis. Rather than thinking in terms of the sequence of losses, families may respond by thinking that the patient has dealt with similar problems in the past so it is unclear why at this point he is having such a negative response.

Assessment of vulnerability factors may help to explain the ability to deal with crises and to predict the possibility of withdrawal, suicidal ideation, depression, or anxiety.

REFERENCES

Aguilera, D. C. (1990). *Crisis intervention: Theory and methodology.* St. Louis, MO: Mosby.

Beck, A. T. (1967). *Depression: Causes and treatment.* Philadelphia: University of Pennsylvania Press.

Beck, A. T. (1976). *Cognitive therapy and the emotional disorders.* New York: International Universities Press.

Beck, A. T., Freeman, A., & Associates. (1990). *Cognitive therapy of personality disorders.* New York: Plenum.

Beck, A. T., Rush, A. J., Shaw, B. F., & Emery, G. (1979). *Cognitive therapy of depression.* New York: Guilford Press.

Burgess, A., & Holstrom, L. (1974). *Rape: Victims of crisis.* Bowie, MD: Robert J. Brady.

Dattilio, F. M. (1984). The mental health delivery system. In M. Braswell & T. A. Seay (Eds.), *Approaches to counseling and psychotherapy* (pp. 229–237). Prospect Heights, IL: Waveland Press.

Dattilio, F. M. (1993). Cognitive therapy with couples and families. *The Family Journal, 1*(1), 51–65.

Dattilio, F. M. (Ed.). (1998). *Case studies in couple and family therapy: Systemic and cognitive perspectives.* New York: Guilford Press.

Dattilio, F. M. (1999, January/February). Cultural sensitivities in forensic psychological evaluations. *The Forensic Examiner, 8*(1&2), 26–27.

Erikson, E. (1950). *Childhood and society.* New York: Norton.

Farberow, N. L., & Schneidman, E. S. (Eds.). (1961). *The cry for help.* New York: McGraw-Hill.

Freeman, A. (1993). A psychosocial approach for conceptualizing schematic development for cognitive therapy. In K. T. Kuhlwein & H. Rosen (Eds.), *Cognitive therapies in action: Evolving innovative practices.* San Francisco: Jossey-Bass.

Freeman, A., & Leaf, R. C. (1989). Cognitive therapy applied to personality disorders. In A. Freeman, K. M. Simon, L. E. Beutler, & H. Arkowitz (Eds.), *Comprehensive handbook of cognitive therapy* (pp. 403–433). New York: Plenum.

Freeman, A., Pretzer, J., Fleming, B., & Simon, K. M. (1990). *Clinical applications of cognitive therapy.* New York: Plenum.

Freeman, A., & Reinecke, M. (1993). *Cognitive therapy of suicidal behavior.* New York: Springer.

Freeman, A., & Simon, K. M. (1989). Cognitive therapy of anxiety. In A. Freeman, K. M. Simon, L. E. Beutler, & H. Arkowitz (Eds.), *Comprehensive handbook of cognitive therapy* (pp. 347–365). New York: Plenum.

Goldenberg, H. (1983). *Contemporary clinical psychology* (2nd ed.). Pacific Grove, CA: Brooks/Cole.

Greenstone, J. L., & Leviton, S. C. (1993). *Elements of crisis intervention*. Pacific Grove, CA: Brooks/Cole.

Holmes, T. H., & Rahe, R. H. (1967). The social readjustment rating scale. *Journal of Psychosomatic Research, 11,* 213–218.

Roberts, A. L. (1990). An overview of crisis theory and crisis intervention. In A. L. Roberts (Ed.), *Crisis intervention handbook* (pp. 3–16). Belmont, CA: Wadsworth.

Rosenbaum, A., & Calhoun, J. F. (1977). The use of the telephone hotline in crisis intervention: A review. *Journal of Community Psychology, 5,* 325–330.

Slaiku, K. A. (1990). *Crisis intervention* (2nd ed.). Boston: Allyn & Bacon.

Spitzer, R. L., & Williams, J. B. W. (1986). *Structured clinical interview for DSM-III-R, Upjohn version (SCID-UP-R)*. New York: New York State Psychiatric Institute, Biometrics Research.

Teichman, Y. (1992). Family treatment with an acting out adolescent. In A. Freeman & F. M. Dattilio (Eds.), *Comprehensive casebook of cognitive therapy* (pp. 331–346). New York: Plenum.

I

TREATMENT OF
CLINICAL PROBLEMS

2

Treating High-Arousal Patients: Differentiating between Patients in Crisis and Crisis-Prone Patients

Arthur Freeman
Gina Fusco

Sherri hated the mornings. It seemed to her that everyone in the world was waking to the new day, showering, dressing, and preparing for work. Sherri lay in bed, unsure, frightened, alone, and worst of all, convinced that things were never going to change, certainly not in any positive way. Losing her job 6 months ago seemed to be the last straw, but it wasn't. It was, in fact, one more issue in a long history of life crises. She seemed to bounce from crisis to crisis without any respite. Her coping style consisted of going from day to day. Her mother's comment was that since Sherri was a young child she always had a *crisis du jour.*

Her main goal would be to try to get through each day without too much damage, pain, or difficulty. The only thing that she remembered from her brief time in an Alcoholics Anonymous (AA) group was, "one step at a time."

Her husband, Bob, left her and their beautiful home 2 weeks earlier to live with his brother in a tiny one bedroom apartment and said he would never come back to her. She thought that she must be a really bad person for him to do that. She always "knew" that he would someday leave her and often berated him for not being adequately supportive and attentive. Now she had no one. Sure, her friends *said* they cared, but they didn't really understand.

She felt no hope, and was overwhelmed by her loneliness, her failures, her fears, and her experience of what she labeled as the horrible

27

emptiness. She felt she no longer wanted to feel any of the pain anymore. She wanted to disappear. She went into the bathroom, poured a glass of water, and swallowed an unknown amount of medication that she found in her medicine cabinet.

She was found by her mother who came by each day to see how Sherri was doing. Her mother called 911 and a Fire Department Emergency Squad brought her to the hospital emergency room. After she was medically cleared she was referred to a crisis worker for evaluation and follow-up treatment planning.

Working with patients in crisis is not new to psychotherapists. People come to therapy because of the four D's—discomfort, dysfunction, dyscontrol, and disorganization. Discomfort relates to the patient's subjective experience of uncomfortable feelings, discontent, and general distress. Dysfunction, a more objective measure, indicates how the patient is functioning in all aspects of his/her life. Dyscontrol indicates both the subjective and objective experience of being out of control or being unable to control life events. This includes both the internal and external experience. Finally, disorganization relates to the inability to formulate or activate a given plan to effect a change, or to prioritize problems in such a way that goals are attainable.

Normal and common life stressors can have the effect of becoming life crises for any individual, either as a single episode or a part of a series of episodes. When individuals experience one or more of the D's and cannot resolve the difficulty intrapersonally or with the help and intervention of significant others, they may seek therapy. When there is a premorbid history of high-arousal, emotional or behavioral dyscontrol, or of life being a series of "brushfires" that periodically erupt into major conflagrations, the psychotherapeutic treatment may need to be structured differently than with the individual who has a history of generally coping well and for whom the current difficulty is atypical.

Sherri is typical of high-arousal crisis patients. These individuals are not simply responding to life crises. Their baselines are more generally susceptible to being overwhelmed or unable to cope and experiencing difficulty in problem solving. Their personality style, affective state, and behavior are more typical of individuals who meet criteria for disorders coded by the therapist on Axis II, cluster B (borderline, histrionic, narcissistic, or antisocial personality disorders). For these individuals, the issues of being in crisis are bidirectionally exacerbated by the individual's being excitable, erratic, and agitated. With "neurotic" patients who are reactive to a stressful life context, situational management or change can bring about significant relief. When being in crisis is a way of life, the therapy is far more complicated. The high-arousal individuals are either in crisis, about to go into crisis, or live their lives with crisis always on the horizon. Whether they welcome the crises as way of getting an adrenaline rush or as a result of their tendency to self-victimize, these individuals may be therefore more demanding of the therapist's time, energies, effort, and attention than are other patients. Because of this personality style, high-arousal patients frequently elicit a major negative response from therapists.

The excitability and crisis-prone style of these individuals is emblematic of the cluster B patient (Millon, 1999). The therapist must take care in that the crisis-prone style may be used (incorrectly) as a major diagnostic indicator for assigning a borderline, histrionic, antisocial, or narcissistic diagnosis. Meeting the required number of DSM-IV criteria is still essential for diagnosis.

We want to differentiate between two types of patient. The first is the patient who is in crisis due to some natural disaster or traumatic life circumstance. The other patient type is the crisis-prone patient for whom awakening in the morning and having to cope with life's daily events is fraught with crisis and resulting angst. The focus of this chapter will be the latter type. These patients, in addition, have met the DSM-IV criteria of a personality disorder within the cluster B spectrum. These disorders include the borderline, antisocial, histrionic, and narcissistic disorders.

The format of this chapter is to describe each cluster B disorder, offer a proposed conceptualization of the disorder, and then offer a cognitive-behavioral therapy (CBT) model to assist the clinician in understanding, applying, and preparing for both the crisis work and the ensuing treatment. At times, an individual may not fall cleanly within a single diagnostic category. By recognizing the cluster B spectrum, wherein elements of all of the disorders may be present, one can assign the individual to the cluster. For the purposes of this chapter, however, we deal with each diagnosis separately because individuals will generally respond to the stress of crisis in a typical or predictable manner that is consistent with their disorder. In addition, a series of therapeutic interventions are outlined as examples of how to manage this group of patients.

Personality disorders are defined as "an enduring pattern of inner experience and behavior that deviates markedly from the expectations of the individual's culture, is pervasive and inflexible, has an onset in adolescence or early adulthood, is stable over time, and leads to distress or impairment" (American Psychiatric Association, 1994, p. 629). Patients diagnosed with these disorders have typically experienced difficulties in their relationships, socialization, employment, and overall functioning.

Inasmuch as their style is egosyntonic, they may generally avoid psychotherapy. Their frequent referrals are when they are experiencing a crisis and/or through family or externalized pressure to seek help. While they will verbalize the pain and discomfort of the crisis, they often appear reluctant or unable to change. The nature of their crisis may involve fundamental safety issues related to suicidal and homicidal threats, gestures, or attempts, which clearly complicate and confound the treatment process. They generally see crises that they encounter in life as a product of other people's negative behavior, neglect, or ill will and therefore negate their own ability to influence the given situation. Given the long-term nature of the patients' characterological problems, they are often well experienced in being in crisis.

Typical of the personality disorders in an egosyntonic nature, these individuals often come into therapy puzzled as to how they so often end up in crisis despite their frequent experience of it. Though patients with personality disorders may be aware of the self-defeating nature of their personality problems (e.g., overdependence, lack of empathy, excessive avoidance, and demands for attention), they are at a total loss as to how to change these patterns. They may make statements indicating they have no or little control over their behaviors and reactions. Still other patients may have the motivation to change but do not have the skills to change.

In sum the patient with a cluster B personality disorder who is experiencing crisis will often see the difficulties that they encounter as tasks as outside of them and independent of their behavior. They may have little idea about how they got to be the way they are, how they contribute to their stress, crises, perceived life problems, and how to change.

Individuals vary in their reactions to crisis. Some individuals may not be aware that they are either in crisis or will be so imminently. They are often taken aback when a situation finally explodes. Up to that point they may have had no inkling of what was clear and obvious to others. They may have missed what others might have seen as warning signs or the escalation of the situation. Others are aware of potential difficulty but see the trigger or threshold point as being far more distal than it actually is. Still others are aware of the nature and extent of the crisis but chooses to deal with crises by ignoring the problems hoping that the crises will abate of their own accord. There are also those that see themselves as innocent victims of a malevolent world. They may have forfeited any notion of control to the "horror" of everyday living. Some people seem to take a sadistic delight in pushing life situations to precipitate crises thereby fulfilling their prophesies about the world. Finally, some individuals appear to be in no objective crisis, but nevertheless live the life of Chicken Little, and perceive the world as a source of crises.

SOURCES OF LIFE STRESS

Clearly, stress can come from any source inasmuch as stress is subjectively experienced. Most commonly, however, for the crisis-prone individual life operates by the equation "STRESS = DISTRESS." There appears to be no discrimination of stressful events, therefore, the patient tends to respond with the same reaction to any perceived pressures. The stressor event or circumstances typically include relationship problems or discord, occupational difficulties, and family conflicts. The sequelae of the crisis can include substance abuse, eating disorders, depression, anxiety disorders, suicidal ideation and action, self-injurious behaviors, or behavior injurious to others. In some cases there can be a loss of reality significant enough to be labeled as psychosis.

Part of the difficulty for the crisis-prone individual comes from the normal and reasonable reaction that when under stress individuals perceive they have or will lose control of voluntary behavior. There is an automaticity to their responses that allows them to escape from the stressful and/or crisis situations. This movement toward a more automatic (or autonomous response) will be influenced by the individual's style. This might be one of the "three F's," fight, flight, or freeze. Getting the patient in crisis to take back control of thoughts and actions is essential. This is complicated by the patient's vulnerability.

VULNERABILITY FACTORS

Each individual has a threshold or trigger point above which they can control their responses to external or internal stressors. When the individual's response to internal or external stimuli are out of control, we label that as crisis. The crossover point is the threshold. There are factors that serve to lower the threshold and thereby increase the individual's vulnerability and problem-solving difficulties, thereby maintaining the crisis situation.

These are all circumstances, situations, or deficits that have the effect of decreasing the patient's ability to effectively cope with life stressors. The patient may lose options or fail to see available options and result in crises. Alone or in combination these factors may serve to increase the patient's suicidal thinking or actions, lower threshold for anxiety stimuli, or increase the patient's vulnerability to depressogenic thoughts and situations (Freeman & Simon, 1989) These factors include:

1. *Acute illness.* This may span the range from a severe and debilitating illness to more transient illnesses such as headaches, virus infections, irritable bowel syndrome, and so on.
2. *Chronic illness.* When the health problem is chronic, there can be an acute exacerbation of the suicidal thinking.
3. *Deterioration of health.* There may a loss of activity due to aging.
4. *Hunger.* During times of food deprivation, the individual is often more vulnerable to a variety of stimuli. There has been in recent studies, evidence linking a depressive diagnosis to those with an eating disorder. Studies have indicated that in times of hunger, individuals should not attempt to shop for food because of the probability of over purchasing food.
5. *Anger.* When individuals are angry, they can lose problem-solving ability. They may also lose impulse control or overrespond to stimuli that they are usually able to ignore.
6. *Fatigue.* In a similar fashion, fatigue decreases both problem-solving strategies and impulse control, and can therefore increase feelings of hopelessness.
7. *Loneliness.* When individuals see themselves as isolated, leaving this unhappy world may seem to be a reasonable option. They may have

made the determination that they would not be missed if they were not in this world.

8. *Major life loss.* Following the loss of a significant other through death, divorce, or separation, individuals often see themselves as having reduced options, or they don't care about what happens to them. They may begin to question their purpose and future direction without the other.

9. *Poor problem-solving ability.* Certain individuals may have impaired problem-solving ability. This deficit may not be obvious until the individual is placed in situations of great stress. The ability to deal with minor problems may never test the individual's ability to manage more complicated issues or a crisis.

10. *Substance abuse.* The abuse of many substances can cause two types of problems: acute, in which the patient's judgment is compromised during periods of intoxication, and more chronic, in which judgment may be impaired more generally. Such problems can increase suicidality.

11. *Chronic pain.* Chronic pain may have the effect of causing the individual to see suicide as one method for achieving release from the pain. They may have viewed each treatment failure as cause or additional reason to commit suicide.

12. *Poor impulse control.* Certain patients have poor impulse control because of organic (hyperactivity) or functional problems. Patients with bipolar illness, borderline, antisocial, or histrionic personality disorders may all have impulse control deficits.

13. *New life circumstance.* Changing jobs, marital status, homes, or family status are all stressors that are vulnerability factors. Assessment of the vulnerability factors may help to explain crisis behaviors, intense reactions to crises, suicidal ideation, and actions that predict the possibility of bouts of suicidal ideation or other poor coping strategies.

STAGES OF READINESS FOR CHANGE

The clinician dealing with a patient in crisis may be able to see the crisis situation clearly, conceptualize the crisis objectively, understand the nature of the patient's stressful life circumstances, be aware of how the patient's life experience (summarized by their acquired schemata), and have suggestions for coping. However, the patient's ability to respond to therapeutic interventions developed collaboratively with the therapist depends on the patient's stage of readiness to change. Readiness to change is a combination of motivation to change, schemata related to changing, and the requisite skills to effect change. Early research in this area identified five stages of change (Prochaska & DiClemente, 1982, 1992). This model is as follows:

Precontemplation. Here, there is no intention to change behavior in the foreseeable future. Many individuals in this stage are unaware or underaware of their problems. Families, friends, neighbors, or employees, however, are often well aware that the precontemplators have problems. When precontemplators present for psychotherapy, they do so often because of pressure from others.

Contemplation. People at this stage are aware that a problem exists and are seriously thinking about overcoming it but have not yet made a commitment to take action.

Preparation. This stage combines intention and developing behavioral criteria for what the change would "look like." Individuals in this stage are intending to take action in the next month and have unsuccessfully taken action in the past year. As a group, individuals who are prepared for action report some small behavioral changes (DiClemente et al., 1991).

Action. Individuals now modify their behavior, experiences, or environment in order to overcome their problems. Action involves the most overt behavioral changes and requires a considerable commitment of time and energy.

Maintenance. During maintenance, people work to prevent relapse and to consolidate the gains attained during the action stage. Traditionally, maintenance has been viewed as a static stage. However, maintenance is a continuation, not an absence, of change. For some behaviors, maintenance can last a lifetime. Stabilizing behavior change and avoiding relapse are the hallmarks of maintenance.

Prochaska and DiClemente (1983, 1992) believe that a person's stage of change provides proscriptive as well as prescriptive information on treatments of choice. They see action-oriented therapies as being quite effective with individuals who are in the preparation or action stages. These same programs may be ineffective or detrimental, however, with individuals in precontemplation or contemplation stages. They believe that it is critical to assess the stage of a patient's readiness for change and to tailor the therapeutic interventions accordingly. A more explicit model would enhance efficient, integrative, and prescriptive treatment plans.

REVISED STAGES OF CHANGE

The revised stages of change model (Freeman & Dolan, in press) is built on the same platform as the original model. Change occurs in a series of specified stages. The therapist must assess the patient's stage as part of the initial evaluation. It is from this point that the treatment plan will be initiated. The revised stages are:

Noncontemplation. Individuals in crisis at this stage of change are not considering or even thinking about changing. They often seem oblivious to their need to change what they do, how they process stress, the content of their schemata, or the effect their behavior has on others. Their global level of functioning is considerably less than it might be were they more attentive or cognizant of the need to change.

Anticontemplation. This stage involves the process of becoming reactive and violently opposed to the notion of needing to change. This response is often seen in those individuals who are in the midst of a crisis but see the source of their distress as external to them. The active or inactive schemata often revolve around the need to be self-protective at any cost. These individuals are often mandated for therapy by the courts, or required to come to therapy by family or significant others. Most simply, the attendant frame of mind is stated by the patient as, "Screw you! I don't want to be here, you can't make me change, and I think that I'm fine just the way that I am," "I refuse to change or don't want to change," or, "My crises are the result of what others do to me."

Precontemplation. In this revised model, precontemplation is the stage in which a person begins to consider the consequences, purpose, and the possibility of change. It is a metacognitive state in which the patient is thinking about thinking about his/her crisis state and the need to change something (cognition, affect, or behavior). The typical internal statement is, "I may really need to consider the possibilities of doing something differently than I do now to relieve the crisis."

Contemplation. This is the point in the change process when a person is directly and actively considering change. At the point of contemplation, the patient has reached a point of readiness to engage in the change process.

Action planning. At this stage, the therapist and patient have collaboratively developed a treatment focus and treatment plan. The therapeutic process has begun and the patient is beginning to make plans for how change will occur. The key phrase with this group is, "I plan to change."

Action. Now there is behavioral progress toward change. A patient described the difference as having now shifted himself from "neutral into drive."

Lapse activation. The skills needed to maintain the action stage decrease or are ignored, and the changes developed in therapy begin to decrease. Although there has not been an actual return to pretreatment behavior and affect, the processes are in place for lapse to occur. In cognitive terms, it is a return to the old thinking or perceptions that put the person at risk for difficulty in the first place. The patient ends up questioning if the changes are real or even beneficial to continue.

Relapse. This is a return to the behaviors that were the cause of the original referral and which were, ideally, altered in the action stage. This is a critical stage in the change process because the definition of addiction includes the probability of relapse as one of its components. The relapse stage is usually a crisis stage for most patients. Immediate intervention is crucial in order for the patient to continue to progress in the change process. The patient states, "I'm right back where I started from."

Redirection. Right after the crisis of relapse, redirection is a stage in which new skills and cognitions must be developed and old skills practiced to ensure continued recovery. The question that the patient asks is, "How can I get back on track?"

Maintenance. This is the final stage in the continuous process of maintaining and developing the skills of the previous stages. The goal is to (1) fine tune and adjust changes, (2) support growth, (3) encourage stability, and (4) help the patient be his/her own therapist.

UNDERSTANDING THE ROLE OF SCHEMATA

The personality disorder is probably one of the most striking representations of Beck's concept of schemata (Beck, Rush, Shaw, & Emery, 1979; Beck, Freeman, & Associates, 1990; Freeman, 1993; Freeman, Pretzer, Fleming, & Simon, 1990; Layden, Newman, Freeman, & Byers-Morse, 1993). A therapist might begin to understand the individual in crisis, for example, by focusing on the clinically relevant and schemata. The schemata are the basic rules of life. The specific rules that govern and influence information processing and behavior can be classified into a variety of useful categories, such as personal, familial, cultural, religious, gender, or occupational schemata. Normally, schemata can be inferred from behavior or assessed through a complete and thorough intake, interview, and history-taking process. For the patient in crisis however, the clinician needs to adapt his/her interview style to include an in-depth evaluation eliciting activated schemata related to the current situation and its related and precipitating factors. Through empathic questioning, the clinician can elicit the automatic thoughts or processes engendering the distress felt by the patient. The points on the continuums from active to inactive and unchangable to changable occupied by particular schemata are essential data in conceptualizing the patient's problems. The active schemata govern the usual integration of information and result in everyday behavior. These schemata have to do with how we integrate other people's behavior, and how we generally relate to people and tasks. Inactive schemata become active when the individual experiences subjective distress, often labeled as "crisis." At that threshold point, these dormant schemata become active and govern behavior. When the crisis situation (subjectively or objectively perceived) is no longer present, the inactive schemata will typically recede to their previous state of dormancy.

> For example, Mary, a 32-year-old female, was very well able to deal with the day-to-day performance of her job. Her active schemata included rules such as "I am competent"; "I am good at my job"; and "My coworkers can be called upon to help me." When confronted by significant stress in interpersonal intimate relationships, Mary experienced a crisis situation in her personal life. The previously inactive schemata that she learned as a child—which had been superseded over the years—would become more active. These schemata included ideas such as, "People can't be trusted"; "I

am alone"; and "I'm incompetent." As her behavior was now governed by these newly exposed rules, her work functioning suffered, her ability to relate to others became strained, and she ultimately responded by withdrawing.

Additionally, schemata may be classified as noncompelling or compelling. A noncompelling schema is one that the individual believes in but can relatively easily challenge and/or surrender. Compelling schemata are not easily challenged and are modified only with great difficulty, or not at all. When a cluster B patient presents in crisis, typically the activated schema will be of a compelling nature, therefore more difficult to question or challenge. Historical examples would be the religious or political martyrs who chose to die rather than surrender their compelling views. Table 2.1 shows the typical schemata of various cluster B disorders.

TABLE 2.1. Typical Schemata of the Cluster B Disorders

Antisocial personality disorder

Rules are meant for others.
Only fools follow all of the rules.
Rules are meant to be broken.
Look out for number 1.
My pleasure comes first.
If others are hurt, offended, or inconvenienced by my behavior, that's their problem.
Do it now! I will not allow myself to be frustrated.
I will do whatever I must to get whatever I want.
I'm really smarter than most everybody else.

Borderline personality disorder

I am not sure who I am.
I will eventually be abandoned.
My pain (psychic) is so intense that I cannot bear it.
My anger controls me, I cannot modulate my behavior.
My feelings overwhelm me, I cannot modulate my feelings.
He/she is so very, very good that I am so lucky; or (alternately and quickly) he/she is so very, very awful that I cannot bear them.

When I am overwhelmed I must escape (by flight or suicide).
I am not able to control my life.
No one can help me or understand me.

Histrionic personality disorder

Appearances are important.
People are judged on external appearances.
I must be noticed.
I must never be frustrated in life.
I must get everything I think that I want.
Emotions should be expressed quickly and directly.
Beauty is the most important consideration in judging someone.
If people don't notice me, I am nothing and therefore don't exist.

Narcissistic personality disorder

I must have my way in every interaction.
I must not be, in any way, foiled in seeking pleasure or status.
I am more special than anyone else.
I should only have to relate to special people like me.
I must be admired.
No one should have more of anything than I have.
Few people can really understand me.

CRISIS FOR THE CLUSTER B PATIENT

Crisis for the cluster B patient will most likely have occurred due to the triggering of an inactive or active schematic pattern that causes the patient unbearable distress. Overwhelmed with a flood of emotions and impulsivity characteristic to the cluster, these patients tend to be reactive to the crisis rather than assessing their resources, supports, or strengths. Unarmed with coping skills or strategies, they often resort to dramatic or impulsive gestures to decrease the anxiety brought about by the crisis situation. Highly sensitive, they may perceive events in a manner greatly exaggerated from what is actually occurring. Their assumptions and automatic thoughts may initiate a cascade of events leading to erratic behaviors, often to their own detriment. These behaviors may cause a further break down in relationships, difficulties in their work life, and internal stress culminating in potential self-harm.

SCHEMATIC SHIFT POTENTIAL

For effective crisis intervention, it is imperative to assess the patient's ability to address, challenge, and dispute the schematic material that has initiated the crisis response. This in turn allows the crisis intervention to be targeted toward the appropriate level in which the patient is functioning. The ability to shift or alter schemata can be viewed as a continuum. The points of the continuum are schematic paralysis, schematic rigidity, schematic stability, schematic flexibility, and schematic instability. They can each be defined in the following way:

Schematic paralysis. In this state, the beliefs are ossified. The individual will maintain the beliefs regardless of the situation, context, or requirements of the circumstance.

Schematic rigidity. The rules at this state are dogmatic. The individual will not easily change what they do or how they respond. They can, in crisis situations, alter the beliefs, but when the crisis abates, they return to their dogmatic insistence that things be the way they expect things to be.

Schematic stability. The individual whose rules are stable is far more steady and predictable. Predictability does not necessarily imply that their functioning is improved. The individual with stable schemata will predictably respond to stress over many different times or situations. During a crisis, their schemata may be altered; however, they will largely respond in a predictable fashion.

Schematic flexibility. Flexibility is required for creativity and for problem solving. These individuals may look for new answers to old problems. When confronted by crisis, they look for new ways to cope.

Schematic instability. These individuals are in a state of chronic chaos. They have poor problem-solving strategies. Life is filled with unexpected assaults to which they respond without attempting to develop a coping strategy. They may appear more erratic and unpredictable to others as their schemata continually fluctuate as a response to internal and external influences. These individuals may be thought of as having a more externalized locus of control.

COGNITIVE DISTORTIONS AND THERAPEUTIC INTERVENTIONS

We recognize that an individual can distort in a positive or negative way. The patient in crisis may be there because he/she is an individual who distorts in a positive direction. He/she may be the "fool who rushes in where angels fear to tread" and is now in crisis because he/she is in over the head in business, social, familial, educational, or relationship difficulties. The distortions are just as often negative. Whether positive or negative, the distortions become the initial focus of the therapy. The therapist works to help make the distortions manifest in content, degree of patient belief, style, and the impact on life. The distortions become the thematic directional signs that can then be used to point to the underlying schema. The distortions presented in Table 2.2 are in no way a comprehensive list of all of the possible distortions the therapist might encounter with any patient because the distortions occur in many combinations and permutations. They are presented in isolation for the sake of discussion with

TABLE 2.2. Cognitive Distortions Often Encountered in Therapy

1. *All-or-nothing thinking.* "I'm either a success or a failure." "The world is either black or white." The therapeutic response needs to move the patient from the extremes to a more moderate belief. The modification here is minimal. Accept the patient's position and try to offer the smallest possible modification.

2. *Mind reading.* "They probably think that I'm incompetent." "I just know that he/she disapproves." The therapist needs to offer a challenge by asking the patient to identify the evidence of their mind-reading ability.

3. *Emotional reasoning.* "Because I feel inadequate, I am inadequate." "I believe that I must be funny to be liked, so it is fact." Challenging the patient to produce evidence that supports this distortion can effectively break down this irrational belief style.

4. *Personalization.* "That comment wasn't just random, it must have been directed toward me." "Problems always emerge when I'm in a hurry."

5. *Overgeneralization.* "Everything I do turns out wrong." "It doesn't matter what my choices are, they always fall flat."

6. *Catastrophizing.* "If I go to the party, there will be terrible consequences." "I better not try because I might fail, and that would be awful." The therapist may suggest the patient to produce a "disaster" continuum and realistically identify the exact consequences of each perceived catastrophe.

continued

TABLE 2.2. Continued

7. *Should statements.* "I should visit my family every time they want me to." "They should be nicer to me." Challenging the patient to "leave all shoulds outside" can assist the patient in identifying what their own needs are versus what has been expected or dictated by other's rules.

8. *Control fallacies.* "If I'm not in complete control all the time, I will go out of control." "I must be able to control all of the contingencies in my life." Encouraging the patient to view a less-controlled atmosphere creates additional options and may assist the patient to feel less constricted and hopeless in their situation.

9. *Comparing.* "I am not as competent as my coworkers or supervisors." "Compared to others, there is clearly something flawed about me." The therapist may encourage self-appraisal versus other-appraisal as a mechanism to challenge the patient to progress on an internal rather than external basis.

10. *Heaven's reward fallacy.* "If I do everything perfectly here, I will be rewarded later." "I have to muddle through this life, maybe things will be better later." The patient needs to be redirected to experience life's events in the "here and now" versus putting all his/her eggs in the future basket.

11. *Disqualifying the positive.* "This success experience was only a fluke." "The compliment was unwarranted." "I'm really a fraud and everyone will find out." The therapist can challenge the patient to list the positives or achievements that have actually occurred.

12. *Perfectionism.* "I must do everything perfectly or I will be criticized and a failure." "An adequate job is akin to a failure."

13. *Selective abstraction.* "The rest of the information doesn't matter. This is the salient point." "I must focus on the negative details while I ignore and filter out all the positive aspects of a situation."

14. *Externalization of self-worth.* "My worth depends on what others think of me." "They think, therefore I am."

15. *Fallacy of change.* "You should change your behavior because I want you to." "They should act differently because I expect it."

16. *Fallacy of worrying.* "If I worry about it enough, it will be resolved." "One cannot be too concerned."

17. *Fallacy of ignoring.* "If I ignore it maybe it will go away." "If I don't pay attention I will not be held responsible."

18. *Fallacy of fairness.* "Life should be fair." "People should all be fair."

19. *Being right.* "I must prove that I am right because being wrong is unthinkable." "To be wrong is to be a bad person."

20. *Fallacy of attachment.* "I can't live without a man." "If I was in a relationship, all of my problems would be solved."

the specific attention to the patient in crisis. Therapist response is also noted. Although all of these distortions are stated in the first person, they can also apply to expectations of others, including family, social, religious, or gender groups.

THE GENERAL COGNITIVE–BEHAVIORAL THERAPY APPROACH

The establishment of a discrete problem list as quickly as possible helps both patient and therapist to have an idea of the nature, content, context, duration, frequency, dynamics, and population of the crisis situation. Later on, this list will help determine where the therapy is going and how the therapy is progressing.

The structure of agenda setting is essential in crisis work. Rather than having the therapy session meander, the therapist must work with the patient to set an agenda for the session, help focus the therapy work, make better use of time, energy, and available skills. Agenda setting at the beginning of the session allows both patient and therapist to put issues of concern on the agenda for the session. We emphasize that often the reason individuals are in crisis is that they have lost their ability to organize and problem solve. By setting an agenda, a problem-solving focus is modeled by the therapist and an imposed structure creates a sense of safety and predictability for the patient. The collaboration with the patient is crisis is not likely to be 50:50, but may be 70:30 or even 90:10, with the therapist providing most of the energy and structure within the session. Having the patient use the session time for abreaction, review of the crisis situation without taking a problem-solving approach is not recommended.

Crisis intervention, depending on the nature of the situation, can either be a one-shot evaluation to determine level of care requirements, or a series of brief therapy sessions designed to assist the patient to return to a previous level of functioning. Imperative in crisis intervention is to ascertain the safety of the patient, both to him/herself and to others. This aspect of crisis intervention involves the in-depth evaluation of a patient and requires rapid development of the therapeutic relationship. The initial session therefore is both an evaluation and a beginning of the therapeutic process.

Slaiku (1990) offers a synthesis of definitions of what a crisis actually is: a temporary state of upset and disorganization, characterized chiefly by an individual's inability to cope with a particular situation using customary methods of problems-solving, and by the potential for a radically positive or negative outcome.

Slaiku's definition encompasses all relative aspects to crisis work. By breaking down the definition, several avenues of treatment can be readily identified:

1. *Temporary state.* Crises are usually transitory phenomena, however, for those individuals who tend to perceive stimuli as dangerous or threatening (personality disorders), life can be a series of "brushfires."

2. *Crisis involves upset.* The patient is uncomfortable. This can be expressed in many ways: depression, anxiety, and disorganization. Disorganization can lead to or precipitate a decline in problem-solving ability, and in worst cases, psychosis. Disorganization can be cognitive, behavioral, or emotional.

3. *Inability to cope.* Crisis situations also may render the individual unable to cope. As both internal and external resources may be compromised, cognitive flexibility may also decrease. The patient may not be able to identify alternative avenues of choice, or may be expressing avoidance or denial or may be completely overwhelmed. Coping methods the patient may have used previously may now be ineffective.

4. *Life-changing consequences.* A crisis situation provides the potential for life-changing positive or negative consequences. How the clinician manages the crisis can impact the patient's future views of self-esteem, new experiences, manner of starting over, and in some cases actually save a life. Sometimes the individual seen in crisis is actually encountering the mental health field for the first time. This provides the opportunity for the professional to set the stage for further effective treatment offered with great empathy. Often, the patient may view a crisis clinician as the only link to getting well or "taking a last stand."

In crisis intervention treatment using cognitive-behavioral therapy, discerning and manifesting relative schemata assists the therapist in examining the advantages and disadvantages to maintaining schemata and introduces ways to dispute/alter held schemata (through assimilation and accommodation).

Overall the immediate goals of cognitive-behavioral therapy in crisis intervention are:

1. Evaluating and assessing the immediacy of the crisis situation.
2. Assessing the individual's coping repertoire to deal with the crisis.
3. Generating options of thought, perception, and behavior (includes problem-solving skills).

Integrating Slaiku's definition of crisis, the following are points to remember in crisis intervention and again provide several avenues to intervention: (1) crisis is a temporary state, (2) the patient will be upset (perceptions can be questioned or challenged), (3) the patient will be experiencing disorganization (offer structure and format for problem solving), and (4) assist the patient in reducing the potential for radical negative change. For those patients who may not require hospitalization or partial hospitalization, the following treatment outline addresses the management of a patient attending outpatient therapy who has indicated that they are in a crisis.

Five Steps of Crisis Intervention (Nonemergency)

The following lists five steps of crisis intervention with cognitive-behavioral therapy (Dattilio & Freeman, 1990) included with specific treatment interventions.

Develop Relationship with the Patient and a Build Rapport

1. Set agenda to include introduction of yourself, what you hope to achieve through this assessment, and the possibility that you might include family members if necessary.
2. Adopt a nonjudgmental attitude.
3. Communicate reframing.
4. Use metaphors to convey understanding (e.g., black hole, swallowed up, towel wringing, telescope filter).
5. Mirror patient's language, voice, and body communications.
6. Use assured voice (the patient is seeking structure and guidance).
7. Maintain good eye contact with patient.
8. Do not convey surprise, disgust, or other negative reactions.
9. Be consistent with style (especially if the patient is manic).
10. Set limits (patient is seeking structure).
11. Take history and elicit information while maintaining connection.

Make Initial Evaluation of Severity of Crisis Situation

1. Assess immediate physical danger to the patient or from the patient (offers avenue into held schemata).
2. Assist the patient in identifying the specific problem he/she is having. This is achieved by providing a structured and reframed synopsis of dilemma(s). Confusion and disorganization often render patients unable to actually define their problem. The therapist assists the patient to focus on the specific areas creating problems rather than deal with the vagaries of their actual symptoms. This provides a directive approach to setting the stage for treatment plan that outlines and options. In the initial session with a patient in crisis, you are not likely to make a huge impact on actual symptoms of depression, anxiety, or communication problems (especially vegetative symptoms and panic). However if you tend to focus more on the identification of problems, the patient will most likely gain some relief at having his/her issues clearly identified. However, be sure to not focus on an overly specific problem too early as you may miss bigger more complicated or dangerous problems. A specific problem list will help with this.

Help the Patient Assess and Mobilize His/Her Strengths and Resources

1. Identify support networks, friends, family, church, employee assistance programs (EAPs), employees, support groups, 12-step groups, sponsors, hotlines.

2. If possible and if patient agrees (if emergency, no waiver is needed), bring support network into initial evaluation to activate or challenge held beliefs regarding worth and other issues. If you are seeing a patient in crisis for the first time, most likely a family member or friend has came along to the session.

3. Help identify the patient's own internal resources and strengths which may be overlooked (schema activation). The patient may readily identify held beliefs ("I can't do anything right," "I'm a loser, no one loves me," "There's no hope," "I'd be better off dead than trying something new," etc). These beliefs offer data and information as to areas to challenge, dispute, or modify.

4. Call on previous challenges that the patient was able to overcome (maintaining employment despite this debilitating illness, completing a course, taking care of children, getting self up and dressed, caring for home, etc.).

5. Imagine role model managing problem and ask "How is X able to do this?" Be specific. For instance, "How would your best friend handle this?"

Work Together to Develop a Positive Plan of Action

1. Elicit commitment from patient to the plan of action.
2. Bring supports in to provide backup and motivation to complete plan.
3. Advocate for patient; for instance in accessing social services or treatment options, or providing alternative options of support (shelters, etc.).
4. Use imagery (imagine completion of goals, seeing self attempting and completing stepwise tasks).
5. Be very concrete and specific in identifying future plans and related goals. The more specific, the more the patient can affirm that he/she is actually accomplishing something.

Test Ideas and New Behaviors

1. See how plan is working.
2. Evaluate strategies.
3. Redefine mechanisms if not appropriate.
4. Elicit feedback from supports to assist in better definition of goals.
5. Elicit feedback from supports to help patient gather evidence that he/she is succeeding in his/her goals.

After the crisis has subsided, continue with the predetermined treatment plan.

Crisis Intervention in an Emergency

If you are advised by the patient or a family member by phone, or, if in session, you suspect that a patient is in crisis, follow the steps below. (This section includes both telephonic crisis management and in-session management.)

1. Always ascertain the patient's address (for instance, get apartment number in case emergency services need to be called).

2. Always verify phone number to patient in event you need to call back.

3. Refer the patient to the nearest emergency room if any suicide or self-injury attempt may have occurred.

4. Never believe amounts of medications or depth of cuts the patient admits to with an attempt. Exercise clinical judgment if family members report seriousness of attempt (they may have motives for nondisclosure of seriousness—denial or belief that they can handle patient or situation).

5. Elicit from the patient the exact nature of the attempt (what medications were taken (name and amount), what was used to make cuts, where were cuts made, and so on.

6. Listen closely and, if in session, observe patient's behaviors (slurring, disorganization, hesitations, breathing difficulties, rapid speech) that may indicate a suicide attempt or gesture.

7. If you suspect that the patient has made a suicide attempt, call 911.

8. Advise the responding emergency teams if the patient has access to firearms or has expressed paranoid ideation or homicidal ideation.

9. If you fear that the patient may flee while you call emergency services, try to keep the patient on the phone or in the room until services arrive (it's helpful to have a cellular phone available).

10. If the the patient is able to tolerate services' being called, advise him/her what you are doing. Because the patient has made the initial call for help, he/she will most likely be relieved that help is on the way.

11. If the patient sounds disorganized or hysterical, have the patient focus on the closed-ended questions you are presenting.

12. Asked closed-ended questions that do not aggravate the patient's distress, for instance, "I'm going to ask you some questions so you can help me out a little bit. I want you to focus on the questions I'm asking only . . . OK? Let's start with where do you live? How old are you? Are you alone? Are you on any medications?" Keep questions brief and to the point as you assess the potential danger of the situation.

13. Set very tight limits: if you suspect the patient has made a suicide attempt or is a danger to him/herself or others, whatever he/she might say, tell the patient that you would like to speak with a family member. If the patient disagrees, advise him/her that you will need to call the police or emergency services. Do not get caught in the "I'm not sure I won't hurt myself but I'm not

going anywhere" cycle. Set limits: "Either you're going for emergency evaluation, or I'm calling the police."

14. If you contact emergency services, be sure to give your full name, title, and return phone number. Police officers generally call the referring therapist once they have arrived at a home.

15. If a child/early adolescent calls with an emergency, be sure to tell him/her to open the door for the ambulance or police officers.

16. If you are evaluating a patient who presents as paranoid or has homicidal ideation, be sure to position yourself closer to the door than the patient and advise staff members.

17. If you are evaluating a paranoid patient, be sure to elicit whether the patient has felt the need to protect him/herself (this often identifies those who attack first due to their perceptions that they are in danger). "Have you ever felt the need to protect yourself from this individual who is watching you?" or "Have you ever protected yourself from the neighbors whom you are convinced want to hurt you?"

Once the patient has been sent to the emergency room, the process of managing the patient can be helped by the following suggestions:

1. Inform medical emergency room of pending arrival of patient. Include any medications the patient may be taking (if you know) and any medical problems that the patient has. Provide a brief synopsis of the case to the triage desk in the emergency room and make yourself available to the emergency physician if any questions arise. Advise the emergency personnel of the exact nature of the suicide attempt, and, if patient has overdosed, let them know what medications the patient said he/she ingested. Advise the emergency personnel of the name of the patient's psychiatrist and primary care physician if you know.

2. Contact the patient's attending psychiatrist to consult.

3. Contact the patient's primary care physician to advise him/her of the situation.

4. Contact the patient's managed care or insurance company (if applicable).

For patients who are suicidal, a complete and intensive evaluation is warranted to assist in making an appropriate decision regarding the level of care or disposition needed for the patient.

IMPULSE CONTROL

The impulse control model diagram (Figure 2.1) illustrates a hierarchical sequence that requires the therapist to help the patient deal with each step in the

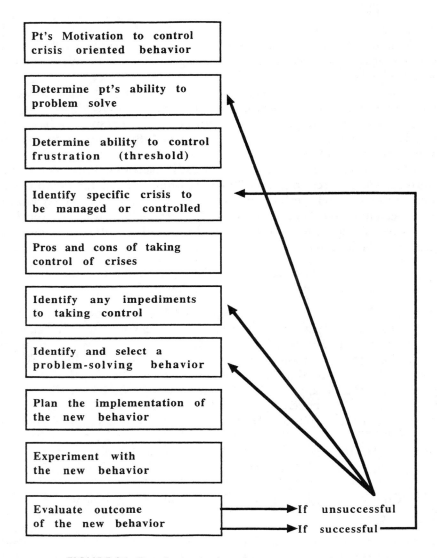

FIGURE 2.1. Developing an impulse management program.

sequence. The ultimate goal is a psychoeducational skill building so that the present crisis becomes an arena in which to practice crisis resolution.

The first step in the sequence is to ascertain the individual's motivation to control his/her life crises. If the motivation is poor or limited, that is, the patient believes that the crises are not his/her fault but due to the malice of others or to the confluence of the planets, little more can be done with the patient. Until the therapist helps to generate the motivation for change. A key question must be, "What is the value to you of being in crisis?" The therapist should stay with that question and not be side-tracked into discussions of all of the "thems" that create the crises. The patient must be motivated to do something about the "its" and the "thems."

Once there is some motivation to change, the next step is to determine the patient's ability to solve problems. Any of several problem-solving protocols can be used, including the work of Nezu and Nezu (1989) and Nezu and D'Zurilla (1981). For many patients, the basic work of Spivak and Shure (1976) can be used. The problem-solving training is a major part of the therapy work and will continue throughout the other stages. The individual's level of frustration (threshold) must be established. The question here is, "At what point do you stop trying?" or, "At what point do you revert to the same old techniques for coping with crises that haven't worked in the past?" In addition, posing to the patient, "What has worked for you before?" encourages the patient to be receptive to the fact that he/she has been able to manage prior events. Once the threshold and vulnerability factors have been addressed, the therapist can work with the patient to identify a crisis on which to practice.

The choice of a single, specific crisis situation is essential. Here again, the patient or therapist may want to deal with broad crisis situations or even classes of crises. This must be resisted. Using a specific situation allows for clear delineation of goals, problems, and interventions. Once this is done, the process continues.

The simple problem-solving technique of looking at the pros and cons of crisis management is introduced. This is done for two reasons. The first is to identify the relative weighting of how the individual sees the goals and purposes of crisis management. The second is to model how one can look at choices and options. The weighting may be against taking a crisis management approach, for instance, "I shouldn't have to be the one to change." The therapist can look at the advantages and disadvantages with the patient.

The patient's resistance or impediments to change must be evaluated. Too often, the best therapeutic work is sabotaged or subverted because scant attention was paid to the possible impediments. These include impediments from four sources: the patient, the therapist, the pathology, and the environment. These sources, or factors, are outlined in Table 2.3.

The next step is to identify and select a more appropriate, prosocial, assertive coping response or behavior. The premise is that having a patient give up one behavior without having an appropriate replacement will ultimately lead to relapse. It is said that nature abhors a vacuum. This is especially true when you ask a patient to stop one behavior without having a substitute behavior that fills the void.

The therapist and patient must then plan a careful implementation of the new behavior and to then experiment with the new behavior in a careful and controlled manner. After a reasonable trial (to be determined by the patient and

TABLE 2.3. Impediments to Successful Therapy

Patient factors

1. Lack of patient's problem-solving or crisis management skills
2. Cognitions regarding failure in previous crisis management
3. Cognitions regarding the consequences to others of the patient's being able to manage crises better
4. Secondary gain by maintaining problems
5. Fear of changing one's style
6. Lack of motivation to change
7. Negative cognitive set
8. Limited or poor self-monitoring
9. Limited or poor monitoring of others
10. Narcissistic and other-blaming style

Problem or pathology factors

1. Patient rigidity foils compliance
2. Existence of medical/physiological problems impede change
3. Difficulty in establishing trust in people
4. Autonomy press (need for independence and lack of reliance on others)
5. Poor impulse control
6. Confusion and/or limited cognitive ability
7. Symptom profusion (multiple symptoms on several axes)
8. Dependence

9. Self-devaluation regarding ability to cope
10. Dissociation
11. Substance abuse

Environmental factors

1. Environmental stressors preclude changing
2. Significant others foil therapy
3. Agency reinforcement of pathology to maintain compensation and/or benefits
4. System homeostasis
5. Financial constraints
6. Housing

Therapist factors

1. Lack of therapist skill
2. Patient and therapist distortions are congruent regarding life situations and circumstances
3. Poor socialization to the cognitive-behavioral therapy problem-solving model
4. Lack of collaboration/alliance
5. Lack of data
6. Poor timing of interventions
7. Lack of experience in therapist
8. Therapy goals are unstated, unrealistic, or vague
9. Lack of agreement with therapy goals
10. Lack of limit setting

---

therapist), the new behavior can be evaluated in terms of how well the new more coping behavior meets the needs of the individual and the circumstances.

If the new behavior is successful, the therapist and patient can then choose another crisis issue to be resolved. The patient may not be able to generalize his/her success, and each crisis situation may have to be dealt with separately.

If the new behavior is unsuccessful, there are three key areas to review: (1) Did the patient have the ability to control the crisis? (2) Were the impediments and resistances dealt with? (3) Was the alternative crisis management strategy appropriate?

THE TREATMENT CONCEPTUALIZATION

This conceptualization must meet several criteria. It must be useful, simple, coherent, able to explain past behavior, and able to predict future behavior. Part of the conceptualization process is the compilation of a problem list. This list can then be prioritized in terms of identifying a sequence of problems to be dealt with in therapy. The reasons for choosing one problem as opposed to another as the primary, secondary, or tertiary foci of the therapy depends on many factors. A particular problem may be the primary focus of therapy because of its debilitating effect on the individual. In another case the focus may be on the simplest problem. In a third case, the choice of a primary focus might be a "keystone" problem, that is, a problem whose solution will cause a ripple effect in solving other problems.

Patients may readily verbalize "This is who I/we are and this is the way I have always coped." By asking them to challenge or directly dispute their beliefs, we are then asking them to directly challenge their very being. When the challenge to self is perceived, the individuals usually respond with anxiety. They are then placed in a conflict situation as to whether they would prefer to maintain their particular dysfunctional symptoms or to experience anxiety. As they see themselves defined by the problem, they hesitate to give up the problem—doing so would leave them nothing but an empty shell. Thus any challenge to the self needs to be the result of a careful, guided discovery based on collaboration as opposed to a direct, confrontational, and disputational stance.

TREATMENT INTERVENTIONS

Several cognitive and behavioral techniques can be used by the therapist to help question both the distortions and the schemata that underlie them. These techniques can be taught to the patients to help them respond in more functional ways. A rule of thumb in treating severely depressed patients would be that the greater the severity of the depression, the greater the proportion of behavioral to cognitive interventions the therapist will use (Figure 2.2). The precise mix of cognitive and behavioral techniques will depend on the patient's level of functioning.

Cognitive Techniques

Idiosyncratic Meaning

A term or statement used by a patient is not completely understood by the therapist until the patient is asked for meaning and clarification. It is essential to question the patient directly on the meanings of verbalizations. This also models for the patient active listening skills, increased communication, and a means for checking out assumptions.

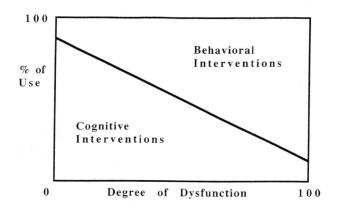

FIGURE 2.2. Use of cognitive and behavioral interventions.

Questioning the Evidence

It is essential to teach patients to question the evidence that they are using to maintain and strengthen an idea or belief. Questioning the evidence also requires examining the source of data. Many patients are able to ignore major pieces of data and focus on the few pieces of data that support their dysfunctional view.

Reattribution

A common statement made by patients is, "It's all my fault," especially in situations of relationship difficulty, separation, or divorce. Although one cannot dismiss this out of hand, it is unlikely that a single person is totally responsible for everything going wrong within a relationship. The therapist can help the patient distribute responsibility among all the relevant parties to a crisis. If the therapist takes a position of total support, for instance, "It wasn't your fault," "She isn't worth it," "You're better off without her," or "There are other fish in the ocean," the therapist ends up echoing friends and family that the patient has already dismissed as being a cheering squad. By taking a middle ground, the therapist can help the patient reattribute responsibility and not take all of the blame, nor unrealistically shift all blame to others.

Examining Options and Alternatives

Many individuals see themselves as having lost all options. Perhaps the prime example of this lack of options appears in the suicidal patient. They see their options and alternatives as so limited that among their few choices, death might be the easiest or simplest choice. This cognitive strategy involves working with the patient to generate additional options.

Decatastrophizing

Also called the "What if" technique, this involves helping patients evaluate if they are overestimating the catastrophic nature of a situation. Questions that might be asked include, "What is the worst thing that can happen?" or "And if it does occur, what would be so terrible?" This technique has the therapist working against a "Chicken Little" style of thinking. If the patient sees an experience (or life itself) as a series of catastrophes and problems, the therapist can work toward reality testing.

Fantasized Consequences

In this technique the individual is asked to fantasize a situation and to describe his/her images and attendant concerns. Often the patient describes concerns and, in the direct verbalization, can see the irrationality of his/her ideas. If the fantasized consequences are realistic, the therapist can work with the patient to realistically assess the danger and develop coping strategies. This technique allows the patients to bring imaged events, situations, or interactions that have happened previously into the consulting room.

Advantages and Disadvantages

As described above, asking that patients examine both the advantages and the disadvantages of both sides of an issue, a broader perspective can be achieved. Although patients will often claim that they cannot control their feelings, actions, and thoughts, it is precisely the development of this control that is the strength of cognitive therapy.

Turning Adversity to Advantage

There are times that a crisis can be used to advantage. Losing one's job can be a disaster but may, in some cases, be the entry point to a new job or even a new career.

Guided Association/Discovery

Through simple questions such as, "Then what?", "What would that mean?", "What would happen then?", the therapist can help the individual explore the significance in events. The therapist provides the conjunctions to the patient's verbalizations. The use of statements such as "And then what?", "What evidence do we have that that is true?", allows the therapist to guide the patients along various therapeutic paths, depending on the conceptualization and therapeutic goals.

Use of Exaggeration or Paradox

By taking an idea to its extreme, the therapist can often help to move the individual to a more central position vis-à-vis a particular belief. Care must be taken to not insult, ridicule, or embarrass the patient. Given a hypersensitivity to criticism and ridicule, some patients may experience the therapist who uses paradoxical strategies as making light of their problems. The therapist who chooses to use the paradoxical or exaggeration techniques must have (1) a strong working relationship with the patient, (2) good timing, and (3) the good sense to know when to back away from the technique.

Scaling

For those patients who see things as "all or nothing," the technique of scaling or seeing things as existing on a continuum can be very helpful. The scaling of a feeling can force patients to utilize the strategy of gaining distance and perspective. Because patients may be at a point of extreme thoughts and extreme behaviors, any movement toward a midpoint is helpful.

Direct Disputation

Although we do not advocate arguing with a patient, there are times when direct disputation is necessary. A major guideline for necessity is the imminence of a suicide attempt. The therapist must directly and quickly work to challenge hopelessness. Disputation might appear to be the treatment technique of choice, but the therapist risks becoming embroiled in a power struggle or argument with the patient. Disputation coming from outside the patient may, in fact, engender passive resistance and a passive–aggressive response that might include suicide. Disputation, argument, or debate are potentially dangerous tools. They must be used carefully, judiciously, and with skill. If the therapist becomes one more harping contact, the patient may turn the therapist off completely.

Behavioral Techniques

The goals in using behavioral techniques within the context of cognitive-behavioral therapy are manifold. The first goal is to utilize direct behavioral strategies and techniques to test dysfunctional thoughts and behaviors. By having the patient *try* feared or avoided behaviors, old ideas can be directly challenged. A second use of behavioral techniques is to practice new behaviors as homework. Certain behaviors can be practiced in the office, and then practiced at home. Homework can range from acting differently, practicing active listening, being verbally or physically affectionate, or doing things in an new way.

Activity Scheduling

The activity schedule is perhaps the most ubiquitous form in the therapist's arsenal. For patients who are feeling overwhelmed, the activity schedule can be used to plan more effective time use. The activity schedule is both a retrospective tool to assess past time utilization and a prospective tool to help plan better time use.

Mastery and Pleasure Ratings

The activity schedule can also be used to assess and plan activities that offer patients both a sense of personal efficacy (mastery, 1–10), and pleasure (1–10). The greater the mastery and pleasure, the lower the rates of anxiety and depression. By discovering the low- or high-anxiety activities, the therapist and patient can plan to increase the former and decrease the latter.

Social Skills Training

If reality testing is good, and patients actually lack specific skills, it is incumbent upon the therapist to either help them gain the skills or to make a referral for skills training. The skill acquisition may involve anything from teaching patients how to properly shake hands to practicing conversational skills.

Assertiveness Training

As with social skills training, assertiveness training may be an essential part of the therapy. Patients who are socially anxious can be helped to develop responsible assertive skills (Jakubowski & Lange, 1978).

Bibliotherapy

Several excellent books can be assigned as readings for homework. These books can be used to socialize or educate patients to the basic cognitive therapy model, emphasize specific points made in the session, or introduce new ideas for discussion at future sessions. Some helpful patient resources are listed at the end of this contribution.

Graded Task Assignments

Graded task assignments involve a shaping procedure of small sequential steps that lead to the desired goal. By setting out a task and then arranging the necessary steps in a hierarchy, patients can be helped to make reasonable progress with a minimum of stress. As patients attempt each step, the therapist can be available for support and guidance.

Behavioral Rehearsal/Role Playing

The therapy session is the ideal place to practice many behaviors. The therapist can serve as teacher and guide offering direct feedback on performance. The therapist can monitor the patient's performance, offer suggestions for improvement, and model new behaviors. In addition, anticipated and actual road blocks can be identified and worked on in the session. There can be extensive rehearsal before the patient attempts the behavior *in vivo*.

In Vivo Exposure

There are times that the practice in the consulting room needs to be expanded. The therapist can go with patients into feared situations. The therapist can drive with a patient across a feared bridge, go to a feared shopping mall, or travel on a feared bus. The *in vivo* exposure can join the office-based practice and the patient-generated homework into a laboratory experience.

Relaxation Training

The anxious patient can profit from relaxation training inasmuch as the anxiety response and the quieting relaxation response are mutually exclusive. The relaxation training can be taught in the office and then practiced by the patient for homework. Ready-made relaxation tapes can be purchased or the therapist may easily tailor a tape for a patient. The therapist-made tape can include the patient's name and can focus on particular symptoms. The tape can be modified, as needed.

Challenging Dysfunctional Thinking

One of the most powerful techniques in cognitive therapy involves using the various cognitive techniques to challenge dysfunctional thinking. The cognitive-behavioral therapy model posits an interaction between the individual's thoughts and the emotions but *does not* posit a direct causal relationship between thoughts and feelings. The daily record of dysfunctional thoughts is an ideal form for this purpose. The goal is to have them develop a model for problem solving.

Often, patients phrase their thoughts as questions, for instance, "Why does this always happen to me?", "Why can't I maintain a relationship?", or "Why doesn't my life turn out better?" A heuristic view is that questions are generally functional. It is important to ask questions, and then to answer them, for instance, "Does this always happen to me?", "Why do I have difficulty in maintaining relationships?", or "What has caused my life to be less than I had hoped for?" The dysfunctional thoughts are more generally declarative rather than interrogatory, for instance, "This always happens to me," "I can't maintain a relationship," and "My life is less than I had hoped for." The several cognitive techniques can be used to question the patient's conclusions.

The utilization of the techniques are limited only by the creativity of the therapist. The techniques need to be learned so that the therapist can move quickly and easily among the appropriate techniques.

Homework

Therapy, of necessity, needs to take place beyond the confines of the consulting room. It is important for the patient to understand that the extension of the therapy work to the nontherapy hours allows for a greater therapeutic focus. The homework can be either cognitive or behavioral. It might involve having the patient complete an activity schedule (an excellent homework for the first session), complete several dysfunctional thought records, or try new behaviors. The homework needs to flow from the session material, rather than being tacked onto the end of the session simply because cognitive therapy "should" include homework. The more meaningful and collaborative the homework, the greater the likelihood of patient compliance with the therapeutic regimen.

The homework should be reviewed at the next session. If the homework is not part of the session agenda, the patient will quickly stop doing the homework. The more the patient is helped to do homework, the better. When therapy ends, everything will be homework for the patient.

Follow-Up

For many patients, therapy will need to be a lifelong endeavor. This does not necessarily mean that they must come for therapy on a weekly schedule. For some patients a session once a month as a "check-in" session to review and deal with the problems and solutions of the past month will suffice. For other patients, a check-in phone call on some scheduled basis may be what is required. For some patients the therapy sessions might be "as-needed." It will be important to move the patient from the regular sessions to the maintenance phase of therapy.

SUMMARY

The patient in crisis experiences discomfort, dysfunction, dyscontrol, and disorganization—one in great measure or several in combination. For patients who are experiencing a crisis and have adequate intrapersonal and interpersonal resources, a crisis period need not be a time for only negative results or consequences. These patients may take advantage of their experiences to formulate change, growth, and adaptation to life's circumstances in a positive way. However, for those patients diagnosed with a cluster B personality disorder, added or additional stressors—whether internal or external—can create a "crossover" through threshold or trigger points. Thresholds for these patients are invariably lower than for those patients who are not crisis-prone. This is particularly so for the cluster B patient. Sensitive, erratic, and at times subject to extreme periods of lability, these patients often respond to stressors from an emotional standpoint. Unarmed with adequate coping or modulating strategies to manage these emotional states, an already vulnerable system can be thrown into crisis by minimal amounts of stress. High-arousal patients such as these usually have additional vulnerability factors that compound and complicate an already chaotic system. These include those factors from the patients themselves, their environment, supports or inadequate supports, and—characteristic to these disorders—unstable relationships.

By understanding and eliciting the patient's primary or underlying schematic material related to their personality style, the therapist can approach each crisis situation armed with an understanding of the cognitive processes or thought pathways in which the patient is reacting. For the cluster B patient, all of these disorders will react in an egosyntonic emotionally charged manner. It will be difficult for these patients to comprehend their role in the crisis, and likewise, their ability to create an effect or change within the crisis.

By applying, the revised stages of change proposed by Freeman and Dolan (in press), the therapist can understand and conceptualize the readiness or ability for the patient to engage in schematic shifts. Often these patients are operating within schematic paralysis and are therefore not accessible to shifting, adapting, or assimilating change to schemata. Being challenged with therapeutic interventions aimed at cognitive distortions, the patients can begin to create options for themselves, rather than making negative assumptions that no other choices are available to them. This is particularly true for the suicidal patient who has designated death as an option to manage unbearable pain. By creating a continuum of options other than suicide, the patient can begin to see the alternatives, rather than the sheer hopelessness that creates, feeds, and worsens suicidal ideation.

For the cluster B patient, the application of the defined schematic patterns will often assist the therapist in defining, creating, and refining therapeutic interventions. By framing basic schematic representations in a nonpejorative style to the patient, the patient can therefore feel understood. For example to the narcissistic patient, the therapist might say, "You have special needs right now that you feel aren't getting met. Maybe there are some other options to having those needs met." This statement reframes the narcissist's basic schematic pattern of being different or special, however it also creates an inroad to intervention by suggesting options. In other words, we encourage therapists to use the personality pathology as a guide or aid in creating therapeutic interventions.

Imperative to crisis intervention is a thorough and complete evaluation, assessment, and triage of the patient. This includes a comprehensive suicide and homicide inquiry. As many cluster B patients often react in a dramatic or emotional style, threats of harm to themselves or others can be easily made. We strongly advise that all threats be taken seriously, and to apply the patient's history and current mental status to the conceptualization and determination of the lethality of the patient.

All assessments should also include whether the patient can demonstrate good impulse control. By utilizing the cogntive-behavioral therapy approach encouraging self/other monitoring, the patient can learn to target their own impulses by being aware or cognizant of their escalation. They will then create for themselves a choice of behaviors to utilize as a response to the impulse and also to avert a crisis. For those patients largely more depressed and unable to access their cognitive resources as readily, more behavioral treatment approaches are encouraged.

Throughout treatment, challenging dysfunctional beliefs through a myriad of techniques creates options and alternatives and ultimately fosters hope for the patient, The method of these challenges is an opportunity for the therapist to utilize creativity and apply the patient's strengths to the task set forth. For the cluster B crisis-prone patient, the therapist can utilize and reframe schematic personality patterns to guide and cognitively intervene, thwart, and divert a crisis situation into an opportunity to collaboratively generate options, alternatives, and attempt new coping strategies ultimately improving the quality of life these patients experience.

REFERENCES

American Psychiatric Association. (1994). *Diagnostic and statistical manual of mental disorders* (4th ed.). Washington, DC: Author.

Beck, A. T., Freeman, A., & Associates. (1990). *Cognitive therapy of personality disorders.* New York: Guilford Press.

Beck, A. T., Rush, A. J., Shaw, B. F., & Emery, G. (1979) *Cognitive therapy of depression.* New York: Guilford Press.

Dattilio, F. M., & Freeman, A. (Eds.). (1994). *Cognitive-behavioral strategies in crisis intervention.* New York: Guilford Press.

DiClemente, C. C., Prochaska, J. O., Fairhurst, S. K., Velicer, W. F., Velasquez, M. M., & Rossi, J. S. (1991). The process of smoking cessation: An analysis of precontemptation, contemplation, and preparation stages of change. *Journal of Consulting and Clinical Psychology, 59,* 295–304.

Freeman, A. (1993). *A psychosocial approach for conceptualizing schematic development for cognitive therapy.* In K. T. Kuhlwein & H. Rosen (Eds.), *Cognitive therapies in action.* San Francisco: Jossey-Bass.

Freeman, A., & Dolan, M. (in press). Revisiting Prochaska and DiClemente's stages of change theory: An expansion and specification to aid in treatment planning and outcome evaluation. *Cognitive and Behavioral Practice.*

Freeman, A., Pretzer, J., Fleming, B., & Simon, K. M. (1990). *Clinical applications of cognitive therapy.* New York: Plenum.

Freeman, A., & Simon, K. M. (1989). Cognitive therapy of anxiety. In A. Freeman, K. M. Simon, L. Beutler, & H. Arkowitz (Eds.), *Comprehensive handbook of cognitive therapy* (pp. 347–366). New York: Plenum.

Jakubowski, P., & Lange, A. J. (1978.) *Responsible assertive behavior.* Champaign, IL: Research Press.

Layden, M. A., Newman, C. F., Freeman, A., & Byers-Morse, S. (1993). *Cognitive therapy of borderline personality disorder.* Boston: Allyn & Bacon.

Millon, T. (1999). *Personality guided therapy.* New York: Wiley.

Nezu, A. M., & D'Zurilla, T. J. (1981). Effects of problem definition and formulation on the generation of alternatives in the social problem-solving process. *Cognitive Therapy and Research, 5,* 265–271.

Nezu, A. M., & Nezu, C. M. (1989). *Clinical decision making in behavior therapy: A problem-solving perspective.* Champaign, IL: Research Press.

Prochaska, J. O., & DiClemente, C. C. (1982). Transtheoretical therapy: Toward a more integrative model of change. *Psychotherapy: Theory Research and Practice, 20,* 161–173.

Prochaska, J. O., & DiClemente, C. C. (1983). Stages and processes of self-change of smoking: Toward an integrative model of change. *Journal of Consulting and Clinical Psychology, 5,* 390–395.

Prochaska J. O., & DiClemente, C. C. (1992). Stages of change in the modification of problem behaviors. In M. Hersen, R. M. Eisler, & P. M. Miller (Eds.), *Progress in behavior modification* (pp. 184–214). Sycamore, IL: Sycamore Press.

Slaiku, K. (1990). *Crisis intervention* (2nd ed.). Boston: Allyn & Bacon.

Spivak, G., Platt, J. J., & Shure, M. B. (1976). *The problem-solving approach to adjustment.* San Francisco: Jossey-Bass.

3

Panic Disorder

Frank M. Dattilio
Philip C. Kendall

Howard decided to take the spur route home on this particular day because he had heard that it was much faster and more pleasant than the
crowded interstate. A less stressful commute was especially welcome after
another hectic day of sales calls. As he sped along the open road in a push
to get home early, Howard experienced an abrupt increase in heart rate
along with difficulty breathing. Thinking that perhaps he needed some
fresh air, he began to roll down the window when his symptoms suddenly
worsened. He felt a hot flash radiate through his entire body like a bolt of
lightning. He began sweating profusely with a tingling feeling invading his
hands and feet—all symptoms he never experienced before.

Howard's thought at that moment was "My God, I must be having a
heart attack—I'm not going to make it." As his symptoms intensified, he
became increasingly distressed and unable to concentrate. Overwhelmed
by anxiety, he turned off at the next exit, where he spotted a little blue sign
reading "Hospital ¼ mile West." Howard sped down the off ramp and
onto the avenue, which led him to the entrance way to the hospital.

He swiftly pulled into the parking lot and rushed into the emergency
room where he received immediate attention. Although Howard may
have been correct in thinking that his symptoms indicated a heart attack,
an arterial blood gas determination and an electrocardiogram (EKG) both
yielded normal results. Howard was told that he had experienced an
"anxiety attack" and was given alprazolam (Xanax) 0.5 mg p.r.n. (as
needed) and released to the care of his family physician with no further instructions.

The above scenario is a common example of crises situations involving a psychological disorder—panic attacks. The victim experienced symptoms that he
believed to be life-threatening and, as a consequence, sought immediate medical attention.

According to the *Diagnostic and Statistical Manual of Mental Disorders,* fourth edition (DSM-IV; American Psychiatric Association, 1994), panic attacks are diagnosed by the presence of at least four of the following symptoms: (1) shortness of breath or suffocating sensation; (2) dizziness, unsteady feelings, or faintness; (3) palpitations or accelerated heart rate; (4) trembling or shaking; (5) sweating; (6) choking; (7) nausea or abdominal distress; (8) depersonalization or derealization—a feeling that the sufferer's body or environment, respectively, is not real; (9) numbness or tingling sensations in one or more parts of the body; (10) hot flashes or chills; (11) chest pain or discomfort; (12) fear of dying; and (13) fear of going crazy or losing self-control. A condition of these criteria involves "unexpected panic attacks," which is required for a diagnosis of panic disorder as well as the symptoms' reaching a peak within 10 minutes (American Psychiatric Association, 1994).

Panic disorder is one of the most common and disabling psychological disorders encountered in both mental health and general medical settings and for some time has continued to rank among the top 10 disorders found in psychiatric emergencies (Wayne, 1966; Goldenberg, 1983). In past studies, investigators have estimated that the 1-month prevalence of panic disorder among primary care patients was 1.4% (Von Korff et al., 1987). This appears to hold true with a slight increase to date (Dattilio & Salas-Auvert, 1999). In addition, statistics derived from a study assessing community-based epidemiological catchment areas estimate that in any given month 0.5% of the population will be diagnosed with panic disorder (Regier et al., 1988).

Panic is reportedly a common diagnosis among hospital emergency room patients (Rosenman, 1985; Dunner, 1985). This situation is in part due to the fact that heart palpitations are among the most common symptoms expressed during a panic attack (Ehlers & Breuer, 1992; Dattilio & Salas-Auvert, 2000), and panic episodes are particularly common in cardiology patients (Beitman, DeRosear, Basha, Flaker, & Corcoran, 1987). Outpatient mental health clinics also report a high frequency of complaints of panic, with estimated incidences in the general population of 1.6% to 2.9% among women and 0.4% to 1.7% among men (Crowe, Noyes, Pauls, & Slymen, 1983; Boyd, 1986).

Although the literature on crises and crises intervention in general is abundant (e.g., Kocmur & Zavasnik, 1991; Aguilera, 1990; Roberts, 1990), very little has been devoted to specifically addressing crisis intervention for panic disorder (Diez, Gastó, & Vallejo, 1989; Aronson & Logue, 1988; Dattilio & Kendall, 1994). This situation is surprising, because it is well documented that physicians have, for the past 120 years, experienced difficulty in differentially diagnosing panic disorder from a variety of physiological disorders (DaCosta, 1871; Westphal, 1871; Prince & Putnam, 1912; Oppenheimer & Rothschild, 1918; Skerrit, 1983). Moreover, because the primary goal of crisis intervention is to reduce the patient's self-reported emotional distress (Kendall & Norton-Ford, 1982), it is not surprising that panic would appear near the top of the list of disorders targeted in crises intervention.

The scarcity of crisis intervention literature regarding panic may be because panic attacks are often viewed as crisis manifestations of some other underlying problem. In the medical setting, for example, a physician will usually focus immediately on any chronic underlying condition suspected of precipitating the panic symptoms, such as temporal lobe epilepsy, coronary artery disease, alcohol or tranquilizer withdrawal, hyperthyroidism, pheochromocytoma, electrolyte abnormalities, or stimulant medications/decongestants (see Katon, 1992, for a more extensive list). In addition, symptoms of panic can be secondary to other mental disorders such as major affective disorders (Breir, Charney, & Heninger, 1984), personality disorder (Barlow, 1988; Beck, Freeman, & Associates, 1990) and alcohol withdrawal (Katon, 1992). For a more extensive review of this subject, the reader is referred to Dattilio and Salas-Auvert (2000).

TWO THEORIES OF PANIC

There have been several attempts to explain the etiology of panic. The psychobiologists have contributed a number of hypotheses, which include the septohippocampal theory (Gray, 1982), the locus coeruleus theory (Svensson, 1987; Charney, Heninger, & Breier, 1984) and the gamma-aminobutyric acid–benzodiazepine hypothesis (Skolnick & Paul, 1983). More recently, cholecystokinin tetrapeptide (cck-4) has been studied as a panicogenic agent (Bradwejn, Koszycki, Payeur, Bourin, & Borthwick, 1992). These theories seek to explain panic by the action of certain neurochemicals in the brain.

Another possibility is that there is a specific genetic basis for inheriting a predisposition to panic disorder. Recent research on deoxyribonucleic acid (DNA) has analyzed the genetic structure of panic victims and members of their families who also reported a history of experiencing panic or related symptoms.

A genetic linkage among individuals diagnosed with panic disorder has been hypothesized for some time (Knowles & Weissman, 1995; Weissman, 1993; Weismann & Merikangas, 1986). Such a linkage is most likely to be true of individuals who describe an early onset of panic (Goldstein, Wickramaratne, Horwath, & Weissman, 1997). Recently, a series of studies were undertaken in order to test this hypothesis (Hamilton et al., 1999; Knowles et al., 1998).

In one particular study, the investigators used a family-based design to test for genetic association and linkage between panic disorder and a functional polymorphism in the promoter of the gene 5-HTT. In this study, 340 individuals in 45 families, as well as 75 haplotype relative risk "trios" were genotyped at the polymorphic locus, which consists of 44 base pair deletion/insertion. The results yielded no significant differences in allele frequencies or occurrence of genotypes within the triads. Furthermore, no linkage between the 5-HTT polymorphism and panic disorder was observed in the multiplex families, using a variety of simulations for dominant and recessive models of inheritance. The results of this study suggest that the genetic basis of panic disorder may be distinct from anxiety-related traits assessed by personality inventories in normal populations (Hamilton et al., 1999).

One of the more popular theories is the sodium lactate theory proposed as a result of the early studies by Pitts and McClure (1967). This study examined the effects of sodium lactate infusion, which induced panic attacks only in subjects who had a history of panic and not in others in the study who had no history of panic. Other studies were repeated yielding similar results (Appleby, Klein, Sachar, & Levitt, 1981; Dager, Cowley, & Dunner, 1987). On the other hand Ley (1986), in his reexamination of the original data of the 1967 Pitts and McClure study, uncovered that the 1967 panic subjects actually experienced an increase in a sensitivity to uncomfortable symptoms. This requires a determination as to whether it was an actual chemical chain reaction that occurred, or catastrophic misinterpretation that caused the subjects in the study to panic.

Even more convincing is the study conducted by Margraf and Ehlers (1989), which investigated panic-disordered individuals' reactions to hyperventilation and compared them to a normal population. The influence of subjects' expectancies was tested by manipulating instructions that were presented during an exercise. Two groups (panic and normals) were informed that they were participating in a "biological panic attack test" as opposed to the others, who were told that they were involved in a "fast-paced breathing task." Apparently, the increase in panic subjects' anxiety and arousal depended on what they were told. The expectation that they were taking a panic test produced physiological reactions and self-reported elevations in both anxiety and arousal. Conversely, the manipulation of the instructions and expectations had no effect on normal subjects' responses. As a consequence of these biology-based theories, the treatment of choice in medical settings involves a pharmacological regimen of high-potency benzodiazepines, tricyclic antidepressants, or monoamine oxidase inhibitors (Sheehan, 1982) coupled with behavior therapy (Brown, Rakel, Well, Downs, & Akisdal, 1991).

Although the psychobiological explanation of panic has merit, it retains several drawbacks. For one, there is little evidence to prove a psychobiological etiology for panic disorder—that is, there is no sure method to test for chemical imbalances or other difficulties in the brain. In fact, additional evidence recently reviewed in Kendall and Hammen (1999) has suggested that the biological model of panic disorder does not explain as much as once thought. In an interesting study at Vanderbilt University, researchers had individuals diagnosed with panic disorder inhale carbon dioxide either with or without an accompanying safe person who was chosen by the individual. The researchers hypothesized that if panic was solely biological in nature, a person's presence should have little effect on the panic episode. The results indicated that those panic-disordered individuals who were without a "safe person" reported greater distress, more catastrophic cognitions, and an increase in physiological arousal than did those who were accompanied by a "safe person." These results support the cognitive-behavioral theory of panic (Clark, Salkovskis, & Chalkley, 1985). The explosion of research relying on magnetic resonance imaging (MRI), positron emission tomography (PET) scans, and brain electrical area mapping (BEAM) studies have generated tremendous interest in psychobiological research of panic disorders. Nevertheless, the complexity of brain-related behavior continues to stall a comprehensive understanding of brain mechanisms involved in panic and anxiety. Although pharmacotherapy can expeditiously alleviate symptoms and possibly reduce the likelihood of phobic avoidance by reducing or ameliorating spontaneous panic attacks, it remains less than a cure. Pharmacotherapy provides the inflicted individual with little in the way of true coping mechanisms other than the reliance on simply taking the prescribed compound as instructed. In addition, individuals with panic disorder can be among the most difficult groups of patients to treat with medication—all pharmacologic compounds have side effects and panic attack patients are often hypersensitive to bodily sensations (Katon, 1992).

Pharmacological compounds have offered the most expedient treatment in crisis settings and have long been the treatment of choice for emergency situations involving panic and acute anxiety symptoms. The medical literature still suggests, however, that the first stage of treatment in primary care and emergency settings should be to negotiate explanatory models of the illness with the patients (Katon & Kleinman, 1980) and to elicit patients' beliefs about their illness prior to the actual treatment intervention. Open-ended questions such as "What do you believe is the problem?" and "What reasons would you give for the onset of symptoms at this particular time?" are recommended (Katon, 1992). Unfortunately, questioning can be limited to gathering some background information about the patient's relevant medical history subsequent to a blood profile and/or electrocardiogram (EKG), and medication is often dispensed without further exploration or explanation.

Psychobiological theories argue that panic is essentially the result of biochemical abnormalities associated with genetic predispositions (Sheehan, 1982; Weiss & Uhde, 1990); however, more recent literature suggests that psychological theories are better supported by empirical research (Beck, Emery, & Greenberg, 1985; Dattilio & Salas-Auvert, 2000).

A cognitive-behavioral theory of panic contends that it is psychological factors rather than solely psychobiological factors that precipitate panic symptoms. Whereas the cognitive-behavioral theories do acknowledge the neurochemical components of autonomic symptoms, they place more emphasis on the perception of threat or danger whether it involves internal (bodily sensations) or external (environmental) events (Raskin, Peeke, Dickman, & Pinsker, 1982; Dattilio, 1986; Ottaviani & Beck, 1987). Specifically, the misattribution theory introduced in the literature within the last two decades has proposed that specific symptoms resulting in hyperventilation elicit panic in individuals who are predisposed, whether genetically or psychologically, to catastrophic misattribution of internal bodily sensations (Ley, 1985; Clark, 1986). According to this theory, the most commonly occurring physical sensations during a panic attack include dizziness, vertigo, blurred vision, tachycardia, palpitations, numbness, tingling in the hands and feet, nausea and breathlessness (Clark, Salkovskis, & Chalkey, 1985; Hibbert, 1984; Kerr, Dalton, & Gliebe, 1937). Clark et al. (1985) noticed that these sensations bear similarity to sensations produced by hyperventilation. Thus it was hypothesized that hyperventilation may play an important role in the initiation of panic attacks (Clark et al., 1985). The theory purports that some individuals increase their respiratory ventilation when under stress. This increase causes carbon dioxide to be expelled from the lungs, triggering a decrease in the partial pressure of carbon dioxide (pCO_2) in the blood with an increase of pH in the blood. Such changes in the blood's chemistry manifests uncomfortable body sensations such as the aforementioned to which the individuals respond with startle and apprehension. This increased apprehension elicits further augmentation in ventilation, which spirals into a full-blown panic attack.

Clark et al. (1985) contend that it is either the perception of the feared stimuli itself or the induction of fear already elicited by other stimuli that contributes to the catastrophic reaction during this event that precipitates panic. Hence, teaching individuals how to avoid hyperventilation when under stress via breathing retraining, is the crux of the treatment.

Although panic attacks have often been reported as occurring "spontaneously," Beck, Emery, and Greenberg (1985) have found that some particular experiences appear to activate a person's "alarm system" (p. 112) involving cognitive-affective and physiological components. In addition, the aspect of perceived control has received increasing attention in explaining outcome effects in the treatment of panic (Borden, Clum, & Salmon, 1991; Dattilio & Salas-Auvert, 1999).

ASSESSMENT AND DIAGNOSIS

A comprehensive assessment protocol for diagnosing panic is quite complex and usually involves a structured interview. Such interviews may be performed with the use of assessment instruments such as the SCID (Structured Interview Schedule for DSM-III-R; Spitzer, Williams, & Gibbon, 1985) or the ADIS-R (Anxiety Disorders Interview Schedule–Revised; DiNardo et al., 1985). Unfortunately, such comprehensive assessment usually requires a considerable amount of time, which is not always available during crisis situations. Some abridged versions have been developed in recent studies to provide a more expedient method of assessment in crisis situations, for example, the Upjohn version of the SCID (SCID-UP-R; Spitzer & Williams, 1986; Swinson, Soulios, Cox, & Kuch, 1992).

It is recommended that a brief clinical interview be conducted, including an excerpt from the panic section of the ADIS-R and screening questions that elicit the individual's medical history (particularly cardiac or seizure disorders) along with all medication currently in use.

Some of the briefer diagnostic questionnaires may also help to pinpoint specific symptoms and to support information that has been obtained from the patient verbally. Such quick screening questionnaires include the Beck Anxiety Inventory (BAI; Beck, 1987), Body Sensations Questionnaire (BSQ; Chambless, Caputo, Bright, & Gallagher, 1984), Anxiety Sensitivity Index (ASI; Reiss, Peterson, Gursky, & McNally, 1986), and the Zung Anxiety Scale (Zung, 1975), any of which can be completed in a matter of minutes. In addition, Table 3.1 includes some of the more important questions to ask during crisis situations.

Because much of the cognitive-behavioral literature stresses the importance of relating symptoms to the misinterpretation of interoceptive cues and catastrophic cognitions (Alford, Beck, Freeman, & Wright, 1990; Ottaviani & Beck, 1987; Dattilio, 1986, 1987, 1990, 1992a, 1994a), a formal system for linking panic symptoms to thoughts and emotional-behavioral responses is essential. A recently developed assessment technique known as the SAEB system (Symptoms–Automatic Thoughts–Emotions–Behavior) is recommended as an approach for helping panic sufferers recognize the link between their panic symptoms and their catastrophic responses to their initial bodily sensations (Dattilio, 1990, 1992a, 1992b, in press; Dattilio & Berchick, 1992).

The unique design of the SAEB system allows the treating clinician to align specific catastrophic thoughts and misinterpretations of symptoms with the onset of subsequent symptoms in a quick, expedient fashion. The system thus allows the panic victim to see the connections between stages of the escala-

---

TABLE 3.1. Questions for Crisis Intervention

---

1. Have you recently adjusted, discontinued, or changed any medications, either prescription or nonprescription?

2. Have you experienced any illness or deaths or changes in relationships, job, or financial situation in the past 6 months?

3. Have you recently experienced childbirth, surgery, or a change in menstrual pattern?

4. Has anyone in your immediate family or family of origin experienced symptoms similar to those you are experiencing now?

5. Have you recently commenced or discontinued any use of tobacco, drugs, or alcohol?

6. Do you have any history of medical disorders such as hypoglycemia, cardiac abnormalities, seizure disorder, etc.?

7. Have you experienced these types of symptoms in the past?

8. Are you currently using stimulant/diet drugs such as crank, speed, cocaine, crack, etc.?

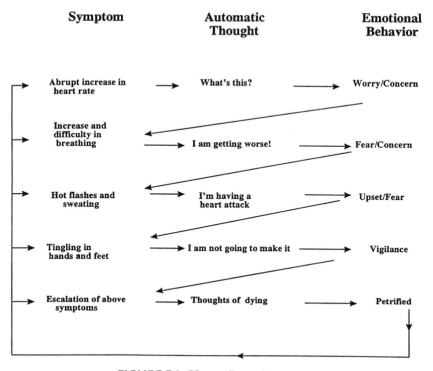

FIGURE 3.1. Howard's panic sequence.

tion process setting the stage for the next step, which involves the treatment intervention (see Figure 3.1).

This system is applied by having patients identify the beginning symptom of the panic episode. If the individual has experienced more than one attack, the repetitive sequence of each attack is more credible. For example, in Figure 3.1, a "spontaneous increase in heart rate" was the initial symptom experienced by Howard, the gentleman depicted in the case study, at the onset of each attack. This was followed by "difficulty breathing" and subsequently by "hot flashes and sweating," and so on. Once the symptoms have been aligned, the automatic thoughts accompanying each symptom are indicated along with the associated emotion and behavior. Vectors are then drawn in order to demonstrate to the patient in a collaborative fashion how the catastrophic thought content may be in reaction to the autonomic symptoms experienced and how these thoughts contribute to the subsequent behavior and possibly to the subsequent escalation of the symptoms (Dattilio, 1990). This technique is demonstrated in detail in a videotape (Dattilio, 1994b) as well as in Dattilio and Salas-Auvert (2000).

This SAEB system sets the stage for the implementation of several cognitive-behavioral treatment interventions that are explained later in this chapter. It is recommended as a quick method of assessment for tracking the cognitive, affective, behavioral, and physiological sequence of panic. Pinpointing specific triggers of panic symptoms (e.g., stress; hot, stuffy climates; and excessive exercise) is also another important aspect of assessment that has been emphasized in the literature (Beck, Emery, & Greenberg, 1985; Dattilio & Berchick, 1992).

COGNITIVE-BEHAVIORAL INTERVENTION TECHNIQUES

A great deal of professional literature has focused on the use of cognitive-behavioral techniques and their effectiveness in treating panic and anxiety disorders (Beck, Emery, & Greenberg, 1985; Barlow, 1988). Specifically, exposure-based treatments have been quite successful in reducing panic (Clark & Ehlers, 1993; Barlow, 1988), particularly when used in concert with pharmacological interventions (Zitrin, Klein, & Woerner, 1978). Cognitive-behavioral treatment focusing on panic control through education, cognitive restructuring, interoceptive exposure, and breathing retraining have been reported in some cases with success in a group format (Telch et al., 1993). More recently, large didactic group approaches have been used in Scotland by White, Keenan, and Brooks (1992) to accommodate the large number of anxiety-disordered patients referred to primary care services. The therapy sessions employ a combination of cognitive-behavioral techniques and elements of traditional group therapy with a psychoeducational self-help package. The goal is to turn the individual into his/her own therapist, providing him/her with the education and skills necessary to recognize and overcome anxiety or panic. In a recent study with panic-disordered patients, 90% of the patients at posttherapy and 70% at 6-month follow-up were panic free and coping better on a range of measures (White, in press).

Most recently, brief treatments of panic attacks in emergency situations have used exposure instruction with relative effectiveness (Swinson et al., 1992). In this particular study, 33 patients with panic attacks were seen in two emergency room settings. Forty percent (40%) of the patients had been diagnosed with the SCID as meeting the criteria for panic disorder with agoraphobia. Patients were randomly assigned to groups receiving either reassurance or exposure instruction. Outcome measures demonstrated significant improvement over a 6-month period for individuals of the exposure group. Individuals of the reassurance group showed no improvement on any measure and, in fact, reported increased symptomatology (Swinson et al., 1992). The specific treatment involved informing patients that the most effective way to reduce their fear was to confront the situation in which the attack occurred. Patients were advised to return to the situation as soon as possible after the interview and to wait until their anxiety decreased (p. 945). Although this approach improves upon the sole use of pharmacologic interventions, it still falls short of providing the individual with any specific set of coping techniques, especially for dealing with future panic episodes. It also relies on extinction procedures and appears to require more time for reducing symptoms and may not always be practical depending on the circumstances in which the individual experienced the attack.

A number of additional cognitive-behavioral techniques may prove to be more satisfactory alternatives in the treatment of panic in crisis settings by providing the individual with specific coping mechanisms to apply during future episodes or attacks.

Controlled Breathing

Early studies on anxiety refer to the use of progressive muscle relaxation and controlled breathing as well as carbon dioxide inhalation (Wolpe, 1958). These techniques are based on the premise that a state of relaxation and a state of anxiety cannot coexist. Some view these techniques as being all that is necessary to put a stop to recurrent panic attacks (Lum, 1981; Clark, Salkovskis, & Chalkley, 1985).

The concept of controlled breathing is an offshoot of the hyperventilation hypothesis mentioned previously, which contends that individuals commonly hyperventilate prior to panicking (Hibbert, 1984). Individuals who hyperventilate tend to breathe through their mouth, taking short shallow breaths of air or sighing frequently. Diaphragmatic breathing is one form of breathing retraining for counteracting hyperventilation. Individuals are instructed to breathe through the nose normally and to count the number of breaths while at rest, keeping the frequency to 9 to 16 times per minute. They are also told to place both hands over the abdomen while breathing, noticing the movement of the diaphragm. Individuals are instructed to practice the exercise during both panic and nonpanic periods (Clum, 1990).

If, during a severe panic attack, the diaphragmatic method does not enable the individual to obtain a full breath, which is often the case, breathing into a paper bag or cupped hands may be used in order to increase the level of carbon dioxide (Dattilio, 1990). An alternative is to exhale through the mouth as much as possible and then slowly inhale through the nose, repeating the process several times. While practicing these techniques, distraction may be used to divert one's attention from the panic symptoms to enhance the positive effects of the breathing exercise.

Symptom Induction and Deescalation

The cognitive-behavioral model of panic contends that individuals' misinterpretations of bodily sensations play an integral role in the escalation of panic symptoms. Consequently, such misinterpretations can be responsible for maintaining the vicious panic cycle (Argyle, 1988; Beck, Emery, & Greenberg, 1985; Dattilio, 1987; Ottaviani & Beck, 1987). During this period of vulnerability, individuals tend to overestimate perceived danger and to underestimate their capacity for coping (Dattilio, 1987, 1990; Greenberg, 1989).

In symptom induction, clients are presented with a therapeutic exercise whereby they are instructed to follow the therapist in taking short successive breaths of air, inhaling and exhaling, for approximately 2 to 3 minutes. This procedure serves to reproduce the symptoms of panic by activating the autonomic nervous system and disrupting the balance of oxygen and carbon dioxide levels, sometimes causing hyperventilation as well (Dattilio, 1990). Symptom induction allows the therapist to obtain a direct report of the client's thought processes as the attack develops and to assist the client first-hand in controlling the attack through progressive breathing and thought restructuring. The goal here is to reproduce the type of situation that may precipitate an attack and then show the client that he/she can "turn on" as well as "turn off" the attacks.

Once the symptoms have been induced, the therapist records the sequence of events that occur, paying particular attention to the specific symptoms, the automatic thoughts, and the emotional reaction experienced as a result. Figure 3.1 provides an example of how to track the client's panic sequence during an attack. In response to the initial symptom, spontaneous increase in heart rate, the automatic thought is overreactive in the sense that it is assumed that "something is wrong" or that the client "could faint."

It is essential that all clients who are candidates for this technique receive medical clearance prior to the exercise in order to ensure that the technique is not contraindicated by an existing medical condition. The therapist can then begin to intervene with the deescalation techniques by collaboratively focusing with the client on the initial symptoms.

In the case presented in Figure 3.1, a spontaneous increase in heart rate followed by the thought, "something is wrong" or "I'm going to faint," translated into increased fear. By identifying the early onset of symptoms in the panic cycle, the therapist can aid clients in the deescalation of symptoms. This is done by having patients downplay the severity of the symptoms by altering their misinterpretations. For example, the individual in Figure 3.1 had developed a pattern of responding to increased heart rate by perceiving it as dangerous and a sure sign that "something is wrong." In restructuring their thoughts, clients are asked to consider an alternative response that may involve a less catastrophic implication. For instance, "Just because I have an increase in heart rate doesn't mean that this is necessarily dangerous or that something is wrong. It is perhaps just benign autonomic activity which will last for a limited time." This cognitive response is then supported by having the client log each attack and review the log for reassurance that because nothing dangerous has occurred in the past, it is unlikely to occur in the future. Clients are then taught controlled breathing in order to regulate their oxygen intake level and reduce autonomic activity.

The purpose of this type of restructuring is to lessen the likelihood that the individual's automatic thoughts are fueling the subsequent increase in symptoms and emotional reaction and to persuade them that their fear ("I might faint") is unsubstantiated. This point can be affirmed with cognitive correction via factual information (e.g., in order to faint, one must experience a decrease in blood pressure; blood pressure increases with increased heart rate and anxiety). In addition, this serves to improve their perceived sense of bodily control, which reduces the intensity of threat and danger.

This type of thought correction is followed throughout the entire panic cycle and then reinforced by virtue of reexposure to symptoms through the use of the panic induction exercise. It is the combination of the artificial induction of symptoms (e.g., purposely increasing heart rate), as well as the reinterpretation of these symptoms, (e.g., it will not hurt me), deescalation of the catastrophic thoughts, (e.g., this will not last forever), and eventual reduction of symptom severity that makes the technique effective. In addition, follow-through on having clients expose themselves to real-life situations is also an important component to treatment so that the ability to generalize the techniques to a variety of situations can develop.

This technique is usually well received by panic sufferers, particularly after they have overcome their initial apprehension about raising their autonomic activity level. With those clients who sometimes do not benefit from the intervention (e.g., they become too overwhelmed or are unable to increase their autonomic activity level), it is recommended that the same technique of cognitive restructuring be used without the symptom induction exercise.

Paradoxical Intention

Paradoxical intention, originally developed by Frankl (1984), is similar to symptom induction in that it involves a behavioral prescription for clients to perform responses that seem incompatible with the goal for which they are seeking help. The specific difference, however, is that in paradoxical intention clients are asked to exaggerate their anticipations rather than behaviorally induce the symptoms by deliberately hyperventilating. For example, individuals who experience panic attacks and fear that they may die suddenly or become "overwhelmed" would be instructed to "go ahead and let themselves die" or do whatever they fear they might do (Dattilio, 1987). After several attempts, they often discover that they are unable to achieve the feared response, and their anxiety then diminishes. At this point, many clients are able to perceive the absurd or irrational aspect of their apprehensions, which is strongly encouraged by the therapist. They are then instructed to repeat this same procedure in selected settings at graded levels of panic-evoking situations until they experience few or no symptoms. This technique also differs from symptom induction and deescalation in that there is no deescalation of symptoms and no instruction in the use of controlled breathing as an anxiety-reducing agent. In fact, it poses the opposite approach to the client with the reliance on the paradoxical focus itself as the trigger in reducing anxiety (Dattilio, 1987, 1994a; Dattilio & Salas-Auvert, 2000).

Paradoxical intention has at times been rather loosely defined in the literature, particularly as it has been utilized by therapists of varying theoretical orientations who conceptualize it quite differently (Dell, 1981; Efran & Caputo, 1984; Ascher, 1984; Dowd & Trutt, 1988; Sexton, Montgomery, Goff, & Nugent, 1993). More specifically, the debate appears to center around whether or not the "intention" referred to is the patient's or the therapist's. This issue is fully discussed by Dowd and Trutt (1988), and the intention was clearly defined earlier by Frankl (1975) as being the patient's. Thus, the technique of paradoxical intention may fall more clearly within the bounds of a cognitive intervention, because it first forces a behavioral change, which is followed by a restructuring of cognition upon reflection on the implication of the behavioral change. This point has been challenged, however, by others (Bandura, 1977) arguing that the behavioral change precedes the restructured cognition.

Paradoxical intention appears antithetical to the other cognitive-behavioral treatments for panic, such as symptom induction, deescalation, and the relaxation-based techniques, mainly because it seems to provide patients with few coping techniques for anxiety. However, at times certain individuals may prove to benefit more from paradoxical treatments than others because of the extinction-based philosophy. It may be recommended for individuals who may experience relaxation-induced anxiety (Heide & Borkovec, 1983; Cohen, Barlow, & Blanchard, 1985; Lazarus & Mayne, 1990), in which many of the more traditional anxiety-reducing techniques are less effective. side effects such as tingling, numbness, dizziness, paradoxical increases in tension, increased heart rate, and other untoward reactions have been reported with relaxation-based treatment (Borkovec & Grayson, 1980; Edinger & Jacobsen, 1982). Patients have reportedly often lost interest in progressive muscle relaxation or have repeatedly fallen asleep. Relaxation techniques may at times even evoke seizure activity or traumatic memories, which may undermine the intention of the treatment (Kiselica & Baker, 1992).

Paradoxical intention would also be recommended in patients who appear resistant to techniques that involve actual symptom induction, as well as patients with a history of cardiovascular disorders. Even though paradoxical intention encourages the symptoms to worsen, there is no direct induction of symptoms (e.g., overbreathing); thus, the likelihood of cardiovascular stress is reduced. It is therefore suggested as an alternative treatment when induction is contraindicated and when an expedient intervention is required such as with crisis situations.

Symptom induction, deescalation, breathing retraining, and paradoxical intention are all nonpharmacologic techniques that may be applied for rapid amelioration of panic symptoms in emergency and crisis situations. In combination with exposure and/or pharmacological interventions, these techniques may prove to be the most efficacious (Brown et al., 1991).

Eye Movement Desensitization and Reprocessing

Shapiro and Forrest propose a new method that has shown benefit in the treatment of traumatic memories and has recently been explored as a potential intervention in panic disorder. This approach has been called eye movement desensitization and reprocessing (EMDR; Shapiro & Forrest, 1997).

Shapiro reports initially developing EMDR while working with some 70 people over the course of about 6 months, with refinements added over the past 10 years. As a result of her work, she reports developing a standard procedure that alleviated patients' complaints. Because the primary focus of EMDR was on reducing anxiety, this has become Shapiro's targeted population. Shapiro has reported results of EMDR in the treatment of posttraumatic stress disorder (PTSD; Shapiro, 1996, 1998).

It was fairly recently that Goldstein and Feske (1994) reported on the use of EMDR in the treatment of panic disorder. They initially selected seven panic-disordered subjects who were patients at anxiety disorder clinics. The patients were treated with EMDR for memories of past and anticipated panic attacks and other anxiety-evoking memories of personal reference. Standardized report inventories and behavioral monitoring instruments were employed to measure changes with treatment. After only five sessions of EMDR, subjects reported a considerable decrease in the frequency of panic attacks, fear of experiencing a panic attack, general anxiety, fear of body sensations, depression, and other measures of pathology. These results sparked the authors' further investigation of the effectiveness of EMDR for panic.

In a subsequent study, the same authors (Feske & Goldstein, 1997) randomly assigned 43 outpatients diagnosed with panic disorder to six sessions of EMDR. A control group was assigned to the same treatment, but with the omission of the eye movement and with a waiting list. Posttest comparisons showed EMDR to be more effective in alleviating panic and panic-related symptoms than the waiting-list procedure. Compared with the same treatment without the eye movement, EMDR led to a greater improvement on two of five primary outcome measures at posttest. EMDR's advantages had dissipated 3 months after treatment. Consequently, this study fails to support the eye movement component of the treatment of panic disorder (Feske & Goldstein, 1997). Shapiro (1998) argued that Feske and Goldstein removed part of the treatment package (e.g., self-control imagery, attention to physical stimuli, and log reporting), which may have made a crucial difference in the maintenance of effectiveness. This was the issue of debate regarding the efficacy of eye movement in the Feske and Goldstein (1997) article.

Pharmacotherapy

Because medication is so widely used in many crisis settings, it is essential that it be addressed in this chapter. As mentioned earlier, pharmacotherapy has been the medical treatment of choice in most crisis or emergency settings involving acute anxiety or panic. This is particularly due to the quick-acting effects of many of the pharmacological agents, particularly the benzodiazepines, which act more rapidly than any other antipanic agents (Liebowitz, Fyer, & Goman, 1986). Alprazolam is probably the most widely used benzodiazepine (Ballenger, Burrows, & Dupont, 1988). A variety of other benzodiazepines, including clonazepam, lorazepam and diazepam, also have antipanic effects when administered in significant doses (Brown et al., 1991).

Tricyclic antidepressants, most notably imipramine hydrochloride, have been studied in depth as antianxiety agents (Brown et al., 1991). Imipramine has been found to be more effective in the long run in treating panic, particularly when it is accompanied by depression. Other tricyclic antidepressants such as trimipramine, amitriptyline, doxepin, nortriptyline, and maprotiline have also been documented as effective in the treatment of panic (Lydiard & Ballenger, 1987).

As an alternative to tricyclic antidepressants, the monamine oxidase inhibitors (MAOIs) have been successful with individuals who suffer from panic associated with atypical depressive features. MAOIs, while effective, carry a number of serious side effects and require strict dietary restrictions that exclude foods containing tyramine. MAOIs, like the tricyclic antidepressants, require an onset period before any therapeutic effects may be gained.

Additional compounds, such as beta-adrenergic blockers and serotonin reuptake inhibitors, have also been used to treat panic with only minimal or no success.

The combination of cognitive-behavioral techniques and pharmacologic agents have been successful in treating panic disorder. A recent study was undertaken involving a randomized double-blind, placebo-controlled clinical trial with 326 subjects carefully screened for a diagnosis of panic disorder (Barlow, Gorman, Shear, & Woods, 1998). Subjects received either imipramine (IMI), cognitive-behavior therapy (CBT) or a combination. The results indicate that both treatments were significantly better than placebos, and individual CBT and IMI worked approximately equally well at the end of acute treatment and after 6 months of maintenance. Response to placebos was short-lived. Among those completing treatment, IMI produced a response of higher quality. Six months following treatment discontinuation, more patients responding to IMI, whether combined with CBT or not, had deteriorated compared to those responding to CBT alone or CBT combined with placebos where subjects tended to retain their gains.

These investigators conclude that there seems little advantage to combining drug and cognitive-behavioral therapy, and each individual treatment works approximately equally well immediately following treatment and during maintenance. Follow-up data after termination indicates that cognitive-behavioral therapy is more durable. When pharmacologic agents are used in conjunction with nonpharmacologic techniques, it is recommended that a multicomponent treatment package be used such as the one described by Craske and Barlow (1990). This program consists of four major components: (1) education and corrective information concerning the nature, etiology, and maintenance of panic; (2) cognitive therapy techniques aimed at helping the patient identify, monitor, and alter faulty appraisals of threat that contribute to panic occurrence; (3) framing in methods of slow diaphragmatic breathing as a way of reducing or eliminating physical symptoms that often trigger panic attacks; and (4) interoceptive exposure exercises designed to reduce patients' fear of somatic sensations through repeated exposure to feared bodily sensations. It is suggested that it might also apply to emergency settings as well.

Bibliotherapy

One of the adjunct techniques that has been found to be helpful with anxiety disordered individuals is the use of assigned readings on the topic of panic. This is otherwise known as bibliotherapy (Gould, Clum, & Shapiro, 1993; Lidren et al., 1994). As a behavioral technique, bibliotherapy is a continuous reinforcement of many of the principles and concepts promoted in therapy regarding coping skills. Literature may also help individuals who are suffering from panic feel less isolation and become aware that others experience these symptoms and struggle with the same reactions.

There are a number of excellent self-help books available on the market for panic sufferers, among them are *Don't Panic* (Wilson, 1986) and *Coping with Panic* (Clum, 1990). Both of these books have been written by professionals skilled in the cognitive-behavior therapies. As a result, they are fine supplemental reading and supportive aids to many of the techniques described in this chapter. Individuals should be directed to read these books as they are receiving treatment and may even benefit from them following the termination of therapy. For a more comprehensive listing of self-help books along with annotation, the reader is referred to Dattilio and Salas-Auvert (2000).

Homework

Homework is a very important aspect of cognitive-behavioral treatment of panic. Many of the coping skills that are taught require practice in order to become part of the individual's work repertoire of skills. Such homework assignments as practicing breathing exercises and cognitive coping skills are necessary to learn how to respond effectively when a spontaneous panic attack occurs.

Recording information on forms such as the "panic diary" developed by Dattilio and is reprinted in Dattilio and Salas-Auvert (2000) is also vital in allowing both the client and the therapist to track the occurrence and progress with the clients' panic occurrences.

Finally, homework is also a prelude to the eventual coping skills that will be used in relapse prevention. Whereas homework assignments vary during the course of treatment, typical assignments may include practicing methods of progressive muscle relaxation training, breathing exercises, practicing challenging automatic thought statements during periods of automatic activity, self-exposure to stimuli that may cause automatic arousal and/or recording catastrophic thought statements.

Relapse Prevention

Panic relapse after treatment occurs in the majority of cases as a result of the discontinuation of skills practice and exposure as well as poor follow-up in therapy. In fact, treatment is often ended abruptly by the client because their symptoms have subsided.

It is essential that clients contract with the therapist to complete their treatment and include all of the follow-up visits. The follow-up visits should focus on a skills check and anticipation of the use of techniques in the event of a spontaneous reoccurrence of panic symptoms. Other issues that should be addressed are psychosocial and internal stressors that may serve to trigger panic.

Finally, it is also recommended that clients be instructed to not delay in contacting the therapist for booster sessions when they are experiencing difficulty coping on their own. It is often the extreme delay that facilitates the return of the panic cycle in full force.

SUPPORT GROUPS

A distinction must be made between group psychotherapy and support groups. Support groups typically are groups of individuals who have been through treatment and need to rely on group meetings as booster sessions. These groups usually are conducted by a trained professional or a paraprofessional and are designed primarily to support patients in utilizing what they have learned in the course of treatment. Although topics such as backsliding and stumbling blocks are often discussed, emphasis is placed on a support system as opposed to any specific intervention or treatment (Dattilio & Salas-Auvert, 2000).

Quite often, recovered panic-disordered individuals will form their own patient support groups and conduct them primarily as leaderless groups. These may be beneficial to some degree, but a useful caveat is that untrained professionals may face difficulties depending on the condition of other group members. These groups are not recommended unless there is professional supervision, and it may behoove clinicians to have their patients avoid groups that are not so monitored.

Typically, support sessions are conducted on a monthly basis. Members may attend to talk about achieving their goals or to celebrate their successes. Generally, they can attend group meetings as long as sessions are available. Group support systems are recommended for individuals who have had serious relapses, but only after they have reentered treatment. Some support groups may also involve the spouse or other relatives of a person with panic disorder, and these can be very helpful to family members in their struggle to understand panic.

It is important to remember that support groups are not a substitute for effective treatment, but are designed to complement treatment.

FAMILY/SPOUSAL SUPPORT

Even though panic is a disorder of the individual, it undoubtedly has a ripple effect on families. However, little research exists on the role of relationships and their contribution to panic disorder. Marital and family difficulties were ranked high on lists of stressors by panic-disordered subjects who were surveyed by researchers Thorpe and Burns (1983). Clearly, families may play a major role in accelerating the treatment process as well. Much of the professional literature supports the concept of educating spouses and family members to the treatment of panic and contributing to their understanding of why and how the disorder develops (Barlow, 1988). What is more, it is important for treating clinicians to coach spouses and immediate family members on their roles in the treatment process. This should be executed with care and only after it has been determined that the patient's spouse or other family member is not facilitating an unhealthy dependency that may be enabling the patient's disorder, particularly because research has indicated that marital relations play a key role in the development and maintenance of panic and agoraphobia (Goldstein & Chambless, 1978; Wolpe, 1970). Further studies have focused on the relationship characteristics of agoraphobics and their partners (Epstein & Dutton, 1997; Epstein, Dutton, Dattilio, & Vittore, in progress) and suggest that agoraphobics are in more maladjusted marriages than are other couples; however, agoraphobics differ from other groups, in that their degree of marital maladjustment falls in the middle between that of highly distressed and of nondistressed couples (Arrindell & Emmelkamp, 1986; Lange & Van Dyck, 1992). Unfortunately, little in the literature addresses the benefits of including the spouse in treatment, and the results of doing so are mixed (Himadi, Boice, & Barlow, 1986; Barlow, O'Brien, & Last, 1984; Arnow, Taylor, & Agras, 1985). Spouses are often trained by the treating clinician on how to coach their partners through difficult periods, as well as how to support the recovery process in general. Clinicians can and should take the opportunity to address any relationship issues that may be contributing to the panic cycle (e.g., overprotectiveness, dependency) and assess the need for further conjoint therapy. Because no research studies are available on the use of marital or family therapy alone or with medication for the treatment of panic, no conclusions can be drawn about the efficacy of the approach.

CONCLUSION

The treatment of panic in crisis settings is ripe for the application of cognitive-behavioral interventions that build on coping skills. The techniques proposed in this chapter are suggested as adjuncts and alternatives to the sole reliance on pharmacotherapy in treating panic in crisis settings. Cognitive-behavioral techniques may prove to be most efficacious when used in conjunction with pharmacotherapy (Sharp, Power, & Simpson, 1996; Barlow et al.,1998).

It is recommended that the cognitive-behavioral techniques described in this article be considered prior to the use of pharmacologic agents whenever possible (Solkol, Beck, Greenberg, Wright, & Berchick, 1989). Medication may serve as an adjunct to cognitive-behavior therapy rather than the reverse. Continued research in this area is certainly warranted.

REFERENCES

Aguilera, D. C. (1990). *Crises intervention: Theory and methodology*, St. Louis, MO: Mosby.

Alford, B. A., Beck, A. T., Freeman, A., & Wright, F. (1990). Brief focused cognitive therapy of panic disorder. *Psychotherapy, 27*(2), 230–234.

American Psychiatric Association. (1993). *Diagnostic and statistical manual of mental disorders* (4th ed.). Washington, DC: Author.

Appleby, I. L., Klein, D. F., Sachar, E., & Levitt, M. (1981). Biochemical indices of lactate-induced panic: A preliminary report. In D. F. Klein & J. G Rabkin (Eds.), *Anxiety: New research and changing concepts.* New York: Raven Press.

Argyle, N. (1988). The nature of cognitions in panic disorder. *Behaviour Research and Therapy, 26,* 261–264.

Arnow, B. A., Taylor, C. B., & Agras, W. S. (1985). Enhancing agoraphobia treatment outcomes by changing couple communication patterns. *Behavior Therapy, 16,* 452–467.

Aronson, T. A., & Logue, C. M. (1988). Phenomenology of panic attacks: A descriptive study of panic disorder patients' self-reports. *Journal of Clinical Psychiatry, 49,* 8–13.

Arrindell, W., & Emmelkamp, P. (1986). Marital quality and general life adjustment in relation to treatment outcome in agoraphobia. *Advances in Behaviour Research and Therapy, 8,* 139–185.

Ascher, M. (1984). Paradox in behavior therapy: Some data and some possibilities. *Journal of Behavior Therapy and Experimental Psychiatry, 15*(5), 187.

Ballenger, J. C., Burrows, G. D., & Dupont, R. L. (1988). Alprozolam in panic disorder and agoraphobia: Results from a multicenter trial: Efficacy in short-term treatment. *Archives of General Psychiatry, 45,* 413–422.

Bandura, A. (1977). Self-efficacy: Toward a unifying theory of behavioral change. *Psychological Review, 84,* 191–215.

Barlow, D. H. (1988). *Anxiety and its disorders.* New York: Guilford Press.

Barlow, D. H., Gorman, J. M., Shear, M. K., & Woods, S. W. (1998, November). Study design and pretreatment attrition. In D. Barlow (Chair), *Results from the multicenter clinical trial on the treatment of panic disorder: Cognitive-behavior treatment versus imipramine versus their combination.* Symposium presented at the 32nd annual convention of the Association for Advancement of Behavior Therapy, Washington, DC.

Barlow, D. H., O'Brien, G. T., & Last, C. G. (1984). Couples treatment of agoraphobia in relation to marital adjustment. *Archives of General Psychiatry, 36,* 807–811.

Beck, A. T. (1987). *Anxiety inventory.* Philadelphia: Center for Cognitive Therapy.

Beck, A. T., Emery, G., & Greenberg, R. L. (1985). *Anxiety disorders and phobias.* New York: Guilford Press.

Beck, A. T., Freeman, A., & Associates. (1990). *Cognitive therapy of personality disorders.* New York: Guilford Press.

Beitman, B. D., DeRosear, L., Basha, I., Flaker, G., & Corcoran, C. (1987). Panic disorder with cardiology patients with atypical or non-anginal chest pain. *Journal of Anxiety Disorders, 1*(3), 277–282.

Borden, J. W., Clum, G. A., & Salmon, P. G. (1991). Mechanisms of change in the treatment of panic. *Cognitive Therapy and Research, 15*(4), 257–272.

Borkovec, T. D., & Grayson, J. B. (1980). Consequences of increasing the functional impact of emotional stimuli. In K. Blankstein, P. Pliner, & J. Polivy (Eds.), *Assessment and modification of emotional behavior* (pp. 328–343). New York: Plenum Press.

Boyd, J. H. (1986). Use of mental health services for the treatment of panic disorder. *American Journal of Psychiatry, 143,* 1569–1574.

Bradwejn, J., Koszycki, D., Payeur, R., Bourin, M., & Borthwick, H. (1992). Replication of action of cholecystokinin tetrapeptide in panic disorder: Clinical and behavioral findings. *American Journal of Psychiatry, 149,* 962–964.

Breir, A., Charney, D. S., & Heninger, G. B. (1984). Major depression in patients with agoraphobia and panic disorder. *Archives of General Psychiatry, 41,* 1129–1135.

Brown, C. S., Rakel, R. E., Well, B. G., Downs, J. M., & Akiskal, H. S. (1991). A practical update on anxiety disorders and their pharmacologic treatment. *Archives of Internal Medicine, 151,* 873–884.

Chambless, D. L., Caputo, G. C., Bright, P., & Gallagher, R. (1984). Assessment of fear in agoraphobia: The Body Sensations Questionnaire and the Agoraphobic Questionnaire. *Journal of Consulting and Clinical Psychology, 52,* 1090–1097.

Charney, D. S., Heninger, G. R., & Breier, A. (1984). Noradrenergic function of panic anxiety: Effects of yohimbine in healthy subjects and patients with agoraphobia and panic disorder. *Archives of General Psychiatry, 41,* 751–763.

Clark, D. M. (1986). A cognitive approach to panic. *Behaviour Research and Therapy, 24,* 461–470.

Clark, D. M., & Ehlers, A. (1993). An overview of the theory and treatment of panic. *Applied and Preventive Psychology, 2,* 131–139.

Clark, D. M., Salkovskis, P. M., & Chalkley, A. J. (1985). Respiratory control as a treatment for panic attacks. *Journal of Behavior Therapy and Experimental Psychiatry, 16,* 23–30.

Clum, G. A. (1990). *Coping with panic.* Pacific Grove, CA: Brooks/Cole.

Cohen, A. S., Barlow, D. H., & Blanchard, E. B. (1985). Psychophysiology of relaxation-associated panic attacks. *Journal of Abnormal Psychology, 94,* 96–101.

Craske, M. G., & Barlow, D. H. (1990). *Therapist guide for the mastery of anxiety and panic.* Albany, NY: University of Albany, State University of New York, Center for Stress and Anxiety Disorders.

Crowe, R. R., Noyes, R., Pauls, D. L., & Slymen, D. J. (1983). A family study of panic disorder. *Archives of General Psychiatry, 40,* 1065–1069.

DaCosta, J. M. (1871). On irritable heart: A clinical study of a functional cardiac disorder and its consequences. *American Journal of Medical Science, 61,* 17–52.

Dager, S. R., Cowley, D. S., & Dunner, D. L. (1987). Biological markers in panic states: Lactate-induced panic and mitral valve prolapse. *Biological Psychiatry, 22,* 339–359.

Dattilio, F. M. (1986). Differences in cognitive responses to fear among individuals diagnosed as panic disorder, generalized anxiety disorder, agoraphobia with panic attacks and simple phobia (Doctoral Dissertation, Temple University, 1986). *Dissertation Abstracts International, 48,* O3A.

Dattilio, F. M. (1987). The use of paradoxical intention in the treatment of panic attacks. *Journal of Counseling and Development, 66,* 66–67.

Dattilio, F. M. (1990). Symptom induction and de-escalation in the treatment of panic attacks. *Journal of Mental Health Counseling, 12*(4), 515–519.

Dattilio, F. M. (1992a). Interoceptive sensations during sexual arousal and panic. *The Behavior Therapist, 15*(9), 231–233.

Dattilio, F. M. (1992b). "The SAEB System"–Crises intervention techniques with panic. In *Crisis intervention.* Symposium presented at the 26th annual meeting of the Association for the Advancement of Behavior Therapy, Boston, MA.

Dattilio, F. M. (1994a). SAEB: A method of conceptualization in the treatment of panic. *Cognitive and Behavioral Practice, 1*(1), 179–191.

Dattilio, F. M. (1994b). *The use of the SAEB system and symptom induction in the treatment of panic* [Videotape, 58 minutes]. Sarasota, FL: Professional Resource Press.

Dattilio, F. M. (1994c). Paradoxical intention as a proposed alternative in the treatment of panic disorder. *Journal of Cognitive Psychotherapy, 8(1), 33–40.*

Dattilio, F. M., & Berchick, R. M. (1992). Panic disorder with agoraphobia. In A. Freeman & F. M. Dattilio (Eds.), *Comprehensive casebook of cognitive therapy,* (pp. 89–98). New York: Plenum.

Dattilio, F. M., & Kendall, P. C. (1994). Panic disorder. In F. M. Dattilio & A. Freeman (Eds.), *Cognitive-behavioral strategies in crisis intervention* (pp. 46–66). New York: Guilford Press.

Dattilio, F. M., & Salas-Auvert, J. A. (1999). Heart attack or panic attack? *ADAA Reporter, X*(3), 1–3.

Dattilio, F. M., & Salas-Auvert, J. A. (2000). *Panic disorder: Assessment and treatment through a wide-angle lens.* Phoenix, AZ: Zeig/Tucker.

Dell, P. F. (1981). Some irreverent thoughts on paradox. *Family Process, 20,* 37–42.

Diez, C., Gastó, C., & Vallejo, J. (1989). Desarrollo de conductas de evitación en un sujeto con crisis de angustia atipicas [Development of behavioral avoidance in a subject with atypical anxiety crisis]. *Revista de Psiquiatría de la Facultad de Medicina de Barcelona, 16*(6), 329–332.

DiNardo, P. A., Barlow, D. H., Cerny, J., Vermilyea, B. B., Vermilyea, J. A., Himadi, W., & Waddell, M. (1985). *Anxiety Disorders Interview Schedule–Revised (ADIS-R).* Albany, NY: Phobia and Anxiety Disorders Clinic, State University of New York at Albany.

Dowd, E. T., & Trutt, S. D. (1988). Paradoxical interventions in behavior modification. In M. Hersen, C. Eisler, & D. Miller (Eds.), *Progress in behavior modification* (Vol. 12, pp. 96–130). New York: Pergamon Press.

Dunner, D. L. (1985). Anxiety and panic: Relationship to depression and cardiac disorders. *Psychosomatics, 26,* 18–21.

Edinger, J. D., & Jacobsen, R. (1982). Incidence and significance of relaxation treatment side effects. *The Behavior Therapist, 5,* 137–138.

Efran, J. S., & Caputo, C. (1984). Paradox in psychotherapy: A cybernetic perspective. *Journal of Behavior Therapy and Experimental Psychiatry, 15*(3), 235–240.

Ehlers, A., & Breuer, P. (1992). Increased cardiac awareness in panic disorder. *Journal of Abnormal Psychology, 101*(3), 371–382.

Epstein, N. B., & Dutton, S. S. (1997, November). Relationship characteristics of agoraphobics and their partners. Paper presented at the 31st annual meeting of the Association for Advancement of Behavior Therapy, Miami, FL.

Epstein, N. B., Dutton, S. S., Dattilio, F. M., & Vittore, B. (in progress.) An analysis of relationship characteristics of agoraphobics and their spouses.

Feske, U., & Goldstein, A. J. (1997). Eye movement desensitization and reprocessing treatment for panic disorder: A controlled outcome and partial dismantling study. *Journal of Consulting and Clinical Psychology, 65*(6)1–10.

Frankl, V. E. (1975). Paradoxical intention and de-reflection. *Psychotherapy: Theory, research and practice, 12,* 226–237.

Frankl, V. E. (1984). Paradoxical intention. In G. R. Weeks (Ed.), *Promoting change through paradoxical therapy.* Homewood, IL: Dow Jones-Irwin.

Goldenberg, H. (1983). *Contemporary clinical psychology.* Pacific Grove, CA: Brooks/Cole.

Goldstein, A. J., & Chambless, D. L. (1978). A reanalysis of agoraphobia. *Behavior Therapy, 9,* 47–59.

Goldstein, A. J., & Feske, U. (1994). Eye movement desensitization and reprocessing for panic disorder: A case series. *Journal of Anxiety Disorders, 8,* 351–362.

Goldstein, R. B., Wickramaratne, P. J., Horwath, E., & Weissman, M. M. (1997). Familial aggregation and phenomenology of "early onset" (at or before age 20 years) panic disorder. *Archives of General Psychiatry, 54,* 271–278.

Gould, R. A., Clum, G. A., & Shapiro, D. (1993). The use of bibliotherapy in the treatment of panic: A preliminary investigation. *Behavior Therapy, 24,* 241–252.

Gray, J. A. (1982). *The neuropsychology of anxiety.* Oxford: Clarendon.

Greenberg, R. L. (1989). Panic disorder and agoraphobia. In J. Scott, J. M. G. Williams, & A. T. Beck (Eds.), *Cognitive therapy in clinical practice: An illustrative casebook* (pp. 25–49). London: Routledge & Kegan Paul.

Hamilton, S. P., Heiman, G. A., Haghighi, F. G., Mick, S., Klein, D. F., Hodge, S. E., Weissman, M. M., Fyer, A. J., & Knowles, J. A. (1999). Lack of genetic linkage or association between functional serotonin transporter polymorphism and panic disorder. *Psychiatric Genetics, 9,* 1–6.

Heide, F. J., & Borkovec, T. D. (1983). Relaxation-induced anxiety: Paradoxical anxiety enhancement due to relaxation training. *Journal of Consulting and Clinical Psychology, 51,* 171–182.

Hibbert, G. A. (1984). Hyperventilation as a cause of panic attacks. *British Medical Journal, 288,* 263–264.

Himadi, W. G., Boice, R., & Barlow, D. H. (1986). Assessment of agoraphobia–II: Measurement of clinical change. *Behaviour Research and Therapy, 24*(3), 321–332.

Katon, W. (1992). *Panic disorder in the medical setting.* Rockville, MD: NIMH Publication.

Katon, W., & Kleinman, A. M. (1980). Doctor–patient negotiation and other social science strategies in patient care. In L. Eisenberg & A. M. Kleinman (Eds.), *The relevance of social science for medicine* (pp. 253–259). Datrecht, Holland: D. Reidel.

Kendall, P. C., & Hammen, R. (1999). *Abnormal psychology.* Boston: Houghton-Mifflin.

Kendall, P. C., & Norton-Ford, J. D. (1982). *Clinical psychology: Scientific and professional dimensions.* New York: Wiley.

Kerr, W. J., Dalton, J. W., & Gliebe, P. A. (1937). Some physical phenomena associated with anxiety states and their relation to hyperventilation. *Annals of Internal Medicine, 11,* 961–992.

Kiselica, M. S., & Baker, S. B. (1992). Progressive muscle relaxation and cognitive restructuring: Potential problems and proposed solutions. *Journal of Mental Health Counseling, 14*(2), 149–165.

Knowles, J. A., Fyer, A. J., Vieland, V. J., Weissman, M. M., Hodge, S. E., Heiman, G. A., Haghighi, F., deJesus, G. M., Rassnick, H., Preud'homme-Rivelli, X., Austin, T., Cunjak, J., Mick, S., Fine, L. D., Woodley, K. A., Das, K., Maier, W., Adams, P. B., Freimer, N. B., Klein, D. F., & Gillima, T. C. (1998). Results of a genome-wide genetic screen for panic disorder. *American Journal of Genetics, 81,*139–147.

Knowles, J. A., & Weissman, M. M. (1995). Panic disorder and agoraphobia in J. M. Oldham & M. B. Riba (Eds.), *Review of psychiatry* (Vol. 14, pp. 383–404). Washington, DC: American Psychiatric Press.

Kocmur, M., & Zavasnik, A. (1991, April). Patients' experience of the therapeutic process in a crisis intervention unit. *Crises, 12*(1), 69–81.

Lange, A., & Van Dyck, R. (1992). The function of agoraphobia in marital relationship. *Acta Psychiatrica Scandinavica, 85,* 89–93.

Lazarus, A. A., & Mayne, T. J. (1990). Relaxation: Some limitations, side effects and proposed solutions. *Psychotherapy, 27*(2), 261–266.

Ley, R. A. (1985). Blood, breath and fears: A hyperventilation theory of panic attacks and agoraphobia. *Clinical Psychology Review, 5,* 271–285.

Ley, R. A. (1986). Hyperventilation and lactate infusion in the production of panic attacks. *Clinical Psychology Review, 8,* 1–18.

Liebowitz, M. R., Fryer, A. B., & Goman, J. M. (1986). Alprazolam in the treatment of panic disorder. *Journal of Clinical Psychopharmacology, 6,* 13–20.

Lidrin, D. M., Watkins, P., Gould, R. A., Clum, G. A., Asterino, M., & Tulloch, H. L. (1994). A comparison of bibliotherapy and group therapy in the treatment of panic disorder. *Journal of Consulting and Clinical Psychology, 62,* 865–869.

Lum, L. (1981). Hyperventilation and anxiety state. *Journal of the Royal Society of Medicine, 74,* 1–4.

Lydiard, R. B., & Ballenger, T. C. (1987). Antidepressants in panic disorder and agoraphobia. *Journal of Affective Disorders, 13,* 153–168.

Margraf, J., & Ehlers, A. (1989). Etiology models of panic: Medical and biological aspects. In R. Baker (Ed.), *Panic disorder: Theory, research, and therapy.* Chichester, UK: Wiley.

Oppenheimer, B. S., & Rothschild, M. A. (1918). The psychoneurotic factor in irritable heart of soldiers. *Journal of the American Medical Association, 70,* 1919–1922.

Ottaviani, R., & Beck, A. T. (1987). Cognitive aspects of panic disorders. *Journal of Anxiety Disorders, 1,* 15–28.

Pitts, F. N., & McClure, J. N. (1967). Lactate metabolism in anxiety neurosis. *New England Journal of Medicine, 277,* 1329–1336.

Prince, M., & Putnam, J. J. (1912). A clinical study of a case of phobia: A symposium. *Journal of Abnormal Social Psychology, 7,* 259–292.

Raskin, M., Peeke, H. V., Dickman, W., & Pinsker, H. (1982). Panic and generalized anxiety disorders: Developmental antecedents and precipitants. *Archives of General Psychiatry, 39,* 687–689.

Regier, D. A., Boyd, J. H., Burke, J. D., Rae, D. S., Myers, J. K., Kramer, M., Robins, L. N., Karno, M., & Locke, B. Z. (1988). One-month prevalence of mental disorders in the United States: Based on five epidemiologic catchment area sites. *Archives of General Psychiatry, 45,* 977–986.

Reiss, S., Peterson, R. A., Gursky, D. M., & McNally, R. J. (1986). Anxiety sensitivity, anxiety frequency and the prediction of fearfulness. *Behaviour Research and Therapy, 24,* 1–8.

Roberts, A. R. (Eds.). (1990). *Crises intervention handbook: Assessment, treatment and research.* Belmont, CA: Wadsworth.

Rosenman, R. H. (1985). The impact of anxiety on the cardiovascular system. *Psychosomatics, 26,* 6–17.

Roy-Byrne, P. P., Cowley, D. S. and Katon, W. (in press) Pharmacotherapy of anxiety disorders. In *Textbook of therapeutic medicine for practicing physicians.*

Sexton, T. L., Montgomery, D., Goff, K., & Nugent, W. (1993). Ethical, therapeutic and legal considerations in the use of paradoxical techniques: The emerging debate. *Journal of Mental Health Counseling, 15*(3), 260–277.

Shapiro, F. (1986). Eye movement desensitization and reprocessing: Evaluation of controlled PTSD research. *Journal of Behavior Therapy and Experimental Psychiatry, 27,* 209–218.

Shapiro, F. (1998). Eye movement desensitization and reprocessing (EMDR): Historical context, recent research, and future directions. In L. VandeCreek & T. Jackson (Eds.), *Innovations in clinical practice: A sourcebook* (Vol. 16, pp. 211–217). Sarasota, FL: Professional Resource Press.

Shapiro, F., & Forrest, M. S. (1997). *EMDR: The breakthrough therapy.* New York: Basic Books.

Sharp, D. M., Power, K. G., & Simpson, R. J. (1996). Fluvoxamine, placebo, and cognitive behaviour therapy used alone and in combination in the treatment of panic disorder and agoraphobia. *Journal of Anxiety Disorder, 10,* 219–242.

Sheehan, D. V. (1982). Panic attacks and phobias. *New England Journal of Medicine, 307,* 156–158.

Skerrit, P. W. (1983). Anxiety and the heart—A historical review. *Psychological Medicine, 13,* 17–25.

Skolnick, P., & Paul, S. M. (1983). New concepts in the neurobiology of anxiety. *Journal of Clinical Psychiatry, 44,* 12–19.

Solkol, L., Beck, A. T., Greenberg, R. L., Wright, F. D., & Berchick, R. J. (1989). Cognitive therapy of panic disorder: A nonpharmacological alternative. *Journal of Nervous and Mental Disease, 177,* 711–716.

Spitzer, R. L., & Williams, J. B. W. (1986). *Structured Clinical Interview for DSM-III-R, Upjohn Version (SCID-UP-R).* New York: New York State Psychiatric Institute, Biometrics Research.

Spitzer, R. L., Williams, J. B. W., & Gibbon, M. (1985). *Instructional manual for the Structured Clinical Interview Schedule for DSM-III (SCID, 7/1/85 Revision).* New York: New York State Psychiatric Institute.

Svensson, T. H. (1987). Peripheral, autonomic regulation of locus coeruleus noradrenergic neurons in the brain: Putative implications for psychiatry and psychopharmacology. *Psychopharmacology, 92,* 1–7.

Swinson, R. P., Soulios, C., Cox, B. J., & Kuch, K. (1992). Brief treatment of emergency room patients with panic attacks. *American Journal of Psychiatry, 149,* 944–946.

Telch, M. J., Lucas, J. A., Schmidt, N. B., Hanna, H. H., Jaimez, T. L., & Lucas, R. A. (1993). Group cognitive-behavioral treatment of panic disorder. *Behaviour Research and Therapy, 31*(3), 279–287.

Thorpe, G. L., & Burns, L. E. (1983). *The agorgaphobic syndrome.* New York: Wiley.

Von Korff, M., Shapiro, S., Burke, J. D., Teitelbaum, M., Skinner, E. A., German, P., Turner, R. W., Klein, L., Burns, B. (1987). Anxiety and depression in a primary care clinic: Comparison of Diagnostic Interview Schedule, General Health Questionnaire, and practitioner assessments. *Archives of General Psychiatry, 44,* 152–156.

Wardle, J. (1990). Behavior therapy and benzodiazepines: Allies or antagonists? *British Journal of Psychiatry, 156,* 163–168.

Wayne, G. J. (1966). The psychiatric emergency: An overview. In G. J. Wayne & R. R. Koegler (Eds.), *Emergency psychiatric and brief therapy* (p. 321). Boston: Little, Brown.

Weiss, S. R. B., & Uhde, T. W. (1990). Annual models of anxiety. In J. C. Ballanger (Ed.), *Neurobiology of panic disorder* (pp. 3–27). New York: Wiley-Liss.

Weissman, M. M. (1993, Supp. 1). Family genetic studies of panic disorder. *Journal of Psychiatric Research, 27,* 69–78.

Weissman, M. M., & Merikangas, K. R. (1986, June, Supp. 1). The epidemiology of anxiety and panic disorders: An update. *Journal of Clinical Psychiatry, 47,* 1–7.

Westphal, C. (1871). Die Agoraphobie, eine Neuropathische Erscheinung [Agoraphobia, A neurological discovery]. *Archiv für Psychiatrie und Nervenkrankheiten, 3,* 138–161.

White, J. (in press). "Stress control" large group therapy for generalized anxiety disorder: Two year follow-up. *Journal of Mental Health.*

White, J., Keenan, M., & Brooks, N. (1992). Stress control: A controlled comparative investigation of large group therapy for generalized anxiety disorder. *Behavioral Psychotherapy, 20,* 97–114.

Wilson, R. (1986). *Don't panic: Taking control of anxiety attacks.* New York: Rawson.

Wolpe, J. (1958). *Psychotherapy by reciprocal inhibition.* Stanford, CA: Stanford University Press.

Wolpe, J. (1970). Identifying the antecedents of an agoraphobic reaction: A transcript. *Journal of Behavior Therapy and Experimental Psychiatry, 1,* 229–304.

Zitrin, C. M., Klein, D. F., & Woerner, M. G. (1978). Behavior therapy, supportive psychotherapy, imipramine and phobias. *Archives of General Psychiatry, 35,* 107–116.

Zung, W. W. K. (1975). A rating instrument for anxiety disorders. *Psychosomatics, 12,* 371–379.

SUGGESTED READINGS

Dattilio, F. M. (1994a). SAEB: A method of conceptualization in the treatment of panic. *Cognitive and Behavioral Practice, 1*(1), 179–191.

Dattilio, F. M., & Salas-Auvert, J. A. (2000). *Panic disorder: Assessment and intervention through a wide-angle lens.* Phoenix, AZ: Zeig/Tucker.

Wilson, R. (1986). *Don't panic: Taking control of anxiety attacks.* New York: Rawson.

4

Suicide and Depression

Mark A. Reinecke

How small a thought it takes to fill someone's whole life! Just as a man can spend his life traveling around the same little country and think there is nothing outside it! You see everything in strange perspective (or projection): the country that you keep traveling around strikes you as enormously big; the surrounding countries all look like narrow border regions. If you want to go down deep you do not need to travel far; indeed, you don't have to leave your most immediate and familiar surroundings.

—WITTGENSTEIN (1946/1980, p. 50)

When Ludwig Wittgenstein wrote the above passage in 1946, he was commenting on the ways in which focusing on a specific philosophical issue can lead to a misperception of the larger world. One can come to view everything from the perspective of the issue or thought (which, from an external point of view may appear relatively small and unimportant). One becomes focused upon it. Traveling deeper and deeper, one becomes fixated on the issue, and the outer world becomes a narrow borderland. His point is well taken. Our experience of ourselves and our world is guided by our inner language and the issues we identify as important. As a small thought may fill a life with meaning, value, and richness, so too can it end it. "I just can't take it anymore and there's nothing I can do, I might as well be dead." Simple statements such as this are frightening, both for individuals who feel that there is no solution for their problems other than their own destruction and for the therapist who must address them. Decisions about patients who are considering suicide, or who have made a suicide attempt, must be made rapidly. There is little room for error. Suicidality can, as such, represent a crisis for the therapist as it is for the patient.

Slaiku (1990) defined a crisis as "a temporary state of upset and disorganization, characterized chiefly by an individual's inability to cope with a particular situation using customary methods of problem solving, and by the potential for a radically positive or negative outcome." The four components of a crisis— its transient nature, the accompanying state of disorganization and distress, the failure of customary solutions or problem-solving skills, and the opportunity for reintegration and a positive outcome—apply both to our understanding of suicidality and to its treatment. Suicidal crises are, in most cases, time limited. Although suicidal thoughts may persist for extended periods of time, the intense and highly charged "urge to act," as well as the internal sense of being unable to control or resist the impulses, often subsides after a relatively short period. With support and strategic interventions, the accompanying feelings of distress can be alleviated. New problem-solving skills can be developed such that there is an opportunity for a positive outcome. With preparation and the refinement of coping skills, future crises can be averted. The goal of this chapter, is threefold: first, to review the recent literature on factors associated with suicidal risk; second, to provide clinicians with useful tools and recommendations for managing suicidal crises; and third, to provide guidelines for treating suicidal patients. The latter, crisis management and longer-term treatment, can be viewed as separate but related processes. The primary goal in managing a suicidal crisis is to protect patients from themselves—to ensure their survival. Protection can be accomplished in several ways: hospitalization, medications, intensive outpatient therapy, alleviation of stressors or problems that may have precipitated the crisis, and development of a more supportive and secure environment. Treatment of suicidal patients involves identification and resolution of factors that have contributed to their suicidality. It is not sufficient to simply alleviate the stressors that have contributed to the current suicidal episode. Other problems or stressors may arise in the future. Rather, the goal of treatment is to identify factors that lead individuals to consider suicide a viable alternative and to develop other strategies for coping with the problems and stresses of life. This is a longer-term goal and is typically addressed once the patient has been stabilized and the immediate crisis has passed.

Crisis situations are varied and highly personal, and they tend to fluctuate over time. Thus it would be difficult to prepare a list of specific "rules" for their management. Rather, an attempt will be made to draw on contemporary cognitive-behavioral theory for guidelines that can be used in a flexible, creative manner. Suicidality among children and adolescents is an increasingly important problem; however, a review of the literature is beyond the scope of this chapter. (See Berman & Jobes, 1991; Brent & Kolko, 1990; Freeman & Reinecke, 1993; Overholser & Spirito, 1990; Piacentini, Rotheram-Borus, & Cantwell, 1995; Spirito, Overholser, & Vinnick, 1995; and Trautman, 1995, for thoughtful discussions of cognitive-behavioral approaches for assessing and treating suicidal youth.)

COGNITIVE MODELS OF DEPRESSION AND SUICIDE

At the most basic level, cognitive models of psychopathology are based on the assumption that there is an interaction between how individuals think and how they subsequently feel and behave. Individuals' assumptions, schemata, memories, beliefs, goals, attributions, expectations, wishes, plans, inferences, and perceptual biases all influence how they respond, behaviorally and emotionally, to events in their world. These cognitive processes are adaptive, selective, and automatic. Emotional and behavioral problems, including suicidality, are seen as stemming from distorted or maladaptive mental representations and thought processes that were learned at an earlier point in time.

Clinically, the therapist's objective is to assist the patient to identify these maladaptive cognitive processes and dysfunctional beliefs, and to encourage the development of more adaptive or functional beliefs and coping skills. Although the emphasis is on understanding and changing beliefs, expectations, assumptions, and schemata, cognitive therapy acknowledges the importance of attending to social, environmental, biological, emotional, and behavioral factors that may be contributing to the patient's distress.

Both research and clinical observation suggest a strong link between depression and suicidality. More than 80% of persons who commit suicide are depressed at the time of their attempt (Murphy, 1985), and an early review of follow-up studies by Guze and Robins (1970) suggested that the lifetime incidence of suicide among clinically depressed persons is 15%. A more recent study by Klerman (1987) indicated that fully 30% of patients with a major affective disorder die by suicide. This rate is three to four times higher than that for other psychiatric conditions, and is more than 20 times higher than seen in the general population (Pokorny, 1964; Roy, 1986; Sainsbury, 1986). Why might this be?

Research initiated by Aaron Beck in the early 1960s (1967, 1973, 1976) suggests that depressed individuals experience a range of negativistic thoughts about themselves, their world or experience, and their future. They tend to view themselves as flawed in important ways and believe that others are rejecting or unsupportive. As a consequence, they tend to believe that they do not possess the resources to resolve their difficulties and they view their future as hopeless. In an attempt to preserve what resources they retain, they become passive or withdrawn and tend to seek reassurance from others. Their depressed affect biases their memory, such that they selectively recall other instances of failure in their past (Bower, 1981), as well as their perceptions of current events (Beck, Rush, Shaw, & Emery, 1979). The dark lens of negativistic beliefs leads depressed individuals to perceive that they lack control over important events in their life, leading them to feel helpless (Abramson, Metalsky, & Alloy, 1989). Recent prospective studies indicate that cognitive factors may increase an individual's vulnerability to both depression and suicide (Abramson et al., 1998; Alloy, Abramson, Murray, Whitehouse, & Hogan, 1997; Alloy et al., 1999; Priester & Clum, 1993).

Depressed individuals tend to pay attention to the immediate (rather than the delayed) consequences of their behavior and may make inappropriate attributions about their responsibility for negative events. Depressed individuals tend not to reward themselves for their successes and can become highly self-punitive when they fail to meet their standards or goals (Fuchs & Rehm, 1977; Rehm, 1977). They tend to view themselves in negative ways and demonstrate high levels of discrepancy between how they view themselves and how they feel they "ought" to be or should "ideally" be.

Given these beliefs, expectations, self-appraisals, and attributions, highly depressed individuals can become suicidal. They feel that their current predicament is intolerable and believe there is no hope for it to change. As a consequence, suicide becomes a viable solution. They believe that their attempt will communicate their distress to others and so may effect a change in the environment, or that it will provide them with a sense of relief from their problems. As Shneidman (1985) cogently observed, "The common stimulus in suicide is unendurable psychological pain" (p. 124), and the "common purpose is to seek a solution" (p. 129). Cognitive therapy, as such, is directed toward alleviating specific cognitive biases and distortions, developing behavioral skills, reducing environmental stress, developing supports, and assisting patients to communicate their concerns to others more clearly and adaptively.

Suicide, from this perspective, is a state of mind. We must adopt this perspective if we are to understand and address it. In addition to the cognitive distortions often associated with feelings of depression, there are several other cognitive distortions that appear to contribute to the risk of suicide. Most prominent among these is "tunnel vision" or "constriction" (Shneidman, 1985)—the inability to see alternative courses of action and outcomes—and "dichotomous thinking." Studies suggest that suicidal individuals tend to categorize events or experiences into polar extremes. They rigidly adopt an absolutistic, black-or-white perspective and experience difficulty acknowledging nuances, subtleties, or relativistic alternatives (Neuringer, 1968; Neuringer & Lettieri, 1971; Wetzel, 1976). Moreover, suicidal individuals appear to manifest increased levels of irrational or dysfunctional beliefs (Prezant & Neimeyer, 1988), and behave in an impulsive manner (Ellis & Ratliff, 1986; Linehan, Camper, Chiles, Strosahl, & Shearin, 1987; Patsiokas, Clum, & Luscomb, 1979; Schotte & Clum, 1987). Recent work indicates that they may also experience deficits in "positive future thinking" (MacLeod et al., 1998). The cognitive model posits that an individual's beliefs are heavily influenced by his/her social experiences, and that dysfunctional attitudes develop in a social context. Depressed and suicidal patients tend to withdraw from others and report feeling that their families are not cohesive or supportive. These social difficulties serve to exacerbate their feelings of alienation and provide further evidence for their beliefs that others are rejecting.

A number of studies indicate that suicidal individuals may demonstrate deficits in social problem solving. It has been postulated that these difficulties may interact with hopelessness and stressful life events in placing individuals at risk for suicidal thoughts and behavior. Specific deficits have been observed in problem-solving orientation, confidence in being able to solve problems, generating alternative solutions, and use of "active" problem-solving strategies (Bonner & Rich, 1988; Clum & Febbraro, 1994; Dixon, Heppner & Anderson, 1991; Linehan et al., 1987; Orbach, Bar-Joseph, & Dror, 1990; Pollock & Williams, 1988; Priester & Clum, 1993; Rudd, Rjab, & Dahm, 1994; Schotte & Clum, 1987). Although it is not clear that problem-solving deficits are stable predictors of suicidal behavior (Schotte, Cools, & Payvar, 1990), they can play an important role in the treatment process (Lerner & Clum, 1990; Salkovskis, Atha, & Storer, 1990).

THE ROLE OF HOPELESSNESS

An extensive body of research suggests that hopelessness is an important mediator of suicide among adults. Hopelessness, which may be defined as a general set of negative expectancies about oneself and the future, appears to be both a concomitant of depression and a predictor of suicidal behavior (Beck, 1967, 1986; Dyer & Kreitman, 1984; Weishaar & Beck, 1992). Hopelessness has been found, for example, to be a more powerful predictor of suicidal intent than is depression among suicidal ideators (Bedrosian & Beck, 1979; Nekanda-Trepka, Bishop, & Blackburn, 1983; Wetzel, Margulies, Davis, & Karam, 1980) and nonreferred adults (Cole, 1988; Joiner & Rudd, 1996). It has been found to predict eventual suicide among individuals diagnosed with major affective disorders (Fawcett et al., 1987), schizophrenia (Drake & Cotton, 1986), and alcohol abuse (Beck, Weissman, & Kovacs, 1976). Moreover, it appears to discriminate suicidal from nonsuicidal patients with equivalent levels of depression (Ellis & Ratliff, 1986). Hopelessness appears to be a strong predictor of suicide among patients who have made a prior suicide attempt (Beck, Kovacs, & Weissman, 1975; Dyer & Kreitman, 1984; Goldney, 1979; Kovacs, Beck, & Weissman, 1975; Minkoff, Bergman, Beck, & Beck, 1973; Petrie & Chamberlain, 1983; Weissman, Beck, & Kovacs, 1979; Wetzel, 1976). Finally, longitudinal studies suggest that hopelessness may be a useful long-term predictor of completed suicide (Beck, Brown, & Steer, 1989; Beck & Steer, 1989; Fawcett et al., 1990).

Taken together, these findings are impressive and compelling. They suggest that hopelessness may be a useful predictor of suicidal risk among adults, and that feelings of pessimism may be an important target for therapy (Freeman & Reinecke, 1993). In a prospective study of 1958 outpatients, for example, hopelessness was found to be strongly associated with eventual suicide (Beck, Brown, Berchick, Stewart, & Steer, 1990). Given the large sample employed, the authors were able to use statistical techniques derived from signal detection theory to determine optimum cutoff scores for both the Beck Depression Inventory (BDI) and the Beck Hopelessness Scale (HS) for predicting suicide. Employing receiver operating characteristic curves, they found that a cutoff score of 9 or above on the HS and 23 or above on the BDI yielded an accurate prediction of suicidal risk. Although the BDI had greater specificity, the HS had superior sensitivity in predicting ultimate suicide. The authors suggest that these findings indicate that hopelessness "is more directly related than is depression alone to suicidal intent" (Beck et al., 1990, p. 193). These findings are congruent with those of an earlier prospective study of 165 adults who had been hospitalized due to suicidal ideations (Beck et al., 1985). Of the 11 patients who committed suicide over a 10-year follow-up period, 10 (90%) had HS scores greater than 9. Only one patient who ultimately committed suicide received a hopelessness score below 10. Similar results have been found in prospective studies of psychiatric outpatients. In a study of 2,174 adults, Beck (1986) found that a cutoff score of 10 correctly identified 9 of 10 eventual suicides, yielding a false negative rate of 10%. Of concern, however, was the fact that 1,137 of the 2,164 patients who did not commit suicide (52.5%) also received HS scores of 10 or above. The specificity rate for this cutoff score, then, was 47.5%—unacceptably high for most clinical practices. Beck observed that a more stringent criteria—a cutoff score of 17 or above—identifies a "high-risk group" whose rate of eventual suicide is 15 times greater than that of other outpatients.

Recent work suggests that there may be both state and trait components to scores on the HS (Young et al., 1996). In a study of 316 adults, they found that patients manifest a relatively stable, "trait" level of hopelessness when they are not depressed, as well as an incremental, "state-dependent" increase in pessimism that accompanies the depressive episode. Patients' baseline or "trait" level of hopelessness predicted future suicide attempts, whereas the incremental increase and total score did not. It appears, then, that patients who maintain a chronic, pessimistic outlook may be at higher risk for suicidal gestures and attempts than are patients who do not. This study suggests that it may be useful to assess "how pessimistic is this patient when not depressed, and how much more hopeless do they become during the depressive episode?" Taken together, these findings indicate that hopelessness might best be viewed as a predictor of suicidal potential rather than a predictor of a specific behavior at a specific time. It can be used, in conjunction with other clinical information, in estimating suicidal risk.

It is worth acknowledging that although hopelessness appears to be a strong predictor of suicidal risk among adults, equivocal findings have been reported (Kennedy & Reinecke, 1998). Robust relationships between hopelessness and suicidality are most often found among patients with a history of suicidal gestures and among more severely depressed inpatients and outpatients. Research with the elderly (Uncapher, Gallagher-Thompson, Osgood, & Bongar, 1998), adolescents (Rotheram-Borus & Trautman, 1988), prison inmates (Ivanoff & Jang, 1991), and college students (Bonner & Rich, 1987; Rich & Bonner, 1987), however, are less consistent. Taken together, these findings highlight the importance of considering depression and hopelessness simultaneously when assessing and treating suicidal adults, and of viewing hopelessness within the context of a broader range of cognitive, social, and psychiatric risk factors.

TOWARD AN INTEGRATED MODEL OF RISK

A number of psychiatric, social, environmental, and cognitive factors are associated with severity of suicidal thoughts, and they may serve as predictors of suicidal risk. Although studies have tended to examine these variables in isolation, recent work based upon diathesis-stress models of psychopathology suggests that these factors may interact in contributing to vulnerability for suicide. In an early attempt to evaluate an integrative model, Rudd (1990) found that stressful life events were significant predictors of both depression and hopelessness, which, in turn, mediated the relationship between negative life events and severity of suicidal thoughts. Significant relationships were also observed between perceived social support, life events, and suicidality. In a similar manner, Clum and Febbraro (1994) found that stressful life events, social support, and social problem-solving skills interacted in predicting severity of suicidality in a sample of 59 chronically suicidal college students. This was congruent with observations by Yang and Clum (1994), who found that social support and problem-solving skills may mediate relationships between stressful life events and suicidal ideations among young adults. Attributional style has also been found to interact with stressful life events in predicting levels of depression, hopelessness, and suicidality among college students (Joiner & Rudd, 1995).

It has been nearly 15 years since Ellis (1986) suggested that the pattern of cognitive deficits observed among suicidal patients may distinguish them from other individuals, and that these differences may warrant developing distinct treatment programs for suicidal patients. It appears that the cognitive characteristics of suicidal patients he described—problem-solving deficits, cognitive rigidity, cognitive distortions, a view of suicide as a viable solution, and hopelessness—may interact with stressful life events, behavioral impulsivity, and the perceived lack of social supports in placing individuals at risk. Although the specific relationships among these factors are not yet known, the general outlines of an integrated model of vulnerability and treatment are beginning to emerge.

SOCIAL AND PSYCHIATRIC RISK FACTORS

A number of social and psychiatric factors have also been identified that place a person at risk for suicide. As Pokorny (1986) observed, however, suicidality does not represent a singular entity but reflects a continuum from ideation to attempt to completed suicide. Research suggests that meaningful differences exist between individuals who think about suicide (ideators) and those who attempt or complete the act. These three groups—ideators, attempters, and completers—are, in important ways, independent and distinct. It is worth keeping in mind, then, that different factors may be associated with risk for each of these groups. Moreover, differences appear to exist within each of these groups with regard to the individual's level of intent, lethality of means, the presence of mitigating circumstances, and the availability of deterrents. As such, it is essential that one adopt an individualized or idiographic approach to assessing suicidality.

Finally, it is important to define what is meant by a risk factor or predictor. Risk factors may be thought of as experiences, events, or propensities that make a particular outcome—in this case, an attempted or completed suicide—more likely. They may play causal roles in the development of the crisis—that is, they may be necessary and/or sufficient for the person to become suicidal. On the other hand, they may simply be contributory. That is, they increase the likelihood of a suicide attempt but are neither necessary nor sufficient for the act to occur. Causal factors may be proximal or distal. That is, they may have occurred immediately before the onset of the suicidal crisis (e.g., an executive who is fired for embezzlement then borrows a gun to commit suicide) or more remote in the patient's past. Both prospective and retrospective studies suggest, for example, that stressful life events (including work or legal problems, humiliating social events, the recent loss of a loved one, and changes of residence) are associated with an increased risk of suicide (Hagnell & Rorsman, 1980). It is also known that the loss of a parent during childhood increases the risk of suicide years later (Adam, Bouckoms, & Streiner, 1982; Adam, Lohrenz, Harper, & Streiner, 1982; Goldney, 1981; Roy, 1984). These findings are important in that negative early experiences—including family psychopathology, negative peer relationships, abuse and neglect, family instability, and a chaotic home environment—appear to be associated with both cognitive markers of vulnerability and later suicidal behavior (Yang & Clum, 1996).

Factors that are predictive of suicide in the short term differ from those that are associated with risk over longer periods. With these considerations in mind, consider Tuckman and Youngman's (1968) list of risk factors for suicide. Based on a 5-year follow-up of 3,800 persons who attempted suicide, they identified 17 variables that are associated with a later completed suicide:

Over 45 years of age
Male
Caucasian
Separated, divorced, or widowed
Lives alone
Unemployed or retired
Medical problems during the past 6 months
Mood disorder, alcoholism, or other mental problems
Has received medical care during the past 6 months
Attempted suicide by firearms, jumping, or drowning
Attempt made during warm months
Attempt made during daylight
Attempt made at own or other's home

Person reported the attempt almost immediately
Person denies the intent to kill self
Suicide note
Prior suicide attempt

One point is scored for each of the risk factors identified, with the total score indicative of the degree of risk of a completed suicide. A score of 5 to 9 was seen as suggestive of moderate risk, whereas a score of 9 or higher indicated high risk. As can be seen, demographic variables, stressful life events, and psychiatric history are predictive of suicidal risk among individuals who made a prior attempt.

Several years later, Weisman and Worden (1974) developed a second scale for assessing suicidal risk among individuals who made a suicide attempt. Their scale includes both risk and rescue factors and is unique in that weighted values are assigned to each item. Risk factors center on the nature and lethality of the means employed in the suicide attempt, whether it resulted in an impaired consciousness, the severity and reversibility of the damage actually inflicted by the attempt, and the nature of the treatment required. Rescue factors include the location of the attempt, the availability of "rescuers," and the length of time that elapsed between the attempt and its discovery. A ratio of risk/rescue is then derived that can be used, in conjunction with other scales and clinical data, in estimating suicide risk. This study expands on research into demographic and social variables associated with suicide by suggesting that factors associated with the suicide attempt itself may be useful in predicting later attempts. In a provocative study of individuals who attempted suicide by overdose, Buglass and Horton (1974) identified six factors associated with an increased risk of future suicide attempts:

1. Problems with the use of alcohol
2. Sociopathic personality disorder
3. Previous inpatient psychiatric treatment
4. Previous outpatient psychiatric treatment
5. Previous suicide attempts resulting in hospital admission
6. Not living with a relative

The probability of an additional suicide attempt during a 1-year follow-up period ranged from 5% for individuals who received a score of 0 to approximately 45% for those who scored 5 or 6. This scale was cross-validated by Garzotto, Siani, Zimmerman-Tansella, and Tansella (1976) and Siani, Garzotto, Zimmerman-Tansella, and Tansella (1979). Once again, psychiatric and social factors (in this case, social isolation) were found to be strong predictors of suicidal behavior. More recently, Fawcett et al. (1987), in a prospective study of 929 clinically depressed patients, found that hopelessness, anhedonia, and mood cycling were predictive of completed suicide during the 12 months after a suicide attempt.

Taken together, these studies suggest that a number of variables—including demographic, social, environmental, behavioral, psychiatric, and psychological factors—are associated with risk of suicide (Buerk, Kurz, & Moeller, 1985). In a suicidal crisis, each of these domains should be assessed. Caution should be taken, however, when employing such scales because the limited reliability of individual items may reduce the utility of the scales for predicting suicide attempts in some populations (Spirito, Brown, Overholser, & Fritz, 1991).

As noted, individuals with a diagnosable psychiatric disorder are at an increased risk of attempting suicide. The risk is greatest among individuals with depression, schizophrenia, alcoholism, substance abuse, or a personality disorder (Caldwell & Gottesman, 1990; Holding, Buglass, Duffy, & Kreitman, 1977; Klerman, 1987; Miles, 1977; Morgan et al., 1975; Robins, 1985, 1986; Roy & Linnoila, 1986; Roy, Lamparski, DeJong, Moore, & Linnoila, 1990). Although discrepant findings have been reported (Beck, Steer, Sanderson, & Skeie, 1991; Friedman, Jones, Chernen, & Barlow, 1992), recent studies suggest that individuals suffering from panic disorder may also be at an increased risk of attempting suicide (Friedman, Smith, & Fogel, 1999; Korn, Plutchik, & Van Praag, 1997; Agarguen & Kara, 1996; Hornig & McNally, 1995; Appleby, 1994). With this in mind, a careful diagnostic assessment is recommended as part of an evaluation of suicide risk.

Recent research with a nonpsychiatric sample of young adults suggests that many chronically suicidal individuals have a history of childhood psychiatric problems, and that severity of suicidal ideations among adults may be associated with early psychopathology (Clum & Weaver, 1997). These findings are both complex and intriguing. They suggest that developmental continuities may exist in vulnerability for chronic suicidality, and that an assessment of early psychopathology may play a role in a comprehensive evaluation of suicidal risk.

Whereas demographic, social, psychiatric, and psychological factors are useful in identifying groups of individuals who are at increased risk of suicide, they have not been found useful in predicting the behavior of individuals. Given the relatively low incidence of completed suicide in the general population (and even among a number of high-risk groups), rating scales based on demographic, social, and psychological characteristics are accompanied by unacceptably high false-positive and false-negative rates. Suicide risk for an individual appears to be more strongly related to clinical and proximate risk factors than to demographic characteristics. As Lester (1974) observed, scales based on demographic variables tend, by their very nature, to overlook individual differences. This is not meant to minimize the value or the usefulness of these scales. In practice, risk scales such as those described and clinical ratings complement one another. Together, they form the foundation of a comprehensive and sensitive evaluation of suicide risk. Suicide risk scales might best be used as a guide, and information derived from them should be integrated with the results of clinical interviews and a review of the patient's history in estimating current risk. Inasmuch as the likelihood of making a successful suicide attempt is greater during the months after an initial attempt, clinicians working with suicidal patients should be particularly attentive immediately following their attempt or their discharge from the hospital.

SUBTYPES OF MOTIVATION FOR SUICIDE

Freeman and Reinecke (1993) described four groups of suicidal patients: (1) hopeless suicide, (2) psychotic suicide, (3) rational suicide, and (4) histrionic or impulsive suicide. The hopeless subtype refers to individuals who believe that their predicament is intolerable and that there is no hope that the situation will improve. They become highly pessimistic and view suicide as a reasonable solution to their problems. Quite often, these individuals are motivated by a desire for relief from their difficulties and consider suicide "adaptive." Although they are often ambivalent about ending their life, their pervasive sense of personal helplessness presses them toward action. Although suicidal patients often feel other emotions—including anger or rage, guilt, shame, fear, isolation, and loneliness—it is their feelings of hopelessness and impotence, their belief that they cannot effect a change, that lead them to death. Clinical experience suggests that hopeless individuals do envision a future but one that is worse than their current state. They believe that their suffering will continue, that the canyon into which they have fallen is bottomless, and that suicide is their only solution.

The second group, psychotic suicides, includes patients who experience command hallucinations or delusions (Caldwell & Gottesman, 1990; Gardner & Cowdry, 1985; Roy, 1982, 1986; Roy, Mazonson, & Pickar, 1984). Although suicide is the leading cause of premature death among individuals with a history of schizophrenia, research does not support the belief that delusional patients attempt suicide in response to command hallucinations (Nathan & Rousch, 1984). Rather, schizophrenic individuals attempt suicide during periods of relative lucidity. It is the chronicity of the illness and the inexorable recurrence of psychotic episodes that place the individuals at risk for suicide. As they become aware of their deteriorating condition and lose confidence in the effectiveness of their treatment, feelings of pessimism develop and suicide risk increases.

Rational suicides constitute a third subgroup of patients. Most often, these individuals suffer from a terminal illness or a progressive disease and view suicide as a reasonable course of action. Like "hopeless" patients, these individuals are typically motivated by a desire for relief from their illness or by a desire to avoid pain or hardship stemming from their deteriorating condition. Only a small percentage of suicidal patients, about 2%, are terminally ill at the time of their attempt. Of these, the majority also manifest an acute mental disorder, such as depression. As such, it is unclear that these attempts are "rational" in the traditional sense of the term.

Histrionic or manipulative individuals constitute a fourth subgroup of suicidal patients. They are motivated not by a desire for relief but by a desire for stimulation or excitement. They do not tend, as a group, to feel particularly hopeless or pessimistic. Rather, often they are motivated by a desire for attention or revenge—they want to "make someone pay" for a perceived wrong. Although their attempts are often impulsive and may be seen by others as "attention seeking," they should not be overlooked or their significance minimized.

It should be acknowledged that there is some overlap between these alternatives, and that other conceptual schemes for understanding suicidal behavior have been proposed (Arensman & Kerkhof, 1996; Reynolds & Berman, 1995). Typologies such as this can be clinically useful tools for rapidly assessing suicidal motivation and for developing a treatment plan. Of particular interest is the fact that of the four subtypes, in all but one (the histrionic-manipulative) suicide is mediated by feelings of pessimism or hopelessness. This typology is consistent with the results of a study of 200 adults hospitalized after making a suicide attempt (Kovacs, Beck, & Weissman, 1975). Of these patients, 56% reported that they attempted suicide as a means of gaining a sense of relief from their problems, whereas 13% had attempted suicide "for the sole purpose of taking a chance on effecting some change in others or in the environment" (p. 365).

This conceptual scheme of suicidal subtypes is similar in many ways to one proposed by Beck, Rush, et al. (1979). They also suggested that suicidal individuals may be differentiated with regard to their motivation for considering suicide. They proposed that some individuals are motivated by a "desire for escape or surcease," whereas others are motivated by a "desire to communicate" their concerns to others. They suggested that those who are motivated by a desire for escape may be more hopeless or pessimistic than those motivated by a desire to express their concerns to others. An assessment of a patient's motivation for considering suicide is clinically important in that treatment goals may differ for each of the groups. Feelings of pessimism might, for example, be a reasonable target for the hopeless or rational individual, whereas appropriate communication and regulation of anger might be the focus of treatment for the histrionic-manipulative patient.

ASSESSMENT

Although suicidal risk should regularly be assessed when working with depressed individuals, there are two situations in which a more formal evaluation is needed—when patients express suicidal thoughts and after they have made a suicidal gesture or attempt (Williams & Wells, 1989). Given the range of factors that are associated with risk of completed suicide, a comprehensive evaluation will include a diagnostic and developmental interview, an assessment of suicide risk indicators, completion of objective rating scales, and a more extended assessment of risk and protective factors.

Clinical Interviews

Assessing suicidal risk typically begins with clinical interviews of the patient and family members. As we have seen, factors that are associated with an increased risk of suicide have been identified. As a consequence, a number of issues should be addressed in a clinical interview (Freeman & Reinecke, 1993; Yufit & Bongar, 1992). These include the following:

1. What reasons do the patients have for contemplating suicide? Was it motivated by a desire for relief from their problems, or by a wish to manipulate others, to get attention, or to seek revenge?
2. Do they manifest a specific psychiatric disorder?
3. Do they currently experience significant feelings of depression or hopelessness? Do they appear highly anxious, agitated, hostile, suspicious, or evasive?
4. Do they feel that their predicament is intolerable and requires an immediate solution?
5. What is the degree of their suicidal intent? Was the attempt carefully planned or impulsive? Did they believe it would be successful? Was "rescue" anticipated or likely?
6. What situational or social factors contributed to the attempt? Are these problems long-standing or intractable?
7. Do they possess adaptive coping capabilities, or, conversely, do they employ maladaptive coping strategies such as alcohol or substance abuse? Have they been able to manage serious problems or stressful situations in the past?
8. What resources and social supports are available to the patients? Are there people they feel they can turn to and in whom they can confide? What do they think that others, such as their family and friends, think about their plan or attempt? Are they lonely, isolated, or withdrawn?
9. What is their attitude toward death and suicide?
10. Are there deterrents or reasons for living? (Hope for the future would be seen as a strong deterrent.) Do they believe that it may be possible for their predicament to change and that they may be able to bring this about?
11. Are there unstated beliefs, attitudes, or expectations that are maintaining their desire to die?
12. Are they able to generate and evaluate alternative solutions? Are they flexible or rigid in their cognitive style? Do they accept alternatives suggested by the clinician, or do they reject these out of hand as untenable?

Similar recommendations were made by Motto (1989), who observed that factors associated with suicidal risk can be assessed by directly asking patients about their recent experiences. Empathic, sensitive questioning can be useful in identifying factors contributing to the suicidal crisis. Recommended questions include the following:

1. Do the patients experience periods of feeling depressed or despondent about their life?
2. How long do these periods last? How frequent are they? How severe? Are associated symptoms of depression evident?
3. Do they feel hopeless, discouraged, or self-critical?
4. How are these feelings managed?
5. Are suicidal ideations present? What is their nature?
6. What supports are available?

If patients express suicidal thoughts, it is essential to determine their specific reasons or motives for considering suicide. The strength of their desire to attempt suicide as well as the development of a specific plan should be assessed. Have they developed a specific plan? What is their understanding of the lethality of their plan? Do they have the means and opportunity to kill themselves? Have they made a suicide attempt before? Further questioning might focus on the availability of effective deterrents to making an attempt. Do they have reasons for wanting to live? How strong or important are these reasons? The evaluation would continue with a discussion of stresses and supports they perceive and an assessment of their typical approach to solving problems. It would conclude with a review of their medical and psychiatric history and an evaluation of their current mood. Particular attention would be given to assessing their current levels of depression, hopelessness, anxiety, and anger.

Rating Scales

Assessing suicidal risk can be a complex endeavor. Standardized rating scales can be quite useful in this regard and are a valuable adjunct to a clinical interview. Many of the measures available are concise and easy to administer and have proven clinical utility. In addition to providing a quantitative index of the patient's mood and suicidality, the specific items endorsed can provide the clinician with important insights into areas that are most problematic. Although many of these scales have received extensive empirical support, it is worth keeping in mind that they are face valid. As such, they are subject to distortion should patients wish to minimize or exaggerate their current distress. Corroborating evidence should be sought from the patient's family or friends.

Among the most useful measures for assessing suicidality is the Scale for Suicidal Ideation (SSI; Beck, Kovacs, & Weissman, 1979). The scale contains 19 items, which are rated by a clinician on a scale of 0 (least severe) to 3 (most severe). Total scores are derived for both the current episode and a time in the patient's past when he/she "felt the worst." The scale is administered as a semi-structured interview and yields a quantitative estimate of the intensity of the patient's suicidal thoughts and impulses. The assessment of suicidal ideation at its worst point is of particular interest as recent work suggests that this may identify a subgroup of patients at relatively high risk for eventual suicide (Beck, Brown, Steer, Dahlsgaard, & Grisham, 1999). A modified version of this scale, the MSSI (Miller, Norman, Bishop, & Dow, 1986; Clum & Yang, 1995), is also available. Both scales are useful qualitatively as well in that they provide information about the patient's motivations for considering suicide and deterrents that are available.

The Suicide Intent Scale (SIS; Beck, Schuyler, & Herman, 1974) is a 15-item questionnaire assessing the intensity of an attempter's wish to die at the time of his/her attempt. This information can serve as an index of the risk of future attempts. The authors suggest that suicidal intent—the seriousness of the wish to end one's life—is one of several components of suicidal risk. Other factors include the availability of means, the presence of deterrents or "protective individuals," and knowledge about the lethality of the method selected. Suicidal intent is conceptualized as reflecting a balance between the wish to die and life-protective wishes, and it is believed to be based on the estimates made by patients about the probability that their attempt will be successful. Suicidal intent or risk may be viewed, then, as a continuum. As Beck, Rush, et al. (1979) observed, "At one extreme is an absolute intention to kill oneself and at the other extreme is an intention to go on living" (p. 210). One's position on this continuum is not static but varies in accord with one's perceptions and beliefs. Suicidal intent is conceptually independent, as such, from the lethality of an attempt. This is clinically important in that individuals may possess a high degree of suicidal intent yet may make an ineffective, nonlethal attempt (e.g., they might take a relatively small number of aspirin). The SIS includes items about the suicidal gesture, as well questions about the patients' thoughts and feelings at the time of their attempt. The Lethality of Suicide Attempt Rating Scale (LSARS; Smith, Conroy, & Ehler, 1984) is another useful measure for estimating the lethality of an attempt. It differs from the SIS in that it does not incorporate judgments about patients' intent, premeditation, or understanding of the lethality of their attempt. As a result, it is less susceptible to biases in reporting by the patient. Rather, a clinician estimates the degree of lethality of the attempt on an 11-point (0–10) scale, using a table of risk variables and a set of nine well-defined anchor points as a guide.

Other measures of suicidal risk include the Los Angeles Suicide Prevention Scale/Suicidal Death Prediction Scale (LASPS/SDPS; Lettieri, 1974), the Suicide Risk Assessment Scale (SRAS; Motto, Heilbron, & Juster, 1985), the Scale for Assessing Suicidal Risk (SASR; Tuckman & Youngman, 1968), the Suicide Probability Scale (SPS; Cull & Gill, 1982), the Suicide Risk Measure (Plutchik, van Praag, Conte, & Picard, 1989), the Short Risk Scale (SRS; Pallis, Barraciough, Levey, Jenkins, & Sainsbury, 1982), the Suicide Potential Scale

(SPS; Dean, Miskimins, DeCook, Wilson, & Maley, 1967), and the Index of Potential Suicide (IPS; Zung, 1974).

The Reasons for Living Inventory (RLI; Linehan, Goodstein, Nielsen, & Chiles, 1983; Linehan, 1985; Osman et al., 1999) is an interesting and valuable instrument. It does not assess suicidal ideations; rather, it is a 48-item self-report scale that taps feelings and beliefs about *not* attempting suicide. The scale is useful in identifying deterrents that may be meaningful for patients as well as the strength of the deterrents. As such, it can assist in identifying targets for clinical intervention.

Among the most valuable measures currently available for assessing pessimism is the Beck Hopelessness Scale (HS; Beck, Weissman, Lester, & Trexler, 1974). As noted, hopelessness or pessimism is a strong predictor of suicidal risk among adults and stands as an important target for therapy.

The BDI (Beck, Ward, Mendelson, Mock, & Erbaugh, 1961) is a 21-item self-report scale assessing depressive attitudes, feelings, and symptoms. It is the most widely used depression rating scale in the world and has become "the standard in its class" (Rabkin & Klein, 1987, p. 64) and "a touchstone against which to compare assessments derived from other measures" (Steer, Beck, & Garrison, 1986, p. 123). Items are scored from 0 (not at all) to 3 (severe) and are summed to yield a total score. Scores on the BDI and its recent revision, the BDI-II, are highly correlated with suicidal intent and measures of self-esteem, pessimism, and anxiety.

As noted, recent research suggests that anxious patients, particularly those with a history of recurrent panic attacks, may be at an increased risk of suicide. Moreover, depressed and suicidal patients are often highly anxious and agitated. With this in mind, it is often helpful to assess levels of anxiety among depressed or suicidal patients. Questionnaires such as the Beck Anxiety Inventory (Beck, Epstein, Brown, & Steer, 1988) are useful in this regard.

INTERVENTIONS

As Bongar (1991) observed in his discussion of outpatient management of suicidal crises:

> If the clinician becomes preoccupied with the issue and threat of a patient's suicide, it can divert the clinician from the primary task of attending to more disposition-based treatment-therapeutics that are solidly grounded in an understanding of the power of a sound therapeutic alliance and on a well-formulated treatment plan. (p. 104)

Quite true. Effective treatment of suicidality, as with other clinical problems, begins with the establishment of a trusting therapeutic collaboration and the development of a clear, simple, and parsimonious conceptualization and treatment plan.

Beck, Rush, et al. (1979) described a series of steps in working with suicidal individuals. After assessing suicidal risk and gaining an understanding of the patient's motives for considering suicide, the therapist's first goal is to "step into his world and view it through the patient's lens" (p. 212). A phenomenological stance is an integral part of the cognitive model (Freeman & Reinecke, 1995) and forms a foundation for understanding and addressing the patient's most pressing concerns. Empathizing with patients' despair, understanding their motives for considering their own destruction, and acknowledging their belief that there are no other alternatives can provide them with a sense of being understood and accepted.

As Freeman and Reinecke (1993) noted, it can be helpful to acknowledge that "suicide is an option, things are bad for you, and death is something that might be considered" (p. 61). As one suicidal patient said,

> "You're the first person who ever really understood that. Everybody else just tries to talk me out of it, or tells me things could be worse. . . . God, that would be something."

This acknowledgment should be followed by a discussion of other available alternatives and the development of a list of concrete steps that might be taken. In addition to enhancing rapport, this approach may reduce manipulative gains some patients seek through suicidal threats. Patients may be reassured by your candor in discussing their most terrifying thoughts and concerns. Suicidal persons typically view death as a reasonable solution to their predicament. In fact, they may view it as the only solution available. A therapeutic goal is to enhance their sense of hope by demonstrating that although suicide remains an option, it is not their only option. Moreover, it is not their best option.

The goal of crisis management is simple—to preserve the patient's life. This is achieved by restoring the patient's hope, developing effective deterrents, alleviating stressors, and providing support. When faced with a suicidal crisis, therapists adopt an active, problem-oriented stance. In contrast to traditional psychotherapy, minimal emphasis is placed on the interpretation of the therapeutic relationship or an examination of developmental events. As noted, impaired problem solving and cognitive distortions often contribute to the suicidal crisis. The therapist attempts to serve, then, as a supportive "rational guide"—an external ego, if you will, to supplement the patient's limited cognitive resources. Whereas suicidal patients typically see few alternatives, the therapist actively assists in developing solutions. When patients report feeling that their problems are numerous and overwhelming, the therapist breaks them into smaller units that can be attacked individually. When patients engage in maladaptive attempts to cope (such as using alcohol or drugs), the therapist works to develop more effective coping skills.

Suicidal patients frequently feel isolated from others and believe there is no one to whom they can reliably turn for support. Therapist availability, as such, is essential. Regular sessions should be scheduled as frequently as necessary, and patients might be given a card with emergency telephone numbers that they can call day or night. This might include the therapist's pager or home telephone number, an emergency room or crisis center number, and a backup therapist's telephone number. The provision of reliable and unwavering support is often quite reassuring to suicidal patients. The therapeutic message that someone will be reliably available to ensure their security is paramount. A calm, active therapeutic stance is employed to demonstrate that problems are endurable and solutions can be developed.

Family or friends, if available, might be recruited to assist with crisis management. They might be asked, for example, to accompany the patient home, or to allow the patient to stay with them until the next therapy session. The objectives are to ensure the patient's safety and provide them with an experience that is inconsistent with their belief that others are uncaring or unsupportive. If conflicts at home have contributed to the crisis (which is not uncommon), these should be directly addressed. As Fremouw, de Perczel, and Ellis (1990) stated, "A therapist's assistance in defining problems, articulating feelings, communicating wishes, and engineering solutions can prove invaluable in helping resolve stressful interpersonal conflicts" (pp. 104–105).

If a patient has a means for attempting suicide, it should be removed. Guns should be locked and removed, and the patient's access to knives, prescription medications, poisons, and the like should be strictly monitored.

Given the central role of hopelessness in suicidality, an immediate goal is to address the source of the patient's sense of pessimism and demoralization. This goal should be accomplished in the first session, during subsequent sessions, and throughout the follow-up period, through cognitive and behavioral exercises or assignments and by the therapist's modeling of effective problem solving and optimism in the face of difficult problems. If the patient feels he/she will be unable to resist the impulse to attempt suicide until the next therapy session, or the patient will be returning to a stressful, conflict-laden home, hospitalization should be considered. Hospitalization protects the patient and provides the therapist with the opportunity to complete a more thorough assessment of factors contributing to the crisis. Medication trials can be initiated and patients can participate in intensive individual and group psychotherapy (Davis & Schrodt, 1992).

Once the crisis has passed, longer-term treatment can begin. The issues and concerns that contributed to the emergency can be addressed. Strategic cognitive therapy of depression and anxiety can be initiated (Beck, Rush, et al., 1979), with the goal of providing the patient with more effective cognitive and behavioral tools for coping with life's problems. Goals of therapy might include developing stable and supportive interpersonal relationships and learning more effective or adaptive ways of communicating one's concerns to others. Social skills training and marital or family therapy might prove useful in this regard (Epstein, Schlesinger, & Dryden, 1988).

Attempts also might be made to address problems with alcohol or substance abuse (Beck, Wright, & Newman, 1992). Therapy might be directed toward reducing behavioral impulsivity, developing a positive attitude toward addressing life problems, and promoting flexible problem solving, given the important role these factors play in suicide (Lerner & Clum, 1990). Patients should be encouraged to recognize their ability to influence events in their life, and their belief that suicide is a viable solution directly disputed. An objective is to enhance the patients' sense of control and personal effectiveness. As patients become better able to generate solutions that might be pursued in lieu of suicide, the link between thought and impulsive action is broken. Patients' reasons for living and dying can be openly discussed, and patients encouraged to envision alternative, positive future scenarios. As Markus and Nurius (1986) observed, an individual's beliefs, goals, and expectations for the future—the individual's sense of a "possible self"—have important behavioral and emotional implications. These beliefs and expectations affect not only an individual's motivation but also his/her self-concept. Direct attempts should be made to identify and alleviate depressogenic beliefs and cognitive distortions. The focus is on changing dysfunctional schemata and interpersonal behavioral patterns (Linehan, 1987; Young, 1991).

There is a subtle but important distinction being made here: The therapist wants to acknowledge patients' belief that their problems are both significant and unresolvable, and empathize with the associated affect, but not validate the legitimacy of the meaning they attach to that belief. On the one hand, the therapist is acknowledging patients' despair and desperation, but on the other encouraging them to step back from this perception and acknowledge the possibility of constructing another point of view. This is similar, in some ways, to the distinction Linehan (1993) draws between "normative" and "cognitive validation." Cognitive therapy of suicidal patients is multidimensional and acknowledges the importance of behavioral, affective, social, and environmental factors in suicide. Cognitive interventions include rational responding, thought monitoring, cognitive distraction, guided imagery, thought stopping, self-instruction, scaling, guided association, reattribution, and examination of idiosyncratic meanings. Behavioral interventions are directed primarily toward developing coping skills, and they include activity scheduling, assertiveness or relaxation training, graded task assignments, mastery and pleasure ratings, behavioral rehearsal, *in vivo* exposure, and bibliotherapy. These and other techniques have been discussed at length by Beck, Rush, et al. (1979), Freeman and Reinecke (1995), and McMullin (2000).

No-suicide contracts are commonly employed in work with suicidal patients and may, in fact, be viewed as "standard practice" in some settings. Unfortunately, there is relatively little empirical support for their effectiveness in reducing suicidal gestures and attempts among acutely suicidal patients. The possibility exists, then, that they serve as much to alleviate the clinician's anxiety as to reduce the patients' distress. As Mahrer and Bongar (1993) note, there are some situations in which the use of this approach may be contraindicated. Although we regularly use no-suicide contracts or agreements in our clinical work, they are not a substitute for sensitive, ongoing assessment of suicidal risk or a systematic program of treatment.

Efficacy of Cognitive Therapy

The question remains—is cognitive therapy clinically useful in reducing suicidal behavior? Whereas a substantial body of research indicates that cognitive-behavioral therapy can be effective for treating clinically depressed adults, relatively few controlled studies have focused specifically on the prevention of suicidal behavior. Although research on the treatment of suicidal patients is limited, recent findings have been promising.

In an early study, Patsiokas and Clum (1985) examined the effectiveness of three forms of treatment—cognitive-restructuring, problem-solving training, and nondirective therapy—for reducing suicidal ideations in a sample of 15 psychiatric inpatients admitted after having made suicide attempts. Results indicated that all three treatments were effective in reducing the intensity of patients' suicidal thoughts. More recently, Lerner and Clum (1990) reported that social problem-solving therapy was more effective than supportive psychotherapy in reducing depression, hopelessness, and loneliness among suicidal young adults, and that these gains were maintained at 3-month follow-up. This approach was not significantly better, however, at reducing suicidal ideations. Social problem-solving training was, however, found to be effective in reducing suicidality in a study of 39 patients who had attempted to poison themselves (McLeavey, Daly, Ludgate, & Murray, 1994). The study reported that interpersonal problem-solving training (IPSST) was effective in reducing levels of hopelessness, enhancing self-perception, improving social problem-solving skills, and improving patients' perceived ability to cope with ongoing problems. As importantly, patients in this condition reportedly made fewer suicidal gestures during a 1-year follow-up period than did patients in a control treatment condition.

The efficacy of cognitive-behavioral interventions in reducing suicidality among patients diagnosed with borderline personality disorder (BPD) has been explored by Marsha Linehan and her colleagues at the University of Washington (Linehan, 1993, 1999; Linehan et al., 1991; Linehan, Heard, & Armstrong, 1993). In a study of 39 women with BPD who had a history of suicidal gestures, for example, a combination of intensive individual and group cognitive-behavioral therapy was contrasted with community treatment. During the initial 6 months of the follow-up period, patients who had received cognitive-behavioral therapy reportedly made fewer suicidal gestures, were less angry, and demonstrated better social adjustment than those in the control condition. Moreover, during the subsequent 6 months they had fewer inpatient days and better interviewer-rated social adjustment.

These findings are consistent with other controlled studies (Evans et al., 1999; Salkovskis, Atha, & Storer, 1990), and with the results of a recent meta-analytic review of randomized controlled trials of interventions for suicide attempters (van der Sande, Buskens, Allart, van der Graaf, & van Engeland, 1997). Their results indicated that only the cognitive-behavioral approach demonstrated a consistent preventive effect on repeated suicide attempts.

Taken together, these findings indicate that cognitive-behavioral therapy may be more effective than community-based "treatment as usual" in reducing the frequency of suicidal gestures and in improving psychosocial adjustment of patients with a history of suicide attempts. Are these gains maintained over time? It is difficult to know. Results thus far are generally positive, but the long-term stability of gains observed has not been examined. Moreover, it is not clear whether the gains observed are clinically meaningful, or what factors discriminate those patients who are best able to benefit from these interventions. Given the limited number of studies completed, additional research is required before we can have confidence in the effectiveness of these approaches for treating suicidal patients.

CASE STUDY

Presenting Problems

G. L. was 41 years old at the time of her referral to our clinic. She had recently been discharged from an inpatient psychiatric treatment program and was experiencing recurrent, subjectively severe feelings of depression, anxiety, and anger. She was completing her doctorate in history and worked part time as a college instructor. Although G. L. had been raised in a devout Jewish home, she and her husband were atheists. G. L. had been divorced twice and now lived with her husband of 16 years and their three teenage children.

Presenting concerns included feelings of irritability, fear, anxiety, and depression. Although G. L. reportedly had lost 30 pounds during the past 3 months, medical tests revealed no physical basis for her loss of appetite or weight. She was, nonetheless, quite concerned that she might have a serious physical illness. She had been diagnosed with breast cancer approximately 8 months before, and the treatment had been successful. The node of cancerous cells reportedly was quite small and was excised completely. As there was no evidence of metastasis, radiation treatments and chemotherapy were not recommended. G. L.'s brother-in-law had, however, died of cancer several years before, leading her to suspect that she might be vulnerable to a physical illness. G. L. was highly sensitive to bodily sensations and reported experiencing a range of vague somatic problems. G. L. reported that she had felt depressed "all of her life," and that these feelings had become progressively more severe during the past 5 years. This worsening of her condition coincided with the beginning of her doctoral studies. She stated that she felt "frustrated about being alive" and commented that "everything I touch is destroyed." When asked to elaborate, she stated, "I mess up people's lives, I'm not fun, I make people miserable, and I can't stand myself." As a consequence, she observed that she "doesn't like to be alone; but I'm not able to be with others either." G. L. reported that she experienced a "lack of joy and fulfillment in life" and that this was "just the way I am." She recalled having struggled with feelings of guilt since her childhood, and remarked that she felt she "needed to be believed . . . and validated by others." G. L.'s specific symptoms, then, included the following:

Affective: dysphoria, irritability, guilt, anxiety, anger, fear, worrying, anhedonia, hopelessness, helplessness

Cognitive: ruminations about past mistakes, depersonalization, feelings of unreality, low self-esteem, confusion, suicidal ideations, impaired concentration and memory.

Physiological: fatigue, decreased libido, loss of appetite, severe weight loss, nausea, insomnia, nightmares, early-morning awakening, dry mouth

Behavioral: severe psychomotor retardation, agitation, hand wringing, frequent crying, social avoidance, angry outbursts, restless, yelling at children

G. L. stated that these difficulties were worse just prior to taking exams, and she reported fearing that she was "going to fail." She reportedly became depressed and anxious prior to appointments with physicians or psychologists and when she was away from her children. She became quite fearful at those times and said that she experienced images of her children being killed in an accident. G. L. also became depressed while on vacations with her family. She stated that she "always had difficulty with unstructured time" and was fearful that she would "ruin it for everyone else." A structured diagnostic interview revealed that G. L. met the criteria in the *Diagnostic and Statistical Manual of Mental Disorders,* fourth edition (DSM-IV; American Psychiatric Association, 1994), for major depression—recurrent, dysthymia, and generalized anxiety disorder. These difficulties were superimposed on a range of borderline and dependent traits. The latter observation was of some concern given recent research suggesting that borderline personality disorder may be associated with an increased risk of both attempted and completed suicide (Kjellander, Bongar, & King, 1998).

Assessment

A clinical interview, including the SSI, was completed to assess G. L.'s current level of suicidal risk. She stated that she had "no wish to live" and felt a "strong desire to die"—she simply "felt like being dead." Her thoughts of suicide were frequent and persistent. Although she stated that she was "ambivalent" about attempting suicide, she had no sense of control over these impulses. G. L. was deterred from attempting suicide by thoughts of the effects of her death on her family and a fear of pain or serious injury if she failed. She later acknowledged feeling, however, that she was a "bad mother and wife," and that her family would soon forget her if she were dead. She was motivated to consider attempting suicide by a desire for relief from her problems. Although G. L. had considered writing a suicide note, she had not developed a plan and did not have a lethal means available for attempting suicide. Moreover, she did not feel she would be able to carry out an attempt and had a supportive and caring family. She was able to agree not to make a suicide attempt prior to our next therapy session and was comfortable making this promise. With these considerations in mind, and given the fact that there was no history of prior suicidal gestures or attempts, rehospitalization was not indicated.

G. L. reported that there were no acute stressors or problems in her life. Because her husband was a successful attorney, finances were not a concern. Although she characterized her graduate program as "difficult," she noted that she had earned A's in all her courses. Her children reportedly were polite and well mannered and were doing reasonably well in school. G. L. remarked, however, that she had few close friends and so felt isolated and estranged. Although she had numerous acquaintances and friendly neighbors, she felt she did not have anyone she could confide in. As a consequence, G. L. felt isolated and alienated. She stated that her husband was supportive, but she characterized her marriage as "living with a saint"—a situation she resented. She remarked that her husband was rarely critical of her, and that given her recent behavior was "either a saint or the biggest masochist in the world."

G. L.'s responses on a battery of objective rating scales were consistent with the results of the clinical interview and suggested that she was highly depressed, anxious, and pessimistic and was moderately suicidal. Her self-esteem was low, and she acknowledged being fearful of many situations. G. L.'s responses on the Young-Brown Schema Questionnaire (Young, 1991) revealed that she believed that others would not be able to provide emotional support or protection for her and that she was vulnerable to harm or illness. She viewed herself as incompetent and unable to handle day-to-day problems without support and felt that she was fundamentally flawed and unlovable. G. L. acknowledged that she had very high standards for herself, and that she felt she could never meet them. As a consequence, she continually felt discouraged and dissatisfied. A summary of G. L.'s scores on the self-report questionnaires and clinician rating scales is presented in Table 4.1.

As noted, G. L. was highly depressed, anxious, agitated, and pessimistic at the time of her referral. Of particular concern was the fact that she was experiencing moderately severe suicidal thoughts and demonstrated a number of significant cognitive distortions. A summary of her suicide risk indicators is presented in Table 4.2.

TABLE 4.1. Summary of Objective Rating Scales

	Scale	Score	Level
Depression	BDI	55	Severe
	CES-D	54	Severe
	Hamilton (HRSD)	52	Severe
Anxiety	BAI	38	Severe
	Zung	30	Severe
	Hamilton (HARS)	38	Severe
Hopelessness	HS	20	Severe
Suicidality	SSI (Current)	19	Moderate
	(Past)	15	Moderate

Summary of Developmental and Medical History

When asked what may have led her to become so depressed, G. L. remarked, "I blame my mother . . . I wasn't meant to be born." She recounted that she was the youngest of two children (her sister was approximately 15 years older) and that her mother was 45 years old when she became pregnant. Her mother reportedly had several abortions during the preceding years and had "attempted to miscarry me by throwing herself down a ladder." G. L. stated that her mother "never forgave me for being born," and she recalled her mother admonishing her to act appropriately or she would be "abandoned on a street corner . . . or in the park." Although G. L. was quiet, polite, and studious during her childhood, she recalled her mother berating her as "a bad child" and "an idiot." She described her mother as "angry and tense" and characterized her relationship with her mother as "frightening." These experiences may have contributed to G. L.'s belief that people are rejecting and unpredictable and that she was fundamentally unlovable, defective, and vulnerable. They are consistent, as well, with the possibility that she manifested an insecure attachment with her mother, and that this may have contributed to the development of her negativistic beliefs.

There is now some evidence, with both clinical and nonclinical populations, that the relationship between early negative events and later depression may be mediated by insecure attachment style and the consolidation of dysfunctional attitudes (Reinecke & Rogers, 1999; Roberts, Gotlib, & Kassel, 1996). As a case study, this is, of course speculative, but G. L.'s history and presentation is consistent with these findings.

TABLE 4.2. Summary of Risk Indicators

Indicator	Interpretation
Daily functioning	Moderately good
	Cares for children; well respected at work
	Frustrated, angry at children
Lifestyle	Stable, but engages in no enjoyable activities; few social activities
Supports	Caring husband and family; few close friends; tends to withdraw
Stressors	Moderate stress at work; good performance, but avoids tasks
Coping	Adequate resources available; intelligent; motivated; good sense of humor
Psychiatric history	Extensive psychotherapy and medications
	Cooperative with treatment, but poor response
	No prior suicide attempts
Family history of suicide	None
Medical history	Breast cancer (in remission)
	Chronic fatigue and somatic complaints
Recent losses	None
Depression	Severe
Anxiety	Severe
Pessimism	Severe
Positive future thinking	Negligible; severe
Anger/irritability	Moderate
Impulsivity	Low
Alcohol/drug use	None
Suicidal ideations	Moderate to severe
Prior suicide attempts	None
Problem solving	Poor; negative problem orientation
Cognitive distortions	Severe
Constriction/dichotomizing	Severe
Self-focused attention	Severe
Ruminative style	Severe

G. L. described her father in somewhat different terms. Her father was employed as a watchmaker and worked in a small jewelry shop attached to their house. G. L. characterized her father as a "political and social activist" and noted that he was "full of life when he was away from home." She described her relationship with him as "distant" and recalled him stating that "life

at home doesn't exist . . . one should always be working for society." She recalled feeling that he was unresponsive to her concerns during her childhood,
and noted that "no one was allowed to become upset at home . . . that was a
sign you were self-centered." G. L.'s father is now almost 90 years old and lives
several thousand miles away. Although she frequently sends him money, G. L.
feels guilty that she is not able to be more supportive. She visits her father
every several years but describes these visits as "tense."

G. L. lived at home until she was 18 years old, when she married. She
stated that she was "never separated" from either of her parents during her
childhood, and that she was frightened of being left alone. As she stated,
"Even now I can't tolerate being separated from my family." As noted, G. L.
has been married three times. She said that she divorced her first two husbands "just because," and remarked that "I think I get afraid they will leave
me because I'm horrible, so I quit before they fire me." She continued by observing, "I never had a good reason for believing they'd leave me . . . I'm just
too afraid."

G. L. reported that her parents had emigrated from Poland, and that
many of her relatives were killed in the Holocaust. In addition, many of G. L.'s
relatives and friends were arrested, tortured, and killed during military coups
in South America during the 1970s. These experiences contributed to her belief
that "individuals have no value in society," and to her feelings of guilt.

G. L. had participated in individual and family therapy for approximately
5 years but did not find the interventions helpful. In addition, she has received
trials of numerous medications, including imipramine, nortriptyline, trazodone, phenelzine sulfate (Nardil), fluoxetine hydrochloride (Prozac), lorazepam
(Ativan), diazepam, chlorpromazine hydrochloride (Thorazine), and lithium.
The medications were ineffective, however, and were discontinued due to adverse side effects. The fact that she had not benefited from prior therapy is of
concern given observations that unfavorable response to treatment may be a
predictor of completed suicide (Dahlsgaard, Beck, & Brown, 1998).

Cognitive Conceptualization

Several cognitive-behavioral models of depression relevant to this case have
been proposed during recent years, each emphasizing a specific facet of clinical depression (Ingram, Miranda, & Segal, 1998). Cognitive theorists and researchers have noted the importance of cognitive errors, distortions, and
negativistic beliefs (Beck, Rush, et al., 1979), impaired problem solving and
self-reinforcement (Fuchs & Rehm, 1977; Rehm, 1977), depressogenic schemata
(Beck, Rush, et al., 1979; Guidano & Liotti, 1983; Segal, 1988), reduced social
reinforcement (Lewinsohn, 1975), attributional style (Abramson, Metalsky, &
Alloy, 1989; Alloy, Abramson, Metalsky, & Hartlage, 1988; Barnett & Gotlib,
1988); helplessness, reduced perceptions of control over important outcomes

(Seligman, 1975), hopelessness (Weishaar & Beck, 1992), and behavioral activity (Freeman, Pretzer, Fleming, & Simon, 1990) in depression.

G. L. demonstrated features of many of these models. A range of cognitive distortions was readily apparent as she described herself and her relationships with others, and she appeared to maintain highly negative views of herself, the world, and her future. She believed that she was essentially unlovable, that others were unsupportive and rejecting, and that she lacked the attributes or abilities necessary to succeed. Moreover, she actively avoided social activities and behaved in ways that might elicit rejection from her friends and family. G. L. demonstrated little "social interest" or empathy for others. Rather, she tended to ruminate about her concerns and experienced difficulty identifying possible solutions. As a consequence, she felt both hopeless and helpless. G. L. avoided challenging tasks and engaged in few activities that would provide her with a sense of competence or pleasure. She maintained high standards for her personal performance (both as a mother and a graduate student) and was highly self-critical when she did not meet these standards. She gave herself little credit for her successes ("Anyone can get a Ph.D. . . . it's easy," she noted) and believed that she would be punished ultimately if she allowed herself to feel happy. These beliefs, expectations, attributions, behavioral skills deficits, and difficulties in problem solving became the focus of treatment. A cognitive-behavioral conceptualization of G. L.'s difficulties includes the following components:

> *Behavioral coping strategies:* Avoidance, withdrawal, excessive reassurance seeking
>
> *Cognitive processes:* Dichotomizing, personalization, magnification/minification, selective abstraction, should statements, self-focused attention, ruminative style, dependent/sociotropic stance
>
> *Automatic thoughts:* I'll never be as good as others; They don't care . . . they won't want to see me again; I destroy everything I touch; I'm a horrible, castrating person; I'll be punished for feeling happy; There's no one who can help; All people care about is money . . . people have no value; I can't function . . . I'll never be as capable as I should be; Something bad is going to happen . . . I just know it; Life isn't worth living; I can't manage on my own; I'm too old to get a job.
>
> *Assumptions:* If I stay with my family, I can feel secure; One should never be happy—the letdown afterward is worse.
>
> *Schemata:* I'm defective and unlovable; People are uncaring and rejecting; The world is a dangerous place.
>
> *Problem solving:* Negative problem orientation; capable of solving problems rationally, but does not anticipate that efforts will be effective

Treatment

The first goal of crisis intervention is to ensure the patient's immediate safety. With that in mind, a comprehensive review of G. L.'s concerns and a systematic assessment of suicide risk factors were completed. Given G. L.'s poor response to psychodynamic therapy in the past, as well as her tendency to magnify and personalize problems, it was felt that insight-oriented approaches or anxiety-provoking interventions could further disorganize her and might exacerbate the suicidal risk. With this in mind, the initial focus of therapy was on addressing the sources of her feelings of hopelessness and on providing her with cognitive and behavioral skills for managing her feelings of depression.

At the outset of the first treatment session, G. L. noted that it was normal to feel afraid and scared and that she did not believe that therapy would be effective. As she stated, "This treatment won't work . . . it never works." Given her limited improvement over the years, there may have been some support for this belief. These thoughts—that it was normal to feel afraid and that treatment would not work—were particularly important in that if they were true, they would undermine G. L's motivation for participating in cognitive therapy. Our first interventions, then, were straightforward, demonstrating the relationship between her thoughts and current mood and examining evidence for and against these beliefs. G. L. readily recognized that she felt "despondent . . . and paralyzed" when she thought about therapy in these terms and acknowledged that many people did not feel anxious or depressed—it was not "normal" for others. She noted, however, that if her mood improved, others would "expect more of her." As she stated, "I'm hiding behind my depression." Her comment raised the possibility that there were secondary gains from her problems—an issue that would be addressed later in treatment. G. L. reported that she was worried about an upcoming exam, and that she had not been studying due to a fear of failing the test. She agreed that a behavioral homework assignment might be helpful and made plans to study for the test for 1 hour that night. Although this assignment was, admittedly, small and would have little effect on her grade, it served her well in that it demonstrated that she could return to work on her degree. Not surprisingly, she passed the test.

G. L. continued to believe that it was impossible to consciously influence one's mood. She felt that moods "were hormonal" and regularly commented on how her feelings of depression had worsened "for no real reason." She experienced difficulty identifying automatic thoughts and was unable to recall times when she had not felt depressed. The latter difficulty may have been related to the effects of her dysphoria on her ability to recall mood-incongruent events (Bower, 1981) or to an actual paucity of enjoyable experiences during recent years. With this in mind, G. L. was asked to recall her early childhood. She began smiling, and described images of playing with her relatives. "It was wonderful," she stated, "I was happy, I felt human . . . that was the way it should be." G. L.'s mood had improved, if only for a few moments, in response to a conscious intervention. Our clinical goal had been met; G. L. learned that she did have the capacity to influence her feelings of depression.

A goal in crisis intervention is to actively help the patient to respond to the specific negativistic perceptions or beliefs that contributed to the crisis. This process is quite selective. The objective is to identify and resolve only those beliefs that are exacerbating or maintaining the crisis.

This involves several steps:

1. Identify and label the negative emotion
2. Identify thoughts or events that triggered this feeling
3. Identify automatic thoughts that are maintaining this emotional state (e.g., "What is going through your mind that leads you to feel this way?")
4. Have the patient recognize the central importance of this perception or belief
5. Collect evidence that is inconsistent with this belief
6. Identify the most persuasive evidence against the belief or perception
7. Develop an alternative, more adaptive, conceptualization of the triggering event
8. Assist patients to see how their mood would shift if they were to accept this alternative viewpoint
9. Develop a behavioral plan for using this information to cope with the situation.

It is often helpful to provide patients with more adaptive and objective "coping statements" and to help them to decatastrophize the situation by pointing out that it is, in fact, possible to endure the problem. G. L. noted, for example, that she "couldn't tolerate" her feelings of depression any longer. When asked how long she had felt this way she remarked "all my life." When it was pointed out that it seemed she had been able to tolerate these feelings for quite some time, she smiled and responded, "Sure, I just don't like it. . . . I wish it would end, but I don't know what to do . . . just tell me what to do."

The emphasis in crisis intervention is on resolving current problems rather than addressing past losses or failures. In working with G. L., our focus was on two particularly malignant beliefs—that "nobody really cares" and "I'm not able to function." She came to see that there were a number of people in her life (including her husband, children, friends, and therapist) who were concerned about her well-being, and that she had, in fact, done quite well in her studies and as a teacher. G. L. was asked to read a number of books and articles on cognitive therapy during the next several weeks and to think about how they might apply to her concerns. She read *Coping with Depression* (Beck & Greenberg, 1978), a pamphlet describing cognitive and behavioral tools for managing depression, but found it "simplistic." She next read *Reinventing Your Life* (Young & Klosko, 1993), a book on the development and treatment of maladaptive beliefs, and "Possible Selves" (Markus & Nurius, 1986), a review article on the role of expectations and goals in human behavior. G. L. found these readings interesting and useful. Moreover, they demonstrated that she was, in fact, able to assimilate and remember fairly complex material—something she had felt unable to do in class. Although there are risks in providing patients with readings that have been prepared for a professional audience, it is important to select articles that meet the patient's specific needs. Flexibility in developing homework assignments and selecting readings for bibliotherapy is essential. In this case, the readings not only served a didactic function (teaching G. L. about cognitive therapy and its procedures), they also provided G. L. with an experience that was inconsistent with a central belief—that she was unable to function intellectually.

Subsequent sessions focused on identifying and changing negativistic assumptions and schemata. The downward arrow procedure (Beck, Rush, et. al., 1979) was introduced to identify depressogenic assumptions. We began for example, with the thought, "I can't do my dissertation." When asked, "What comes to mind when you think of that?" she remarked, "I won't move forward." The remainder of the downward arrow is presented below.

I can't do my dissertation. I won't move forward.
I'll never finish my degree.
Everything I start is unfinished.
My mother told me I couldn't finish things. I can't help others.
I'm a terrible person.
I'll never support myself. I'll wind up in the streets.
I have to depend on others. What if they die? I'll be a burden.

G. L. recognized a number of themes in her statements, including the beliefs that "I'm incapable" and "People will abandon me." As noted, these were long-standing beliefs and seem to have stemmed from early experiences with her mother. At this point, G. L. became angry at the therapist and remarked, "Are you married? . . . I don't know how anyone could stand to be with you." When asked what had gone through her mind at that point, she remarked tersely, "I'm the biggest failure." She reportedly experienced an image of her mother sitting near her admonishing her that she was "making a fool" of herself and that she should "shut up and go to the corner." She stated that she heard the voice of her mother telling her that her participation in therapy was "proof that [she'd] failed" and that she had "failed because [she] wasn't strong." G. L. became quite agitated at the outset of the following therapy session. She reported feeling that the therapist would "test her" and that she would be "thrown out" if she did not "do therapy right." Upon questioning, she noted that there was nothing the therapist had done or said to suggest that she might "fail therapy," and that these thoughts and feelings were internally generated. The therapeutic relationship, then, served as evidence that was inconsistent with her belief that she would ultimately be abandoned. This theme reemerged several weeks later when she asked for assistance in processing an insurance claim. She reported that she had received a denial of coverage, which served as proof that "people have no value" and "I'm just another policy to you . . . I don't matter." Once again, a patient reappraisal of the event led her to conclude that the therapist was concerned for her well-being and that "maybe not everyone will abandon you." Interventions directed toward activating tacit beliefs can be quite powerful and should be undertaken only after the initial crisis has passed and a strong therapeutic rapport has developed. G. L.'s feelings of anger toward her husband and children were examined during subsequent sessions. The beliefs that she had "damaged the children beyond repair" and that she "had become just like her mother" were discussed at length, as were her feelings of anxiety when apart from her family. She acknowledged that it was necessary for her teenage children to become more independent, but she resented their increasing autonomy. As she stated, "I do a lot for them. . . . Kids ask more and more, then they leave you . . . they abandon you." Upon examination, she noted that her children were not "abandoning her," and that her belief that "I have nothing except my children" was both untrue and maladaptive. Behavioral interventions, including relaxation training and scheduling of pleasurable activities, were introduced. G. L. was also asked to resume work on her dissertation—an activity that she felt would provide her with a sense of accomplishment. She began by reading a short research article but experienced a great deal of difficulty understanding it. The experience was taken as further evidence of her "defectiveness." A behavioral experiment was developed to assess the validity of this belief. G. L. asked a colleague to review the article and to share his thoughts with her. He reportedly felt the article was "an awful piece . . . poorly written," leading G. L. to recognize that her difficulties may have stemmed, at least in part, from the quality of the article.

After 10 weeks of therapy, G. L. reported, with some surprise, that her mood was "reasonably good" and that she was "feeling better" about her classes and teaching. Her scores on each of the objective rating scales had improved dramatically and she reportedly felt less isolated, defective, and dependent on others. As she stated, "Life isn't always horrible." Although the suicidal crisis had passed and important therapeutic gains had been made, much work remained to be accomplished. G. L. continued to feel emotionally depleted and pessimistic about her future. Moreover, her anxiety about separation from her family was not fully resolved. She still feared abandonment and experienced difficulty separating from her children. These became the focus of her ongoing therapy.

CONCLUSION

This chapter reviewed the assessment and management of suicidality among depressed adults. In concluding, several general statements can be made. First, the general outline of an integrated model of suicidality is beginning to emerge. Studies indicate that a number of cognitive, social, environmental, and psychiatric factors are associated with an increased risk of suicidal thoughts and gestures. These variables can serve as targets of intervention in a comprehensive treatment program. The specific manner in which these variables interact over time in contributing to vulnerability to suicide, however, is not yet known.

Second, the prediction of suicidal behavior remains a daunting clinical task. Although progress has been made in understanding the social, psychiatric, cognitive, and emotional concomitants of suicidal ideations, the astute reader will note that prediction of suicidal behavior for individual patients remains an imprecise endeavor. Additional research into the clinical prediction of suicidal ideations and behavior is warranted.

The primary goal in addressing a suicidal crisis is, of course, to ensure the patient's safety. This is accomplished by alleviating environmental pressures or stresses, recruiting the support of others, and helping the patient to cope with immediate problems. Attention is directed only toward those perceptions, beliefs, attributions, or expectations that are contributing to the crisis. Other maladaptive cognitions are not addressed at that time. After the crisis has been resolved, the therapeutic focus can shift to identifying and changing ancillary maladaptive beliefs as well as dysfunctional schemata or assumptions that contributed to the suicidal crisis. The goals of therapy are to identify the cognitive, behavioral, and social factors that placed the patient at risk and to provide the patient with alternative ways of coping with problems that arise. Certainly cognitive and behavioral techniques are useful, but the importance of a trusting, reliable, and supportive therapeutic relationship should not be minimized. Clinicians should be aware of their beliefs or expectations and sensitive to the ways that these can influence the course of therapy. Negative biases—including thoughts that a patient "looks untreatable" or is "just being manipulative"—can affect both the tone of the therapeutic relationship and the nature of the interventions that are made. As when examining the validity or utility of a patient's beliefs, it is often helpful to examine the evidence for and against the therapist's perceptions, whether there is a more reasonable interpretation, and how one's behavior is affected by it (Rudd & Joiner, 1997). Although the results of recent controlled outcome studies are promising, it is not clear, at this point, that psychotherapy can reliably reduce the frequency and severity of suicidal ideations, reduce the risk of suicide attempts among ideators, or prevent further attempts by individuals with a history of suicidal behavior. Nonetheless, cognitive models of depression and suicide have empirical support, and interventions derived from them can be clinically useful. In the absence of evidence for the effectiveness of specific interventions, clinicians would do well to adopt a broad view and use a range of cognitive and behavioral techniques when working with acutely suicidal patients.

Working with acutely suicidal patients can be both challenging and anxiety provoking. With this in mind, regular consultation with colleagues can be quite helpful. Consultation is viewed by some, in fact, as an essential component of effective care and risk management (Bongar, 1993; Linehan, 1993). It can provide clinicians with a sense of support as well as recommendations for providing more effective care. Therapists can have confidence that cognitive models have proven useful for conceptualizing depression and suicidality. The interventions derived from the model are clinically powerful. Cognitive and behavioral interventions can be of value in alleviating suicidal patients' feelings of depression, pessimism, anxiety, and anger. They are useful in reducing impulsivity, enhancing social relationships, and in improving their ability to cope with reality-based problems. For the acutely suicidal patient there is, in short, hope.

REFERENCES

Abramson, L., Alloy, L., Hogan, M., Whitehouse, W., Cornette, M., Akhavan, S., Chiara, A. (1998). Suicidality and cognitive vulnerability to depression among college students: A prospective study. *Journal of Adolescence, 21,* 157–171.

Abramson, L., Metalsky, G., & Alloy, L. (1989). Hopelessness depression: A theory-based subtype of depression. *Psychological Review, 96*(2), 358–372.

Adam, K., Bouckoms, A., & Streiner, D. (1982). Parental loss and family stability in attempted suicide. *Archives of General Psychiatry, 39,* 1081–1085.

Adam, K., Lohrenz, J., Harper, D., & Streiner, D. (1982). Early parental loss and suicidal ideation in university students. *Canadian Journal of Psychiatry, 27,* 275–281.

Alloy, L., Abramson, L., Metalsky, G., & Hartlage, S. (1988). The hopelessness theory of depression: Attributional aspects. *British Journal of Clinical Psychology, 27,* 5–21.

Alloy, L., Abramson, L., Murray, L., Whitehouse, W., & Hogan, M. (1997). Self-referent information processing in individuals at high and low cognitive risk for depression. *Cognition and Emotion, 11,* 539–568.

Alloy, L., Abramson, L., Whitehouse, W., Hogan, M., Tashman, N., Steinberg, D., Rose, D., & Donovan, P. (1999). Depressogenic cognitive styles: Predictive validity, information processing and personality characteristics, and developmental origins. *Behaviour Research and Therapy, 37,* 503–531.

American Psychiatric Association. (1994). *Diagnostic and statistical manual of mental disorders* (4th ed.). Washington, DC: Author.

Arensman, E., & Kerkhof, A. (1996). Classification of attempted suicide: A review of empirical studies, 1963–1993. *Suicide and Life-Threatening Behavior, 26*(1), 46–67.

Barnett, P., & Gotlib, I. (1988). Psychosocial functioning in depression: Distinguishing among antecedents, concomitants, and consequences. *Psychological Bulletin, 104,* 97–126.

Beck, A. (1967). *Depression: Clinical, experimental, and theoretical aspects.* New York: Harper & Row.

Beck, A. (1973). *The diagnosis and management of depression.* Philadelphia: University of Pennsylvania Press.

Beck, A. (1976). *Cognitive therapy and the emotional disorders.* New York: International Universities Press.

Beck, A. (1986). Hopelessness as a predictor of eventual suicide. *Annals of the New York Academy of Science, 487,* 90–96.

Beck, A., Brown, G., Berchick, R., Stewart, B., & Steer, R. (1990). Relationship between hopelessness and ultimate suicide: A replication with psychiatric outpatients. *American Journal of Psychiatry, 147,* 190–195.

Beck, A., Brown, G., & Steer, R. (1989). Prediction of eventual suicide in psychiatric inpatients by clinical ratings of hopelessness. *Journal of Consulting and Clinical Psychology, 57,* 309–310.

Beck, A., Brown, G., Steer, R., Dahlsgaard, K., & Grisham, J. (1999). Suicide ideation at its worst point: A predictor of eventual suicide in psychiatric outpatients. *Suicide and Life-Threatening Behavior, 29*(1), 1–9.

Beck, A., Epstein, N., Brown, G., & Steer, R. (1988). An inventory for measuring clinical anxiety: Psychometric properties. *Journal of Consulting and Clinical Psychology, 56*(6), 893–897.

Beck, A., & Greenberg, R. (1978). *Coping with depression.* Unpublished manuscript, University of Pennsylvania, Philadelphia.

Beck, A., Kovacs, M., & Weissman, A. (1975). Hopelessness and suicidal behavior: An overview. *Journal of the American Medical Association, 234,* 1146–1149.

Beck, A., Kovacs, M., & Weissman, A. (1979). Assessment of suicidal intention: The scale for suicidal ideation. *Journal of Consulting and Clinical Psychology, 47,* 343–352.

Beck, A., Rush, A., Shaw, B., & Emery, G. (1979). *Cognitive therapy of depression.* New York: Guilford Press.

Beck, A., Schuyler, D., & Herman, I. (1974). Development of suicidal intent scales. In A. Beck, H. Resnick, & D. Lettieri (Eds.), *The prediction of suicide* (pp. 45–56). Philadelphia: Charles Press.

Beck, A., & Steer, R. (1989). Clinical predictors of eventual suicide: A 5- to 10-year prospective study of suicide attempters. *Journal of Affective Disorders, 17,* 203–209.

Beck, A., Steer, R., Kovacs, M., & Garrison, B. (1985). Hopelessness and eventual suicide: A 10-year prospective study of patients hospitalized with suicidal ideation. *American Journal of Psychiatry, 142,* 559–563.

Beck, A., Steer, R., Sanderson, W., & Skeie, T. (1991). Panic disorder and suicidal ideation and behavior: Discrepant findings in psychiatric outpatients. *American Journal of Psychiatry, 148*(9), 1195–1199.

Beck, A., Ward, C., Mendelson, M., Mock, J., & Erbaugh, J. (1961). An inventory for measuring depression. *Archives of General Psychiatry, 4,* 561–571.

Beck, A., Weissman, A., & Kovacs, M. (1976). Alcoholism, hopelessness, and suicidal behavior. *Journal of Studies on Alcohol, 37,* 66–77.

Beck, A., Weissman, A., Lester, D., & Trexler, L. (1974). The measurement of pessimism: The Hopelessness Scale. *Journal of Consulting and Clinical Psychology, 42,* 861–865.

Beck, A., Wright, F., & Newman, C. (1992). Cocaine abuse. In A. Freeman & F. Dattilio (Eds.), *Comprehensive casebook of cognitive therapy* (pp. 185–192). New York: Plenum.

Bedrosian, R., & Beck, A. (1979). Cognitive aspects of suicidal behavior. *Suicide and Life-Threatening Behavior, 9*(2), 87–96.

Berman, A., & Jobes, D. (1991). *Adolescent suicide: Assessment and intervention.* Washington, DC: American Psychological Association.

Bongar, B. (1991). *The suicidal patient: Clinical and legal standards of care.* Washington, DC: American Psychological Association.

Bongar, B. (1993). Consultation and the suicidal patient. *Suicide and Life-Threatening Behavior, 23*(4), 299–306.

Bonner, R. & Rich, A. (1987). Toward a predictive model of suicidal ideation and behavior: Some preliminary data in college students. *Suicide and Life-Threatening Behavior, 17*(1), 50–63.

Bonner, R., & Rich, A. (1988). Negative life stress, social problem-solving, self-appraisal, and hopelessness: Implications for suicide research. *Cognitive Therapy and Research, 12*(6), 549–556.

Bower, G. (1981). Mood and memory. *American Psychologist, 36,* 129–148.

Brent, D., & Kolko, D. (1990). The assessment and treatment of children and adolescents at risk for suicide. In S. Blumenthal et al. (Eds.), *Suicide over the life cycle: Risk factors, assessment, and treatment of suicidal patients* (pp. 253–302). Washington, DC: American Psychiatric Press.

Buerk, F., Kurz, A., & Moeller, H. (1985). Suicide risk scales: Do they help to predict suicidal behaviour? *European Archives of Psychiatry and Neurological Sciences, 235*(3), 153–157.

Buglass, D., & Horton, J. (1974). A scale for predicting subsequent suicidal behaviour. *British Journal of Psychiatry, 124,* 573–578.

Caldwell, C., & Gottesman, I. (1990). Schizophrenics kill themselves too: A review of risk factors for suicide. *Schizophrenia Bulletin, 16*(4), 571–589.

Clum, G., & Febbraro, G. (1994). Stress, social support, and problem-solving appraisal/skills: Prediction of suicide severity within a college sample. *Journal of Psychopathology and Behavioral Assessment, 16*(1), 69–83.

Clum, G., & Weaver, T. (1997). Diagnostic morbidity and its relationship to severity of ideation for a nonpsychiatric sample of chronic and severe suicide ideators. *Journal of Psychopathology and Behavioral Assessment, 19*(3), 191–206.

Clum, G., & Yang, B. (1995). Additional support for the reliability and validity of the Modified Scale for Suicide Ideation. *Psychological Assessment, 7*(1), 122–125.

Cole, D. (1988). Hopelessness, social desirability, depression, and parasuicide in two college student samples. *Journal of Consulting and Clinical Psychology, 56,* 131–136.

Cull, J., & Gill, W. (1982). *Suicide probability scale.* Los Angeles: Western Psychological Services.

Dahlsgaard, K., Beck, A., & Brown, G. (1998). Inadequate response to therapy as a predictor of suicide. *Suicide and Life-Threatening Behavior, 28*(2), 197–204.

Davis, M., & Schrodt, G. (1992). Inpatient treatment. In A. Freeman & F. Dattilio (Eds.), *Comprehensive casebook of cognitive therapy* (pp. 293–301). New York: Plenum.

Dean, R., Miskimins, W., DeCook, R., Wilson, L., & Maley, R. (1967). Prediction of suicide in a psychiatric hospital. *Journal of Clinical Psychology, 23,* 296–301.

Dixon, W., Heppner, P., & Anderson, W. (1991). Problem-solving appraisal, stress, hopelessness and suicide ideation in a college population. *Journal of Counseling Psychology, 38*(1), 51–56.

Drake, R., & Cotton, P. (1986). Depression, hopelessness, and suicide in chronic schizophrenia. *British Journal of Psychiatry, 148,* 554–559.

Dyer, J., & Kreitman, N. (1984). Hopelessness, depression, and suicidal intent in parasuicide. *British Journal of Psychiatry, 144,* 127–133.

Ellis, T. (1986). Toward a cognitive therapy for suicidal individuals. *Professional Psychology: Research and Practice, 17*(2), 125–130.

Ellis, T., & Ratliff, K. (1986). Cognitive characteristics of suicidal and nonsuicidal psychiatric patients. *Cognitive Therapy and Research, 1,* 625–634.

Epstein, N., Schlesinger, S., & Dryden, W. (1988). *Cognitive-behavioral therapy with families.* New York: Bruner/Mazel.

Evans, K., Tyrer, P., Catalan, J., Schmidt, U., Davidson, K., Dent, J., Tata, P., Thornton, S., Barber, J., & Thompson, S. (1999). Manual-assisted cognitive-behaviour therapy (MACT): A randomized controlled trial of a brief intervention with bibliotherapy in the treatment of recurrent deliberate self-harm. *Psychological Medicine, 29*(1), 19–25.

Fawcett, J., Scheftner, W., Clark, D., Hedeker, D., Gibbons, R., & Coryell, W. (1987). Clinical predictors of suicide inpatients with major affective disorders: A controlled prospective study. *American Journal of Psychiatry, 144,* 35–40.

Fawcett, J., Scheftner, W., Fogg, L., Clark, D., Young, M., Hedeker, D., & Gibbons, R. (1990). Time-related predictors of suicide in major affective disorder. *American Journal of Psychiatry, 147*(9), 1189–1194.

Freeman, A., Pretzer, J., Fleming, B., & Simon, K. (1990). *Clinical applications of cognitive therapy.* New York: Plenum.

Freeman, A., & Reinecke, M. (1993). *Cognitive therapy of suicidal behavior.* New York: Springer.

Freeman, A., & Reinecke, M. (1995). Cognitive therapy. In A. Gurman & S. Messer (Eds.), *Essential psychotherapies: Theory and practice* (pp. 182–225). New York: Guilford Press.

Fremouw, W., de Perczel, M., & Ellis, T. (1990). *Suicide risk: Assessment and response guidelines.* New York: Pergamon Press.

Friedman, S., Jones, J., Chernen, L., & Barlow, D. (1992). Suicidal ideation and suicide attempts among patients with panic disorder: A survey of two outpatient clinics. *American Journal of Psychiatry, 149*(5), 680–685.

Fuchs, C., & Rehm, L. (1977). A self-control behavior program for depression. *Journal of Consulting and Clinical Psychology, 45,* 206–215.

Gardner, D. L., & Cowdry, R. W. (1985). Suicidal and parasuicidal behavior in borderline personality disorder. *Psychiatric Clinics of North America, 8,* 389–403.

Garzotto, N., Siani, R., Zimmerman-Tansella, C., & Tansella, M. (1976). Cross-validation of a predictive scale for subsequent suicidal behaviour in an Italian sample. *British Journal of Psychiatry, 128,* 137–140.

Goldney, R. (1979). *Attempted suicide: Correlates of lethality.* Unpublished doctoral dissertation, University of Adelaide, Australia.

Goldney, R. (1981). Parental loss and reported childhood stress in young women who attempt suicide. *Acta Psychiatrica Scandinavica, 64,* 34–59.

Guidano, V., & Liotti, G. (1983). *Cognitive processes and emotional disorders: A structural approach to psychotherapy.* New York: Guilford Press.

Guze, S., & Robins, E. (1970). Suicide and primary affective disorders. *British Journal of Psychiatry, 117*(539), 437–438.

Hagnell, O., & Rorsman, B. (1980). Suicide in the Lundby study: A controlled prospective investigation of stressful life events. *Neuropsychobiology, 6,* 319–332.

Holding, T., Buglass, D., Duffy, J., & Kreitman, N. (1977). Parasuicide in Edinburgh: A seven year review. *British Journal of Psychiatry, 130,* 534–543.

Ingram, R., Miranda, J., & Segal, Z. (1998). *Cognitive vulnerability to depression*. New York: Guilford Press.

Ivanoff, A., & Jang, S. (1991). The role of hopelessness and social desirability in predicting suicidal behavior: A study of prison inmates. *Journal of Consulting and Clinical Psychology, 59*(3), 394–399.

Joiner, T., & Rudd, M. (1995). Negative attributional style for interpersonal events and the occurrence of severe interpersonal disruptions as predictors of self-reported suicidal ideation. *Suicide and Life-Threatening Behavior, 25*(2), 297–304.

Joiner, T., & Rudd, M.(1996). Disentangling the interrelations between hopelessness, loneliness, and suicidal ideation. *Suicide and Life-Threatening Behavior, 26*(1), 19–26.

Kennedy, J., & Reinecke, M. (1998). *Hopelessness and suicide among adults: A review and meta-analysis*. Paper presented at the 10th Annual Convention of the American Psychological Society, Washington, DC.

Kjellander, C., Bongar, B., & King, A. (1998). *Suicidality in borderline personality disorder. Crisis, 19*(3), 125–135.

Klerman, G. (1987). Clinical epidemiology of suicide. *Journal of Clinical Psychiatry, 48,* 33–38.

Kovacs, M., Beck, A., & Weissman, A. (1975). Hopelessness: An indicator of suicidal risk. *Suicide, 5,* 98–103.

Lerner, M., & Clum, G. (1990). Treatment of suicide ideators: A problem-solving approach. *Behavior Therapy, 21*(4), 403–411.

Lester, D. (1974). Demographic versus clinical prediction of suicidal behaviors: A look at some issues. In A. Beck, H. Resnik, & D. Lettieri (Eds.), *The prediction of suicide* (pp. 71–84). Philadelphia: Charles Press.

Lettieri, D. (1974). Research issues in developing prediction scales. In C. Neuringer (Ed.), *Psychological assessment of suicidal risk*. Springfield, IL: Charles C. Thomas.

Lewinsohn, P. (1975). The behavioral study and treatment of depression. In M. Hersen, R. Eisler, & P. Miller (Eds.), *Progress in behavior modification* (Vol. 1, pp. 19–64). New York: Academic Press.

Linehan, M. (1985). The reasons for living inventory. In P. Keller & L. Ritt (Eds.), *Innovations in clinical practice: A sourcebook* (pp. 321–330). Sarasota, FL: Professional Resource Exchange.

Linehan, M. (1987). Dialectical behavior therapy: A cognitive-behavioral approach to parasuicide. *Journal of Personality Disorders, 1,* 328–333.

Linehan, M. (1993). *Cognitive-behavioral treatment of borderline personality disorder*. New York: Guilford Press.

Linehan, M. (1999). Standard protocol for assessing and treating suicidal behaviors for patients in treatment. In D. Jacobs et al. (Eds.), *The Harvard Medical School guide to suicide assessment and intervention* (pp. 146–187). San Francisco: Jossey-Bass.

Linehan, M., Armstrong, H., Suarez, A., Allmon, D., & Heard, H. (1991). Cognitive-behavioral treatment of chronically parasuicidal borderline personality. *Archives of General Psychiatry, 48*(12), 1060–1064.

Linehan, M., Camper, P., Chiles, J., Strosahl, K., & Shearin, E. (1987). Interpersonal problem-solving and parasuicide. *Cognitive Therapy and Research, 11*(1), 1–12.

Linehan, M., Goodstein, J., Nielsen, S., & Chiles, J. (1983). Reasons for staying alive when you are thinking of killing yourself: The Reasons for Living Inventory. *Journal of Consulting and Clinical Psychology, 51,* 276–286.

Linehan, M., Heard, H., & Armstrong, H. (1993). Naturalistic follow-up of a behavioral treatment for chronically parasuicidal borderline patients. *Archives of General Psychiatry, 50*(12), 971–974.

MacLeod, A., Tata, P., Evans, K., Tyrer, P., Schmidt, U., Davidson, K., Thornton, S., & Catalan, J. (1998). Recovery of positive future thinking within a high-risk parasuicide group: Results from a pilot randomized controlled trial. *British Journal of Clinical Psychology, 37*(4), 1998, 371–379.

Mahrer, J., & Bongar, B. (1993). Assessment and management of suicide risk and the use of the no-suicide contract. In L. VandeCreek, S. Knapp, et al. (Eds.), *Innovations in clinical practice: A sourcebook* (Vol. 12, pp. 277–293). Sarasota, FL: Professional Resource Press/Professional Resource Exchange.

Markus, H., & Nurius, P. (1986). Possible selves. *American Psychologist, 41,* 954–969.

McLeavey, B., Daly, R., Ludgate, J., & Murray, C. (1994). Interpersonal problem-solving skills training in the treatment of self-poisoning patients. *Suicide and Life-Threatening Behavior, 24*(4), 382–394.

McMullin, R. (2000). *The new handbook of cognitive therapy techniques.* New York: Norton.

Miles, C. (1977). Conditions predisposing to suicide: A review. *Journal of Nervous and Mental Disease, 164,* 231–246.

Minkoff, K., Bergman, E., Beck, A, & Beck, R. (1973). Hopelessness, depression, and attempted suicide. *American Journal of Psychiatry, 130,* 455–459.]

Miller, I., Norman, W., Bishop, S., & Dow, M. (1986). The Modified Scale for Suicidal Ideation: Reliability and validity. *Journal of Consulting and Clinical Psychology, 54*(5), 724–725.

Morgan, H., Burns-Cox, C., Pocock, H., & Pottle, S. (1975). Deliberate self-harm: Clinical and socioeconomic characteristics of 368 patients. *British Journal of Psychiatry, 126,* 564–574.

Motto, J. (1989). Problems in suicide risk assessment. In D. Jacobs & H. Brown (Eds.), *Suicide: Understanding and responding: Harvard Medical School perspectives on suicide.* Madison, CT: International Universities Press.

Motto, J., Heilbron, D., & Juster, R. (1985). Development of a clinical instrument to estimate suicide risk. *American Journal of Psychiatry, 142*(6), 680–686.

Murphy, G. (1985). Suicide and attempted suicide. In R. Michels (Ed.), *Psychiatry.* Philadelphia: Lippincott.

Nathan, R., & Rousch, A. (1984). Which patients commit suicide? *American Journal of Psychiatry, 141,* 1017.

Nekanda-Trepka, C., Bishop, S., & Blackburn, I. (1983). Hopelessness and depression. *British Journal of Clinical Psychology, 22,* 49–60.

Neuringer, C. (1968). Divergencies between attitudes towards life and death among suicidal, psychosomatic, and normal hospitalized patients. *Journal of Consulting and Clinical Psychology, 32,* 59–63.

Neuringer, C., & Lettieri, D. (1971). Cognition, attitude, and affect in suicidal individuals. *Suicide and Life-Threatening Behavior, 1,* 106–124.

Orbach, I., Bar-Joseph, H., & Dror, N. (1990). Styles of problem-solving in suicidal individuals. *Suicide and Life-Threatening Behavior, 20*(1), 56–64.

Osman, A., Kopper, B., Linehan, M. Barrios, F., Gutierre, P., & Bagge, C. (1999). Validation of the adult suicidal ideation questionnaire and the reasons for living inventory in an adult psychiatric inpatient sample. *Psychological Assessment, 11*(2), 115–123.

Overholser, J., & Spirito, A. (1990). Cognitive-behavioral treatment of suicidal depression. In E. Feindler et al. (Eds), *Adolescent behavior therapy handbook. Springer series on behavior therapy and behavioral medicine* (Vol. 22, pp. 211–231). New York: Springer.

Pallis, D., Barraciough, B., Levey, A., Jenkins, J., & Sainsbury, P. (1982). Estimating suicide risk among attempted suicides: 1. The development of new clinical scales. *British Journal of Psychiatry, 141,* 37–44.

Patsiokas, A., & Clum, G. (1985). Effects of psychotherapeutic strategies in the treatment of suicide attempters. *Psychotherapy, 22*(2), 281–290.

Patsiokas, A., Clum, G., & Luscomb, R. (1979). Cognitive characteristics of suicide attempters. *Journal of Consulting and Clinical Psychology, 47,* 478–484.

Petrie, K., & Chamberlain, K. (1983). Hopelessness and social desirability as moderator variables in predicting suicidal behavior. *Journal of Consulting and Clinical Psychology, 51,* 485–487.

Piacentini, J., Rotheram-Borus, M. & Cantwell, C. (1995). Brief cognitive-behavioral family therapy for suicidal adolescents. In L. VandeCreek et al. (Eds.), *Innovations in clinical practice: A sourcebook* (Vol. 14, pp. 151–168). Sarasota, FL: Professional Resource Press.

Plutchik, R., van Praag, H., Conte, H., & Picard, S. (1989). Correlates of suicide and violent risk: 1. The Suicide Risk Measure. *Comprehensive Psychiatry, 30,* 296–302.

Pokorny, A. (1964). Suicide rates in various psychiatric disorders. *Journal of Nervous and Mental Disease, 139,* 499–506.

Pokorny, A. (1986). A scheme for classifying suicidal behaviors. In A. Beck, H. Resnick, & D. Lettieri (Eds.), *The prediction of suicide* (pp. 29–44). Philadelphia: Charles Press.

Pollock, L., & Williams, J. M. G. (1988). Problem solving and suicidal behavior. *Suicide and Life-Threatening Behavior, 28*(4), 375–387.

Prezant, D., & Neimeyer, R. (1988). Cognitive predictors of depression and suicide ideation. *Suicide and Life-Threatening Behavior, 18*(3), 259–264.

Priester, M. & Clum, G. (1992). Attributional style as a diathesis in predicting depression, hopelessness, and suicide ideation in college students. *Journal of Psychopathology and Behavioral Assessment, 14*(2), 111–122.

Priester, M., & Clum, G. (1993). Perceived problem-solving ability as a predictor of depression, hopelessness, and suicide ideation in a college population. *Journal of Counseling Psychology, 40*(1), 79–85.

Rabkin, J., & Klein, D. (1987). The clinical measurement of depressive disorders. In A. Marsella, R. Hirschfeld, & M. Katz (Eds.), *The measurement of depression* (pp. 30–83). New York: Guilford Press.

Reinecke, M., & Rogers, G. (1999). *Dysfunctional attitudes mediate relations between adult attachment and depressive symptoms in a mixed clinical sample.* Paper presented at the 33rd annual convention of the Association for the Advancement of Behavior Therapy, Toronto, Ontario.

Rich, A., & Bonner, R. (1987). Concurrent validity of a stress-vulnerability mode of suicide ideation and behavior: A follow-up study. *Suicide and Life-Threatening Behavior, 17*(4), 265–270.

Rehm, L. (1977). A self-control model of depression. *Behavior Therapy, 8,* 787–804.

Reynolds, F., & Berman, A. (1995). An empirical typology of suicide. *Archives of Suicide Research, 1*(2), 97–109.

Roberts, J., Gotlib, I., & Kassel, J. (1996). Adult attachment security and symptoms of depression: The mediating roles of dysfunctional attitudes and low self-esteem. *Journal of Personality and Social Psychology, 70,* 310–320.

Robins, E. (1985). Psychiatric emergencies: Suicide. In H. Kaplan & B. Sadock (Eds.), *Comprehensive textbook of psychiatry* (pp. 1311–1315). Baltimore: Williams & Wilkins.

Robins, E. (1986). Psychosis and suicide. *Biological Psychiatry, 21,* 665–672.

Rotheram-Borus, M., & Trautman, P. (1988). Hopelessness, depression, and suicidal intent among adolescent suicide attempters. *Journal of the American Academy of Child and Adolescent Psychiatry, 27*(6), 700–704.

Roy, A. (1982). Suicide in chronic schizophrenia. *British Journal of Psychiatry, 141,* 171–177.

Roy, A. (1984). Suicide in recurrent affective disorder patients. *Canadian Journal of Psychiatry, 29,* 319–322.

Roy, A. (1986). Suicide in schizophrenia. In A. Roy (Ed.), *Suicide.* Baltimore: Williams & Wilkins.

Roy, A., Lamparski, D., DeJong, J., Moore, V., & Linnoila, M. (1990). Characteristics of alcoholics who attempt suicide. *American Journal of Psychiatry, 147,* 761–765.

Roy, A., & Linoilia, M. (1986). Alcoholism and suicide. *Suicide and Life-Threatening Behavior, 16,* 244–273.

Roy, A., Mazonson, A., & Pickar, D. (1984). Attempted suicide in chronic schizophrenia. *British Journal of Psychiatry, 144,* 303–306.

Rudd, M. (1990). An integrative model of suicidal ideation. *Suicide and Life-Threatening Behavior, 20*(1), 16–30.

Rudd, M., & Joiner, T. (1997). Countertransference and the therapeutic relationship: A cognitive perspective. *Journal of Cognitive Psychotherapy, 11*(4), 231–250.

Rudd, M., Rjab, M., & Dahm, P. (1994). Problem-solving appraisal in suicide ideators and attempters. *American Journal of Orthopsychiatry, 64*(1), 136–149.

Sainsbury, P. (1986). The epidemiology of suicide. In A. Roy (Ed.), *Suicide.* Baltimore: Williams & Wilkins.

Salkovskis, P., Atha, C., & Storer, D. (1990). Cognitive-behavioural problem solving in the treatment of patients who repeatedly attempt suicide: A controlled trial. *British Journal of Psychiatry, 157,* 871–876.

Schotte, D., & Clum, G. (1987). Problem-solving skills in suicidal psychiatric patients. *Journal of Consulting and Clinical Psychology, 55,* 49–54.

Schotte, D., Cools, J., & Payvar, S. (1990). Problem-solving deficits in suicidal patients: Trait vulnerability or state phenomenon? *Journal of Consulting and Clinical Psychology, 58*(5), 562–564.

Segal, Z. (1988). Appraisal of the self-schema construct in cognitive models of depression. *Psychological Bulletin, 103*(2), 147–162.

Seligman, M. (1975). *Helplessness: On depression, development, and death.* New York: Freeman.

Shneidman, E. (1985). *The definition of suicide.* New York: Wiley-Interscience.

Siani, R., Garzotto, N., Zimmerman-Tanselia, C., & Tansella, N. (1979). Predictive scales for parasuicide repetition: Further results. *Acta Psychiatrica Scandinavica, 59,* 17–23.

Slaiku, K. (1990). *Crisis intervention* (2nd ed.). Boston: Allyn & Bacon.

Smith, K., Conroy, R., & Ehler, B. (1984). Lethality of suicide attempt rating scale. *Suicide and Life-Threatening Behavior, 14*(4), 215–242.

Spirito, A., Brown, L., Overholser, J., & Fritz, G. (1991). Use of the risk-rescue rating scale with adolescent suicide attempters: A cautionary note. *Death Studies, 15*(3), 269–280.

Spirito, A., Overholser, J., & Vinnick, L. (1995). Adolescent suicide attempters in general hospitals: Psychological evaluation and disposition planning. In J. Wallander et al. (Eds.), *Adolescent health problems: Behavioral perspectives. Advances in pediatric psychology* (pp. 97–116). New York: Guilford Press.

Steer, R., Beck, A., & Garrison, B. (1986). Applications of the Beck Depression Inventory. In N. Sartorius & T. Ban (Eds.), *Assessment of depression* (pp. 123–142). New York: Springer-Verlag.

Steer, R., Ranieri, W., Beck, A., & Clark, D. (1993). Further evidence for the validity of the Beck Anxiety Inventory with psychiatric outpatients. *Journal of Anxiety Disorders, 7,* 195–205.

Trautman, P. (1995). Cognitive behavior therapy of adolescent suicide attempters. In J. Zimmerman et al. (Eds.), *Treatment approaches with suicidal adolescents* (pp. 155–173). New York: Wiley.

Tuckman, J., & Youngman, W. (1968). A scale for assessing suicide risk of attempted suicides. *Journal of Clinical Psychology, 24,* 17–19.

van der Sande, R., Buskens, E., Allart, E., van der Graaf, Y., & van Engeland, H. (1997). Psychosocial intervention following suicide attempt: A systematic review of treatment interventions. *Acta Psychiatrica Scandinavica, 96*(1), 43–50.

Uncapher, H., Gallagher-Thompson, D., Osgood, N., & Bongar, B. (1998). Hopelessness and suicidal ideation in older adults. *Gerontologist, 38*(1), 62–70.

Weishaar, M., & Beck, A. (1992). Hopelessness and suicide. *International Review of Psychiatry, 4,* 185–192.

Weisman, A., & Worden, J. (1974). Risk-rescue rating in suicide assessment. In A. Beck, H. Resnick, & D. Lettieri (Eds.), *The prediction of suicide* (pp. 193–213). Philadelphia: Charles Press.

Weissman, A., Beck, A., & Kovacs, M. (1979). Drug abuse, hopelessness, and suicidal behavior. *International Journal of Addiction, 14,* 451–464.

Wetzel, R. (1976). Hopelessness, depression, and suicide intent. *Archives of General Psychiatry, 33,* 1069–1073.

Wetzel, R., Margulies, T., Davis, R., & Karam, E. (1980). Hopelessness, depression, and suicide intent. *Journal of Clinical Psychiatry, 4*(5), 159–160.

Williams, J., & Wells, J. (1989). Suicidal patients. In J. Scott, J. Williams, & A. Beck (Eds.), *Cognitive therapy in clinical practice: An illustrative casebook* (pp. 206–226). London: Routledge.

Wittgenstein, L. (1946/1980). *Culture and value.* Chicago, IL: University of Chicago Press.

Yang, B., & Clum, G. (1994). Life stress, social support, and problem-solving skills predictive of depressive symptoms, hopelessness, and suicide ideation in an Asian student population: A test of a model. *Suicide and Life-Threatening Behavior, 24*(2), 127–139.

Yang, B., & Clum, G. (1996). Effects of early negative life experiences on cognitive functioning and risk for suicide: A review. *Clinical Psychology Review, 16*(3), 177–195.

Young, J. (1991). *Cognitive therapy of personality disorders: A schema-focused approach.* Sarasota, FL: Professional Resource Exchange.

Young, J., & Klosko, J. (1993). *Reinventing your life.* New York: Dutton.

Young, M., Fogg, L., Scheftner, W., Fawcett, J., Akiskal, H., & Maser, J. (1996). Stable trait components of hopelessness: Baseline and sensitivity to depression. *Journal of Abnormal Psychology, 105*(2), 155–165.

Yufit, R., & Bongar, B. (1992). Structured clinical assessment of suicide risk in emergency room and hospital settings. In B. Bongar et al. (Eds.), *Suicide: Guidelines for assessment, management, and treatment* (pp. 144–159). New York: Oxford University Press.

Zung, W. (1974). Index of Potential Suicide (IPS): A rating scale for suicide prevention. In A. Beck, H. Resnick, & D. Lettieri (Eds.), *The prediction of suicide* (pp. 221–249). Philadelphia: Charles Press.

SUGGESTED READINGS

Bongar, B., Berman, A., Maris, R., Silverman, M., Harris, E., & Packman, W. (Eds.). (1998). *Risk management with suicidal patients.* New York: Guilford Press.

Ellis, T. (1987). A cognitive approach to treating the suicidal client. In P. A. Keller et al. (Eds.), *Innovations in clinical practice: A sourcebook* (Vol. 6, pp. 93–107). Sarasota, FL: Professional Resource Exchange.

Freeman, A., & Reinecke, M. (1993). *Cognitive therapy of suicidal behavior.* New York: Springer.

Freeman, A., & White, D. (1989). The treatment of suicidal behavior. In A. Freeman, K. Simon, H. Arkowitz, & L. Beutler (Eds.), *Comprehensive handbook of cognitive therapy* (pp. 321–346). New York: Plenum.

Greenberger, D. (1992). The suicidal patient. In A. Freeman & F. M. Dattilio (Eds.), *Comprehensive casebook of cognitive therapy* (pp. 139–146). New York: Plenum.

Hawton, K. (1997). Attempted suicide. In D. M. Clark et al. (Eds.), *Science and practice of cognitive behaviour therapy. Oxford medical publications* (pp. 285–312). Oxford, UK: Oxford University Press.

Hawton, K., & Catalan, J. (1982). *Attempted suicide: A practical guide to its nature and management.* Oxford, UK: Oxford University Press.

Overholser, J. (1995). Cognitive-behavioral treatment of depression: I. Assessment of depression and suicide risk. *Journal of Contemporary Psychotherapy, 25*(3), 185–204.

Weishaar, M., & Beck, A. (1990). The suicidal patient: How should the therapist respond? In K. Hawton et al. (Eds.), *Dilemmas and difficulties in the management of psychiatric patients. Oxford medical publications* (pp. 65–76). Oxford, UK: Oxford University Press.

Williams, J., & Wells, J. (1989). Suicidal patients. In J. Scott, J. Williams, & A. Beck (Eds.), *Cognitive therapy in clinical practice: An illustrative casebook* (pp. 206–226). London: Routledge.

5

Substance Abuse

J. Russell Ramsay
Cory F. Newman

Treating clients who abuse drugs or alcohol is particularly challenging. Ongoing substance abuse produces a progressive dysregulation of brain reward systems, which distorts both adaptive information and emotional processing (Koob & Le Moal, 1997; Nesse & Berridge, 1997). Left untreated, the effects of substance abuse can lead to compulsive use such that it enervates most aspects of a person's life and becomes a primary coping strategy for emotional distress and life problems (Follette, 1998; Koob & Le Moal, 1997). The environmental and relational effects of substance abuse serve to undermine the very coping resources—ego strength, will power, social support, employment, physical health, among others—that are crucial to recovery (Newman & Wright, 1994; Seligman, 1993). Furthermore, the substance abuser's problem-solving skills and emotional resilience are compromised and their emotional reactions to typical stressors become unpredictable as a result of the neurological impairments mentioned above (Nesse & Berridge, 1997). The role as substance abuser and its corollary behaviors progressively becomes more of a central and defining identity role for the individual and, in turn, better defended and more resistant to change (Klion & Pfenninger, 1997). As a result, drug and alcohol abuse predictably becomes a precipitant for life crises.

In spite of experiencing the aforementioned detrimental effects, substance-abusing clients often participate in therapy with great ambivalence about changing their behaviors. There is a frustrating approach–avoidance of this issue even among clients who have been legally mandated for treatment as a result of substance-related offenses. Due to the pervasive and negative effects of drugs and alcohol in the lives of such clients, their therapists will face clinical management crises that can be intimidating and exasperating in both their frequency and their severity.

When substance abuse has led to legal intervention or participation in a structured drug rehabilitation program, the therapist usually functions as part of a larger professional team, including parole officers, halfway house counselors, and other addiction counselors. This arrangement helps provide increased therapeutic contact for the client and corroborative information sources for the therapist. When clinical crises occur, the client and treatment team members have ready access to support.

A different challenge for the therapist is the client who presents for treatment either at the prompting of another person or for a reason other than their substance use problem. Clients who minimize or deny the effects of substance use require a cautious approach in which the clinician does not collude with the denial, yet maintains a collaborative alliance in an attempt to constructively address the client's presenting issues. Despite the fact that such clients have not yet experienced legal repercussions as a result of their substance use, they are at risk for experiencing crises during the course of treatment, which significantly impacts the therapeutic agenda.

This chapter suggests techniques for assessing and managing the treatment of substance-abusing clients who deny or minimize the effects of their substance use. We review the stages of change model pertinent to addictive behaviors, discuss the clinical signs of active substance abuse, and highlight active interventions that ideally work toward abstinence but maintain a collaborative therapeutic alliance. The chapter concludes with a case example illustrating a client moving from denial to identifying substance abuse as problematic as a result of a crisis. Of particular interest is the management of the crisis situation, and how the client's substance abuse becomes a central treatment issue.

STAGES OF CHANGE

Prochaska, DiClemente, and Norcross (1992) proposed an empirically generated, transtheoretical model describing the process through which addictive behaviors are modified. The five stages apply to intentional change both with and without treatment. Successful modification of addictive behavior requires progression through all five stages, although individuals frequently recycle through these stages several times before the addiction is considered in remission. This model of change has been widely adopted as a clinical heuristic for understanding addictive behaviors and formulating interventions.

Precontemplation represents the stage in which there is no intent to change an addictive behavior and little insight about the ramifications of substance use. If individuals in this stage are in treatment, it is usually by mandate (i.e., court-ordered treatment) or at the urging of significant others (e.g., spouse).

Contemplation is the stage in which clients become more aware of problems related to their substance use and consider potential actions to change, but have no commitment to a systematic modification. A hallmark of this stage is the client's passive weighing of the pros and cons of drinking and using, or not drinking and using. At this level of change, clients often look as if they are giving lip service to their problems, but they are not following through in doing anything about it.

In the *preparation* stage, individuals have taken some partial steps to cease their substance use or have somehow altered their habitual pattern (e.g., reduction of use, or avoiding use at certain times). Further, they may express their intent to attain the goal of abstinence in the near future. At this point, clients have a plan, and they intend to use it soon.

Action is the stage in which individuals have taken active steps toward achieving their target goals for altering their substance use. This stage is classified by significant and specific efforts to modify addictive behavior, with tangible results. Clients who reach this stage often feel a significant boost in hope and self-efficacy, although they may still be vulnerable to relapse at any time.

Finally, *maintenance* is the stage in which individuals have maintained abstinence and engaged in positive lifestyle changes for more than 6 months. Relapse prevention and the solidification of treatment gains mark the primary tasks of this stage.

This five-stage model of change does not represent a linear trajectory of change. As Prochaska et al.'s (1992) data suggest—and as clinical experience will corroborate—clients move through these stages in a cyclical fashion, complete with regressions to previous stages, and advancements anew to higher stages. Newman and Wright (1994), in the first edition of this volume, illustrated how to use crisis-intervention strategies to minimize stage regression; that is, how to keep a drug relapse from becoming a total life collapse. By contrast, the current chapter highlights the clinical use of naturally occurring substance-abuse crises as opportunities to promote *progression* to higher stages of change.

The stages of precontemplation and contemplation are characterized by denial or strongly rationalized substance use. Clients in treatment may falsely claim that they do not drink or use, or they may minimize their substance use and its effects on functioning. The extent of the clients' drinking or using may be congruent with their maladaptive beliefs about substance use (e.g., "Cocaine isn't harmful if you only snort it.") and about themselves (e.g., "Real men can handle their booze."). When such beliefs are strongly held they are difficult to change. These beliefs interact with the chemical addiction such that they adversely influence the client's ongoing interactions with others, their sense of identity, and behavioral choices. Substance use and its related belief systems can become central to the client's core identity or schema (Klion & Pfenninger, 1997; Young, 1994), with denial representing efforts to protect these systems. A clinical challenge is to be able to focus on what the client wishes to avoid, without unduly endangering the therapeutic alliance. The next section will illustrate how denial manifests itself in sessions with substance-abusing clients, and will provide suggestions for constructively dealing with this common problem.

MANIFESTATIONS OF DENIAL

In the sections that follow, we discuss some of the forms of denial that are relatively common among substance-abusing clients. Left unchallenged, therapy may fail to address one of the client's most serious clinical problems, resulting in an absence of meaningful change. Furthermore, the client will continue to be a proverbial walking crisis waiting to happen.

Concealment/Minimization

Some clients may not mention their substance use unless it is explicitly assessed. Even if the clients acknowledge that they drink or use drugs, their clinicians must be careful to sift through casual, light-hearted descriptions and euphemisms that may camouflage more extensive substance use. For example, when a client describes having "a few drinks" each week, it is important to get specific numbers, sizes, and types of drinks as well as the time frame in which these drinks are consumed. Other words that should serve as red flags are "only" and "just," such as when clients say that they "*Only* had one or two drinks before getting into the car," or "I *just* wanted to get a pleasant buzz, that's all."

The more detailed and comprehensive the assessment, the more likely the diligent clinician will be able to understand the fuller extent of a client's level of substance use. This process also would include asking about the clients' experiences with legal problems (including driving offenses due to intoxication), participation in 12-step groups, and family history. Additionally, clients should be asked whether anyone among their family, friends, or colleagues has expressed concern about the clients' drinking or using.

Rationalization/Justification

When clients present with undeniable consequences of their substance abuse, they may offer arguments in which they rationalize or justify their use. For example, a client who is in legally mandated treatment may rail against the system impinging on his rights, claiming that what he puts in his body is his business and nobody else's. Another client who is addicted to cocaine may speak derisively of his friends who are addicted to heroin stating, "At least I don't do that. They're serious addicts." Yet another client lamented that she knew smoking marijuana made her inattentive to her responsibilities, but she explained that "[Smoking] weed is my only joy in life." These expressed attitudes about substance use—and similar others—serve as *permission-giving beliefs* (Beck, Wright, Newman, & Liese, 1993) that facilitate further substance use and impede the efforts of the therapist.

Resistance

Resistance reflects behaviors that seem to work in opposition to the goals of therapy. Consequently, it is important to address these issues, conceptualize them, and to structure interventions that engender motivation to make desired changes. It is generally acknowledged that resistance serves a self-protective function for the psychotherapy client (Mahoney, 1991; Newman, 1994; Wachtel, 1982). In the case of the substance-abusing client it serves to protect the addictive behavior and lifestyle. Resistance may appear in the form of non-participation or limited participation in therapy. For example, a client may only respond to questions with "Yes," "No," or "I don't know" answers and not spontaneously contribute to the therapy dialogue. Other clients may superficially comply with therapy through regular attendance and some interaction but not follow through on homework tasks and not make changes in their behavior. Some clients may avoid the topic of substance abuse by presenting an alternative topic (i.e., "My real problem is my relationship with my girlfriend. I can't talk about this other stuff until I know what's going on with her.").

Resistance also may manifest itself in the therapeutic alliance. The client may make overt efforts to align with the therapist in the manner of a personal friend who will look the other way (e.g., "Come on 'doc,' you've been cool with me up to now. Why are you worried about me partying a little?") or, conversely, react with hostility and blame (e.g., "You're just like the rest of the system and you're trying to control me. If you're gonna keep making a big deal about nothing then maybe I'm just gonna stop talking!"). One of our clients wanted treatment for her depression, but failed to see that her alcohol abuse was a significant part of the problem. Unfortunately, she stated up front that if the therapist even mentioned alcohol as an issue, she would leave therapy on the spot. The therapist nicely replied that while he would try to respect her wishes and boundaries wherever possible, he could not responsibly promise to eliminate a potentially vital clinical topic from therapy as a precondition to working together. The client chose not to make a second appointment.

Strategies for Managing Denial and Resistance

Therapists who treat substance-abusing clients who deny their use or resist interventions that address their use face quite a dilemma. On the one hand, it is inadvisable to be immediately, gratuitously confrontational toward outpatient clients who can easily leave therapy at any time.[1] Anybody can point fingers, criticize, and proselytize, and clients have probably seen and heard it all before. Therefore, if the therapist does the same, the client likely will react with the same avoidance and disdain. On the other hand, if the therapist—in an attempt to forge a positive therapeutic relationship—does nothing but validate the client's views, he/she runs the risk of colluding with the client's denial, missing vital information from the assessment and treatment plan, providing inadequate care, and doing nothing to help the client avert imminent but preventable crises.

So what are therapists to do? First, in keeping with the cognitive model, they must adopt a constructive mindset and generate a plan of action. This mindset has many variations, but the gist is as follows:

"I am not going to ignore vital clinical data, but neither will I shame or berate my clients. I will act respectfully toward my clients, but I will not shy away from gently addressing the unpleasant realities that need our attention. I will carefully assess the clients' situation as fully as possible, ask as many specific, open-ended questions as the clients can tolerate, examine all of their answers as useful data for the case conceptualization, and ask them to assist me in this process by agreeing to self-monitor during the week. I will try to determine where they are in their readiness for change, and meet them just slightly ahead, with a helping hand outstretched in their direction."

As the above example illustrates, the therapist strives to find a balance between acceptance and change. This territory becomes thinner and thinner as the clients become more and more dysfunctional (see Layden, Newman, Freeman, & Morse, 1993), to the point where—in the most difficult cases, the therapist practically has to walk a tightrope. The mindset presented above also points to the need to use the Prochaska et al. (1992) model to assess the clients' stage of change. Clearly, clients in the precontemplative or contemplative stages will not be as responsive to aggressive treatment to reduce or eliminate drinking or drug use as will clients in the preparation or action stages. Similarly, clients who are in the preparation or action stages may become more restless and dissatisfied with nondirective, supportive approaches to therapy than may clients in the precontemplative or contemplative stages.

As this chapter focuses on crises that are related to the earlier stages of change, we will comment on clinical strategies that therapists can use to overcome denial, minimization, permission giving, and other forms of avoidance. The case example presented below will reflect a client who is at a rudimentary stage of change, and whose life crisis provides an opportunity to come to grips with his chemical dependency in a constructive way.

The Client's Distress Is a Starting Point

Although clients with substance abuse problems may not wish to discuss the issues surrounding their addictions, they may be more receptive to discussing their general states of dissatisfaction in life. For example, there is evidence that antisocial drug abusers who are clinically depressed are *more* responsive to treatment than are nondepressed, antisocial drug abusers (Woody et al., 1983;

Woody, McLellan, & O'Brien, 1990). By focusing on the clients' distress, thera-pists communicate that they are concerned about them as people, and are not just labeling them as substance abusers. This facilitates the forming of a posi-tive alliance in which the clients may be more willing to come forward with in-formation about the full extent of their difficulties with drugs and alcohol.

Use Socratic, Open-Ended Questions

When therapists suspect that their clients are being less than forthcoming about the true nature of their problems, it can lead to awkward moments in therapy. The therapists, upon hearing—but not fully believing—the things their clients say, may find themselves at a loss as to how to proceed. They may think, "Should I just nod empathically, and move on, and act as though I'm be-ing duped; or should I express my misgivings and disbelief?" Either way, the therapists may be more uncomfortable than their clients, which represents a problematic role reversal.

Instead of the two choices above, therapists can respond to these awkward moments by asking Socratic, open-ended questions. This is less confrontational than expressing doubts about the veracity of the clients' self-report, but it puts a share of the burden of the work of therapy back on the clients' shoulders, where it needs to be. For example, if clients state they're "doing fine," thera-pists can ask for the specifics about *how* the clients are coping and under *what* conditions. If the clients continue to be vague and evasive, or appear uneasy, the therapists can then ask open-ended questions about the clients' "perplex-ing" reaction, such as, "I notice that you're not too thrilled that I'm asking all these questions. What do you think I'm driving at, and what makes this dis-concerting to you?"

Use the Clients' Own Words to Make Clinical Observations

In order to lessen the likelihood of problematic power struggles with substance-abusing clients, it is important to use the clients' own words to make your clini-cal point whenever possible. When clients lie and deny, they almost invariable wind up contradicting themselves at some point. Astute therapists who listen well and take good notes will be in the best position to spot these inconsisten-cies and point them out to the clients.

For example, Newman (1997) writes of a client who flatly denied that she had been using crack cocaine, but then spoke of "losing track of days at a time." The therapist countered by saying, "You once told me that one of the side effects of your crack addiction was that you couldn't account for your time. You may have just spotted your own crack use right now, and you didn't even realize it. Well done." One of the benefits of this approach is that it allows the therapist to imply that the client is using alcohol and drugs, but without shaming or blaming the client. In general, it is wise to give the clients a face-saving way to discuss their problems. Respectfully reflecting on the comments that clients themselves have made is one such method.

Explore the Pros and Cons of Stasis and Change

One of the most fundamental difficulties in treating substance abusers who are in the early stages of change is that therapists and clients may not be on "the same page." Simply put, the therapists will believe that it is in the clients' best interest to change—that is, to become abstinent from alcohol and other drugs—whereas the clients may believe that they are "just fine" remaining the way they are. In such situations, therapists would do well to explore the pros and cons of changing, and the pros and cons of staying the same (Grilo, 1993; Miller & Rollnick, 1991; Newman, 1994).

This procedure has several advantages over straight confrontation in addressing denial and resistance. First, the intervention brings important information to the fore for discussion, without seeming as though the therapist is interrogating the client. Second, clients appreciate when their therapists try to understand their thoughts and feelings about matters that may not have social approval in everyday life. Therefore, the degree of felt empathy is increased. Third, this technique highlights the clients' *ambivalence* about changing, including the thoughts, feelings, behaviors, and physiological components of their approach–avoidance conflicts regarding alcohol and drugs. Additionally, when clients engage in a pros and cons analysis of their own functioning, they can feel more in charge of the exploration and change process (see also, Prochaska, 1994). This is potentially more motivating, and less stigmatizing than when they are given directives about what to do.

Infuse Caring in the Confrontation

Beck et al. (1993) note that it is sometimes necessary to confront substance-abusing clients directly. This is so because some clients are so adamant in their denials that it seems to render the rest of therapy moot. In other words, the attitude of the client can be summed up the following way, "This cognitive therapy for substance abuse seems pretty interesting, but what does it have to do with me, and why should I remain in this office?" Here, therapists have to state opinions that the clients likely will not appreciate. By the same token, however, there is no reason the therapists cannot be respectful and caring in the process.

For example, Beck et al. (1993) present a number of ways for therapists to "nicely" state the equivalent of the phrase, "I think you're lying." For example, a therapist may simultaneously confront yet show empathy and respect for a client by saying something such as:

"Mr. X., I have come to respect the things you say, and to expect that they will make sense to me. You have the knowledge and skill to figure out what's truly going on, and to explain it to me well. That's why I'm troubled by today's conversation—because things don't make sense and don't add up, and that's so out of character for you. Something's up. Mr. X., I'm hoping that you will level with me."

Newman (1997) also shows that it is useful to get out of the false dichotomy of "trust versus mistrust" in the therapeutic relationship, and instead to talk to the clients about the fact that "trust is not a perfect thing." When the client who lost track of days denied her drug use—even though there was incontrovertible evidence that she had relapsed—the therapist asserted his belief that there was enough good will in the therapeutic relationship to survive this one episode where the two of them were having a tough time trusting the other's comments and intentions. He expressed a "we can work it out" philosophy, thus reaffirming that he wanted to continue his very important work with this client, even through a period of stress and strain on the therapeutic relationship.

CRISIS SITUATIONS

In the previous edition of this book, Newman and Wright (1994) listed some of the commonly encountered crises related to the use of alcohol and illicit drugs. Though not an exhaustive list, the following offers a summary of the most commonly encountered life crises associated with the problems of addiction.

Overdose and Suicidality

Whether by accident or a deliberate suicide attempt, an overdose of illicit drugs (perhaps in combination with alcohol, prescribed medications, and/or over-the-counter products) represents a life-threatening crisis.

In many instances, the therapist of a drug-abusing client who overdoses will not know of the episode until after the damage is done. On rarer occasions, the client will contact the therapist to inform him/her of a drug overdose. When the overdose is unintentional, the client is likely to be in a state of agitation and confusion. The therapist's first order of business is to confirm (1) the client's location and telephone number, (2) the types and amounts of drugs used, and (3) the time elapsed since the drugs were used. Next, the therapist must explain to the client that the therapist now will call for an emergency vehicle to meet the client at his/her present location.

When the client calls the therapist while in the process of a suicide attempt (either by overdose or by other means), it is imperative that the therapist speaks calmly and empathically in order to keep the client on the line. This is particularly necessary when the client is unwilling to reveal his/her whereabouts at first. If possible, the therapist may write a note to alert a colleague to call for an ambulance or to contact the operator and the police in order to trace the call. In the meantime, the therapist should work to assess the severity of the suicide attempt, try to instill a sense of hope, and solicit the client's cooperation in the rescue. Modern technology in communications has made this process a little less daunting, in that telephone options such as "caller ID" can help therapists track down a client's location even if he or she is not forthcoming, and/or doesn't remain on the line very long.

In the case of a suicidal emergency in which the client has not yet taken self-harming actions, the therapist can afford to respond a bit more cautiously and methodically. If a client is feeling hopeless as a result of continued drug problems (or losses related to drug use) the suicidal wishes may be reduced by attacking the hopelessness directly. If successful, the therapist may not have to contact a third party. In this case, a face-to-face therapy appointment should be arranged as soon as possible, preferably the same day or first thing the next morning.

The situation is a bit more tricky and serious when the client has not yet taken self-harming actions but is actively suicidal *and* cognitively impaired as a result of being intoxicated with drugs and/or alcohol. Drugs and alcohol are notorious for exacerbating a person's suicidal intentions (Marzuk et al., 1992) and for rendering the person less able to respond to others' attempts to help. Therefore, if the client calls the therapist in this state but does not seem to be able to understand the therapist's questions, the therapist is warranted in breaking confidentiality in order to take the safest course of action (e.g., contacting a relative of the client or calling directly for an ambulance).

Loss of Domicile/Disappearance from Domicile

Therapists sometimes are witness to their drug-abusing clients' expulsion from their household, usually by a relative, housemate, or landlord who has gone beyond the limits of toleration for the clients' drug-related behaviors. When such clients cannot find another friend or relative with whom to live, they may have no alternative but to go out on the streets, in shelters for the homeless, in drug houses, or (if they are resourceful and lucky) an inpatient facility.

The therapist can assist during this crisis by eliciting the client's permission to consult with other professionals, such as a case worker or a parole officer, in order to arrange for the client's admission to an inpatient detoxification and drug rehabilitation program. Although the inpatient setting may provide only a short-term solution to a long-term problem (McLellan et al., 1991), it is far better for the client to be receiving medical supervision than to be languishing on the streets. Furthermore, the client's participation in an inpatient program may help the client to regain favor with family members, as well as to establish a program of outpatient cognitive therapy after discharge.

Clients who are on a drug binge sometimes disappear from their homes for days at a time, usually while taking "shelter" with other drug abusers who are also "on a run." While such clients are away, they may be losing money, jobs, family ties, and physical health, but they often do not seem to notice or care about their crises until the "run" is over and they begin to crash (Gawin & Ellinwood, 1988). At this point, clients are forced to wake up to the harsh reality of losses and possible legal consequences (e.g., breaking the terms of their parole).

Clients who leave their homes to go on prolonged drug binges may be almost impossible to locate. Still, it is important for therapists to continue to try to reach them by telephone or mail, and to be prepared to resume treatment with them once they return. However, much work will need to be done in order to reduce the risk of a repetition of such an episode. This work includes emphasizing the importance (perhaps the necessity) of the client's contacting the therapist on a regular and frequent basis (especially whenever cravings for drugs are elevated), and learning relapse prevention strategies (Carroll, Rounsaville, & Keller, 1991; Marlatt & Gordon, 1985; Washton, 1988).

Loss of Employment

A client who loses a job, whether or not as a direct result of drug use, often reacts with an accentuation of hopelessness and negative affect. For example, a client who derives most of his sense of self-esteem from his job may respond to the loss of the job by believing that now he has nothing to lose by going out and getting "ripped" or "wasted." We have encountered clients who have endorsed variations on the following theme: "I worked so hard to stay off drugs, and look what it got me—nothing! If that's the way it's going to be, I might as well just go out and get messed up!"

When a therapist learns that a substance-abusing client has lost a job, swift and concerted effort is called for in order to help the client solve this life-disrupting problem. Obtaining new legal sources of income such as unemployment insurance, public assistance, or a new job, becomes a high-priority agenda item for therapy. Therapists must be aware of the newly fired client's propensity for giving up, abdicating all financial responsibilities, seeking money via illegal means, and "self-medicating" (Castaneda, Galanter, & Franco, 1989; Khantzian, 1985) with drugs and alcohol. Naturally, in addition to helping the client cope with the loss of the job, the therapist must also focus on the substance abuse problem per se; otherwise, the client's poor work habits will result in prolonged and/or serial unemployment.

Rifts and Losses in Close Personal Relationships

Conflict, separation, and loss in significant relationships are common sources of crisis for substance-abusing clients. We have seen clients become extremely dysphoric, angry, and hopeless when parents have "disowned" them, mates have broken up with them, contact with their children has been denied them (by an ex-spouse or the courts), and members of their family or circle of friends die.

New breaks in romantic and marital relationships in particular puts clients at risk for renewed or continued drug use. Clients may seek solace in their drugs of choice, hoping to deaden the pain of interpersonal loss. Or, they deliberately may engage in self-destructive behavior out of anger, hopelessness, guilt, or a desire to manipulate the other party. For example, one of our clients started an alcohol and cocaine binge in order to make his ex-girlfriend feel guilty and responsible for his "fall." He admitted later that he believed that she would take him back if he could convince her that the breakup "drove (him) to drink and drug again."

A particularly disturbing form of interpersonal crisis related to substance abuse is domestic violence. When the client is the victim of violence in the home, the therapist will need to have ready access to telephone numbers of protective shelters and support groups. Therapists should pay close attention to their women patients who are involved with substance-abusing men, as this type of relationship is significantly correlated with domestic violence and with the victim's retreat into heavier drug and alcohol abuse as a coping mechanism (Amaro, Fried, Cabral, & Zuckerman, 1990).

When the client is the perpetrator of physical or sexual abuse of a minor, the therapist is legally obligated to inform child protection authorities. In order to keep the client in treatment, and thereby help to control this serious problem, we strongly advise therapists to encourage their clients to report themselves to the appropriate agencies while in the therapist's supportive presence. The therapist who is willing and able to remain collaborative under these most trying of circumstances stands the best chance of helping abusive clients to work toward change.

Finally, when a client's loved one has died, the therapist must react with great sensitivity to the client's grief, yet still be willing to call attention to the client's now increased risk for drug abuse. In Newman and Wright (1994), the therapist dealt with a client's grief by suggesting that the deceased person would not have wanted the client to harm herself in any way. In fact—the therapist opined—the woman who died would have felt terribly guilty if she knew that the client were relapsing and considering suicide in response to her grief.

Medical Emergencies

Clients who abuse drugs and alcohol are at substantially greater risk for incurring acute medical crises than are members of the general population (Frances & Miller, 1991; Grossman & Schottenfeld, 1992; O'Connor, Chang, & Shi, 1992; Schleifer, Delaney, Tross, & Keller, 1991). Examples include the alcohol abuser who becomes critically jaundiced as a result of liver atrophy, the pregnant crack abuser who goes into premature labor, the diabetic who shoots heroin instead of his insulin and becomes comatose, the asthmatic woman who smokes free-base cocaine and begins to asphyxiate, and others.

Tragically, these individuals also are at significantly increased risk of contracting the AIDS virus (Chiasson et al., 1989; Fullilove, Fullilove, Bowser, & Gross, 1990; Goldsmith, 1988).

> After learning that he was seropositive for HIV, Roland called the therapist in an extreme state of agitation, saying over and over again, "I'm going to die, I'm going to die!" First, the therapist responded by offering a great deal of sympathy and allowed Roland the opportunity to vent. Next, the therapist assessed whether there was any immediate likelihood of drug use or suicidal behavior. Finally, after 30 minutes on the telephone, the client was calmed down sufficiently that he could be engaged in looking for ways to maintain hope. Specifically, the therapist noted that although Roland was seropositive, he was asymptomatic for AIDS and might remain that way for many years to come. They agreed that in order to maximize the symptom-free period, Roland would have to live as healthy a lifestyle as possible, as exemplified by staying off drugs. They reasoned that this strategy would increase Roland's chances of surviving long enough to see the day when more effective treatments would be developed.
>
> Later, when Roland arrived for a face-to-face therapy session, the issue of sexual responsibility was addressed. All the while, the therapist continued to be empathic toward Roland, thus disproving the client's expectation that even the therapist would now treat him as a leper.

When therapists surmise that their clients are experiencing serious, acute medical difficulties, it is imperative that they instruct their clients to seek emergency treatment as soon as possible. This may be accomplished by the clients' calling their physicians, transporting themselves to the nearest hospital, arranging for a friend or relative to take them to the hospital, or simply calling for an ambulance if the situation is critical.

At times, clients will resist the therapist's pleas to seek medical help, because they *want* to worsen the crisis (perhaps due to hopelessness and resultant passive suicidality), because they resent the implied "weakness" or loss of control over their bodies, or because they fear that hospital tests will reveal their active drug abuse. In such cases, when the therapist's suggestions fall on deaf ears, the therapist may need to call for help without the client's consent and hope to repair the therapeutic alliance after the medical crisis abates.

Legal Crises

When clients actively abuse drugs, they run the risk of criminal apprehension, especially when "clean" urinalyses are required on a regular basis as a condition of parole. In addition to the legal hazards incurred by using illicit substances in and of themselves, active drug abusers are prone to engage in other illegal activities as well. For example, one of our clients was arrested when she was caught trying to cash forged checks. Another client served time in prison as a result of stealing and fencing shipments of electronics equipment from the docks where he worked. In both of these cases, the motive for the crimes was to obtain money to feed expensive cocaine habits.

When therapists learn that a client is involved in illegal activities, they must first determine whether other parties are at risk of being harmed. If so, there is an obligation to alert the police as well as the intended victim(s). Ideally, this situation can be averted if the client (1) is willing to work with the therapist to cease and desist from the criminal actions in question, (2) agrees to voluntarily inform his/her parole office, or (3) is amenable to inpatient supervision for the substance abuse problem that fuels the criminal behavior.

If no others are at risk (and the therapist is still bound by the principle of confidentiality), the therapist must find a way to enlist the client's cooperation in doing the kinds of problem solving necessary to find legal alternatives to the criminal behavior. The therapist will also need to help the patient test and challenge dysfunctional beliefs, such as "There's nothing I can do about this problem"; "There ain't no way out of this situation except (to engage in the illegal activities)"; "There's nothing wrong with what I'm doing"; and "It's okay to do what I'm doing because if I'm careful I won't get caught." Without moralizing, the therapist also can help the client to examine the pros and cons of the illegal behaviors, as well as the advantages and disadvantages of prosocial methods of goal attainment.

COMMON FACTORS ACROSS SUBSTANCE-RELATED CRISES

Although each crisis needs to be assessed individually, it is instructive to review some of the factors that are common across substance-related crisis situations. These factors can serve as useful guideposts in doing an individual case formulation at times of crisis.

Urgency and Immediacy

Although the precipitants for the crisis may have been festering for some time and been addressed in therapy, when the crisis occurs the substance-abusing client presents for a session desiring a quick and tidy solution. It is easy for the therapist to pick up on the client's sense of urgency and abandon a structured approach to the session. However, it is during this "crisis mode" that a session agenda is all the more important. The session structure helps the clinician and client to stay problem focused and to ensure that problems are prioritized appropriately. By identifying specific problems and prioritizing them, the therapist models effective problem solving and the client may modify overgeneralized, catastrophic thoughts (e.g., "I've failed again, everything is going wrong—my life is over!") to more constructive construals of their situation (e.g., "The urinalysis required for my job application was positive because I slipped and used marijuana a few days ago. I may not get this job because of that, but I can use therapy to help me to stay clean so that my next urinalysis is clean").

Skill Deficit/Problem Solving

The clients' psychological skills deficits become highly exposed during crises, thus hindering effective crisis management. Simultaneously dealing with a crisis and developing problem-solving skills is akin to reading the directions for a fire extinguisher when you are surrounded by flames. Nevertheless, crises can be used as opportunities to learn or practice problem-solving skills.

> Juan had been making good progress in his recovery from heroin addiction and was pursuing his GED. He presented for a session in obvious distress and shared that he was considering returning to selling drugs. It eventually emerged that Juan was unable to balance and maintain his checkbook, and some of his checks had bounced. This triggered his sense of shame and failure. Juan's first—and "easiest" reaction—was to give up and use drugs again. The more adaptive—though difficult reaction—was to think about how to learn to manage his money, and his financial records as part of his overall recovery and lifestyle change.

Trigger for Use/Hopelessness

Even when a substance-abusing client seems to be making progress and developing a lifestyle congruent with abstinence, the permission-giving beliefs and a sense of hopelessness that may lie dormant can be triggered by a crisis. In such a scenario, clients typically minimize or overlook the therapeutic gains they have made, focusing instead on their current hardship. This leads to a magnification of their pessimism, and an activation of their all-or-none belief that their work in therapy was entirely for naught. At such times, it is critical that therapists focus the clients' attention on their strengths and progress to date. This will help them to feel supported, boost their morale, and orient them toward constructively dealing with the crisis. Clients need to learn that setbacks are not synonymous with abject failure, and that doing effective "damage control" in times of crisis is a very important part of long-term maintenance of therapeutic gains.

Affective Arousal

Along with the sense of urgency listed above, substance-abusing clients often respond to crises with extreme affective arousal. The level of affect and agita-

tion can be disconcerting for even the most experienced, level-headed therapist. This may be especially so if the clients perceive that the therapist will report them to the authorities (e.g., parole officer), and therefore the clients direct
their anger toward the therapist.

It is often the case that the client's reaction to a life crisis is exacerbated by
the dysregulation of emotional processing and reliance on drugs and/or alcohol
to suppress strong affect. The client in crisis may present for session with unmodulated emotions and the desire to have them "go away." When substance-
abusing clients react in this manner, they run the risk of spiraling into relapse,
dropping out of treatment, violating parole, or attempting suicide. Simply managing the crisis without a worsening of the relapse is a therapeutic success.

For clients who have been ambivalent about change or who minimize or
deny a substance abuse problem, the crisis, handled deftly and compassion-
ately, may represent an opportunity to initiate a progression through the stages
of change. In the parlance of 12-step approaches to recovery, crises can be
thought of as moments of "hitting bottom," when the clients realize their pre-
dicaments and increase their motivation to change. It must be remembered,
however, that this desire to change is by no means automatic. Quite to the contrary, it requires great degrees of motivation, know-how, and support to make
significant life improvements in the throes and aftermath of a crisis. This is
where a well-executed course of cognitive therapy is invaluable.

Crisis and Emotional Arousal as Stimuli
for Progressive Change

Emotions can be thought of as action dispositions (Greenberg, Rice, & Elliot,
1993; Lang, Cuthbert, & Bradley, 1998). Emotions both direct experience and
are changed by it. That is, emotional arousal may provide a catalyst to generate
novel reactions to and interpretations of situations. In turn, situations that elicit
intense affective experiences provide opportunities to revise one's cognitive, affective, and behavioral reactions.

When substance-abusing clients present with crises, their affect is often extreme and unmodulated. From a clinical standpoint, these crisis situations
bring to light the very addictive patterns that had been obfuscated by denial
and resistance. Prochaska et al. (1992) noted that consciousness raising, dramatic relief, and environmental reevaluation are primary interventions at the
precontemplation stage. These can be addressed in a crisis situation such that
the immediate crisis can be managed and the client is able to use the experience
to foster stage progression.

Prioritizing the relevant issues and engaging in prescriptive problem solving helps to break down the crisis into component parts. This process serves to
decatastrophize the situation, to develop more manageable tasks, and to foster
a sense of efficacy for personal change. Specific skill deficits may also emerge
from this process, which are prime targets for therapeutic attention.

CASE STUDY

Kevin is a 26-year-old male who sought therapy following a promotion and re-location in his job. He and his wife moved away from their hometown so that Kevin could pursue this promotion. Kevin stated that the move and new job were intimidating but "there was no way I could say 'no.'" Kevin sought therapy about 6 months after the move at the urging of his wife who, according to Kevin's intake report, claimed that he had changed and appeared more depressed and isolated. His symptoms met DSM-IV criteria for adjustment disorder with depressed mood, as well as social phobia (American Psychiatric Association, 1994) following the promotion. Kevin acknowledged that his new position required more exposure to group presentations, consulting with unfamiliar people, and more frequent performance reviews.

The intake evaluation indicated that Kevin denied any drug or alcohol use problems. Considering the comorbidity of social phobia and substance use (i.e., Heckelman & Schneier, 1995; Rapee, 1995), the therapist (J. R. R.) performed a brief assessment during the first session. When asked how he relaxed after dealing with the pressure of the day, Kevin said that he and his wife had a stocked home bar and that he enjoyed a drink with dinner. He said that drinking helped him unwind, but he denied getting drunk or drinking outside the home.

Kevin and his therapist met for weekly sessions over the next 3 months. Kevin, though initially evasive and nervous, began to grow more trusting and disclosed the intensity of his discomfort in his current position. Kevin seemed to respond well to cognitive therapy and improved his ability to recognize his automatic thoughts in stressful situations, and to test his theories rather than assume them to be true and avoid situations on the basis of those assumptions.

Kevin arrived for the thirteenth session and handed his mood scales to the therapist. His depression and anxiety scores, which had been steadily improving, had skyrocketed into the severe range. Kevin also endorsed an item that stated "I would like to kill myself." Kevin's face was forlorn and he seemed to choke back tears as the therapist commented on the scores and his affect. A summary of the ensuing therapeutic dialogue is as follows:

THERAPIST: From the looks of these scores and the look on your face it seems like this might have been a difficult week for you. Would you like to share what's been going on with you?

KEVIN: It's over. I've screwed up everything. I don't even know why I bothered coming here today. I'm so stupid. [Leans forward and starts to sob.] Everything's ruined and there's nothing that can help me.

THERAPIST: Kevin, it's obvious that whatever happened was very important. I would imagine it was very difficult for you to come in here today and I'm glad you did. Let's take our time today. Let me know when you're ready to talk about whatever happened. Please, take your time. Then let's put our heads together and use the rest of this hour to see what we can accomplish. If we need to, we can schedule an additional meeting as soon as possible, even later this evening if you think it would be helpful. How does that idea sound?

The therapist's response was meant to reduce the sense of urgency and hopelessness, while maintaining a problem focus. The implicit message from the therapist was, "Whatever you are about to tell me, we will collaboratively find some way to work through it."

Kevin went on to report that he had been arrested for drunk driving the night before and had been released from jail that morning. During the previous day at work his department had received feedback that they needed to "pick up the pace" on a project, and Kevin's boss wanted him to make a presentation at the next month's meeting to report on the progress. Later, Kevin overheard two coworkers questioning management's decision to promote him to their office. Kevin reported that these two occurrences were blows to his confidence and triggered his core belief of inadequacy. He said that he had three mixed drinks in 30 minutes at a bar near the train station. Then, he bought a six-pack of beer during his ride home from the train station because he wanted to calm down so that his wife would not suspect that he was having problems at work. He admitted that, contrary to his earlier assertions in session, he had increasingly frequented bars on his way home from work over the past few months. This particular evening he misjudged a turn and hit a parked car in a residential community near his home. He was arrested for driving while intoxicated.

THERAPIST: Kevin, I'm sorry that you've had to endure all this in the past 24 hours. That would be overwhelming for anyone. How are you feeling now that you've shared your story?

KEVIN: I can't believe that it happened. It seems like a dream. . . . I'd do anything to undo last night. I don't know how I'm going to get past all this. I'm sorry to dump all this on you.

THERAPIST: Kevin, this is what therapy is all about—handling the tough stuff. Of course, I wish that you didn't have to endure all that happened last night. But, I'm glad you made it here today so that we can roll up our sleeves and handle these issues. Before we begin, I want to check with you about this item you circled on the mood scale, "I would like to kill myself."

KEVIN: I wish I could make all these problems go away. Tina [Kevin's wife] was so upset last night. . . . I can't believe all of this happened.

THERAPIST: I know I can only guess how you're feeling right now and please know that I'm not dismissing the seriousness of the situation. That being said, what would killing yourself accomplish?

KEVIN: I wouldn't have to feel the way I'm feeling. I wouldn't have to face Tina and to go back to work. Now I'm going to face a whole bunch of other people. I don't know if I can handle that. . . . I've never felt so ashamed.

Though Kevin had no history of suicidality, the therapist wanted to take his current comments seriously. It quickly emerged that Kevin's reason for contemplating suicide was to escape from his problems and the "shame" of facing others. The therapist encouraged Kevin to consider some of the treatment gains he had made up to this point in therapy with regard to overcoming his tendency to make assumptions about how others would react to him and to catastrophize potential outcomes. The therapist was careful to communicate that he was not trying to minimize or invalidate Kevin's reaction but rather to remind him that there were steps he could take other than killing himself to mitigate the situation. Kevin soon acknowledged that he had no intent to harm himself and agreed to a plan for safety.

Kevin and the therapist proceeded to develop a plan for handling the most immediate problems resulting from the arrest (i.e., arrangements to have the car repaired, making an appointment with an attorney). The therapist then took the opportunity to address the issue of Kevin's drinking.

THERAPIST: What are your thoughts about scheduling another session in the next day or two in order to touch base about the things you have to take care of tomorrow and to discuss some of the longer-range issues?

KEVIN: [sighing] I guess we should. If I know I'm coming to see you tomorrow I'll be more likely to follow through and call the lawyer.

THERAPIST: Kevin, I imagine that this has been a difficult meeting for you, and I appreciate the fact that you came in for our meeting when it would have been easy to avoid it. With that in mind, I would like to suggest that we place the issue of alcohol at the top of our list tomorrow. [Notices Kevin's face redden and his eyes tear slightly.] How are you feeling about this suggestion? By your expression it looks like I've triggered some thoughts.

KEVIN: I guess I've been fooling myself about my drinking. Now I'm a drunk driver and I've really messed up a lot of stuff in my life. Have you ever worked with anyone as screwed up as me?

THERAPIST: It sounds like you're already concluding that you must be pretty "screwed up," to use your words. It also sounds as if you are feeling regret and maybe shame about what has happened. Am I capturing some of how you're feeling?

KEVIN: Yeah, it's gonna be hard to face reality when I leave here.

THERAPIST: How was it to face me today?

KEVIN: To be honest, I thought about not showing up but I had to. something.

THERAPIST: Did you have any thoughts about what my reaction would be to the drunk driving offense?

KEVIN: I knew that you wouldn't come out and criticize me for it, but I'm sure you're disappointed and must think I'm some sort of lying loser.

THERAPIST: Your "mind reading" of my thoughts is similar to what you do with other people in your life. I'm guessing that the citation only listed the offense of "driving while intoxicated" and did not make any added judgments about you as a person. I view this incident as a mistake, an important one with some important consequences, but one which we'll work together to help you to overcome. Have you ever had some other challenge in your life and wondered if you'd be able to handle it?

KEVIN: [pause] Now that I think about it, I had to drop a chemistry course in college because I failed the midterm miserably and I didn't want my GPA to take a hit. I'd never failed an exam like that before. I never even told my parents because I felt so bad about that.

THERAPIST: How did you decide to handle the situation?

KEVIN: Well, it was a required course so I enrolled for it again the next semester, I made sure I reviewed the notes I already had, even before the first class, and I made sure I kept up with all the work and studied hard before exams. I didn't do great in the class but I got a B and was quite pleased with that.

THERAPIST: My hope is that we will work together to handle your drunk driving arrest in a similar manner. We need to have you break some old patterns and start with some new perspectives and behaviors. It strikes me that the first step you took with the chemistry class was to recognize the problem and take a step. I'm guessing that was a difficult but pivotal step for you. You then made some important changes in your study habits that paid off and it sounds like you even had some pride about that B. Am I right?

KEVIN: Yeah. I came close to giving up a few times until I got back the midterm and learned that I did all right.

THERAPIST: So there may have been some thoughts prior to the midterm such as, "This new study plan isn't helping, I might as well just give up." It sounds as if you handled those urges to stop studying and stayed the course. To tie this in with our current session and the issue of drinking, do you have any urges to drink right now?

KEVIN: No way! That's the last thing I need on top of everything else.

THERAPIST: The next few sessions will provide important opportunities for us to reconceptualize our work together. Our job will be to put our heads together and understand the role of drinking in your life, and to come up with ways to make positive changes. What are your thoughts about making a commitment to focus on the alcohol problem?

KEVIN: It's hard to hear it put that way, but I guess there's no getting around it now.

THERAPIST: Well, for starters, it would be very important for you to keep tabs of situations when you typically have a drink or when you feel an urge to have a drink. This is important information for both of us so that we can be aware of these patterns and learn how to manage them. That would be my suggestion for a homework assignment—to monitor and document the situations in which you typically have a drink or whenever you notice a desire to drink.

Thus, the immediate crisis was managed, and the tasks of therapy were redefined and upgraded to reflect Kevin's alcohol problem as a therapeutic priority. The therapist set the pace for the session by stating that not every issue could be addressed or solved that day. However, options for scheduling additional sessions and concrete plans of action were addressed. The therapist gently reintroduced Kevin's alcohol use as an undeniable element of the treatment plan in a nonjudgmental, collaborative way. Using the stages of change model, Kevin was confronted with his denial through the drunk driving arrest. In the session above he experienced relief from his emotional distress and gained a new sense of direction and hope. The therapist attempted to decatastrophize the driving offense without minimizing its seriousness. Kevin may be considered to have moved from precontemplation to contemplation, considering the possibility of change and taking some initial steps. The therapist set up an agenda for the next session to "contemplate" the role of alcohol use within the ongoing cognitive conceptualization and to explore with Kevin the prospects for making changes in his lifestyle. Further, by giving Kevin a self-monitoring homework assignment, the therapist constructively breached the preparation stage as well.

CONCLUSION

The treatment of clients who abuse drugs and/or alcohol is fraught with many challenges. Developing a therapeutic alliance while addressing issues related to denial of substance use requires the right blend of accurate empathy and forthright confrontation. Furthermore, life crises precipitated by substance use—either directly or indirectly—are almost inevitable in the course of therapy. Handled skillfully, however, the management of a substance-related crisis can serve as a turning point in therapy, particularly for clients who are ambivalent about change. The cognitive-behavioral model provides an efficacious and flexible approach for managing crises as well as other clinical issues associated with substance abuse. This approach not only helps clients to manage the problems at hand, but also empowers them with coping skills to make long-term lifestyle changes conducive to overcoming substance abuse.

NOTE

1. By contrast, some inpatient settings provide fertile ground for confrontation, in that the clients cannot easily drop out of treatment, and therefore must learn to adapt to critical feedback about their denials and minimizations. Furthermore, group therapy settings can also be conducive to a more confrontational approach, in that the clients face both the power of peer pressure to admit a problem, and the nurturing support of many people. Yes, it is possible for individual outpatient therapists to provide both critical feedback and support at the same time, but a one-on-one relationship of this sort, in this setting, requires a much more delicate balance.

REFERENCES

Amaro, H., Fried, L. E., Cabral, H., & Zuckerman, B. (1990). Violence during pregnancy and substance use. *American Journal of Public Health, 80,* 575–579.

American Psychiatric Association. (1994). *Diagnostic and statistical manual of mental disorders* (4th ed.). Washington, DC: Author.

Beck, A. T., Wright, F. D., Newman, C. F., & Liese, B. S. (1993). *Cognitive therapy of substance abuse.* New York: Guilford Press.

Carroll, J. M., Rounsaville, B. J., & Keller, D. S. (1991). Relapse prevention strategies for the treatment of cocaine abuse. *American Journal of Drug and Alcohol Abuse, 17,* 249–265.

Castaneda, R., Galanter, M., & Franco, H. (1989). Self-medication among addicts with primary psychiatric disorders. *Comprehensive Psychiatry, 30,* 80–83.

Chiasson, R. E., Bacchetti, P., Osmond, D. Moss, A., Onishi, R., & Carlson, V. (1989). Cocaine use and HIV infection in intravenous drug users in the United States. *Journal of the American Medical Association, 261,* 2677–2684.

Follette, W. C. (1998). Expanding the domains of clinical behaviorism: A comment on Dougher. *Behavior Therapy, 29*(4), 593–601.

Frances, R. J., & Miller, S. I. (Eds.). (1991). *Clinical textbook of addictive disorders.* New York: Guilford Press.

Fullilove, R. E., Fullilove, M. T., Bowser, B. F., & Gross, S. A. (1990). Risk of sexually transmitted disease among black adolescent crack users in Oakland and San Francisco, California. *Journal of the American Medical Association, 263,* 851–857.

Gawin, F. H., & Ellinwood, E. H. (1988). Cocaine and other stimulants: Actions, abuse and treatment. *New England Journal of Medicine, 318,* 1173–1182.

Goldsmith, M. F. (1988). Sex tied to drugs = STD spread. *Journal of the American Medical Association, 260,* 2009.

Greenberg, L. S., Rice, L. N., & Elliot, R. (1993). *Facilitating emotional change: The moment by moment process.* New York: Guilford Press.

Grilo, C. M. (1993). An alternative perspective regarding "Non-compliance: What to do?" *The Behavior Therapist, 16*(8), 219–220.

Grossman, J., & Schottenfield, R. (1992). Pregnancy and women's issues. In T. R. Kosten & H. D. Kleber (Eds.), *Clinician's guide to cocaine addiction: Theory, research, and treatment* (pp. 374–388). New York: Guilford Press.

Heckelman, L. R., & Schneier, F. R. (1995). In R. G. Heimberg, M. R. Liebowitz, D. A. Hope, & F. R. Schneier (Eds.), *Social phobia: Diagnosis, assessment, and treatment* (pp. 3–20). New York: Guilford Press.

Khantzian, E. J. (1985). The self-medication hypothesis of addictive disorders: Focus on heroin and cocaine dependence. *American Journal of Psychiatry, 142,* 1259–1264.

Klion, R. E., & Pfenninger, D. T. (1997). Personal construct psychotherapy of addictions. *Journal of Substance Abuse Treatment, 14*(1), 37–43.

Koob, G. F., & Le Moal, M. (1997). Drug abuse: Hedonic homeostatic dysregulation. *Science, 278*(5335), 52–58.

Lang, P. J., Cuthbert, B. N., & Bradley, M. M. (1998). Measuring emotion in therapy: Imagery, activation, and feeling. *Behavior Therapy, 29*(4), 655–674.

Layden, M. A., Newman, C. F., Freeman, A., & Morse, S. B. (1993). *Cognitive therapy of borderline personality disorder.* Needham Heights, MA: Allyn & Bacon.

Mahoney, M. J. (1991). *Human change processes: The scientific foundations of psychotherapy.* New York: Basic Books.

Marlatt, G. A., & Gordon, J. R. (Eds.). (1985). *Relapse prevention: Maintenance strategies in the treatment of addictive behaviors.* New York: Guilford Press.

Marzuk, P. M., Tardiff, K., Leon, A. C., Stagis, M., Morgan, E. R., & Mann, J. J. (1992). Prevalence of cocaine use among residents of New York City who committed suicide during a one-year period. *American Journal of Psychiatry, 149,* 371–375.

McLellan, A. T., O'Brien, C. P., Metzger, D., Alterman, A. I., Cornish, J., & Urschel, H. (1991). How effective is substance abuse treatment—Compared to what? In C. P. O'Brien & J. H. Jaffe (Eds.), *Understanding the addictive states* (pp. 231–252). New York: Raven Press.

Miller, W. R., & Rollnick, S. (1991). *Motivational interviewing: Preparing people to change addictive behavior.* New York: Guilford Press.

Nesse, R. M., & Berridge, K. C. (1997). Psychoactive drug use in evolutionary perspective. *Science, 278*(5335), 63–66.

Newman, C. F. (1994). Understanding client resistance: Methods for enhancing motivation to change. *Cognitive and Behavioral Practice, 1*(1), 47–69.

Newman, C. F. (1997). Substance abuse. In R. Leahy (Ed.), *Practicing cognitive therapy: A guide to interventions* (pp. 221–245). Northvale, NJ: Aronson.

Newman, C. F., & Wright, F. D. (1994). Substance abuse. In F. Dattilio & A. Freeman (Eds.), *Cognitive-behavioral strategies in crisis intervention* (pp. 119–136). New York: Guilford Press.

O'Connor, P. G., Chang, G., & Shi, J. (1992). Medical complications of cocaine use. In T. R. Kosten & H. D. Kleber (Eds.), *Clinician's guide to cocaine addiction: Theory, research, and treatment* (pp. 241–272). New York: Guilford Press.

Prochaska, J. O. (1994). Strong and weak principles for progressing from precontemplation to action on the basis of twelve problem behaviors. *Health Psychology, 13*(1), 47–51.

Prochaska, J. O., DiClemente, C. C., & Norcross, J. C. (1992). In search of how people change: Applications to addictive behaviors. *American Psychologist, 47*(9), 1102–1114.

Rapee, R. M. (1995). Descriptive psychopathology of social phobia. In R. G. Heimberg, M. R. Liebowitz, D. A. Hope, & F. R. Schneier (Eds.), *Social phobia: Diagnosis, assessment, and treatment* (pp. 41–66). New York: Guilford Press.

Schleifer, S. J., Delaney, B. R., Tross, S., & Keller, S. E. (1991). AIDS and addictions. In R. J. Frances & S. I. Miller (Eds.), *Clinical textbook of addictive disorders* (pp. 299–319). New York: Guilford Press.

Seligman, M. E. P. (1993). *What you can change and what you can't: The complete guide to successful self-improvement.* New York: Knopf.

Wachtel, P. L. (Ed.) (1982). *Resistance: Psychodynamic and behavioral approaches.* New York: Plenum.

Washton, A. M. (1988). Preventing relapse to cocaine. *Journal of Clinical Psychiatry, 49,* 34–38.

Woody, G. E., Luborsky, L., McLellan, A. T., O'Brien, C. P., Beck, A. T., Blaine, J., Herman, I., & Hole, A. (1983). Psychotherapy for opiate addicts: Does it help? *Archives of General Psychiatry, 40,* 1081–1086.

Woody, G. E., McLellan, A. T., & O'Brien, C. P. (1990). Research on psychopathology and addiction: Treatment implications. *Drug and Alcohol Dependence, 25,* 121–123.

Young, J. E. (1994). *Cognitive therapy for personality disorders: A schema-focused approach* (rev. ed.). Sarasota, FL: Professional Resource Press.

SUGGESTED READINGS

Beck, A. T., Wright, F. D., Newman, C. F., & Liese, B. S. (1993). *Cognitive therapy of substance abuse.* New York: Guilford Press.

Marlatt, G. A., & Gordon, J. R. (Eds.). (1985). *Relapse prevention: Maintenance strategies in the treatment of addictive behaviors.* New York: Guilford Press.

Woody, G. E., McLellan, A. T., & O'Brien, C. P. (1990). Research on psychopathology and addiction: Treatment implications. *Drug and Alcohol Dependence, 25,* 121–123.

6

Rape Trauma

Elizabeth Muran
Raymond DiGiuseppe

Current research underscores the imposing effects of experiencing the trauma of rape. The *Diagnostic and Statistical Manual of Mental Disorders,* fourth edition (DSM-IV; American Psychiatric Association, 1994) describes "trauma" as an event that involves perceived or actual threat and elicits an extreme emotional response. The psychological sequelae that is frequently seen in survivors of the trauma of rape is called *posttraumatic stress disorder* (PTSD). Traumatic events, especially rape, occur in tremendous numbers, and a significant proportion of of survivors will develop PTSD. Moreover, PTSD-like syndromes have been described in the literature for more than 100 years under various labels such as nervous shock, compensation neurosis, hysteria, traumatophobia, and others (Foa, Steketee, & Rothbaum, 1989; Dancu & Foa, 1992). Despite the magnitude and long-standing history of PTSD and rape, the treatment of PTSD is a relatively new territory for clinicians. It has only been recognized as a diagnosis since 1980 when it first appeared in the DSM-III (American Psychiatric Association, 1980). Subsequently, several cognitive-behavioral treatment programs for PTSD have been developed and studied.

In the last decade, treatment outcome studies have approached better methodological standards (e.g., Rothbaum, Foa, Murdock, Riggs, & Walsh, 1992), bringing important issues and strategies to the foreground and developing an empirical foundation for clinical practice. Cognitive-behavioral treatments have proven to be efficacious, having been the subject of the greatest number of well-controlled outcome studies.

Despite the growing number of rigorous treatment studies, there remains very little information and a serious paucity of empirical findings about crisis intervention strategies with rape survivors (Calhoun & Atkeson, 1991). Crisis intervention counseling is short term, often limited to one or two sessions. It is the earliest and often the only intervention that many rape survivors experience. However, its effects on recovery and prevention of long-term psychopathology have yet to be studied. In light of the inherent limitations due to both the brevity of therapeutic contact in crisis intervention and the lack of empirical data, the goal of this chapter is to provide a practical guide for clinicians who are working with rape trauma survivors[1] in crisis.

POSTTRAUMATIC STRESS DISORDER

DSM-III-R (American Psychiatric Association, 1987) described PTSD as an anxiety disorder including a criterion of a precipitating trauma, a stressor that is beyond the range of usual human stressors. Although both acute and chronic reactions following exposure to trauma vary along a continuum of adjustment, some survivors do not recover to their pretrauma level of functioning (Fairbank & Brown, 1987). Only a minority of these survivors seek crisis intervention or longer-term treatment. Within this group, many develop symptoms of PTSD. The hallmark symptoms include persistent, distressing, and intrusive recollections of the trauma, numbing of responsiveness to the environment, avoidance or escape in the presence of trauma-related cues, and a variety of autonomic, dysphoric, or cognitive symptoms that persist longer than 1 month after the trauma (Fairbank & Brown, 1987).

DSM-IV has retained the symptoms of PTSD delineated in DSM-III-R, but it has modified the "trauma" to include characteristics of the actual trauma, as well as the perception of threat to self. Because PTSD cannot be diagnosed until the required symptom constellation has lasted beyond 1 month, DSM-IV has introduced a new disorder called acute stress disorder (ASD), which overlaps PTSD considerably. The differences in criteria between PTSD and ASD are both the duration of symptoms and the emphasis in ASD on dissociative symptoms. ASD can be diagnosed in the immediate aftermath of a trauma, with the disturbance lasting for at least 2 days and less than 1 month. In order for ASD to be diagnosed, the individual must also experience three of five dissociative symptoms (derealization, depersonalization, dissociative amnesia, subjective sense of numbing, reduction in awareness of surroundings) immediately after the trauma.

In this chapter, we address rape, a trauma specifically acknowledged by the DSM-IV as a potential precipitant of PTSD. It has been found that shortly after the assault, 94% of rape survivors met criteria for PTSD; 3 months after the assault, 47% of survivors still suffered from PTSD; 17 years later, 16.5% of survivors still experienced PTSD (Rothbaum et al., 1992). This prospective study is indicative of the high prevalence of PTSD following rape. Most relevant to this chapter, almost all the rape survivors seen in the Rothbaum et al. (1992) study initially demonstrated symptoms of PTSD shortly after the assault. Given these findings, we may assume the presence of PTSD symptoms (now formally diagnosed as ASD) during initial contact or crisis intervention with these survivors.

GOALS OF CRISIS INTERVENTION WITH RAPE TRAUMA

Recounting the Trauma

Although many treatment approaches have been suggested for PTSD, cognitive-behavioral interventions rely primarily on exposure to help PTSD clients. The first step in exposure treatment often entails the verbal revelation of the traumatic event. It is important that this initial stage occur as early as possible. Many psychologists believe that the more successful an individual is at avoiding the stimuli, the more the individual's anxiety will be reinforced. Military psychologists have a long history of treating combat-related PTSD. Their experience indicates that early intervention is crucial to successful treatments. Animal and human learning studies indicate that successful avoidance of a conditioned stimulus results in the strengthening of both the anxiety to that stimuli and the avoidance of that stimuli. Thus, based on well-established learning principles, early intervention is crucial.

During the crisis period, most survivors of rape trauma experience high autonomic arousal and are, therefore, more inclined to disclose their traumatic experience to an attentive and supportive listener. The survivor is often driven to repeat descriptions of the assault as a need to retell her[2] experience. The therapist should encourage the recapitulations and the cathartic expressions, sensitively reinforcing the client to continue. It is important at this time that the therapist normalize the intense initial reactions of the survivor, while encouraging completion of the story. Of course, complete disclosure will be a difficult process, because many survivors may be unable to recall the entire experience and may also avoid confrontation with the painful memory details.

Many survivors have been inadvertently discouraged by friends and family from sharing their entire experience and their painful emotions. It can be extremely uncomfortable for friends and family members to listen to a recapitulation of the gruesome experience. They may also believe it is in the survivor's best interest to put this negative experience behind, not dwell on it, and carry on with life. Therefore, describing the assault and expressing related cognitions and emotions may be the first complete imaginal exposure for the survivor. Incomplete or spontaneous exposures (e.g., flashbacks, nightmares, and intrusive recollections) can be less therapeutic because they do not include all the conditioned stimuli. As a result, the incompleteness of such recollections may account for the lack of extinction of the PTSD responses. Complete exposure or more conditioned stimuli, on the other hand, may lead to extinction of PTSD responses. Moreover, Keane, Zimmerling, and Caddell (1985) have suggested that providing more cues (conditioned stimuli) during *in vitro* exposure may improve memory and enhance confrontation with the trauma. Furthermore, the subsequent increase in arousal following this memory will lead to better recall and ultimately a better match between the affect at the time of the trauma and at the time of recall; this improved match will facilitate the retrieval of memory details leading to complete exposure.

As the client is relating her experiences, the therapist should assess for PTSD symptoms and the degree to which she has difficulty or avoids recalling and retelling parts of the traumatic event. The therapist should also attend to the maladaptive thoughts and feelings regarding the client's role in the rape, reinforce adaptive thoughts and feelings, gently begin challenging inappropriate thoughts and feelings, and finally substitute more adaptive ones.

Drawing upon cognitve theories, Resick and Schnicke (1992) have suggested an information-processing model whereby the experience of trauma conflicts with preexisting assumptions about the self and the world, and this conflict is manifested in PTSD-like responses. The theory that processing an event requires a modification in existing beliefs is derived from Piaget's (1954) model of cognitive development. He proposed that assimilation and accomodation were two mechanisms used to modify beliefs about an experience. In other words, to reconcile the conflict, the survivor must distort the trauma experience to be more consistent with prior beliefs (assimilation) or alter her beliefs to adjust to this new information (accomodation). In view of this suggestion, the goal of crisis intervention is to help the survivor to neither assimilate (e.g., blaming self for rape) nor overaccommodate (e.g., never feeling safe again). Instead, the therapist's goal is to support the survivor in recalling the trauma, accept that it happened, and begin processing the related emotions.

Establishing and Maintaining a Therapeutic Alliance

The therapeutic alliance is just as critical to success (and often more difficult to establish) in crisis intervention as it is to any other therapeutic intervention, even though crisis therapy is brief. In fact, this is a limitation that may make the establishment of a therapeutic alliance more difficult, as the therapist, having minimal contact with the client, must be adept at establishing rapport and communicating effectively in a very short time. The therapist should employ both verbal and nonverbal strategies to validate the client's experience and to convey sensitivity, understanding, support, and a positive outlook toward recovery. These strategies are particularly critical with a survivor of rape, whose trust of self and others has been shaken. Another limitation in establishing a therapeutic alliance and inherent in treatment with trauma survivors is their high attrition rate, resulting from their inclination to avoid confrontation with the memory of the trauma and, therefore, the therapy process. Helping the survivor explore and, ultimately, overcome the resistance to confront the painful memories should again be done through a supportive and validating approach.

After normalizing the survivor's experience and defining a course of recovery, it is important here to get a clear agreement on the goals of therapy. Two important aspects of Bordin's (1979) model of the therapeutic alliance are agreement on the goals and agreement on the tasks, which are interdependent with a third aspect, the affective bond between client and therapist. The therapist may see the goals as reducing the anxiety and the avoidance behavior. However, the client may not agree. She may wish to keep the anxiety because it helps motivate avoidance. The client may believe that if she avoids well enough, she can prevent such an event from recurring.

Reaching an agreement on the goals of therapy may not be easy. The client may believe that continued and complete avoidance is achievable and the only reaction likely to bring a sense of safety. The therapist may need to first discuss the appropriateness and achievability of the client's goal. Then the therapist can help the client explore alternative goals. This needs to be done in a sensitive, nonforceful way. The therapist should be checking in regularly with the client for her experience of the therapy process and the therapist (Safran & Muran, 2000), which will serve to give some control to the survivor who has just undergone a trauma that violated her.

Once agreement on the goals is reached, the therapist can work toward achieving agreement on the tasks. This refers to the procedures the therapist will utilize to help the client reach the agreed-on tasks. The therapist may need to discuss the importance of verbal exposure. Some clients may find the procedure too threatening. Again, it may be necessary for the therapist to stop and address any issue and explore the resistance the client has about the procedures before implementing them. Even though the client may agree to the goals of therapy, as well as to the importance of talking about the rape trauma, she may still be resistant. Talking about the traumatic experience produces a great deal of anxiety. We have found that two possible anxiety reactions that may inhibit the process of therapy at this point are discomfort anxiety and shame.

If a client is resistant to recounting her story, we recommend that the therapist validate the client's experience and report that many survivors of rape have experienced similar difficulty recounting their trauma. Next, the therapist should ask the client how she feels about proceeding with her story. Some clients will have no difficulty reporting that they feel shame, or that the task is too hard for them. If they are able to express these emotions, the therapist can proceed by discussing the importance of targeting these emotions because they block the client's ability to proceed in therapy. However, we find that many clients are unable to acknowledge their emotional blocks. Patiently awaiting for the client's insight through reflective or nondirective techniques can be costly. The costs result from the fact that continued avoidance may reinforce the anxiety, and the client may not return for further sessions.

Therefore, we recommend a more active approach to assessing the resistance by hypothesis drive assessment (DiGiuseppe, 1991). Using this strategy, the therapist offers hypotheses concerning the emotions or thoughts the client is experiencing. In such a situation, the therapist could say, "Many women who have gone through similar experiences find they are too upset to talk about what happened to them. Does that sound like you?" The therapist waits for the client to respond, and if she affirms the question, the therapist continues, "Some women feel too much shame. They believe others will think badly of them for what happened. Others believe that it is just too hard to discuss these things. After all, the trauma was painful enough. Reliving it is just more painful. Which one of these sounds like a reaction you may be having? The first, the second, both, or neither?"

Notice that the client does not have to say much to answer. If she is unwilling to talk about an issue because of an emotional block, a lengthy reply would be unlikely. Providing the possibility for a curt reply makes it easier for her to proceed. In our experience, most clients reply honestly, and there seems to be little risk of leading the client.

Restructuring Cognitions Underlying Resistance

If the client reports that she experiences shame, the therapist would then proceed to uncover the belief that coexists with that shame. Perhaps she believes the therapist will think less of her, or that she was responsible for the rape. It is most important for the therapist to challenge these maladaptive thoughts and to share with the client the fact that he/she does not harbor any such thoughts of the client. Regardless of any poor judgment the client may believe she displayed by putting herself at risk for the rape, it could not have been predicted. The therapist should make clear to the client that she in no way "made" the rapist act as violently as he did. It is also important that the therapist challenge the client's feelings of worthlessness that resulted from the trauma. The experience of the rape in no way undoes all the positive aspects of the client's personality.

The client's discomfort anxiety emotions may be more difficult to change. Ellis (1985) maintains that discomfort anxiety is a frequent cause of resistance in psychotherapy. The recommended therapeutic strategy is to challenge the client's low frustration tolerance (Ellis, 1985, 1986) and replace it with the notion that they can tolerate any level of discomfort that they believe they can handle. We have generally found this strategy to be useful with most clients who resist talking about their emotional upset. However, suggesting to rape survivors—who have experienced an event beyond the range of usual human experiences—that they have a low tolerance for frustration because they resist recounting the trauma may be perceived as an invalidation of the traumatic experience.

Marie Joyce (personal communication, 1992) has proposed a variation on Ellis's (1986) concept of low frustration tolerance. She argues that many clients, blocked by discomfort anxiety from completing a goal, have failed despite levels of frustration and discomfort greater than those of most people in their reference group. The frustration they have tolerated may be average or higher.

The problem is that they are just not willing to experience a high enough frustration level that is required to complete the desired task.

Joyce (personal communication, 1992) recommends that we label such cognitive–emotional reactions as frustration intolerance. This frustration intolerance problem seems to arise with most PTSD clients and clients with physical disabilities, chronic illnesses, or other challenging and enduring stressors. Such clients endure greater frustration than the average person. Suggesting that they have low frustration tolerance is inaccurate and invalidating. Joyce recommends that we acknowledge the high degree of frustration they have endured while focusing on the belief that their task is "too difficult" to tolerate.

Thus, we wish to help survivors of rape develop greater frustration tolerance. Discussing the painful memories of the rape is very difficult, but it is also critical for recovery. It is in their best long-term interest to experience more discomfort temporarily in order to suffer less in the long run.

Gathering and Providing Information

After the client has recounted the trauma experience, it is important to gather information about immediate presenting problems, daily functioning, and available social support. Assessing suicidal risk should be done at this juncture, and steps must be taken as appropriate. Finally, information should be taken about the client's premorbid adjustment, interpersonal relationships, and any previous traumatic experiences.

Following the initial interview, the presence of PTSD symptoms can be efficiently assessed by the PTSD Symptom Scale (PSS; Foa, Riggs, Dancu, & Rothbaum, 1993). Although PTSD cannot be diagnosed before at least 1 month's duration of the symptoms listed here (ASD is the appropriate diagnosis), a preliminary assessment is important for an early measure of the PTSD responses that are present. This can serve as a baseline on which to contrast future changes or treatment gains. Most significantly, such an interview is an important vehicle to normalize the posttrauma experience for the survivor. The client needs to be educated about the most frequently experienced symptoms following a rape. Further, these PTSD responses and the responses specific to rape-related trauma can be normalized by communicating information to the client as follows:

"Symptoms of posttraumatic stress disorder can develop after a person has experienced a very upsetting event, especially one that is life-threatening, as rape is. These symptoms may affect your normal daily functioning as well as your relationships with others. They can affect you when you reexperience the rape in your thoughts and in your dreams. You may want to avoid activities, situations, feelings, and thoughts that you associate with the rape. You may become easily startled or aroused by anything that reminds you of the rape. You will probably be scared and cry often; you may have difficulty with your appetite and your sleep. You may feel somatic pain or soreness throughout your body, as well as physical symptoms specific to the attack—for example pain in the anal or vaginal area. Even if you try to block the rape from your mind, there may be a strong desire for you to think about how you could have changed or prevented the rape from happening. After being raped, most women experience diminished self-esteem, degradation, depression, sadness, guilt, shame, embarrassment, self-blame, and anger. Any or all these feelings could affect you intensely and often simultaneously. You could have mood swings, which inhibit social relatedness. If the rapist was someone you knew, your trust in people can be shattered. Whether or not the rapist is someone you knew, the world may no longer feel safe. Sometimes it will seem as though withdrawing is the best way to protect yourself emotionally. Try to remember, though, that it is now more than ever that you need support from your friends and family. Rape can be a very isolating experience, but you are not alone in what you are feeling, and there are people who can help you."

Information about the symptoms that are commonly experienced by other survivors of a rape trauma will normalize the experience, reduce distress over symptoms, and help the client begin to regain a sense of control and normalcy. There is a great deal of information to be provided, and it is understandably difficult for the survivor to concentrate, listen, and assimilate all or even parts of that which has been discussed. Therefore, in addition to the factual information communicated verbally, it may be helpful to provide the client with written handouts concerning rape-related responses as well as common myths about rape.

Coping Strategies

In view of the psychological sequelae of rape, the survivor's daily functioning, interpersonal relationships, and sexual functioning may reflect the negative aftereffects of the rape trauma. Therefore, coping strategies should be provided despite the brevity of the crisis intervention phase.

Stress Inoculation Training

Stress inoculation training (SIT) was originally developed by Meichenbaum (1985) in the early 1970s and adapted for use with rape survivors by Kilpatrick, Veronen, and Resick (1982). It is currently the most comprehensive and well-researched program for survivors of sexual assault (Calhoun & Atkeson, 1991). The objective of this program is to provide the survivor with a sense of control over her fears and anxiety by teaching her coping strategies to overcome her fears and improve her functioning in distressing situations.

Although it may not be possible to cover the entire training program within the limited time frame of crisis intervention, the program is well suited for adaptation to various needs and objectives. Ideally, the SIT program is designed to train clients within a course consisting of approximately 12 weekly 90-minute sessions. However, a more realistic goal, depending on the time provided, would be to shorten the educational phase and modify the skills training phase by not teaching all the skills. Possibly, follow-up sessions will be discussed after the initial meeting, and further training can be provided.

SIT is presented in two phases. The first phase is educational, in which learning theory (e.g., principles of stimulus generalization or higher order conditioning) is presented to the client as it applies to the development of her rape-related responses (i.e., PTSD symptoms). These responses are explained as occurring along three channels (Lang, 1968): (1) physical or autonomic responses, (2) behavioral or motoric responses, and (3) cognitive responses. The interrelationship among these channels can be discussed, using specific examples from the client's experience. The goals of crisis intervention already comprised, in effect, the first phase described earlier in this chapter.

The second phase of SIT is coping skills training, in which a variety of strategies (discussed below) are taught for coping with fear and anxiety.

Controlled Breathing

Deep diaphragmatic breathing is taught and practiced at a rate of approximately 4 seconds each for inhaling and exhaling. The initial instruction is to place one hand on the chest and the other hand on the abdomen. The next step is to expand the stomach like a balloon, with as little movement as possible from the hand on the chest. The procedure should be demonstrated and practiced to attain a smooth and fluid breathing cycle.

Muscle Relaxation

Jacobson's (1938) progressive muscle relaxation technique, more recently refined and modified by Bernstein and Borkovec (1973), demonstrates the contrast of tensing and relaxing major muscle groups of the whole body. It should be introduced through simultaneous instruction and demonstration. Typically, a muscle group is tensed for 5 to 10 seconds, attending to the sensation of the tension. Then the muscle is relaxed, and attention is focused on differentiating between the sensation of tensing and that of relaxing. The procedure is practiced in session and taped for daily home practice.

Covert Modeling

The client is instructed to imagine an anxiety-producing situation and imagine herself confronting it successfully, using the coping strategies she has learned to manage her anxiety.

Role Playing

The therapist models the desired behavior or communication; then the roles
are switched. The client practices a desired response to a rape-related problem.
Assertion training can be an important aspect of this skill, as interpersonal situations are often involved. For example, the client may need to communicate
her sexual discomfort or fears with her sexual partner. Education and role playing in assertive communication would help to countercondition the potential
anxiety in these situations.

Cognitive Restructuring

Survivors of sexual assault will often endorse maladaptive thoughts of self-
blame, future uncontrollability, and the futility of future responses. Cognitive
restructuring can help a survivor correct her beliefs that the world is dangerous and that she is incompetent. The goal is to reduce distress by teaching the
survivor to identify, evaluate, and change negative and dysfunctionl thinking
(Foa & Rothbaum, 1998). Cognitive restructuring of their negative self-blam-
ing thoughts should be done in a manner similar to that with other clients
(Beck & Emery, 1985; Walen et al., 1992). Our clinical experience suggests
that some areas of traditional cognitive-behavioral therapy may be more helpful than others. Both Beck (1976; Beck & Emery, 1985) and Ellis (1962; Ellis &
Dryden, 1987) have identified catastrophizing or "awfulizing" as dysfunctional beliefs leading to anxiety disorders. Challenging this belief has been an
important part of therapy for both these pioneers. Rape survivors are likely to
report the presence of such beliefs after their trauma and when they experience PTSD symptoms. However, it has been our professional experience that
targeting such catastrophizing beliefs in rape survivors and other PTSD clients is not helpful. Regardless of the theory proposed by Beck and Ellis that
such beliefs are irrational, antiempirical, and lead to emotional disturbance,
we have found that focusing on these beliefs results in a rupture of the therapeutic alliance. Survivors perceive such an intervention as insensitive and invalidating. Given the social context of the prevailing reactions to rape, most
people would agree with the following statements: "It is awful to have been
raped" and "It would be awful to be raped again." Challenging these specific
thoughts is socially unacceptable and will, undoubtedly, result in a broken
therapeutic alliance. We suggest that it would be preferable to focus on other
dysfunctional beliefs.

Ellis (1994) proposes that dysfunctional beliefs are undergirded by deeper
cognitive structures. He suggests that therapists target this "deeper" level,
where survivors hold absolutistic shoulds, oughts, and musts that go beyond
existent reality (e.g., "Really bad things must never happen to me"), driving
them into severe states of panic and depression. When investigating a survivor's attributions and inferences, it may be more thorough to further examine

the absolutistic demands underlying the automatic thoughts. Resick and Schnicke (1992) devised an effective procedure, cognitive processing therapy (CPT), for treating PTSD. Ellis (1994) suggests that CPT be coalesced with his rational-emotive behavior therapy (REBT), where core cognitive structures, as well as dysfunctional thoughts, are examined.

Regarding awfulizing beliefs, we have also found that it is helpful to restructure awfulizing statements in a manner to increase the client's frustration tolerance or self-efficacy. In other words, a revised thought could be, "I lived through an awful experience, and I'm strong enough to survive." This strategy acknowledges the trauma of the rape but redefines the reaction in an adaptive manner. We find that maladaptive thoughts of self-blame are much more fertile ground for intervention. Given that individuals often derive comfort from the belief that the world is fair and predictable, there is subsequently a search for explanation and meaning. This search predisposes individuals to attribute explanations in the face of trauma, which ultimately may account for responses of self-blame, helplessness, frustration, depression, and anger. Consonant with this theory of causal attribution is one advanced by Janoff-Bulman (1979), who proposes that directing blame for victimization at one's behavior rather than at one's character would result in fewer deficits. In other words, assigning some responsibility for the rape to a changeable behavior (e.g., "I could have walked home with someone from work") may enable the client to regain a sense of control. Assigning blame to one's character (e.g., "I'm a bad person") is maladaptive and has been correlated positively with fear and depression (Meyer & Taylor, 1986). Survivors should be guided toward restructuring their maladaptive thinking accordingly.

Thought Stopping

The purpose of thought stopping is to end obsessive maladaptive self-statements. The client is instructed to think about a feared stimulus, which the therapist interrupts by yelling "Stop!" and clapping simultaneously. The client is instructed to repeat the thought and verbalize "Stop!" first aloud and then subvocally. She learns to use thought stopping covertly. This skill provides a good opportunity to assess the client's maladaptive thoughts, followed by a discussion of why these thoughts are dysfunctional. Some examples of typical maladaptive self-statements following a sexual assault are:

"I'm damaged goods now."
"It must have been my fault."
"Nobody must know that I was raped."
"I will never be the same again."
"If I was aroused during the assault, I must be sick."

"I shouldn't cry this much."
"I will never trust anyone again."

Guided Self-Dialogue

This technique involves assessing maladaptive cognitions, such as the examples listed above, and substituting them with adaptive ones. Adaptive self-statements are taught in the face of a distressing situation in the following four phases:

1. *Preparation:* Identifying the problem and appraising the negative outcome
2. *Confrontation:* Breaking down the goal into manageable steps
3. *Management:* Imagining anxiety as manageable and temporary
4. *Reinforcement:* Making positive self-statements after taking action

Social, Medical, and Legal Support

The critical role that family and friends can play in the recovery stage should be emphasized to the survivor. The survivor should be encouraged to depend on the social network she has identified, to confide in others who can provide emotional support. Some survivors may feel safer by moving in with a friend or relative or by having someone move in with them temporarily. Other ways to increase perceptions of safety (e.g., installing a security system) can be explored. It is also important to discuss potential difficulties with intimacy and sexual functioning with the survivor and possibly her sexual partner, facilitating realistic expectations concerning the aftermath of a sexual assault. If possible, any intervention with the survivor's significant others would be helpful.

A rationale for seeking medical treatment should be presented. There may be external and/or internal physical injuries that should receive medical attention immediately. Factual information about potential sexually transmitted diseases and pregnancy should be discussed. Medical intervention may also be necessary (if given immediately following the assault) for forensic evidence. The survivor will often experience the medical intervention received immediately following the assault as extremely invasive and, therefore, she may react as though she is reliving the trauma experience. If the survivor is about to confront this situation, potential adverse reactions should be discussed.

Many survivors will be as reluctant to seek medical attention as they are to report the assault to the police. Factual information concerning the procedures necessary in reporting a sexual assault, as well possible outcomes, should be discussed (Calhoun & Atkeson, 1991).

Follow-Up Treatment

During the immediate aftermath of crisis, cognitive-behavioral techniques that include exposure can be dangerous, as exposure procedures create temporarily high levels of arousal. Instead, because crisis intervention is time limited, the focus needs to be on helping the survivor stabilize and develop adaptive coping strategies for the short term. Other cognitive-behavioral treatments that include exposure can, however, be recommended to clients as a follow-up to crisis intervention and for longer-term therapy.

Two cognitive-behavioral therapies, besides SIT, that have been shown to be effective through well-controlled studies are prolonged exposure (PE) and cognitive processing therapy (CPT), both of which include an exposure component. In a recent review of the literature on treatment outcome for PTSD, Foa and Meadows (1997) consider PE to be the treatment of choice for long-term gains, having been the most rigorously tested procedure to date. SIT is more likely to produce immediate symptom relief; PE has been shown to be the most effective treatment over the long term; CPT shows promising initial findings (Foa & Meadows, 1997). These positive results may suggest that a combination of these programs may be optimal, but there is no empirical evidence at this time to substantiate this implication for follow-up treatment.

Support without Resistance

Working with rape survivors can be very difficult for the therapist. It has been our experience in supervising therapists that their own maladaptive beliefs often get in the way of their helping clients. Working with rape survivors often shatters a therapist's own sense of security or just-world beliefs (Janoff-Bulman, 1992). Anyone (male or female) is a potential target for rape. Working with survivors often reminds therapists of their own vulnerability to danger. Realizing that the survivors cannot bring this on themselves results in the knowledge that anyone could be attacked. Many therapists have difficulty accepting this. Therapists need to be careful not to inadvertently reinforce a survivor's self-blame (e.g., "What were you doing walking alone in the park that late at night?") *or* the belief that life is fair and we can control our fate. A therapist's verbal or nonverbal reactions can hold a judgment that is subtly conveyed, creating an atmosphere of distrust for the survivor.

Another problem that therapists encounter is their strong empathy with rape survivors. Some therapists do believe that these clients have endured too much suffering and should, therefore, not be asked to reexperience any additional pain by recounting the trauma. Such an empathic attitude may result in supportive therapeutic strategies, but it can also result in protecting the client from exposure interventions, thereby impeding potential therapeutic gains. It is important for therapists to monitor their own beliefs or myths about rape, as these beliefs will, undoubtedly, be communicated one way or the other to the client. If the therapist believes that the traumatic experience is too difficult to face, the client's avoidance will be reinforced.

Working with rape survivors, as with any PTSD client, requires a fine balance between empathy and support on one hand and encouragement and faith in the survivor's ability on the other hand.

ACKNOWLEDGMENT

We gratefully wish to acknowledge the contribution that the book *Treatment of Rape Victims: Facilitating Psychological Adjustment*, by Karen S. Calhoun and Beverly M. Atkeson (1991), made to the development of this chapter.

NOTES

1. We choose to use the term *rape survivor* instead of *rape victim* in order to emphasize the implication of active coping and recovery.
2. Because the majority of rape victims are women, the female pronoun is used throughout this chapter, although we acknowledge that anyone is vulnerable to rape.

REFERENCES

American Psychiatric Association. (1980). *Diagnostic and statistical manual of mental disorders* (3rd ed.) Washington, DC: Author.

American Psychiatric Association. (1987). *Diagnostic and statistical manual of mental disorders* (3rd ed., rev.). Washington, DC: Author.

American Psychiatric Association. (1994). *Diagnostic and statistical manual of mental disorders* (4th ed.). Washington, DC: Author.

Beck, A. T. (1976). *Cognitive therapy and emotional disorders.* New York: International Universities Press.

Beck, A. T., & Emery, G. (1985). *Anxiety disorders and phobias: A cognitive perspective.* New York: Basic Books.

Bernstein, D., & Borkovec, T. (1973). *Progressive relaxation training: A manual for the helping professions.* Champaign, IL: Research Press.

Bordin, E. (1979). The generalizability of the psychoanalytic concept of the working alliance. *Psychotherapy, 16,* 252–260.

Calhoun, K. S., & Atkeson, B. M. (1991). *Treatment of rape victims: Facilitating psychosocial adjustment.* New York: Pergamon Press.

Dancu, C. V., & Foa, E. B. (1992). Post-traumatic stress disorder. In A. Freeman & F. M. Dattiho (Eds.), *Comprehensive casebook of cognitive therapy* (pp. 79–88). New York: Plenum.

DiGiuseppe, R. (1991). A rational-emotive model of assessment. In M. E. Bernard (Ed.), *Doing rational-emotive therapy effectively* (pp. 88–96). New York: Plenum.

Ellis, A. (1962). *Reason and emotion in psychotherapy.* New York: Lyle Stuart.

Ellis, A. (1985). *Overcoming resistance: Rational-emotive resistance with difficult clients.* New York: Springer-Verlag.

Ellis, A. (1986). Discomfort anxiety: A cognitive-behavioral construct. In A. Ellis & Grieger (Eds.), *Handbook of rational-emotive therapy* (Vol. 2, pp. 105–120) New York: Springer-Verlag.

Ellis, A. (1994). Post-traumatic stress disorder (PTSD): A rational emotive behavioral theory. *Journal of Rational-Emotive and Cognitive Behavior Therapy, 12,* 3–25.

Ellis, A. & Dryden, W. (1987). *The practice of rational-emotive therapy.* New York: Springer-Verlag.

Fairbank, J. A., & Brown, T. A. (1987). Current behavioral approaches to the treatment of posttraumatic stress disorder. *Behavior Therapist, 3,* 57–64.

Foa, E. B. & Meadows, E. A. (1997). Psychosocial treatments for posttraumatic stress disorder: A critical review. *Annual Review of Psychology, 48,* 449–480.

Foa, E. B., Riggs, D. S., Dancu, C. V., & Rothbaum, B. O. (1993). Reliability and validity of a brief instrument for assessing post-traumatic-stress disorder, *Journal of Traumatic Stress, 6,* 459–473.

Foa, E. B., & Rothbaum, B. O. (1998). *Treating the trauma of rape: Cognitive-behavioral therapy for PTSD.* New York: Guilford Press.

Foa, E. B., Steketee, G., & Rothbaum, B. O. (1989). Behavioral/cognitive conceptualizations of post-traumatic stress disorder. *Behavior Therapy, 20,* 155–176.

Jacobson, E. (1938). *Progressive relaxation.* Chicago: University of Chicago Press.

Janoff-Bulman, R. (1979). Characterological versus behavioral self-blame: Inquiries into depression and rape. *Journal of Personality and Social Psychology, 37,* 1798–1809.

Janoff-Bulman, R. (1992). *Shattered assumptions: Towards a new psychology of trauma.* New York: Free Press.

Keane, T. M., Zimmerling, R. T., & Caddell, J. M. (1985). A behavioral formulation of post-traumatic stress disorder in Vietnam veterans. *Behavior Therapist, 8,* 9–12.

Kilpatrick, D. G., Veronen, L. J., & Resick, P. A. (1982). Psychological sequelae to rape: Assessment and treatment strategies. In D. M. Doleys, R. L. Meredith, & A. R. Ciminero (Eds.), *Behavioral medicine: Assessment and treatment strategies* (pp. 473–498). New York: Plenum.

Lang, P. J. (1968). Fear reduction and fear behavior: Problems in treating a construct. *Research in Psychotherapy, 3,* 90–102.

Meichenbaum, D. H. (1985). *Stress inoculation training.* Elmsford, NY: Pergamon Press.

Meyer, C. B., & Taylor, S. E. (1986). Adjustment to rape. *Journal of Personality and Social Psychology, 50,* 1226–1234.

Piaget, J. (1954). *The construction of reality in the child.* New York: Basic Books.

Resick, P. A. & Schnicke, M. K. (1992). Cognitive processing therapy for sexual assault victims. *Journal of Consulting and Clinical Psychology, 60,* 748–756.

Rothbaum, B. O., Foa, E. B., Murdock, T., Riggs, D., & Walsh, W. (1992). A prospective examination of post-traumatic stress disorder in rape victims. *Journal of Traumatic Stress, 5,* 445–475.

Safran, J. & Muran, J. C. (2000). *Negotiating the therapy alliance: A relational treatment guide.* New York: Guilford Press.

Walen, S. R., DiGiuseppe, R., & Dryden, W. (1992). *The practitioners' guide to rational-emotive therapy* (2nd ed.). New York: Oxford University Press.

SUGGESTED READINGS

Calhoun, K. S., & Atkeson, B. M. (1991). *Treatment of rape victims: Facilitating psychosocial adjustment*. New York: Pergamon Press.

Foa, E. B., & Meadows, E. A. (1997). Psychosocial treatments for posttraumatic stress disorder: A critical review. *Annual Review Psychology, 48,* 449–480.

Foa, E. B. & Rothbaum, B. O. (1998). *Treating the trauma of rape: Cognitive-behavioral therapy for PTSD*. New York: Guilford Press.

Foa, E. B., Steketee, G., & Rothbaum, B. O. (1989). Behavioral/cognitive conceptualizations of post-traumatic stress disorder. *Behavior Therapy, 20,* 155–176.

Resick, P. A., & Mechanic, M. B. (1995). Brief cognitive therapies for rape victims. In A. R. Roberts (Ed.), *Crisis intervention and time-limited cognitive treatment* (pp. 91–126). Newbury Park, CA: Sage.

7

Child Sexual Abuse

Anne Hope Heflin
Esther Deblinger
Craig D. Fisher

Child sexual abuse (CSA) is a highly prevalent public health problem that affects children in all ethnic, racial, educational, and socioeconomic groups (Sedlak & Broadhurst, 1996; Wyatt & Peters, 1986). Unfortunately, most graduate programs in mental health disciplines offer little or no formal training in how to recognize, evaluate, and intervene in cases of child sexual abuse. Because of this lack of training, mental health professionals often do not respond in the most effective way to the crisis precipitated by a child's disclosure of sexual abuse. Thus, they may miss a crucial opportunity to influence the response of the family as well as the system of professionals involved with the child in ways that facilitate a positive outcome for the child.

This chapter is written to provide professionals with some of the information that is needed to respond effectively to the crisis of a child sexual abuse disclosure. The chapter is divided into three parts. In the first part, information is provided regarding the phenomenon of child sexual abuse, professional responses to abuse, recognition and reporting of abuse, and the subsequent investigations. In the second portion of the chapter, a guide to practice is offered, which provides suggestions for the clinician faced with assisting the child and his/her family through the crisis of a child sexual abuse disclosure. Finally, in the third section of the chapter, a case study is provided, which illustrates the process of responding to clients who are in the midst of the crisis of a disclosure of child sexual abuse.

PREVALENCE

The Third National Incidence Study of Child Abuse and Neglect (NIS-3) was a congressionally mandated study designed to provide estimates of the incidence of child abuse and neglect in the United States during the year 1993. The study relied on reports from child protective services as well as from professionals in public schools and day care centers, hospitals, public health departments, and law enforcement agencies (Sedlak & Broadhurst, 1996). The findings of this study indicated that approximately 300,200 children (4.5 per 1,000) in the United States experienced sexual abuse during 1993. This incidence rate had more than doubled since the Second National Incidence Study, which was conducted in 1986. However, these figures undoubtedly still underestimated the actual rates of child sexual abuse. The study did not include cases of sexual abuse perpetrated by noncaretakers. Furthermore, the study did not include the many cases of child sexual abuse of which professionals are not aware.

More accurate statistics concerning the lifetime prevalence rates of CSA may be gleaned from retrospective surveys of adult community samples. For example, Finkelhor, Hotaling, Lewis, and Smith (1990) conducted a national telephone survey and found that 27% of adult females and 16% of adult males surveyed suffered contact sexual victimization by the age of 18. Similarly, Elliott and Briere (1992) mailed a questionnaire to a stratified random sample of professional women throughout the United States and found that 26.9% of women reported experiencing sexual abuse prior to the age of 16. Boney-McCoy and Finkelhor (1995) looked at prevalence rates in a nationally representative sample of youth between the ages of 10 and 16 in the United States. During telephone interviews, 15.3% of the females and 5.9% of the males in that age group reported that they had experienced sexual assault. The discrepancy between the incidence rates reported by professionals during a given year and the lifetime prevalence rates reported retrospectively by child sexual abuse victims highlights the need for increased recognition and reporting of suspected cases of CSA. These steps are critical both to prevent further victimization and to lessen the long-term impact of CSA.

IMPACT

The psychosocial sequelae associated with CSA have been documented by numerous investigations. The findings suggest that CSA survivors seem to be affected by their abusive experiences in different ways and to different degrees. Indeed, research has not found evidence for a specific post–sexual abuse syndrome (Beitchman et al., 1992; Kendall-Tackett, Williams, & Finkelhor, 1993). Some survivors appear to suffer minimal or no apparent effects; others develop severe social and/or psychiatric problems including behavior problems (such as aggression or sexualized behaviors during childhood), substance abuse, sexual dysfunction during adulthood, major depression, suicidal tendencies, fears, and posttraumatic stress disorder (PTSD) (Beitchman et al., 1992; Boney-McCoy & Finkelhor, 1995; Briere & Elliott, 1994; Kendall-Tackett, Williams, & Finkelhor, 1993; McLeer, Deblinger, Henry, & Orvaschel, 1992; Neumann, Housekamp, Pollock, & Briere, 1996). Studies also have demonstrated that certain patterns of cognitions, such as self-blame for negative events, feelings of being different from peers, lower interpersonal trust, belief that the world is a dangerous place, negative views of sexuality, and negative body image are more common among children who have been sexually abused than among those who have not (Cohen, Deblinger, Maedel, & Stauffer, 1999; Heflin, Mears, Deblinger, & Steer, 1997; Mannarino & Cohen, 1996).

Numerous researchers have attempted to identify factors that might explain the differential effects of CSA. Although the findings have been somewhat inconsistent, several variables have been associated repeatedly with more severe reactions. Sexual abuse perpetrated by a person who is in a close relationship with the child appears to result in more severe postabuse symptomatology than abuse by someone in a more distant relationship with the child (Beitchman et al., 1992; Briere & Runtz, 1988; Kendall-Tackett, Williams, & Finkelhor, 1993; Wyatt & Newcomb, 1990). However, closeness has not been defined in any consistent way. Often, it is determined by degree of kinship, though it might be more appropriate to measure the degree of emotional connection between the child and the perpetrator (Kendall-Tackett, Williams, & Finkelhor, 1993). The threat of force or the use of force during the course of CSA also has been associated consistently with more negative outcomes (Beitchman et al., 1992; Briere & Elliott, 1994; Kendall-Tackett, Williams, & Finkelhor, 1993; Russell, 1986). In addition, more invasive or intimate sexual contact has been linked to more traumatic reactions (Beitchman et al., 1992; Kendall-Tackett, Williams, & Finkelhhor, 1993; Peters, 1988; Tufts New England Medical Center, 1984). Again though, the invasiveness of the abuse has been operationalized in a variety of ways, making it difficult to compare the findings of some studies. The most common means of measuring invasiveness is to categorize the abuse as to whether or not it involved penetration (which might be vaginal, anal, or oral). There also is some suggestion that greater duration and higher frequency of abuse may be associated with increased postabuse symptomatology (Kendall-Tackett, Williams, & Finkelhor, 1993; Steel, Wilson, Cross, & Whipple, 1996). However, solitary violent sexual assaults also are associated with high levels of postabuse symptoms, making it difficult to identify simple, linear relationships between duration and frequency of abuse and subsequent symptoms (Beitchman et al., 1992). Unfortunately, although the information described above is useful in identifying abuse-related variables that may influence the child's postabuse adjustment, these abuse-related variables are inherent and immutable aspects of the abuse and, therefore, cannot be targets for intervention (Conte & Schuerman, 1987).

However, support provided by nonoffending parents to children who have suffered sexual abuse has been identified as a moderating variable that may be amenable to change. The findings of a series of investigations, in fact, show that children's postabuse adjustment may be influenced significantly by the level of support they receive from nonoffending adults following disclosure of the abuse (Conte & Schuerman, 1987; Everson, Hunter, Runyon, Edelson, &

Coulter, 1989; Feiring, Taska, & Lewis, 1998; Friedrich, Luecke, Beilke, & Place, 1992; Spaccarelli & Fuchs, 1997). Indeed, the study by Everson and colleagues (1989) found that children's postabuse adjustment was more closely linked to maternal support than to the nature or duration of abuse or to the child's relationship to the offender.

Recent evidence also indicates that maternal levels of psychiatric symptoms or distress may be linked to children's postabuse outcomes (Deblinger, Steer, & Lippmann, 1999; Deblinger, Taub, Maedel, Lippmann, & Stauffer, 1997; Runyon, Hunter, & Everson, 1992). Runyon, Hunter, and Everson (1992) reported that in addition to support variables, maternal psychiatric symptoms appeared to contribute significantly to the prediction of sexually abused children's adjustment difficulties. Deblinger, Steer, and Lippman (1999) found that mother's severity of depression was positively related to children's PTSD symptoms and parent-reported internalizing behaviors.

Researchers have recently extended the examination of the influence of parental support and emotional distress to the outcome of treatment for children who have been sexually abused. Friedrich and colleagues (1992) found that initial levels of maternal support and depression were significantly related to the outcome of therapy with sexually abused boys. Similarly, Cohen and Mannarino (1996) found that parental emotional distress was significantly related to the presence of both internalizing symptoms and behavior problems among sexually abused preschool children at the end of treatment, regardless of whether the children received cognitive behavioral treatment or nondirective supportive therapy.

More general assessments of family functioning also indicate that the overall quality of family relationships may be associated with the adjustment of sexually abused children. For example, Friedrich, Urquiza, and Beilke (1986) found that increased family conflict and less cohesive family functioning were related to greater behavioral symptoms in sexually abused children. Similarly, Oates, O'Toole, Lynch, Stern, and Cooney (1994) found that family functioning was a critical variable influencing the adjustment of CSA victims. Friedrich, Luecke, Beilke, and Place (1992) found that a high degree of family conflict was associated with a negative outcome of therapy with sexually abused boys.

Finally, preliminary evidence indicates that the type of parenting style utilized may be related to the symptoms exhibited by children who have been sexually abused. Deblinger, Steer, and Lippman (1999) found that in a sample of 100 children who had been sexually abused, those who perceived their mothers' parenting style to be rejecting reported increased levels of depressive symptomatology. In addition, the perceived use of guilt and anxiety provoking parenting methods was associated with higher levels of PTSD symptoms and parent-reported externalizing behavior problems.

In summary, these findings suggest that nonoffending parents play a crucial role in influencing their children's postabuse adjustment as well as their response to therapy. Indeed, the nonoffending parents may be their children's greatest potential "natural resource." Thus, one of the most effective ways in which mental health professionals can assist sexually abused children may be by helping their nonoffending parents to overcome those psychosocial difficulties that impede their ability to be therapeutic and supportive to their children.

PROFESSIONAL RESPONSE

Although there have been enormous advances in the last several decades in our recognition of and response to CSA, many professionals continue to find themselves ill prepared for the events precipitated by a child's disclosure of sexual abuse. Frequently such a disclosure creates a crisis for the child and his/her family, which requires an appropriate and effective response from the clinician. Although a child's disclosure may set off a significant period of psychological turmoil, it also represents a new beginning free from the secrecy and shame associated with the sexual abuse. Moreover, during such a crisis, the child and his/her family may be more amenable to outside help, providing the therapist with a unique opportunity to stimulate positive growth and change.

Given the widespread prevalence and the highly disruptive impact of CSA, it is essential for all human services professionals to be prepared to respond to a suspicion and/or disclosure of CSA. Unfortunately, few graduate programs offer formal training in the area of child abuse. Thus, many clinicians find themselves poorly prepared on a professional level to assist a child during this crisis. In addition to the lack of appropriate training regarding sexual abuse, professionals may experience personal discomfort regarding the issue of child sexual abuse, which can compromise their response to this situation. As a result, many well-meaning professionals may be unprepared to identify and/or inquire about such childhood trauma. They may also find it difficult to respond calmly and effectively to a spontaneous disclosure. Thus, in addition to obtaining formal training regarding CSA, the clinician preparing to offer crisis intervention in the area may need to explore his/her professional attitudes and personal feelings regarding this disturbing problem.

Professional attitudes that may interfere with recognition and effective intervention in cases of CSA may stem from personal biases as well as common misconceptions. Perhaps the most fundamental bias may be reflected in personal perceptions regarding the prevalence of CSA. Clearly, individuals who continue to view CSA as a rare phenomenon, despite the prevalence data reported earlier, are less likely to recognize and/or inquire about this childhood trauma. Because many survivors of sexual abuse do not spontaneously report CSA as a presenting complaint (Femina, Yeager, & Lewis, 1990), clinicians who do not routinely screen for such trauma are less likely to identify victimization in their clients. In fact, the findings of two investigations demonstrated that when clinicians were given specific instructions to inquire directly about CSA, the rates of sexual abuse reports increased elevenfold for adult psychiatric patients (Briere & Zaidi, 1989) and fourfold for child psychiatric patients (Lanktree, Briere, & Zaidi, 1991). These findings strongly suggest that direct inquiry is essential to (1) the identification of CSA victims, (2) the formulation of appropriate diagnoses and treatment plans, and (3) the possible prevention of further victimization.

Social biases also can interfere with effective recognition, reporting and intervention in child abuse cases. Kelley (1990), for example, found that such biases influence the practices and attitudes of professionals in the field. Specifically, many professionals demonstrated more tolerance and recommended less severe punishments for offenders with high social status. In addition, they considered the effects of the sexual abuse to be more severe when the offender represented a lower social status. Suspected cases of CSA should be evaluated and treated equally regardless of the alleged offender's social and demographic characteristics. This may be accomplished only if clinicians make active efforts to acknowledge and counter their personal biases and prejudices. Sex offenders are not easily identifiable and they do not generally fit the "dirty old man" or "perverted stranger" stereotypes. Rather, many offenders are trusted individuals who appear to be highly regarded in their communities, successful in their work, and particularly engaging with children.

There is also evidence that gender bias may influence professional and personal attitudes toward CSA victims. The findings of several investigations suggest a tendency to minimize the impact of CSA on male victims as opposed to female victims (Eisenberg, Owens, & Dewey, 1987; Kelley, 1990). Kelley (1990), for example, found that professionals tended to recommend less severe punishment for offenders who sexually abused boys. In addition, Stauffer and Deblinger (1996) found that mothers of sexually abused boys were less likely to participate in therapy than mothers of victimized girls, perhaps due to their underestimation of the impact of CSA on boys. To date, however, the empirical evidence that exists generally has not demonstrated that CSA is any less traumatic for boys than for girls (Beitchman et al., 1992; Boney-McCoy & Finkelhor, 1995; Jumper, 1995; Kendall-Tackett, Williams, & Finkelhor, 1993). Unfortunately, there has been relatively little attention given to possible differences across gender, perhaps in part due to the bias described above, which may cause professionals to minimize the impact of CSA on boys and also due to difficulties in obtaining adequate samples of boys.

Biases and misconceptions concerning nonoffending mothers of children who have been sexually abused also appear to be widespread. The early clinical literature regarding child sexual abuse often depicted mothers in quite negative ways, implicating them as being indirectly responsible for the sexual abuse of their children based on a pattern of denial and collusion (Cormier, Kennedy, & Sangowicz, 1962; Sarles, 1975). However, there is little, if any, empirical data to support that depiction. In fact, the vast majority of mothers appear to believe and support their children following disclosures of CSA (Deblinger, Stauffer, & Landsberg, 1994; Sirles & Franke, 1989).

Mothers who have their own histories of child sexual abuse often have been the subject of particular concern from clinicians. Some clinicians have been concerned that mothers who have such a personal history will be unable to acknowledge and respond appropriately to their child's experience of sexual abuse. On the other hand, other clinicians have suggested that mothers with a personal history of abuse may be predisposed to suspect sexual abuse, even when the evidence does not support such concerns. Several studies have explored the relationships between mothers' personal histories of child sexual abuse and maternal levels of emotional distress following their child's disclosure of sexual abuse as well as maternal responses to the child's disclosure (Deblinger, Stauffer, & Landsberg, 1994; Hiebert-Murphy, 1998; Timmons-Mitchell, Chandler-Holz, & Semple, 1996). The findings of the studies generally do indicate that mothers who have a personal history of child sexual abuse tend to experience greater levels of emotional distress when confronted with their child's abuse experience than do mothers without such a personal history of abuse (Deblinger, Stauffer, & Landsberg, 1994; Hiebert-Murphy, 1998; Timmons-Mitchell, Chandler-Holtz, & Semple, 1996). However, a personal history of sexual abuse does not appear to be related to the mother's belief in her child's disclosure or to her support for the child (Deblinger, Stauffer, & Landsberg, 1994). These findings underscore the need to design interventions that allow nonoffending parents to assist a child during a crisis of child sexual abuse and that also help the parents cope successfully with their own emotional distress.

There is also a common misconception that mothers frequently raise false allegations of CSA to get back at ex-spouses during divorce and custody disputes (Humphreys, 1997). Actually, sexually abused children may be particularly motivated to disclose sexual abuse during separation proceedings due to (1) increased feelings of safety, (2) reduced control by the perpetrator, (3) increased time and enhanced communication with the nonoffending parent, and (4) fear of unsupervised visits with the perpetrator. Interestingly, findings of an empirical investigation revealed that CSA allegations arising during custody disputes were just as likely to be substantiated as sexual abuse allegations in the general population (Thoennes & Tjaden, 1990). However, allegations brought during divorce proceedings often appear to require a greater degree of evidence before they are considered seriously, than do allegations of child sexual abuse brought outside of divorce proceedings (Humphreys, 1997). Disclosures made during divorce proceedings deserve the same professional response and rigorous investigation afforded to children who disclose abuse under other circumstances. Although false allegations do occur, it is inappropriate for clinicians to assume that disclosures made during custody disputes are less valid than others.

Of course, there are many other biases and misconceptions that can interfere with the appropriate management of suspected cases of CSA. To maintain as much objectivity as possible, it is important that professionals in the field keep abreast of the empirical literature and periodically explore and examine their professional attitudes and potential biases. Such exploration is likely to lead to more effective and responsible practice by enhancing one's awareness of and sensitivity to factors that may inappropriately influence professional responses.

RECOGNITION

Many articles in the clinical literature list signs and symptoms of sexual abuse. However, symptoms that are unique to sexual abuse, such as anogenital injury, sexually transmitted diseases, or evidence of seminal fluids, generally are not observed and are rarely present at the time of the child's disclosure. On the other hand, many children who have experienced sexual abuse do exhibit fears, regression, withdrawal, behavioral problems, and school difficulties. However, these problems also are exhibited by children who have suffered other childhood traumas and/or family difficulties. In fact, studies comparing children who have been sexually abused to other psychiatrically disturbed, nonabused children demonstrate few differences (Friedrich, Beilke, & Luecke, 1988; Goldston, Turnquist, & Knutson, 1989). Based on their review of the literature, Kendall-Tackett, Williams, and Finkelhor (1993) suggest that children who have been sexually abused may be no more symptomatic than other clinical, nonabused, children except in their levels of PTSD symptoms and sexualized behaviors.

Even PTSD symptoms do not consistently differentiate these children from other nonabused children. PTSD is not specific to sexual abuse. In fact, any number of traumatic childhood experiences may lead to this disorder. However, the type and quality of the PTSD symptoms exhibited by a child may offer clues regarding the nature of the underlying trauma. Thus, sexually abused children may be more likely to exhibit unusual and persistent fears in response to sexual abuse reminders such as bathing, undressing, or displays of physical affection. For example, one might carefully evaluate the possibility of sexual abuse for a child who insists on wearing several layers of clothing to bed each night.

The behavioral symptom that is most likely to differentiate sexually abused from non–sexually abused children is sexually inappropriate and sexually abusive behaviors (Deblinger, McLeer, Atkins, Ralphe, & Foa, 1989; Friedrich, 1993; Kendall-Tackett, Williams, & Finkelhor, 1993; Kolko, Moser, & Weldy, 1988). Children exhibit a range of normal sexual behaviors that tend to reflect age-appropriate sexual curiosity and exploration. However, sexual knowledge inappropriate to the child's age and sexual behaviors that are imitative of adult sexual activity (i.e., oral, anal, and vaginal intercourse) should be considered suggestive of sexual abuse and further explored. Still, it is important for clinicians to recognize that such behaviors are not always the consequence of child sexual abuse. Indeed, there are alternative explanations for such be-haviors and symptoms that must be considered, including accidental exposure to adult sexual activity and/or pornography. In summary, the presence of sexualized fears and behaviors should encourage the exploration of underly-ing sexual abuse in the context of a comprehensive psychological evaluation, but should not be viewed as unequivocally indicative of a sexually abusive experience.

Although the behaviors and symptoms described above may raise suspi-cions concerning sexual abuse, ultimately a child's disclosure is the most essen-tial piece of evidence in cases of alleged CSA. Numerous factors, however, mo-tivate children to remain silent about their abusive experiences. Many children are verbally and/or physically threatened into secrecy by their perpetrators; others remain silent out of embarrassment, shame, and/or fear that no one will believe them. Some children may maintain the secret in order to avoid family disruption and/or to protect the perpetrator from imprisonment.

Studies examining the process of disclosure have demonstrated that it may be a complex process including a mixture of denials, acknowledgments or reve-lations, and recantations (Nagel, Putnam, & Noll, 1997). The findings of these studies generally indicate that some disclosures occur without intention on the part of the victimized child, for example, through medical examinations, a dis-closure by a sibling, or a confession by the perpetrator. Other disclosures are made in response to a precipitant such as a television show or educational pro-gram regarding child sexual abuse. Finally, another group of disclosures is made purposefully, without clear precipitants. In general, those children whose disclosures occur accidentally tend to be younger than those children who make purposeful disclosures (Nagel, Putnam, & Noll, 1997; Sorenson & Snow, 1991). Another factor that may influence a child's willingness to disclose sexual abuse is the presence of supportive caretakers. Lawson and Chaffin (1992) found that among children with confirmed cases of sexually transmitted dis-eases, 63% of those with supportive caretakers (who acknowledged that abuse was a possibility) disclosed, whereas 17% of those with nonsupportive caretak-ers disclosed. The amount of information and detail provided in a disclosure also may vary significantly. Factors that predict an increased level of detail pro-vided in children's disclosures include being female, being older, and experi-encing more invasive degrees of abuse (Heflin, Finkel, Deblinger, & Brown, 1996).

Researchers have documented that even when there is strong evidence that sexual abuse occurred (such as positive medical evidence or a confession by the perpetrator) a certain percentage of children will deny the abuse. How-ever, the rates of denial vary significantly across studies from as low as 6% (Bradley & Wood, 1996) to as high as 72% (Sorenson & Snow, 1991). Similarly, a number of studies have demonstrated that even in clearly substantiated cases, a significant portion of the children will recant their original disclosures, with studies reporting rates of recantation from lows of 4% to 8% (Bradley & Wood,

1996; Jones & McGraw, 1987) to highs of 22% to 27% (Gonzalez, Waterman, Kelly, McCord, & Oliveri, 1993; Sorenson & Snow, 1991). Regardless of the rate of occurrence, the data from these studies suggest that clinicians should be cautious about dismissing CSA allegations based on children's initial denials and/or later recantations.

REPORTING

All states have laws that require human services professionals to report suspected CSA to the appropriate child protection authorities. The statutes in most states further indicate that any person making such a report in "good faith" will be immune from any civil or criminal liability, whereas professionals who knowingly fail to report suspected CSA will be subject to a penalty in the form of a fine and/or imprisonment. While the states' laws stipulate that reports are mandated on the basis of reasonable suspicions, not concrete evidence, it is well documented that many professionals fail to report suspected cases (Kalichman, Craig, & Follingstad, 1988; Swoboda, Elwork, Sales, & Levine, 1978). Indeed, the Third National Incidence Study (Sedlak & Broadhurst, 1996) reported that child protective services only investigated 42% of the cases of sexual abuse that were identified by professionals. The 58% of cases that were not investigated include both cases in which professionals failed to make a needed report as well as cases in which the child protection agency screened out the case before an investigation was initiated.

Empirical investigations indicate that professionals who fail to report suspected abuse frequently offer the following explanations: (1) lack of certainty that the alleged abuse had occurred, (2) concerns regarding the disruption of the therapeutic process, (3) lack of confidence in the child protection system, and (4) belief that the suspected abuse was not ongoing (Kalichman, Craig, & Follingstad, 1988). Although these concerns are reasonable, they do not mitigate one's responsibility to report suspected abuse. Indeed, mandated reporters such as clinicians cannot ignore the opportunity as well as the responsibility to engage the child protection agency in an effort to assist the child. Flango (1991) found that allegations from mandated reporters were substantiated 40% to 64% of the time, whereas those made by anonymous reporters were validated 3% to 25% of the time, suggesting that the allegations described by mandated reporters may be particularly valuable in eliciting assistance for the child. The clinician should make the required report and then allow the child protective agency as well as any law enforcement agencies involved to conduct the investigation. The clinician typically is not responsible for the investigation of past or present abuse and indeed usually is not able to adequately investigate possible abuse while also ensuring the safety of any children exposed to the alleged perpetrator. Clinicians, therefore, must rely on the child protection and law enforcement agencies in their communities to address these concerns.

MULTIDISCIPLINARY COLLABORATION

When CSA is suspected, a report initiates an investigation that requires the involvement of professionals from many different disciplines, including child protective services, law enforcement, medicine, and mental health. The multidisciplinary response to an allegation of CSA involves a number of different components. The order in which the various processes occur will vary depending on the needs of the child and the policies of the agencies involved. Ideally, the child protection agency and the law enforcement agencies work collaboratively in pursuing the investigation of possible abuse. In some locales, multidisciplinary teams work together as formal units, with common work facilities. These facilities are often called child advocacy centers. In other locations, the agencies cooperate in joint investigations in less formal ways, without pooling their resources. Finally, in some locations the agencies work fairly independently, which sometimes has the unfortunate consequence of adding to the child's trauma by requiring multiple interviews. These interviews also may lead to conflicting evidence, which may be challenged by the defense in court (Pence & Wilson, 1994). Thus, whenever possible, it is useful to advocate for the coordination of services by the various agencies involved.

Investigation by the Child Protection Agency

When the child protection agency investigates an allegation of sexual abuse, its purpose is to determine whether sexual abuse actually occurred, so that the agency can intervene, if necessary, to assure the child's safety and well-being (Sgroi, Porter, & Blick, 1982). Such an investigation may begin under the auspices of a crisis unit or, in less urgent cases, with the assignment of a specific intake worker to the case. Typically the investigation consists of a series of interviews with the child, the alleged perpetrator, the person to whom the child first disclosed the abuse (if such a disclosure has been made), and other persons involved in the situation. Depending on the results of that initial investigation, the child protection agency may formulate a variety of plans ranging from placing the child in foster care (if the presence of the alleged perpetrator in the home jeopardizes the child's safety) to monitoring the situation to closing the case. At the time of the investigation, the child protection agency may also make a referral to a mental health professional for a psychological evaluation and/or psychotherapy.

Investigation by Law Enforcement Officials

In many cases, law enforcement officials also will launch an investigation into the allegations of sexual abuse. The general purpose of that investigation is to determine whether the alleged perpetrator has violated any laws and, thus, whether he/she should be prosecuted legally (Sgroi, Porter, & Blick, 1982). Again, the nature of the investigation by law enforcement officials depends in part on the urgency of the situation. If the alleged abuse is ongoing and the child is currently at risk, the local police may intervene immediately. In other cases, when the allegations are focused on previous events, the police and/or the local prosecutor's office may initiate an investigation without immediate intervention. The specific procedures used in those interviews vary from area to area. In some offices, anatomically correct dolls and/or drawings may be used to facilitate the child's interview. In many offices, the interviews are videotaped or audiotaped for possible use later in the legal process.

Medical Examination

Another phase of the multidisciplinary response to an allegation of CSA is the medical examination. In almost all cases of CSA, it is appropriate for the child to receive a thorough medical examination, preferably by a pediatrician or gynecologist (if the victim is a late adolescent) experienced in issues of child sexual abuse. This examination is of value for a variety of reasons. First, the examination should be done in order to diagnose and/or treat physical injuries and/or sexually transmitted diseases resulting from the alleged sexual abuse. Second, the examination allows the doctor to answer any worries or concerns that the child might have as a result of the alleged sexual contact. Most often the sexual abuse does not result in any residual physical damage or health problems. Thus, the examination can concretely establish that there are no problems resulting from the abuse, and the physician can provide reassurance that the child's body is healthy and intact. If a child or adolescent is aware of any residual problems that do exist, he/she may benefit by learning the facts about what those difficulties are and how they will be addressed. Third, medical findings that substantiate the allegations of sexual abuse can be important in the legal prosecution of the case.

Although it is important that the child receive a medical examination, rarely does that examination need to be scheduled immediately. In most cases, the sexual abuse has been ongoing and the most recent episode may have occurred some time ago. In such situations, an urgent trip to a local hospital emergency room is not indicated. Instead, it would be more appropriate to have the child seen by a physician skilled in the assessment of alleged sexual abuse, if possible, as soon as the physician's schedule permits. In a few cases, there is a more urgent need for an examination. For example, a medical examination should be pursued immediately if the child clearly is suffering physical problems resulting from the abuse. Similarly, if the child reports that an episode of abuse occurred during the previous 72 hours, the medical examination should be conducted immediately as it may yield important forensic medical evidence such as evidence of semen (American Academy of Pediatrics, 1991).

The procedures used in the medical examination will vary somewhat depending on the specific needs of the child and the practice of the physician. Most often the child will receive a head-to-toe examination, which allows the physician to complete a full health assessment while looking for any extragenital indications of trauma (Finkel & DeJong, 1992). The child's genital and anal areas will be inspected for any evidence of acute or chronic trauma (Finkel & DeJong, 1992). That examination may be completed with the use of a colposcope, an instrument that provides light, magnification, and the capacity to obtain photographic and/or video documentation. During the examination, the physician will collect oral, vaginal, and rectal cultures as indicated by history. Depending on the types of sexual activities alleged, blood samples may be collected. In addition, a test for pregnancy may be completed for postmenarchal girls.

Psychological Evaluation

An additional component sometimes included in the multidisciplinary response to a CSA allegation is a psychological evaluation. In some communities, mental health professionals will conduct the initial interviews with suspected victims of child sexual abuse as members of the investigating team. In other communities, a psychological evaluation may only be requested when the findings of the initial investigation by child protection and/or law enforcement are inconclusive. The purposes of such an evaluation are to gather history about the alleged sexual activity, assess the credibility of the allegations, and assess the child's emotional and behavioral status, both currently and historically. A variety of techniques may be used during this evaluation, including interviews with the child, his/her parents, and other significant persons in the child's life, the use of anatomically correct dolls and/or drawings, objective and projective assessment instruments, and structured play sessions. When possible, this evaluation should be completed by a mental health professional skilled in pursuing such evaluations, as the evaluation may be a crucial component in criminal or family court proceedings. *The evaluation should be conducted by a professional who has not been seeing the child in therapy previously.* This allows the evaluating professional to offer an unbiased and objective opinion and preserves the confidentiality of the ongoing therapeutic relationship. Based on the findings, the evaluator will likely offer treatment recommendations. If the findings indicate that the child has been sexually abused, at least a brief course of therapy is likely to be recommended to help the child process his/her thoughts and feelings about the abusive experience. Recent research also suggests that when a child has suffered sexual abuse, it is important to actively involve the nonoffending parent(s) in treatment particularly when the child presents with depressive symptomatology and/or acting out behavior problems (Deblinger, Lippmann, & Steer, 1996).

GUIDE TO PRACTICE

Based on the information provided above regarding the phenomenon of child sexual abuse and the investigatory process, the following guide to practice offers suggestions regarding how a clinician might most effectively assist a child and his/her family through the crisis precipitated by a disclosure of child sexual abuse.

Reporting the Abuse

As was described above, when CSA is suspected, the professional has a legal responsibility to make certain that a report is made to the appropriate authorities. While responding to the client in a calm and supportive way, the professional should communicate decisively that the necessary report must be made. Often clients are relieved to make that report in order to have some action taken regarding the sexual abuse. In some cases, however, clients may be reluctant to make such a report because of fear of the alleged perpetrator, love for the perpetrator, hesitancy to disrupt the family, fear that child protective services will assume custody of the child, embarrassment, or shame. If the clients express such reluctance, the clinician may empathize with their concerns but also should state that filing such a report is not optional. Further, the therapist may encourage the clients by saying that filing the necessary report is the first step toward resolving this difficult situation for everyone involved.

Typically it is most appropriate to have the necessary telephone call reporting the alleged abuse made from the professional's office. In that way, the clinician is afforded the opportunity to support the client(s) while verifying that the report has been made. The most appropriate person to place that initial telephone call may vary from situation to situation. Typically, the investigating professionals will need to speak with the person to whom the child made the initial disclosure of sexual abuse. Thus, in cases in which the child initially disclosed to the clinician, the clinician him/herself should make the telephone call to report the abuse allegations. In other situations, the child will have made an initial disclosure to a nonoffending parent, who will then need to provide investigating professionals with information regarding that disclosure. However, in either case there appears to be some merit to having the professional place the telephone call, if only to introduce the parent and inform the investigating professionals that a report of alleged abuse is forthcoming. As was indicated previously, there is some indication that reports of CSA are more likely to be substantiated when made by professionals than when made by the general public. For example, 47.6% of the reports of child abuse and neglect made by health professionals in New Jersey were substantiated in 1988, compared with a substantiation rate of 38% for all reports filed (New Jersey Governor's Task Force on Child Abuse and Neglect, 1990).

All mental health professionals should familiarize themselves with their state laws governing the reporting of suspected child abuse. The ways in which child abuse is defined and the requirements in terms of the timing and agencies to which these reports should be made differ somewhat across the states. Initial reports of suspected child abuse are most often made to child protection agencies. During business hours, that report can be filed by calling the local office of the child protection agency. In many states, a toll-free number can be used to make such a report during evenings and weekends. That agency may then determine whether a report needs to be filed with the law enforcement agency as well and if necessary may initiate that report. In such cases, an investigation of the allegations may be conducted jointly by the child protection agency and the law enforcement agency.

Child abuse reporting laws may not necessarily pertain in cases in which the perpetrator was not functioning in a caretaking capacity (i.e., an adolescent raped on a date). In those situations, the child protection agency may not have the authority to investigate. However, law enforcement officials could pursue the investigation. Depending on the practices of the local community, the report of such incidents may be filed by the child's parents or legal guardians with the area police department or with the local prosecutor's office. Professionals should acquaint themselves with the policies of their professions and the practices of their communities so that they can provide accurate information, referrals, and support to clients facing this type of crisis. In some instances, clinicians may find it useful to contact the child protection agency to determine whether the concerns regarding possible child maltreatment are sufficient to warrant a child abuse investigation. Finally, given the complexity of this field, at times it may be helpful for the mental health professional to consult an attorney familiar with the laws pertaining to child abuse and mental health practice.

Responding to the Child's Initial Disclosure

While making sure that the report has been made to the appropriate agency, the clinician simultaneously must focus attention on helping the child and the child's family cope with this crisis. If the child makes the initial disclosure to the clinician, the professional should respond to the child in a calm and supportive manner. For example, the clinician might respond to the child's disclosure by saying, "I'm really glad you told me about that. Sometimes it is hard to talk about experiences like that and I think you were really brave to tell me." Although the clinician should not discourage the child from sharing any information about the abusive experience, the clinician need not attempt to gather detailed and specific information regarding the abuse from the child. As was described earlier, unless specifically trained for this purpose and requested to do so, the clinician is not responsible for conducting the evaluation of the abuse allegations. If the clinician hearing the initial disclosure does wish to ask a few questions to clarify the child's experience, those questions should be phrased in a general and nonleading way, in an attempt to elicit a free narrative account. For example, the clinician might simply ask, "Can you tell me more about that?" It is important not to ask questions in leading ways that may suggest responses to the child. Furthermore, it is preferable to avoid asking closed-ended questions that can be answered with a simple yes or no. If a child misinterprets such a question and unintentionally responds erroneously, it may create confusion and weaken the credibility of the rest of his or her disclosure. The child's disclosure is most credible and meaningful when it is provided in the child's own words, without a great deal of prompting from an interviewer. In general, unless the clinician has been trained specifically in how to appropriately interview a child regarding a disclosure of sexual abuse, the investigatory questioning is better left to the professionals from child protective services or law enforcement agencies, or to a mental health clinician skilled in the assessment of children's allegations of sexual abuse. In any situation in which a child does make a disclosure about sexual abuse to the clinician or provides new details about the abuse, the clinician should keep careful records of both what the child said as well as any questions or comments offered by the clinician. These records may be critical in helping the clinician recall exactly what was said and may be incorporated in a report that might eventually be submitted to the court as evidence.

It is important to inform the child that other people will need to be told about this experience. For example, in initiating a discussion of the need to make a report to child protective services, initially the clinician might say, "We're going to need to talk with some other people so that we can help you with this." In addition, if the child has not disclosed to his or her nonoffending parent(s), the child may be told that the nonoffending parent(s) should be informed about the disclosure so that they can assist the child during the investigatory process. With children who are particularly anxious about their nonoffending parent's response, the clinician should offer whatever support he/she can provide. For example, it may be appropriate to suggest, "I would be glad to be here with you while you tell your Mom, if you would like." In cases in which the clinician shares the child's concerns about the nonoffending parent's initial response to this information, it may even be helpful for the clinician to offer to talk with the parent privately about the child's disclosure before asking the child and parent to discuss the issue. In that way, the therapist provides the parent(s) with the opportunity to process their emotional distress regarding this disclosure privately in order to facilitate their ability to respond to the child in the most effective way possible. In most cases, however, it may be helpful to provide an opportunity for the parent and child to talk about the child's disclosure briefly together, with the clinician facilitating that discussion, in order to help them begin to learn how to communicate effectively about this experience. In the event that the nonoffending parent is overtly unsupportive and disbelieving of the child's disclosure, it would be inadvisable to ask the parent and child to discuss the disclosure together, as it would expose the child to that disbelief and might provide pressure that would influence the child's further disclosure of details regarding the alleged abuse. In situations in which it is not clear whether it would be helpful to include the nonoffending parent in a discussion of the disclosure, it may be useful to talk with the investigating personnel from the child protection agency or the law enforcement agencies to be certain that such a discussion would not hinder their investigation.

In general, it is most appropriate to wait until the child has been interviewed by investigatory professionals before involving the child in therapeutic or educational activities specific to the issue of sexual abuse. It is most useful if the investigating professionals are able to elicit the child's disclosure without having it be altered significantly by information the child has obtained from a therapist. However, it is important to note that simply by having the clinician respond to the child's initial disclosure in a calm, supportive, and accepting way the child is learning that it is safe to talk about this experience, that he/she is believed, and that people still accept the child without blame or criticism.

Education about the Investigatory Process

Another way in which the professional can assist both the nonoffending parents and the child is to educate them so that they know what to anticipate after the disclosure is made. The clinician may explain to the clients the typical process of investigations conducted by the child protection agency and law enforcement agencies. Because the procedures in those investigations vary from one community to another, clinicians should educate themselves about the investigatory procedures followed in their community. If the professional has questions about the procedures at the time of the investigation, he/she should ask the investigators to clarify what will happen next. Simply having the clinician take the initiative in gathering some of that information may give the clients a sense of support.

Some clients have significant concern about the child protection agency becoming involved in the life of their family. These concerns may be based in a variety of different issues. At the most extreme, parents and children may be worried that the child protection agency will remove the child from the care of the nonoffending parent. Other clients may be angry about what they perceive as an implication that they are inadequate parents who require the intervention of the child protection agency. Yet another basis for frustration may be the perception of parents that the child protection agency is unnecessarily intruding in their lives and in their decision-making role as parents. Although it is important not to offer false reassurance to clients, it may be possible to dispel some unnecessary anxiety simply by providing accurate information about the role of the child protection agency. For example, the clinician might describe the child protection agency's role as intervening when necessary to provide for the safety and well-being of children. The clinician might further describe how the child will benefit most if parents can view the professionals from the child protection agency as allies in their efforts to protect their child. It is important that if at all possible, the clinician encourage the parent(s) to work in a cooperative way with the child protection professionals and to avoid any adversarial relationships.

Clients also frequently have significant anxiety about the legal process. For example, they may question: Will the alleged perpetrator be arrested? When will that happen? Will the case go to trial? When will that happen? Will my child have to testify? Typically the professional will not be able to answer most of these questions right away. However, he/she can educate clients regarding the variety of courses the legal process can take, depending on the practices specific to that community or state. It also may be possible to facilitate contact between clients and other professionals who may be better able to respond to legal questions. For example, in many communities a victim witness advocate is available to assist victims of crime. That person may be invaluable in assisting clients through the legal system. It also is important to inform clients that although the first interview with law enforcement officials may occur shortly after the initial disclosure, the rest of the legal process often proceeds slowly, with many delays. Thus, it is rarely useful to focus the child's attention initially on the legal process as that focus may unnecessarily heighten the child's anxiety.

Another aspect of the investigatory process that may be anxiety provoking for clients is the medical examination. It is important to discuss the medical examination in a calm, matter-of-fact way, so that it is not presented as a threatening experience. When talking with nonoffending parents it is useful to highlight the benefits of an examination. For example, the examination provides the opportunity to treat any physical complications from the sexual abuse, to educate the child about his/her body, to offer reassurance that the child's body is intact, or to educate the child appropriately about any medical problems he/she is experiencing (Sgroi, Porter, & Blick, 1982).

It is difficult to predict for clients exactly what procedures will be involved in the medical examination without being familiar with the practices of the examining physician. Thus, in most cases, the referring clinician may simply provide the child with some general information such as, "The doctor will check you from head to toe to make sure that you are okay." Then just prior to the actual examination, a professional familiar with the particular physician (such as a nurse or counselor in the physician's office, or the physician him/herself) should provide the child with more detailed information about what to anticipate during the examination.

Finally, the clinician will need to provide clients with some education regarding the psychological evaluation that may be done following a disclosure of CSA. When talking with nonoffending parents, the clinician may explain that the evaluation is needed to help clarify the sexual abuse allegations and to assess the impact of the alleged abuse on the child's psychosocial functioning. Furthermore, the evaluator will attempt to determine how the child is coping with the crisis precipitated by the disclosure and may make some recommendations for treatment.

When discussing the psychological evaluation with the child, the clinician may simply tell the child that he/she will be going to see a person who will help the child talk about his/her thoughts and feelings. It is important not to be too leading in preparing the child to discuss the abuse allegations. For example, it would be inappropriate for the referring professional to say, "You can tell this doctor all about how the perpetrator touched you and you touched him."

Acting as an Advocate for the Child

As clients move through the investigatory process, the professional needs to be comfortable assuming an advocacy role for the child. The child and his/her nonoffending parent(s) will be negotiating through unfamiliar systems and agencies and may be overwhelmed by all the processes involved in the investigation of CSA. They may benefit greatly from having a professional available as a source of support and information regarding the systems involved. Furthermore, the clinician may assist them significantly by serving as the child's advocate among all the investigating professionals and agencies involved. Although it is certainly the intent of virtually all the professionals involved in the investigation of CSA to assist the child, in reality the child's needs occasionally may get lost in systems overloaded with too many cases and too few resources. Thus, having an advocate within the system who can speak to the child's needs can be invaluable.

Preliminary Therapeutic Interventions with the Child

Once the child has been interviewed by the investigating professionals, it may be useful to engage the child in some preliminary therapeutic work regarding the sexual abuse and the subsequent disclosure. If unsure whether or not such therapeutic work would interfere with an ongoing investigation, the clinician might discuss the issue with the investigating professionals, with the client's consent. A thorough discussion of a complete treatment plan for victims of CSA is beyond the scope of this chapter. (A comprehensive description of a treatment approach for sexually abused children that has received some initial empirical support is provided in Deblinger & Heflin, 1996.) This chapter, however, offers some guidelines for crisis management for clinicians who are already working with children and/or parents at the time of disclosure. Even if the clinician working with the child during this time is not the therapist who ultimately provides a full course of therapy regarding the sexual abuse, the therapeutic interventions offered during this crisis may yield significant benefits.

Therapist as Role Model

Most children are acutely sensitive to the reactions of other people when they learn of the sexual abuse. Indeed, children often avoid discussing the abuse because they anticipate negative responses. Thus, a clinician working with a child at the time of disclosure has both an opportunity and a responsibility to model for the child how to communicate effectively regarding the abuse. The therapist should communicate both verbally and behaviorally that he/she is available to talk about any of the child's thoughts, questions, or concerns regarding the abuse. Although many adults are uncomfortable hearing a child describe a sexually abusive experience and seeing a child experience significant emotional distress, it is crucial that the clinician not model avoidance for the child. A clinician who avoids discussions of the sexual abuse communicates to the child that those discussions are not appropriate. A child may interpret such avoidance in many different negative ways; for example, that the abuse is shameful, that it is too horrible to discuss, or that the child was responsible for the abuse. If the clinician models avoidance, the child is likely to cope with the abuse in a similar way. Such a behavior pattern will only make later therapeutic work more difficult. Although it is important for the clinician to model openness and a willingness to discuss the sexual abuse, at this point it is not appropriate to push a child to discuss the experience unless the clinician has committed to providing a full course of treatment around this issue. The difficult work of confronting painful thoughts and memories associated with the sexual abuse is best pursued in the context of an ongoing therapeutic relationship.

Education Regarding Child Sexual Abuse

In addition to serving as a model for the child, the clinician working with a child in the midst of the crisis of disclosure has the opportunity to provide some basic education regarding CSA. Again, it is important to wait to provide this education until after the child has been interviewed by the investigating professionals, so that the information does not influence the child's disclosure. In providing the education, it is usually helpful to provide some basic facts such as a definition of CSA, its prevalence, who is affected, who is responsible, why it occurs, and how children feel who have been abused. Often it is useful initially to elicit from the child his/her own responses to those questions. In that way it may be possible to identify any misconceptions that the child has so that they may be corrected. For example, if when asked why CSA occurs, a girl responds that it occurs because the child was dressed in inappropriately revealing clothing, the clinician has the opportunity to educate the child in a way that could have significant therapeutic effect. In explaining that CSA occurs because the perpetrator has a problem with being sexually attracted to young children and has nothing to do with any style of dress or behavior exhibited by the girl, the clinician may afford the child significant relief and diminished distress. In general, the clinician can describe how children may be confused by such an experience and have thoughts and emotions regarding the experience that adults would not necessarily anticipate. Thus, it is important that the child talk about his/her thoughts and feelings so that the professional can help the child correct any erroneous thoughts and can help the child cope with any emotional distress he/she is experiencing.

Preliminary Therapeutic Interventions with Parents

Similarly, the professional should attempt to serve as a source of support and a therapeutic agent for the nonoffending parents. Unfortunately, parents' needs are not always recognized. When the parents' needs are ignored, professionals lose a valuable opportunity to intervene in ways that ultimately could benefit the child significantly. As discussed earlier in this chapter, a number of studies have demonstrated that children's postabuse adjustment may be related to the ways that their nonoffending parents cope with the crisis of CSA (Conte & Schuerman, 1987; Deblinger, Steer, & Lippmann, 1999; Deblinger et al., 1997; Everson et al., 1989; Spaccarelli & Fuchs, 1997). Thus, any interventions that help the parent(s) cope with this crisis probably will benefit the child as well.

Parents as Role Models

It is important to inform parents that they will serve as models for their child with respect to how he/she should respond to the sexual abuse. Thus, the parents' responses to the sexual abuse may be very influential in determining how their child copes with this situation. The clinician should encourage the parents to remain as calm and supportive of the child as possible. The parents should avoid any tendencies to overreact and catastrophize the situation, as that type of response is likely to heighten the child's anxiety. Similarly, parents should be encouraged to be open to any discussions of the abuse that the child may initiate. Parents should be cautioned not to model avoidance, in the same way that clinicians should be careful about that issue. On the other hand, parents should also be discouraged from pushing a child to provide details regarding the abuse, unless the child initiates those conversations. A well-intentioned parent may inadvertently ask the child leading questions or respond to the child's disclosure in a way that inhibits further discussion. Thus, it is more appropriate if the parent waits to pursue detailed abuse-related conversations with the child until he or she can do so with the guidance of a therapist who is pursuing a course of treatment with the child specifically focused on the abuse allegations.

Cognitive Coping Strategies

While working with the parents during the crisis of the disclosure, the clinician also may offer the parents a variety of coping strategies to assist them in effectively managing their own emotional responses. One such strategy involves providing a combination of education regarding CSA and cognitive coping skills training. Often parents have misconceptions about sexual abuse that serve to intensify their own emotional distress. The clinician can educate the parents in a way that dispels some of those misconceptions. Moreover, the clinician can teach the parents how to use that new information to dispute their own dysfunctional and distressing thoughts. For example, parents may feel very guilty for not recognizing "the signs" that indicated that the alleged perpetrator was a sexual offender. The first step in helping the parents cope more effectively with those feelings is to educate the parents about the fact that there is no typical psychological or physical profile of a sexual offender and thus there are no specific signs that can be recognized. Subsequently, the clinician can help the parents practice replacing their erroneous and dysfunctional thoughts with more accurate and effective thoughts. In this example, a parent might replace the thought, "It's all my fault because I should have been able to tell what kind of pervert that coach is," with the thought, "Even professionals usually cannot recognize sex offenders because there is no consistent psychological profile, so there was no way I could have anticipated this." This combination of education and cognitive coping skills may help significantly to reduce the parent's feelings of guilt.

This same combination of techniques may be used effectively to help parents cope with other distressing emotions such as anger, sadness, anxiety, and fear. In teaching parents how to use these skills, it is important to elicit from them which distressing emotions they are experiencing and what thoughts are underlying those emotions. Only by focusing on their specific dysfunctional thoughts and effectively replacing them will the client experience significant symptom relief.

Psychotherapy

Following the CSA investigation, it is usually important for the child to participate in psychotherapy focused specifically on helping him/her cope with the experience of sexual abuse. When the child already has been participating in psychotherapy regarding other issues, a decision must be made as to whether the child should continue with the previous clinician or see a new therapist to deal with this specific issue. One obvious advantage to continuing with the previous therapist is that a trusting relationship already may have been established. Although that is an important factor, it is only one of several factors that must be considered. Another important consideration is the current clinician's level of comfort and expertise in dealing with the issue of CSA. Such expertise and personal comfort are important in conducting successful therapy and probably should outweigh the issue of a previously established relationship. However, in many communities it may be difficult to find clinicians with true expertise in the field of CSA. In such situations, one must rely on the therapist's own judgment as to his/her level of comfort in dealing with these issues.

Another issue to be considered in deciding whether to continue working with a current therapist is that clinician's relationship with family members. It must be clear to the child that the clinician helping him/her cope with the sexual abuse experience is truly an advocate for that child. Thus, if the clinician previously has had a working relationship with another family member, which might make the child doubt the therapist's commitment to the child, that clinician may not be the best choice to continue work with the child at this time. For example, if the therapist's previous work with the child has included work with a parent or sibling later accused of being the sexual abuse perpetrator, or with a parent who is unsupportive and disbelieving of the child, it would be more helpful for the child to form a new therapeutic relationship that is not complicated with those previous relationships. In addition, it seems to be preferable, at least initially, for the child to be seen by an individual therapist rather than a family therapist whose allegiances and objectives may be confusing for the child. Eventually, it may be very useful to have some therapy sessions involving multiple members of the family to discuss the impact of the abuse on all members of the family. However, to move into that type of work prematurely may inappropriately minimize the impact of the experience on the child who was actually abused.

When it is available, group therapy can be very useful, both for children who have experienced CSA and for their nonoffending parents (Stauffer & Deblinger, 1996). These groups can be used alone or in various combinations with individual therapy. Often it is effective to have the clients work in individual therapy initially and then move into a group therapy program once they have made progress in dealing with their individual issues. In a group setting, clients enjoy benefits such as receiving support from other group members, realizing that CSA is a relatively common and shared experience, sharing effective coping strategies, and having opportunities both to learn from the modeling of other group members who are coping well with their abusive experiences and to serve as models themselves for members who are not as far along in the adjustment process.

CASE STUDY

The following case study is offered to illustrate how a clinician might help a nonoffending parent and her children cope with the crisis which may be precipitated by a disclosure of child sexual abuse.

Diane, a 32-year-old mother, contacted a counselor in order to obtain help for her 5-year-old daughter, Lisa, and her 2-year-old son, Michael. She reported that she had been having great difficulty managing her children's behavior ever since she and her husband separated approximately 6 months earlier. Diane indicated that her husband, Tom, was the disciplinarian in the family. Although she maintained physical custody of the children, Tom frequently visited during the week and took the children for overnight visits every other weekend without fail. Diane hesitantly acknowledged that she and her husband had some problems with domestic violence. Although she admitted that the children had been exposed to some of the violence, Diane denied their exposure to any other childhood traumas. Diane described the children's emotional and behavioral difficulties, noting that the children behaved better for their father and seemed to enjoy his attention and playfulness. The counselor asked Diane to complete a child behavior checklist for each of her children. Although Diane had expressed concerns about managing her son's temper tantrums, her responses to the child behavior checklist revealed that his overall behavior fell within the normal range. However, the child behavior profile for her 5-year-old daughter showed significant elevations with respect to somatic complaints and sexualized behaviors. When Diane was asked to describe the sexualized behaviors in greater detail, she reported that her daughter frequently masturbated in public and had been caught several times playing with her brother's penis with her hands and her mouth. Diane reported that she handled the incidents poorly; she yelled at Lisa and sent her to her room for punishment. When asked if she talked to Lisa about the incidents, Diane indicated that Lisa refused to talk about it. However, she recalled that on one occasion Lisa tearfully complained that her daddy let her play with his "peepee." Diane explained that she considered the possibility of sexual abuse, but she feared that she might be overreacting. In response to questioning, Diane reported that to her knowledge, her daughter had never been exposed to any type of adult sexual activity or pornography.

The counselor indicated to Diane that she was not overreacting and, in fact, the information she provided indeed raised concern. The counselor further explained that, as a mental health professional, she was legally responsible to report a suspicion of sexual abuse so that an investigation could be initiated. This did not mean that her daughter had been sexually abused, but that the possibility needed to be fully explored by a team of trained professionals.

Diane reacted with shock, dismay, and self-blame. She insisted that although she and her husband had their differences, he always seemed to be a caring and involved father. She could not imagine that he would sexually abuse their daughter. At the same time, she blamed herself, fearing that she was responsible due to her inability to satisfy her husband sexually. While acknowledging Diane's feelings, the counselor corrected her misconceptions, offering some basic information about CSA. She explained to Diane that there is no evidence that a father will choose to sexually abuse his daughter out of frustration regarding his sexual relationship with his wife. The counselor also explained the components of the CSA investigation. She informed Diane that the initial report would be made to the child protection agency. However, if they determined that an investigation was warranted, they would likely conduct a joint investigation with the law enforcement agency.

Subsequently, the counselor placed the call to the child protection agency while Diane was in the office. The counselor identified herself to the child protection worker and briefly described the behaviors Lisa had exhibited as well as her statement regarding her father. Then, Diane spoke on the phone to the child protection worker and provided further information about Lisa's behaviors. Because Lisa would not be seeing her father for several days, the child protection worker scheduled an appointment to meet with Diane, Lisa, and Michael the following day. The child protection worker added that she anticipated that an investigator from the county prosecutor's office would observe the interview with Lisa from behind a one-way mirror. After the telephone call was completed, Diane was obviously shaken. When the counselor asked exactly what her concerns were, Diane reported that she could not believe that this was happening, that she never wanted her husband to go to jail. The counselor explained that it was too early to try to guess what the outcome of the investigation would be. She further explained that the reason the investigator would be observing the interview is to try to minimize the number of interviews Lisa would have to experience. She explained that the decision to prosecute a case of alleged sexual abuse is complicated and that the investigator's presence does not indicate that that decision has been made yet.

Diane also expressed concern about how to prepare Lisa for the interview, questioning, "What should I tell her?" The counselor cautioned Diane against trying to prepare Lisa in any formal way. She reassured Diane that the investigating professionals will be skilled in working with children and will want to elicit any information Lisa has to share in a spontaneous way. The counselor and Diane discussed what Diane might tell Lisa about the appointment the next day. Diane requested that the counselor help her talk with Lisa about it, so they asked Lisa to join them in the office. When Lisa joined them, the counselor and Diane explained to her that just as she had met with the counselor today, she would be meeting with another person tomorrow at a different office. They explained that she will be talking with a social worker whose job it is to help kids. Lisa did not seem disturbed by that explanation, rather she appeared to accept it without significant concern.

After they spoke with Lisa for a few minutes, Lisa returned to the playroom next door, where her brother was playing. The counselor then explained to Diane that she would like to continue to provide support and advocacy for Diane and her children during the course of the investigation. She also offered the mother some coping assistance as well as guidelines for responding to her daughter's questions and behavioral reactions. For example, she encouraged Diane to call her or to talk with a trusted friend about her own emotional responses to this situation, but cautioned her strongly against discussing the situation at a time when the children could overhear her. Diane expressed concern about how she should handle it if Lisa began talking about any instance of sexual abuse. The counselor suggested that she should allow Lisa to discuss anything, as long as Lisa brought it up spontaneously. It was explained that Diane could be a tremendous source of support to her daughter by simply listening to what her daughter had to say rather than questioning her in any way. However, she discouraged Diane from questioning Lisa about any type of sexual contact, explaining that at this point, it is important not to influence Lisa's disclosure of information in any way. At the end of the session, the counselor and Diane agreed to meet weekly for several sessions to help Diane and her children cope with the immediate crisis. During these sessions, they agreed to formulate a plan for treatment with the current counselor or, if necessary, with a counselor who had more expertise in the area of child sexual abuse.

CONCLUSION

Given the widespread prevalence of child sexual abuse, all mental health professionals should be prepared to identify and appropriately intervene on behalf of suspected child victims. This chapter provides basic information that may assist clinicians in recognizing and reporting suspected CSA. In addition to outlining reporting requirements, the chapter describes the components of the multidisciplinary investigation that generally ensues once a report is made. Guidelines are also offered for responding to the emotional reactions and coping needs of the child and his/her nonoffending parent(s) in the immediate aftermath of a CSA disclosure. By providing support and advocacy, the mental health professional may critically influence the investigatory process while also reducing the stress experienced by the child and his/her family during this crisis period.

REFERENCES

American Academy of Pediatrics. (1991). Guidelines for the evaluation of sexual abuse in children. *Pediatrics, 87*(2), 254–260.

Beitchman, J. H., Zucker, K. J., Hood, J. E., DaCosta, G. A., Akman, D., & Cassavia, E. (1992). A review of the long-term effects of child sexual abuse. *Child Abuse and Neglect, 16,* 101–118.

Boney-McCoy, S., & Finkelhor, D. (1995). Psychosocial sequelae of violent victimization in a national youth sample. *Journal of Consulting and Clinical Psychology, 63*(5), 726–736.

Bradley, A. R., & Wood, J. M. (1996). How do children tell? The disclosure process in child sexual abuse. *Child Abuse and Neglect, 20*(9), 881–891.

Briere, J. N., & Elliott, D. M. (1994). Immediate and long-term impacts of child sexual abuse. *The Future of Children, 4*(2), 54–69.

Briere, J., & Runtz, N. (1988). Symptomatology associated with childhood sexual victimization in a nonclinical adult sample. *Child Abuse and Neglect, 12,* 51–59.

Briere, J., & Zaidi, L. Y. (1989). Sexual abuse histories and sequelae in female psychiatric emergency room patients. *American Journal of Psychiatry, 146,* 1602–1606.

Cohen, J. A., & Mannarino, A. P. (1996). Factors that mediate treatment outcome of sexually abused preschool children. *Journal of the American Academy of Child and Adolescent Psychiatry, 34*(10), 1402–1410.

Cohen, J. B., Deblinger, E., Maedel, A. B., & Stauffer, L. B. (1999). Examining sex-related thoughts and feelings of sexually abused and nonabused children. *Journal of Interpersonal Violence, 14*(7), 701–712.

Conte, J. R., & Schuerman, J. (1987). Factors associated with an increased impact of child sexual abuse. *Child Abuse and Neglect, 11,* 201–211.

Cormier, B. M., Kennedy, M., & Sangowicz, J. (1962). Psychodynamics of father–daughter incest. *Canadian Psychiatric Association Journal, 1,* 203–217.

Deblinger, E., & Heflin, A. H. (1996). *Treating sexually abused children and their nonoffending parents: A cognitive-behavioral approach.* Thousand Oaks, CA: Sage.

Deblinger, E., Lippmann, J., & Steer, R. (1996). Sexually abused children suffering posttraumatic stress symptoms: Initial treatment outcome findings. *Child Maltreatment, 1*(4), 310–321.

Deblinger, E., McLeer, S., Atkins, M., Ralphe, D., & Foa, E. (1989). Posttraumatic stress in sexually abused, physically abused, and nonabused children. *Child Abuse and Neglect, 13,* 403–408.

Deblinger, E., Stauffer, L., & Landsberg, C. (1994). The impact of a history of child sexual abuse on maternal response to allegations of sexual abuse concerning her child. *Journal of Child Sexual Abuse, 3*(3), 67–75.

Deblinger, E., Steer, R., & Lippmann, J. (1999). Maternal factors associated with sexually abused children's psychosocial adjustment. *Child Maltreatment, 4*(1), 13–20.

Deblinger, E., Taub, B., Maedel, A., Lippmann, J., & Stauffer, L. (1997). Psychosocial factors predicting parent reported symptomatology in sexually abused children. *Journal of Child Sexual Abuse, 6,* 35–49.

Eisenberg, N., Owens, R. G., & Dewey, M. E. (1987). Attitudes of health professionals to child sexual abuse and incest. *Child Abuse and Neglect, 11,* 109–116.

Elliott, D. M., & Briere, J. (1992). Sexual abuse trauma among professional women: Validating the Trauma Symptom Checklist-40 (TSC-40). *Child Abuse and Neglect, 16*(3), 391–398.

Everson, M. D., Hunter, W. M., Runyon, D. K., Edelson, G. A., & Coulter, M. L. (1989). Maternal support following disclosure of incest. *American Journal of Orthopsychiatry, 59*(2), 197–207.

Feiring, C., Taska, L., & Lewis, M. (1998). Social support and children's and adolescents' adaptation to sexual abuse. *Journal of Interpersonal Violence, 13,* 240–260.

Femina, D. D., Yeager, C. A., & Lewis, D. O., (1990). Child abuse: Adolescent records vs. adult recall. *Child Abuse and Neglect, 14,* 227–231.

Finkel, M. A., & DeJong, A. R. (1992). Medical findings in child sexual abuse. In R. M. Reece (Ed.), *Child abuse: Medical diagnosis and management* (pp. 185–247). Philadelphia: Lea & Febiger.

Finkelhor, D., Hotaling, G., Lewis, I., & Smith, C. (1990). Sexual abuse in a national survey of men and women: Prevalence, characteristics, and risk factors. *Child Abuse and Neglect, 14,* 19–28.

Flango, V. E. (1991). Can central registries improve substantiation rates in child abuse cases? *Child Abuse and Neglect, 15,* 408–415.

Friedrich, W. N. (1993). Sexual victimization and sexual behavior in children: A review of the recent literature. *Child Abuse and Neglect, 17*(1), 59–66.

Friedrich, W. N., Beilke, R. L., & Luecke, W. J. (1988). Behavior problems in young sexually abused boys: A comparison study. *Journal of Interpersonal Violence, 2,* 21–28.

Friedrich, W. N., Luecke, W. J., Beilke, R. L., & Place, V. (1992). Psychotherapy outcome of sexually abused boys: An agency study. *Journal of Interpersonal Violence, 7*(3), 396–409.

Friedrich, W. N., Urquiza, A. J., & Beilke, R. (1986). Behavioral problems in sexually abused young children. *Journal of Pediatric Psychology, 11*(1), 47–57.

Goldston, D. B., Turnquist, D. C., & Knutson, J. F. (1989). Presenting problems of sexually abused girls receiving psychiatric services. *Journal of Abnormal Psychology, 98,* 314–317.

Gonzalez, L. S., Waterman, J., Kelly, R. J., McCord, J., & Oliveri, M. K. (1993). Children's patterns of disclosures and recantations of sexual and ritualistic abuse allegations in psychotherapy. *Child Abuse and Neglect, 17,* 281–189.

Heflin, A. H., Finkel, M., Deblinger, E., & Brown, G. (1996, November). *Factors predicting children's disclosures of sexual abuse and related concerns during forensic medical exams.* Paper presented at the annual meeting of the Association for Advancement of Behavior Therapy, New York, NY.

Heflin, A. H., Mears, C., Deblinger, E., & Steer, R. (1997, June). *A comparison of body images and views of sexuality between sexually abused and nonabused girls.* Paper presented at the annual meeting of the American Professional Society on the Abuse of Children, Miami, FL.

Hiebert-Murphy, D. (1998). Emotional distress among mothers whose children have been sexually abused: The role of a history of child sexual abuse, social support, and coping. *Child Abuse and Neglect, 22*(5), 423–435

Humphreys, C. (1997). Child sexual abuse allegations in the context of divorce: Issues for mothers. *British Journal of Social Work, 27,* 529–544.

Jones, D. P. H., & McGraw, J. M. (1987). Reliable and fictitious accounts of sexual abuse in children. *Journal of Interpersonal Violence, 2,* 27–45.

Jumper, S. A. (1995). A meta-analysis of the relationship of child sexual abuse to adult psychological adjustment. *Child Abuse and Neglect, 19*(6), 715–728.

Kalichman, S. C., Craig, M. E., & Follingstad, D. R. (1988). Mental health professionals and suspected cases of child abuse: An investigation of factors influencing reporting. *Community Mental Health Journal, 23*(1), 43–5 1.

Kelley, S. J. (1990). Responsibilities and management strategies in child sexual abuse: A comparison of child protective workers, nurses and police officers. *Child Welfare, 69*(l), 43–51.

Kendall-Tackett, K. A., Williams, L. M., & Finkelhor, D. (1993). Impact of sexual abuse on children: A review and synthesis of recent empirical studies. *Psychological Bulletin, 113*(1), 164–180.

Kolko, D. J., Moser, J. T., & Weldy, S. R. (1988). Behavioral emotional indicators of sexual abuse in child psychiatric inpatients: A controlled comparison with physical abuse. *Child Abuse and Neglect, 12,* 529–541.

Lanktree, C., Briere, J., & Zaidi, L. Y. (1991). Incidence and impact in a child outpatient sample: The role of direct inquiry. *Child Abuse and Neglect, 15,* 447–453.

Lawson, L., & Chaffin, M. (1992). False negatives in sexual abuse disclosure interviews: Incidence and influence of caretaker's belief in abuse in cases of accidental abuse discovery and diagnosis of STD. *Journal of Interpersonal Violence, 7,* 532–542.

Mannarino, A. P., & Cohen, J. A. (1996). Abuse-related attributions and perceptions, general attributions, and locus of control in sexually abused girls. *Journal of Interpersonal Violence, 11*(2), 162–180.

McLeer, S. V., Deblinger, E., Henry, D., & Orvaschel, H. (1992). Sexually abused children at high risk for post-traumatic stress disorder. *Journal of the American Academy of Adolescent and Child Psychiatry, 31*(5), 875–879.

Nagel, D. E., Putnam, F. W., & Noll, J. G. (1997). Disclosure patterns of sexual abuse and psychological functioning at a 1-year follow-up. *Child Abuse and Neglect, 21*(2), 137–147.

Neumann, D. A., Housekamp, B. M, Pollock, B. M., & Briere, J. (1996). The long-term sequelae of childhood sexual abuse in women: A meta-analytic review. *Child Maltreatment, 1*(1), 6–16.

New Jersey Governor's Task Force on Child Abuse and Neglect. (1990). *Report on New Jersey's child protection system.* Unpublished report.

Oates, R. K., O'Toole, B. I., Lynch, D. L., Stern, A., & Cooney, G. (1994). Stability and change in outcomes for sexually abused children. *Journal of the American Academy of Child & Adolescent Psychiatry, 33*(7), 945–953.

Pence, D. M., & Wilson, C.A. (1994). Reporting and investigating child sexual abuse. *The Future of Children, 4*(2), 70–83.

Peters, S. D. (1988). Child sexual abuse and later psychological problems. In G. E. Wyatt & G. J. Powell (Eds.), *Lasting effects of child sexual abuse.* Newbury Park, CA: Sage.

Runyon, D. K., Hunter, W. M., & Everson, M. D. (1992). *Maternal support for child victims of sexual abuse: Determinants and implications.* Final report for the National Center for Child Abuse and Neglect. Washington, DC: U.S. Department of Health and Human Services.

Russell, D. (1986). *The secret trauma: Incest in the lives of girls and women.* New York: Basic Books.

Sarles, R. M. (1975). Incest. *Pediatric Clinics of North America, 22,* 633–642.

Sedlak, A. J., & Broadhurst, D. D. (1996). *Third national incidence study of child abuse and neglect: Final report.* Washington, DC: U.S. Department of Health and Human Services.

Sgroi, S. M., Porter, F. S., & Blick, L. C. (1982). Validation of child sexual abuse. In S. M. Sgroi (Ed.), *Handbook of clinical intervention in child sexual abuse* (pp. 39–79). Lexington, MA: Lexington Books.

Sirles, E., & Franke, P. (1989). Factors influencing mothers' reactions to intrafamily sexual abuse. *Child Abuse and Neglect, 13,* 165–170.

Sorensen, T., & Snow, B. (1991). How children tell: The process of disclosure in child sexual abuse. *Child Welfare, 70*(l), 3–15.

Spaccarelli, S., & Fuchs, C. (1997). Variability in symptom expression among sexually abused girls: Developing multivariate models. *Journal of Clinical Child Psychology, 26*(1), 24–35.

Stauffer, L. B., & Deblinger, E. (1996). Cognitive behavioral groups for nonoffending mothers and their young sexually abused children: A preliminary treatment outcome study. *Child Maltreatment, 1*(1), 65–76.

Steel, J. L., Wilson, G., Cross, H., & Whipple, J. (1996). Mediating factors in the development of psychopathology in victims of childhood sexual abuse. *Sexual Abuse: A Journal of Research and Treatment, 8*(4), 291–316.

Swoboda, J., Elwork, A., Sales, B., & Levine, D. (1978). Knowledge of and compliance with privileged communication and child abuse reporting laws. *Professional Psychology, 9,* 448–458.

Thoennes, N., & Tjaden, P. (1990). The extent, nature and validity of sexual abuse allegations in custody/visitation disputes. *Child Abuse and Neglect, 14,* 151.

Timmons-Mitchell, J., Chandler-Holtz, D., & Semple, W. E. (1996). Post-traumatic stress symptoms in mothers following children's reports of sexual abuse: An exploratory study. *American Journal of Othopsychiatry, 66*(3), 463–467.

Tufts New England Medical Center. (1984). *Sexually exploited children: Service and research project.* Final report for the Office of Juvenile Justice and Delinquency Prevention. Washington, DC: U.S. Department of Justice.

Wyatt, G. E., & Newcomb, M. (1990). Internal and external mediators of women's sexual abuse in childhood. *Journal of Consulting and Clinical Psychology, 58*(6), 758–767.

Wyatt, G. E., & Peters, S. D. (1986). Methodological considerations in research on the prevalence of child sexual abuse. *Child Abuse and Neglect, 10,* 241–251.

SUGGESTED READINGS

Berliner, L., & Elliott, D. M. (1996). Sexual abuse of children. In J. Briere, L. Berliner, J. A. Bulkley, C. Jenny, & T. Reid (Eds.), *The APSAC handbook on child maltreatment* (pp. 51–71). Thousand Oaks, CA: Sage.

Deblinger, E., & Heflin, A. H. (1996). *Treating sexually abused children and their nonoffending parents: A cognitive behavioral approach.* Thousand Oaks, CA: Sage.

Pence, D. M., & Wilson, C. A. (1994). Reporting and investigating child sexual abuse. *The Future of Children, 4*(2), 70–83.

8

Assessment and Crisis Intervention with Older Adults

Helen M. DeVries
Dolores Gallagher-Thompson

Whether one has planned to or not, working with older adults is an increasing likelihood for all clinicians unless they limit their practice to children and adolescents. Demographic data tell us that the fastest growing segment of the population is adults over the age of 75, with the over-85 group increasing more than sixfold by 2050 (Belsky, 1999). As baby boomers age, the number of adults living well into their 80's and even 90's will jump exponentially. Yet, few clinicians are prepared by their academic or clinical training to assess and treat this unique population.

Older adults are a diverse population. They experience the same broad array of psychological issues and disorders that affect younger adults. However, differences in education, health status, economic status, and life experiences are often greater than in younger clients. Gerontologists often break old age into three categories: the "young old" (ages 65–75), the "old" (75–85), and the "oldest old" (age 85+). Current generations of the "young old" and the aging baby boomer population are healthier and better educated than those entering old age a generation ago. They are entering old age with more resources and different expectations than earlier generations of the elderly. However, the current cohort of older adults, especially those over 70, have generally had little experience with psychotherapy and consequently are reluctant to seek out psychological services when faced with emotional distress. This failure to access services at an early stage of crisis often means that the older adult client may be quite overwhelmed by the time they actually present for treatment.

The majority of older adults do manage to face problems and overcome them effectively, but some will need help facing the challenges of aging. Several researchers have noted the increase in stressful life events associated with the process of aging (Duffy & Iscoe, 1990; Kirsling, 1986; Wilson & Schulz, 1983). As the number and frequency of these stressors pile up, the older adult becomes increasingly at risk for psychological crisis. Taxonomies for categorizing life stressors have noted four types of stressful life events (Reese & Smyer, 1983; VandenBos, 1998): (1) biological factors (e.g., physical and sensory disabilities, illness), (2) physical and environmental factors (e.g., retirement, loss of income, changes in housing or living conditions), (3) psychological factors (e.g., changes in cognitive ability, loss and bereavement), and (4) social/cultural factors (e.g., changes in role or expected behavior). These stressors frequently occur simultaneously or in close succession, thus complicating efforts to cope. In addition, older adults often have reduced resources for coping compared to other age groups. Wilson and Schulz (1983) point out that many elderly "have fewer economic, health, personal, and social resources on which to call" (p. 122) when faced with a crisis event.

Although stressful life events often act as precipitating forces in "crisis" situations, it is the individual's subjective experience of that stress that signals whether a crisis exists. Duffy and Iscoe (1990) argue that crisis experience is related to the way in which life stressors or events are perceived by the individual. Drawing on Seligman's "learned helplessness" model, they define crisis as "the subjective experience of loss of control, helplessness, and perceived inability to cope"(p. 304). Therefore, many older adults encounter increasing life stressors (death of a spouse, mandatory retirement, etc.), but only those who perceive these events as threats or beyond their coping abilities will go into crisis. This definition of crisis (the subjective experience of feeling out of control) provides a framework for understanding individual differences in responding to stressful situations and identifying those in crisis.

Psychological crisis, therefore, is not the inevitable outcome of the multiple stressors associated with aging. Rather, the interaction between stressful events and the person's perception of those events predicts outcome. When an individual makes the appraisal that the stressors exceed the resources needed to cope, a crisis situation exists. For each individual, the threshold is different. Yet, when that threshold is crossed, the individual experiences psychological crisis.

Despite the multiple stressors and risk factors confronting older adults, most do adapt and do not exhibit psychiatric symptoms. "Normal" aging is not characterized by pathological reactions or hopelessness and despair. However, coping is a process that must take place over time. Assessing where individuals are in the coping process and identifying those who have exceeded their coping threshold are essential. Differentiating normal patterns of reaction to stressful events from pathological reactions is critical in anticipating and intervening in crisis situations.

Of particular importance is the need to identify older adults who are at risk for suicide, the most devastating extreme of psychological crisis. Epidemiological evidence indicates that approximately one fourth of all suicides are carried out by persons age 60 or older (Richardson, Lowenstein, & Weissberg, 1989). In addition, the number of suicides among those over age 65 increased by 36% from 1980 to 1992, with the largest relative overall increase occurring in 80- to 84-year-olds (U.S. Centers for Disease Control & Prevention, 1996). Conwell et al. (1998) report that older adults were more likely than other populations to engage in determined and planned self-destructive acts and to give fewer warnings of suicidal intent. In addition, there is growing concern about frequently undetected "silent" suicides among older adults who determine to die through self-starvation or noncompliance with essential medical treatment (Simon, 1989).

Age alone, however, is not a sufficient predictor of suicide in late life. Like other forms of psychological crisis, suicide is the consequence of multiple and interacting stressors that exceed the individual's perceived ability to cope. Depression is frequently cited as the principal risk factor for suicide (Blazer, Bachor, & Manton, 1986; Kirsling, 1986; Lindesay, 1991; Losee, Parham, Auerbach, & Teitelman, 1988; Richardson, Lowenstein, & Weissberg, 1989). Other commonly identified risk factors include social isolation, losses, physical illness, a past history of suicide attempts, and psychiatric illness (Conwell, 1997). In addition, Blazer (1991) identified seven demographic factors that interact with age to increase risk for suicide: sex, race, marital status, economic status, mental illness, suicide attempts, and biochemical factors. For example, the rate for males over the age of 65 who commit suicide is significantly higher than the rate for females in this age group. Thus, the apparent relationship between suicide and age is due almost entirely to the association between suicide and elderly males (Blazer, 1991). Awareness of psychosocial and demographic risk factors that interact with age to increase the possibility of suicidal behavior is a beginning step toward effective assessment and intervention.

This chapter focuses on two main components of crisis intervention with older adults: assessment and intervention. The goal is to enable the reader to evaluate whether an older adult is at risk for experiencing a crisis, to provide information and identify measures useful in assessing psychological crisis in this population, to describe cognitive-behavioral strategies for intervening with this group, and to provide case studies.

ASSESSMENT

Diagnosing psychological crisis in the elderly is difficult because of the hesitancy of older adults to seek psychiatric or psychological services or to employ typical psychiatric vocabulary. Somatic distress is the most common presenting problem and indicator of psychological distress in older adults. Typically, the older patient seeks treatment for a medical condition rather than for emotional distress. In fact, data indicate that many older adults who commit suicide have consulted a primary care physician (rather than psychiatric services) in the month preceding their suicide attempt (Liptzin, 1991). Alternatively, many older adults prefer to turn to the clergy for help when they experience personal problems (Weaver & Koenig, 1996). Thus, both physicians and clergy need to be sensitive to the possibility of psychological illness. Eliciting information regarding stressful life events and the patient's perception of those events is a necessary part of the assessment of psychological well-being.

Because feelings of loss of control and inability to cope are often triggers for catastrophic or crisis reactions, recognizing situations that would increase the risk for these reactions is essential. As older adults face the multiple stressors associated with aging, some will cross the coping threshold and experience psychological crisis. In particular, older adults who present with the following complaints or situations may be at high risk for experiencing psychological crises: depression, complicated bereavement, alcohol or drug abuse, cognitive impairment, chronic or serious illness, and changes in family roles/dynamics. Examination of these multiple domains is critical to the effective assessment of risk for psychological crisis in the elderly.

Depression

The relationship between depression and psychological crisis is particularly acute among the elderly, for whom depression is the most frequently noted functional (nonorganic) mental disorder (Koenig & Blazer, 1992; Losee et al., 1988). Although most older adults acknowledge some depressive symptoms, the majority are not clinically depressed (Gallagher & Thompson, 1983). Research indicates that more women than men are diagnosed with a depressive disorder in early adulthood and old age, whereas more males are severely depressed in late midlife (ages 55 to 64; Leaf et al., 1988). A major depressive episode that occurs for the first time in patients age 60 or older is sometimes referred to as late-onset depression. Koenig and Blazer (1992) suggest that late-onset depression is less linked to genetic factors and more likely associated with situational or illness-related biological factors. This distinction is important in assessing depression in older adults and has significant treatment implications. Differentiating symptoms of depression from symptoms indicating underlying medical problems is particularly critical in the elderly. Although many of the symptoms of depression among the elderly are similar to those found in other age groups, several differences exist. As previously mentioned, older adults are more likely to report somatic rather than psychological symptoms and to seek medical services rather than psychiatric services for treatment of depression. In addition, older adults more frequently evidence symptoms of apathy and agitation, as well as increased problems with concentration and memory, and report lower prevalence of dysphoria and ideational symptoms, such as guilt or suicidal ideation (Kasl-Godley, Gatz, & Fiske, 1998; Koenig & Blazer, 1992). Cavanaugh (1990) reports that depressed older adults are more likely than are younger adults to withdraw, confine themselves to bed, and neglect bodily functions.

Standard self-report measures are frequently used as tools to assess symptoms of depression, although accurate diagnoses cannot be made without a thorough clinical interview. Most commonly used are the Beck Depression Inventory (BDI; Beck, Ward, Mendelson, Mock, & Erbaugh, 1961) and the Center for Epidemiological Studies Depression Scale (CES-D; Radloff, 1977). Caution should be exercised in interpreting results, however, as these scales are weighted heavily with physical symptoms that are not always reliable indicators of depression in an older population. The Geriatric Depression Scale (GDS; Yesavage et al., 1983) attempts to remedy this difficulty by focusing primarily on the psychosocial aspects of depression. Structured interviews, such as the Hamilton Rating Scale for Depression (Hamilton, 1967), may also be useful. (See Gallagher, 1986, 1987, and Thompson, Futterman, & Gallagher, 1988, for comprehensive reviews of the psychometric properties of these scales, along with discussion of their utility with older persons.) In general, the BDI is recommended for elders who have at least an eighth-grade reading level and who present with psychiatric difficulties, whereas the GDS is more widely used with less educated elders or medically ill and/or cognitively impaired elders.

Complicated Bereavement

The multiple losses, especially loss of spouse, associated with aging appear to put older adults at greater risk for psychological crisis. Epidemiological data indicate that married people have the lowest suicide rate, whereas the divorced and widowed have the highest (Blazer, 1991). Yet, studies of bereavement in older spouses have found that most cope well with loss but that the affective and cognitive effects of bereavement may continue for at least 2 to 7 years after the loss (Thompson, Gallagher-Thompson, Futterman, & Peterson, 1991; Lund, 1989). While acknowledging the highly stressful nature of spousal bereavement, Lund (1998) argues that "older adults are quite resilient and find ways to manage the many losses that they experience throughout their lives" (p. 108).

Nevertheless, there are those older adults who lack the resources (external or internal) to effectively weather the bereavement process. The most intense psychological impact appears to occur within the first several months, with gradual improvement over time (Thompson, Gallagher, Cover, Gilewski, & Peterson, 1989). At risk for psychological crisis are those who continue to experience high levels of psychological distress 1 to 2 years after the death of their spouse (Thompson, Gallagher-Thompson, Futterman, & Peterson, 1991). In particular, low levels of internal resources (independence, self-efficacy, self-esteem) have been found to correlate with poor adjustment to loss and risk for psychological crisis (Lund, 1989). Also, older bereaved persons who remain significantly depressed following their spouse's death are particularly vulnerable to other kinds of symptoms (Gilewski, Farberow, Gallagher-Thompson, &

Thompson, 1991). Identifying those who are not adapting or coping adequately with loss is critical to effective crisis assessment.

Measures such as the Texas Revised Inventory of Grief (TRIG; Faschingbauer, 1981) and the Grief Experience Inventory (GEI; Sanders, Mauger, & Strong, 1979) can be helpful in this regard, although normative data for older adults are still being developed. Of particular clinical usefulness is the ability to distinguish normal grief from grief complicated by a serious depressive disorder. Research by Breckenridge, Gallagher, Thompson, and Peterson (1986) compared BDI profiles of older bereaved persons with those who were sociodemographically comparable but had not lost a spouse within 5 years of the evaluation. They found that certain symptoms reliably distinguished the two groups (such as frequency of crying, dissatisfaction with self, and various somatic disturbances). Other symptoms, such as guilt and a sense of failure as a person, were uncommon in the normal bereaved group and were, in fact, more typically associated with a significant depressive disorder that warranted treatment in its own right.

Alcohol or Drug Abuse

The high rate of prescribed medication use, increased physiological sensitivity to drug effects, and the danger of interaction effects of multiple medications and/or alcohol place older adults at high risk for deliberate or accidental misuse of drugs or alcohol. In addition, the use of alcohol to help cope with stressful life events increases the risk of addiction and/or toxic interactions. Data indicate that about 10% of older adults have a notable substance abuse problem (Kemp, Brummel-Smith, & Ramsdell, 1990), although good epidemiological data are hard to find and estimates vary widely across studies. Regardless of age, more men than women (approximately 12 to 1) are diagnosed with a substance abuse problem (Hopson-Walker, 1990). In later life, data indicate that elderly widowers have the highest rate of alcoholism of any group (Freund, 1984).

Detection of alcohol abuse, however, can be difficult. Factors such as the isolation of the older adult, absence of social or work schedules and demands, and the tendency of the older adult to drink at home rather than in public all conspire to mask the problem (Solomon, Manepalli, Ireland, & Mahon, 1993). In addition, substance abuse in older adults involves a different set of substances, with the exception of alcohol, than those abused by younger adults (Atkinson, Ganzini, & Bernstein, 1992). Specifically, older adults are less likely to use illicit drugs, but rather to be at risk for abuse of prescribed or over-the-counter medications. The danger, of course, is that alcohol and/or drug abuse will increase the possibility for depression, illness (including risk for falls and accidents), and cognitive impairment.

To assess the potential for substance abuse in the elderly, the professional must explore at least the following factors: whether medication use is being coordinated and monitored by a primary physician for interaction effects, whether the older adult is able to manage the administration of multiple medications, and whether alcohol abuse exists. Because alcohol is metabolized differently in the older person, smaller amounts may cause problems. (See Lamy, 1988, and Shimp & Ascione, 1988, for fuller discussion of this issue.)

At present, unfortunately, no reliable or valid self-report scales exist for the assessment of substance abuse in the elderly. As Solomon et al. (1993) point out, many patients are reluctant or even completely unwilling to be evaluated, and their denial can prevent important information from coming to light. They recommend honesty and directness in questioning both the patient and others involved in the patient's care, along with careful history taking and a urinary drug screen for all new patients. They believe that even with these measures, some patients may not be able to be adequately evaluated for these problems.

In contrast, Willenbring and Spring (1988) describe an interview technique called "giving patients the HEAT," which they recommend for rapid routine screening of all elders. Four questions are asked (using the HEAT mnemonic) about alcohol use, and a positive response to any question leads to further questioning. They recommend that this simple method be used whenever older adults present themselves for care. Similar suggestions for eliciting medication use (and possible intentional or unintentional misuse) are provided by LeSage and Zwygart-Stauffacher (1988). They also emphasize that all health care providers should be knowledgeable about common adverse reactions to drugs frequently used by the elderly.

Cognitive Impairment

Cognitive impairment is not an automatic consequence of "normal" aging. Research has demonstrated that cognitive functions, such as intelligence and memory, remain relatively stable across adulthood, with only selective normative changes with age. When cognitive impairments are noted, they are usually the result of a dementing illness, cerebralvascular accident, physical illness, toxic reaction to medication, or depression. Approximately 15% of people over age 65 have some type of dementia (Davies, 1988). Fortunately, many of the conditions leading to cognitive impairment are treatable if they are properly diagnosed.

Often, however, older adults experiencing a problem with memory or cognitive functioning assume that the problem is irreversible and become depressed, anxious, frightened, or hopeless about the future. The fear of dementia may prevent their seeking appropriate diagnosis and treatment. A medical exam to rule out possible underlying illness, neuropsychological testing, functional assessment, and psychosocial history are all critical in establishing a diagnosis of dementia. Appropriate assessment provides information for identifying possible causes for noted impairments, planning intervention strategies, and addressing psychological distress.

Many comprehensive reviews of the specifics of such assessments have been published in recent years. We particularly recommend two that contain good reviews of measures and information regarding age-appropriate norms: a special issue of the *Psychopharmacology Bulletin* (National Institute of Mental Health, 1988), which presents a thorough review of well-known (and lesser-known) measures of cognition, functional status, and mood for geropsychiatric patients; and a chapter on neuropsychological assessment of the elderly (Crawford, Venneri, & O'Carroll, 1998) found in Volume 7 of *Comprehensive Clinical Psychology,* edited by Bellack and Hersen. In addition, a special issue of *International Psychogeriatrics* (Miller, Lipowski, & Lebowitz, 1991) focuses on assessment of delirium in its various forms. It provides excellent information about behavioral and neuropsychiatric measures that can be used to assist clinicians in making a differential diagnosis between delirium (which is treatable) and the dementias (which are not). In short, when some type of dementia, such as Alzheimer's disease, has been diagnosed, this can create a crisis for the patient or the family (family crisis is discussed later in the chapter).

Chronic Illness

Approximately 80% to 85% of the present cohort of older adults have some type of chronic illness, such as arthritis, diabetes, hypertension, respiratory problems, cardiac problems, etc., which cannot be cured and which cause at least mild levels of disability (Cavanaugh, 1990; Knight, 1996). For example, epidemiological data indicate that approximately 85% of persons ages 75 to 79 have osteoarthritis, 59% of persons in their 70's or 80's have chronic obstructive pulmonary disease (COPD), 32% of those over age 75 have some form of heart disease, and 39% of those over the age of 65 have hypertension (Cavanaugh, 1990; Mongan, 1990; Ries, 1990).

Often, the consequence of chronic illness for the person means permanent changes in lifestyle to accommodate restrictive medical schedules and regimens. In addition, many must endure chronic pain and adjust to physical limitations. These demands cause stress, strain coping resources, and challenge the person's sense of self-worth and control. Assessing the individual's beliefs about changes in body image, competence, and sense of self is critical in identifying those at risk for psychological distress.

Those who hold negative beliefs about themselves and their ability to cope with their illness are likely to develop symptoms of depression. In fact, depression is more common among medical inpatients than with the population as a whole (Knight, 1996). It is these persons who are at greatest risk for psychological crisis. Data suggest that among physically ill older adults, suicidal thoughts are more closely associated with depression than with the illness per se (Lindesay, 1991). Another risk facing older adults with a chronic illness is the risk for "increased disability." This term refers to the added impact of a psychological disorder (such as depression or anxiety)that exacerbates the limitations imposed by the medical condition itself. For example, a person with cataracts may become too depressed to seek alternative ways to enjoy reading, such as books on tape or large print editions (Knight, 1996). Assessment of psychological crisis in the elderly must not ignore the impact of chronic illness on the individual's mental health and coping resources.

Changes in Family Roles/Dynamics

Normative changes in family structure occur as the family moves through developmental stages (i.e., no children, preschool children, school-age children, adolescents, launching, and postparental phases). Although much attention has been paid to the impact of early family transitions, less has been paid to understanding the dynamics of late-life families. In particular, older adults and their adult children face multiple shifts in relationships that require adjustments to new roles and responsibilities. In addition, data suggest that by age 85 years, 60% of the population has at least some degree of disability that requires regular, ongoing assistance, a need most often met within the family context (Zarit, Davey, Edwards, Femia, & Jarrott, 1998).

Retirement, loss of a spouse, geographic distance from adult children, or physical illness of an elderly parent exemplifies ways in which family roles and dynamics may be challenged or require restructuring. Data suggest that many older adults prefer to maintain independence from their children (Brody, Johnsen, Fulcomer, & Lang, 1983; Lee, 1985). However, financial constraints or a parent's physical frailty/illness may force dependence on adult children as caregivers. Shanas (1980) reported that approximately 18% of those over age 65 who have living children do live with them. Although most caregiving is provided by spouses, adult children usually serve as secondary caregivers, or if there is no surviving spouse, as primary caregivers. Pilisuk and Parks (1988) report that approximately 80% of care for elders is provided by families, with less than 10% relying on formal support services. Females (daughters and daughters-in-law) assume the major share of responsibility for parental caregiving (Stone, Cafferata, & Sangl, 1987). Complicating this picture is the increase in divorce and remarriage, which blurs family lines and adds complexity to the situation.

Intergenerational differences and conflicts are bound to emerge when elderly parents and adult children negotiate new roles and responsibilities. For example, elderly parents may become distraught if forced to become dependent on children or, conversely, if they perceive that their children are not willing or available to care for them (Loebel, Loebel, Dager, & Centerwall, 1991). So, too, adult children may experience depression, resentment, anger, guilt, or burden when confronted with caring for frail or needy parents. Some of the stresses on the family may be unexpected, such as reappearance of sibling rivalries as adult children are forced to work together to make decisions about parent care. In fact, these types of conflict are often more difficult to manage than the actual parent care itself. In addition, long-term successful marriages can be thrown into chaos when one spouse becomes disabled due to illness or injury, thus disrupting set patterns of functioning. Due to the importance of family support for many elders, assessment of family functioning and dynamics is critical. Specific issues that should be explored include level of caregiver stress, meaning of role reversal to elder and to adult child, and elder's fears regarding "abandonment" or nursing home placement. High levels of distress regarding any of these issues put the elder and family at risk for potential crisis.

Due to the increased stress on families caring for an elderly relative, the clinician should always be careful to assess the risk for elder abuse. Elder abuse includes physical abuse, neglect, and chronic verbal aggression most commonly at the hands of a spouse, adult child, grandchild, or professional caregiver. It occurs at all economic levels and among all age groups in later adulthood. Abuse is much more likely to occur when the older person is experiencing physical, emotional, or cognitive problems (American Psychological Association, 1997). It is important for the mental health professional to question the cause of any physical injuries or bruises. Many states require reporting by health care, social service, or other professionals if abuse is suspected in the home. All states require reporting when abuse occurs in an institution.

COGNITIVE–BEHAVIORAL APPROACHES TO CRISIS INTERVENTION WITH THE ELDERLY

One of the most important and consistent findings of recent studies is that psychotherapy is as effective with older adults as with younger adults in treating depression and other mental disorders (Engels & Vermey, 1997; Gallagher-Thompson, 1992; Gallagher-Thompson, Hanley-Peterson, & Thompson, 1990; Gallagher-Thompson & Thompson, 1995; Scogin & McElreath, 1994; Thompson, Gallagher, & Breckenridge, 1987). In addition, psychotherapy may be particularly helpful to older adults for whom medication is not appropriate or contraindicated because of health problems. Although psychotherapy can be helpful to this population, some modifications and adaptations may be necessary (see Zeiss & Steffen, 1996). Given the information that has been presented on various problems and risk factors that predispose elders to developing psychological crises, we now discuss intervention strategies that have proven useful in our work with elders in crisis. We primarily operate from a cognitive-behavioral perspective, partly because of the strong empirical base documenting its effectiveness in the treatment of major affective disorders in the elderly. A recent review of this literature found that, as of 1992, seven published papers provided descriptions of treatment and case reports of cognitive-behavioral therapy with depressed elders, fourteen separate publications presented empirical data on the comparative effectiveness of cognitive-behavioral therapy with the elderly, and five additional studies pointed to the usefulness of cognitive-behavioral therapy with physically or cognitively disabled depressed elders (Teri, Curtis, Gallagher-Thompson, & Thompson, 1994).

Carefully controlled clinical trials have indicated, overall, that cognitive-behavioral therapy is at least as effective as other forms of psychotherapy to which it has been compared (e.g., short-term psychodynamic psychotherapy). Recently, a project was completed comparing cognitive-behavioral therapy and pharmacotherapy alone and in combination for the treatment of major depression in elderly outpatients. It was found that, on most outcome measures, the cognitive-behavioral therapy alone did as well as the combination condition, but the drug treatment alone did not (Thompson & Gallagher-Thompson, 1991). In addition, there have been some studies evaluating the efficacy of other forms of treatment, such as family therapy, for dealing with various psychological or psychiatric problems in the elderly. Only a small body of literature has accumulated to date, but it has been reviewed in Futterman, Gallagher-Thompson, Thompson, and Ferris (1995). It should be noted that no particular form of crisis intervention therapy has been developed for use with the elderly, but modifications have been made to existing approaches as clinically indicated.

We assume that the reader has basic familiarity with the theory and techniques of cognitive-behavioral therapy, and so we do not go into great detail here. (See Thompson, Gantz, et al., 1991; Gallagher, Thompson, Lovett, & Rose, 1991; and Thompson, 1996 for a discussion of techniques and useful adaptations of traditional cognitive-behavioral therapy to maximize its effectiveness with older adults.) Briefly, cognitive-behavioral therapy utilizes a combination of cognitive and behavioral techniques (such as those found in Burns, 1980, 1989; Lewinsohn, Munoz, Youngren, & Zeiss, 1986), including the recording of dysfunctional thoughts on a regular basis; learning to identify consistent, unhelpful thinking patterns; learning to generate alternative views of a particular situation (and alternative thoughts along with that); and learning to evaluate the evidence for and against a given cognition. The behavioral methods focus more on techniques such as daily mood monitoring, identification of specific pleasant events to be increased on a daily basis, and learning a consistent method for relaxation. For the patient really to improve, and to remain improved over time, the skillful blending of both cognitive and behavioral techniques seems to be essential.

Therapy typically begins with a few sessions devoted to socializing the patient into treatment. This is particularly important for older adults as they often have negative thoughts about being told to change and may fear psychological or psychiatric treatment, thinking that it means that they are "crazy." They also typically have very little experience in participating in any kind of psychotherapy, and so do not know what to expect or how to behave. When working with an elderly patient in a crisis situation, the socialization period must necessarily be shortened in order that treatment can begin as quickly as possible. Nevertheless, it should not be glossed over, because misunderstandings at the outset are very common and can certainly impede the development of a therapeutic relationship.

We have conceptualized treatment as generally consisting of "early, middle, and late stages" using a 16- to 20-session model (see Thompson, 1996; Thompson, Gantz, et al., 1991). In our crisis intervention work, where the initial goal is to stabilize the patient, the therapy does not proceed in quite the same fashion. Rather, in consultation with other colleagues (most notably, the elderly patient's primary care physician), a plan will be developed to assess the overall situation, to establish the various currently active diagnoses, and to provide limited cognitive-behavioral therapy until the immediate crisis has passed and further evaluation can be done. In most cases, the immediate crisis situation will be resolved within 1 to 2 weeks, and at that point the decision is frequently mutually reached to continue cognitive-behavioral therapy, along with other medical or psychiatric regimens, as appropriate. In that case, the more usual model of short-term cognitive-behavioral therapy would then be followed.

In other instances (which are far less common) a referral will need to be made after the initial period of stabilization is completed. This can occur for several reasons, but most typically occurs when the individual's presenting complaints are so complex that an inpatient hospital stay (either medical or psychiatric) is really needed to sort out various contingencies. In very few instances have we found it necessary to refer the patient for other forms of therapy, such as electroconvulsive therapy (ECT), but this has occurred occasionally in our practice with intractably depressed elders who had a poor history of responding to other forms of treatment.

CASE STUDIES

The following examples illustrate some of the issues that trigger crisis in the elderly and provide assessment and treatment approaches that were useful in addressing the crisis situation. The first case addresses suicide risk and the second case addresses caregiving burnout. While these are only two examples of the kinds of crises that bring older adults in for treatment, they provide a framework for the two tasks of crisis intervention: stabilizing the immediate crisis and providing follow-up support and skills training for more adaptive future functioning.

Case 1: Suicide Risk

Mr. A. is a 72-year-old widowed Caucasian male whose wife died of heart disease within the past year. He was not psychologically prepared for her death, nor did he feel that he could make the necessary adjustments to live alone. He had little experience with household management tasks such as cooking and cleaning and was not used to setting up the social calendar. These things had been done by his wife and now that she was gone, his life was quite empty and, to him, meaningless. He had two grown children in the area with whom he had good relationships, but he did not feel that it was appropriate to turn to them often in his time of grief. Rather, he waited for them to visit him and to talk about their absent mother. Only then did he respond in kind. He found it difficult to cry or to be demonstrative in the expression of any of his feelings regarding the loss of his wife.

About 3 months previous to coming in for treatment, he had been diagnosed with Parkinson's disease. He was a retired English professor at a local college and, unfortunately, knew several colleagues who developed dementia from Parkinson's disease after having the illness for a number of years. He knew that dementia was not inevitable, but he was very frightened of the possibility. He felt that it would make him totally dependent on his daughters, and this was something he did not believe he could tolerate. About 1 month before coming for treatment, Mr. A. was forced to move out of the apartment in which he and his wife had lived for more than 40 years because the building was to be demolished for new construction. This seemed to him to be "the last straw" and sent him into a very deep depression. Mr. A. acknowledged being depressed and also talked about feeling hopeless with regard to the future. Being retired and on a fixed income, he could not really afford to move or pay current rents. His declining health, although it was not precipitous, made him very fearful of the future. He thought about using alcohol to block out some of his painful feelings but said that he did not do that too often. By the time one of his daughters brought him for therapy, he was talking about "ending it all" and seemed to be taking steps to put his affairs in order, as if he were planning to commit suicide in the relatively near future.

The assessment process revealed a BDI score in the "severe" range, a diagnosis of major depressive disorder with questionable alcohol abuse, and a man with few emotional and social resources at the time of the evaluation. He had very negative ideas about his ability to live on his own and about what life held in store for him. He could not seem to visualize a more positive life for himself and was able to acknowledge that he had developed a concrete plan for committing suicide. He kept a gun in the apartment and was a World War II veteran, so he knew quite well how to use the weapon appropriately. He felt that the only deterrent was the shame that this would bring on his daughters, and if it were not for that he would commit suicide without hesitation.

Following this assessment the patient's primary care physician was contacted, and the patient agreed to a voluntary psychiatric hospitalization. This was arranged, and he was treated with cognitive-behavioral therapy during a 2-week stay in the hospital. During this time his psychiatrist prescribed a low dosage of fluoxetine (Prozac), recognizing that it would probably not help him immediately, but it would be beneficial in the long run. He also received milieu therapy and participated in group therapy nearly every day of his inpatient stay. However, he attributed a significant change in his outlook to the individual cognitive-behavioral therapy sessions with the author (D. G. T.).

Some of his cognitive distortions (which we have noted in other patients with suicidal ideation) included the belief that suicide would bring an end to his suffering. He saw it as a respite or a solution to his problems rather than as an untenable way to deal with his life. For this patient, as well as for many others (see Worden, 1992), suicide may represent a way to be reunited with the deceased loved one. This belief became apparent after several sessions, when Mr. A.'s intense loneliness was revealed and his sadness was more apparent. Mr. A. was asked to keep daily thought records so that he could become more aware of his dysfunctional thoughts. He was able to identify negative automatic thoughts and began to learn how to challenge them. Specifically, the thought record helped to point out that he was not as alone as he thought he was, as his daughters were very supportive, and that he did not have dementia, only the fear that someday he would develop it. He was asked to read information about Parkinson's disease so that he could see for himself that dementia was not an inevitable consequence of the disease.

He also worked very hard to overcome his belief that "I can't go on anymore." By challenging his all-or-nothing thinking, he realized that even though he felt overwhelmed, there were some positive things going on in his life. For example, he acknowledged that his former apartment was actually quite large and difficult to maintain. Moving into a smaller unit would make the practical housekeeping chores easier for him. Also, he disclosed that he had previously played golf and had several male friends with whom he had lunch on a fairly regular basis. He was encouraged to contact these men again to let them know of his situation and to see what kind of support they would be willing to provide. This more behavioral assignment resulted in a very surprising (to him) outpouring of support from his friends. This, in turn, helped to challenge the thought that suicide was the only solution to his current problems.

Finally, we spent considerable time examining the consequences of the suicidal action. He was able to discuss the strong negative impact that it would have on his daughters and other family members and finally to realize that he would think of himself as "a quitter" if this really were the path that he chose. Through some structured reminiscence work, he shared with the therapist many of his prior successes in life and began to realize that he had coped with previous difficult situations in a much more adaptive manner. Throughout the course of treatment, he was given a great deal of emotional support, as he clearly felt overwhelmed by the number of negative life circumstances to which he had to adjust.

Following his discharge from the inpatient unit, he was seen once a week for outpatient therapy with the same cognitive-behavioral therapist for approximately 1 year, rather than the more typical 16 to 20 sessions, in order to be sure that he was integrated into the community. During that year, he had a total of 35 sessions of individual therapy, with the final 15 being spread out at more than weekly intervals so that he had ample opportunity to practice becoming reengaged with his friends and his social activities. In fact, over the course of treatment, the emphasis shifted from the more cognitive approach to a more behavioral approach, with gradual reengagement in pleasant activities and development of age-appropriate friendships. He continued to be seen periodically by his psychiatrist during that time and remained on a low dose of fluoxetine. Follow-up 2 years later indicated that he continued to maintain himself well in his new apartment, and that his health had declined somewhat but not in a major way. At the very last follow-up contact, Mr. A. indicated that he was glad to be alive and had found new purpose in life. He said that he was ready to live out the remainder of his days and to die when his creator called him. This seemed to us to be a most satisfactory resolution of this particular client's crisis.

Case 2: Family Caregiving Crisis

Mrs. B. is a 67-year-old married woman who is the primary caregiver for her 93-year-old mother, who is physically frail but cognitively alert. Mrs. B.'s presenting complaint was that she felt overwhelmed with the relentless demands of caregiving and unable to cope any longer. In particular, she voiced frustration that she and her husband were unable to enjoy the type of retirement they had anticipated due to her caregiving responsibilities. She said that she had not taken a vacation in several years because she could not leave her mother alone. In addition, she felt hurt by her mother's critical remarks and lack of appreciation and described their interactions as negative and unpleasant. In fact, due to her anger and resentment, she had begun avoiding conversations with her mother and limiting interactions to necessary caregiving tasks. Mrs. B. stated that she had "no personal life" and had given up many enjoyable activities as the demands of caregiving increased. She described herself as a bitter, resentful, unhappy person. The crisis occurred one day when she found herself becoming enraged while she was assisting her mother on the usual slow and tedious walk from the bedroom to the bathroom. It became clear to her that she needed help when such a small thing could trigger such a powerful emotional reaction. She expressed fear that she was "out of control."

A critical component of the assessment process was to determine whether there was any indication of elder abuse by Mrs. B. She acknowledged that many times she felt "ready to burst" with frustration, but she denied having acted on these feelings, although she voiced concern that she might do so if the stress continued. Clearly, the prevention of inappropriate expressions of anger and frustration was an immediate treatment goal. In addition, it was deemed that Mrs. B. would benefit from the acquisition of coping skills that would help her manage the caregiving responsibilities with less resentment and frustration.

Treatment approaches included both cognitive and behavioral components. To help reduce the risk of elder abuse, Mrs. B. was asked to maintain a record of the thoughts that accompanied the bursts of anger at her mother. Examination of her thought record indicated that most of the negative feelings were associated with thoughts regarding implied criticism from her mother. For example, the mother owned several rental properties, which Mrs. B. was managing for her. When the mother would ask repeatedly whether tasks associated with the rental property had been taken care of, Mrs. B. would tell herself, "She thinks I'm irresponsible" or "She's treating me like a child." Mrs. B. learned to challenge these unhelpful thoughts and to generate more helpful ones (e.g., "Mother is feeling helpless and needs reassurance that everything is okay"). Once Mrs. B. recognized the way her own thoughts were fueling her anger and resentment, she felt empowered to challenge other automatic thoughts and to develop more adaptive alternatives.

The second component of treatment was to help Mrs. B. increase the pleasant activities in her life. The initial focus was to increase positive interactions between the two women. Mrs. B. enjoyed writing and frequently used family history as the source of her stories. She was encouraged to reframe her time with her mother as an "opportunity" to gather stories about her childhood and her mother's childhood as background for her writing. Although initially skeptical about her mother's willingness to share stories with her, Mrs. B. was pleasantly surprised to find her mother cooperative. She began to tape record her mother's reminiscences and found that both of them began to look forward to sharing memories. Although the caregiving tasks remained demanding, the introduction of a pleasant common activity eased the tension between the two and improved the quality of their interactions.

A longer-term goal of treatment was to help Mrs. B. get some respite from caregiving by going on a long-wished-for vacation with her husband. The initial task was to challenge her beliefs that she should be the one to care for her mother, that she should never ask any of her family for relief, and that none of her family would be willing to help. She acknowledged that she had no evidence for these beliefs and agreed to talk with her grown children about the need for a short break from caregiving. Once again, she was pleasantly surprised to learn that they were not only aware of her distress but were more than willing to provide temporary relief so she and her husband could take a short vacation. Mrs. B. entered into the planning of the vacation with enthusiasm. She even built into the plans an insurance policy that would refund 90% of her money if she had to cut her vacation short due to an emergency with her mother. The vacation was a great success and provided needed respite from the strain of caregiving.

At a 1-year follow-up, Mrs. B. reported continued positive coping despite the deteriorating health of her mother and increased caregiving demands. She reported that she was still able to take occasional short "get-aways" of an afternoon or weekend with her husband and no longer felt as though her life had disappeared.

CONCLUSION

In summary, this chapter has emphasized the value of cognitive-behavioral techniques and strategies in assessing and treating psychological crisis in older adults. Whereas many older adults face life-altering events, including chronic illness; death of loved ones and friends; and changes in work, living, and financial status, most cope effectively with these events. However, for some older adults the resources for coping with multiple stressors are not available, and they become overwhelmed. Health care professionals need to be sensitive to the needs of these individuals and to provide services to help them cope with crisis. It is hoped that this chapter has identified the factors that put older adults at risk for crisis, has described the signs of psychological crisis in the elderly, and has provided cognitive-behavioral strategies that would be useful in crisis intervention with the elderly.

REFERENCES

Atkinson, R., Ganzini, L., & Bernstein, M. (1992). Alcohol and substance-use disorders in the elderly. In J. Birren, R. B. Sloane, & G. Cohen (Eds.), *Handbook of mental health and aging* (2nd ed., pp. 515–555). San Diego: Academic Press.

American Psychological Association Working Group on the Older Adult. (1997). *What practitioners should know about working with older adults.* Washington, DC: American Psychological Association.

Beck, A. T., Ward, C. H., Mendelson, M., Mock, J., & Erbaugh, J. (1961). An inventory for measuring depression. *Archives of General Psychiatry, 4,* 561–571.

Belsky, J. (1999). *The psychology of aging: Theory, research, and interventions.* Pacific Grove, CA: Brooks/Cole.

Blazer, D. (1991). Suicide risk factors in the elderly: An epidemiological study. *Journal of Geriatric Psychiatry, 24,* 175–190.

Blazer, D., Bachar, J., & Manton, K. (1986). Suicide in late life: Review and commentary. *Journal of the American Geriatrics Society, 34,* 513–525.

Breckenridge, J. N., Gallagher, D., Thompson, L. W., & Peterson, J. (1986). Effects of bereavement on self-perceptions of physical health in elderly widows and widowers. *Journal of Gerontology, 39*(3), 309–314.

Brody, E. M., Johnsen, P. T., Fulcomer, M. C., & Lang, A. M. (1983). Women's changing roles and help to elderly partners: Attitudes of three generations of women. *Journal of Gerontology, 38,* 597–607.

Burns, D. D. (1980). *Feeling good: The new mood therapy.* New York: Morrow.

Burns, D. D. (1989). *The feeling good handbook.* New York: Penguin Books.

Cavanaugh, J. C. (1990). *Adult development and aging.* Belmont, CA: Wadsworth.

Conwell, Y. (1997). Management of suicidal behavior in the elderly. *Psychiatric Clinics of North America, 20*(3), 667–683.

Conwell, Y., Duberstein, P., Cox, D., Herrmann, J., Forbes, N., & Caine, E. (1998). Age differences in behaviors leading to completed suicide. *American Journal of Geriatric Psychiatry, 6*(2), 122–126.

Crawford, J. R., Venneri, A., & O'Carroll, R. E. (1998). Neuropsychological assessment of the elderly. In A. Bellack & M. Hersen (Eds.), *Comprehensive clinical psychology* (Vol. 7, pp. 133–169). New York: Elsevier Science.

Davies, P. (1988). Alzheimer's disease and related disorders: An overview. In M. K. Aronson (Ed.), *Understanding Alzheimer's disease* (pp. 3–14). New York: Scribner's.

Duffy, M., & Iscoe, I. (1990). Crisis theory and management: The case of the older person. *Journal of Mental Health Counseling, 12,* 303–313.

Engels, G., & Vermey, M (1997). Efficacy of nonmedical treatments of depression in elders: A quantitative analysis. *Journal of Clinical Geropsychology, 3*(1), 17–35.

Faschingbauer, T. R. (1981). *Texas Revised Inventory of Grief manual.* Houston, TX: Honeycomb.

Freund, G. (1984). Current research directions on alcohol problems and aging. *Alcohol Health and Research World, 8,* 11–15.

Futterman, A., Gallagher-Thompson, D., Thompson, L. W., & Ferris, R. (1995). Depression in later life. In E. E. Beckham & W. R. Leber (Eds.), *Handbook of depression* (2nd ed., pp. 494–525). New York: Guilford Press.

Gallagher, D. (1986). The Beck Depression Inventory and older adults: Review of its development and utility. *Clinical Gerontologist, 5,* 149–163.

Gallagher, D. (1987). Assessing affect in the elderly. *Clinics in Geriatric Medicine, 3*(1), 65–85.

Gallagher, D., & Thompson, L. W. (1983). *Elders' maintenance of treatment benefits following individual psychotherapy for depression: Results of a pilot study and preliminary data from an ongoing replication study.* Paper presented at the annual meeting of the American Psychological Association, Washington, DC.

Gallagher-Thompson, D. (1992). The older adult. In A. Freeman & F. Dattilio (Eds.), *Comprehensive casebook of cognitive therapy* (pp. 193–200). New York: Plenum.

Gallagher-Thompson, D., Hanley-Peterson, P., & Thompson, L. (1990). Maintenance of gains versus relapse following brief psychotherapy for depression. *Journal of Consulting and Clinical Psychology, 58,* 371–374.

Gallagher-Thompson, D., Lovett, S., & Rose, J. (1991). Psychotherapeutic interventions for stressed family caregivers. In W. Myers (Ed.), *New techniques in the psychotherapy of older patients* (pp. 61–78). Washington, DC: American Psychiatric Association.

Gallagher-Thompson, D., & Thompson, L. (1995). Psychotherapy with older adults in theory and practice. In B. Bonger & L. Beutler (Eds.), *Comprehensive textbook of psychotherapy* (pp. 357–379). New York: Oxford University Press.

Gilewski, M., Farberow, N., Gallagher-Thompson, D., & Thompson, L. (1991). Interaction of depression and bereavement on mental health in the elderly. *Psychology and Aging, 6,* 67–75.

Hamilton, M. (1967). Development of a rating scale for primary depressive illness. *British Journal of Social and Clinical Psychology, 6,* 278–296.

Hopson-Walker, S. D. (1990). Substance abuse in older persons with disability: Assessment and treatment. In B. Kemp, K. Brummel-Smith, & J. W. Ramsdell (Eds.), *Geriatric rehabilitation* (pp. 279–293). Austin, TX: Pro-Ed.

Kasl-Godley, J., Gatz, M., & Fiske, A. (1998). Depression and depressive symptoms in old age. In I. Nordhus, G. VandenBos, S. Berg, & P. Fromholt (Eds.), *Clinical geropsychology,* (pp. 211–217). Washington, DC: American Psychological Association.

Kemp, B., Brummel-Smith, K., & Ramsdell, J. W. (1990). *Geriatric rehabilitation.* Austin, TX: Pro-Ed.

Kirsling, R. (1986). Review of suicide among elderly persons. *Psychological Reports, 59,* 359–366.

Knight, B. (1996). *Psychotherapy with older adults* (2nd ed). Thousand Oaks, CA: Sage.

Koenig, H., & Blazer, D. (1992). Mood disorders and suicide. In J. Birren, R. B. Sloane, & G. Cohen (Eds.), *Handbook of mental health and aging* (2nd ed.). San Diego: Academic Press.

Lamy, P. P. (1988, Summer). Actions of alcohol & drugs in older people. *Generations,* 9–13.

Leaf, P. J., Berkman, C. S., Weissman, M. M., Holzer, C. E., Tischler, G. L., & Myers, J. K. (1988). The epidemiology of late-life depression. In J. A. Brody & G. L. Maddox (Eds.), *Epidemiology and aging: An international perspective* (pp. 117–133). New York: Springer-Verlag.

Lee, G. R. (1985). Kinship and social support of the elderly: The case of the United States. *Aging and Society, 5,* 19–38.

LeSage, J., & Zwygart-Stauffacher, M. (1988, Summer). Detection of medication misuse in elders. *Generations, 12*(4), 32–36.

Lewinsohn, P. M., Munoz, R., Youngren, M. A., & Zeiss, A. M. (1986). *Control your depression* (rev. ed.). New York: Prentice Hall.

Lindesay, J. (1991). Suicide in the elderly. *International Journal of Geriatric Psychiatry, 6,* 355–361.

Liptzin, B. (1991). The treatment of depression in older suicidal persons. *Journal of Geriatric Psychiatry, 24,* 203–215.

Loebel, J. P., Loebel, J. S., Dager, S., & Centerwall, B. (1991). Anticipation of nursing home placement may be a precipitant of suicide among the elderly. *Journal of the American Geriatrics Society, 39,* 407–408.

Losee N., Parham, I., Auerbach, S., & Teitelman, (1988). *Crisis intervention with the elderly: Theory, practical issues, and training procedures.* Springfield, IL: C. C. Thomas.

Lund, D. A. (Ed.). (1989). *Older bereaved spouses: Research with practical applications.* New York: Hemisphere.

Lund, D. A. (1998). Bereavement. In A. Bellack & M. Hersen (Eds.), *Comprehensive clinical psychology* (Vol. 7, pp. 95–112). New York: Elsevier Science.

Miller, N. E., Lipowski, Z. J., & Lebowitz, B. D. (Eds.). (1991). Delirium: Advances in research and clinical practice. *International Psychogeriatrics, 3,* 97–414.

Mongan, E. (1990). Arthritis and osteoporosis. In B. Kemp, K. Brummel-Smith, & J. W. Ramsdell (Eds.), *Geriatric rehabilitation* (pp. 91–105). Austin, TX: Pro-Ed.

National Institute of Mental Health. (1988). Assessment in diagnosis and treatment of geropsychiatric patients. *Psychopharmacology Bulletin, 24*(4).

Pilisuk, M., & Parks, S. H. (1988). Caregiving: Where families need help. *Social Work, 33,* 436–440.

Radloff, L. S. (1977). The CES-D Scale: A self-report depression scale for research in the general population. *Applied Psychological Measurement, 1,* 385.

Reese, H. W., & Smyer, M. A. (1983). The dimensionalization of life events. In E. J. Callahan & K. A. McCluskey (Eds.), *Life-span developmental psychology: Non-normative life events* (pp. 1–33). New York: Academic Press.

Richardson, R., Lowenstein, S., & Weissberg, M. (1989). Coping with the suicidal elderly: A physician's guide. *Geriatrics, 44,* 43–47.

Ries, A. L. (1990). Pulmonary rehabilitation. In B. Kemp, K. Brummel-Smith, & J. W. Ramsdell (Eds.), *Geriatric rehabilitation* (pp. 107–120). Austin, TX: Pro-Ed.

Sanders, C. M., Mauger, P. A., & Strong, P. N. (1979). *A manual for the Grief Experience Inventory*. Belmont, NC: Sacred Heart College.

Scogin, F., & McElreath, L. (1994). Efficacy of psychosocial treatments for geriatric depression: A quantitative review. *Journal of Consulting and Clinical Psychology, 62,* 69–74.

Shanas, E. (1980). Older people and their families: The new pioneers. *Journal of Marriage and the Family, 42,* 9–15.

Shimp, L. A., & Ascione, F. J. (1988, Summer). Causes of medication misuse and error. *Generations, 12*(4), 17–21.

Simon, R. (1989). Silent suicide in the elderly. *Bulletin of the American Academy of Psychiatry and the Law, 17,* 83–95.

Solomon, K., Manepalli, J., Ireland, G., & Mahon, G. M. (1993). Alcoholism and prescription drug abuse in the elderly: St. Louis University grand rounds. *Journal of the American Geriatrics Society, 41,* 57–69.

Stone, R., Cafferata, G. L., & Sangl, G. (1987). Caregivers of the frail elderly: A national profile. *The Gerontologist, 27,* 616–626.

Teri, L., Curtis, J., Gallagher-Thompson, D., & Thompson, L. W. (1994). Cognitive-behavior therapy with depressed older adults. In L. S. Schneider, C. F. Reynolds, B. D. Lebowitz, & A. J. Friedhoff (Eds.), *Diagnosis and treatment of depression in late life: Results of the NIH consensus development conference* (pp. 279–291). Washington, DC: American Psychiatric Press.

Thompson, L. (1996). Cognitive-behavioral therapy and treatment for late-life depression. *Journal of Clinical Psychiatry, 57,* 29–37.

Thompson, L. W., Futterman, A., & Gallagher, D. (1988). Assessment of late-life depression. *Psychopharmacology Bulletin, 24*(4), 108–117.

Thompson, L., Gallagher, D., & Breckenridge, J. (1987). Comparative effectiveness of psychotherapies for depressed elders. *Journal of Consulting and Clinical Psychology, 55,* 385–390.

Thompson, L. W., Gallagher, D., Cover, H., Gilewski, M., & Peterson, J. (1989). Effects of bereavement on symptoms of psychopathology in older men and women. In D. Lund (Ed.), *Older bereaved spouses: Research with practical applications* (pp. 17–24). New York: Hemisphere.

Thompson, L. W., & Gallagher-Thompson, D. (1991). *Comparison of desipramine and cognitive/behavioral therapy in the treatment of late-life depression: A progress report.* Paper presented at the annual meeting of the Gerontological Society of America, San Francisco.

Thompson, L. W., Gallagher-Thompson, D., Futterman, A., & Peterson, J. (1991). The effects of late-life spousal bereavement over a thirty-month interval. *Psychology and Aging, 6,* 434–441.

Thompson, L. W., Gantz, F., Florsheim, M., DelMaestro, S., Rodman, J., & Gallagher-Thompson, D. (1991). Cognitive/behavioral therapy for affective disorders in the elderly. In W. Myers (Ed.), *New techniques in the psychotherapy of older patients* (pp. 3–19). Washington, DC: American Psychiatric Association.

U.S. Centers for Disease Control and Prevention (1996). Suicide among older persons— United States, 1980–1992. *Journal of the American Medical Association, 275*(7), 509.

VandenBos, G. (1998). Life-span developmental perspectives on aging: An introductory overview. In I. Nordhus, G. VandenBos, S. Berg, & P. Fromholt (Eds.), *Clinical geropsychology* (pp. 3–14). Washington, DC: American Psychological Association.

Weaver, A., & Koenig, H. (1996). Elderly suicide, mental health professionals, and the clergy: A need for clinical collaboration, training, and research. *Death Studies, 20*(5), 495–508.

Willenbring, M., & Spring, W. D., Jr. (1988, Summer). Evaluating alcohol use in elders. *Generations, 12*(4), 27–31.

Wilson, K., & Schulz, R. (1983). Criteria for effective crisis intervention. In M. Smyer & M. Gatz (Eds.), *Mental health and aging: Programs and evaluations* (pp. 121–142). Beverly Hills, CA: Sage.

Worden, J. W. (1992). *Grief counseling and grief therapy: A handbook for the mental health practitioner.* New York: Springer-Verlag.

Yesavage, J. A., Brink, T. L., Rose, T. L., Lum, O., Huang, V., Adey, M., & Leirer, V. O. (1983). Development and validation of a geriatric depression scale: A preliminary report. *Journal of Psychiatric Research, 17,* 37–49.

Zarit, S., Davey, A., Edwards, A., Femia, E., & Jarrott, S. (1998). Family caregiving: Research findings and clinical implications. In A. Bellack & M. Hersen (Eds.). *Comprehensive clinical psychology* (Vol. 7, pp. 499–523). New York: Pergamon Press.

Zeiss, A. M., & Steffen, A. (1996). Treatment issues with elderly clients. *Cognitive and Behavioral Practice, 3*(2), 371–389.

SUGGESTED READINGS

Belsky, J. (1999). *The psychology of aging: Theory, research, and interventions.* Pacific Grove, CA: Brooks/Cole.

Cavanaugh, J. C. (1990). *Adult development and aging.* Belmont, CA: Wadsworth.

Duffy, M., & Iscoe, I. (1990). Crisis theory and management: The case of the older person. *Journal of Mental Health Counseling, 12,* 303–313.

Gallagher-Thompson, D. (1992). The older adult. In A. Freeman & F. Dattilio (Eds.), *Comprehensive casebook of cognitive therapy* (pp. 193–200). New York: Plenum.

Kemp, B., Brummel-Smith, K., & Randell, J. W. (1990). *Geriatric rehabilitation.* Austin, TX: Pro-Ed.

Thompson, L., Gallagher, D., & Breckenridge, J. (1987). Comparative effectiveness of psychotherapies for depressed elders. *Journal of Consulting and Clinical Psychology, 55,* 385–390.

U.S. Centers for Disease Control and Prevention. (1996). Suicide among older persons—United States, 1980–1992. *Journal of the American Medical Association, 275*(7), 509.

II

SPECIAL TOPICS

9

Traumatic Brain Injury

Mary R. Hibbard
Wayne A. Gordon
Lynne M. Kothera

Individuals often present to mental health professionals in psychological crisis following a significant traumatic event. The origin of these traumatic events can vary—for example, a motor vehicle accident (MVA), pedestrian accident, sports-related accident, whiplash injury, serious fall or an act of violence (e.g., abuse, assault, etc.)—but many individuals will report a combination of anxiety and stress-related symptoms (Green, McFarlane, Hunter, & Griggs, 1993; Koren, Arnon, & Klein, 1999; Mayou, Bryant, & Duthie, 1993). The events surrounding the trauma will, by their nature, place the individual at increased risk of having experienced a simultaneous, and potentially undiagnosed, traumatic brain injury (TBI). The physical, cognitive, and affective changes following TBI will complicate the clinical presentation of anxiety symptoms, and necessitate shifts in traditional cognitive-behavioral approaches to assessment and treatment. An understanding of TBI is essential for clinicians to effectively diagnose and treat individuals with dual diagnoses. This chapter provides (1) an overview of the prevalence, etiology, and functional changes following TBI; (2) approaches to screening for a TBI; (3) the psychiatric disorders observed following TBI; and (4) suggested modifications of cognitive-behavioral approaches to assessment and treatment of individuals with dual diagnoses of an anxiety disorder and a TBI. Case vignettes will highlight suggested modifications in assessment and treatment approaches.

TRAUMATIC BRAIN INJURY—THE SILENT EPIDEMIC

Traumatic brain injury has been called the "silent epidemic" (Marino, 1999). A review of the most recent statistics presented by the Centers for Disease Control and Prevention (CDC) validates this label. According to CDC statistics, an estimated 5.3 million Americans, or slightly greater than 2% of the population of the United States, currently live with disabilities resulting from a TBI (Marino, 1999). Each year, approximately 1 million people are treated and released from hospital emergency rooms: 230,000 of these individuals are hospitalized and survive, 80,000 will experience the onset of acquired disabilities resulting from brain injury, and 50,000 will die from brain injury (Marino, 1999). To gain perspective on the impact of TBI in America, one needs only to compare the prevalence of TBI with other medical conditions: AIDS: 350,000 people living in the United States today; breast cancer: 182,000 women and 1,000 men diagnosed each year; and 7,800 Americans will sustain spinal cord injuries every year (Marino, 1999). TBI is more frequently diagnosed in men, with peak ages of occurrence noted in adolescence and young adulthood and in persons over the age of 75. The leading causes of TBI are motor vehicle accidents, violence, and falls (Centers for Disease Control and Prevention, 1997; U.S. Department of Transportation, 1995).

UNDERSTANDING A TRAUMATIC BRAIN INJURY

Traumatic brain injury refers to the effects of a significant blow to the head that result in either a loss of consciousness or a period during which mental status is altered and the person feels "dazed and confused" following this event. Many individuals subsequently experience changes in physical functioning, thinking, mood, and behavior. TBI exists along a continuum of severity. The severity of TBI is typically estimated by the duration of loss of consciousness (LOC), or the duration of altered mental status following a blow to the head. Severity of brain injury can also be inferred from the depth and/or length of coma that follows a blow to the head. Approximately 15% of individuals who are diagnosed with TBI will have experienced a *moderate to severe injury*. The vast majority of these individuals are hospitalized with many of these individuals experiencing coma of varying durations following TBI. Typically, such individuals receive intensive medical and rehabilitation services to address their residual cognitive, physical and emotional sequelae, and thus, are "known" to the medical system.

The remaining 85% of individuals who experience a TBI will have a *mild injury*. A mild injury is defined by a loss of consciousness of less than 20 minutes and/or an altered mental status (i.e., feeling dazed, confused, or disoriented) following a blow to the head (Kay et al., 1993; Mitil et al., 1993). Many individuals with a mild TBI present to local emergency rooms or local physicians' offices for evaluation, are diagnosed with a "concussion" and told that they will be "fine" in a couple of days. An even larger number of individuals with mild TBI fail to seek medical attention and therefore remain undiagnosed (Bernstein, 1999). Although the negative consequences of a mild brain injury tend to dissipate over time, approximately 15% of such individuals will continue to experience residual cognitive, physical, and emotional changes

(Brown, 1998). Without proper identification of the underlying brain injury pathology, these individuals begin to develop secondary affective reactions due to their ongoing difficulties with cognitive functioning. It is then of little surprise that these individuals with potentially undiagnosed TBI present to the mental health professional with predominant anxiety symptoms post trauma (Green et al., 1993; Koren, Arnon, & Klein, 1999; Mayou, Bryant, & Duthie, 1993). According to the literature, the most prevalent anxiety disorder following an MVA is posttraumatic stress disorder (PTSD; Blanchard et al., 1995; Green et al., 1993; Koren, Arnon, & Klein, 1999; Mayou, Bryant, & Duthie, 1993). Although the potential of a prior TBI was not directly examined in these later studies, an LOC at the time of the MVA was significantly related to the later development of PTSD (Blanchard et al., 1995). Given that anxiety disorders, in general, and PTSD in particular, are common diagnoses following a known TBI (Hibbard, Uysal, Kepler, Bogdany, & Silver, 1998; Rattock, 1996; Ohry, Rattokm, & Solomon, 1996; Silver, Rattok, & Anderson, 1997), the presence of an undiagnosed TBI in at least a proportion of individuals presenting to mental health settings following an MVA appears to be likely.

THE ETIOLOGY OF TRAUMATIC BRAIN INJURY

When an individual experiences a TBI, there is a traumatic blow to the head or rapid movement of the head resulting in damage and destruction of brain tissue. Two types of injuries to the head resulting in brain injuries are commonly seen: an open head injury and a closed head injury (Bernstein, 1999). In *open head injury*, the individual experiences a blow to the head in which the skull is penetrated, for instance, by a bullet or a falling or flying object. Damage following an open head injury tends to be localized with subsequent impairment limited to the areas of the brain damaged by the path of the object entering the head and the specific location within the brain at point of impact (Brown, 1998). The most common etiologies of an open head injury are gunshot wounds and falling objects (Centers for Disease Control and Prevention, 1997).

In *closed head injury*, damage to the brain occurs by inertial forces created within the brain (Bernstein, 1999). A closed head injury can result from any event in which the brain is set in rapid motion within the skull and then comes to an abrupt stop, for instance, during a car crash. In these types of injuries, inertia throws the head forward and creates equal momentum in the opposite direction. The extent of damage is usually related to the initial severity or force of the blow and the part of the head that has been hit. For example, the unbelted passenger's head that is slammed into a car windshield during a high speed impact will probably experience more severe brain injury than a seatbelted passenger's head who is involved in a similar MVA during a lower speed impact. In closed head injuries, the brain is also injured by the rotational movement of the brain against the spinal cord and within the skull (Cecil et al., 1998). Thus, the head does not have to actually hit a surface to incur a closed brain injury. For example, in a whiplash injury, the head is "whipped" forward and back and from side to side causing the brain to collide at high velocity with the rough inner surfaces of the skull. These rapid movements cause the brain to move in two or more different directions at once, resulting in stretching and tearing of nerve cells throughout the brain. The most common etiologies of closed head injury are MVAs, pedestrian accidents, sports accidents, falls, and violence (e.g., shaken baby syndrome, abuse, assault, etc.; Centers for Disease Control and Prevention, 1997).

TYPICAL SEQUELAE OF TRAUMATIC BRAIN INJURY

The impact of brain injury on an individual's functioning will depend on many factors: the severity of the initial injury, the areas of the brain that have been damaged, the rate and completeness of physiological recovery, the nature and extent of deficits following brain injury, the individual's awareness of these changes, and the unique meaning these changes have to an individual. Typically, functional changes are grouped into three major domains: physical, cognitive, and affective or behavioral changes. Most individuals experience symptoms across the three domains, however, the relative severity of symptoms and the degree of interference with everyday life will vary from person to person.

The most common *physical changes* reported by an individual after brain injury include: extensive fatigue, clumsiness, decreased or altered sensory functioning (i.e., changes in hearing, vision, smell, and touch), difficulties with sleep, body temperature changes, seizures, change in appetite and weight (Brown, 1998). The *cognitive changes* will significantly interfere with everyday functioning and successful resumption of many former life roles. These symptoms include impaired attention and concentration, reduced processing speed, word-finding difficulties, altered academic abilities (i.e., errors in simple math computation, spelling, reading and comprehension), decreased memory and learning abilities, and impaired executive functioning (i.e., reduced ability to plan, sequence, prioritize, think flexibly, abstract, or problem solve; Brown, 1998). *Affective changes* following TBI include changes in mood and alterations in behavioral control and interpersonal relationships (Brown, 1998). Mood changes typically reflect symptoms of depression, mood lability, and anxiety. Behavioral changes include an inability to manage the unexpected and a reduced ability to control anger. Impaired interpersonal communication (e.g., an inability to follow conversations, being rude, interrupting people, talking too fast or too slowly), although more subtle, may seriously impact the person's ability to develop and maintain meaningful relationships.

SCREENING FOR A PRIOR TRAUMATIC BRAIN INJURY

When an individual presents to the mental health professional with an anxiety disorder secondary to a traumatic event, screening for a prior TBI should be a routine part of the intake interview. The purpose of this screening is to rule out a possible, but heretofore unidentified, TBI.

If upon questioning, an individual reports that the traumatic event involved a blow to the head accompanied by either a period of loss of consciousness or an altered mental state, the clinician is encouraged to probe for potential changes in functioning that the individual has experienced since the traumatic event. These functional changes include the physical, cognitive, and affective symptoms described earlier. When changes are reported, the probability of a previously undiagnosed TBI at the time of the trauma is significantly increased.

Joint discussion of this probable secondary diagnosis is an important therapeutic intervention. In our clinical experiences, an individual whose TBI remains undiagnosed is often quite aware of his/her affective distress (and hence is seeking psychological help), however, the individual remains perplexed and frightened by the seemingly random and inexplicable changes in his/her physical, cognitive, and affective functioning since the traumatic event. The process of relating these functional changes to a possible undiagnosed TBI is often comforting to the individual who, until then, felt he/she was truly "going crazy." A referral for neuropsychological evaluation should be discussed with the individual at this juncture. A neuropsychological evaluation will confirm (or possibly rule out) the diagnosis of TBI and will provide a specific profile of the individual's cognitive strengths and weaknesses, which can then be integrated in effective treatment planning for the individual.

PSYCHIATRIC DISORDERS FOLLOWING TRAUMATIC BRAIN INJURY

In addition to known physical, cognitive, and behavioral changes that occur following TBI, the majority of individuals with TBI are diagnosed with one or more newly acquired DSM-IV Axis I diagnoses (American Psychiatric Association, 1994; Hibbard et al., 1998). The presence of a psychiatric disorder poses additional challenges for an individual with TBI as he/she attempts to reintegrate into the community and resume former life roles. During the 1980s, psychopathology following TBI was clinically described by family members and care providers. Early studies produced divergent results with depressive symptoms found in anywhere from 6% to 77% of individuals following TBI (Brooks, Campsie, Symington, Beattie, & McKinley, 1986; Kinsella, Moran, Ford, & Ponsford, 1998; Rutherford, Merritt, & McDonald, 1979; Van

Zomeren, & Vandenberg, 1985); anxiety symptoms were noted in 18% to 60% of individuals following TBI (Brooks et al., 1986; Dikman, McLean, & Temkin, 1989; Tyerman, & Humphrey, 1984). In the 1990s, research efforts shifted assessment to the use of DSM criteria (American Psychiatric Association, 1994) to determine psychiatric disorders post-TBI. The most prevalent Axis I disorder following TBI was major depression, with the frequency of this disorder increasing over time post trauma. Major depression was noted in 26% of individuals at 1 year (Jorge, Robinson, Starkstein, & Arndt, 1994), 50% to 77% at 3 to 5 years (Fann, Katon, Uomoto, & Essleman, 1995; Van Reekum, Bolango, Finlayson, Garner, & Links, 1996; Varney, Martz, & Roberts, 1987), and 61% at 8 years (Hibbard et al., 1998) following TBI. Robust rates of resolution have been reported for this affective disorder (Fann et al., 1995; Hibbard et al., 1998; Van Reekum, Bolango, Finlayson, Garner, & Links, 1996) suggesting a time-limited nature to the depressive episodes and the probable efficacy of psychotherapy and medication for this disorder.

Anxiety disorders following TBI have received less systematic attention. Despite the limited research available, anxiety disorders appear to be common reactions following TBI. Generalized anxiety disorder (GAD) has been frequently documented after TBI—that is, 11% of individuals at 1 year post-TBI (Jorge et al., 1994), in slightly over 20% of individuals at 3 and 5 years post-TBI (Fann et al., 1995; Van Reekum et al., 1996), and in 9% of individuals at 8 years post-TBI (Hibbard et al., 1998). Panic disorder (PD), appears to increase over time; PD was found in 4% to 6% of individuals at 3 and 5 years post-TBI (Fann et al., 1995; Van Reekum et al., 1996), and 14% at 8 years post-TBI (Hibbard et al., 1998). Obsessive–compulsive disorder (15%) and phobia (10%) have also been reported (Hibbard et al., 1998). Of interest to this chapter, PTSD following TBI has received considerable research attention. The specific issue debated in the literature is whether an individual with no recall of a traumatic event (due to LOC) can meet full criteria for a PTSD (Bontke, 1996). Despite this controversy, there is general agreement that individuals with mild TBI do experience PTSD, with frequency rates as high as 20% to 30% post TBI (Hibbard et al., 1998; Ohry, Rattokm, & Solomon, 1996; Silver, Rattok, & Anderson, 1997). When anxiety disorders develop post-TBI, they are more likely to coexist with other Axis I disorders (Hibbard et al., 1998; Silver, Rattok, & Anderson, 1997) and appear to be more chronic in nature.

MODIFICATIONS OF COGNITIVE-BEHAVIORAL ASSESSMENT FOR INDIVIDUALS WITH TRAUMATIC BRAIN INJURY AND ANXIETY DISORDERS

Individuals with potentially undiagnosed TBI are likely to present to mental health settings with anxiety symptoms. Additional diagnostic considerations are necessary when assessing such individuals. A multimethod approach is suggested, which includes obtaining pertinent information from a variety of sources about the TBI, the events surrounding the trauma and functional changes since the TBI (Hibbard, Grober, Stein, & Gordon, 1992; Hibbard, Gordon, Stein, Grober, & Sliwinski, 1993; Lyons, Gerardi, Wolfe, & Keane, 1989). Suggested areas of investigation include:

1. *A detailed history of events surrounding the traumatic episode.* Due to a potential loss of consciousness or alteration in memory surrounding the trauma, information from multiple sources may be necessary to round out a detailed history of the actual event. Direct questioning of the individual, his/her family and a review of available medical documentation should be utilized to maximize the clinical picture. Specific issues to explore include the individual's last memories before the traumatic event, the earliest memories following the event, a description of events that occurred after the trauma, and feeling/reactions of the individual during the traumatic event itself. This information is important for later planning of cognitive and behavioral interventions.

2. *An evaluation of TBI-related changes.* It is important to identify the nature and relative severity of physical, cognitive, and behavioral challenges experienced by the individual secondary to the TBI. These self-reports should be corroborated by other family members' impressions as well as a neuropsychological evaluation whenever possible. Test results should be incorporated into treatment planning.

3. *Pretrauma psychosocial factors.* Essential areas to be explored include prior personality traits, previous stressful events and subsequent coping abilities, prior sexual or physical abuse, and prior substance/drug usage.

4. *A structured clinical interview to determine DSM-IV diagnoses.* The cornerstone of the assessment remains the structured clinical interview to determine if the individual meets criteria for a DSM-IV Axis I diagnosis (American Psychiatric Association, 1994). Individuals with TBI are more likely to exhibit comorbid Axis I disorders, such as a major depression and an anxiety disorder (Hibbard et al., 1998). As a result, the clinician should screen for these coexisting psychiatric difficulties as well.

The clinician should also be aware of the potential overlap of symptoms that can occur in individuals who present with TBI and comorbid Axis I psychopathology. More specifically, anxiety disorders, major depression, and TBI can *all* result in symptoms of fatigue, sleep difficulties, problems with concentration, sensitivity to noise, and irritability. However, clear differences do exist in symptoms among the various diagnoses. For example, TBI does not result in a reexperiencing phenomenon (e.g., flashbacks, nightmares), numbing of general responsiveness or hyperarousal seen in individuals with PTSD (Silver, Rattok, & Anderson, 1997). Neither does TBI result in specific avoidance behaviors that are often core to diagnoses such as PTSD and phobia. Conversely, anxiety disorders and major depression do not typically result in severe impairments in memory, attention, information processing speed, executive functioning, and/or affective control; these symptoms are commonly observed following TBI. Hence, the clinician needs to assess the full range of affective, cognitive, and behavioral symptoms when attempting to diagnose coexisting TBI and other comorbid Axis I psychopathology.

COGNITIVE-BEHAVIORAL TREATMENT OF ANXIETY DISORDERS IN INDIVIDUALS WITH TRAUMATIC BRAIN INJURY

Cognitive-behavioral therapy has been suggested as an effective approach to treatment of major depression in individuals with brain injury (Hibbard et al., 1992). Fourteen principles of cognitive-behavioral therapy are suggested (see Table 9.1) and are derived from earlier work by the present authors in treating individuals with depression following stroke (Hibbard et al., 1992). Because many individuals with TBI and anxiety disorders also present with comorbid major depression (Hibbard et al., 1998), these principles are especially relevant.

TABLE 9.1. Principles of Cognitive-Behavioral Therapy in the Treatment of Individuals with Brain Injury

1. Cognitive functioning moderates the treatment strategies used.
2. Cognitive remediation enhances the individual's ability to profit from therapy.
3. New learning and generalization are difficult for individuals with brain injury.
4. An individual's awareness of affective symptomatology moderates therapeutic strategy.
5. Mourning is an important component of treatment.
6. Premorbid lifestyle and interests provide a context for understanding current behavior.
7. Understanding the discrepancy between actual and perceived losses is essential to treatment.
8. Reinforcing even small therapeutic gains improves mood.
9. Emphasis on the collaborative nature of the therapeutic relationship facilitates a working alliance.
10. To ensure continuity of treatment, session flexibility is essential.
11. Fluctuations in medical status impact the course of treatment.
12. The distortions of family members must be addressed in therapy.
13. Family members' mourning must be addressed in therapy.
14. Family members are important therapeutic helpers.

Note. Adapted from Hibbard, Grober, Stein, & Gordon (1992), p. 306. Copyright 1992 by Plenum Publishing Corp. Adapted by permission.

Traditional approaches to treatment of anxiety disorders include the use of behavioral exposure techniques, anxiety management techniques, and anti-anxiety medications (Rothbaum, & Foa, 1992). When addressing anxiety disorders in individuals with TBI, additional treatment considerations must include the extent with which compensatory strategies need to be utilized within treatment (Hibbard, Grober, et al., 1992; Hibbard, Gordon, et al., 1993). In general, the more severe the cognitive impairments, the greater the emphasis on the use of compensatory strategies within treatment. The severity of coexisting cognitive deficits will also impact the selection of behavioral techniques and anxiety management tools utilized.

Two behavioral procedures have been traditionally used in the treatment of anxiety disorders: exposure-based procedures and anxiety management techniques (Rothbaum & Foa, 1992). Both approaches are highlighted below.

Exposure Techniques

Exposure techniques are used when an anxiety disorder involves excessive avoidance; treatment is intended to activate and modify the fear structure (Rothbaum & Foa, 1992). Exposure-based procedures share a common approach in that all strategies utilize confrontation of the feared situations. These techniques can be classified along three dimensions: the medium of exposure (imagined or *in vivo*), the length of exposure (short vs. long) and the level of arousal during exposure (low vs. high). At one end of the continuum is systematic desensitization (Wolpe, 1958), during which an exposure is imagined, brief, and minimally arousing. At the other end of the continuum is *in vivo* flooding (Marks, 1987), during which an exposure is prolonged and designed to elicit high levels of anxiety. In individuals with TBI, exposure techniques must be considered within the context of the individual's recall of the precipitant event and the cognitive limitations of the individual secondary to TBI. For example, in an individual with severe cognitive impairments and no recall of the events surrounding the trauma, systematic desensitization techniques would not be utilized. The individual's avoidant behaviors would be better addressed using *in vivo* flooding combined with both antianxiety medications and anxiety management techniques.

Anxiety Management Techniques

Anxiety management techniques focus on anxiety reduction by provision of skills to control fears in an individual (Rothbaum & Foa, 1992). Such techniques include relaxation training (Bernstein & Borkovec, 1973; Jacobsen, 1938), stress inoculation training (Meichenbaum, 1974), cognitive restructuring (Beck, 1972; Ellis, 1977), guided self-dialogue (Meichenbaum, 1974), breathing retraining (Clark, Salkovskis, & Chaukley, 1985; Wolpe, 1985), and distraction techniques (Wolpe, 1973). Perhaps the most widely used technique is deep muscle relaxation training as described by Wolpe (1985). Given the limited attention span and memory difficulties of many individuals with TBI (particularly individuals with more severe TBI), relaxation training and stress inoculation training may offer the least effective approaches to anxiety reduction. Cognitive restructuring, guided self-dialogue, and breathing relaxation techniques appear to be the most effective tools for symptom control. Each of these latter techniques are described below.

Cognitive Restructuring

Cognitive restructuring techniques (Beck, Rush, Shaw, & Emery, 1979) are utilized when the goal of treatment is to challenge and restructure an individual's automatic thoughts into more rational self-statements. In this paradigm, a therapist provides an A-B-C (where A = antecedent, B = belief, C = consequence) model to address automatic thoughts, has the individual focus on these automatic subjective thoughts, helps the individual assess the rationality of the beliefs and consequently assists the individual to challenge and replace these beliefs with more rational self-statements. Once learned in a neutral setting, these techniques are then applied to avoidant experiences.

Guided Self–Dialogue Techniques

Guided self-dialogue techniques (Meichenbaum, 1974) are utilized when the goal of treatment is to focus on internal self-statements (i.e., what an individual is saying to oneself), and creation of dialogue substitution. In this approach, the therapist teaches the individual to focus on internal dialogues in order to identify irrational, faulty, or negative statements. More rational and facilitative self-statements are then substituted. Unique statements to use in confrontation and management of anxiety, for coping with feelings of being overwhelmed, and for reinforcement are generated and then applied to the specific avoidant problem. Self-statements generated within session are written on cue cards and practiced within session and outside session. Use of individualized cue cards is particularly helpful for individuals who present with cognitive difficulties following TBI.

Breathing Relaxation

Breathing relaxation technique (Clark, Salkovskis, & Chaukley, 1985) are utilized as a behavioral countercondition to anxiety. In this approach, the individual is taught to practice taking a normal breath, exhaling slowly while saying the word CALM, pausing briefly between breaths and performing a distraction counting task (i.e., counting to four slowly), before taking the next breath. The entire sequence is practiced in session, with the individual asked to practice the exercise between sessions. Breathing techniques can then be applied later in treatment when imaginary or *in vivo* exposure techniques are implemented.

These techniques are extremely useful for individuals with TBI but these individuals typically require written cue cards to help remember and/or sequence this multistep task.

CASE STUDIES

Two vignettes are presented to illustrate the challenges of assessing and treating anxiety disorders in individuals with coexisting TBI. Modifications in traditional cognitive-behavioral approaches based on the nature and severity of an individual's cognitive functioning secondary to a TBI will be highlighted. In Vignette 1 (Ms. D.), an individual's TBI was undiagnosed at the time of the initial referral for treatment for severe anxiety symptoms. Identifying the TBI required shifts in both assessment and cognitive-behavioral treatment approaches. In Vignette 2 (Mr. S.), an anxiety disorder was diagnosed during the course of treatment for his major depression. In this vignette, the individual's severe memory impairments required significant modification of traditional cognitive-behavioral approaches to address his anxiety disorder.

Vignette 1

Client's name:	Ms. D.
Reason for referral:	Severe anxiety secondary to MVA
Time posttrauma:	4 months

Description of Traumatic Event

During a winter ski vacation, Ms. D. was involved in an MVA. She was a front seat passenger in a van that skidded on a mountain road, turned over, and fell into a ditch overhanging the mountain edge. She was brought by ambulance to a local hospital where she was diagnosed with a concussion and soft tissue injuries of her neck secondary to whiplash. Neuroradiological evaluations (CT scans, MRI) were negative. On subsequent follow-up by her local physicians, a variety of postaccident physical complaints were identified: impairments in her walking, severe photophobia (i.e., sensitivity to light), frontal headaches, occipital head pain, numbness and tingling in her left hand and foot, a retinal hemorrhage and a temporomandibular joint (TMJ) disorder.

Prior Psychosocial History

Ms. D. was a 49-year-old married female who was involved in a longstanding and stable marriage. She had four grown children with two still living at home. Ms. D. was a college graduate who worked as the general office manager for her husband in his large real estate office. In that capacity, she oversaw a staff of five persons. She had been unable to return to work since her MVA. Her medical history was negative for drug or alcohol abuse and/or prior emotional difficulties.

Recall of Events Surrounding the Trauma

Since Ms. D. was involved in an MVA in which she was diagnosed with a concussion, the possibility that Ms. D. was experiencing residual functional changes of a TBI as well as anxiety symptoms was explored in further detail. On detailed questioning about events related to her MVA, Ms. D. related the following story:

> "I remembered getting into a van at the top of a mountain, and falling asleep as the van slowly went down a rather sharp and winding mountain road. The next thing I remember is being jolted awake by the jerky movements of the van as it careened down a twisty part of the road. The van flipped over and then headed over the side of the mountain. I don't know what happened next, but the next thing I remember is that the van had come to a standstill and was now hovering off the top of a cliff with the front half of the van dangling freely above a deep ravine. I remember feeling totally overwhelmed with the fear that if I moved, the van would topple off the cliff and kill us all."

Upon further questioning, Ms. D. reported that she had hit her head during the MVA but was unsure if she experienced a loss of consciousness. She did remember that she felt "dazed and confused," had terrible headaches and severe neck pains for several days following the MVA.

Brain Injury Symptoms

Given her positive history of a blow to the head, combined with an altered mental state post event, questions about potential TBI related changes were explored. The patient reported a variety of physical complaints: headaches, dizziness and vertigo, balance and coordination problems, a weight gain of 25 pounds since the MVA, neck and TMJ pain, sensitivity to light, numbness and tingling in her left extremities, fatigue, and sleep disturbances. Her cognitive complaints included significant problems with concentration, memory, thinking, and decision making. She spontaneously reported that she often would go through the day "unable to accomplish anything because [she was] totally unable to structure [herself]." Her affective changes were her largest complaints with frequent symptoms of anxiety and depression reported.

The patient was referred for a neuropsychological evaluation in order to determine her relative cognitive strengths and weaknesses. Test findings suggested that Ms. D. was functioning in the high-average range of intelligence. Testing also validated her self-reports of significant deficits in the domains of visual and verbal memory, motor planning, attention, and organization secondary to a mild TBI.

DSM-IV Diagnoses

On the basis of a structured clinical interview for DSM-IV diagnoses (American Psychiatric Association, 1994), the patient met criteria for major depression. She endorsed severe depressive symptomatology on the Beck Depression Inventory (BDI = 36; Beck, 1987). The patient was also diagnosed with PTSD. Her PTSD symptoms included intrusive symptomatology, that is, a recurrent nightmare about falling off a bridge while she was driving a car. Her nightmares were accompanied by panic (i.e., palpitations) and autonomic (i.e., profuse sweating) responses. The frequency of her nightmares had gradually increased with a growing dread of going to bed at night for fear of having the nightmare. Her avoidance symptoms included efforts to avoid any activity that involved being in a car—for instance, she would take subways or walk whenever possible—or to participate in a car trip where travel over a bridge was required to reach a destination. In addition, she began to notice her conscious avoidance of any physical structure that had height—a small walk bridge in a park, an escalator in a store, a ramp, etc. Her hyperarousal symptoms included severe sleep difficulties, problems with concentration, marked irritability, and an exaggerated startle response. Her symptoms worsened rather than improved over the preceeding 2 months, resulting in her self-referral for medication and psychological treatment. The patient had seen her local physician who had prescribed Prozac for her mood and trazodone for her sleep disturbance 2 weeks prior to her initial intake interview with the current therapist.

Initial diagnoses

Axis I	Major depression, PTSD
Axis III	Mild TBI
GAF	60

Formulation of Cognitive-Behavioral Treatment Plan

Ms. D. presented with PTSD symptoms of avoidant behaviors, nightmares, and hypervigilance related to her MVA. Ms. D. also presented with major depression and mild to moderate cognitive impairments in memory, attention, and executive functioning secondary to her TBI. Given Ms. D.'s combined affective and cognitive profile, a multimodal approach to treatment was formulated (Hibbard, Grober, et al., 1992; Hibbard, Gordon, et al., 1993), which included an initial combination of pharmacological treatment, anxiety management techniques, compensatory strategies for her cognitive challenges, with the later use of exposure techniques to address her avoidant behaviors.

Initial Phase of Treatment

Ms. D.'s ongoing level of depression and her response to prescribed medications for mood and sleep were monitored during weekly cognitive-behavioral psychotherapy sessions. Treatment of her PTSD focused on detailed education about PTSD and the relationship of her PTSD to her traumatic MVA. The initial anxiety management technique introduced in session was breathing relaxation exercises. Ms. D. had minimal trouble learning this technique; however, cue cards were written and used in both her subsequent sessions and when she was practicing this technique as a homework assignment. Cognitive restructuring and guided self-dialogue were next introduced.

Sessions focused on helping Ms. D. understand the A-B-C paradigm and learn basic techniques to reality test and reformulate her self-statements with neutral and less affect-laden responses to her everyday life. For example, Ms. D. presented to treatment with the preconceived and automatic thought that she was unable to do "anything" around the house. Many of her ongoing difficulties in everyday functioning were due to cognitive failures, but her reactions to these failures were extreme and only served to further limit her abilities to organize herself following her TBI. Early sessions were spent in helping Ms. D. cognitively organize her day-to-day activities. A daily planner was introduced into session as a compensatory tool for her coexisting executive functioning difficulties. Sessions were spent in preplanning activities she wanted to accomplish daily and having her write them in her planner. She was then taught how to use her planner as an ongoing organizer of her daily activities.

Once the patient was able to use her planner more effectively at home, sessions shifted to identifying her automatic thoughts related to her reduced level of current functioning. These critical self-statements were reanalyzed, less critical counter statements were created, and alternative approaches to minimize her cognitive confusion during such situations were developed. All facilitative statements were written on cue cards and organized by areas of potential problems encountered in her home (e.g., problems in cooking, problems when shopping, difficulties on the phone, etc). To enhance her recall and use of these facilitative cue cards, she was asked to review the cards each morning, and prior to any activity that had previously challenged her. As a source of potential reinforcement, she was also asked to record any and all tasks she accomplished each day, regardless of the relative merit of the accomplishment.

Middle Phase of Treatment

This phase of intervention focused on Ms. D.'s automatic thoughts as related to avoidant situations and the creation of self-statements to deal with her fears. Personal statements were created in session for use during attempts to engage in previously avoided activity and when she experienced increased anxiety while engaging in the activity. All self-statements were written on cue cards and placed in her daily planner. A hierarchy of avoidant activities was generated, with the least anxiety-producing events becoming the primary target for between session assignments. For Ms. D., these activities included walking over slightly elevated ramps and walk bridges in her local community park. Relaxation and use of previously generated self-statements were combined with systematic desensitization techniques to address Ms. D.'s imagined reactions to avoidant situations within session.

Final Phase of Treatment

Engaging in previously avoided activities in the community via *in vivo* assignments was the focus of the final phase of treatment. Using the hierarchy of avoidant activities, Ms. D.'s *in vivo* assignment was to have her initially walk up and over an elevated ramp followed by a slightly higher walk bridge in her local community park on a daily basis. Ms. D. was asked to review the anxiety management techniques practiced in session before leaving her house, and then utilize her cue cards as reinforcement during her actual attempts at an activity. These repeated assignments exposed Ms. D. to previously avoided activities in order to flood her, thereby decreasing her overall fear of the activity. Ms. D.'s successes in engaging in these activities between sessions were reviewed during each subsequent session with the effectiveness of her anxiety management tools examined. Once a "comfort" zone for engaging in a select activity was achieved, the next avoidant activity in her hierarchy was addressed. Over several months, Ms. D. was able to engage in most activities she had been avoiding since her MVA. Her most positive outcomes were her ability to bike over a bridge at the end of a large reservoir (a favorite weekend biking route for Ms. D. and her husband) and sit in her husband's car as he drove out of the city over a large connecting bridge. She continued to apply anxiety management techniques when engaging in formerly avoided events. She ultimately became able to rely on her own self-generated statements rather than reading her cue cards to successfully engage in these activities.

Vignette 2

Client's name:	Mr. S.
Reason for referral:	Severe depressive symptoms secondary to MVA
Time posttrauma:	6 months

Description of Traumatic Event

Mr. S. was involved in an occupational accident in which he fell 30 feet from a bucket of a tree-cutting truck when it accidentally overturned. During the accident, Mr. S. was ejected from the bucket and fell onto a cement sidewalk. Because Mr. S. was rendered unconscious at the time of the accident, he was unable to provide an adequate history. As a result, his family was interviewed and available medical records were reviewed. Mr. S. was taken to a local hospital by ambulance and admitted to the intensive care unit, where he remained in a coma for approximately 3 hours. He remained hospitalized for a period of 1 month, followed by an additional month of rehabilitation. According to Mr. S.'s medical records, he experienced a closed head injury, a basilar skull fracture, four fractured spinal vertebrae, a fractured scapula, and nerve damage to his left hand secondary to his fall. Neuroradiological evaluations (CT scan findings) documented bilateral frontal lobe contusions, a left subarachnoid hemorrhage, and the basilar skull fracture. Mr. S. evolved from coma in a state of extreme agitation, which required medication. At 6 months post-TBI, the patient presented with numerous complaints including decreased feeling and movement of his left hand, severe frontal and occipital headaches, visual disturbances, depression, irritability, and severe memory loss.

Prior Psychosocial History

Mr. S. was a 35-year-old male who was living with a significant other for the past 6 years. He had three small children by this relationship. Mr. S. completed 11th grade and immigrated to the United States from the Caribbean after being recruited by a major league baseball team. He left baseball after 3 years due to shoulder injuries sustained during play. He worked as a tree cutter for the past 7 years, rising to the rank of foreman at the time of his injury. He had been unable to return to work since his TBI. His medical history was negative except for moderate social use of alcohol on weekends before his accident.

Recall of Events Surrounding the Accident

Because Mr. S. had a clearly documented, severe TBI, attempts to delineate his recall of events were pursued. Mr. S. had no recall of events occurring 3 weeks prior to his work-related accident. Upon interview, the first thing Mr. S. remembered was being in his apartment after discharge from the rehabilitation facility 1 month before the interview. Hence, a period of probable amnesia (lack of continuous memory) for approximately 3 months was noted, a pattern not atypical of individuals who sustain more severe brain injuries. As a result of his severe memory deficits, Mr. S. would ask repeatedly for information about his accident and an explanation for his current functional difficulties.

Brain Injury Symptoms

Mr. S. had a documented severe TBI, so he and his mate were interviewed in order to determine Mr. S.'s current functional difficulties. On self-report, the patient admitted to numerous and severe physical complaints: headaches, dizziness, difficulty lifting heavy objects, a loss of smell, balance and coordination problems, moving slowly, poor sleep, and blurred vision. His cognitive complaints focused primarily on his decreased memory. In contrast, his mate reported significantly more cognitive problems in Mr. S.'s attention, memory and learning, thinking, decision making, and executive functioning. Mr. S. endorsed many affective changes since his TBI with symptoms reflective of severe anxiety and depression. His mate agreed with the patient's self-report, but also reported that Mr. S. had poor control of his behavior and emotions (e.g., throwing things, cursing at others, difficulty coping with change). A neuropsychological evaluation had been completed 1 month prior to his initial intake interview. Testing suggested Mr. S. was functioning in the low-average range of intellectual functioning. Testing further validated the patient's self-reports by documenting significant deficits across all cognitive domains assessed: attention, memory, information processing speed, executive functioning, and language abilities.

DSM–IV Diagnoses

Using a structured clinical interview for DSM-IV diagnoses (American Psychiatric Association, 1994), the patient initially met criteria for a major depression. He endorsed severe depressive symptomatology on the Beck Depression Inventory (BDI = 45; Beck, 1987).

Initial diagnoses

Axis I	Major depression
Axis III	Severe TBI
GAF	40

Mr. S. was referred to a psychiatrist for medication evaluation and placed on antidepressant for his depression, a mood stabilizer for his affective dyscontrol, and a sleep medication. In addition, the patient was seen for weekly cognitive-behavioral psychotherapy and two sessions per week of cognitive remediation. This combined approach (Hibbard, Grober, et al., 1992; Hibbard, Gordon, et al., 1993), resulted in a modest reduction in the severity of his depression and increased learning of compensatory tools for his severe memory and executive functioning deficits.

During the course of treatment, a second Axis I diagnosis was made based on behavioral information that emerged within the context of treatment. Mr. S. was subsequently diagnosed with a phobia when it was observed that the patient was exhibiting particular avoidant behaviors. For example, Mr. S. would frequently cancel appointments because the "elevator in [his] apartment building was broken." Because he was able to climb stairs without difficulty, his reasons for canceling were challenged. Mr. S. replied that he could not take the stairs to exit his apartment because he was "too nervous." In addition, when Mr. S. came to sessions, he would sit as far from the office window as possible. Due to the severity of his memory deficits, Mr. S. never voiced concerns about his avoidant behaviors or the underlying anxiety related to these activities. Quite by accident, the therapist requested Mr. S. to look out of the window of her office at activities that were occurring on the street below. This request was met with an immediate and excessive anxiety reaction and a strong resistance to look downward. Mr. S. could not explain why this was occurring and lacked the insight to relate his behaviors to the etiology of his TBI–a fall from a height of 30 feet.

Mr. S.'s mate was interviewed about these behaviors and validated his avoidance of looking out of any window, his refusal to ride down on an escalator, and his adamant refusal to use the stairs to exit his fifth-floor apartment. (This latter behavior was particularly troublesome as the elevator was often broken, and thus raised an issue about safety for the family in case of fire.) A further concern–Mr. S.'s reluctance to fly given his difficulty with heights–was particularly relevant to treatment planning because relocation to his native country (via plane) was anticipated following his rehabilitation. Prior to his TBI, the patient had no difficulty descending stairs or with air travel.

Mr. S.'s phobic symptoms had remained "hidden" during the early months of treatment due to the severity of his depression and memory deficits. Furthermore, his self-limited involvement with activities in his community offered the patient minimal opportunities to become aware of the functional limitations of his avoidant behaviors. He had simply restricted his activities to minimize situations in which anxiety reactions would occur. In the brain injury literature, two competing theories are proposed for the later development of avoidant reactions despite the fact that the person may be totally amnesic to the traumatic event. One theory posits that behaviors may be "pseudo-memories" derived by the patient in learning details about the accident subsequent to the event (Bryant, 1996). The alternative hypothesis is that symptoms are reflective of "nonverbal" or "nondeclarative memory" traces of the events surrounding the trauma, which in turn become the basis for postevent avoidant behaviors (Bryant, 1996; Layton & Wardi-Zonna, 1995). In Mr. S.'s situation, his lack of memory of events surrounding his fall would suggest that his avoidant symptoms were more reflective of the later hypothesis.

Revised diagnoses

Axis I	Major depression
	Phobia
Axis III	Severe TBI
GAF	45

Formulation of Cognitive–Behavioral Treatment Plan

Due to the severity of his memory and other cognitive deficits, a multimodal approach was used to treat Mr. S.'s severe depression and impairments. This approach combined traditional cognitive-behavioral interventions, a heavy emphasis on the use of psychopharmacological interventions, and aggressive cognitive remediation. Treatment of Mr. S.'s avoidant behaviors and anxiety symptoms related to his phobia for heights were introduced later in treatment. Pharmacological interventions, limited exposure treatment, breathing relaxation training, and behavioral management training for his family were utilized to address his phobic responses.

Initial Phase of Treatment

The initial dual emphasis of cognitive remediation was to reorient Mr. S. to the reasons for his current functional limitations and teach Mr. S. to use a daily planner to record pertinent information about his TBI, his cognitive and mood difficulties, his daily activities, and his taking of prescribed medications for his mood. Mr. S.'s ongoing level of depression and his continued compliance with taking his medications for mood, behavioral control, and sleep were monitored during weekly cognitive-behavioral psychotherapy sessions. Mr. S. was taught to use a daily planner to record all his daily activities, and to keep track of whether he was taking his medication. Cognitive-behavioral psychotherapy focused on behavioral strategies to increase his social activities and enhance his self-esteem. Cognitive restructuring was utilized to help Mr. S. limit his critical self-statements about "being totally useless," with all counterresponses written in his daily planner for later recall and practice within session. His daily planner entries were reviewed in sessions to evaluate the extent of his social involvement, medication compliance, and created self-facilitating statements.

Middle Phase of Treatment

This phase of intervention focused on treatment of Mr. S.'s phobia. Initial sessions focused on providing the family with education about a phobia and its relationship to Mr. S.'s accident. Introduction to anxiety management techniques was limited to training of breathing relaxation exercises. Due to the severity of Mr. S.'s memory deficits, each step in the relaxation exercises was written out, placed in Mr. S.'s daily planner, and then reviewed with Mr. S. following each written step during subsequent sessions. Once he was able to independently locate the written instructions in his daily planner and follow the steps required in the breathing relaxation exercise by himself, he was assigned daily practice sessions at home. Compliance with home practice was monitored through review of Mr. S.'s daily planner entries. Due to the severity of the patient's memory impairments, guided self-dialogue was not attempted.

The next phase of treatment focused on creating a hierarchy of avoidant activities with information obtained from both Mr. S. and his mate. For Mr. S., the hierarchy of anxiety producing activities included walking down stairs, riding down escalators, and looking down from places of increasing height (e.g., looking out of windows on higher floors of a building or from balconies). Because his memory impairments precluded Mr. S. from remembering events surrounding his initial accident, systematic desensitization was not attempted. However, *in vivo* exercises were utilized in combination with antianxiety medications and breathing exercises to help Mr. S. engage in previously avoided activities. On consultation with Mr. S's psychiatrist, "as needed" antianxiety medication was prescribed with Mr. S. instructed to take the medication before attempting *in vivo* exposure techniques in session.

Sessions were preplanned in which Mr. S. would practice *in vivo* exposure with his therapist. On such days, Mr. S. wrote in his daily planner to take the antianxiety medication one half hour before coming to session. For each session, relaxation breathing was practiced in the safety of the therapist's office. Mr. S. was then escorted to the targeted avoidant activity. Using the hierarchy of avoidant activities, the initial target for *in vivo* practice was escorting Mr. S. down a short flight of stairs within the same building. Initially, Mr. S. clung to the stairwell wall, walked sideward down the steps in a hesitant fashion, and began to hyperventilate. Distraction techniques (e.g., focusing on a distant point rather than looking down to the bottom of the stairs), breathing exercises, and direct supervision by this therapist enabled Mr. S. to resume a more normalized stair-descending approach. The therapist gradually faded her direct supervision but remained at the top of the stairs for more distant supervision and support. Over time, the number of flights of stairs attempted was increased.

Once Mr. S. became comfortable with descending stairs, assignments were extended to his own apartment house where he was asked to take the antianxiety medication one half hour before practicing descending flights of stairs with his mate. Once comfortable with this routine, he was encouraged to do the activity independently. His weekly progress was monitored by reviewing entries in his daily planner about the number of flights of stairs he had descended each week. Flooding—repeat exposure to these stair descent activities—combined with antianxiety medications and anxiety management strategies decreased his overall fear of this activity. Once a "comfort" zone for this activity was achieved, the next avoidant behavior in his hierarchy was focused on—looking down from heights. *In vivo* practice within session was again utilized for this task. Initially, Mr. S. was escorted to a second-story window and asked to look at distant objects at eye level across the street. He was then asked to slowly drop his line of vision while at the same time practicing relaxation/breathing exercises. This approach was repeated at gradually greater heights (higher stories of the building) and then transferred to practice overlooking edges of balconies. Premedication, relaxation techniques, and direct supervision were combined for all *in vivo* exposure events. Over a relatively short period of time, Mr. S. was able to descend stairs and tolerate a considerable downward gaze from various heights. He continued to show significant anxiety, however, when asked to redirect his gaze directly downward from a considerable height.

Final Phase of Treatment

As discharge from rehabilitation was imminent and plane tickets had already been purchased for relocation to his country of origin, several additional treatment strategies were implemented to maximize Mr. S.'s ability to take a plane trip without an extreme phobic reaction. His psychiatrist was consulted to increase his dose of "as needed" antianxiety medications in anticipation of his upcoming plane flight. Mr. S. and his mate were seen in joint session to discuss behavioral strategies to help Mr. S. control his anxiety during the flight. Breathing exercises were reviewed with his mate taught to coach Mr. S. proactively during the flight. Additional distracter strategies were suggested to minimize Mr. S.'s awareness of being in the plane itself (and therefore flying at a considerable height). These strategies included reserving a plane seat away from the window, seating Mr. S. in the middle of a row, bringing other family members along on the trip, use of portable tape player and headsets to play Mr. S.'s favorite music, and alerting the plane personnel to the specific needs of Mr. S. Additional behavioral management strategies included increased use of medication and the optimal timing of such medication relative to the plane flight itself. In summary, a combination of behavioral management techniques, breathing exercises, and medication allowed Mr. S. to successfully return to his homeland without an exacerbation of his phobic symptoms.

CONCLUSION

In this chapter, a clinical understanding of the TBI, including its prevalence, etiology, and functional changes are addressed. The importance of screening for TBI in individuals presenting with anxiety disorders is stressed. Frequent and coexisting psychopathologies following TBI are highlighted. Suggestions to broaden traditional cognitive-behavioral assessment and shift cognitive-behavioral treatment when treating individuals with combined cognitive and psychiatric challenges are discussed and illustrated via case studies of individuals with varying severities of TBI. It is hoped that this chapter has served to heighten clinical sensitivity to the potential of a comorbid TBI in individuals who present with anxiety disorders post trauma. A broad approach, which incorporates cognitive strategies, is essential if treatment of anxiety disorders in individuals with TBI is to be effective.

ACKNOWLEDGMENTS

Work at the Research and Training Center on the Community Integration for Individuals with Traumatic Brain Injury was supported by Grant No. H133B30038 from the National Institute on Disability and Rehabilitation Research, U.S. Department of Education to the Department of Rehabilitation Medicine, the Mount Sinai School of Medicine, New York, NY. We would like to express our appreciation to Chantal Sanabria for her careful attention to the preparation of this chapter.

REFERENCES

American Psychiatric Association (1994). *Diagnostic and statistical manual of mental disorders* (4th ed.). Washington, DC: Author.

Beck, A. T. (1972). *Depression: Cause and treatment.* Philadelphia: University of Pennsylvania Press.

Beck, A . (1987). *Beck depression inventory: Manual.* San Antonio, TX: Psychological Corp.

Beck, A. T., Rush, A. J., Shaw, B. F., & Emery, G. (1979). *Cognitive therapy of depression.* New York: Guilford Press.

Bernstein, D. A., & Borkovec, T. D. (1973). *Progressive relaxation training.* Springfield, IL: Research Press.

Bernstein, D. M. (1999). Recovery from mild head injury. *Brain Injury, 13*(3), 151–172.

Blanchard, E. B., Hickling, E. J., Taylor, A. E., Loos, W. R., Forneris, C. A., & Jaccard, J. (1995). Who develops PTSD from motor vehicle accidents. *Behaviour Research and Therapy, 34*(1), 1–10.

Bontke, C. F. (1996). Controversies: Do patients with mild brain injuries have posttraumatic stress disorders too? *Journal of Head Trauma Rehabilitation, 11*(1), 95–102

Brooks, N., Campsie, L., Symington, C., Beattie, A., & McKinley, W. (1986). The five year outcome of severe blunt head injury. *Journal of Neurology, Neurosurgery and Pychiatry, 46,* 336–344.

Brown, M. (1998). *TBI 101: Basic facts about injury and life after injury.* Unpublished document, Research and Training Center on Community Integration of Individuals with Traumatic Brain Injury, NIDRR Grant No. H133B30038 to Mount Sinai School of Medicine, New York.

Bryant, R. A. (1996). Posttraumatic stress disorder, flashbacks, and pseudomemories in closed head injury. *Journal of Traumatic Stress, 9,* 621–629.

Cecil, K. M., Hills, E. C., Sandel, E., Smith, D. H., McIntosh, T. K., Mannon, L. J., Sinson, G. P., Bagley, L. J., Grossman, R. I., & Lenkinski, R. E. (1998). Proton magnetic resonance spectroscopy for detection of axonal injured patients. *Journal of Neurosurgery, 88,* 795–801.

Centers for Disease Control and Prevention. (1997). Traumatic brain injury–Colorado, Missouri, Oklahoma, and Utah, 1990–1993. *MMWR, 46*(1), 8–11.

Clark, D. M., Salkovskis, P. M., & Chaukley, A. J. (1985). Respiratory control as a treatment for panic attacks. *Journal of Behavior Therapy and Experimental Pychiatry, 9,* 109–114.

Dikman, S., McLean, A., & Temkin, N. (1989). Neuropsychological and psychosocial consequences of minor head injury. *Journal of Neurology, Neurosurgery and Pychiatry, 49,* 1227–1233.

Ellis, A. (1977). The basic clinical theory and rational-emotive therapy. In A. Ellis & R. Grieger (Eds.), *Handbook of rational-emotive therapy.* New York: Springer.

Fann, J. R. Katon, W. J., Uomoto, J. M., & Essleman, P. C. (1995). Psychiatric disorders and functional disability in outpatients with traumatic brain injuries. *American Journal of Pychiatry, 152*(1), 1493–1499.

Green, M. M., McFarlane, A. C., Hunter, C. E., & Griggs, W. M. (1993). Undiagnosed post-traumatic stress disorder following motor vehicle accidents. *Medical Journal of Australia, 159,* 529–534.

Hibbard, M. R., Gordon, W. G., Stein, P. S., Grober, S., & Sliwinski, M. (1993). A multimodal approach to the diagnosis of post-stroke depression. In W. A. Gordon (Ed.), *Advances in stroke rehabilitation.* Stoneham, MA: Andova Medical.

Hibbard, M. R., Grober, S. E., Stein, P. N., & Gordon, W. G. Poststroke depression (1992). In A. Freeman & F. M. Datillio (Eds.), *Comprehensive casebook of cognitive therapy* (pp. 303–310). New York: Plenum.

Hibbard, M. R., Uysal, S., Kepler, K., Bogdany, J., & Silver, J. (1998). Axis I psychopathology in individuals with traumatic brain injury. *Journal of Head Trauma Rehabilitation, 13*(4), 24–39.

Jacobsen, E. (1938). *Progressive relaxation.* Chicago: University of Chicago Press.

Jorge, R. E., Robinson, R. G., Starkstein, S. E., & Arndt, S. W. (1994). Influences of major depression on one-year outcome. *Journal of Neurosurgery, 81,* 726–733.

Kay, T., Harrington, D. E., Adams, R., Anderson, T., Berrol, S., Cicerone, K., Dahlberg, C., Gerber, D., Goka, R., Harley, P., Hilt, J., Horn, L., Lehmkuhl, D., & Malec, J. (1993). Definition of mild traumatic brain injury. *Journal of Head Trauma Rehabilitation, 8*(3) 86–87.

Kinsella, G., Moran, C., Ford, B., & Ponsford, J. (1988). Emotional disorders and its assessment within severely head injured populations. *Psychological Medicine, 18,* 57–63.

Koren, D., Arnon, I., & Klein, E. (1999). Acute stress response and post traumatic stress disorder in traffic accident victims: A one-year prospective follow-up study. *American Journal of Psychiatry, 156*(3), 367–373.

Layton, B. S., & Wardi-Zonna, K. (1995). Posttraumatic stress disorder with neurogenic amnesia for the traumatic event. *Clinical Neuropsychologist, 9,* 2–10.

Lyons, J. A., Gerardi, R. J., Wolfe, J., & Keane, T. M. (1989). Multiaxial assessment of PTSD: Phenomenological, psychometric and psychophysiological considerations. *Journal of Traumatic Stress, 1,* 373–394.

Marino, M. (1999). CDC report shows prevalence of brain injury. *Brain Injury Association's TBI Challenge, 3*(3), 1.

Marks, I. M. (1987). Flooding and allied treatments. In W. Agras (Ed.), *Behavior modification: Principles and clinical applications.* Boston: Little, Brown.

Mayou, R., Bryant, B., & Duthie, R. (1993). Psychiatric consequences of road traffic accidents. *British Medical Journal, 307,* 646–651.

Meichenbaum, D. (1974). *Cognitive behavior modification.* Morristown, NJ: General Learning Press.

Mitil, R. L., Grossman, J. F., Hiehle, J. F., Hurst, R. W., Kauder, D. R., Gennarelli, T. A., & Alburger, G. W. (1993). Prevalence of MR evidence of diffuse axonal injury in patients with mild traumatic brain injury and normal CT findings. *American Journal of Neuro-radiology, 15,* 1583–1589.

Ohry, A., Rattokm J., & Solomon, Z. (1996). Posttraumatic stress disorder in brain injury patients. *Brain Injury, 10*(9), 687–695.

Rattock, J. (1996). Do patients with mild brain injuries have posttraumatic stress disorder too? *Journal of Head Trauma Rehabilitation, 11*(1) 95–96.

Rothbaum, B. O., & Foa, E. B. (1992). Cognitive-behavioral treatment of posttraumatic stress disorder. In P. A. Saigh (Ed.), *Posttraumatic stress disorder: A behavioral approach to assessment and treatment* (pp. 85–110). New York: Pergamon Press.

Rutherford, W. H., Merritt, J. D., & McDonald, J. R. (1979). Symptoms at one year following concussion from minor head injury: A relative's view. *Brain Injury, 10,* 225–230.

Silver, J. M., Rattok, J., & Anderson, K. (1997). Posttraumatic stress disorder and traumatic brain injury. *Neurocase, 3,* 1–7.

Tyerman, A., & Humphrey, M. (1984). Changes in self-concept following severe head injury. *International Journal of Rehabilitation Research, 7,* 11–23.

U.S. Department of Transportation. (1995). *Traffic safety facts 1994: A compilation of motor vehicle data from the fatal accident report system and general estimates systems.* Washington, DC: National Highway Traffic Safety Administration.

Van Reekum, R. M., Bolango, I., Finlayson, M. A., Garner, S., & Links, P. S. (1996). Psychiatric disorders after traumatic brain injury. *Brain Injury, 10*(5), 319–327.

Van Zomeren, A., & VandenBerg, W. (1985). Residual complaints of patients two years after severe head injury. *Journal of Neurology, Neurosurgery and Psychiatry, 48,* 21–28.

Varney, N. R., Martz, J. S., & Roberts, R. J. (1987). Major depression in patients with closed head injuries. *Neuropsychology, 1,* 7–8.

Wolpe, J. (1958). *Psychotherapy by reciprocal inhibition.* Stanford, CA: Stanford University Press.

Wolpe, J. (1973). *The practice of behavior therapy.* New York: Pergamon Press.

Wolpe, J. (1985). Deep muscle relaxation. In A. S. Bellack & M. Hersen (Eds.), *Dictionary of behavior therapy techniques.* New York: Pergamon Press.

SUGGESTED READINGS

Hibbard, M. R., Gordon, W. G., Stein, P. S., Grober, S., & Sliwinski, M. (1993). A multimodal approach to the diagnosis of post-stroke depression. In W. A. Gordon (Ed.), *Advances in stroke rehabilitation.* Stoneham, MA: Andova Medical.

Hibbard, M. R., Uysal, S., Kepler, K., Bogdany, J., & Silver, J. (1998). Axis I psychopathology in individuals with traumatic brain injury. *Journal of Head Trauma Rehabilitation, 13*(4), 24–39.

Kay, T., Harrington, D. E., Adams, R., Anderson, T., Berrol, S., Cicerone, K., Dahlberg, C., Gerber, D., Goka, R., Harley, P., Hilt, J., Horn, L., Lehmkuhl, D., & Malec, J. (1993). Definition of mild traumatic brain injury. *Journal of Head Trauma Rehabilitation, 8*(3) 86–87.

Silver, J. M., Rattok, J., & Anderson, K. (1997). Posttraumatic stress disorder and traumatic brain injury. *Neurocase, 3,* 1–7.

Rothbaum, B. O., & Foa, E. B. (1992). Cognitive-behavioral treatment of posttraumatic stress disorder. In P. A. Saigh (Ed.), *Posttraumatic stress disorder: A behavioral approach to assessment and treatment* (pp. 85–110). New York: Pergamon Press.

10

Disaster Trauma

Francis R. Abueg
George W. Woods
Dale S. Watson

The quick and massive destruction wrought by disasters presents a complex challenge to society: how to organize and dispatch resources in the management of that destruction while simultaneously attending to vast human suffering. Victims are typically overwhelmed psychically and often impaired physically. The victim's family network and material resources are compromised if not decimated. The pervasiveness of grief and loss can be marked by early signs of numbing and dissociation. The incidence and future risk of psychopathology is increased and the potential for institutional conflict (e.g., victim communities vs. federal government) is heightened. Clinical behavior therapy in the field of traumatic stress offers a range of approaches to mitigating the psychosocial impact of disaster trauma; moreover, its relevance to improvements in community preparedness, policymaking and institutional change is being demonstrated empirically with greater frequency in a wide variety of catastrophic events.

The central aim of this chapter is to elaborate upon theory and practice of techniques in behavior therapy through an up-to-date review of developments in the disaster and trauma literature. Practical guidelines are offered to help a clinician (1) make rapid, well-reasoned assessments of need; (2) predict client, community, or institutional risk based upon base-rate observations in previous disasters (from the epidemiological to the anecdotal); (3) provide effective, ethical, and culturally sensitive intervention; and (4) evaluate the effects of interventions proffered. An important underpinning to our conceptualization of addressing psychological distress in disaster arises from developments in contextual approaches to human experience and scientific application of contextualism to psychology (Hayes, 1996); and contextual understanding of trauma and traumatic stress disorder (Follette, Ruzek, & Abueg, 1998b; Meichenbaum, 1994).

DISASTER INTERVENTION:
CONTEXTUAL BEHAVIOR THERAPY FOR TRAUMA

A growing anecdotal and scientific concern regarding interventions in disaster is whether in fact disaster counseling is truly necessary. The largest proportion of survivors in most disasters actually return to original or improved functioning as evidenced by large epidemiological sampling (Green, Korol, Grace, et al., 1991) as well as smaller, more in-depth studies of individual differences with particular attention to trauma-related anxiety disorder (Yehuda, 1999). The dearth of outcome studies of psychological interventions in disaster is remarkable but understandable given the challenge of disaster research. Still, our knowledge base is rapidly growing with regard to who is at risk for psychopathology in a sudden catastrophe, and the naturalistic course of adaptation to these life stressors. The vast majority of individuals not only recover from dramatic and horrific losses; they often exhibit heroic altruism, generativity, and existential shifts in appreciation of their survival. How they do it is often the subject of poignant human interest pieces presented in the media. Focused scientific study of resilience or successful coping, quantitative or qualitative, is virtually nonexistent. The little information we have in this regard, appears as a post hoc comparison of low- or no-symptom groups compared with the dysfunctional group.

Another significant shortcoming of the scientific literature on the acute traumatic stress response—aside from the absence of any studies on resilience—is the everpresent temptation toward diagnostic reification. With the advent of DSM-IV, our colleagues are now drawn to not only posttraumatic stress disorder (PTSD) and the dissociative disorders but to the new construct, acute stress disorder (ASD). The meaning lost in studies constrained by such categorization is well summarized in the literature (Haynes & O'Brien, 1990; Hayes & Follette, 1992) and is drawn to a fine point in traumatic stress studies by a number of authors (Follette, Ruzek, & Abueg, 1998a; Naugle & Follette, 1998; Walser & Hayes, 1998). A contextual approach emphasizes the range of contingencies impinging upon an individual—from interoceptive conditioning through broad social, cultural, and communal shaping of behavior—and places a high value on functional analytic techniques in establishing first what is a problem worth treating (see Kohlenberg & Tsai, 1998, for an excellent discussion of this idea in trauma treatment) and how, in the most conservative way, to maximize change with the most parsimonious interventions.

The contextual approach has numerous practical implications for therapy but it is most salient in disaster work for a number of reasons. First, the challenge of resource conservation and impact mitigation is central in disaster work. Contextual-behavioral approaches can assist the helper in identifying risk quickly, based on previous research findings, and devise interventions that are brief but effective. We propose in this discussion a three-tiered risk assessment model that reflects progress in the field while being sensitive to the need for technical parsimony. Instead of static notions of diagnosis matched to treatment, we also propose that timing of interventions in this field—though widely varying—has not heretofore been carefully labeled, described, or studied. Many practitioners have nevertheless employed a heuristic in their work that appears to be mainly utilitarian (i.e., do what works) often at the expense of theory (a way of knowing what works and a systematic strategy to examine outcomes). A matching paradigm, akin to stage models of intervention described elsewhere in the PTSD literature (Abueg & Fairbank, 1992), seems to be very helpful in "titrating intervention dosage" to what we have come to understand as modal progression of clinical problems after a disaster. The contextual model emphasizes acceptance of the survivor narrative (see Hayes, 1991, and Meichenbaum, 1994, for more extensive, general discussion of these notions) while gently orienting the person toward understanding impediments to disclosure (Abueg, 1997a), avoidance conditioning (Levis, 1995), and new ways of making constructive meaning of the experience (Kohlenberg & Tsai, 1998). Once that worldview has been breached or challenged in a substantive way, it can be nurtured in part for its inherent resilience. These beliefs can be challenged and/or corrected for errors in appraisal, processing, judgment, and inference—that is, how an individual makes meaning of in his/her unique sociocultural context will largely determine whether the individual can successfully adapt. One underlying goal of approaches to assisting victims of disaster is to increase their feelings of controllability and predictability.

POSTDISASTER SYMPTOMATOLOGY

Disasters lead to substantial increases in the level of distress and/or psychiatric illness within a community. Rubonis and Bickman (1991) completed a meta-analysis of 52 studies and concluded that major disasters have the potential to increase, on average, the prevalence rate of psychopathology approximately 17% over predisaster levels or in comparable groups. However, the estimates of morbidity can vary widely depending on the extent of destruction. For example, nearly 77% of the population of a village destroyed in the 1978 hurricane in Sri Lanka were found to have psychological impairment (Patrick & Patrick, 1981, cited in Rubonis & Bickman, 1991). It would appear that the level of resultant psychiatric impairment is strongly dependent upon the sheer number of deaths occurring in a given disaster.

Smith, North, McCool, and Shea (1990) found highly different rates of PTSD following an airplane crash depending on the degree of exposure. They found that of employees on-site at the time of the crash (i.e., high exposure), 29% had PTSD as opposed to only 7% of employees who were not at work at the time (low exposure). Freedy and colleagues (Freedy, Kilpatrick & Resnick, 1992; Freedy, Shaw, Jarrell & Masters, 1992), though not examining PTSD specifically, found increased psychological distress among subjects who had experienced greater resource losses following Hurricane Hugo. Green, Grace, Lindy, Titchener, and Lindy (1983) found increased distress among subjects with greater degrees of bereavement after the Beverly Hills supper club fire.

Inclusion of the construct/diagnosis ASD (American Psychaitric Association, 1994), mainly as a precursor condition of PTSD, reflects and has since facilitated further growth in our understanding of the pathogenesis of PTSD. The literature is quite informative with respect to how symptoms of traumatic stress are presented among disaster victims. Intrusive thoughts and memories of the trauma (diagnostic category B of ASD and PTSD in the DSM-IV (American Psychiatric Association, 1994), for example, seem to be the most frequently reported posttrauma symptoms following natural disaster (McFarlane, 1992; Solomon & Canino, 1990; Madakasira & O'Brien, 1987). However, intrusive thoughts seem to be quite frequently experienced during the acute phase—less than 30 days—posttrauma. The presence of these symptoms during the early phase may not predict particularly well the development of chronic PTSD. McFarlane (1988) reported that intrusive memories had a low specificity (63%) for a PTSD diagnosis (i.e., the presence of these symptoms did not predict strongly whether a person had PTSD). Nightmares are another form of intrusive symptoms. Wood, Bootzin, Rosenhan, Nolen-Hoeksema, and Jourden (1992) noted that nightmare frequency was twice as high among college students in the San Francisco Bay area as among control students in Tucson, Arizona, following the 1989 Loma Prieta earthquake. In addition, earthquake content in nightmares was much more frequent among those exposed to the earthquake.

Avoidance symptoms (DSM-IV diagnostic category C)—feelings of numbness, social withdrawal and avoidance of trauma-relevant situations or reminders—tend to be less frequently reported than are intrusive symptoms. Solomon and Canino (1990) report that this finding is uniquely apparent during the acute period following a disaster. However, they propose that measurement may be one reason for this finding. They suggest that certain PTSD instruments, the Diagnostic Interview Schedule (Solomon & Canino, 1990) in particular, frequently used in disaster studies may underreport the presence of category C symptoms and arousal category D. McFarlane (1992) reported that avoidance had no significant relationship with either exposure variables or predicting the development of PTSD. Shalev (1992) noted that in a group of survivors of a terrorist attack avoidant symptoms tended to develop later than did intrusive symptoms, suggesting that avoidance is a way of coping with the presence of disturbing trauma recollections, a strategy used increasingly over time.

The symptoms of arousal in category D seem to be the least studied of PTSD symptoms in disaster samples, although researchers are increasingly suggesting that these symptoms may have more predictive value in identifying those at high risk for development of chronic PTSD after a trauma. Shalev (1992) notes that McFarlane's (1988) data indicate that arousal symptoms have a much better specificity (94%–100%) than do the intrusive symptoms. Our own laboratory has replicated findings of physiological arousal in the presence of salient traumatic cues reported most commonly in the combat trauma literature. We found that earthquake survivors had many PTSD symptoms 18 months following the 1989 Loma Prieta earthquake. They had significantly higher heart rate increases than did controls when exposed to videotaped news footage about the earthquake. This case-control study matched groups on age and degree of earthquake exposure (Drescher et al., 1993). Preliminary examination of psychophysiological data collected by our laboratory following Hurricane Iniki indicates a similar finding of increased arousal to salient cues 6 weeks after the hurricane. One model for PTSD development suggests that certain symptoms may result from a conditioned emotional reaction to environmental cues present during the traumatic event (Barlow, 1988). The question of whether category D symptoms predict development of chronic PTSD problems is one that deserves further exploration.

Another important issue is the change in trauma symptoms over time. A number of studies have noted high rates of PTSD occurrence among subjects in the early weeks (now referred to as acute stress disorder symptoms) and months postdisaster. Smith et al. (1990) report a high incidence (54%) of psychiatric disorder among victims 4 to 6 weeks following a jet plane crash. Of these victims, 72% had a prior history of psychiatric disorder, suggesting that this is a risk factor for symptom development. Fifty-three percent of high-exposure victims met criteria for PTSD, while 21% of the low-exposure group had PTSD. Madakasira and O'Brien (1987) found that 59% of tornado victims met self-report criteria for PTSD at 5 months postdisaster. In contrast, North, Smith, McCool, and Lightcap (1989) found very low rates of psychiatric disorder in general (12%) and PTSD in particular (2%) among victims assessed 1 month following a tornado.

Disasters are somewhat unique among trauma types in that their effect tends to be widespread within a community. This may have both advantages and disadvantages for victims. The fact that many community members share similar trauma experiences may facilitate therapeutic disclosure of feelings and fearful cognitions regarding the trauma. In addition, the community may pull together and provide a higher than usual level of social support for victims, which may be therapeutic. The way in which a community perceives disaster victims and the degree to which individuals feel they are a part of the community as a whole may be important variables in the recovery process. Steinglass and Gerrity (1990) suggest that social support and community variables such as these may have contributed to higher acute and chronic PTSD rates in one community they studied. This study examined two communities that were similar in overall demographics with the exception of level of education and family income. One of the communities was located in an economically depressed region. Findings indicate that the community that had more economic resources and physically rebuilt damaged areas faster but that tended to characterize the disaster in more individual than communitywide terms had higher initial and follow-up rates of PTSD.

It is becoming increasingly clear that more complex models are needed to explain the development and maintenance of traumatic symptoms in survivors of natural disasters. One early model proposed by Green, Wilson, and Lindy (1985) suggested that stressor factors, individual factors, and environmental and recovery factors all affect the development of and recovery from PTSD. A similar model has been proposed since been proposed Freedy, Kilpatrick, et al. (1992). They propose a risk factor model postulating that predisaster, within disaster, and postdisaster factors share an important role in predicting an individual's ability to adjust following the impact. Predisaster factors include demographics, previous traumatization, recent life events, psychiatric history, coping, and social support. Within-disaster factors are degree of trauma exposure and cognitive appraisal of exposure related to perceived control, predictability, and threat; and postdisaster factors are acute-period distress level, life events, resource loss, coping, and social support.

Clearly, the inclusion of ASD in the DSM-IV was warranted given the growing evidence that the full array of PTSD symptoms is presaged by the same symptom picture immediately after the event (and within 4 weeks of disaster; American Psychiatric Association, 1994; Yehuda, 1999). The following interventions have been shown to be successful (in controlled single-case studies and controlled group-outcome studies) in interrupting the downward course of symptoms: psychoeducational interventions, which elucidate the PTSD cluster of symptoms (Osterman & Chemtob, 1999); critical incident stress debriefing (CISD) in acute rape victims; cognitive restructuring and coping skills training, which produce positive results comparable with those of progressive muscle relaxation training alone—though exceed the latter in benefit at 1-year follow-up (Echeburua, de Corral, Sarasua, et al., 1996).

A THREE-TIERED RISK ASSESSMENT

Given the above developments in the field, we propose a hierarchical model of risk assessment, which has as its primary goals: to facilitate a priori hypotheses about severity of symptoms in an affected group, to make judgments about levels and timing of interventions, and to respect the stage at which the survivor presents (and potentially rule out intervention). Table 10.1 illustrates the risk assessment model.

The first tier, or the *low-risk category,* encompasses the majority of disaster survivors for whom modest intervention is sufficient and at times unnecessary. They will manage losses and the psychological shock of the devastation with appropriate grief and loss reactions. They will mobilize their social supports in a way that often enhances them (e.g., engaging friends and loved ones in problem-solving strategies and preventive tactics for the future) as opposed to

TABLE 10.1. Categories of Risk in Disaster and Recommended Level and Timing of Interventions

Risk level	Subject characteristics	Timing	Interventions[a]
I. Low	Resilient; nonsymptomatic and mobilizes social supports Emotionally expressive, grief, mourning, feelings of loss	Primary	Disaster planning[27, 28] Psychoeducation regarding ASD/PTSD[21, 27] School/community-based[22, 23] Education for adaptive behaviors CISD/CISM[24, 25]
II. Moderate	Acute stress disorder symptoms Obsessive rumination Dysphoric; intense grief/mourning Intermittent rage reactions Self-medication History of psychiatric disorder Children and older adults	Secondary	CxBT[1, 21] Acceptance/grief support[2, 3, 6] ASD symptom reduction[4–8, 21] Arousal reduction[9, 10] Focal exposure[11–13, 21] Dissociation management[8, 17, 26] Skills training[14–18] Stress inoculation[6]
III. High	Severe dissociation: amnesia, detachment, depersonalization, dereism, identity disturbance Profound numbing Acutely suicidal Complex PTSD Impoverished; regional targets of armed conflict/terrorism Active comorbid alcohol/drug abuse or recent history of dependence	Secondary Tertiary	Restitutive (housing, water, food)[5, 27] Hospitalization[5] Safety/acceptance[1–3, 20, 21] Long-term treatment[6, 17, 19–21] Relapse prevention[6, 19, 21] Harm reduction[17, 19] Trauma-relevant relapse prevention training[19] Decreasing repeat victimization[17, 20]

Note. ASD, acute stress disorder; CISD, critical incident stress debriefing; CISM, critical incident stress management; CxBT, contextual behavior therapy; PTSD, posttraumatic stress disorder.

[a]References cited: 1, Follette et al., 1998a; 2, Walser & Hayes, 1998; 3, Naugle & Follette, 1998; 4, Young et al., 1998; 5, Johnson & Johnson, 1999; 6, Meichenbaum, 1994; 7, Ruzek, Polusny & Abueg, 1998; 8, Meadows & Foa, 1998; 9, Wolfe, 1991; 10, Baldwin, since 1995; 11, Levis, 1980; 12, Levis, 1995; 13, Stampfl & Levis, 1967; 14, Novaco, 1998; 15, Kubany, 1998; 16, Serafin & Follette, 1998; 17, Wagner & Linehan, 1998; 18, Herman, 1992; 19, Abueg, 1994; 20, Cloitre, 1998; 21, Abueg et al., this volume; 22, Weinberg, 1990; 23, Galante & Foa, 1986; 24, Armstrong, O'Callahan, & Marmar, 1991; 25, Mitchell & Everly, 1994; 26, Abueg, 1999; 27, Myers, 1998; 28, Young et al., 1998.

ways that fatigue them (preseverative frustration and complaint); and they will seek additional help when they perceive the need (as opposed to withdrawing from the prospect or minimizing the problem). Their level of traumatic exposure is mild to moderate. They may show tendencies toward obsessive rumination about the event, mild dysphoria, and increases in arousal and reexperiencing symptoms.

The main intervention strategy for this group is debriefing, ideally in a survivor group context, with just a single long session with 1- to 3-month follow-up. Typically, their medical and restitutive needs (housing) are minimal. Although not empirically evaluated, we have repeatedly observed in our disaster work that this group may well respond to bibliographic and media-based interventions without the need for face-to-face intervention whatsoever. Some individuals may consistently refuse intervention; community or institutional leadership may thwart attempts at organizing debriefing sessions. These boundaries must ultimately be honored as they clearly communicate the degree to which problems are viewed as clinically relevant, or "potentially treatable," behavior. Violation of the boundary is unethical and possibly iatrogenic.

The second tier, or *moderate-risk category,* refers to the group manifesting clinically significant dysfunction. Left untreated, the course is likely to continue or worsen. This group of individuals usually will exhibit at least one of the following: meeting criteria for ASD; exposure to massive or horrific loss of life or property or the perceived sense of overwhelming helplessness and loss of control (truly meeting criterion A, bona fide trauma, as outlined in ASD or PTSD); is a helper-victim who experienced the trauma itself and has an occupation that brings them in repeated contact with other victims. Any combination of these variables increases risk for psychopathology in general (depression, ruminative or obsessive disorder) and posttraumatic problems in particular (PTSD, dissociative identity disorder [DID], phobias, and conversion disorders).

The third tier, or *high-risk category,* refers to individuals exposed to criterion A–level traumatic stress *and* who have any one or more of the following characteristics: loss of significant number of immediate family, friends, coworkers and/or community; currently in an affectively numb, intransigently hopeless and/or dissociative state, as evidenced by one or more of the dissociative symptoms discussed in criterion B, part 1 (amnesia for the event, detachment, dereism, or depersonalization); acutely thought-disordered or disorganized in behavior or affect; and actively suicidal.

INTERVENTION LEVEL AND TIMING

Timing and level of intervention are equal in importance to evaluating risk in meeting the needs of survivors. Timing of disaster work is best delineated in terms of primary, secondary, and tertiary interventions. *Primary* or *preventive in-*

tervention, occurs before the fact of trauma, typically in the form of institutional and family or personal disaster planning. National and international coverage of disaster has facilitated a forum for the education of nonvictims about the psychological effects of these events and how professionals address problems. Behavioral preventive strategies include addressing safety issues in housing and at the workplace through retrofitting in earthquake-prone areas, storm prevention and reinforcement for hurricanes, and stopgap measures for fires and floods. In terms of crime prevention, a whole host of systemic interventions (e.g., community policing) and installation or modification of security systems is in order. The area of greatest impact for contextual behavioral intervention remains in psychoeducational approaches via the Internet and World Wide Web, as well as integrating their message within corporate and governmental disaster agencies.

Secondary intervention encompasses all professional assistance once the disaster has hit. Clearly the earlier the intervention occurs in the succession of events, the more likely these activities will be akin to prevention. Emergency service officials may still be attempting to move individuals, families—perhaps entire communities—in an effort to mitigate further loss of life and property and improve the access for their services (e.g., clearing the roads for fire prevention). Formal and informal transmission of accurate information in the traumatic context is the most effective mode of allaying fears and potential mass hysteria. Formal transmission denotes governmental and emergency agency communications via radio, television, and public announcement. Informal transmission refers to oral communications between individuals, families, and groups. Disaster management in institutional settings emphasizes swift and accurate transmission of death tolls, location of evacuation centers and shelters, and continuous monitoring of the likelihood of reoccurrence. It is rare for information to be consistently available and accurate, however; therein lies another opportunity for the "contextual intervenor/advisor" to shape the communications. After the recent spate of American high school shootings (among them the Columbine High School tragedy of 1999), school psychologists and colleagues around the nation stepped up to the plate in educating their communities about what to expect and what measures might be needed to allay future risk. Brainstorming the problems of violence in school, hatred and rage, and how to feel secure again led to practical changes in policy in schools across the nation.

Tertiary interventions are *launched* during the months after the disaster but may continue in the form of long-term pyschotherapy and intermittent hospital-based treatment. Techniques addressing relapse-prevention skills, elimination or reduction of the use of nonprescribed drugs, and enhancement of the repertoire of positive coping strategies should be emphasized with this category of survivors.

Numerous institutional advancements have been made in the United States and around the world addressing the likelihood of large-scale disaster (Jacobs, 1995). Clear and accurate information regarding onset, course, and types of hazards presented is absolutely critical to laying the foundation for resilient coping of victim communities. For example, knowing which local sirens signify the danger of a hurricane and knowing and practicing how to take cover during an earthquake are important insulators against the effects of the disaster. The media therefore can become a broad instrument for social action and trauma prevention at the primary and secondary stages. The extent of psychologically and physically traumatic exposure can be directly mitigated by adaptive behaviors. As implied earlier, if the dose of the trauma can be lessened, the likelihood of psychiatric sequelae may similarly be reduced.

The type of disaster experience—social, technological, or natural—occurring within specific social contexts may also create unique trauma experiences with characteristic symptom patterns (Aguilera & Planchon, 1995; McMillen, Smith, & Fisher, 1997). For example, it has been suggested that social disasters involving civil and political unrest or criminological intent, such as the 1995 bombing of the Murrah Federal Office Building in Oklahoma City, may be marked by an quicker onset of posttraumatic symptomatology, more intense and dramatic shock, rage, and grief experiences as well as significant physiological manifestations of acute stress such as stroke and headache (Aguilera & Planchon, 1995). In contrast, one might surmise that technological disasters, such as an airplane crash, may lead to a greater sense of isolation inasmuch as the victims and their families have no preexisting social ties or shared identification. In addition, the community response to such a disaster may differ in important ways. McMillen, Smith, and Fisher (1997) note that "a disaster in a small town may be a defining event for that community, whereas a disaster that occurs in a large city affecting the same numbers of people may be seen as a defining event for those directly involved but not for the community itself" (p. 733).

Early secondary intervention can be especially important in protecting a community from the deleterious effects of perceived isolation. Norris and Kaniasty (1997) elucidated a social support deterioration deterrence model in which early support (financial and emotional) led to the perception of support availability, which in turn ameliorated long-term symptomatology. They further made the important point that often "racial and ethnic minorities and persons of lower socioeconomic status have received less help than other victims experiencing comparable levels of need (disaster losses). Because their assets may have been strained even before the event, these victims are especially vulnerable in the face of a disaster" (p. 738).

The capacity to derive meaning from a trauma experience can have important implications for the avoidance of long-term morbidity. Those individuals who, in the early phase of recovery, are able to derive a sense that the event has created some positive good in their lives (personal growth, closer emotional ties, etc.) may be less likely to experience later PTSD. In contrast to the view that a simple dose-response relationship will determine symptomatology, McMillen, Smith, and Fisher (1997) found that perceived benefits altered the expected pattern, such that increased traumatic exposure was associated with increased recovery. It is uncertain whether the act of perceiving benefit itself is protective or whether an inherent resiliency and optimism leads to the perception of benefit. However, those who experienced life-threatening events and those with the largest number of preincident diagnoses were more likely to perceive benefits.

Among the most common of secondary interventions are the various methods of debriefing described in the literature on disaster (Mitchell, 1988; Armstrong, O'Callahan & Marmar, 1991; Wolfe, 1991). The central task common to all these approaches is the disclosure of the individual's story. From a behavioral perspective, conditioned avoidance can be minimized through healthy "reexposure" or extinction of feared cues in the context of the trauma. Feelings of safety can be reclaimed most powerfully through group debriefing methods. Communal debriefings also permit the modification and enhancement of each individual's story to accommodate some shared reality representing the experience of the trauma. Debriefing often corrects frankly inaccurate beliefs. Cognitive distortions of all sorts are common, especially, personalization—one instance of which is feeling as though one has been targeted "by the gods"—and can immediately be minimized by a shared debriefing experience.

Experienced leadership of debriefing groups is critical for a number of reasons. First, the management of affect can be a challenge depending on the collection of traumatic assaults suffered by the participants. Highly disturbing and intrusive imagery is typical for those exposed to massive loss of life, horrific human injury, and the discovery and movement of child victims, then dissociation and even decompensation is likely. Participants may show evidence of this behavior subtly, by fixing their gaze and becoming inattentive in movement or speech. Overt signs of dissociation include alterations in speech or behavior that reflects reexperiencing the original trauma in the here and now of the group. Language may become present tense to describe something past, and body movements may mimic movements in the original context. The person may become highly focused on content or emotion and inattentive to his/her surroundings.

In such instances, experienced debriefers will slow or interrupt the process. In those instances of massive loss of life, brief behavioral and restorative interventions are in order. Rest and attending to physical needs and high-priority recovery tasks (beginning a search for loved ones still unaccounted for) are often the first routes in providing help. Children and the elderly, in particular, will often have basic nutritional or survival needs (e.g., potable water or increased nutritional demands) that differ from those of the average adult (Johnson & Johnson Pediatric Institute, 1999). By the same token, intense affect in debriefing groups is quite common; tolerance and accurate interpretation of such emotional expression can enhance feelings of control immeasurably. Participants can be told that sometimes they will feel detached or disconnected. Quick assurances, such as "That's okay" or "Everyone will space out once in a while," can bolster the ability to stay with the traumatic material.

Most victims of disaster benefit from being educated about the onset and course of posttraumatic symptoms. Using the literature briefly reviewed earlier, the clinician can assay the overall risk of a given group. Each of the symptom categories, especially the most prevalent symptoms postdisaster reexperiencing and hyperarousal, should be explained and couched in the context of an "expected" response to a life-threatening stressor. It should be noted that a standard intervention of the past, "This is a normal reaction to an abnormal stressor," is misleading for the true sufferer of ASD or those who are sufficiently symptomatic to warrant treatment beyond debriefing. Based on current knowledge, such a statement is, in fact, incorrect (see Yehuda & McFarlane, 1995). This conveys to the sufferer that the typical or most common response can be an extreme one, whereas—as indicated earlier—an extreme response is actually infrequent and usually requires further professional assistance. Nonetheless, group debriefings and the therapist's description of others with whom he's worked, allows for the destigmatization of psychopathology and builds a strong base from which a survivor can comfortably seek additional help. This level of clarity and specificity also enhances the clinician's ability to draw a bright distinguishing line between a debriefing, psychoeducational secondary intervention to a level three, tertiary, or longer-term therapy.

Nightmares are common among survivors in the short run and provide clues regarding the "topography" of their fear response. This information will allow victims to integrate what was scariest or most horrifying about the experience at a pace that is tolerable. Nightmare content can become a subject of discussion in therapy or with fellow victims in an effort to provide a new context or narrative for encountering the world. Instead of an intolerable, uncontrollable stressor ("Why did this happen to us?", "What kind of god causes such misery?", etc.), the somatic and psychological traumatic response can, in fact, become anchors to predictability and controllability. These reactions can be construed as biological signs of a struggle to survive, to make meaning of loss. Interventions typical in responding to suicide threat—such as reasons for living (children or the prospect of helping other victims)—are also helpful in this context.

Victims need to be warned of the resurgence of symptoms in the presence of reminders. In many natural disasters, the first impact is not an isolated one. Earthquakes are often followed by numerous aftershocks. Floods and hurricanes rise and fall in intensity, duration, and geographic location. After the period of greatest impact, rain and wind act as vivid reminiscence cues for the original life-threatening experience. In politically motivated acts of terror, the air of suspicion, fear, and urges for reprisal, continues to wear upon the community or nation.

Existing methods for the treatment of chronic PTSD, most notably implosive theory and therapy (Stampfl & Levis, 1967; Levis, 1980, 1995), provide a useful heuristic for the elicitation of the trauma narrative. Levis (1980) describes a systematic approach to constructing an implosive scene, which we have found to be quite successful in helping victims reconstruct their disaster experience. Three types of cues are identified and systematically presented to the individual. They include symptom-contingent cues, serial or contextual cues, and psychodynamic cues. Symptom-contingent cues are obtained through direct questioning regarding current fears, concerns, and problems experienced by the victim. These cues may include thoughts of losing one's children, nightmares of horrific loss, and extreme muscle tension. They are stepping stones in building a picture of the traumatic context. Nightmare content, for example, may be an accurate or at least a symbolic depiction of the most painful part of the trauma.

Serial or contextual cues spontaneously emerge in the discussion of the manifest content proffered by the victim. However, with the clinician's assistance, asking additional questions regarding the environmental context can tap otherwise forgotten or avoided painful traumatic material. This is often a dramatically emotional approach to debriefing, which precipitates feelings of relief from a burden. In our experience, these contextually conditioned fear cues can best be obtained through careful questioning regarding a victim's sensory experiences at the height of the traumatic "insult." By simply asking what the victim saw, heard, felt, touched, or tasted, additional channels of information appear to open and to facilitate additional storytelling. At the same time, the helper minimally intrudes upon the reconstruction of the experience. In addition we have found that proprioceptive and kinesthetic cues—the sensation of position of body and movement in space—also draw forth intense elaborations of the disaster experience (e.g., being crushed, pinned, or cramped). An elaborated cue elicitation technique based on the sensory exposure, called the Multi-Sensory Interview (MSI), is available from this chapter's first author (see Abueg, 1997b).

Some caution is warranted with respect to the complex PTSD sufferer or the highly dissociative person who has suffered numerous traumas—usually with little resolution or treatment—prior to the disaster experience. Although these methods can be highly effective with these patients, care should be taken in assessing the manner in which extreme emotionality arises (i.e., triggers), and safety interventions should already be in place. These include having taught and practiced breathing and self-soothing relaxation techniques, practicing orientation techniques, and heightening discrimination skills in anticipating a dissociative episode. Simple screening via questionnaire (for example with the Dissociative Experiences Scale [DES]; Carlson, 1991) is not adequate. A formal functional analysis of precipitants to dissociation and extreme horror or terror is in order, and recent structured approaches with manualized interviewing techniques are now available (Abueg, 1999). A final caveat regarding the severely symptomatic or patient with a high risk history (e.g., frequent suicide attempts or a history of having been diagnosed with dissociative identity disorder [DID] or schizophrenia), is that pursuit of outpatient treatment requires the clinician's preparedness to hospitalize. Aside from the logistical responsibilities of the therapist, informed consent regarding this prospect is absolutely necessary. We have found that this is usually reassuring to the patient using language such as, "I also want to make sure that your safety is our first concern. If it appears as if you really might hurt yourself or someone else, then I will arrange for a hospitalization."

Finally, hypothesized or psychodynamic cues include themes resonating to early childhood trauma or loss, guilt, shame, and a whole host of other emotions (see Horowitz, 1985, for a discussion of these primitive emotional themes). An understanding of this group of cues is important especially in cases of traumatic reactivation (Hiley-Young, 1992), somewhat distinct from the complex PTSD sufferer, for whom the current disaster resonates specifically with an earlier traumatic experience. Levis (1980) referred to this reliving of an earlier trauma as *reintegration* and it is often marked by unanticipated evocation of memories (the "crooked cue" from Levis, 1995). This can be highly distressing to individuals who for the first time find that they have access to early traumatic memories. Because guilt is so pervasive in the context of trauma, we suggest that victims consistently explore themes such as: Does the individual feel as if he/she did not do enough, made a mistake during the recovery phase, or somehow was responsible for some untoward consequence? If it is a very early childhood trauma, then what sense impressions as opposed to verbal constructions are prominent? Once the complexity of the history of conditioning unfolds, prescriptions regarding what to expect, traditional methods of rational disputation, and skill building in certain areas (e.g., desensitization to feared imagery as homework) can be implemented.

CHILDREN AND FAMILIES

As well as being an etiological factor in the development of PTSD in individual adults, disasters can make a dramatic impact on the psychosocial functioning of children and family groups. Adams and Adams (1984) noted that there were dramatic increases in illnesses, domestic violence, alcohol abuse, and utilization of mental health resources (i.e., psychiatric admissions, mental health appointments, and crisis-line calls) following the eruption of Mount Saint Helens. If at-home functioning is impaired for principal caretakers, it is reasonable to posit that children will also be victimized.

A number of studies have documented empirically, and clinicians have noted anecdotally, that children may be uniquely vulnerable to the trauma of disaster contexts (Honig, Grace, Lindy, et al., 1993). In the acute period following a disaster, one researcher–clinician (Saylor, 1991) noted the presence of "thematic repetitive play associated both with anxiety about a traumatic event and reduction of that anxiety." She describes a spontaneous game called "Hurricane" after Hugo of 1989 hit, in which the children pretended the hurricane is coming, and engaged in various activities designed to protect themselves and repair damage in the aftermath. She describes another child who repeatedly recreated the hurricane damage with her broccoli at dinner.

Burkes, Borus, Burns, Millstein, and Beasley (1982), in a prospective study, found increased anxiety among preschool boys and increased aggressive conduct among children previously identified as having special needs following a severe winter storm. Overall, for the entire group sampled, school behavior improved. Connely and Bromet (1986) found higher rates of behavior disturbance among 5- to 6-year-old children who lived in the vicinity of Three Mile Island nuclear plant at the time of the accident as compared to controls who lived near a fossil fuel facility. The prevalence of children exceeding a cutoff score was 11%. In a retrospective analysis of data collected 2 years following the Buffalo Creek dam collapse, Green et al. (1991) found that 37% of children involved had a probable PTSD diagnosis. Exposure severity, gender, parental distress, and family environment all predicted a number of PTSD symptoms and accounted for 28% of the variance of PTSD symptoms. In a review of family sequelae among combat veterans and rape victims with PTSD, Carroll, Foy, Cannon, and Zwier (1991) suggest that the most frequently identified problems within families that have a member with PTSD are constricted expressiveness, hostility, and global maladjustment.

The intermittent presentation of reminder cues postdisaster creates a tenacious learning context for dysfunctional anticipatory anxiety and vigilance. Training in cognitive reappraisal and mastery appears to have powerful impact on these problems. Galante and Foa (1986) evaluated a seven-session, school-based, small-group intervention for children in grades 1 to 4 following a devastating earthquake in Italy. Each session had cognitive and emotional components as well as an activity (usually drawing while listening or role playing). Children had an opportunity to express their fears freely and to disclose their trauma experiences to other students and facilitators. Cognitive distortions, such as erroneous beliefs and myths about earthquakes, and irrational fears were corrected and opportunities encouraged children to utilize active coping skills and not to see themselves as victims. Results indicated a significant decline in earthquake-related fears among treated children and a decline in the number of children "at risk" for problem behavior.

Large-group, school-based interventions for adolescents have also been described by several authors. Stewart (1992) outlines an intervention that uses both large and small groups in a single 2½-hour session and is designed to lower disaster-related distress and enhance social support among students. The intervention incorporated physical activity and group-enhancing activity. The didactic portion helped explain to students the relationship between unmet needs and stress and attempted to normalize stress-related symptoms. Although the efficacy of this intervention was not formally evaluated, student feedback through evaluation questionnaires was overwhelmingly positive.

Another large-group protocol for adolescents is described by Weinberg (1990). This intervention is designed for school traumas, such as murders or suicides, in which grief and loss issues predominate. Students are convened in a school assembly addressing a number of important issues. Unexpressed grief is described and emotional expression is encouraged. Healthy coping responses, on the other hand, are elaborated in detail and unhealthy reactions are actively discouraged (e.g., rage or extreme isolation). An interesting behavioral observation component is included when at-risk students are identified and encouraged to participate in subsequent small-group sessions. Students evidencing extremely strong emotional reactions and those attempting to leave the meeting met on an individual basis with counselors and are encouraged, when they feel ready, to participate in small-group sessions.

This multilevel assessment and response is crucial especially in high-profile school events such as the Columbine High School tragedy of 1999 in which two students shot and killed a number of fellow students and a teacher in the predominantly white, middle-class community of Littleton, Colorado. The onslaught of media attention focused on numerous accounts of spontaneous public grieving, despite clear and conscious attempts by local officials to protect the students and their families from the intrusiveness of interviewers. The potential for embarrassment and even humiliation is high, for example, with male adolescents who are culturally constrained from exhibiting strong emotions.

Several family interventions are described in the literature as well. Harris (1991) describes a family-based crisis intervention model designed for use within a week of a disaster. Initial sessions are designed to elicit open expression of feelings and development of rapport with the therapist. Cognitive restructuring is used when appropriate to correct distortions and irrational thinking on the part of family members. Next, issues requiring immediate attention are identified. Communication skills are taught and social support systems are mobilized within and outside the family. The family is then encouraged to take concrete, positive problem-solving actions to create a sense of movement and progress toward goals.

Figley (1988) describes a five-phase family treatment approach. A key element of this approach is the development of a "family healing theory." In essence, this theory involves helping the family to reframe and articulate together what happened to them as a result of the trauma and to envision effective coping in the future. It is important that this theory be shared and endorsed by all members of the family. It is a way of normalizing what has happened and assigning meaning to the event.

It must be recognized that the cultural context of trauma significantly shapes the meaning attached to that experience by individuals and groups. Dissociation, for example, has numerous expressions and potential interpretations in other cultures and its adaptive functions may be significantly underemphasized in the psychiatric nosology. Poverty as a traumatic stressor has been the formal subject of study in only the last few years. Much of the world's victimization occurs in the poorest of contexts and the manner in which governments and institutions respond can contribute to insidious, repetitive victimization (World Health Organization, 1993).

CASE STUDIES

Two case studies follow, which illustrate the vulnerability of two disaster providers who were victims themselves. Cathy, in the first case, was involved in a debriefing and became a client in a brief contextual behavior treatment. The case studies are separated by a brief discussion of cultural and forensic variables that no longer appear to be ancillary in the contextual approach to disaster work. Deborah, in the second case, was not formally treated but was alerted to her symptomatology, which engaged her natural resilience coping skills. The backdrop to her experience was an international crisis, the 1998 U.S. Embassy bombing in Nairobi, Kenya.

Loma Prieta Earthquake: The Case of Cathy

Cathy was a head nurse employed at a large hospital in the San Francisco Bay area that was severely damaged by the October, 1989, earthquake. Her duties included management of a small staff and direct patient care on a medical ward. The director of the unit specifically requested a debriefing from the National Center for PTSD within 10 days of the quake. The floor of his ward was among the most seriously affected in terms of structural damage. The staff evacuated the patient tower with only minor injuries, although the 24-hour period that followed the most dramatic shaking presented quite a challenge for them.

In the course of the debriefing, Cathy revealed to the debriefer (F. R. A.) that she was a single parent and also cared for her infirm mother. At the time the earthquake hit, Cathy was working well past the 3:30 P.M. completion of her shift. As she typically did in most of her work settings, in the face of this catastrophe, Cathy took charge. Although internally she felt a great deal of fear for her life once the earthquake hit, she externalized much of this emotion by orchestrating the evacuation of her unit per orders of safety officials and hospital administration. She was in constant communication with the chief of staff's office as well as the nursing chief. Cathy was largely responsible for evacuating 8 staff members and more than 20 patients and helping move beds and medical supplies to a grassy area behind the main part of the hospital. In the midst of a great deal of chaos and confusion, she was able to speak with the house-helper (who cared for Cathy's mother while Cathy was at work), her daughter, and directly with her mother. They confirmed that they were all safe, but they had no electricity and were worried about whether or not to shut off the gas valve. The scariest part of their experience was the heavy, loud crashing sound of the china hutch falling onto the dining room table and the shattering of glass and crystal. The mother and the caretaker were at a safe distance in the living room and the daughter was in her bedroom, so no one was hurt.

With her staff, Cathy attended a 2-hour debriefing held in their relocated ward. She was quite forthcoming about her feelings of vulnerability and helplessness; it was clear, however, that much more emotion was being contained—fear, as she put it, "of making it feel worse."

With reassurance, Cathy disclosed the fact that she had been having nightmares in which she would awaken in the context of the earthquake wondering where her patients were. Themes of being "the good-enough caretaker" were underscored by the debriefer and the group validated her efforts as being not only adequate but "exceptional and heroic." The debriefer supported the group feedback and added, "Sometimes feedback like this is difficult to incorporate because we all are so complex and have histories where we often don't see ourselves as adequate."

The group was able to share cathartic summaries of the challenge of balancing personal fears and family demands with work demands. One staff member's home was completely destroyed, but her cognitive resilience was remarkable and inspiring for the group. "I still have my loved ones and I thank God for that. I know we'll make it." Cathy, however, used that as an opportunity to diminish her own level of coping. The debriefer attempted to mitigate the harshness of this self-evaluation by educating the group about the genesis and maintenance of PTSD symptomatology.

> "All of you are vulnerable to developing symptoms of posttraumatic stress. We know that those of you who have been undergoing other types of stressors may be at greater risk. The more you are directly afraid for your life or for the lives of friends or loved ones, the more you will be at risk. And don't be surprised by a worsening of anxieties or memories when the aftershocks hit. Each response will be quite unique, however, and it is important to use your personal response as a gauge for whether to seek help either from friends, or family, or from a professional. I have often found that brief early discussions with survivors often help prevent more serious problems from developing. The bottom line is that exceptional stress makes us all vulnerable."

Cathy's nonverbal responses were quite revealing although the debriefer suspected that she would be reticent to disclosing anything further to the group. At the completion of the group, the debriefer announced that he would return for at least one follow-up session in a week but would be happy to meet with anyone individually on an as-needed basis. The debriefer then formally approached two members, including Cathy, and gave them his card. "Thank you for being as open as you were. I would like to chat more with you if you would be willing." Cathy readily agreed to setting up an individual appointment.

Cathy was extremely forthcoming in the individual session. She described how the group debriefing was helpful in clarifying what the earthquake meant to her in the context of her life and her perceptions of herself with respect to family and job responsibilities. It became clear that her need to be in control

was a longstanding issue in her family. She saw her father as a loving but unpredictable man with a "moderate alcohol problem." He grudgingly became a
caretaker to Cathy's mother when she developed multiple sclerosis during
Cathy's late adolescence. When Cathy perceived her father as distant and uncaring she would either intervene herself or confront her father unsuccessfully.
Cathy once viewed her mother as "the competent one," but when her mother
became ill that notion was profoundly altered.

Cathy described her first and most significant relationship as a conflicted
one. She had married young and had a child, but she and her husband clashed
on the issues of money and Cathy's ambition to become a nurse and later to
move up the career ladder. When her daughter was 12, Cathy decided to divorce her husband. Within a year of the divorce, her father had a massive coronary and died. Suddenly she was left to care for herself, her daughter, and her
mother, who was in declining health, entirely on her own.

The earthquake marked an opportunity for Cathy to feel and acknowledge unexpressed helplessness and rage. She recounted a longstanding need to
be taken care of. She acknowledged that she went into "hyperdrive" to care for
everyone in her environment after the earthquake and finally realized that she
had nothing left for herself. The debriefing was the first time she had begun to
let go of the control. This realization, in the context of a safe and trusting relationship with the clinician, marked a release, an acceptance of self that Cathy
never allowed herself. Some anger was directed at her mother for becoming ill,
a thought she knew was irrational and for which she felt extreme guilt. This
anger was immediately validated as quite normal for caregivers. The scary possibility of having to finally institutionalize her mother was finally broached
openly. We formally discussed the option of redefining the debriefing relationship in terms of a "brief therapeutic contract," for six sessions, in which many
of these issues could be addressed. Cathy's personal resources and general
competence were emphasized and she consented with enthusiasm.

Psychotherapy centered on themes of control and autonomy versus helplessness and feelings of neglect and abandonment. Specific techniques included
progressive muscle relaxation and extensive use of imagery. From a direct
therapeutic exposure perspective, Cathy's fantasies evoked a great deal of fear
and avoidance and had never fully been examined. We began with symptom-
contingent cues, such as feeling overwhelmed with work duties, and quickly
progressed to serial and psychodynamic cues—the death of her father being the
final marker of abandonment and early feelings of rage regarding his neglect of
the family. With successive exposure in imagery to these memories, Cathy was
able to comfortably discuss how her history shaped her current behavior. For
example, Cathy realized that her workaholism was distancing her from her
family.

She admitted carrying a lifelong resentment toward her father and guilt
about never matching the idealized "good girl" impression most had of her. Finally, the current guilt over what she was not doing began to be understood in

the context of chaos—she was responding to crises in immediate proximity. These were choices—albeit hardly conscious ones—and benefited countless patients and colleagues. As she was able to review the situation with less adverse emotion, she recognized her ability to shape her schedule, take time off, and generally tame the feelings of uncontrollability.

Cathy's situation and our response illustrate the role of preexisting vulnerability, in particular guilt feelings with respect to her father. Fortunately, the measurement of guilt in trauma-related contexts has significantly improved with the advent of the Trauma-Related Guilt Survey (TRGS; Kubany, Abueg, Kilauano, Manke, et al., 1997), and cognitive interventions with trauma survivors has been manualized and subjected to early empirical evaluation (Kubany, Haynes, Abueg, Manke, et al. 1996). Successful exposure work seems to address issues of guilt and shame; we have, however, found great utility in the formal guilt interventions outlined by Kubany, when faced with intransigent guilt and shame. This severe presentation is not at all uncommon among complex PTSD patients, namely, those who have suffered previous unaddressed traumas (cf. Herman, 1992; Shay, 1995).

Discrete prescriptions for self-care emerged in a problem-solving fashion almost without much conscious effort on the part of the therapist or Cathy. Cathy needed to take regular, measured breaks from work—a day per week until she could see an opening for her first real vacation in years. She would hire the home health care worker for an additional number of hours per week to look after the family even when Cathy was at home. This was a "luxury" that Cathy formerly enjoyed only for a few hours per week. She also planned "alone time" during which she simply would not be accountable to anyone but herself.

By the end of this brief therapy, Cathy began to feel remarkably more in control by taking less control, a paradox in which she took great pride. The frequency of her nightmares declined to just one per week (as opposed to many nightly) and, perhaps most importantly, her appraisal was far more positive: "These memories are reminders of work I need to do on myself." At 3 months postdebriefing, Cathy had spontaneously resumed a regular daily regimen of self-relaxation. She had begun to read books with themes of growth and self-examination (e.g., Viktor Frankl's works) and had indicated a greater openness to looking at herself "as a whole person" again.

Cultural Factors

Preexisting vulnerability related to traumatic life circumstance is an area of growth in the clinical and scientific literature. Merely being a member of an American minority group may place a person at higher risk for trauma-related symptomatology than his/her white counterparts (e.g., Kulka et al., 1991; Keane et al., 1996). A replication study of Vietnam veterans who are Asian American, Native Hawaiian, and Native American (specifically Sioux and

Navajo) has suggested similar increased vulnerability. Litz et al. (1997) suggest that African American troops who served in the peacekeeping role in the Somalia conflict exhibited greater severity of PTSD symptoms in part because of their greater affinity, through racial identification, to the Somali combatants. Literature on Asian American veterans who fought in the Vietnam war documents more directly the problem of identifying with the enemy and the guilt and shame that ensues (Abueg & Chun, 1996).

The study of traumatic symptomatology after the 1998 Kenya Embassy Bombing showed that more than 80% of victims met the DSM-IV criteria for PTSD. A smaller sampling verified, however, that significant vulnerability for traumatic stress existed in many victims even before the bombing, due to inherent culture-specific factors—poverty, previous exposure to political terror and other forms of civil unrest (Nyamai, Njenga, Woods, Abueg, & Watson, 1999). Another challenge arises when European or North American professionals attempt to provide services or conduct research in developing nations. It is often the case that the country may actually have a history of being colonized by the home country of the visitor; the obviously sensitive issues of what the visitors intend quickly becomes paramount (e.g., taking data home and improving one's academic status; cf. Holloway, 1999).

The implications of culture studies in trauma extend beyond differential rates of symptom expression. How trauma is construed and even the relevance of Western constructions of the idea of psychiatric sequelae to an event all come into question when the culture is significantly different from our own (Manson et al., 1996). Avoidance symptoms, in particular the lack of psychological expression or numbing, provides a good example of these variations. In those cultures where either the physical or emotional manifestation of grief is discouraged, it becomes difficult to distinguish the avoidance symptoms from culturally established norms in the expression of grief-related emotion. The Tanzanian government was reticent to investigate the psychiatric manifestations of the 1998 embassy bombing for fear that the more traditional institutions, such as family, tribe, and village cohesion, were being undermined by Western psychological paradigms (Nyamai, Njenga, Woods, Abueg, & Watson, 1999). Attention must be paid to the degree to which victims have a voice in their cultural system, and cognitive interventions must be aimed at squarely addressing how to empower victims in those settings (see Marsella, Friedman, Gerrity, & Scurfield, 1996).

Constraints on Responding Due to Forensic Needs

Forensic science has emerged as an often confounding factor in response to both natural disasters and terrorist acts. The tension between the desire to preserve and develop forensic evidence and the need to both save lives and mitigate psychological trauma seems to be more measurable in recent years and, in some specific instances, irreconcilable. These problems were observed in part during the Oklahoma City bombing and later in the August 1999 Turkey earthquake. In the latter natural disaster, many victims and families of victims were concerned that the building failures may have been preventable defects in construction. But a week postearthquake, many of the collapsed structures were bulldozed, likely destroying forensic evidence of building code violations.

Politically motivated disasters, such as the Kenya/Tanzania bombings of 1998, illustrate similar conflicts between the increasing need to understand the crime versus the demands of an emergency health care response (Njenga et al., 1999; Woods et al., 1999). The embassy bombing disasters create a set of politically charged factors, anger, secrecy of documents, maintenance of security versus access, and criminal responsibility. As the diagnosis of PTSD and the impact of trauma is increasingly embraced by the law, further refinements in the interplay between forensic sciences and emergency responses will aid in understanding complex aspects of the traumatic response (cf. Simon, 1995; Woods et al., 1999).

Kenya Embassy Bombing:
Media Debriefing and the Case of Deborah

Deborah was the administrator of one of the hospitals forced into action after the American Embassy in Nairobi, Kenya, was bombed August 7, 1998. She proudly discussed the role that her hospital played in caring for some of the 250 Kenyans killed and over 4,500 injured. One month after the bombing and, while showing the various units where victims were still hospitalized, she suddenly stopped, staring ahead. Quickly recompensating, she started crying and could not continue the tour. Deborah acknowledged that she had, at times like these, not seen the patients recovering, but in the physical state they were in when they came into her hospital immediately after the bombing: ". . . my hands are tied. . . . Ambulances are full, lined up thousands deep, and I keep looking for my house. I can't seem to find my house."

What is striking about this particular terrorist disaster is that it appears to have been the first recorded instance in which an instantaneous media-based debriefing was enacted while the tragedy was occurring (Njenga et al., 1999). Psychiatrist Dr. Frank Njenga was a guest on a radio show being broadcast over the greater Nairobi area when the bomb exploded. As information regarding the disaster interrupted the broadcast, the show returned to its format—a call-in show—but attended to the expected suffering related to traumatic symptomatology. Dr. Njenga shifted his emphasis immediately to content-related posttraumatic symptoms, an area in which he happened to be well versed. Local Kenyans called in with their stories and received immediate help akin to the methods we have described herein. Other news services quickly heard of the show, which in turn led to a cascade of highly informed reporting throughout the region.

Ironically, while many Kenyans were listening to the mass debriefing occurring on both the radio and television, the trauma-response providers were saving lives rather than observing or protecting their own responses to the trauma surrounding them. Deborah's husband commented on the limitation of affect Deborah showed since the bombing. Normally a bright, active woman, she had maintained her business pace, but her face rarely changed expression. As in many emergency preparedness agencies in Africa, there were no formal interventions for health care providers during or after any disaster, natural or terrorist. When interviewed 8 months after the embassy bombing, more than three-quarters of the Kenyan-born psychologists treating victims continued to have intrusive thoughts, avoidance behaviors, and occasional arousal symptoms (Njenga, Nyamai, Woods, Watson, & Abueg, 1999). Her recognition of symptoms came late compared to the numerous victims she and her staff had helped. It was important to acknowledge that not only was she in fact directly victimized by the event (as all local Kenyans were) but the subsequent vicarious exposure was equally painful and, to her, much more of an ongoing burden. One year after the bombing, Deborah still noted occasional nightmares, but continued to function very capably. She chose to be part of a longitudinal study looking at the impact of trauma as well as parameters of resiliency in health care providers during the Nairobi embassy bombing. Much of her symptom relief came in the context of training and educational events, which she at times conducted herself. The supportive prodding of fellow professionals and her husband allowed her to discriminate deep dedication to her work versus posttraumatic immersion and premorbid PTSD.

Internet and Web–Based Resources in Disaster

The advent of Web-based technology and instantaneous access to information has already begun to revolutionize consumer access to health information. Disaster contexts are unusual in that high-quality information needs to be disseminated quickly and often to a large and scattered audience. The technology of the Web provides solutions to all of these challenges (Grohol & Zuckerman, 2000). Those interested in accessing important resources on disaster should be aware of at least two central Web resources, among countless others, available currently. The first is called the Baldwin Trauma Pages (Baldwin [since 1995]), a Web-site dedicated to research and practice in emotional trauma. This informative compendium of online resources, compiled by a research-oriented clinical psychologist with a background in trauma intervention, has already established itself as a reliable and seemingly exhaustive Web resource on trauma and PTSD. The disaster section is particularly useful in that printable educational handouts and pamphlets are immediately retrievable for dissemination in a crisis. Another important resource on disaster intervention, now available through the Walter Reed Army Hospital Web site (look under their Social Work department), is a complete guide to disaster mental health, principally authored by a social worker highly active in disaster services, training and re-search (Young, Ford, Ruzek, Friedman, & Gusman, 1998). Aside from being a scholarly but practical guide to intervention, it guides the reader through the complex maze of disaster logistics and various levels of agency response, bewildering to most first-time responders.

In addition to compilation of information and quick access to disaster colleagues around the world, the Internet provides countless new ways to disseminate information. Creative applications in disaster await full exploration but here are a few immediately implementable ideas. Support groups abound on the Web and may have particular value for the often fractured social networks postcatastrophe. Web-based distance learning with video-streaming applications may be quite promising for all practitioners but especially for rural professionals and international colleagues in academically isolated locales. Finally, data collection techniques can be streamlined via the Web such that survivors can complete questionnaires online while their data are transparently downloaded to the investigator's computer. Advances such as these will no doubt improve service delivery and clinical research in especially challenging contexts. Finally, wireless technologies have the potential for delivering all of the above with on-the-spot access readiness and freedom from the traditional telecommunication infrastructure, typically compromised in times of crisis.

CONCLUSION

Contextual behavior theory and techniques are invaluable not only in stabilizing the suffering of survivors of natural disaster but also in the prevention of posttraumatic stress symptoms, dissociation, and depression. Empirically based assessment of risk aids in the conservation of human resources. This chapter has emphasized vulnerability factors such as degree of traumatic exposure, perceived threat, and social and environmental resources—all contribute to psychological morbidity in victims. Recent findings are incorporated into our rational-behavioral construction of primary and secondary intervention, such as (1) specific attention to dissociative responding as a predictor of later PTSD; and (2) cultural context and indigenous ways of making meaning of a shared catastrophe. The broadening emphasis toward systemic interventions at all levels—community, national and Federal, and international—was broached and considered as part of a contextual assessment of risks and benefits for various programmatic interventions. Prevention and treatment services for emergency medical and health care providers must be a parallel priority to direct victim triage, especially when providers are indeed victims themselves. Last but not least, international terrorism presents an additional order of complexity in disaster clinical practice, which has only begun to be addressed in the behavioral and psychiatric literature. As much as the extant literature has contributed to treatment development, we argue that much remains to be gained from systematic qualitative and ethnographic research as well as greater emphasis on models of resilience.

REFERENCES

Abueg, F. R. (1994). *Impediments to Disclosure Scale (IDS): Development and validation.* Paper presented at the annual meeting of the International Society for Traumatic Stress Studies (ISTSS).

Abueg, F. R. (1997a, July). *Creative strategies in treating PTSD in ethnic minority patients: Applications to the Filipino elder veteran.* Paper presented at a conference entitled "Special Needs of Filipino Elderly Veterans" hosted by the Geriatric Research, Education and Clinical Center of the VA Palo Alto Healthcare System and Stanford Geriatric Education Center, Menlo Park, CA.

Abueg, F. R. (1997b). *Systematic interview format for elicitation of somatic cues in trauma: The Multi-Sensory Interview (MSI).* Los Altos, CA: Trauma Resource Consulting. (Available from the first author at TresCon, 4966 El Camino Real Suite 115, Los Altos, CA 94022.)

Abueg, F. R. (1999). *Functional analysis of dissociative events (FADE): Manual for scoring, administration and application in psychotherapy.* Los Altos, CA: Trauma Resource Consulting. (Available from the first author at TresCon, 4966 El Camino Real Suite 115, Los Altos, CA 94022.)

Abueg, F. R., & Chun, K. (1996). Traumatization stress among Asians and Asian-Americans. In A. J. Marsella, M. J. Friedman, E. Gerrity, & R. M. Scurfield (Eds.), *Ethnocultural aspects of post-traumatic stress disorders.* Washington, DC: American Psychological Association.

Abueg, F. R., & Fairbank, J. A. (1992). Behavioral treatment of co-occurring PTSD and substance abuse: A multi-stage model of intervention. In *PTSD: A behavioral approach to assessment and treatment.* New York: Allyn & Bacon.

Adams, P. R., & Adams, G. R. (1984). Mount Saint Helen's ashfall: Evidence for a disaster stress reaction. *American Psychologist, 39,* 252–260.

Aguilera, D. M., & Planchon, L. A. (1995). The American Psychological Association–California Psychological Association Disaster Response Project: Lessons from the past, guidelines for the future. *Professional Psychology: Research and Practice, 26,* 550–557.

American Psychiatric Association. (1994). *Diagnostic and statistical manual of mental disorders* (4th ed.). Washington, DC: Author.

Armstrong, K., O'Callahan, W., & Marmar, C. R. (1991). Debriefing Red Cross disaster personnel: The multiple stressor debriefing model. *Journal of Traumatic Stress, 4*(4), 581–593.

Baldwin, D. V. (Au./Ed.). (Since 19 May 1995). *Trauma information pages.* WWW URL: www.trauma-pages.com

Barlow, D. H. (1988). *Anxiety and its disorders: The nature and treatment of anxiety and panic.* New York: Guilford Press.

Burkes, D., Borus, J. F., Burns, B. J., Millstein, K. H., & Beasley, M. D. (1982). Changes in children's behavior after a natural disaster. *American Journal of Psychiatry, 139,* 1010–1014.

Carlson, E. B., & Rosser-Hogan, R. L. (1991). Trauma experiences, posttraumatic stress, dissociation, and depression in Cambodian refugees. *American Journal of Psychiatry, 11,* 1548–1551.

Carroll, E. M., Foy, D. W., Cannon, B. J., & Zwier, G. (1991). Assessment issues involving the families of trauma victims. *Journal of Traumatic Stress, 4,* 25–40.

Cloitre, M. (1998). Preventing revictimization in rape survivors. In V. M. Follette, J. I. Ruzek, & F. R. Abueg (Eds.), *Cognitive-behavioral therapies for trauma.* New York: Guilford Press.

Connely, P., & Bromet, E. (1986). Prevalence of behavior problems in three year old children living near Three Mile Island: A comparative analysis. *Journal of Child Psychology and Psychiatry, 27,* 489–498.

Drescher, K. D., Abueg, F. R. & Gusman, F. D., Kubany, E. S., Torigoe, R. & Scurfield, R. M. (1993). *Psychophysiological reactivity to earthquake reminders.* Working paper of the University of Colorado Natural Hazards Research Center, Boulder, CO.

Echeburua, E., De Corral, P., Sarasua, B., & Zubizarreta, I. (1996). Treatment of acute post-traumatic stress disorder in rape victims: An experimental study. *Journal of Anxiety Disorders, 10,* 185–199.

Figley, C. (1988). A five-phase treatment of post-traumatic stress disorder in families. *Journal of Traumatic Stress, 1,* 127–139.

Follette, V. M., Ruzek, J. I., & Abueg, F. R. (1998a). Theory and practice in cognitive-behavioral models of trauma: A contextual approach. In V. M. Follette, J. I. Ruzek, & F. R. Abueg (Eds.), *Cognitive-behavioral therapies for trauma* (pp. 8–18). New York: Guilford Press.

Follette, V. M., Ruzek, J. I., & Abueg, F. R. (Eds.). (1998b). *Cognitive-behavioral therapies for trauma.* New York: Guilford Press.

Freedy, J. R., Kilpatrick, D. G., & Resnick, H. S. (1992). Natural disasters and mental health: Theory, assessment, and intervention. *Journal of Social Behavior and Personality, 7,* 1–55.

Freedy, J. R., Shaw, D. L., Jarrell, M. P., & Masters, C. R. (1992). Towards an understanding of the psychological impact of natural disasters: An application of the conservation resources stress model. *Journal of Traumatic Stress, 5,* 441–453.

Galante, R., & Foa, D. (1986). An epidemiological study of psychic trauma and treatment effectiveness for children after a natural disaster. *Journal of the American Academy of Child Psychiatry, 25,* 357–363.

Green, B. L., Grace, M. C., Lindy, J. D., Titchener, J. L., & Lindy, J. G. (1983). Levels of functional impairment following a civilian disaster: The Beverly Hills supper club fire. *Journal of Consulting and Clinical Psychology, 5,* 573–580.

Green, B. L., Korol, M., Grace, M. C., Vary, M. G., Leonard, A. C., Gleser, G. C., & Smitson-Cohen, S. (1991). Children and disaster: Age, gender, and parental effects on PTSD symptoms. *Journal of the American Academy of Child and Adolescent Psychiatry, 30,* 945–951.

Green, B. L., Wilson, J. P., & Lindy, J. D. (1985). Conceptualizing PTSD: A psychological framework. In C. R. Figley (Ed.), *Trauma and its wake.* New York: Brunner/Mazel.

Grohol, J. M. (2000). *The insider's guide to mental health resources online: 2000/2001 edition.* New York: Guilford Press.

Gusman, F. D., Stewart, J. A., Hiley-Young, B., Riney, S. J., Abueg, F. R., & Blake, D. D. (1996). A multicultural developmental approach for treating trauma. In A. J. Marsella, M. J. Friedman, E. T. Gerrity, & R. M. Seurfield (Eds.), *Ethnocultural aspects of posttraumatic stress disorder: Issues, research, and clinical applications.* Washington, DC: American Psychological Association.

Harris, C. (1991). A family crisis-intervention model or treatment of posttraumatic stress reaction. *Journal of Traumatic Stress, 4,* 195–207.

Hayes, S. C., & Follette, W. C. (1992). Can functional analysis be a substitute for syndromal classification? *Behavioral Assessment, 14,* 345–365.

Hayes, S. C., Hayes, L. J., Reese, H. W., & Sarbin, T. R. (Eds.). (1993). *Varieties of scientific contextualism*. Reno, NV: Context Press.

Haynes, S. N., & O'Brien, W. H. (1990). Functional analysis in behavior therapy. *Clinical Psychology Review, 10,* 649–668.

Herman, J. L. (1992). *Trauma and recovery*. New York: Basic Books.

Hiley-Young, G. (1992). Trauma reactivation assessment and treatment: Integrative case examples. *Journal of Traumatic Stress, 5*(4), 545–555.

Holloway, A. (1999). Disaster awareness and public education in Africa: The problems here are different. *Natural Hazards Observer, 23,* 1–3.

Honig, R. G., Grace, M. C., Lindy, C. J., Newman, C. J., & Titchener, J. L. (1993). Portraits of survival: A twenty-year follow-up of the children of Buffalo Creek. *The Psychoanalytic Study of the Child, 48,* 327–355.

Horowitz, M. J. (1985). Disasters and psychological responses to stress. *Psychiatric Annals, 15,* 161–167.

Jacobs, G. A. (1995). The development of a national plan for disaster mental health. *Professional Psychology: Research and Practice, 26,* 543–549.

Johnson & Johnson Pediatric Institute. (1999). *Special health needs of children critical during disaster relief: Johnson & Johnson Pediatric Institute Partners with leading pediatric associations to improve care of children during crisis*. PR Newswire: Author.

Keane, T. M., Kolb, L. C., Kaloupek, D. G., Orr, S. P., Blanchard, E. B., Thomas, R. G., Hsieh, F. Y., & Lavori, P. W. (1998). Utility of psychophysiology measurement in the diagnosis of posttraumatic stress disorder: Results from a Department of Veterans Affairs cooperative study. *Journal of Consulting and Clinical Psychology, 66,* 914–923.

Kohlenberg, R. J., & Tsai, M. (1998). Healing interpersonal trauma with the intimacy of the therapeutic relationship. In V. M. Follette, J. I. Ruzek, & F. R. Abueg (Eds.), *Cognitive-behavioral therapies for trauma* (pp. 305–320). New York: Guilford Press.

Kubany, E. S., Abueg, F. R., Kilauano, W. L., Manke, F. P., et al. (1997). Development and validation of the sources of Trauma-Related Guilt Survey–War-zone version. *Journal of Traumatic Stress, 10,* 235–258.

Kubany, E. S., Haynes, S. N., Abueg, F. R., Manke, F. P., et al. (1996). Development and validation of the Trauma-Related Guilt Inventory (TRGI). *Psychological Assessment, 8,* 428–444.

Kulka, R. A., Schlenger, W. E., Fairbank, J. A., Jordan, B. K., Hough, R. L., Marmar, C. R., & Weiss, D. S. (1991). Assessment of posttraumatic stress disorder in the community: Prospects and pitfalls from recent studies of Vietnam veterans. *Psychological Assessment, 3,* 547–560.

Levis, D. J. (1980). Implementing the technique of implosive therapy. In A. Goldstein & E. B. Foa (Eds.), *Handbook of behavioral interventions: A clinical guide*. New York: Wiley.

Levis, D. J. (1995). Decoding traumatic memory: Implosive theory of psychopathology. In W. O'Donahue & L. Krasner (Eds.), *Theories of behavior therapy: Exploring behavior change*. Washington, DC: American Psychological Association.

Litz, B. T., King, L. A., King, D. W., Orsillo, S. M., & Friedman, M. J. (1997). Warriors as peacekeepers: Features of the Somalia experience and PTSD. *Journal of Consulting and Clinical Psychology, 65,* 1001–1010.

Madakasira, S., & O'Brien, K. (1987). Acute posttraumatic stress disorder in victims of a natural disaster. *Journal of Nervous and Mental Disease, 175,* 286–290.

Manson, S., Beals, J., O'Nell, T., Piasecki, J., Bechtold, D. W., Keane, E. M., & Jones, M. C. (1996). Cultural constructions of trauma and its consequences: Adapting the DSM to

Native American experience. In A. J. Marsella, M. J. Friedman, E. Gerrity, & R. M. Scurfield (Eds.), *Ethnocultural aspects of post-traumatic stress disorders* (pp. 255–283). Washington, DC: American Psychological Association.

Marsella, A. J., Friedman, M., Gerrity, E., & Scurfield, R. M. (Eds.). (1996). *Ethnocultural aspects of post-traumatic stress disorders.* Washington, DC: American Psychological Association.

McFarlane, A. C. (1988). The phenomenology of posttraumatic stress disorder following a natural disaster. *Journal of Nervous and Mental Disease, 176,* 22–29.

McFarlane, A. C. (1992). Avoidance and intrusion in posttraumatic stress disorder. *Journal of Nervous and Mental Disease, 180,* 439–445.

McMillen, J. C., Smith, E. M., & Fisher, R. H. (1997). Perceived benefit and mental health after three types of disaster. *Journal of Consulting and Clinical Psychology, 65,* 733–739.

Meadows, E., & Foa, E. (1998). Treatment of acute and chronic PTSD in rape and sexual assault victims. In V. M. Follette, J. I. Ruzek, & F. R. Abueg (Eds.), *Cognitive-behavioral therapies for trauma* (pp. 256–277). New York: Guilford Press.

Meichenbaum, D. J. (1994). *A clinical handbook/practical therapist manual for assessing and treating adults with posttraumatic stress disorder.* Waterloo, Ontario: Institute Press.

Mitchell, J. T. (1988). Development and functions of a critical incident stress debriefing team. *Journal of Medical Emergency Services, 13*(12), 43–46.

Mitchell, J. T., & Everly, G. S. (1994). *Human elements training for emergency services, public safety, and disaster personnel: An instructional guide to teaching debriefing, crisis intervention and stress management programs.* Ellicott City, MD: Chevron.

Myers, D. (1998). *Disaster response and recovery: A handbook for mental health professionals* (DHHS Publication No. (SMA) 94-3010). Washington, DC: U.S. Department of Health and Human Services.

Naugle, A. E., & Follette, W. C. (1998). A functional analysis of trauma symptoms. In V. M. Follette, J. I. Ruzek, & F. R. Abueg (Eds.), *Cognitive-behavioral therapies for trauma* (pp. 48–73). New York: Guilford Press.

Njenga, F., Nyamai, C., Woods, G. W., Watson, D. S. & Abueg, F. R. (1999, June). *The Kenya/Tanzania Embassy bombings: When forensic science, politics, and cultures collide.* Paper presented at the International Congress on Law and Mental Health, Toronto, Ontario, Canada.

Nyamai, C., Njenga, F., Woods, G. W., Abueg, F. R., & Watson, D. S. (1999, May). *Research collaboration between East Africa and the United States: Looking at prior trauma in the Embassy Bombing victims.* Paper presented at the first annual conference of the World Psychiatric Association/Kenya Psychiatric Association, Nairobi, Kenya.

Norris, F. H., & Kaniasty, K. (1997). Received and perceived social support in times of stress: A test of the social support deterioration deterrence model. *Journal of Personality and Social Psychology, 71,* 498–511.

North, C. S., Smith, E. M., McCool, R. E., & Lightcap, P. E. (1989). Acute post-disaster coping and adjustment. *Journal of Traumatic Stress, 2*(3), 353–360.

Novaco, R. (1998). Treating PTSD-related anger. In V. M. Follette, J. I. Ruzek & F. R. Abueg (Eds.), *Cognitive-behavioral therapies for trauma* (pp. 256–277). New York: Guilford Press.

Osterman, J. E., & Chemtob, C. M. (1999). Emergency intervention for acute traumatic stress. *Psychiatric Services, 50,* 739–740.

Rubonis, A. V., & Bickman, L. (1991). Psychological impairment in the wake of disaster: The disaster-psychopathology relationship. *Psychological Bulletin, 109,* 384–399.

Saylor, C. F. (1991). Preschooler's post-disaster play: Observations of a clinician researcher and a mother. *Disaster and Trauma Currents, 1,* 5–8.

Shalev, A. Y. (1992). Posttraumatic stress disorder among injured survivors of a terrorist attack: Predictive value of early intrusion and avoidance symptoms. *Journal of Nervous and Mental Disease, 180*(8), 505–509.

Shay, J. (1995). *Achilles in Vietnam: Combat trauma and the undoing of character.* New York: Touchstone Books.

Simon, R. I. (Ed.). (1995). *Posttraumatic stress disorder in litigation: Guidelines for forensic assessment.* Washington, DC: American Psychiatric Press.

Smith, E. M., North, C. S., McCool, R. E., & Shea, J. M. (1990). Acute postdisaster psychiatric disorders: Identification of persons at risk. *American Journal of Psychiatry, 147,* 202–206.

Solomon, S. D., & Canino, G. J. (1990). Appropriateness of DSM-III-R criteria for posttraumatic stress disorder. *Comprehensive Psychiatry, 31*(3) 227–237.

Stampfl, T. G., & Levis, D. J. (1967). The essentials of implosive therapy: A learning-theory based on psychodynamic behavioral therapy. *Journal of Abnormal Psychology, 72,* 496–503.

Steinglass, P., & Gerrity, E. (1990). Natural disasters and post-traumatic stress disorder: Short-term versus long-term recovery in two disaster-affected communities. *Journal of Applied Social Psychology, 20,* 1746–1765.

Stewart, J. S. (1992). Group protocol to mitigate disaster stress and enhance social support in adolescent exposed to Hurricane Hugo. *Issues in Mental Health Nursing, 13,* 105–119.

Wagner, A., & Linehan, M. (1998). Dissociative behavior. In V. M. Follette, J. I. Ruzek, & F. R. Abueg (Eds.), *Cognitive-behavioral therapies for trauma* (pp. 256–277). New York: Guilford Press.

Walser, R. D., & Hayes, S. C. (1998). Acceptance and trauma survivors: Applied issues and problems. In V. M. Follette, J. I. Ruzek, & F. R. Abueg (Eds.), *Cognitive-behavioral therapies for trauma* (pp. 256–277). New York: Guilford Press.

Weinberg, R. B. (1990). Serving large numbers of adolescent victim-survivors: Group interventions following trauma at school. *Professional Psychology: Research and Practice, 21*(4), 271–278.

Wolfe, J. (1991). Applying principles of critical incident debriefing to the therapeutic management of acute combat stress. In National Center for Post-Traumatic Stress Disorder, *Operation Desert Storm clinician packet: ODS-CP.* Palo Alto, CA: Palo Alto VAMC, National Center for Post-Traumatic Stress Disorder.

Wood, J. M., Bootzin, R. R., Rosenhan, D., Nolen-Hoeksema, S., & Jourden, F. (1992). Effects of the 1989 San Francisco earthquake on frequency and content of nightmares. *Journal of Abnormal Psychology, 101*(2), 219–224.

Woods, G. W., Njenga, F., Nyamai, C., Abueg, F. R., & Watson, D. S. (1999, May). *Utilization of mass media for debriefing: Trauma resiliency in East Africa.* Paper presented at the first annual conference of the World Psychiatric Association/Kenya Psychiatric Association, Nairobi.

World Health Organization. (1993). *Psychosocial consequences of natural disaster.* Geneva, Switzerland: Author.

Yehuda, R. (1999). Biological factors associated with susceptibility to posttraumatic stress disorder. *Canadian Journal of Psychiatry, 44,* 34–39

Yehuda, R., & McFarlane, A. (1995). Conflict between current knowledge about posttraumatic stress disorder and its original conceptual basis. *American Journal of Psychiatry, 152,* 1705–1713.

Young, B. H., Ford J. D., Ruzek, J. I., Friedman, M. J., & Gusman, F. D. (1998). *Disaster mental health services: A guidebook for clinicians and administrators.* Menlo Park, CA: National Center for PTSD.

SUGGESTED READINGS

Aguilera, D. M., & Planchon, L. A. (1995). The American Psychological Association–California Psychological Association Disaster Response Project: Lessons from the past, guidelines for the future. *Professional Psychology: Research and Practice, 26,* 550–557.

Armstrong, K., O'Callahan, W., & Marmar, C. R. (1991). Debriefing Red Cross disaster personnel: The multiple stressor debriefing model. *Journal of Traumatic Stress, 4*(4), 581–593.

Follette, V. M., Ruzek, J. I., & Abueg, F. R. (Eds.). (1998). *Cognitive-behavioral therapies for trauma.* New York: Guilford Press.

Green, B. L. (1991). Evaluating the effects of disasters. *Psychological Assessment, 3,* 538–546.

Herman, J. L. (1992). *Trauma and recovery.* New York: Basic Books.

Meichenbaum, D. (1995). *Handbook of cognitive-behavioral treatment of PTSD: A clinical handbook/practical therapist manual for assessing and treating adults with post-traumatic stress disorder (PTSD).* Waterloo, Ontario: Institute Press.

11

Youth Crisis in the Schools

David Castro-Blanco

From ages 6 to 18, most children will typically spend nearly a quarter of their lives in school. The addition of school-related activities and relationships suggest an even greater length of time spent at school or engaged in school-related activities. For most children and adolescents the school serves as the hub around which cognitive, emotional, interpersonal, social and personality development and growth occur. Given the preeminence of school for this age group, it is not surprising that most crises involving children and adolescents either occur at school, are associated with school, or are first detected at school.

Many of these crises first emerge, or are first detected by educational, rather than mental health professionals. It is imperative that school-based personnel have clear models to define crises and appropriate responses in order to identify, triage, and respond to the variety of problems that can impact children, adolescents, and their families. Given the steady decrease in both the frequency and duration of psychiatric hospitalization for children and adolescents (Craig, 1997), schools have become a primary site, not only to identify, but to provide treatment for a variety of high-risk problems (Bostic and Rauch, 1999).

SCOPE OF THE PROBLEM

Suicide is currently the third leading cause of death among adolescents aged 15 and over (Blumenthal, 1990). Among children aged 14 and under, suicide is currently the fourth leading cause of death (Centers for Disease Control and Prevention, 1997). Disruptive behaviors and the disorders associated with them account for the single greatest percentage of referrals for child mental health services (Bird, 1996), though often children and adolescents in this category are at frequent risk for treatment drop out and failure (Trautman, Stewart, & Morishima, 1993). Rates of comorbidity for substance abuse disorders with mood and disruptive behavior disorders among adolescents appear to be similar to those exhibited by adults (Kandel et al., 1999).

A significant problem encountered by many children is exposure to violence. Miller, Wasserman, Neugebauer, Gorman-Smith, and Kamloukos (1999) have reported that exposure to violence is a common occurrence among urban boys. Their research has suggested that in families with low conflict, witnessed violence had a significant impact on later emerging antisocial behaviors. Schwab-Stone et al. (1999) have reported that across a longitudinal sample of urban adolescents exposed to violence, both internalizing and externalizing disorders were seen to increase within 2 years of violence exposure.

Exposure to violence has been an increasingly problematic situation, particularly among urban children and adolescents. The Centers for Disease Control and Prevention (1993) have reported that nearly one-third of junior high school and high school students acknowledged being threatened with physical harm. Significantly greater numbers of inner-city adolescents have directly witnessed physical assaults on others (Gladstein, Rusonis, & Heald, 1992). The toll taken by this exposure has yet to be fully measured or understood, however, it is clear that increasing exposure to violence may directly or by association, influence the thoughts, feelings, and behaviors of young people. Accordingly, such exposure may indeed be related to an increased incidence of crises in and around schools.

Several problems associated with school performance and behavior may be attributable to unrecognized psychopathology. Frequently children and adolescents who manifest a variety of behaviors regarded as "difficult" or "problematic" may, in fact, be exhibiting symptoms of psychopathology that have gone undiagnosed (Jensen & Watanabe, 1999).

Children and adolescents manifesting psychopathology are at increased risk for the development of later occurring psychiatric disorders (Jensen & Watanabe, 1999; Kandel et al., 1999; Cornell, Peterson, & Richards, 1999). Given the increased risks for recurrence of symptoms, or for the development of longer-term problem behaviors stemming from earlier dangerous behaviors (Loeber, Green, Lahey, Christ, & Frick, 1992), interventions offering the promise of active treatment engagement, empirically supported techniques and demonstrated efficacy are strongly indicated.

DEVELOPMENTAL ISSUES IN CHILD AND ADOLESCENT TREATMENT

Children, adolescents, and adults all differ significantly from each other in their style of thought, emotional experience and expression, and behaviors. Children and adolescents tend to manifest several of the thought styles associated with cognitive distortions in adults. Dichotomous thinking, overinclusive thought, idealized rather than realistic appraisal of situations, and catastrophic thought are common among young people. Although such thought styles are considered pathological and commonly treated in adults, they may be developmentally appropriate for children and teens. This strongly suggests that we need to be cautious in our attribution of "dysfunctional" and "irrational" thoughts and beliefs, as well as judicious in modifying conventional treatment approaches with young people.

This is not to imply that a cognitive-behavioral model is inappropriate for use with children and adolescents. To the contrary, the structure, direction and technical clarity of cognitive-behavioral treatment approaches can yield very positive results. It is imperative however, that the clinician working with young people take into account the marked differences in cognitive function that distinguish children from adults.

DEVELOPMENTAL MODIFICATIONS TO COMMON COGNITIVE-BEHAVIORAL TECHNIQUES

Many commonly utilized cognitive-behavioral techniques can easily be modified to suitably account for developmental differences in younger patients.

Testing Idiosyncratic Meaning

A particularly important technique when working with children and adolescents is *testing the idiosyncratic meaning of statements*. Frequently, patients will use words and terms generically, which therapists employ in specific ways. Patients may frequently report feelings of upset, depression, anger, hurt, or anxiety. Though tempting, it is potentially troublesome for the therapist to assume an understanding of the terms used by the patient. This is particularly so when the patient is a child or adolescent.

While imprecision and inconsistency may exist between and among professionals in the use of terminology, school-age patients may utilize terms commonly employed by adults with only a fleeting glimpse at semantic recognition. It is not at all uncommon for children of various ages to develop idiosyncratic terms and phrases, which are readily recognized and accommodated within the peer group but regarded as alien or nonsensical by adults. The clinician has a deceptively simple means at his/her disposal for assessing the idiosyncratic meaning of patient verbalizations. Directly questioning the child or adolescent, and requesting an explanation may result in some annoyance on the child's part but is perhaps the most effective method for assuring a complete understanding of the child's meaning. In so doing, the clinician avoids the risk of assuming that his/her definition of a term coincides with the patient's, and conversely, aids the child in recognizing and articulating the meaning of terms that are often used indiscriminantly.

Given the tendency for young people to think in absolutist and dichotomous terms, the use of Socratic questioning may prove problematic. This is especially so, if a feature of the child or adolescent's presentation is anger

(Dodge, 1993; Dodge & Newman, 1981; Matthys, Cuperus, & Van Engeland, 1999).

Cornell, Peterson, and Richards (1999) have reported that angry adolescents were far more likely to engage in verbal aggression as a precursor to physical aggressivity. The use of Socratic questioning, rather than more directive, and declarative statements with angry teens may be perceived as provocative, and result in an increase in anger, and a higher risk for behavioral dyscontrol (Cornell & Loper, 1998). Challenges to absolutist thinking need to be made with caution, as the rigid, dichotomous view of the world manifested by the adolescent may be developmentally congruent, and not represent a dysfunctional thought process.

Challenging Absolutist Beliefs

As a group, adolescents tend to be particularly vulnerable to absolute beliefs and statements. Simple efforts at negating the absolute beliefs often prove ineffectual and occasionally counterproductive. By reflecting the adolescent's own absolute statements, the therapist can begin the process of questioning, not the root of the belief, but its absolute and extremist nature. In so doing, a moderation of the intensity of the experience can be effected. For example, an adolescent who, following a rejection by a particular peer, states that no one likes or cares about her. Efforts to modify this belief by statements such as, "Many people care" or, "That isn't true," will likely not yield success. However, by reflecting back the absolutist belief to the patient (e.g., "No one in the entire world?") the therapist permits the adolescent to modify the intensity with which the belief is held. Follow-up questions, designed to find exceptions to the absolutist statements then permit the therapist to further call into question these extreme beliefs.

Reattribution

Attributions are assumptions that allow us to identify the causes of various events in our lives. As a kind of "presumptive short-hand," attributions can aid in making sense of events in a seemingly chaotic world. As presumptive statements however, they are also vulnerable to misperception and error. These misattributions may result in erroneous assumptions about the fairness and safety of the world, the motives and behaviors of others, or, the assignment of responsibility for both successes and failures to the self. It is not at all uncommon for children and adolescents to assume sole responsibility for negative outcomes. Often, these assumptions are predicated on views of the self as inadequate or unlucky, and are selectively reinforced by negative events, for which the child or teen assumes the responsibility and blame. Many children and adolescents are over-incorporative in their thinking, and assume responsibility for events and circumstances over which they clearly have little, if any influence.

The clinician can assist the young person to more accurately and realistically apportion responsibility for events. By questioning, designed to elicit the child's perception of his/her control over situations, the therapist can aid the patient in recognizing the limitations of his/her control over life's events. By indicating disconfirmatory events and information, the therapist can help the patient to more accurately assess both the event in question and assign responsibility for it.

In reapportioning responsibility, and moving away from a pattern of reflexively assuming too much or not enough responsibility for actions and events, the patient is in a position to more accurately appraise the world, the self and others, and, perhaps more importantly, to do so with less intensely experienced negative affect. Beliefs related to guilt, anger and disapproval—which are founded on the assumption of responsibility, irrespective of the constraints of reality—can be effectively challenged and changed.

Direct Disputation of Beliefs

Cognitively oriented treatment models commonly feature techniques aimed at disputing strongly held but dysfunctional thoughts and beliefs. Rational-emotive behavior therapy (REBT), as developed by Albert Ellis, advocates the direct disputation of irrational, or self-defeating beliefs. Cognitive therapy, on the other hand prefers to emphasize the process of guided discovery through Socratic questioning.

There are situations that dictate a direct challenge to problematic beliefs. One such situation is the presentation of suicidal ideation and/or behavior by the child or adolescent. In this case, the clinician must actively and directly challenge not only the young person's perception of hopelessness, but the belief that suicide is a viable problem-solving strategy.

Disputation may also prove an effective tool when employed with patients who are actively resistant to treatment intervention, or, as is often the case, when the young person is reluctant to participate in the treatment process. In challenging beliefs or behaviors of the young person, the clinician must be particularly sensitive and alert to the patient's perception that he or she is being *personally* challenged, rather than the thought or action being disputed. The clinician must exercise caution not to be seen as belittling the child for holding potentially self-defeating beliefs.

Adolescents, in particular, are sensitive to having core beliefs challenged. Given the developmental constraints of thinking dichotomously, and of viewing idealized outcomes to situations as normative, adolescents are keenly aware of and sensitive to efforts to challenge their beliefs and often respond to such efforts as personal criticism. The clinician must therefore, employ disputational techniques sparingly, clearly, and judiciously when working with adolescents.

Feeling Thermometer

An adaptation of the Subjective Units of Discomfort Scale (SUDS; Wolpe, 1969), the Feeling Thermometer requires the participant to identify his/her emotional reaction to a variety of situations. Each participant is asked to quantify the degree of feeling on a continuum, ranging from zero (the lowest value for the emotion being evaluated), to 100 (representing the highest possible value for that affect).

When quantifying negative or problem feelings, patients are encouraged to view the zero rating as one of calm, relaxed, and untroubled emotion. The rating of 100, conversely, serves to describe a "boiling point" at which the feeling is at its greatest, and threatens to boil over.

By reporting the intensity of the experienced emotion, the child or adolescent is freed from having to select the appropriate adjective to describe the felt emotion. Adolescents often experience difficulty in verbally expressing and describing their emotional states. Self-consciousness, lack of adequate vocabulary, developmental constraints, and reluctance to express emotionality before family members or peers make it particularly difficult for children, and, especially adolescents, to effectively describe their feeling states. The Feeling Thermometer allows adolescents to express current and past emotional states in a numerical, rather than verbal fashion.

Often, the intensity of an emotion holds greater salience for the individual than the label or term used to describe it. An adolescent may report *anger* when a telephone eats his last coins, as well as when a peer makes an insulting remark about his mother, but the intensity of that anger may be very different for the two situations. The Feeling Thermometer permits the student to indicate the degree to which two experiences of the "same" emotion actually can be very different.

There are several clinical advantages to be gained by using the Feeling Thermometer in treatment. The thermometer provides each participant with a stable means of identifying changing feeling states. A notable aspect of the Feeling Thermometer is the quickness with which a reliable, internally consistent sense of emotional rating is achieved. For adolescents using the Thermometer, there tends to be little variation in their score assignments, and this consistency has been demonstrated to persist over months (Brent, Poling, McKain, & Baugher, 1993).

The Feeling Thermometer provides treatment participants an opportunity to associate feeling states with particular referent events. The recognition of this association is critical to treatment for two key reasons. First, many adolescents report their feelings during events without acknowledging the influence of the situation on the generation of that feeling. Secondly, in associating feeling states with particular events, feelings are demonstrated to be mutable. By showing that feelings can, and often do, change as situations change, the common adolescent perception that a current situation or feeling will persist indefinitely is effectively disputed.

Another important function of the Feeling Thermometer is its ability to serve as an *early warning device*. The analogy of a smoke detector is a useful and apt one when describing this function in treatment. A smoke detector functions by detecting a threshold level of particle density in the air. This density closes a circuit, triggering the detector; which, in turn, sounds an alarm. In a similar manner, the Feeling Thermometer functions by registering changes in the individual's feeling state. By preselecting an intensity level on the thermometer at which risk-taking, and potentially dangerous behaviors are more likely, the individual sets a "threshold." By learning to monitor the feeling state, and quantify its intensity, the participant learns not only to detect the presence of a particular emotion, but its current level of severity.

By self-monitoring changes in the feeling state on the Feeling Thermometer, the patient has the opportunity to recognize the precursors to an emergency, before a crisis is reached. This maximizes the opportunity for the patient to intervene at numerous points before the occurrence of a crisis. This is particularly important for risk-taking adolescents, many of whom report their experience of crises as "coming out of nowhere."

Many adolescents engaging in potentially life-threatening behaviors report "finding" themselves in the midst of a crisis, with no recognition of warning signs, progression of problems, or antecedents. An effective intervention for school-based clinicians is to aid the young person in recognizing these key points:

1. Crises rarely occur spontaneously.
2. Crises typically result from a progression or sequence of events.
3. Warning signs of impending crises are often available but may be overlooked.
4. Self-monitoring can provide the child with instantaneous feedback about his or her feeling state in response to a situation.
5. By monitoring the feeling state, the warning signs of crises can be more easily and more effectively recognized.
6. By recognizing the warning signs of crises, the patient can more effectively intervene to avoid the sequence leading to a particular crisis.

Like a smoke detector, the Feeling Thermometer alone cannot remove the youngster from a dangerous situation. When a smoke detector alarm sounds, the family must still have a plan to evacuate their home. Ideally, the plan should be worked out in advance and each family member should be familiar with it. Similarly, although the self-monitoring effects of the Feeling Thermometer offer considerable aid to the young person and treating clinician, it is still imperative that an effective and comprehensive response plan be

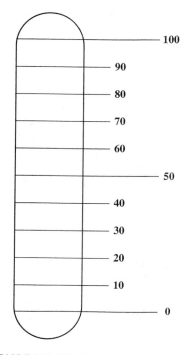

FIGURE 11.1. The Feeling Thermometer.

developed, implemented, and monitored. The Feeling Thermometer is depicted in Figure 11.1.

CRISIS SITUATIONS ENCOUNTERED IN SCHOOLS

Suicide

As noted, suicide is the third leading cause of death for adolescents over age 15 (Blumenthal, 1990), and the fourth leading cause of death for children under age 15 (Centers for Disease Control and Prevention, 1997). Though completed suicide by young people remains a relatively rare event (Rotheram-Borus, Piacentini, Miller, Graae, & Castro-Blanco, 1994), the rate of suicides by young people have more than tripled in the past 25 years (Kruesi et al., 1999; Spirito, Brown, Overholser, & Fritz, 1990).

Suicide among school-age children is a devastating event for the surviving children, relatives, and adult school-based personnel. The most immediate concerns facing the crisis clinician, include aiding adult personnel cope with the tragedy, assist in the formulation of a coordinated school-wide response, directly assist grieving children and, perhaps most importantly, assess the immediate risk for additional suicidal behaviors by other students.

School-based responses to student (or adult) suicides have been designed across two dimensions: system-wide responses (known as "suicide postvention") and clinical responses to individual students at risk. Shaffer, Garland, Gould, Fisher, and Trautman (1988), as well as Gould, Wallenstein, Kleinman, O'Carroll, and Mercy (1990) have written extensively about systemic responses to school suicide. The focus of this chapter is responding to the individual student in crisis, but those interested in the programmatic response to school suicide are referred to those authors.

In response to the suicides of several adolescents in Bergenfield, New Jersey, the Centers for Disease Control and Prevention (CDC; 1994) issued suggested guidelines for responding to the threat of "suicide contagion." Among the suggestions offered by the CDC are coordinating having a single response by the school, avoiding the perceived glorification of the deceased student or the suicidal act, and coordining response with local mental health providers.

Completed suicides by children and adolescents are rare, but suicidal ideation and verbalizations are not (Shaffer et al., 1988). The clinician working with a potentially suicidal child or teenager must directly assess the lethal intent of the child. Direct questioning of adolescents regarding suicidal ideation is recommended as an assessment technique (Kruesi et al., 1999). Among the greatest risk factors for suicidal behavior by adolescents are a prior history of attempt (Rotheram-Borus & Trautman, 1988; Kruesi et al., 1999) and acquaintance with a suicide-attempting relative or peer (Shaffer et al., 1988, Woods, Yin, Middleman, Beckford, Chase, & DuRant, 1997). Cerel, Fristad, Weller, and Weller (1999), have reported a longitudinal study of a sample of children bereaved by parental suicide, who appeared to be at increased risk for behavioral problems and psychopathology.

Clear, direct intervention is required when confronted with a potentially suicidal child or adolescent. It is imperative that the immediacy of risk be assessed and determined. A clear, behaviorally concrete emergency action plan needs to be developed with the student, and immediately implemented. Such a plan should contain strategies for effecting calming, provisions for verbalizing suicidal concerns to a responsible adult (preferably one in the home), as well as establishing access to the clinician and emergency response providers. The Feeling Thermometer provides an extremely useful tool in this regard. By developing use of the thermometer as a self-monitoring strategy, the clinician can aid the child in developing immediate responses to even slight changes in the affective "temperature." Utilization of the thermometer also opens the door to the development and implementation of a coherent response plan that incorporates the family, school-based providers, and, most importantly, the child in the establishment of a treatment plan.

While suicide is arguably the most extreme crisis with which a school-based clinician will be confronted, several other varieties of psychopathology and problematic behaviors can precipitate crises. Among these are depression, disruptive behavior disorders, social anxiety problems, and school refusal.

Depression

Though a sizable minority of adolescent suicide attempters appear to suffer from depression at the time of the attempt (Shaffer et al., 1988), depression is highly prevalent among adolescents (Lewinsohn, Clarke, Seeley, & Rohde, 1994). Given the risk for future recurrence of depressive episodes later in life, adolescent depression is a serious mental health concern. Lewinsohn, Clark, Rohde, Hops, and Seeley (1996) have reported that the cognitive variables of pessimism, negative self-attributions, and lack of coping skills in adolescents appear to be highly predictive of future episodic depression.

Fortunately, a number of cognitively based treatment models have been developed for use with depressed adolescents. Rotheram-Borus et al. (1994), Brent et al. (1993, 1996) and Miller (1999) have all developed cognitive-behavioral models of treatment for depressed adolescents and their families. Mufson, Moreau, Weissman, and Klerman have adapted the Interpersonal Psychotherapy for Depression model for use with adolescents (1993).

Ackerson, Scogin, McKendree-Smith, and Lyman (1999) have reported positive results using a modification of cognitive bibliotherapy with mild and moderately depressed adolescents. Their use of assigned readings, in conjunction with a behavioral journal, appeared to result in significant decreases on a number of depression inventories.

Common to all of these treatment approaches is the use of cognitive restructuring techniques. The use of the Feeling Thermometer provides the clinician with a stable, reliable method of assessing affective arousal. Crisis response to depression must include the assessment of suicidal potential and planning for potential suicidal feelings and thoughts.

Increased self-monitoring through the use of the Feeling Thermometer and a personal journal, linking problem situations with the core cognitions, feelings, and resultant actions associated with them can be especially helpful. The key goal in crisis intervention with depressed children and teens is to establish stability, while assessing and controlling for the variety of comorbid problems associated with depression.

Precise and accurate assessment of depressogenic events, cognitions and symptoms is essential. Unfortunately, such precision is not always achieved when assessing psychopathology in children and adolescents (Angold, Erkanli, Costello, & Rutter, 1996). Recall of dates of symptom onset is vulnerable to error, and the treating clinician must seek as many sources of independent confirmation of information as possible (Angold et al., 1996).

Anger and Aggression

Children and adolescents with oppositional defiant disorder (ODD), conduct disorder (CD), and attention-deficit/hyperactivity disorder (ADHD) are deficient in social problem solving relative to children without those diagnoses (Matthys, Cuperus & Van Engeland, 1999). Unfortunately, these children and teens are also at increased risk for verbally and physically aggressive behaviors (Kazdin, 1997). Although diagnoses of ADHD, ODD, and CD are not, of themselves, predictive of aggressivity, incarcerated juveniles who consistently appeared to have low thresholds for distress and personal restraint were far more likely than others to be recidivists (Steiner, Cauffman, & Duxbury, 1999). Anger appears to play a significant role in the acquisition of aggressive behaviors (Cornell, Peterson, & Richards, 1999), and this affect can certainly be reliably and accurately assessed with the Feeling Thermometer.

Treatment of conduct-disordered children and adolescents is, at best, a daunting task. Brestan and Eyberg (1998) reviewed over 80 treatment studies with conduct-disordered children. Their findings suggest that cognitive-behaviorally based, empirically tested models of treatment proved most efficacious in treating conduct disorder. In contrast, Weiss, Catron, Harris, and Phung (1999) have reported that although children treated with "traditional" (e.g. psychodynamically oriented) psychotherapy fared no better than a control group receiving academic tutoring, parents of the treatment group (vs. non-treatment tutoring) reported greater satisfaction with their children's treatment.

Crisis intervention with disruptive behavior-disordered children and adolescents should feature the assessment of immediate risk for aggressive action. As is the case with suicide assessment, directly questioning the intent and ideation of a potentially aggressive child or adolescent appears to be the most effective means of assessing risk immediacy.

Cognitive-behavioral techniques designed to increase the child's perception of available options, increase self-monitoring and coping behaviors offer an effective treatment package. When coupled with behavioral interventions designed to increase self-control, social skill building, and restraint of aggressive desires, such a cognitive-behavioral model of treatment appears to offer the greatest promise of treatment efficacy.

Anxiety Disorders

Beidel, Turner, and Morris (1999) have suggested that the probable prevalence of social phobia and avoidant disorder is nearly 4%, suggesting that a large number of children and adolescents are vulnerable to some significant form of social anxiety disorder. Children with social phobia have reportedly experienced substantial distress across a variety of social and evaluative situations, and many appear to suffer comorbidly with symptomatology of other anxiety disorders, including specific phobias and generalized anxiety disorder (Beidel, Turner, & Morris, 1999). Surprisingly, a relatively low incidence of comorbid affective disorders is reported for social phobic children. Adolescents with social phobia appear to have higher rates of concurrent affective illness (Strauss & Last, 1993; Last & Strauss, 1990).

Social phobia and related anxiety problems appear to contribute significantly to a variety of problems. Beidel, Turner, and Morris have reported that similar to studied adults, children with social phobia tended to exhibit poorer social skills than did nondiagnosed peers.

Anxiety may pose a crisis situation in schools, particularly for the student who experiences considerable difficulty with attendance and participation. The impairing effects of anxiety may increase significantly the socially phobic child or adolescent's difficulty in maintaining consistent school attendance.

Termed *school phobia,* the phenomenon of missed school attendance as a direct consequence of anxiety and fear is well documented (Hansen, Sanders, Massaro, & Last, 1998; Kearney & Silverman, 1990, 1993). Though frequently written about, no true diagnosis of school phobia exists. It is both more accurate and preferable to refer to *school refusal,* as a consequence of anxiety symptoms.

Unlike conduct- or oppositional-defiant-disordered children and adolescents, or simple truants, these children do not *skip* school as a preference or as a means of avoiding work demands. Rather, school-refusing children and adolescents frequently stay home with the full knowledge, and at least tacit approval, of their parents (Hansen et al., 1998; Kearney & Silverman, 1990).

Although intuitively, it would seem reasonable to assume that children with the greatest degree of fear would exhibit the most severe absenteeism, this is contrary to research findings. Hansen et al. (1998) have reported that the most severe levels of school absenteeism were exhibited by older children and adolescents. These children routinely reported *lower* levels of fear than school-avoidant children with better school attendance. One interesting finding suggests that the children and adolescents exhibiting the most severe school refusal, appear to come from families that do not emphasize out-of-home recreational activities. It has been suggested that children coming from such families may spend an inordinate amount of leisure time at home. Accordingly, spending time at home may be seen as preferable, especially to a youngster who has not had to develop skills to cope with stressors out of the home.

It has been suggested (Hansen et al., 1998) that the most efficacious treatment approach for severely school-avoidant children and adolescents may be familial, rather than individual in basis. Increasing the family's identification of coping skills and reducing familial cooperation with school avoidance are key interventions for the severely school-refusing adolescent or child. Individual treatment aimed at behavioral self-control, increased self-monitoring, disputation of catastrophic cognitions, and social skill acquisition are all essential to reducing the severity of school refusal by the anxious and socially phobic child or teen.

CASE STUDY

Edward is a 16-year-old sophomore in high school. He resides with his parents and sister, age 12. Edward's older brother, aged 23, has not resided with the family for 5 years.

Edward was referred for treatment of severe school refusal. The presenting problem at intake was, "Edward ate a chicken salad sandwich in the Fall, became ill, and has had difficulty attending school since."

On intake, Edward reported having concerns about becoming ill for a number of years. These had crystallized approximately one year earlier, when, shortly after moving from the suburbs to an inner-city neighborhood, Edward visited an uncle's home in his old neighborhood. While there, Edward ate a chicken sandwich, and shortly thereafter, felt ill.

Edward later vomited recurrently both in and out of his home, and experienced considerable gastric distress. He found this to be an extremely distressing event and subsequently has experienced recurrent fears that he will become ill in public and lose control of his digestive functions in front of others.

Subsequently, Edward has missed a considerable amount of school during the past year. He has frequently left home for school, only to abort his efforts to reach school via public transportation. On many occasions, Edward has not even left for school, citing his distress and concerns about becoming physically ill in public. Edward's frequent school avoidance has resulted in concern, both at school and home, and placed him in jeopardy of having to repeat the school year.

Edward has frequently felt "sick" at school; and has, on numerous occasions, obtained a bathroom pass and left school to return home. Edward has reported that his concerns about becoming ill are greatest in public places, where he perceives no viable escape (e.g., a moving bus), or in front of familiar people at school.

Edward was accompanied to most treatment sessions by his parents, who occasionally joined the sessions as collaterals. Although they appeared distressed about the potential negative consequences of Edward's school refusal, both his parents appeared to feel his avoidance of school was justified, given his concerns about becoming physically ill.

Edward's case offers exquisite diagnostic and treatment issues. His frequent avoidance of public places, discomfort in school, and preoccupation with feelings of intense arousal and fear when denied immediate escape suggest a primary diagnosis of panic disorder with agoraphobia. His recurrent, ruminative thoughts about illness and loss of control in public, with the consequent embarrassment or negative evaluation attending such situations, suggest a possible diagnosis of social phobia.

Irrespective of the specific diagnosis, however, Edward was referred for severe school refusal. The focus of treatment with anxiety problems is identification of the specific triggering cues for the anxiety. Edward was able to identify the precursor to his anxiety without difficulty.

More daunting was aiding Edward in describing his affective response to recurrent thoughts threatening illness and loss of control. The Feeling Thermometer was instrumental in this effort. Introduced in the initial intake session, the Feeling Thermometer was readily received and used by Edward. He quickly developed an internally consistent system of calibrating his degree of affective arousal and was able to begin making the connection between events, the thoughts and beliefs inspired by them, the affect influenced by those thoughts, and the actions precipitated by the interaction of situationally driven thoughts and feelings.

Specific techniques utilized in treatment with Edward included Socratic questioning, to elicit his beliefs about the environment and Edward's ability to exercise self-control. More directive disputational interventions were used to counter the generalization of anxiety about becoming ill to situations and places where Edward had never been ill (e.g., school and on the bus, traveling to school).

Edward's positive response to the Feeling Thermomter was accounted for, in part, by his preference to describe affect in numeric, rather than in qualitative, terms. Edward was able to teach his family the use of the thermometer and helped to develop a system whereby he was able to indicate changes in his affective arousal by reporting thermometer scores. Edward found this particularly useful when outside with his parents at family gatherings, as a means of conveying emotional upset without drawing unwanted attention.

Consistent with the concerns noted in Hansen et al. (1998), many of the interventions concentrated not only on Edward's acquisition of new skills, but on the development of more adequate coping skills among his parents. Edward's parents became more skilled at objecting to his school refusal, and at finding negotiated solutions, which increased Edward's ability to attend school consistently, while decreasing the amount of familial friction engendered by Edward's school-avoidant behaviors.

More in-depth cognitive-behavioral treatment would be likely to aid Edward in developing better coping skills and disputational strategies to counter his fears of becoming ill, but the primary purpose of this intervention was to treat the crisis of school avoidance, precipitated by Edward's anxiety. As such, this case serves as a jumping off point for traditional cognitive-behavioral treatment approaches. The alleviation of the immediate crisis resided in use of the Feeling Thermometer, consideration of the developmental issues involved in Edward's presentation, and the recognition that effective crisis intervention requires the setting of goals that can be reached nearly immediately.

CONCLUSION

Effective crisis intervention with children and adolescents requires an understanding of the developmental issues that differentiate children from adults. Although many of the techniques and approaches pioneered with adult patients appear adaptable for effective use with young people, the developmental constraints on cognition, affective experience and expression, and social skills acquisition must be taken into account.

Cognitive-behavioral intervention models, given their long tradition of empirical support, data-based observation, skill building, and emphasis on teaching improved coping skills appear well suited for use with children and adolescents in crisis. Many of the techniques commonly employed in cognitive-behavioral treatment models are readily adaptable for use with younger patients. This developmental adjustment of techniques offers considerable promise for rapid, effective crisis intervention in and around schools.

REFERENCES

Ackerson, J., Scogin, F., McKendree-Smith, N., & Lyman, R. D. (1998). Cognitive bibliotherapy for mild and moderate adolescent depressive symptomatology. *Journal of Consulting and Clinical Psychology, 66*, 685–691.

Angold, A., Ekanli, A., Costello, E. J., & Rutter, M. (1996). Precision, reliability and accuracy in the dating of symptom onsets in child and adolescent psychopathology. *Journal of Child Clinical Psychology and Psychiatry, 37*, 657–664.

Beidel, D. C., Turner, S. M., & Morris, T. L. (1999). Psychopathology of childhood social phobia. *Journal of the American Academy of Child and Adolescent Psychiatry, 38*, 643–650.

Bird, H. R. (1996). Conduct disorder and oppositional defiant disorder. In *21st annual review course in child and adolescent psychiatry* (pp. 118–125). Washington, DC: American Academy of Child and Adolescent Psychiatry.

Blumenthal, S. J. (1990). An overview and synopsis of risk factors, assessment, and treatment of suicidal patients over the life cycle. In S. J. Blumenthal & D. J. Kupfer (Eds.), *Suicide over the life cycle: Risk factors, assessment and treatment of suicidal patients* (pp. 685–733). Washington, DC: American Psychiatric Press.

Bostic, J. Q., & Rauch, P. C. (1999). The 3 R's of school consultation. *Journal of the American Academy of Child and Adolescent Psychiatry, 38*, 339–341.

Brent, D. A., Poling, K., McKain, B., & Baugher, M. A. (1993). A psychoeducational program for families of affectively ill children and adolescents. *Journal of the American Academy of Child and Adolescent Psychiatry, 32*, 770–774.

Brent, D. A., Roth, C. M., Holder, D., Kolko, D. J., Birmaher, B., Johnson, B., & Schweers, J. A. (1996). Psychosocial interventions for treating adolescent suicidal depression: A comparison of three psychosocial interventions. In E. D. Hibbs & P. S. Jensen (Eds.), *Psychosocial treatments for child and adolescent disorders: Empirically based strategies for clinical practice* (pp. 187–206). Washington, DC: American Psychological Association.

Brestan, E. V., & Eyberg, S. M. (1998). Effective psychological treatments of conduct-disordered children and adolescents: 29 years, 82 studies and 5,272 kids. *Journal of Child Clinical Psychology, 27*, 180–189.

Centers for Disease Control and Prevention. (1993). Violence-related suicides and behaviors of high school students—New York City, 1992. *Morbidity and Mortality Weekly Report, 42,* 773–777.

Centers for Disease Control and Prevention. (1994). Suicide contagion and the reporting of suicide: Recommendations from a national workshop. *Morbidity and Mortality Weekly Report, 43,* 13–17.

Centers for Disease Control and Prevention. (1997). *Child suicide surveillance report: Completed child suicide in the U.S. and 25 other industrialized nations.* Atlanta: Author.

Cerel, J., Fridtal, M. S., Weller, E. B., & Weller, R. A. (1999). Suicide-bereaved children and adolescents: A controlled longitudinal examination. *Journal of the American Academy of Child and Adolescent Psychology, 38,* 672–679.

Cornell, D. M., & Loper, A. B. (1998). Assessment of violence and other high-risk behaviors with a school survey. *School Psychology Review, 27,* 317–330.

Cornell, D. M., Peterson, C. S., & Richards, H. (1999). Anger as a predictor of aggression among incarcerated adolescents. *Journal of Consulting and Clinical Psychology, 67,* 108–115.

Craig, C. Q. (1997). Do not go gentle into that good night: When a psychiatric hospital closes. *Psychiatric Services, 48,* 541–542.

Dodge, K. A. (1993). Social-cognitive mechanisms in the development of conduct disorder and depression. *Annual Review of Psychology, 44,* 559–584.

Dodge, K. A., & Newman, J. (1981). Biased decision making processes in aggressive boys. *Journal of Abnormal Child Psychology, 9,* 375–379.

Gladstein, J., Rusonis, E. S., & Heald, F. P. (1992). A comparison of inner-city upper-middle class youths' exposure to violence. *Journal of Adolescent Health, 13,* 275–280.

Gould, M. S., Wallenstein, S., Kleinman, M. H., O'Carroll, P. W., & Mercy, J. A. (1990). Suicide clusters: An examination of age-specific effects. *American Journal of Public Health, 80,* 211–212.

Hansen, C., Saunders, S. L., Massaro, S., & Last, C. G. (1998). Predictors of severity of absenteeism in children with anxiety-based school refusal. *Journal of Clinical Child Psychology, 27,* 246–254.

Jensen, P. S., & Watanabe, H. (1999). Sherlock Holmes and child psychotherapy assessment approaches: The case of the false-positive. *Journal of the American Academy of Child and Adolescent Psychiatry, 38,* 138–146.

Kandel, D. B., Johnson, J. G., Bird, M. R., Weissman, M. M., Goodman, S. H., Lashley, B. B., Regier, D. A., & Schwab-Stone, M. (1999). Psychiatric comorbidity among adolescents with substance use disorders: Findings for the MECA study. *Journal of the American Academy of Child and Adolescent Psychiatry, 38,* 693–699.

Kazdin, A. E. (1997). Practitioner review: Psychosocial treatment for conduct disorder in children. *Journal of Child Psychology and Psychiatry, 38,* 161–178.

Kearney, C. A., & Silverman, W. K. (1990). A preliminary analysis of a functional model of assessment and treatment for school refusal behavior. *Behavior Modification, 14,* 340–366.

Kearney, C. A., & Silverman, W. K. (1993). Measuring the function of school refusal behavior: The School Refusal Assessment Scale. *Journal of Clinical Child Psychology, 22,* 85–96.

Kruesi, M. J. P., Grossman, J., Pennington, J. M., Woodward, P. J., Duda, P., & Hirsch, J. P. (1999). Suicide and violence prevention: Parent education in the emergency department. *Journal of the American Academy of Child and Adolescent Psychiatry, 38,* 250–255.

Last, C. G., & Strauss, C. C. (1990). School refusal in anxiety-disordered children and adolescents. *Journal of the American Academy of Child and Adolescent Psychiatry, 29,* 31–35.

Lewinsohn, P. M., Clarke, G. N., Rohde, P., Hops, H., & Seeley, J. R. (1996). A course in coping: A cognitive-behavioral approach to the treatment of adolescent depression. In E. D. Hibbs & P. S. Jensen (Eds.), *Psychosocial treatments for child and adolescent disorders: Empirically based strategies for clinical practice* (pp. 109–135). Washington, DC: American Psychological Association.

Lewinsohn, P. M., Clarke, G. N., Seeley, J. R., & Rohde, P. (1994). Major depression in community adolescents: Age at onset, episode duration, and time to recurrence. *Journal of the American Academy of Child and Adolescent Psychiatry, 33,* 809–818.

Loeber, R., Green, S. M., Lahey, B. B., Christ, M. A. G., & Frick, P. (1992). Developmental sequences in the age of onset of disruptive child behaviors. *Journal of Child and Family Studies, 1,* 21–24.

Matthys, W., Cuperus, J. M., & Van Engeland, H. (1999). Deficient social problem-solving in boys with ODD/CD with ADHD, and with both disorders. *Journal of the American Academy of Child and Adolescent Psychiatry, 38,* 311–321.

Miller, A. (1999). Dialectical behavior therapy: A new treatment approach for suicidal adolescents. *American Journal of Psychotherapy, 53,* 396–403.

Miller, L. S., Wasserman, G. A., Neugebauer, R., Gorman-Smith, D., & Kamloukos, D. (1999). Witnessed community violence and antisocial behavior in high-risk, urban boys. *Journal of Clinical Child Psychology, 28,* 2–11.

Mufson, L., Moreau, D., Weissman, M., & Klerman, G. (1993). *Interpersonal psychotherapy for depressed adolescents.* New York: Guilford Press.

Rotheram-Borus, M. J., Piacentini, J., Miller, S., Graae, F., & Castro-Blanco, D. (1994). Brief cognitive-behavioral treatment for adolescent suicide attempters and their families. *Journal of the American Academy of Child and Adolescent Psychiatry, 33,* 508–517.

Rotheram-Borus, M. J., & Trautman, P. (1998). Hopelessness, depression and suicidal intent among adolescent suicide attempters. *Journal of the American Academy of Child and Adolescent Psychiatry, 27,* 700–704.

Schwab-Stone, M., Chen, C., Greenberger, E., Silver, D., Lichtman, J., & Voyce, C. (1999). No safe haven II: The effects of violence exposure on urban youth. *Journal of the American Academy of Child and Adolescent Psychiatry, 38,* 359–367.

Shaffer, D., Garland, A., Gould, M., Fisher, P., & Trautman, P. (1988). Preventing teenage suicide: A critical review. *Journal of the American Academy of Child and Adolescent Psychiatry, 27,* 675–687.

Spirito, A., Brown, L., Overholser, J., & Fritz, G. (1989). Attempted suicide in adolescence: A review and critique of the literature. *Clinical Psychology Review, 9,* 335–363.

Steiner, H., Cauffman, E., and Duxbury, E. (1999). Personality traits in juvenile delinquents: Relation to criminal behavior and recidivism. *Journal of the American Academy of Child and Adolescent Psychiatry, 38,* 256–262.

Strauss, C. C., & Last, C. G. (1993). Social and simple phobias in children. *Journal of Anxiety Disorders, 7,* 141–152.

Trautman, P., Stewart, N., & Morishima, A. (1993). Are adolescent suicide attempters non-compliant with outpatient care? *Journal of the American Academy of Child and Adolescent Psychiatry, 37,* 89–94.

Weiss, B., Catron, T., Harris, V., & Phung, T. M. (1999). The effectiveness of traditional psychotherapy. *Journal of Consulting and Clinical Psychology, 67,* 82–94.

Wolpe, J. (1969). *The practice of behavior therapy.* New York: Pergamon.

Woods, E. R., Yin, Y. G., Middleman, A., Beckford, P., Chase, L., & DuRant, R. M. (1997). The associations of suicide attempts in adolescents. *Pediatrics, 99,* 791–796.

SUGGESTED READINGS

Brent, D. A., Roth, C. M., Holder, D., Kolko, D. J., Birmaher, B., Johnson, B., & Schweers, J. A. (1996). Psychosocial interventions for treating adolescent suicidal depression: A comparison of three psychosocial interventions. In E. D. Hibbs & P. S. Jensen (Eds.), *Psychosocial treatments for child and adolescent disorders: Empirically based strategies for clinical practice* (pp. 187–206). Washington, DC: American Psychological Association.

Cornell, D. M., & Loper, A. B. (1998). Assessment of violence and other high-risk behaviors with a school survey. *School Psychology Review, 27,* 317–330.

Rotheram-Borus, M. J., Piacentini, J., Miller, S., Graae, F., & Castro-Blanco, D. (1994). Brief cognitive-behavioral treatment for adolescent suicide attempters and their families. *Journal of the American Academy of Child and Adolescent Psychiatry, 33,* 508–517.

12

Couples in Crisis

Norman B. Epstein
Stephen E. Schlesinger

Couple relationship problems are among the major life stresses that have been shown to be associated with psychological disorders such as depression and anxiety (Daiuto, Baucom, Epstein, & Dutton, 1998; Gotlib & Beach, 1995). Conflict between partners commonly is a chronic state characterized by repetitive behavioral patterns of aversive mutual exchanges, demand–withdraw sequences, or mutual avoidance (Christensen, 1988; Epstein, Baucom, & Rankin, 1993). However, many couples experience acute escalations of conflict and other problems that can result in a crisis state, in which the normal functioning of the couple and its members deteriorates, threatening the well-being of the partners and the stability of their relationship. Unfortunately, it is common for couples to wait until they experience severe disruption in their relationships before they seek professional help.

As will be described in this chapter, many aspects of intervention in couple relationship crises overlap significantly with those cognitive-behavioral procedures commonly used with couples who are engaged in chronic patterns of conflict. However, there are some unique aspects of a crisis state that require specific crisis intervention strategies. Consequently, it is important that clinicians who work with distressed couples be skilled in the assessment and treatment of relationship crises. Often, therapists must intervene quickly to stabilize a couple's disequilibrium before the partners will be able to focus on changing more chronic problematic conditions in their relationship. The following is a description of how crisis theory can be integrated into a cognitive-behavioral approach to the treatment of distressed couples, an outline of couple crisis assessment and intervention procedures, and a case example illustrating this approach.

FAMILY CRISIS THEORY

Hill's (1949, 1958) ABCX model has had a major impact on theoretical and empirical work concerning the development and resolution of crises in family relationships. More recent models such as the Double ABCX Model (McCubbin & Patterson, 1983), the Typology Model (McCubbin & McCubbin, 1989), and the Vulnerability–Stress–Adaptation model (Karney & Bradbury, 1995) have expanded on Hill's original conceptualization. However, the basic components of the ABCX model have remained central in understanding couple and family responses to life stresses. The ABCX model makes an important distinction between stressful life events that place pressure to adapt on members of a relationship and the crisis state of disorganization that results when the couple's or family's attempts to cope with the impinging stressors fail. The model also delineates two major types of factors that influence how well family members cope with stressors: the resources available to the family and the family members' perceptions of the stressors and their abilities to cope with them. The components in couple and family stress and coping models are consistent with psychological theories of individual coping (e.g., Lazarus & Folkman, 1984), which focus on cognitive and behavioral strategies for managing stressful life events. As described below, some forms of coping effectively reduce the impact of stressors whereas other responses are either ineffective or even exacerbate negative effects of stressors. The following is a description of the components of the ABCX family crisis model, including the stressors, the coping factors of resources and perception, and the potential resulting crisis state of disorganized functioning. We also note how recent elaborations of crisis theory address the components of resources and perception in relationship functioning.

Stressors

The "A" component of the ABCX model includes a variety of stressors that place demands on the couple or family system for change in the members' relatively stable interaction patterns, as well as in the individual members' typical response patterns. For example, at the individual level, stressors can impinge on a person's behavioral routines. Thus, Mel reported that for over 10 years he had a comfortable and fairly satisfying routine in his middle management position in an electronics firm. However, when the company reorganized and he was laid off, Mel's familiar daily patterns were disrupted, and he was faced with looking for a new job. These changes affected not only his daily behaviors but also the topics he thought about and the emotions he felt during a typical day. Furthermore, the stressor of the job loss not only influenced Mel's individual functioning, it also affected the functioning of his relationship with his wife Beverly. For example, the couple's conversations shifted from the usual sharing of daily experiences with work, family, and friends to a relatively narrow focus on the negative impacts of unemployment (e.g., worries about paying bills). Consequently, clinicians who work with distressed couples need to identify the ways in which stressors impact functioning at both the individual and dyadic levels.

Stressors are events that vary along a number of dimensions, such as (1) whether they are internal to the relationship (e.g., an individual partner's characteristic, such as substance abuse or violent behavior; a couple's negative dyadic patterns, such as chronic mutual nagging) or external (e.g., a storm that destroys the family's home); (2) the suddenness of their onset; (3) whether or not they are expected; (4) the degree of ambiguity about their onset and characteristics, (5) their severity, (6) their duration, (7) the degree to which the family members chose to be exposed to the stressor (e.g., choosing to move to another city), and (8) how many family members are affected directly (Boss, 1988; McCubbin & Patterson, 1983). The presence of a stressor may involve pressure for the members of a family to make changes in important aspects of their relationships, including their goals, roles, and established patterns of interacting with each other. Whereas some stressors (e.g., the death of a loved one) are clearly negative life events, others (e.g., moving to a new city for a job promotion and raise) are positive events that nonetheless necessitate adjustments in the family's functioning (Boss, 1988).

It is not the stressor event itself that places pressure on a couple or family and its members to adapt, but rather the "hardships" associated with the stressor (McCubbin & Patterson, 1983). For example, moving to another city for a job promotion can involve hardships such as selling one's house, finding and buying a new house, leaving friends and family, finding new doctors and other health care specialists, learning one's way around a new city, and so on. Consequently, clinical assessment requires a careful survey of the idiosyncratic hardships that each couple faces when experiencing a particular stressor.

Furthermore, although any one stressor may not tax the coping abilities of an individual or family, a series of stressors may pile up, providing a significant cumulative impact (McCubbin & McCubbin, 1989). Therefore, assessment of family stressors must include an evaluation of the range of stressors (and their associated hardships) occurring over a period of time.

Many stressors affecting family relationships are normative, in that they are parts of common, predictable developmental changes in the family and its members. Among the normative transitions frequently facing couples are marriage, childbirth and parenthood, occupational stages such as promotions and retirement, and deaths of aging family members (McCubbin & Figley, 1983; Wright, Nelson, & Georgen, 1994). However, there can be significant variations in normative stages of a couple's relationship development, based on factors such as sexual orientation, culture, race, social class, the partners' gender role beliefs, and the presence or absence of children (Carter & McGoldrick, 1999). Changes in partners' experiences of love in their intimate relationships, including inevitable shifts from the emotional "high" of initial romantic love to companionate love (deep attachment and friendly affection) also can be sources of considerable stress (Coleman, 1988).

Other stressors (e.g., sudden separation or divorce, unemployment, or death of a loved one) are nonnormative and even catastrophic, in that they occur often without warning, are threatening to individual and family well-being, and induce a sense of helplessness in family members (Figley, 1983). As described below, the degree to which family members perceive themselves to be helpless in coping with unexpected, catastrophic stressors can influence the likelihood of their entering a crisis state.

Stressors disturb the status quo or steady state of functioning in a couple or family, because they disturb the members' predictable routines and present obstacles that must be overcome. However, stressors are not necessarily negative influences (Boss, 1988). In fact, normal couple and family development involves various desirable changes, such as shifts in family roles as children become more competent and independent of their parents. Family systems theorists have described how healthy family relationships strike a balance between maintaining stability and facilitating growth within and among family members (Leslie, 1988). Therefore, the goal of crisis intervention is not to attempt to minimize stressors in people's lives, but rather to assist individuals, couples, and families in coping effectively with pressures stemming from positive and negative life events.

Resources

The ability of a couple or family to cope with stressful life events is influenced by a variety of resources (the "B" component of the ABCX model) that may be available to them as individuals and as a group. There are three major categories of resources relevant for coping with stressors: (1) the personal resources of each individual; (2) resources of the couple or family system; and (3) resources provided by the environment outside the couple or family relationships. Examples of individual resources include health, intelligence, education, problem-solving skills, job skills, finances, and psychological characteristics such as self-esteem and a sense of mastery (Boss, 1988; McCubbin & Patterson, 1983). Effective coping not only depends on the availability of resources but the manner in which individuals use their available resources. Research findings indicate that even though coping styles that involve avoiding stressors (e.g., denial, distracting oneself) may provide some short-term relief, they result in poorer long-term adaptation than do coping strategies that involve direct attention to using resources for resolving hardships associated with stressors (Suls & Fletcher, 1985).

Resources within a couple's relationship include collaborative problem-solving skills, the degree to which the relationship is characterized by cohesiveness and mutual support, effective communication skills, and adaptability in altering relationship roles and patterns in order to cope with stressors. There is considerable empirical evidence that couples in which the partners provide each other forms of support (e.g., emotional support, information, direct aid in problem solving) experience higher levels of individual well-being and relationship satisfaction (Carels & Baucom, 1999; Pasch, Bradbury, & Sullivan, 1997). Family hardiness, a shared belief that the family is strong and can actively exercise control over life events, is another relationship resource (McCubbin & McCubbin, 1989). Overall, couples can use their relationship resources either to cope directly with stressors they face, or as mechanisms for identifying and accessing resources in their environment. For example, a couple experiencing stress from a tight budget can use their problem-solving skills to brainstorm ways to reduce expenses on their own, or to seek help from community resources such as low-fee money management counselors. Environmental resources are not restricted to direct interactions with other people; they can include archival sources of information, such as books and the Internet.

Social support in a couple's environment includes a variety of resources that they may obtain from their relationships with extended family, friends, neighbors, and community organizations such as social service agencies, health care services, schools, employers, and religious institutions. A growing body of research has identified social support as a major buffer against negative effects of stress on couples and families (Belle, 1989; McCubbin & McCubbin, 1989; McKenry & Price, 1994). Among the forms of social support are emotional support, validation, assistance in problem solving, financial aid, and instrumental support with tasks and roles such as child care. Consequently, crisis intervention strategies commonly include efforts to broaden and strengthen the environmental social support networks of individuals and families who are in crisis. However, clinicians who are intervening with couples in crisis need to be aware of cultural differences in clients' openness to seeking or accepting assistance from outside sources of support. McGoldrick, Preto, Hines, and Lee (1991) describe tendencies for members of different ethnic groups to accept or resist assistance from outsiders, including mental health professionals.

Not only can a couple be at risk for inadequate coping with stressors based on an absence of appropriate resources; they also may be at risk based on the presence of *vulnerability factors*. Stress researchers (e.g., Karney & Bradbury, 1995; McCubbin & McCubbin, 1989) define vulnerabilities as relatively stable characteristics that impede individual, couple, and family adaptation to stressors. At an individual level, members of a couple may have vulnerabilities such as posttraumatic stress disorder from past personal traumas, clinical depression, personality disorders (e.g., borderline personality disorder), and neuroticism or negative emotional overreactivity. At the couple interaction level, vulnerability factors may include partners' tendencies to engage in escalating arguments or mutual avoidance. Recent empirical findings indicate how members of distressed couples often develop global negative emotion that "floods" their experiences with each other (Gottman, 1994). Because negative emotion can inflame relationship distress and become quite aversive, distressed couples commonly have difficulty remaining connected emotionally. Some couples respond to past hurts by actively withdrawing from each other, providing some measure of self-protection but interfering both with their levels of intimacy and cohesion, and with their ability to work together to cope with life stressors. Thus, the couple's way of coping with negative affect in their relationship becomes a vulnerability factor, detracting from their ability to cope with ongoing and future stressors.

Although the "B" factor in Hill's ABCX model originally focused on the presence or absence of resources that members of a relationship could use to cope with stressors, the identification of individual and couple vulnerability factors in more recent conceptualizations broadens the model in an important way. Consequently, assessment of risk factors potentially limiting a couple's coping with stressors should include both the absence of resources and the presence of vulnerabilities.

Perception and Appraisal of the Stressor

The "C" component of the ABCX model involves the family's perception or appraisal of the stressful events occurring in their lives. Boss (1988) notes that although individual family members may have disparate perceptions of a stressor, powerful shared perceptions can supersede variations in individuals' views; for example, the members of a family may share a common denial that an alcoholic member really has a serious drinking problem. Family appraisals of the stressors in their lives increasingly have become important components in models of family coping (cf. Boss, 1988; Karney & Bradbury, 1995; McCubbin & McCubbin, 1989).

A number of writers (e.g., Boss, 1988; McCubbin & McCubbin, 1989) have emphasized the implications for positive coping when family members appraise the stressors in their lives as "challenges" that can be overcome through active effort, rather than as uncontrollable events that must be accepted in a fatalistic, passive manner. Boss (1988) notes that although there are circumstances (e.g., when an individual is a prisoner of war) when it may be adaptive for individuals to adopt a passive mode of coping, passivity leads to the maintenance or exacerbation of most problems facing families. She also describes how there are systematic cultural differences in beliefs about mastery versus fatalism regarding life events that are likely to shape a family's attitudes toward problem solving.

McCubbin and McCubbin (1989) note that when family members are faced with stressors, they tend to identify and weigh the demands inherent in the stressors against their capabilities for meeting those demands. Tension and stress are experienced when it is perceived that the demands of the stressors exceed the family's resources and coping abilities, regardless of whether the perceptions of the demands and coping abilities are accurate. This view that subjective appraisals mediate individuals' responses to life stressors is highly consistent with the tenets of cognitive-behavioral therapies.

McCubbin and McCubbin (1989) differentiate between the above "situational appraisals" of stressors and coping capacities and more global "family schemas," involving the family members' views of their collective cohesiveness, shared purposes, ability to cope with life stressors, optimism for their future, and willingness to accept compromise circumstances. They propose that a family's schemas are shaped by their life experiences, but tend to become relatively stable, thus influencing subsequent situational appraisals.

In summary, subjective cognitive factors are viewed as major influences on how family members cope with stressors in their relationships. Once a couple or family has become destabilized and has entered a crisis state, their appraisals of their situation (e.g., whether they view themselves as helpless to change it) are likely to affect their efforts to adapt and reestablish equilibrium. Boss (1988) argues that in contrast to the considerable work that has been done on stressors and family resources, relatively little attention has been paid to the cognitions that are held by individual members or at times shared by whole families. However, we believe that the substantial existing body of cognitive-behavioral theoretical and empirical knowledge about individual and relationship functioning has much to offer clinicians for assessment and intervention with couples' crises.

The Crisis State

Often couples and families who are faced with the demands for change posed by life stressors are able to cope with the stressors by utilizing their resources and perceiving their potential for exercising mastery in the situation. However, when the resources and appraisals do not result in reduction of the pressure from the stressors and their associated hardships, the relationship system's organization and functioning may become destabilized. Tension resulting from the discrepancy between demands and capabilities produces a crisis state of disorganization (the "X" in the ABCX model), in which roles, typical patterns of interaction, problem solving, and other characteristics that have met the various needs of the family members become immobilized or break down (McCubbin & McCubbin, 1989). When in a crisis state, the individual members of the family are likely to experience a variety of cognitive, affective, physiological, and behavioral symptoms that represent notable departures from their typical functioning (Greenstone & Leviton, 1993). Their cognitive functioning is likely to be impaired by indecisiveness, confusion, and a sense of helplessness. Common emotional symptoms of a crisis state are anxiety, irritability, and depression. Among the physiological symptoms commonly experienced are insomnia, decreased appetite, gastrointestinal disturbances, and headaches. Disorganized behavioral responses include unclear communication, disrupted daily routines, general social withdrawal, and clinging to others for help. In addition to the symptoms experienced by individual members, a crisis state also tends to affect the interpersonal patterns within a couple or family. Thus, a couple's typical patterns of role enactment, communication, and problem solving tend to deteriorate, and their interactions become more characterized by aversive behavior exchanges and/or withdrawal. This state of disorganization at the individual and relationship levels necessitates changes in the couple or family (e.g., changes in roles, development of new resources) in order to restore stability: A crisis state can provide an opportunity for growth in the couple or family and the achievement of a higher level of functioning. However, a crisis also can lead to a dysfunctional outcome in which the functioning of the relationship or its individual members deteriorates (e.g., depression, physical abuse, chronic alienation between partners). Consequently, family crisis intervention focuses on maximizing constructive adaptation through active intervention with family resources and appraisals.

COGNITIVE–BEHAVIORAL COUPLE THERAPY AND THE ABCX MODEL

The ABCX model of stress and coping in couple and family relationships is a useful framework for guiding cognitive-behavioral assessment and intervention with couples in crisis. Although cognitive-behavioral couple therapy (Baucom & Epstein, 1990; Dattilio, Epstein, & Baucom, 1998; Epstein & Baucom, 1989; Epstein, Baucom, & Daiuto, 1997; Schlesinger & Epstein, 1986) commonly is used with couples who have experienced chronic marital conflict and distress, its goals and procedures are well suited for addressing relationship factors that contribute to the disorganized functioning of a crisis state. The following is a description of cognitive-behavioral interventions that can alter the types and intensity of relationship stressors, a couple's utilization of their resources for coping with stressors, and the partners' appraisals of the stressors or crisis state.

Cognitive–Behavioral Interventions for Reducing Relationship Stressors

Among the major stressors commonly contributing to couples' distress are (1) environmental stressors external to the couple's relationship, which place demands on the functioning of the dyad and its two members; (2) stressful aspects of the partners' own interactions with each other; and (3) characteristics of the individual partners. As described earlier, external environmental stressors may include normative events (e.g., birth of a child, job problems) or unexpected nonnormative events (e.g., unemployment, injury, illness). Common stressors in couple interaction include aversive verbal communication (e.g., criticism, escalating exchanges of insults, threats of divorce), behavioral withdrawal, and physical abuse. These interpersonal patterns may have preexisted any external stressors the couple has experienced, or may have developed as dysfunctional responses to particular stressors. For example, a couple may have always relied on criticism and other forms of aversive control to try to influence each other, or they may have developed aversive exchanges in response to conflicts with in-laws. Stressors involving the personal characteristics of the individual partners can include personality traits (e.g., an insecure attachment style, a high level of competitive motivation), temperament (e.g., a generally high activity level), and psychopathology (e.g., depression, anxiety disorders).

When a couple is faced with stressors that either have the potential to overwhelm their coping abilities or actually have produced a crisis state, crisis intervention procedures tend to be focused on reducing the couple's vulnerability factors as much as possible, strengthening their resources, and increasing their adaptive appraisals of the stressors (e.g., mastery cognitions). Because couples who seek help for crises in their relationships commonly present with negative behavioral patterns, either chronic or developed in response to other stressors, crisis intervention work typically begins with a focus on decreasing those stressful behavioral patterns. Cognitive-behavioral couple therapy includes a variety of procedures for accomplishing this goal.

Initially, the clinician conducts an assessment of the couple's presenting problems, their level of distress, and the partners' levels of commitment to working on the problems in therapy. Cognitive-behavioral crisis intervention assessment is similar to traditional cognitive-behavioral assessment of couples (Baucom & Epstein, 1990), in that the clinician places the presenting problems in context by interviewing the couple jointly about the history of their relationship. In particular, attention is paid to the timeline of when various stressors occurred and how the couple coped with them. This assessment identifies a possible pile-up of stressors, as well as the couple's use of available resources. The joint interview also can be used to identify vulnerability factors in the dyad (e.g., vague communication) and the individual partners (e.g., depression). Based on the partners' reports and on observation of the couple's interactions during the interview, the clinician can identify any of the couple's behavioral patterns that need immediate attention to ameliorate the crisis state. Consistent with general crisis intervention practices (e.g., Greenstone & Leviton, 1993), the initial assessment session concludes with the clinician giving the couple feedback to help them understand the disconcerting crisis state they are experiencing and initiating some behavioral changes to produce some quick relief. The feedback includes a summary of the information the clinician collected about the factors in the ABCX model (stressors, resources, vulnerabilities, perceptions) that seem to have contributed to the crisis state. Providing this kind of conceptualization can be reassuring to clients and decrease their sense of helplessness about their problems; such feedback commonly is used in cognitive therapy (e.g., Beck, Rush, Shaw, & Emery, 1979). The following three behavioral interventions can be used to engage the partners in treatment and produce some quick relief from the stressors involved in the couple's aversive behavioral patterns. The goal of these interventions is to focus each partner's attention on the benefits that he or she can accrue if the existing interaction pattern is changed.

Collaborative Agreements

One approach focuses on *engaging a couple in collaborative agreements to reduce their ratio of aversive to pleasant behavioral interactions.* Each partner is asked to report the occurrence of specific positive, neutral, and negative partner behaviors. Although partners could be asked to keep detailed logs of such behaviors, using an instrument such as the Spouse Observation Checklist (SOC; Weiss & Perry, 1983), extensive logs may be too cumbersome and stressful themselves for people in the midst of a crisis state. Consequently, the therapist can identify major aversive behavioral patterns through interviews and direct observations of the couple, as described above. The therapist then collaborates with the couple in devising an agreement for each partner to take some responsibility to increase positive behaviors and decrease negative behaviors involved in the aversive pattern during the next week. The therapist can coach the couple in devising a behavioral contract, in which each spouse explicitly agrees to make specific behavior changes that the other person has requested. Detailed guidelines for constructing different forms of behavioral contracts (quid pro quo, good faith, and holistic) are presented by Baucom and Epstein (1990), Jacobson and Margolin (1979), and Stuart (1980).

For a couple whose negative exchanges are taxing their coping abilities, shifts in frequencies of positive and negative behavior can produce a notable reduction in experienced stress. However, in order to motivate highly distressed couples to make such behavioral changes, it often is necessary for the therapist to provide them a convincing rationale. Especially when spouses are angry with each other, it is important to discuss with them how their present reciprocation of negative behavior is maintaining their high level of stress. The therapist also might coach each spouse in listing the advantages and disadvantages of venting anger toward the partner, with the goal of demonstrating that the costs of such behavior (e.g., eliciting defensiveness and retaliation from the partner) are significant, relative to the rewards (e.g., temporarily gaining compliance from the partner; Neidig & Friedman, 1984).

Communication Training

A second procedure for reducing stress by increasing the percentage of pleasant versus stressful interaction between spouses is to use a variety of forms of *communication training to substitute constructive messages for stressful, aversive ones.* In general, spouses are taught to identify and reduce specific forms of negative messages (e.g., interruptions, fault-finding, focusing on the past), and to replace those with alternatives such as positive requests for behavior change (e.g., "I would appreciate it if you would work on the budget as we had discussed last month."). Neidig and Friedman (1984) help sensitize spouses to various negative forms of communication by providing them with a "Dirty Fighting Techniques Handout," which lists 27 common problematic behaviors (e.g., cross-complaining, blaming) and describes how these exacerbate conflict and distress. Cognitive-behavioral therapists typically give couples specific instructions for communicating more positively, both verbally and nonverbally (cf., Baucom & Epstein, 1990; Bornstein & Bornstein, 1986; Jacobson & Margolin, 1979; Miller, Miller, Nunnally, & Wachman, 1991; Neidig & Friedman, 1984). The instructions may be through verbal descriptions, written materials, videotape examples, or modeling by the therapist. Some of the more common guidelines for sending constructive messages are (1) using "I" statements, (2) expressing thoughts and emotions clearly and specifically, (3) communicating empathy for the partner's position, (4) acknowledging the subjectivity of one's own thoughts and emotions, (5) acknowledging any positives in the situation, and (6) using nonverbal behaviors (e.g., eye contact, facial expressions, gestures) that convey interest and openness. As is described below, these forms of communication also are important for building a couple's resources for coping with stress, but in themselves the behaviors reduce the stressors exchanged during a couple's daily interactions. Training in expressive and listening skills (Baucom & Epstein, 1990; Markman, Stanley, & Blumberg, 1994) accomplishes the dual stress-reducing goals of helping couples focus and pace their communication better and short-circuiting the cycle of reciprocal defensiveness that venting often creates.

Schedule Leisure Activities

The third type of behavioral intervention to modify a couple's distressing interaction pattern is to have them *schedule leisure activities together* (Baucom & Epstein, 1990). Distressed couples often have avoided spending time together, anticipating that shared time will lead to unpleasant interactions. Thus, it is important that the therapist coach them in thinking of activities that both people are likely to enjoy and in structuring the time with ground rules for controlling aversive behavior (e.g., an explicit agreement to focus on the pleasurable activity and to avoid talking about their relationship).

Cognitive–Behavioral Interventions for Building Stress–Buffering Resources

Whether the stressors impinging on a couple originate inside their relationship or outside, a crisis state of disorganization can be prevented or managed to the degree that the couple has a variety of effective stress-buffering resources. Communication and problem-solving skills are among the most important resources that can be strengthened through cognitive-behavioral interventions.

First, the ability of a couple to work together collaboratively to identify and resolve sources of stress in their lives depends on their capacity to exchange information effectively. Some couples communicate in imprecise and confusing ways, resulting in misunderstandings and undesired actions. A couple can be helped to improve and use their expressive and listening skills as a relationship resource through educational, behaviorally oriented procedures that involve specific instructions, modeling of effective behavior, and extensive rehearsal of new skills by the couple (Baucom & Epstein, 1990). The most widely used guidelines and procedures for teaching couples expressive and listening skills are those developed by Guerney (1977). Spouses are instructed in taking turns operating in the modes of expresser and empathic listener. As the expresser, the individual is to follow guidelines such as stating views as subjective, making brief and specific statements, and communicating empathy for the partner's feelings and how one's statements may affect him or her. In the mode of empathic listener, the individual is to focus on verbally and nonverbally communicating attention to the expresser's messages, taking the expresser's perspective and empathizing with his or her thoughts and feelings, and reflecting back (i.e., summarizing and restating) the expresser's thoughts and feelings). In order to practice effective empathic listening, one must avoid various distracting and intrusive behaviors such as expressing one's own opinions and offering solutions (cf., Baucom & Epstein, 1990; Guerney, 1977). Similar programs for enhancing expressive and listening skills have been developed by Markman, Stanley, and Blumberg (1994) and Miller et al. (1991).

Another form of communication training that can assist couples in working collaboratively rather than as distressed adversaries is assertiveness training (Alberti & Emmons, 1986; Epstein, 1981; Neidig & Friedman, 1984). Spouses are assisted in differentiating among assertive, aggressive (including passive aggressive), and submissive forms of behavior and are coached as they rehearse more assertive behavior in their couple interactions. Assertive behaviors include making direct but noncoercive requests of a partner, refusing a partner's request in a nonaggressive manner, and both giving and receiving direct positive messages (e.g., compliments). As a resource for coping with stressors affecting the couple's relationship, assertiveness skills provide the spouses with an important component of constructive negotiation and problem solving, rather than escalation of conflict and hostility. Whereas assertively stating preferences does not necessarily lead to agreement on a solution to a relationship problem, the relative absence of coercive aggression is likely to add to a collaborative atmosphere that may instill some hope in the spouses that they can work together to manage stressors.

Training in problem-solving skills can provide another important resource for couples who are faced with life stressors. Whereas expressiveness and listening skills allow spouses to exchange information about their thoughts and emotions concerning their personal experiences, problem-solving is a specific kind of communication in which spouses are most effective when they take a cognitive approach to identifying workable solutions to issues. In fact, cognitive-behavioral marital therapists coach couples in telling each other when each prefers to communicate for the purpose of expressing feelings versus when he/she wants to work on solving a specific problem (Baucom & Epstein, 1990).

When partners have agreed to engage in problem solving, there is a common set of steps that they are taught to follow: (1) define the problem in specific behavioral terms, (2) generate a set of possible solutions, (3) evaluate the advantages and disadvantages of each solution and then select a feasible solution, and (4) implement the chosen solution and evaluate its effectiveness. For detailed descriptions of problem-solving steps, with some variations in how the steps are broken down, see Baucom and Epstein (1990), Bornstein and Bornstein (1986), and Jacobson and Margolin (1979), as well as the case example in this chapter. It is important that partners avoid blaming each other for the problem or sidetracking from one problem to another (Baucom & Epstein, 1990).

It is common for distressed partners who use good problem-solving skills in other settings (e.g., at work) to fail to use them as a resource for reducing stressors in their home life. Consequently, even though some couples may have a deficit in their *use* of skills rather than in their repertoire of skills per se, coaching couples in problem-solving steps usually is a productive approach to helping them manage stressors in an active manner. When a therapist observes that partners appear to have good problem-solving skills but choose not to use them with each other, the therapist must identify and address such sources of noncompliance (e.g., refusal to act positively toward a partner who behaved in a hurtful manner in the past). Intervening with instances of noncompliance typically involves assessment and modification of cognitive factors, which are discussed below.

Couples can be coached in using the expressive, listening, and problem-solving communication skills described above as resources for addressing stressors in their external environment, within their couple interactions, and resulting from the characteristics of the individual partners. For example, a couple faced with pressures from competing demands of their work and family roles can problem-solve ways to share chores at home and set aside some leisure time together. Similarly, a couple who has stressful arguments over their different preferences for leisure activities can problem-solve about equitable decisions for their shared time. And, a couple in which one member experiences debilitating symptoms of depression can problem-solve ways that the nondepressed partner can behave most helpfully toward the depressed person.

Finally, many couples who are experiencing a pile-up of life stressors benefit from assistance with time and resource management skills. Therapists may coach a couple in listing and prioritizing tasks that demand their attention and energy, scheduling blocks of time to be devoted to one task at a time. The couple also may be assisted in dividing tasks, achieving a distribution of responsibilities that is acceptable to both parties. Of course, for some couples perceived inequities in responsibilities are major sources of distress and conflict, and the resolution of such differences may require problem-solving and cognitive interventions addressing the partners' gender role beliefs.

In addition to these generic cognitive-behavioral approaches to the enhancement of couples' resources, clinicians can use cognitive-behavioral interventions from programs that have been developed for particular problems that commonly produce relationship crises. For example, there is excellent clinical literature on couple therapies for alcohol abuse (McCrady & Epstein, 1995; O'Farrell & Rotunda, 1997), domestic violence (Heyman & Neidig, 1997; Holtzworth-Munroe, Beatty, & Anglin, 1995; Neidig & Friedman, 1984), and marital infidelity (Glass & Wright, 1997; Spring, 1996).

Cognitive–Behavioral Interventions for Addressing Cognitive Appraisals of Relationship Stressors

As noted earlier, the "C" component of the ABCX family crisis model involves cognitive processing of life stressors. A cognitive-behavioral approach to couple and family relationships provides a variety of assessment and intervention procedures for addressing the cognitive factors that can produce or exacerbate stress. The following discussion considers the relevance for crisis intervention of five major types of cognition that have been implicated in marital conflict and distress: selective perception, attributions, expectancies, assumptions, and standards (Baucom & Epstein, 1990; Epstein & Baucom, 1993).

Selective perception (labeled *selective abstraction* by Beck, Rush, Shaw, & Emery, 1979) involves biases in which aspects of couple interaction each partner notices. There is considerable empirical evidence (cf., Epstein & Baucom, 1993) that distressed partners have low rates of agreement about the occurrence of even concrete behaviors during a 24-hour period. Likewise, couple therapists (e.g., Jacobson & Margolin, 1979) have described how distressed couples commonly exhibit *negative tracking,* in which they notice negatives and overlook positives occurring in their relationships. Furthermore, distressed partners commonly perceive linear causality in their interactions (e.g., "I withdraw from him because he nags and pursues me"), rather than circular processes of mutual influence (Baucom & Epstein, 1990). The presence and practice of these processes expose couples to what Gottman (1994) has termed the "Four Horsemen of the Apocalypse" in marriage. This "cascade" or sequence of behaviors—criticism, contempt, defensiveness, and withdrawal—is mutually reinforcing for the two parties and places the couple on a course toward dissolving their relationship.

In order to broaden partners' perceptions of relationship events, cognitive-behavioral couple therapists use a variety of interventions, such as (1) having each person keep logs of daily positive and negative partner behaviors with the Spouse Observation Checklist, (2) drawing the couple's attention to behavioral sequences and circular causality in their interactions, through verbal feedback and videotape playback of interactions during therapy sessions, and (3) teaching partners specific behavioral skills to reduce and counteract the effects of negative "cascades" such as those identified by Gottman (1994). The goals of these interventions are to reduce the sense of hopelessness that often results from perceiving consistent negatives in one's relationship and to reduce the blaming involved in linear explanations of events.

A considerable body of research has indicated that members of distressed couples are more likely than members of nondistressed couples to attribute negative partner behaviors to stable, global traits and negative intent, and to view the behaviors as blameworthy (cf., Baucom & Epstein, 1990; Bradbury & Fincham, 1990). In contrast, members of distressed couples tend to discount positive partner behaviors as due to specific, unstable causes (i.e., factors on which one cannot rely). Furthermore, negative *attributions* have been found to predict subsequent negative partner interaction during problem-solving discussions (e.g., Fincham & Bradbury, 1988). To the extent that partners' attributions contribute to distress (anger, depression, anxiety) and conflict behavior or helplessness responses, they are likely to exacerbate the level of stress and lead to a crisis state. Consequently, it is important for couple therapists to assist partners in examining the validity of their attributions, differentiating between accurate ones that may call for specific behavior change efforts and those that are distorted. Approaches to testing one's attributions include (1) counteracting a trait attribution by identifying any past situations in which a partner behaved differently, (2) altering an attribution of negative partner intent by obtaining direct feedback from the partner about his/her intentions, and (3) coaching an individual in generating and evaluating the plausibility of alternative attributions concerning causes of an upsetting partner behavior (Baucom & Epstein, 1990). When the evidence suggests that an attribution is accurate (e.g., when a partner indeed intended to inflict hurt through sarcastic remarks), the therapist may shift the focus to behavioral interventions such as training the partner in more constructive ways of communicating anger.

Expectancies are the predictions that individuals make about the probabilities that particular events will occur in the future, under particular conditions. Whether accurate or inaccurate, these inferences are likely to influence the individual's emotional and behavioral responses. For example, an individual who anticipates verbal attacks from a partner whenever he or she expresses disagreement with the partner (even when the partner would not have behaved in that manner) may experience anxiety at the thought of disagreeing and then avoid direct communication. Other individuals engage in "preemptive attacks" in order to protect themselves from anticipated aggression from their partners. In terms of the cognitive factors in the ABCX crisis model, negative expectancies can exacerbate stress, because the anticipated stressors can be equally or even more distressing than actual relationship events (similar to negative expectancies in anxiety disorders). Consequently, it is important for the couple therapist to assess each person's expectancies about negative events affecting the couple, including external environmental stressors (e.g., an anticipated job loss), stressors in the couple's interactions (e.g., anticipated couple arguments marked by aversive exchanges), and stressors associated with an individual's characteristics (e.g., a partner's anticipated panic attacks when away from home). Then the couple can be coached in examining the evidence for the predictions, using past experiences in similar situations, considering different kinds of outcomes that have occurred or might occur, and exploring specific actions that the partners could take in order to produce a different outcome (e.g., using new communication skills to discuss disagreements).

Assumptions and *standards* are two forms of cognitive schemata or relatively stable internal representations that an individual has for categorizing things and events, as well as for understanding relationships among them (Seiler, 1984). Cognitive theorists propose that these schemata are formed through an individual's life experiences, including exposure to family relationships as a child. In terms of couples' relationship cognitions, assumptions are beliefs about human nature and the way two people relate to each other in an intimate relationship (e.g., whether partners are able to change a relationship once they have established particular interaction patterns), and standards are beliefs about the characteristics that intimate partners and their relationships "should" have (Baucom & Epstein, 1990). There is evidence that when partners hold extreme assumptions and standards (Epstein & Eidelson, 1981; Eidelson & Epstein, 1982), or when they report that their standards are not met to their satisfaction within their relationship (Baucom, Epstein, Rankin, & Burnett, 1996), they experience greater relationship distress. Couples' assumptions and standards also have been found to be associated with the quality of their current communication and with future marital dissolution (e.g., Bradbury & Fincham, 1993; Gordon, Baucom, Epstein, Burnett, & Rankin, 1999; Kurdek, 1993).

As noted by Boss (1988), family members who accept stressors as uncontrollable (an assumption) are more likely to take a passive approach to coping with their stressors, and McCubbin and McCubbin (1989) have described a number of relatively stable "family schemas" that influence appraisals of specific relationship events. Therefore, the cognitive-behavioral approaches for modifying distressed partners' extreme or unrealistic assumptions and standards are highly relevant for addressing the "C" (perception, appraisal) component of the ABCX model.

Members of a couple can be assisted in exploring how their assumptions and standards were shaped by their life experiences, and they can examine whether such schemata that were realistic or appropriate earlier in their lives "fit" their present relationship circumstances. They also can be coached in identifying the advantages and disadvantages of applying their standards to their current relationship. For example, an individual who grew up in a verbally abusive family and now believes that partners should not express anger toward each other may decide that the disadvantages of this standard (e.g., disappointments and disagreements are not resolved) outweigh its advantages (e.g., daily life is tranquil; Epstein, Baucom, & Rankin, 1993). Therapists can help couples "rewrite" extreme standards and assumptions, devising more moderate views that are still consistent with each person's basic values (see Baucom & Epstein, 1990, for a more detailed description of intervention procedures). Then therapists can help partners devise experiments in which they try living according to the revised standards and assumptions. Thus, the negative impact of life stressors on a couple's relationship can be reduced by modifying the partners' assumptions and standards that are antithetical to effective problem-solving or that themselves produce stress when the couple's relationship fails to match these internalized frames of reference.

Given that relationship distress is associated with the degree to which individuals are satisfied with how their standards are being met in their relationships (Baucom et al., 1996), another relevant cognitive-behavioral intervention is coaching a couple in using problem-solving skills to find better ways to meet both person's standards. The use of problem-solving skills to maximize mutual satisfaction with relationship standards addresses the "B" or resource component of the ABCX crisis model.

An additional cognitive factor that sometimes contributes to a couple's conflict and stress involves differences in the idiosyncratic definitions that two partners attach to particular words and phrases that they use in their conversations. For example, in saying "We have to get *tougher* with Jane," one member of a couple may mean being *more consistent* in enforcing rules about their daughter Jane's behavior around the house, whereas the person's spouse may define "tougher" as meaning applying *more severe punishment*. Consequently, it is important to assist couples in using the resource of their communication skills for clarifying meanings of the words that they use, especially when they attach upsetting definitions to those words.

CASE STUDY

John and Mary had experienced chronic stress in their relationship due to conflicts about appropriate methods of disciplining their adolescent son, Jimmy, an only child. For some time, Jimmy had exhibited a high level of disobedient and defiant behavior at home. John and Mary were both upset about the degree to which Jimmy's behavior was disruptive of their family life and their marriage. Disagreements between John and Mary had escalated over time and focused on their different styles of discipline when Jimmy acted out. These disagreements had led to arguments of escalating intensity and duration, which failed to resolve the spouses' differences or their exasperation. By the time they reached the therapist's office, they had developed a sense of helplessness and hopelessness about Jimmy's behavior, its impact on the family, and most significantly, about their ability to work together as parents. As a result, in their desperation each had threatened the other with divorce.

Initial interviewing of the couple revealed that Jimmy's behavior was variable. He misbehaved regularly at home, but not at school, at friends' homes, or when he was at after-school and weekend activities (e.g., sports, clubs). This situation-specificity suggested that it was unlikely that Jimmy's behavior problem at home was the result of an involuntary dispositional characteristic such as temperament, and it focused the therapist's attention both on John and Mary's interactions with Jimmy and on their interactions as a couple. The therapist decided to conduct a more thorough assessment of couple and family interactions, based on assumptions that (1) John and Mary were using ineffective parenting strategies, contributing to Jimmy's negative behavior at home, (2) conflict between John and Mary likely impeded their ability to work as a parenting team in applying consistent behavior management strategies with their son, and (3) marital conflict may elicit Johnny's behavior. The assessment also was guided by the ABCX crisis model, focusing on stresses in the couple's life, their resources and vulnerabilities, and their perceptions of the situation.

A joint interview with John and Mary revealed that the earlier years in their relationship had been much more positive, with many enjoyable shared activities. When Jimmy was born, the couple decided that Mary would quit her job in order to be home full time with him. Both spouses told the therapist that they still believe that was the best decision, but the loss of Mary's income created some finiancial stress for them over the years. They also reported that Jimmy had been diagnosed with asthma at age 5, and his illness had resulted in stress for them from lost sleep, repeated visits to hospital emergency rooms, and frequent worry about his well-being. Currently, the medical management of Jimmy's asthma was effective, and he administered his own medication independently. Nevertheless, John and Mary reported that in past years there had been frequent aversive exchanges (e.g., yelling) between the two of them, and with Jimmy, when Jimmy was experiencing severe asthma symptoms. Other stressors reported by the couple included much increased work demands at John's job and Mary's mother being diagnosed with Alzheimer's disease. While John was spending more time at the office and working on projects late at night, Mary was increasingly spending time at her parent's nearby home, caring for her mother. Both spouses felt exhausted and easily irritated. The couple reported a steady decline in their time together, as well as in their family time with Jimmy. As Jimmy began to exhibit negative behavior, each busy parent tended to intervene on a "catch as catch can" basis, without consulting with the other parent. They often viewed each other as "working at cross purposes," interfering with each other's attempts to discipline Jimmy.

The therapist discussed the pile-up of stressors in the couple's relationship with them, and they agreed that their ability to parent effectively was impaired by the number of competing demands on each of them. Because their aversive exchanges had become an additional stressor, the therapist initially coached them in using communication skills for reducing exchanges of aversive messages and increasing positive expressive and listening skills. In order to reduce the aversive interactions that had come to dominate their time together and to begin to reverse the deterioration in their intimacy as a couple, the therapist also coached John and Mary in identifying and scheduling some shared pleasant activities (e.g., bowling, taking walks together, socializing with friends), when they would avoid any discussion of their son. It was crucial that the couple separate such positive bonding activities from efforts to solve their parenting problems. The therapist also helped the couple use their problem-solving skills to devise feasible ways to find some leisure time in the midst of the other significant demands on their time. The therapist also determined that the very high standards that both spouses held for performance of their work, parenting and other roles served as a vulnerability factor in their coping with the demands of multiple stressors. Consequently, the therapist used cognitive restructuring techniques to challenge the spouses' perfectionistic standards and help them experiment with living according to more realistic standards for their role performance.

The therapist continued to coach the spouses in constructive expressive and listening skills, so that they would each feel validated in their efforts to discipline their child. Subsequently, they were coached in using problem-solving skills for resolving parenting conflicts, as will be described in more detail later. The therapist also attended to the cognitive factors that impeded collaborative problem solving, such as John's expectancy that Mary would criticize any of his ideas, or Mary's standard that one way of disciplining is "right" while the other way is "wrong." Another intervention that built the couple's resources for managing their son's behavior was expanding their social support network. For example, they were encouraged to join a parenting support group at their church, and to enlist the help of extended family members (Jimmy's paternal grandparents, aunt, and two uncles) in implementing behavioral contracts with their son.

Cognitive restructuring, addressing the "C" component of the ABCX model, also addressed a variety of cognitive factors influencing the couple's responses to their son and their own conflict about him. The spouses' descriptions of selective perceptions of their interactions (e.g., "He *never* supports me when I tell Jimmy to follow my instructions") led the therapist to collect information from both spouses concerning any exceptions to this description of the husband's behavior. John contributed a number of recollections about explicit attempts to support Mary (e.g., "If that's what Mom asked you to do, Jimmy, you need to do it"). Mary recalled several times when John supported her and then talked about the overwhelming frustration they both felt at home.

The spouses had made attributions that Jimmy's behavior problems were caused by inadequacies in themselves as parents, and they tended to blame each other for the problems. They also tended to attribute Jimmy's disobedience to his having a stable personality trait of "aggressiveness." The therapist coached them in considering more benign explanations. For example, they considered evidence that Jimmy had long tended to need considerable structure in order to stay focused on tasks, and that, in spite of their own good intentions, they had disagreed so often about discipline that they had not provided the degree of structure that he tended to respond to favorably at school. Because they also had attributed Jimmy's misbehavior to a global, stable personality trait, the therapist helped them see the contrast between his behavior at home and at school, where there was more imposed structure. They were able to see that he did not behave in an aggressive manner in settings outside their home.

When the couple expressed their frustration about their attempts to deal with Jimmy ("We have tried everything. Nothing will work."), the therapist focused their attention on counteracting this negative expectancy. The therapist inquired about how and for how long they attempted each discipline technique. It became clear that the spouses typically disagreed about their plans, so they were inconsistent with their efforts and gave up when their son failed to change quickly and to behave more positively. Their inconsistency was exacerbated by their busy schedules, and a discussion of this pattern during a therapy session resulted in their joint decision to set aside time each day to "check in" with each other about their childrearing efforts.

Additionally, the therapist addressed the couple's ideas about how changes in Jimmy might occur in response to the consistency of their new efforts. Their expectancies had been that Jimmy's change would occur shortly after they let him know what they expected from him. They were introduced to the diagram that appears in Figure 12.1. "A" represents the degree of Jimmy's objectional behavior at the time when the couple begins a consistently applied approach. They were instructed that Jimmy's misbehavior likely would *increase* at first, and that some parents find this demoralizing. It was emphasized to them that when the behavior increases to point B, parents may conclude that their efforts are not working, as they predict that the rate of misbehavior is increasing unrelentingly. However, the therapist also stressed how the rate of misbehavior was likely to peak at point C and then decrease over time as long as the parents remained consistent in their approach. Use of this educational intervention was intended to "immunize" John and Mary against negative interpretations of initial increases in Jimmy's negative behavior as they implemented their new behavior change program.

As noted above, problem-solving procedures were introduced to assist the couple in devising and carrying out a plan consistently. Specifying the behavioral pattern that the spouses had experienced as a major stressor was a prerequisite for devising new solutions to the parenting problem. The first problem-solving step involved stating the nature of the problem in clear, specific, behavioral terms, rather than global descriptions. John and Mary defined their problem as Jimmy's disobedience when either parent gave him direct instructions (e.g., to clean his room, to do his homework, to limit phone calls with friends to a half-hour). The second step was to "brainstorm" possible solutions to the problem that was identified (e.g., trying to reason with Jimmy about his

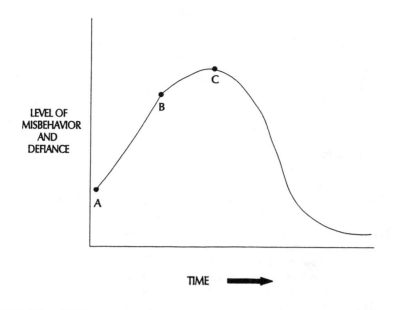

FIGURE 12.1. Child's rate of misbehavior over time as parents implement a consistent behavior management program.

misbehavior; using punishment such as grounding and taking away various privileges; setting up a positive behavioral goal and reward system; spending more positive leisure time with Jimmy). The basic goal in brainstorming is the generation of as many possible solutions without evaluating and censoring any ideas at this point. The therapist coached each spouse in expressing all ideas that occurred to him/her and in refraining from commenting on the partner's solutions. It was stressed that creativity is enhanced when the partners are not inhibited by concerns about each other's evaluations. As in the problem-definition step, solutions needed to be stated in specific behavioral terms, noting who is to do what.

Once a set of possible solutions had been identified, the next step was to evaluate each solution on the list for its costs and benefits. John and Mary were encouraged not to adopt a solution unless it was feasible and acceptable to both of them (Baucom & Epstein, 1990). The therapist coached them in discussing any reservations that they may have about a solution before they decided to try it. The solution that they agreed to implement could be a single one from their list or a composite of two or more solutions.

Finally, the couple's task was to implement the chosen solution at home and to monitor its impact on the problem. They agreed that their response to any new form of misbehavior would be to meet jointly with Jimmy to discuss their expectations for his behavior. If the same behavior occurred again, Mom and Dad would confer with each other privately, decide upon an appropriate consequence, and then meet with Jimmy to announce its implementation. During the next session with the therapist, the spouses reported on their actions. On different occasions, one or the other parent had failed to carry out the planned solution, and the therapist explored sources of noncompliance (e.g., he/she had failed to express ambivalence about the plan to each other and the therapist). Subsequently, the couple successfully implemented the solution, but it did not have the desired effect of reducing Jimmy's negative behavior. The therapist reviewed with the couple the "progress" graph, encouraging them to be patient and consistent when their son at least initially resisted change. In a later session, the therapist assisted John and Mary in modifying the plans for their solution for the following week.

Differences in the spouses' standards for appropriate child behavior were an additional source of conflict and stress. Furthermore, the spouses had different assumptions about the impact of different discipline techniques on children's mental health and development generally (e.g., that withdrawing privileges and thereby upsetting a child harms the child's self-esteem). The therapist helped the couple explore such assumptions and standards through discussions and educational "mini-lectures" on child development, as well as by giving them readings on parenting.

Thus, the goals of a cognitive-behavioral approach to crisis intervention with couples are to (1) reduce the number and intensity of stressors impinging on the couple's coping capacities, including stressors associated with the couple's own negative ways of interacting with each other, (2) broaden and strengthen their resources for coping with stressors arising both outside their relationship and in their own interactions, and (3) modify extreme or distorted cognitions (or discrepancies in partners' cognitions) that exacerbate the impact of stressors or impede the couple's use of stress-managing resources. The active, structured characteristics of cognitive-behavioral couple therapy are well suited to intervening when these factors threaten to destabilize a couple's relationship, and for helping couples already in crisis to regain stability.

REFERENCES

Alberti, R. E., & Emmons, M. L. (1986). *Your perfect right: A guide to assertive living* (5th ed.). San Luis Obispo, CA: Impact.

Baucom, D. H., & Epstein, N. (1990). *Cognitive-behavioral marital therapy.* New York: Brunner/Mazel.

Baucom, D. H., Epstein, N., Rankin, L. A., & Burnett, C. K. (1996). Assessing relationship standards: The Inventory of Specific Relationship Standards. *Journal of Family Psychology, 10,* 72–88.

Beck, A. T., Rush, A. J., Shaw, B. F., & Emery, G. (1979). *Cognitive therapy of depression.* New York: Guilford Press.

Belle, D. (Ed.). (1989). *Children's social networks and social support.* New York: Wiley.

Bornstein, P. H., & Bornstein, M. T. (1986). *Marital therapy: A behavioral-communications approach.* New York: Pergamon Press.

Boss, P. (1988). *Family stress management.* Newbury Park, CA: Sage.

Bradbury, T. N., & Fincham, F. D. (1990). Attributions in marriage: Review and critique. *Psychological Bulletin, 107,* 3–33.

Bradbury, T. N., & Fincham, F. D. (1993). Assessing dysfunctional cognition in marriage: A reconsideration of the Relationship Belief Inventory. *Psychological Assessment, 5,* 92–101.

Carels, R. A., & Baucom, D. H. (1999). Support in marriage: Factors associated with on-line perceptions of support helpfulness. *Journal of Family Psychology, 13,* 131–144.

Carter, B., & McGoldrick, M. (Eds.). (1999). *The expanded family life cycle: Individual, family, and social perspectives.* Boston: Allyn & Bacon.

Christensen, A. (1988). Dysfunctional interaction patterns in couples. In P. Noller & M. A. Fitzpatrick (Eds.), *Perspectives on marital interaction* (pp. 31–52). Clevedon, UK: Multilingual Matters.

Coleman, J. C. (1988). *Intimate relationships, marriage, and family* (2nd ed.). New York: Macmillan.

Daiuto, A. D., Baucom, D. H., Epstein, N., & Dutton, S. S. (1998). The application of behavioral couples therapy to the assessment and treatment of agoraphobia: Implications of empirical research. *Clinical Psychology Review, 18,* 663–687.

Dattilio, F. M., Epstein, N., & Baucom, D. H. (1998). An introduction to cognitive-behavioral therapy with couples and families. In F. M. Dattilio (Ed.), *Case studies in couple and family therapy: Systemic and cognitive perspectives* (pp. 1–36). New York: Guilford Press.

Eidelson, R. J., & Epstein, N. (1982). Cognition and relationship maladjustment: Development of a measure of dysfunctional relationship beliefs. *Journal of Consulting and Clinical Psychology, 50,* 715–720.

Epstein, N. (1981). Assertiveness training in marital treatment. In G. P. Sholevar (Ed.), *Handbook of marriage and marital therapy* (pp. 287–302). New York: Spectrum.

Epstein, N., & Baucom, D. H. (1989). Cognitive-behavioral marital therapy. In A. Freeman, K. M. Simon, L. E. Beutler, & H. Arkowitz (Eds.), *Comprehensive handbook of cognitive therapy* (pp. 491–513). New York: Plenum.

Epstein, N., & Baucom, D. H. (1993). Cognitive factors in marital disturbance. In K. S. Dobson & P. C. Kendall (Eds.), *Psychopathology and cognition* (pp. 351–385). San Diego, CA: Academic Press.

Epstein, N., Baucom, D. H., & Daiuto, A. (1997). Cognitive-behavioral couples therapy. In W. K. Halford & H. J. Markman (Eds.), *Clinical handbook of marriage and couples intervention* (pp. 415–449). Chichester, UK: Wiley.

Epstein, N., Baucom, D. H., & Rankin, L. A. (1993). Treatment of marital conflict: A cognitive-behavioral approach. *Clinical Psychology Review, 13,* 45–57.

Epstein, N., & Eidelson, R. J. (1981). Unrealistic beliefs of clinical couples: Their relationship to expectations, goals and satisfaction. *American Journal of Family Therapy, 9*(4), 13–22.

Figley, C. R. (1983). Catastrophes: An overview of family reactions. In C. R. Figley & H. I. McCubbin (Eds.), *Stress and the family: Vol. II. Coping with catastrophe* (pp. 3–20). New York: Brunner/Mazel.

Fincham, F. D., & Bradbury, T. N. (1988). The impact of attributions in marriage: An experimental analysis. *Journal of Social and Clinical Psychology, 7,* 147–162.

Glass, S. P., & Wright, T. L. (1997). Reconstructing marriages after the trauma of infidelity. In W. K. Halford & H. J. Markman (Eds.), *Clinical handbook of marriage and couples interventions* (pp. 471–507). Chichester, UK: Wiley.

Gordon, K. C., Baucom, D. H., Epstein, N., Burnett, C. K., & Rankin, L. A. (1999). The interaction between marital standards and communication patterns: How does it contribute to marital adjustment? *Journal of Marital and Family Therapy, 25,* 211–223.

Gotlib, I. H., & Beach, S. R. H. (1995). A marital/family discord model of depression: Implications for therapeutic intervention. In N. S. Jacobson & A. S. Gurman (Eds.), *Clinical handbook of couple therapy* (pp. 411–436). New York: Guilford Press.

Gottman, J. M. (1994). *What predicts divorce? The relationship between marital processes and marital outcomes.* Hillsdale, NJ: Erlbaum.

Greenstone, J. L., & Leviton, S. C. (1993). *Elements of crisis intervention.* Pacific Grove, CA: Brooks/Cole.

Guerney, B. G., Jr. (1977). *Relationship enhancement.* San Francisco: Jossey-Bass.

Heyman, R. E., & Neidig, P. H. (1997). Physical aggression couples treatment. In W. K. Halford & H. J. Markman (Eds.), *Clinical handbook of marriage and couples intervention* (pp. 589–617). Chichester, UK: Wiley.

Hill, R. (1949). *Families under stress.* New York: Harper & Row.

Hill, R. (1958). Generic features of families under stress. *Social Casework, 49,* 139–150.

Holtzworth-Munroe, A., Beatty, S. B., & Anglin, K. (1995). The assessment and treatment of marital violence: An introduction for the marital therapist. In N. S. Jacobson & A. S. Gurman (Eds.), *Clinical handbook of couple therapy* (pp. 317–339). New York: Guilford Press.

Jacobson, N. S., & Margolin, G. (1979). *Marital therapy: Strategies based on social learning and behavior exchange principles.* New York: Brunner/Mazel.

Karney, B. R., & Bradbury, T. N. (1995). The longitudinal course of marital quality and stability: A review of theory, method, and research. *Psychological Bulletin, 118,* 3–34.

Kurdek, L. A. (1993). Predicting marital dissolution: A 5-year prospective longitudinal study of newlywed couples. *Journal of Personality and Social Psychology, 64,* 221–242.

Lazarus, R. S., & Folkman, S. (1984). *Stress, appraisal, and coping.* New York: Springer.

Leslie, L. A. (1988). Cognitive-behavioral and systems models of family therapy: How compatible are they? In N. Epstein, S. E. Schlesinger, & W. Dryden (Eds.), *Cognitive-behavioral therapy with families* (pp. 49–83). New York: Brunner/Mazel.

Markman, H. J., Stanley, S., & Blumberg, S. (1994). *Fighting for your marriage.* San Francisco: Jossey-Bass.

McCrady, B. S., & Epstein, E. E. (1995). Marital therapy in the treatment of alcohol problems. In N. S. Jacobson & A. S. Gurman (Eds.), *Clinical handbook of couple therapy* (pp. 369–393). New York: Guilford Press.

McCubbin, H. I., & Figley, C. R. (Eds.). (1983). *Stress and the family: Vol. 1. Coping with normative transitions.* New York: Brunner/Mazel.

McCubbin, M. A., & McCubbin, H. I. (1989). Theoretical orientations to family stress and coping. In C. R. Figley (Ed.), *Treating stress in families* (pp. 3–43). New York: Brunner/Mazel.

McCubbin, H. I., & Patterson, J. M. (1983). Family transitions: Adaptation to stress. In H. I. McCubbin & C. R. Figley (Eds.), *Stress and the family: Vol. 1. Coping with normative transitions* (pp. 5–25). New York: Brunner/Mazel.

McGoldrick, M., Preto, N. G., Hines, P. M., & Lee, E. (1991). Ethnicity and family therapy. In A. S. Gurman & D. P. Kniskern (Eds.), *Handbook of family therapy* (Vol. II, pp. 546–582). New York: Brunner/Mazel.

McKenry, P. C., & Price, S. J. (Eds.). (1994). *Families and change: Coping with stressful events.* Thousand Oaks, CA: Sage.

Miller, S., Miller, P., Nunnally, E. W., & Wachman, D. B. (1991). *Talking and listening together.* Littleton, CO: Interpersonal Communication Programs.

Neidig, P. H., & Friedman, D. H. (1984). *Spouse abuse: A treatment program for couples.* Champaign, IL: Research Press.

O'Farrell, T. J., & Rotunda, R. J. (1997). Couples interventions and alcohol abuse. In W. K. Halford & H. J. Markman (Eds.), *Clinical handbook of marriage and couples interventions* (pp. 555–588). Chichester, UK: Wiley.

Pasch, L. A., Bradbury, T. N., & Sullivan, K. T. (1997). Social support in marriage: An analysis of intraindividual and interpersonal components. In G. R. Pierce, B. Lahey, I. G. Sarason, & B. R. Sarason (Eds.)., *Sourcebook of theory and research on social support and personality* (pp. 229–256). New York: Plenum.

Seiler, T. B. (1984). Developmental cognitive theory, personality, and therapy. In N. Hoffmann (Ed.), *Foundations of cognitive therapy: Theoretical methods and practical applications* (pp. 11–49). New York: Plenum.

Schlesinger, S. E., & Epstein, N. (1986). Cognitive-behavioral techniques in marital therapy. In P. Keller & L. Ritt (Eds.), *Innovations in clinical practice: A sourcebook* (Vol. 5, pp. 137–155). Sarasota, FL: Professional Resource Exchange.

Spring, J. A. (1996). *After the affair.* New York: HarperCollins.

Stuart, R. B. (1980). *Helping couples change: A social learning approach to marital therapy.* New York: Guilford Press.

Suls, J., & Fletcher, B. (1985). The relative efficacy of avoidant and nonavoidant coping strategies: A meta-analysis. *Health Psychology, 4,* 249–288.

Weiss, R. L., & Perry, B. A. (1983). The Spouse Observation Checklist: Development and clinical applications. In E. E. Filsinger (Ed.), *Marriage and family assessment: A sourcebook for family therapy* (pp. 65–84). Beverly Hills, CA: Sage.

Wright, D. W., Nelson, B. S., & Georgen, K. E. (1994). Marital problems. In P. C. McKenry & S. J. Price (Eds.), *Families and change: Coping with stressful events* (pp. 40–65). Thousand Oaks, CA: Sage.

SUGGESTED READINGS

Baucom, D. H., & Epstein, N. (1990). *Cognitive behavioral marital therapy.* New York: Brunner/Mazel.

Carter, B., & McGoldrick, M. (Eds.). (1999). *The expanded family life cycle: Individual, family, and social perspectives.* Boston: Allyn & Bacon.

Dattilio, F. M., & Padesky, C. A. (1990). *Cognitive therapy with couples.* Sarasota, FL: Professional Resource Exchange.

Epstein, N., Baucom, D. H., & Rankin, L. A. (1993). Treatment of marital conflict: A cognitive-behavioral approach. *Clinical Psychology Review, 13,* 45–57.

Figley, C. R. (1989). *Treating stress in families.* New York: Brunner/Mazel.

McKenry, P. C., & Price, S. J. (Eds.). (1994). *Families and change: Coping with stressful events.* Thousand Oaks, CA: Sage.

13

Families in Crisis

Frank M. Dattilio

One of the most intense and explosive situations encountered during crisis intervention involves the family in crisis. Nowhere else is the interaction of a single unit more complex—and at times volatile—than with family dynamics.

However, compared to the literature on crisis intervention as a whole, relatively few studies or reports have been devoted to addressing crisis within the family context (Gold, 1988; Langsley & Kaplan, 1968; Pittman, 1976). The literature on cognitive-behavioral approaches to families in crisis is even more limited. This is surprising because cognitive-behavior therapy has repeatedly demonstrated its effectiveness as a short-term treatment intervention with a broad range of emotional and behavioral disorders (Beck, 1991, 1993). This is also true of its specific application to couples and families (Epstein, Baucom, & Rankin, 1993; Baucom & Epstein, 1990; Dattilio, 1989, 1992, 1998b; Dattilio & Padesky, 1990; Teichman, 1984; Wright & Beck, 1993). As the cognitive approach to couples in crisis is addressed extensively by Epstein and Schlesinger (Chapter 12, this volume), this chapter focuses primarily on the family context.

Cognitive therapy, as it applies to families in general, developed as an extension of its application to couples in conflict in the early 1980s (Epstein, 1982). Although Ellis (1977) has stated that he adapted his model of rational-emotive therapy (RET) to work with couples as early as the late 1950s, little was written on this topic prior to 1980 (Ellis, 1977, 1978, 1986). The later studies developed as offshoots of the behavioral approach, which first described interventions with couples and families in the late 1960s and early 1970s.

Principles of behavior modification were applied to interactional patterns of family members only subsequent to their successful application to couples in distress (Bandura, 1977; Patterson & Hops, 1972; Stuart, 1969, 1976). This work with couples was followed by several single case studies involving the use of family interventions in treating children's behavior. For the first time, behaviorists recognized family members as highly influencing the child's natural environment and so should be included directly in the treatment process (Faloon, 1991).

Several years later, a more refined and comprehensive style of intervention with the family unit was described in detail by Patterson, McNeal, Hawkins, and Phelps (1967) and Patterson (1971). Since that time, the professional literature has addressed applications of behavioral therapy to family systems, with a strong emphasis on contingency contracting and negotiation strategies (Gordon & Davidson, 1981; Jacobson & Margolin, 1979; Liberman, 1970; Patterson, 1982, 1985). Its reported applications remain oriented toward families with children who are diagnosed with specific behavioral problems (Sanders & Dadds, 1993).

Since its introduction almost 30 years ago, behavioral family therapy has received only minimal attention from practitioners of marriage and family therapy as an intervention of choice. This neglect of an effective modality occurs for a number of reasons: First, because of the overwhelming popularity of the strategic, structural, and more recently the postmodern approaches to family therapy, many practitioners have been influenced primarily by noted theorists such as Minuchin (1974), Bowen (1978), Satir (1967), Madanes (1981), and White and Epston (1990) to the exclusion of more empirically tested interventions. In addition, the behavioral approach may be perceived in some circles as too rigid and rigorous in methodology to apply to families, and as failing to capture some of the commonly occurring dynamics of a family's interaction (Dattilio, 1998a).

In fact, it does appear that the behavior therapies' strength lies more in addressing specific behavioral problems such as poor communication or acting out (common among children and adolescents) than in understanding the comprehensive system of family dynamics (Sanders & Dadds, 1993; Goldenberg & Goldenberg, 1991). Specifically, the behavior therapies focus on observable behavior (symptoms) rather than on efforts to establish any intrapsychic or interpersonal causality. Certain targeted behaviors are directly manipulated through external means of reinforcement. Families are also trained to monitor these reinforcements and make modifications where necessary. Also, an ongoing assessment of observable behavior is made in the interest of empirically evaluating the effects of the therapeutic interventions. This is clearly highlighted in a recent article by Jacobson and Addis (1993), which reviews the outcome studies available in the literature.

Regarding the development of cognitive family therapy, a cognitive approach or cognitive component to behavioral marital therapy subsequently received attention as providing a supplement to behavioral-oriented couple and family therapy (Margolin, Christenson, & Weiss, 1975). In addition to the work of Ellis (1977), an important study by Margolin and Weiss (1978), which suggested the effectiveness of a cognitive component to behavioral marital therapy, sparked further investigation of the use of cognitive techniques with dysfunctional couples (Baucom & Epstein, 1990; Baucom & Lester, 1986; Beck, 1988; Dattilio, 1989, 1990a, 1990b, 1992, 1993a, 1993b; Dattilio & Padesky, 1990; Doherty, 1981; Ellis, Sichel, Yeager, DiMattia, & DiGuiseppe, 1989; Epstein,

1992; Finchman, Bradbury, & Beach, 1990; Schindler & Vollmer, 1984; Weiss, 1984). This interest in behavioral approaches to couple therapy also led behavioral family therapists to recognize that cognition plays a significant role in the events that mediate family interactions as well (Alexander & Parsons, 1982; Bedrosian, 1983). The important role of cognitive factors not only in determining relationship distress, but also in mediating behavioral change has become a topic of increasing interest (Epstein, Schlesinger, & Dryden, 1988; Alexander, 1988; Dattilio, 1993a).

Marital and family therapists began to realize decades ago that cognitive factors were very important in the alleviation of relationship dysfunction (Dicks, 1953), but it took some time before cognition was formally included as a primary component of treatment (Munson, 1993).

As research continues on the significance of cognition in couple therapy, so will its integration with other modalities (Bedrosian, 1983; Baucom & Lester, 1986; Dattilio, 1993a, 1994, 1998; Dattilio & Bevilacqua, 2000).

A COGNITIVE-BEHAVIORAL APPROACH TO FAMILY THERAPY

Cognitive-behavioral couple therapy grew out of the behavioral approach, first as a supplemental component and later as a more comprehensive system of intervention. The same progression holds true to some degree for cognitive-behavioral family therapy (Dattilio, 1998b). Munson (1993) notes that there are at least 18 distinct subtypes of cognitive therapy used by various practitioners, with the result that it would be impossible to discuss cognitive family therapy broadly in a single chapter. This discussion is therefore limited to those approaches proposed by the rational-emotive theories (Ellis et al., 1989; 1978; DiGiuseppe & Zeeve, 1985) and the cognitive-behavioral theories (Beck, 1988; Epstein, Schlesinger, & Dryden, 1988; Dattilio, 1993a, 1998a; Teichman, 1984, 1992).

The rational-emotive approach to family therapy,[1] as proposed by Ellis (1978), places emphasis on each individual's perception and interpretation of the events that occur in the family environment. The underlying theory assumes that "family members largely create their own world by the phenomenological view they take of what happens to them" (p. 310). The therapy focuses on how particular problems of the family members affect their well-being as a unit. During the process of treatment, family members are treated as individuals, each of whom subscribes to his or her own particular set of beliefs and expectations (Huber & Baruth, 1989; Russell & Morrill, 1989). The family therapist helps members realize that illogical beliefs and distortions serve as the foundation for their emotional distress.

The use of the A-B-C theory is introduced. According to this theory, family members blame their problems on certain activating events in the family environment (A) and are taught to probe for irrational beliefs (B), which are then to be logically challenged by each family member and finally debated and disputed (C). The goal is to modify the beliefs and expectations to fit a more rational basis (Ellis, 1978). The role of the therapist, then, is to teach the family unit in an active and directive manner that the causes of emotional problems lie in irrational beliefs. By changing these self-defeating ideas, family members may improve the overall quality of the family relationship (Ellis, 1978).

The cognitive-behavioral approach, which balances the emphases on cognition and behavior, takes a more expansive and inclusive approach by focusing in greater depth on family interaction patterns and by remaining consistent with elements derived from a systems perspective (Epstein et al., 1988; Leslie, 1988). In fact, cognitive-behavioral family therapy is conducted against the backdrop of systems theory and relies on a systemic approach. Within this framework, family relationships, cognitions, emotions, and behavior are viewed as exerting a mutual influence on one another, so that a cognitive inference can evoke emotion and behavior, and emotion and behavior can likewise influence cognition. Teichman (1992) describes in detail the reciprocal model of family interaction, proposing that cognitions, feelings, behaviors, and environmental feedbacks are in constant reciprocal process among themselves and sometimes maintain the dysfunction of the family unit. For a more detailed explanation of this concept, see Dattilio (1998a).

Consistent and compatible with systems theory, the cognitive-behavioral approach to families includes the premise that members of a family simultaneously influence and are influenced by each other. Consequently, a behavior of one family member leads to behaviors, cognitions, and emotions in other members, which, in turn, elicit cognitions, behaviors, and emotions in response in the former member (Epstein & Schlesinger, 1996). As this cycle continues, the volatility of the family dynamics escalates, rendering family members vulnerable to a negative spiral of conflict. As the number of family members involved increases, so does the complexity of the dynamics, adding more fuel to the escalation process. Epstein and Schlesinger (1991, 1996) cite four ways in which family members' cognitions, behaviors, and emotions may interact and build to a volatile climax. Each serves as stimulus or combinations of stimuli during family interactions that often become ingrained in family patterns and permanent styles of interaction.

1. The individual's own cognitions, behaviors, and emotion regarding family interaction (e.g., the person who notices him/herself withdrawing from the rest of the family)
2. The actions of individual family members toward the individual
3. The combined (and not always consistent) reactions that several members have toward the individual
4. The characteristics of the relationships among other family members (e.g., noticing that two other family members usually are supportive of each other's opinion)

Cognitive therapy, as set forth by Beck (1976), places a heavy emphasis on schemata or what have otherwise been defined as core beliefs (Beck, Rush, Shaw, & Emery, 1979; DeRubeis & Beck, 1988). As this concept is applied to family treatment, the therapeutic intervention is based on the assumptions with which family members interpret and evaluate one another and the emotions and behaviors that are generated in response to these cognitions. Although cognitive-behavioral theory does not suggest that cognitive processes cause all family behavior, it does stress that cognitive appraisal plays a significant part in the interrelationships existing among events, cognitions, emotions, and behaviors (Epstein, Schlesinger, & Dryden, 1988; Dattilio, 1998b). In the cognitive therapy process, restructuring distorted beliefs has a pivotal impact on changing dysfunctional behaviors.

Schemata are also very important in the application of cognitive-behavior therapy with families. Just as individuals maintain their own basic schemata about themselves, their world, and their future, they maintain a schema about their family. I believe that heavier emphasis should be placed on examining cognitions among individual family members as well as on what may be termed the *family schemata* (Dattilio, 1993a). These are jointly held beliefs that the family has formed as a result of years of integrated interaction among members of the family unit. I suggest that individuals basically maintain two separate sets of schemata about families. These are family schemata related to the parents' family of origin and schemata related to families in general or what Schwebel and Fine (1994) refer to as personal theory of family life. It is the experiences and perceptions from the family of origin that shapes the schemata about both the immediate family and families in general. These schemata have a major impact on how the individual thinks, feels, and behaves within the family setting. Epstein, Schlesinger, and Dryden (1988) propose that these schemata are "the longstanding and relatively stable basic assumption that he or she holds about how the world works and his or her place in it" (p. 13). Schwebel and Fine (1994) elaborate on the term *family schemata* as used in the family model by describing it as

> all of the cognitions that individuals hold about their own family life and about family life in general. Included in this set of cognitions are an individual's schema about family life, attributions about why events occur in the family, and beliefs about why events occur in the family, and beliefs about what should exist within the family unit (Baucom & Epstein, 1990). The family schema also contains ideas about how spousal relationships should work, what different types of problems should be expected in marriage and how they should be handled, what is involved in building and maintaining a healthy family, what responsibilities each family member should have, what consequences should be associated with failure to meet responsibilities or to fulfill roles, and what costs and benefits each individual should expect to have as a consequence of being in a marriage. (p. 50)

Elsewhere (Dattilio, 1993a, 1998b), I have suggested that the family of origin of each partner in a relationship plays a crucial role in the shaping of the immediate family schema. Beliefs funneled down from the family of origin may be both conscious and unconscious and contribute to a joint schema or blended schema that leads to the development of the current family schema (see Figure 13.1).

This family schema then is disseminated and applied in the rearing of the children, and, when mixed with their individual thoughts and perceptions of their environment and life experiences, contributes to the further development of the family schema. Family schemata are subject to change as major events occur during the course of family life (e.g., death, divorce), and they also continue to evolve over the course of ordinary day-to-day experience.

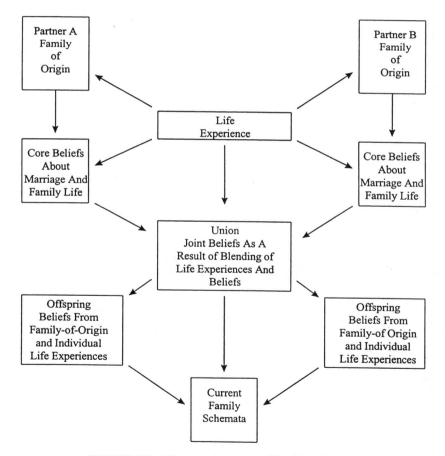

FIGURE 13.1. The development of family schemata.

CRISIS INTERVENTION

Normally, when a family enters into family therapy, the standard procedure is to take a detailed history, which includes gathering information from both parents' families of origin and following a procedure of clinical assessment that may involve individual interviews with family members (Dattilio & Padesky, 1990; Dattilio, 1993a, 1998a). This process may require as many as four to six sessions before the assessment is complete. Crisis situations do not usually afford the therapist the luxury of accumulating such information. Essentially the therapist is obliged to "cut to the chase" by targeting current thoughts and behaviors that are contributing to the family's immediate dysfunction and escalating its crisis. It is important that some family background be gathered, but in such cases the therapist may have to make initial assumptions and interventions in order to stabilize the family as quickly as possible. This, of course, depends on the situation at hand. The focus, once again, must be placed on defusing the immediate crisis. This may involve the use of behavioral strategies up front such as instituting contracts or teaching some emergency problem-solving skills so that the volatility may be reduced. This is analogous to wafting away the smoke in order to determine the extent of the flames, and it paves the way for the identification of individual schema and later family schema, at which point the restructuring process may begin.

Schwebel and Fine (1994) outline four assumptions that they state are central to implementing the cognitive-behavioral model with families. Below is a modified version of these assumptions that may also be applied to crisis situations.

Assumption 1

Individuals seek to maintain their environment in order to fulfill their needs and wants. They try to understand their environment and how they can function most effectively in it.[2] "As they gather data about how the family works, they use the information to guide their behaviors and to aid in building and refining family-related cognitions. This process lends itself to the development of their personal theory of family life and family relationships" (Schwebel & Fine, 1994, p. 41). The personal theory shapes how individuals think and perceive and serves as the central organizer to the mass of life events that they are exposed to (internally and externally).

Assumption 2

Individual members' cognitions affect virtually every aspect of family life. These are determined by five categories of cognitive variables identified by Baucom, Epstein, Sayers, and Sher (1989):

1. *Selective attention* (which is noticed)
2. *Attributions* (how individuals explain why any given event occurs)
3. *Expectancies* (what individuals predict will occur in the short-, middle- or long-term future)
4. *Assumptions* (individuals' perceptions about how the world works)
5. *Standards* (how individuals think the world should be)

Assumption 3

This assumption proposes that certain "obstacles" block healthy family functioning. The roots of these obstacles lie within individual family members' personal theories: specifically the cognitions in the personal theories.

Assumption 4

Members need to become more aware of the family-related cognitions—how these cognitions affect them in certain situations, noting when such cognitions are causing distress and replacing unhealthy ones with healthy ones.

These four assumptions serve as guides for the therapist's intervention with the family, and may be modified to suit the specific situation or the level of crisis at hand. With these assumptions as a philosophical guideline, the therapist attempts to enter the family's world and to help the members, in a collaborative fashion, to identify the areas of dysfunction and to institute the restructuring process.

SUGGESTED STEPS

The strategies used in a crisis setting should be similar to those typically suggested for inpatient units (Miller, Keitner, Epstein, Bishop, & Ryan, 1993) but adapted for the crisis situation:

1. Define the current problem or crisis at hand. Attempt to establish some level of agreement among the family members about the definitions of the problem at hand and the characterization of the family in general.
2. Maintain a definite, directive stance in entering into the family unit and actively introducing change.
3. Attempt to establish some general understanding of the history and family of origin with the parents.
4. Identify schemata derived from the parents' families of origin and determine how these have filtered into the immediate family schema and the expectations of family members.

5. Ascertain automatic thoughts and schemata of family members via Socratic questioning.
6. Introduce the concept of testing automatic thoughts and challenging underlying beliefs of individual family members. Also, make some suggestions for alternative behaviors and the modification of family interactions.
7. Introduce the concept of agreeing to a behavioral contract in an attempt to defuse the current crisis. The time frame should extend from session to session, with a new contract developed at each session.
8. Move toward permanent schema restructuring and behavioral change/enactment.
9. Focus on communication skills and improved problem-solving strategies.
10. Reinforce the implementation of the above-mentioned strategies for future crises. (p. 159)

It is essential to defuse the volatility of a family crisis prior to focusing on permanent schema change. Depending on how well the family learns to deal effectively with crises, their therapy is less likely to be derailed by any other crises that may arise and can focus on permanent change.

The following case example may aid in demonstrating how this approach is implemented during a crisis situation.

CASE STUDY

As a clinical psychologist and family therapist, I was called to the a hospital emergency room on a Friday afternoon to attend to a family who was perceived by the emergency room staff to be "falling apart." This family was said to be exhibiting volatile/aggressive behaviors with one another as they gathered in the waiting area of the emergency room while the youngest member of the family was being examined by the emergency room team.

Brief History

Matt and Joeleen Fredricks were a couple in their late 30s who had a 15-year-old daughter and an 18-month-old son. Mr. and Mrs. Fredricks were not embarrassed to admit that they had not desired any more children after Lisa, the older child, was born. When the family learned that Joeleen was pregnant with Jason, it was an unexpected surprise. Jason's birth obviously changed the dynamics of the family after 13 years of a triadic relationship and caused some intrafamilial adjustment, particularly with regard to the Frederickes' lifestyle and distribution of responsibilities.

What brought this middle class family to the local hospital emergency room this late spring afternoon was the breakdown in communication and familial responsibility over a crisis situation.

Apparently, Mr. Fredricks received a telephone call from his wife just prior to leaving the office for the weekend. Joeleen had locked herself out of the house and had the children with her. She called Matt from the neighbor's home requesting that he leave work right away and come home because she had no other way of getting into the house. Upon arriving home, Matt went directly over to the neighbor's home and met his wife and children. Everyone sat around and chatted a bit while the kids played in the backyard. Lisa, the 15-year-old, who was supposed to be watching the children while the parents were engaged in conversation, decided to leave and go back over to their home now that her father had arrived with the keys. She claimed to have told her mother that she was leaving; however, apparently there was a miscommunication and Joeleen failed to receive the message.

Consequently, the young children were left to run about in the yard unattended. Eighteen-month-old Jason Fredricks wandered into the adjoining yard and inadvertently fell into an open septic tank shaft that had carelessly been left open by another neighbor. Upon hearing the neighbor girl scream, everyone ran to the site, where Matt tore off his jacket and dove into the ominous tank, feeling around for his child who had submerged in the murky water. After about 30 seconds of blind frantic search, Matt pulled Jason out of the water by his shirttail and an ambulance was summoned to take the child to the emergency room of a nearby hospital for examination.

While seated in the emergency room's lobby, the Fredrickses began arguing violently about the carelessness that led to the incident. The fighting became so heated that the emergency room personnel called security and the hospital emergency social worker intervened. After assessing the intensity of the situation, the social worker contacted me for an emergency family consultation. Even though 18-month-old Jason had recovered nicely, the attending physician decided to hospitalize him overnight for further observation and to ensure that he had not ingested too much of the contaminated water. The Fredrickses decided to remain on site for the next 24 hours in anticipation of Jason's release.

During this time, I agreed to meet with the family for an extended session at the hospital and attempted to first defuse the situation by addressing the tension that unfolded in the emergency room lobby.

THERAPIST: I understand that the baby is okay, but you are all pretty shaken and upset right now?

FATHER: I am more than just upset, I am so pissed off at both of those two right now that I could strangle them both [gesturing at his wife and daughter] right here! We almost lost our baby!

MOTHER: Don't you dare blame me. You're not going to pass this all off on me—not this time.

FATHER: Okay, she's just as big of an asshole as you are for letting this happen . . . [pointing to his daughter] and how the hell could you misplace your goddamn keys?

DAUGHTER: Dad, lay off will you. Nobody wanted this to happen. You're always blaming everybody else—get real!

THERAPIST: Listen, I realize that you are all very traumatized by what happened, but I think that we need to collect ourselves a bit and try to get a handle on what happened here. Being agitated with each other is only going to make matters worse and that's the last thing we need. Can we all agree to do that for the time being? To just put your anger on hold a bit so that I can learn more about what's going on here?

MOTHER: I agree that we need to do that right now. I know I need to just talk about what I am feeling or I am going to explode.

As Joeleen spoke, I noticed that Matt was sitting in silence with a sardonic look on his face. I found myself becoming increasingly curious as to what was really going on with this family beyond the obvious crisis. The silence was suddenly broken by the Fredrickes' teenage daughter sobbing, with her face huddled between her hands. As she cried, her mother jumped to comfort her and Matt's disquieting look turned to rage.

THERAPIST: Dad, you're awfully quiet. What's going through your mind right now?

FATHER: I am disgusted by the entire ordeal. This is just the culmination of the ongoing chaos that we live with on a daily basis. One hand is never sure what the other is doing. And now it results in almost losing our baby boy. When the hell is it going to end?

THERAPIST: So, am I correct in understanding that you perceive today's incident as being a direct result of the chaos that you claim exists within your family's context?

MOTHER: [to father] How can you say that? This was an accident. It might have happened to anyone. We didn't leave the lid off of that septic tank. You're really something else—I don't believe you!

THERAPIST: [to father] How do you perceive this connection?

FATHER: I don't know—it's just the thing with the keys and locking herself out of the house. Two weeks ago she almost burns up the engine in our station wagon because she never has the oil checked. It's craziness and I'm tired of it!

DAUGHTER: Dad, you said you would take care of that. In fact, you even screamed at me before about not letting anyone else do anything to the cars because you would handle it. So, don't blame mom.

THERAPIST: There seems to be a major issue with responsibility as well as communication with your family. I think that we need to understand in more detail about what our family schemata or family beliefs are regarding responsibility and most importantly the delegation of that responsibility. [to daughter] Would you like to go first and tell me about how responsibility works in the family?

DAUGHTER: You tell me! I don't know, I'm confused. It seems that my parents give me responsibility at times, but then it's taken away. Half of the time I never know what I am supposed to be responsible for and then I always end up getting yelled at. . . .

MOTHER: [interrupting] My husband has trouble with control, Doctor. If he delegates a responsibility and he doesn't feel that it's being done the way he believes it should be done, he just intervenes and does it himself.

FATHER: No I don't! Don't exaggerate!

MOTHER AND DAUGHTER: Yes you do. We can never do anything right according to you.

THERAPIST: Okay, let me get this straight. Your perceptions [to mother and daughter] are that Dad is very conscientious about having things done the way that he expects them to be done and if that is not accomplished, he just steps in and does it himself.

MOTHER: Yes, you said it exactly—he's like a dictator.

FATHER: Oh, give me a break—you make me sound like a Mussolini or something.

DAUGHTER: But sometimes you are, Dad—really!

THERAPIST: [to father] Are you surprised that your family perceives you this way?

FATHER: Well, yes and no—I mean, I don't believe that I am as bad as they make me out to be, but I do want things to be done properly.

THERAPIST: Why is it so important that they are always done "properly"?

FATHER: Well, because I just think that mistakes can sometimes be very costly—as we have just experienced today. [Breaks down and begins to tear; mother and daughter begin to sob profusely.]

THERAPIST: Well, this is true in this particular case, but is it always the case that it is so crucial? I think that what your family is referring to is more of the run-of-the-mill issues such as chores and so forth. I think I hear them saying that there is no room for error.

FATHER: Well, maybe I get a little carried away, but I am the man of the house and it's my duty and love for my family to see that things run the way they are supposed to.

THERAPIST: You keep referring to some "rule of thumb." This is my sense when you make statements like "the way they are supposed to." Do you have some guideline for things in mind that you follow?

FATHER: No, just what I reflect on from my own upbringing—the way my father ran things at home.

THERAPIST: Tell me more about that.

MOTHER: [interrupting] Oh boy, are you in for a treat, doc. Wait 'til you hear about this nut. Talk about a dictator.

FATHER: [to mother] Don't talk about my father like that.

MOTHER: Why? He was a nut—and you know it—relentless—he drove his family into the ground—and that's what you are doing with us.

THERAPIST: All right, I think we need to let Dad finish here. I would like to hear more about his family of origin and more importantly, his beliefs about his role in your family. But first, I'd like to say that we appear to have a major problem with interrupting one another in this family and in order to attempt to gain some control over that I would like to make a suggestion. [to mother] Is that your son's little baseball cap you have been clutching in your hand?

MOTHER: Yes, it's his favorite cap—he looks so cute in it. [Begins to tear.]

THERAPIST: Okay, may I borrow it for a while?

MOTHER: Sure. [Hands me her son's cap without reluctance.]

THERAPIST: This has been somewhat of an important symbol here today hasn't it? It's a symbol that represents a member of our family whom we all love and cherish and are all here to support today while he recovers. So, I am going to pass this hat around so that it may symbolize respect. When one of you has the floor, I would like to suggest that you hold this hat and the other members of the family will respect your speech by not interrupting you while you are talking. When you are finished speaking, then pass the hat on to the next speaker. This should help us to gain some control over things a little better for the time being. What do you say?

MOTHER: Well, I don't know. It's going to be tough to hold myself back—I am angry right now.

THERAPIST: I can appreciate that and I do want to hear what you have to say. So, let's do this, would it help if you wrote your angry thoughts on paper?

MOTHER: I don't understand.

THERAPIST: Here, let's take a few pieces of paper and I'll give you each a pen. Why don't you write down what is going through your mind at the time instead of blurting it out through an interruption? That way, you won't lose what you have to say and then we can review your automatic thoughts later. Can we all agree to that?[3]

MOTHER AND DAUGHTER: We'll try.

FATHER: [Nods affirmatively.]

THERAPIST: Great! Now Dad, let's go back to what you were saying before about your father.

FATHER: Well, my father was the boss at home. He sort of did rule with an iron fist. Sometimes, he may have been a little too stern, but he kept us all together now that I look back on things. We had respect for him.

THERAPIST: So, do you view your role in this family as being similar?

FATHER: Absolutely, only they don't listen. It's like they just resent it and for the life of me, I can't understand it. Don't I deserve their respect?

THERAPIST: What kind of things do you tell yourself about it? What thoughts go through your mind about why they don't show you the same respect that you demonstrated to your own father?

FATHER: I don't know—maybe that I am ineffective. She doesn't help matters either. [pointing to his wife] She never stands behind me or backs me up on anything. So, I think that the kid picks up on that and then she [referring to daughter] snubs me too.

THERAPIST: Do you believe that your wife does this consciously or intentionally?

FATHER: Yes, I do.

THERAPIST: Well, let's find out. [to mother] Do you do this deliberately, Joeleen, to ally with your daughter against your husband?

MOTHER: No—he thinks that everything is intended to go against him. I just think that at times he comes off too strong and alienates everybody. So, of course the "alienated" stick together, naturally.[4]

THERAPIST: What thought goes through your mind when you see your husband act in this manner?

MOTHER: I feel the need to protect the children as my mother did against my father.

THERAPIST: Was your own father like your husband in that regard?

MOTHER: Yes, but much worse. He was physically abusive to us.

THERAPIST: So perhaps you view your husband in the same light as your father and possibly see your role as mother in this situation as that of your own mother when you were growing up.

MOTHER: I guess you could say that—it's a way to survive.

THERAPIST: I find it very interesting that as problematic as this has become, both of you [to mother and father] are operating under similar assumptions—which is to protect the family. I also see each of you attempting to sustain your identities in this family unit as you have perceived them in your own families of origin. [Father and mother both nod in agreement.] So, I guess it must be very frustrating to you both as you proceed in doing what you believe to be correct and then to experience conflict with each other. It is sort of a violation of your expectations of the way things should operate at home. [to daughter] I would also think that this is all terribly confusing to you.

DAUGHTER: Yes, I sometimes don't know what end is up and it's horrible to be in the position of not knowing who to side with or to listen to.

THERAPIST: So, what do you do? How do you cope in such a situation?

DAUGHTER: Well, I just assume that Mom is right because she screams at me less. At least I can talk to her.

FATHER: [interrupting] You know, that's really something. My sister used to say the same thing about my father—and she was very close to my mother.

THERAPIST: [to everyone] Ah . . . interesting, the scenario almost tends to repeat itself—only things may work differently than they did in your respective families of origin due to it being a different generation and different family members. What is important is that we begin to accept the notion that while certain rules existed in our families of origin, when applied to our immediate family, they may be causing conflict and need to be modified. Sometimes couples bring certain expectations with them to a marriage and as the family grows, so do the expectations. Only, these expectations may be unrealistic. We reflect on our own upbringing, whether positive or negative, and at times may almost force fit our immediate family into what we expect it to be. It sounds as though that is what is going on here.

DAUGHTER: Can I say something?

THERAPIST: Sure.

DAUGHTER: I am sometimes confused because Mom always says to me, "Well your father is the boss, listen to him," but then she does the opposite. I feel almost like she's being a hypocrite at times.

MOTHER: Well, you know why I say that—it's to keep him happy so that he doesn't make a scene. It's to keep peace!

THERAPIST: I think that this is a valid point. You see mother really needs to work things through with your father so that there is more harmony between them. They need to write their own set of rules for the family. Rules that they can mutually agree on. In order to do that, they must begin to examine their needs and beliefs as well as some of the statements that they make to themselves and to identify the distortions that they engage in. But this is something that we are going to need to spend some time on later. For now, I need some type of agreement that will stabilize things until we can look into these issues more and begin to examine our thoughts and perceptions. I want to ask the family to agree to a truce.

FATHER: A truce? What kind of a truce?

THERAPIST: Well, a truce of peace, at least until we meet again and can continue our discussion.

FATHER: Well, I feel more settled, but I don't know about my wife.

MOTHER: I am better, but still shook up. I just can't believe that all of this has happened—are we really that bad?

THERAPIST: No, we just have some changing to do.

DAUGHTER: I need a break.

THERAPIST: Okay, I think we need to take some time out for a few hours and should reconvene later this evening, perhaps after dinner. We can then resume for some more discussions. In the meantime, we all agree to keep things cool and, if need be, just give each other some space. [Family agrees and breaks for several hours.]

Initially, it was my goal to attempt to defuse the intense combativeness of this family by engaging them in a discussion about family responsibility. In this initial session, information was gathered about the families of origin to begin to pinpoint family members' *attributions* as well as the *expectations* and *assumptions* made of one another. Several automatic thoughts about responsibility were identified as well as underlying beliefs about how the family works and how members perceive each other's motives. What is crucial here is that both parents appear to be operating according to what they believe is the correct manner based on their perceptions during their upbringing. It will be important in the next session to begin to work with the family members in identifying cognitive distortions underlying their thoughts and to introduce the concept of alternative styles of thought. What's essential is that family members begin to realize that they have freedom to choose their style of thinking, which is best predicated on substantial evidence. Several hours later, the family reconvenes.

THERAPIST: I hope that everyone had a good dinner and is feeling refreshed to some degree. [Everyone affirms nonverbally.]

MOTHER: Our baby is doing fairly well—he's sleeping now.

THERAPIST: Great—I'm glad that he's going to be okay. Dad, a while ago, when we were talking about receiving respect from your immediate family here, you mentioned that you question your effectiveness. Do you recall that?

FATHER: Certainly—I question it all of the time.

THERAPIST: Why? What makes you believe that you are ineffective?

FATHER: When they don't listen to me, it makes me think that I carry no weight at all. I am . . . disregarded.

THERAPIST: And how does that make you feel?

FATHER: Infuriated—because I try so damn hard and this is what I end up with.

THERAPIST: Is it possible that your wife and daughter actually feel differently?

FATHER: I wouldn't think so.

THERAPIST: Why is that? Do you know for sure?

FATHER: No, but I would assume, just by the way they act.

THERAPIST: How about if I would ask you to test that assumption by gathering information either for or against it? Would you tend to think differently if you came up with information that was contrary to your belief?

FATHER: Well, I don't know. I just find it hard to believe that they don't hold a low opinion of me. It's just something that I've felt for a long time.

THERAPIST: But you said "felt." You in fact don't really know for sure if that's what they really think do you?

FATHER: No. . . .

THERAPIST: Well then, let's gather some evidence and see if we can substantiate that notion. [to mother and daughter] Can you provide some feedback to Dad as to whether or not you view him as being effective as a father and husband?

MOTHER: He's effective. It's just that he ruins it by the way he gives us feedback. He makes us feel so . . .

THERAPIST: Inadequate?

MOTHER: Yes—at times, like we can't do anything right.

DAUGHTER: According to Dad, we can't do anything right!

THERAPIST: So, it's not a matter of him being ineffective, but that you don't respect the condescending manner with which he addresses you.

MOTHER AND DAUGHTER: Yes, that's right.

THERAPIST: Aside from that, does he do a good job of being a provider and protector?

DAUGHTER: Yeah—in that area, he's great!

MOTHER: I have never complained about that part . . . never once in 15 years.

THERAPIST: [to father] Okay, so does this change anything in your mind?

FATHER: Yes—I guess—I am surprised to hear that!

THERAPIST: So, perhaps you were operating under a distortion—one of "all or nothing"—that everything was lumped together. But, in fact, it's only the way that you talk to them that they disrespect—not you, the entire person. Does this change your thinking in any way?

FATHER: Maybe. I just have trouble accepting the fact that things will not always be done right and there will be careless mistakes, etc.

THERAPIST: Well, that's something that we are going to have to work on, but this is a start. What we all need to do is to begin to examine some of our thoughts and perceptions that we carry about each other and begin to weigh out how much hard evidence actually exists to substantiate what we tell ourselves. This is important since much of what we think effects how we feel and behave. This is how we can begin to change some of the conflict in our family interaction for the better. Once we can begin to change our thinking and some of our behaviors, we will begin to feel much differently about each other. I think we also need to look at some other aspects of our family's system—namely power and control issues. This is something that we'll need to address later on as we discuss more about the tension in the family.

CONCLUSION

In the above case, it was decided to target the father because he was perceived by the therapist as being the center of the conflict in this particular crisis. The therapist thought that attempting to restructure the father's thoughts first might have a significant impact on the rest of the family members and diffuse the volatility of the situation. Unfortunately, this has its drawbacks and surely would empower the mother in many ways. Eventually, in subsequent sessions, the focus would be on having each member restructure his/her thoughts as well as on trying some alternative behaviors as a specific therapeutic exercise. This would serve to balance the system and place equal emphasis on each family member. It would also be suggested that they continue in family therapy for an extended period of time subsequent to the crisis intervention.

It is important to note that cognitive-behavior therapy works best with families when it is used within a systems approach (Dattilio, 1998c). It differs from a strict traditional systems approach in that more emphasis is placed on targeting cognitions, particularly belief systems in order to facilitate change.

Most important, one of the strengths of the cognitive-behavior modality of family therapy is that it is readily integrated with other therapeutic modalities and is likely to be utilized more actively in the future, particularly in crisis settings. For the short run, however, it is suggested that cognitive-behavioral strategies be introduced early in order to stabilize the crisis situation such as in the aforementioned case. Clinicians can utilize cognitive-behavioral strategies effectively as an adjunct to just about any modality of family treatment and are encouraged to do so as a measure of both short- as well as long-term intervention.

NOTES

1. This has been renamed "rational-emotive-behavior therapy."
2. I contend that, in addition, family members draw from their own family of origin a model or a frame of how the family system should run. This may at times be a conscious or unconscious process.
3. These two techniques, the passing of the hat and the use of the pad and pencil, are already two behavioral interventions designed to introduce control in this family system as well as to serve as behavioral diffusing agents so that some headway may be gained in a briefer period of time.
4. This statement that Joleen made is very interesting and something I would plan to explore later when discussing the issue of loyalties with the family.

REFERENCES

Alexander, P. (1988). The therapeutic implications of family cognitions and constructs. *Journal of Cognitive Psychotherapy, 2*(4), 219–236.

Alexander, J., & Parsons, B. V. (1982). *Functional family therapy*. Pacific Grove, CA: Brooks/Cole.

Bandura, A. (1977). *Social learning therapy*. Englewood Cliffs, NJ: Prentice Hall.

Baucom, D. H., & Epstein, N. (1990). *Cognitive-behavioral marital therapy*, New York: Brunner/Mazel.

Baucom, D. H., Epstein, N., Sayers, S., & Sher, T. (1989). The role of cognition in marital relationships: Defunctional, methodological, and conceptual issues. *Journal of Consulting and Clinical Psychology, 57,* 31–38.

Baucom, D. H., & Lester, G. W. (1986). The usefulness of cognitive restructuring as an adjunct to behavioral marital therapy. *Behavior Therapy, 17,* 385–403.

Beck, A. T. (1976). *Cognitive therapy and the emotional disorders*. New York: International Universities Press.

Beck, A. T. (1988). *Love is never enough*. New York: Harper & Row.

Beck, A. T. (1991). Cognitive therapy: A 30 year retrospective. *American Psychologist, 46*(4), 368–375.

Beck, A. T. (1993). Cognitive therapy: Past, present and future. *Journal of Consulting and Clinical Psychology, 61*(2), 194–198.

Beck, A. T., Rush, J. A., Shaw, B. F., & Emery, G. (1979). *Cognitive therapy of depression.* New York: Guilford Press.

Bedrosian, R. C. (1983). Cognitive therapy in the family system. In A. Freeman (Ed.), *Cognitive therapy with couples and groups* (pp. 95–106). New York: Plenum.

Bowen, M. (1978). *Family therapy in clinical practice,* Northvale, NJ: Jason Aronson.

Dattilio, F. M. (1989). A guide to cognitive marital therapy. In P. A. Keller & S. R. Heyman (Eds.), *Innovations in clinical practice: A sourcebook* (Vol. 8, pp. 27–42). Sarasota, FL: Professional Resource Exchange.

Dattilio, F. M. (1990a). Cognitive marital therapy: A case study. *Journal of Family Psychotherapy, 1*(1), 15–31.

Dattilio, F. M. (1990b, July). Una guida all teràpia di coppia àd orientàsmente cognitivistà. *Terapia Familiare, 33,* 17–34.

Dattilio, F. M. (1992). Les thérapies cognitives de couple. *Journal de Thérapie Comportmentale et Cognitive, 2*(2), 17–29.

Dattilio, F. M. (1993a). Cognitive techniques with couples and families. *The Family Journal, 1*(1), 51–65.

Dattilio, F. M. (1993b). Un abordaje cognitivo en la terapia de parejas. *Revista Argentina de Clínica Psicologica, 2*(1), 45–57.

Dattilio, F. M. (1994). *Cognitive therapy with couples: The initial phase of treatment* [Videotape]. Sarasota, FL: Professional Resource Press.

Dattilio, F. M. (Ed.). (1998a). *Case studies in couple and family therapy: Systemic and cognitive perspectives.* New York: Guilford Press.

Dattilio, F. M. (1998b). Cognitive-behavior family therapy. In F. M. Dattilio (Ed.), *Case studies in couple and family therapy: Systemic and cognitive perspectives* (pp. 62–84). New York: Guilford Press.

Dattilio, F. M. (1998c, July/August). Finding the fit between cognitive-behavioral and family therapy. *The Family Therapy Networker, 22*(4), 67–73.

Dattilio, F. M., & Bevilaqua, L. J. (Eds.). (2000). *Comparative treatment of relationship dysfunction.* New York: Springer.

Dattilio, F. M., & Padesky, C. A. (1990). *Cognitive therapy with couples.* Sarasota, FL: Professional Resource Exchange.

DeRubeis, R. J., & Beck, A. T. (1988). Cognitive therapy. In K. S. Dobson (Ed.), *Handbook of cognitive-behavioral therapies.* New York: Guilford Press.

Dicks, H. (1953). Experiences with marital tensions seen in the psychological clinic in "Clinical studies in marriage and the family: A symposium on methods." *British Journal of Medical Psychology, 26,* 181–196.

DiGiuseppe, R., & Zeeve, C. (1985). Marriage: Rational-emotive couples counseling. In A. Ellis & M. Bernard (Eds.), *Clinical applications of rational-emotive therapy* (pp. 72–95). New York: Springer.

Doherty, W. J. (1981). Cognitive processes in intimate conflict: 1. Extending attribution theory. *American Journal of Family Therapy, 9,* 5–13.

Ellis, A. (1977). The nature of disturbed marital interactions. In A. Ellis & R. Grieger (Eds.), *Handbook of rational-emotive therapy* (pp. 77–92), New York: Springer.

Ellis, A. (1978). Family therapy: A phenomenological and active-directive approach. *Journal of Marriage and Family Counseling, 4*(2), 43–50.

Ellis, A. (1986). Rational-emotive therapy applied to relationship therapy. *Journal of Rational-Emotive Therapy, 12*(2), 4–21.

Ellis, A., Sichel, J. L., Yeager, R. J., DiMattia, D. J., & DiGiuseppe, R. (1989). *Rational-emotive couples therapy.* Needham Heights, MA: Allyn & Bacon.

Epstein, N. (1982). Cognitive therapy with couples. *American Journal of Family Therapy, 10*(1), 5–16.

Epstein, N. (1992). Marital therapy. In A. Freeman & F. M. Dattilio (Eds.), *Comprehensive casebook of cognitive therapy* (pp. 267–275). New York: Plenum.

Epstein, N., Baucom, D. H., & Rankin, L. A. (1993). Treatment of marital conflict: A cognitive-behavioral approach. *Clinical Psychology Review, 13,* 45–57.

Epstein, N., & Schlesinger, S. E. (1991). Marital and family problems. In W. Dryden & R. Rentoul (Eds.), *Adult clinical problems: A cognitive-behavioral approach* (pp. 288–317). London: Routledge.

Epstein, N., & Schlesinger, S. E. (1996). Treatment of family problems. In M. Reinecke, F. M. Dattilio, & A. Freeman (Eds.), *Cognitive therapy with children and adolescents: A casebook for clinical practice.* New York: Guilford Press.

Epstein, N., Schlesinger, S., & Dryden, W. (1988). Concepts and methods of cognitive-behavioral family treatment. In N. Epstein, S. Schlesinger, & W. Dryden (Eds.), *Cognitive-behavior therapy with families,* New York: Brunner/Mazel.

Faloon, I. R. H. (1991). Behavioral family therapy. In A. S. Gurman & D. P. Kniskern (Eds.), *Handbook of family therapy* (pp. 65–95). New York: Brunner/Mazel.

Fincham, F. D., Bradbury, T. N., & Beach, S. R. H. (1990). To arrive where we began: A reappraisal of cognition in marriage and in marital therapy. *Journal of Family Psychology, 4*(2), 167–184.

Gold, J. R. (1988). An integrative psychotherapeutic approach to psychological crises of children and families. *Journal of Integrative and Eclectic Psychotherapy, 7*(2), 135–151.

Goldenberg, I., & Goldenberg, H. (1991). *Family therapy: An overview.* Pacific Grove, CA: Brooks/Cole.

Gordon, S. B., & Davidson, N. (1981). Behavioral parenting training. In A. S. Gurman & D. P. Kniskern (Eds.), *Handbook of family therapy* (pp. 517–577), New York: Brunner/Mazel.

Huber, C. H., & Baruth, L. G. (1989). *Rational-emotive family therapy: A systems perspective.* New York: Springer.

Jacobson, N. S., & Addis, M. E. (1993). Research on couples and couples therapy: What do we know? Where are we going? *Journal of Consulting and Clinical Psychology, 61*(1), 85–93.

Jacobson, N. S., & Margolin, G. (1979). *Marital therapy: Strategies based on social learning and behavior exchange principles.* New York: Brunner/Mazel.

Langsley, D. G., & Kaplan, D. M. (1968). *The treatment of families in crisis.* New York: Grune & Stratton.

Leslie, L. A. (1988). Cognitive-behavioral and systems models of family therapy: How compatible are they? In N. Epstein, S. E. Schlesinger, & W. Dryden (Eds.), *Cognitive-behavioral therapy with families* (pp. 49–83). New York: Brunner/Mazel.

Liberman, R. P. (1970). Behavioral approaches to couple and family therapy. *American Journal of Orthopsychiatry, 40,* 106–118.

Madanes, C. (1981). *Strategic family therapy.* San Francisco: Jossey-Bass.

Margolin, G., Christenson, A., & Weiss, R. L. (1975). Contracts, cognition and change: A behavioral approach to marriage therapy. *Counseling Psychologist, 5,* 15–25.

Margolin, G., & Weiss, R. L. (1978). Comparative evaluation of therapeutic components associated with behavioral marital treatments. *Journal of Consulting and Clinical Psychology, 46*, 1476–1486.

Miller, I. W., Keitner, G. I., Epstein, N. B., Bishop, D. S., & Ryan, C. E. (1993). Inpatient family therapy, Part A. In J. H. Wright, M. E. Thase, A. T. Beck, & J. W. Ludgate (Eds.), *Cognitive therapy with inpatients: Developing a cognitive milieu*. New York: Guilford Press.

Minuchin, S. (1974). *Families and family therapy*. Cambridge, MA: Harvard University Press.

Munson, C. E. (1993). Cognitive family therapy. In D. K. Granvold (Ed.), *Cognitive and behavioral treatment: Methods and applications* (pp. 202–221). Pacific Grove, CA: Brooks/Cole.

Patterson, G. R. (1971). *Families: Applications of social learning to life*. Champaign, IL: Research Press.

Patterson, G. R. (1982). *Coercive family processes: A social learning approach* (Vol. 3). Eugene, OR: Castalia.

Patterson, G. R. (1985). Beyond technology: The next stage in developing an empirical base for parent training. In L. L'Abate (Ed.), *Handbook of family psychology and therapy* (Vol. 2). Homewood, IL: Dorsey Press.

Patterson, G. R., & Hops, H. (1972). Coercion, a game for two: Intervention techniques for marital conflict. In R. E. Urich & P. Mounjoy (Eds.), *The experimental analysis of social behavior* (pp. 424–440). New York: Appleton.

Patterson, G. R., McNeal, S., Hawkins, N., & Phelps, R. (1967). Reprogramming the social environment. *Journal of Child Psychology and Psychiatry, 8*, 181–195.

Pittman, F. S. (1976). Brief guide to office counseling: Counseling incestuous families. *Medical Aspects of Human Sexuality, 10*, 54–58.

Russell, T., & Morrill, C. M. (1989). Adding a systematic touch to rational-emotive therapy for families. *Journal of Mental Health Counseling, 11*(2), 184–192.

Sanders, M. R., & Dadds, M. R. (1993). *Behavioral family intervention*, Needham Heights, MA: Allyn & Bacon.

Satir, V. (1967). *Conjoint family therapy*. Palo Alto, CA: Science and Behavioral Books.

Schindler, L., & Vollmer, M. (1984). Cognitive perspectives in behavioral marital therapy: Some proposals for bridging theory, research and practice. In K. Hahlwag & N. S. Jacobson (Eds.), *Marital interaction: Analysis and modification* (pp. 146–162). New York: Guilford Press.

Schwebel, A. I., & Fine, M. A. (1994). *Understanding and helping families: A cognitive-behavioral approach*. Hillsdale, NJ: Erlbaum.

Stuart, R. B. (1969). Operant-interpersonal treatment of marital discord. *Journal of Consulting and Clinical Psychology, 33*, 675–682.

Stuart, R. B. (1976). Operant interpersonal treatment for marital discord. In D. H. L. Olsen (Ed.), *Treating relationships* (pp. 675–682). Lake Mills, IA: Graphic Press.

Teichman, Y. (1984). Cognitive family therapy. *British Journal of Cognitive Psychotherapy, 2*(1), 1–10.

Teichman, Y. (1992). Family treatment with an acting-out adolescent. In A. Freeman & F. M. Dattilio (Eds.), *Comprehensive casebook of cognitive therapy* (pp. 331–346). New York: Plenum.

Weiss, R. L. (1984). Cognitive and strategic interventions in behavioral marital therapy. In K. Hahlwag & N. S. Jacobson (Eds.), *Marital interaction: Analysis and modification* (pp. 337–355). New York: Guilford Press.

White, M., & Epston, D. (1990). *Narrative means to therapeutic ends.* New York: Norton.

Wright, J. H., & Beck, A. T. (1993). Family cognitive therapy with inpatients: Part II. In J. H. Wright, M. E. Thase, A. T. Beck, & J. W. Ludgate (Eds.), *Cognitive therapy with inpatients: Developing a cognitive milieu.* New York: Guilford Press.

SUGGESTED READINGS

Dattilio, F. M. (Ed.). (1998a). *Case studies in couple and family therapy: Systemic and cognitive perspectives.* New York: Guilford Press.

Dattilio, F. M. (1998b). Cognitive-behavior family therapy. In F. M. Dattilio (Ed.), *Case studies in couple and family therapy: Systemic and cognitive perspectives* (pp. 62–84). New York: Guilford Press.

Dattilio, F. M., & Padesky, C. A. (1990). *Cognitive therapy with couples.* Sarasota, FL: Professional Resource Exchange.

Epstein, N., Schlesinger, S., & Dryden, W. (1988). Concepts and methods of cognitive-behavioral family treatment. In N. Epstein, S. Schlesinger, & W. Dryden (Eds.), *Cognitive-behavior therapy with families.* New York: Brunner/Mazel.

Schwebel, A. I., & Fine, M. A. (1994). *Understanding and helping families: A cognitive-behavioral approach.* Hillsdale, NJ: Erlbaum.

14

Partner Violence

L. Kevin Hamberger
Amy Holtzworth-Munroe

Marital violence is a serious problem in the United States. Data from a recent national survey indicate that, each year, one out of eight husbands engages in violence toward his wife, and at least 1.8 million wives are beaten by their husbands (Straus & Gelles, 1986). Partner violence often begins early in a relationship; for example, in one study, over one third of couples who were planning to marry reported the occurrence of relationship aggression (O'Leary et al., 1989). In addition, O'Leary, Vivian, and Malone (1992) observed that whereas only about 6% of women seeking marital therapy identified violence as a presenting problem, when directly asked about domestic violence via a structured domestic violence inventory, between 44% and 53% were found to be victims of partner violence.

Relationship violence often continues to occur without intervention. In a longitudinal study of newly married couples, if a partner had been violent at one point in time, there was a 46% to 72% probability that he/she would also be violent at the next follow-up assessment (O'Leary et al., 1989). Feld and Straus (1989) studied couples who experienced violence in the past year. Among couples who reported three severe assaults by the husband in the past year, 67% reported ongoing violence one year later. In a longitudinal study, Aldarondo (1992) found that from the first to the second year, 61% of violent men stopped their violence, and from the second year to the third year, 56% of the men reported cessation of violence; however, 37% of the men who discontinued their violence at one point in time subsequently resumed violent acts. Quigley and Leonard (1996) observed, during a three-year longitudinal study of domestic violence, that desistance rates varied with violence severity. Specifically, husbands with only one incident of minor violence at year 1 were most likely to be violence free in years 2 and 3. Men with the most severe and frequent violence in year 1 were most likely to be violent in years 2 and 3. These data support retrospective, anecdotal reports indicating that, for many couples, violence not only continues but also escalates, in frequency and severity, over time (e.g., Pagelow, 1984; Walker, 1979).

The potential costs of marital violence are high. Marital violence always carries a risk of physical injury, with the most extreme consequence being either homicide or suicide. In addition, initial violence is related to relationship distress (e.g., O'Leary et al., 1989) and has been found to predict marital dissolution (Rogge & Bradbury, 1999). A comprehensive review of the psychological impact of partner violence demonstrated that individual victims suffer many psychological problems, including depression, alcohol abuse, and posttraumatic stress disorder (Holtzworth-Munroe, Smutzler, & Sandin, 1997). Moreover, perpetrators also exhibit a variety of psychological problems (Gleason, 1997; Holtzworth-Munroe, Bates, Smutzler, & Sandin, 1997). These problems include depression and anger (Feldbau-Kohn, Heyman, & O'Leary, 1998; Vivian & Langhinrischen-Rohling, 1994), alcohol problems, and personality disorder (Hamberger, Lohr, Bonge, & Tolin, 1996). In addition, child abuse and other negative effects on the children of such relationships (e.g., Holtzworth-Munroe, Smutzler, & Sandin, 1997) are notable.

Although females report rates of assault perpetration comparable to males (Straus & Gelles, 1986), there are a number of reasons to focus on male violence. Most important, men are more likely to injure their partners than women are, given their greater size and strength (Pagelow, 1984). Research demonstrates that wives are more likely than husbands to require medical care, to take time off from work, and to spend more time in bed due to illness as a consequence of a physical attack from a partner (e.g., Cantos, Neidig, & O'Leary, 1994; Stets & Straus, 1990). Husband violence also results in more psychological problems than does wife aggression, including stress, depression, and psychosomatic symptoms (Cascardi, Langhinrischen, & Vivian, 1992; Vivian & Langhinrischen-Rohling , 1994). In addition, emerging data indicate that women's violence tends to be self-defensive or retaliatory, whereas men's violence is more often motivated by its instrumental value (i.e., to control or punish the wife; Hamberger, 1997; Hamberger, Lohr, Bonge, & Tolin, 1997). The interested reader should refer to Holtzworth-Munroe, Smutzler, and Bates (1997) for a comprehensive review of the differential consequences of partner violence for men and women. Therefore, given the serious consequences of husband violence, our primary focus is male-to-female violence.

Given the prevalence of husband violence, the likelihood that it will continue or escalate once initiated, and the resulting negative consequences, the occurrence of partner violence offers many opportunities for cognitive-behavioral crisis management interventions. In this chapter, three main areas of crisis management in the treatment of partner violence are discussed: (1) understanding and intervening in the general crisis, broadly defined, of ongoing (or past) violence in a relationship; (2) the immediate, acute crisis involved when a perpetrator or victim calls for help in a situation with imminent potential for violence; and (3) the crisis created when a therapist is directly confronted by an angry, agitated perpetrator.

THE CRISIS OF PARTNER VIOLENCE

In a broad sense, relationships in which one partner batters the other always constitute a crisis state. This is not to imply that perpetrators constantly batter their wives (although this is true in some cases). However, we consider even relationships with relatively infrequent violence and in which violence is currently not occurring to be in a state of crisis. To understand this point, one must understand the dynamics of battering and the enduring effects of violence on the perpetrator and victim.

Effects of Violence on the Victim

Partner violence affects many aspects of a victim's life. As reviewed above, battered women have been found to suffer from psychological and health problems. Even during periods when there is no physical violence, battered women are often "on edge" due to the offender's ongoing use of psychological terror tactics. Pence (1989) has outlined some of these tactics. Some are obviously abusive, such as threats of violence, constant name calling, and lengthy verbal tirades. In contrast, others (e.g., criticizing the wife's appearance or complaining that she talks with her mother too much) appear relatively subtle and mundane. Indeed, in nonviolent relationships, the occurrence of such behaviors is perhaps hurtful and irritating but do not have the same impact as they do for battered women. For battered women, such tactics have often accompanied violence; they have been paired with physical violence (the unconditioned stimulus) and its effects (i.e., fear, pain, and injury—the unconditioned response), such that these nonphysical behaviors become conditioned stimuli resulting in conditioned fear responses (Ganley, 1987; Pence, 1989).

In addition to the stress of psychological abuse, an ongoing stressor for battered women is the set of cognitive "rules" they have learned from a variety of sources, including societal messages, formal and informal "helpers," and the batterer (Douglas & Strom, 1988). Such cognitions may include attributions of responsibility for the violence ("It's my fault; I made him hit me") and for keeping the relationship together ("It's a woman's responsibility to keep the family together"), and assumptions about her inability to survive outside the violent relationship ("I can't make it without him"). These cognitions may increase the psychological stress (e.g., depression or anxiety) of victims. In addition to intrapsychic factors, battered women frequently face many situational barriers that lead to futility and entrapment in violent relationships, including being physically prevented from leaving or calling the police, and being threatened with violence if such attempts are made (Fleury, Sullivan, Bybee, & Davidson, 1998).

Thus, even between acute battering episodes, battered women can be conceptualized as being in a relatively constant state of stress. They are always vigilant for the signs of impending attack and constantly engage in violence-avoidant behaviors. However, they are never actually able to control their partner's behavior and are constantly at risk for further abuse.

Effects of Violence on the Perpetrator

Partner violence also affects the male offender. As outlined by Hamberger and Lohr (1989), battering behavior has functional value. Although many offenders report feeling remorse and sorrow following a battering incident, violence is often reinforced through either negative (e.g., the victim stopping some behavior perceived as noxious by the offender) or positive (e.g., tension release or the acquisition of sexual gratification) reinforcement. This reinforcement increases the probability of further violence. Through such processes, various language-cognitive patterns are also reinforced. These include labeling/appraisal and attributional processes. For example, Holtzworth-Munroe and her colleagues found that, relative to nonviolent men, violent husbands attribute more hostile intent to nonviolent, negative wife behavior; such attributions may make it easier for men to view their violence as justified retaliation against a "hostile" wife (Holtzworth-Munroe & Hutchinson, 1993). In addition, domestically violent men often avoid the negative consequences of their behavior by externalizing responsibility for the violence (e.g., "She caused all the trouble"); minimizing their aggression ("We had a little spat"); and denying their behavior ("I never hit her, she bruises easily"). Waltz, Babcock, Jacobson, and Gottman (1991) found a positive correlation between batterers' minimization and victims' reports of psychological abuse. Thus, the cognitions of violent husbands increase the risk of continued abusive behaviors.

Whereas the victim/partner is constantly "on edge" due to threats to her actual safety, the offender is on edge due to perceived threats to his sense of authority, in his relationship. He often views the world as a dangerous, threatening place against which he must take extraordinary steps, including violence, to maintain a sense of integrity and keep his wife "in line" (Hamberger et al., 1997). As a result, the batterer is often depressed and anxious. However, due to his defensiveness, he may have little awareness of his destructive behavior patterns or their impact on his partner.

Effects of Violence on the Relationship

Needless to say, the impact of ongoing violence on the relationship of an offender and a victim is likely to be profound. As outlined above, partner violence is related to relationship distress (e.g., Langhinrischen-Rohling, Schlee, Monson, Ehrensaft, & Heyman, 1998), and marital dissolution (Rogge & Bradbury, 1999). In addition, such violence is often repeated and chronic. For example, in the batterer counseling program conducted by one of the authors (L. K. H.), the average duration of violence prior to attending treatment is 3.8

years and the average frequency of violence is 15 episodes per year. A survey of battered women (Avni, 1991) reported that the duration of violence ranged from 2 to 30 years, and the first occurrence of violence took place within the first month of marriage.

It seems clear, then, that even without an *acute* episode of violence, it is appropriate to conceptualize intervention in such relationships as crisis management. By confronting the overall crisis of partner violence, the therapist can take steps to prevent further, possibly more severe, violence and injury from taking place.

MANAGEMENT OF THE PARTNER VIOLENCE CRISIS

There is no specific "technique" for managing the crisis of partner violence, but a number of useful guidelines have been developed. Although many of these guidelines have emerged from the medical literature on interventions with battered women in emergency and outpatient settings (American College of Emergency Physicians, 1995; American Medical Association, 1992; National Medical Association, 1995; Saunders, 1989a; Hamberger, 1992), they are sufficiently flexible to be applicable to mental health settings as well.

The fundamental tools required for managing the crisis of partner violence are (1) a willingness to ask clients about partner violence as part of routine screening and assessment; (2) an adequate knowledge of local services for battered women and battering men; (3) a clear moral (though not moralistic) position that violence toward one's partner is wrong, unacceptable, and the sole responsibility of the perpetrator; and (4) a willingness to collaborate with the perpetrator, the victim, or both to enhance safety and stop the violence.

The Battered Woman

Inquiry

Battered women do not easily volunteer that they are being battered (Goldberg & Tomlanovich, 1984). In fact, they frequently go to great lengths to avoid disclosure. Often they fear retaliation should the offender/partner learn of the disclosure. Another reason for their reticence is that prior attempts to get help may have resulted in inappropriate or indifferent responses may that have implied that the violence was not a serious problem and may have blamed the victim for her plight rather than assigning responsibility for the violence to the offender (Hamberger, Ambuel, Marbella, & Donze, 1998; Harway & Hansen, 1990; Harway, Hansen, & Cervantes, 1997).

Given the victim's reticence, inquiry should proceed at a gradual pace, beginning with general questions about relationship conflict resolution styles and gradually proceeding to questions about verbal and physical abuse. For exam-

Examples

ple, one line of questioning might be: "When you and your partner argue, how does he act when he becomes angry? Does he ever call you names? During arguments, are you ever afraid for your safety? Sometimes, when men get angry with their partner, they become physical and may push or shove. Has that ever happened to you? What other types of physical aggression has your partner used when he's been angry or otherwise upset? Have you ever been injured by your partner's aggression?" O'Leary, Vivian, and Malone (1992) found that, among marital therapy clients, direct questioning about abuse resulted in higher identification rates than relying on client self-disclosure. Feldhaus et al. (1997) found that a single, direct question such as, "Have you been hit, kicked, punched, or otherwise hurt by someone within the past year? If so, by whom?", was nearly as sensitive and specific as the Conflict Tactics Scale (Straus, 1979) in detecting partner violence victims in an emergency department.

Dangerousness Assessment

Risk

Assessment and prediction of violence and dangerousness in the field of partner violence is controversial. On the one hand, Hart (1994) argues that battered women have informed the field of many aspects of perpetrator behavior that can lead to decision making about potential dangerousness in given cases. On the other hand, Gondolf (1994) argues that many commonsense risk markers, such as gun ownership, previous severe violence, prior police contact, and alcohol and drug abuse have not been shown empirically to predict domestic homicide. Gondolf and Hart both suggest that the situation and behaviors of batterers and victims should be carefully monitored on an ongoing basis, and appropriate action should be taken to protect potential victims when risk markers are evident. Once violence has been reported, one should gather in-depth information on the frequency and severity of violence, the maximum severity that has occurred, changes in frequency and severity, the duration of violence in the relationship, and the impact of the violence on the victim. This information can be gathered via interview.

Information must be gathered to assess dangerousness and lethality. Browne (1987) has enumerated characteristics that differentiated battered women who killed their partners from those who did not. These included high levels of severe and injurious violence, sexual abuse of the woman by the perpetrator, drug and alcohol intoxication by the perpetrator, threats to kill by the perpetrator, and suicide attempts by the battered woman. Hart (1991) also has offered a list of risk markers for lethality to either partner. These include the centrality of the battered woman in the batterer's life, the batterer's sense of ownership of the battered woman, and sudden changes in the batterer's behavior, especially risk taking, such as breaking into an estranged partner's residence. We have found that identifying the characteristics outlined by Browne and Hart provide an opening to express our concern for the safety, welfare, and life of each partner. From a practical perspective, expressions of concern about danger should not be contingent upon the presence of a certain number of observed risk markers; the presence of any risk markers should be cause for concern.

Responding to the Battered Woman's Report

Because a battered woman will often disclose her victimization only reluctantly, inappropriate or insensitive responses to such disclosures could destroy an opportunity for effective intervention. Therefore, on learning of the occurrence of violence, it is important that the therapist clearly and unequivocally communicate to the woman that (1) her story is believed, (2) she is not responsible for the violence or for stopping it, and (3) her disclosure will remain confidential and will only be released with her informed consent (Ambuel, Hamberger, & Lahti, 1997).

The violence must be identified as a problem in its own right, not portrayed as part of communication or other marital problems or a deficiency on the victim's part. Although it is true that violent relationships often involve many other problems, Sonkin, Martin, and Walker (1985) and Holtzworth-Munroe, Beatty, and Anglin (1995) argue that more general marital problems cannot be effectively treated without first stopping the violence and achieving safety for the battered woman. They use the analogy of suicidal intentions in depression. Although psychological interventions into the underpinnings of depression are important, such interventions must follow reduction of suicidal ideation to a safe, manageable level. In addition, there is no evidence supporting the notion that victimization is a function of victim psychopathology. Battered women are not masochistic (Kuhl, 1984) and are no more likely than nonbattered women to exhibit other forms of psychopathology (Hotaling & Sugarman, 1986), although they may exhibit symptoms suggestive of trauma (Holtzworth-Munroe, Smutzler, & Bates, 1997).

Safety Planning

Although the therapist must help a battered woman exonerate herself from culpability for her victimization, it is simultaneously important to help her take responsibility for her safety (and that of any children; Ambuel, Hamberger, & Lahti, 1997; Hamberger et al., 1998). To do so, one must have knowledge of the resources, agencies, and legal options in one's community to support the safety needs of battered women. Such resources include informal supports (e.g., family, friends, medical practitioners, and clergy), more formal resources (e.g., local battered women's shelters and advocacy programs), and social services systems for assisting in acquisition of housing, food stamps, and other necessities if a woman leaves her partner. If there is a shelter in the area, it is important to provide the battered woman with the telephone number, along with encouraging her to use its counseling and shelter services. Legal resources and options should be explored. If there is a mandatory arrest law in the area, it should be described. The availability and function, as well as the limitations, of restraining orders should be discussed.

To further enhance safety planning, many practical steps can be discussed and tailored to the individual needs and situation of the battered woman. Examples include not arguing with the offender when he comes home intoxicated; identifying, when possible, predictors of dangerous situations; and using these cues to seek safety immediately (Hamberger & Potente, 1996). Developing and rehearsing escape plans from numerous locations within the residence can be important. Storing extra clothing, money, and copies of important papers in easily accessible places in the event of a necessary quick exit is recommended. The possibility of storing important items at a friend's or relative's residence should also be explored. To aid in developing and rehearsing a comprehensive, self-relevant safety plan, Hart and Stuehling (1992) have developed a personalized safety plan workbook; the therapist can help the battered woman to use this guide. Through collaboration, rather than prescription, the therapist begins to help the battered woman develop and trust her own problem-solving skills for seeking safety.

Follow-Up

Although it is important to coordinate with other services for battered women, there are several reasons it is also important for the therapist to maintain continuity of care with the battered woman client (Ambuel, Hamberger, & Lahti, 1997; Hamberger & Ambuel, 1997). First, leaving a batterer to seek safety is a very complex process that often requires many attempts before it happens; frequent follow-up is needed to review and revise safety plans as well as to provide support for the battered woman's efforts. Second, follow-up is often necessary to monitor safety when a battered woman leaves her violent relationship, as relationship dissolution is often the single most dangerous time for a battered woman. Rasche's (1988) research indicated that a maximum risk of homicide for battered women continues for up to two years after leaving the relationship.

Another reason for continued follow-up is to discuss the woman's cognitive-related blocks to escaping a violent relationship. Strube (1988) has reviewed many reasons battered women have difficulty leaving a violent relationship. For example, cost-benefit analysis may lead the woman to conclude that it is less costly to stay than to leave. In addition, some battered women truly feel that they are to blame for their partner's violence, and others do not believe they could survive on their own, even if they possess resources to do so. These and other cognitions can be explored, challenged, and modified. This exploration, like all cognitive-behavioral interventions, works best in a collaborative relationship with the therapist in which the therapist engages in a dialogue with the battered woman, rather than trying to analyze and prescribe (Dutton, 1992). Such collaboration cannot occur without follow-up.

Documentation

There are important reasons to document violence when it is reported by a client. First, battered women are at high risk for being injured and/or killed, as well as for committing or attempting homicide or suicide. Therefore, it is important to document assessed dangerousness as well as steps taken to reduce risk, protect potential victims, and enhance safety (Ambuel, Hamberger, & Lahti, 1997).

Second, because battered women are often isolated and tell few people of their plight, careful documentation of their victimization and its impact may constitute the only official record of the situation. Such information may have limited impact in criminal proceedings but may be helpful in civil proceedings such as custody hearings. Battered women often appear as less than optimal parents, but with documentation of the battering, it can be argued that many of the problems of the woman and her children are related to her partner's violence and not to a "defect" within her.

Finally, careful documentation provides validation to the battered woman. Without detailed documentation, the battered woman can become simply a diagnosis without a context. Warshaw (1993) has argued that diagnosing a battered woman without documenting her context dehumanizes and isolates her in the same way that her batterer/partner does when he beats her.

The Offender

Methods of assessment and crisis intervention with male offenders are in many ways similar to those for assisting battered women. That is, it is important to ask about violence, assess dangerousness, develop safety/control plans, conduct follow-up, and provide careful documentation. Nevertheless, working with offenders requires different strategies than does working with battered women.

Inquiry

Asking men about their use of violence should proceed at a gradual pace. Hence, the interview techniques described earlier apply to men as well. Of particular importance in working with men is understanding that male batterers typically deny and minimize their violence relative to the reports of their female partners (Sugarman & Hotaling, 1997). Thus, questions should be structured in a way that facilitates disclosure and minimizes denial. For example, we have found that men are more likely to admit having engaged in specific aggressive actions (e.g., "Have you ever pushed your wife?" "Have you ever slapped your wife?"; see Straus, 1979; Straus, Hamby, Boney-McCoy, & Sugarman, 1996) than to respond affirmatively to global questions that negatively label such actions as "violence" and "abuse" (e.g., "Have you been violent?" "Have you ever abused your wife?").

However, even when a man admits to having engaged in partner violence, he may defensively blame his wife or portray her as the primary instigator or as being more violent than he is; in these ways, he can justify his violent actions as necessary self-defense. Given the goal of getting the perpetrator to take responsibility for his actions, it is tempting for a therapist to become argumentative when faced with such reasoning. However, we have found that it is helpful to avoid such confrontation, at least initially. It is often more useful to explore collaboratively, with the offender, several parameters of his use of force. For example, in addition to assessing violence duration, frequency, and severity, one can ask the man more detailed questions about his partner's use of force against him, both in self-defense and as an initiation of violence. Specific actions should be carefully probed, because it is not uncommon to discover that the man's description of his partner's "initiation" of force involves obnoxious, undesired behaviors (e.g., verbal assault) but not physical aggression. If he reports that she has initiated violence, questions can be asked about what percentage of the time each partner initiates the use of force and whether his partner was the first to initiate violence in the relationship. Preliminary data from various laboratories (Hamberger, 1997; Saunders, 1989b) indicate that men usually report initiating violence a greater percentage of time than do their partners and are more likely to have been the first to initiate violence in the relationship. Men can be asked to consider this information and reexamine their belief that their violence is self-defensive or "mutual."

With male offenders, the goal is to maximize their sense of responsibility for the violence and for stopping it. Therefore, even if the offender gives credible accounts of his partner's negative behavior, his stressful life, his drinking problem, or his poor childhood, it is important to empathize with his experience but also confront his violence as unjustified.

Assessing Dangerousness

All violence should be considered dangerous, but as described in the section on battered women, certain factors indicate a risk of highly injurious or even lethal violence. If any of these variables are observed, it is important to respond with concern. It must be emphasized to the man that although the primary concern is the woman's safety, he is also at risk for injury and even death. Under any circumstance of violence, it is imperative to develop, with the offender, appropriate plans for maximizing safety for his partner and minimizing the risk of violence.

Safety and Control Planning

The goal of safety and control planning for offenders is to stop their violence to ensure safety for their partner. There are several steps that can be taken toward this goal.

If the therapist has, up to this point, interviewed only the offender, it is important to contact the victim to conduct an independent, corroborative assessment and initiate crisis management and safety planning with her, as outlined earlier. Although it is important to let the offender know that his partner will be contacted, it is also important to inform him that the therapist will meet with her separately from him and that the information provided by her will not be disclosed to him. These procedures are important for two reasons. First, she must be provided with safety if she is to be asked to discuss her partner's violence; to ask her to report the violence in front of the offender could place her at risk for further violence after the session. Second, an independent report from the wife can provide information on the extent to which the man is minimizing or denying his use of force. Third, meeting separately highlights individual responsibility for stopping the violence and decreasing the possibility of in-session attempts to control his partner.

A stopgap "time-out" procedure (see Holtzworth-Munroe, Beatty, & Anglin, 1995, for a detailed description of the procedure and its rationale) is an effective step toward achieving safety and control. "Time-out" entails a number of steps that culminate in the man taking a "break" from his violence. The first step involves helping the man to identify the internal and external cues that indicate that he is becoming angry and that his behavior is escalating toward violence. These cues are signals to the man that he needs to take a time-out; at that point, he should verbally tell his partner that he will take a break to "cool down," and he should give her an estimate of how long he will be away. While out of the situation, the man should take appropriate steps to decrease his arousal and probability of engaging in aggressive behaviors (e.g., reevaluate the situation, his escalating behavior pattern and develop strategies to avoid the occurrence of violence). Once cooled down, he should return to his partner. The procedure is repeated as often as necessary to avoid battering. It is important to instruct the man that the sole function of time-outs is to avoid becoming violent or abusive. Many men view time-outs as "running away" from a problem that will be there when they return. This interpretation must be changed. Although it is true that time-outs do not solve specific relationship conflicts, they can facilitate a safer environment in which the couple can work toward nonviolent resolution of such conflicts.

Another step that should be taken to facilitate safety is to motivate the man to enter treatment to end his battering behavior. If violence is discovered in the context of an ongoing therapy relationship, treatment can occur in that context if the therapist is comfortable with, and experienced in, dealing with the problem of partner violence. Alternatively, referral to a batterers' treatment program is recommended. In either case, two issues are important to consider. First, any treatment, regardless of format, must focus on violence as the primary target of intervention, not as a symptom of some other pathology or couple systems problem: Adams (1988) has provided an in-depth critique of therapeutic approaches that do not target violence directly. Vivian and Heyman (1996) have provided guidelines for integrating a sociopolitical and social learning analysis into conjoint treatment formats. Second, one must realize that many violent men are extremely reluctant to enter treatment for their violence. Hamberger and Hastings (1986) found that only 14% of men who attended an initial orientation session actually entered treatment, even when therapy was offered for no charge. Gondolf and Foster (1991) found an attrition rate of over 90% in a batterers treatment program from the time of initial inquiry to completion of a cycle of treatment. In addition, Hamberger and Hastings (1986) observed that report of having witnessed parental violence as a child was characteristic of those men who did enter treatment. Thus, Hamberger and Hastings suggest using such victimization experiences to motivate men to break the cycle of violence by getting help.

In order to facilitate safety and violence control, the therapist must collaborate with the batterer to respect any separation his partner has imposed, with or without a court order. Because many violent men are socially and psychologically isolated, relationship separation can be overwhelming, leading to inappropriate, premature efforts to reconcile with their partner. Two steps can be taken to help men avoid such contact. First, the therapist can help the man to interpret the separation not as a threat but rather as an opportunity for both partners to work on their problems, find safety, and stop violence so that decisions about the relationship can be made in a safe, rational manner. Second, it may be helpful to collaborate with the man to identify formal and informal social supports to assist him through this difficult time; these supports could include friends, family members, counselors and, if relevant, 12-step program sponsors and clergy. Miles (1999) has provided guidelines for clergy to follow in working with families struggling with abuse.

In summary, safety planning for battering men differs in at least one fundamental way from that for battered women: With battering men, the goal of safety and control planning is to foster and develop a sense of personal responsibility for stopping the violence and ensuring safety for their partner. Without acceptance by the man of his responsibility, the woman will remain at risk and other treatment will be ineffective.

Follow-Up

As with battered women, follow-up with the offender is essential. It is also advisable to conduct periodic follow-up with the victim to corroborate the man's report. Follow-up visits with the offender allow for ongoing assessment of the safety/control plan. Stopping violence and giving up control is seldom a one-session phenomenon. Therefore, through many visits, a therapeutic alliance can be developed to facilitate change. A highly confrontational and prescriptive approach, without such collaboration, will likely be perceived by the offender as a moralistic attack, resulting in his leaving therapy.

Documentation

It is important to provide detailed documentation of interactions with domestically violent men. Because of the risks of reoffending and homicide, it is important to document the assessment of violence, steps taken to warn and protect potential victims, and other steps taken to ensure safety. Because many offenders come to treatment under a court order, it is important to develop enough documentation to provide appropriate assistance to the courts in monitoring the offender's accountability, including instances of noncompliance. Finally, as with battered women, documentation of violence may prove important in civil proceedings such as child custody hearings.

CALLS IN THE NIGHT: ACUTE CRISES

When a therapist works with battered women or male offenders, he/she must understand that in addition to intervening in the more "general" crisis discussed above, clients will sometimes call outside regular appointment times. Such calls are usually during an acute, extreme crisis—a situation in which the caller is either very worried that violence could occur or in which an assault has occurred and the caller is distraught, frightened, and possibly hurt. These are difficult calls to take, but the steps taken in such situations can be crucial in stopping or preventing an assault and possibly saving a life. As with managing the broadly defined crisis of domestic violence, management of acute crises requires a willingness to listen, to collaborate with the caller to define the problem, and to develop alternative solutions to achieve safety and avoid violence.

The Battered Woman

When a battered woman calls in crisis, the first priority is to assess her immediate safety and determine whether she or the children have been assaulted. Questions such as "Have you or your kids been assaulted?" and "Is your partner there with you right now? Can he hear you? Is he listening to this conversation? Is it okay for you to talk right now?" help convey the message that her call is taken seriously and her safety is of paramount importance.

If the batterer is nearby and she wishes to continue talking, it may be helpful to pose mainly close-ended questions so that she is not required to provide details in front of a partner who is agitated and struggling with control. If the batterer is present, at some point it is appropriate to ask the victim about the advisability of the therapist speaking with him directly; often, if the offender is present when the woman calls, she is interested in having him participate in the conversation at some point. The specifics of such a conversation are detailed in the next section.

If her partner is not present, try to ascertain whether she knows where he went and whether she expects him back soon. It is also wise to plan with her what will happen should he return to the residence while you are on the telephone. For example, we have often worked with a woman to develop a plan that called for hanging up at her signal and agreeing that she will call back again when she feels safe.

Once it is determined that it is safe to talk, inquire about injuries. If she has been injured, determine whether she would like to go to an emergency room and whether she would like assistance in facilitating the call for emergency services. It is generally believed that health care providers should not "do too much" for battered women so as to further disempower them. In more extreme cases, however, making a call can be helpful, particularly if the choice to do so was made by the client and if medical danger is a possible consequence of inaction. Some states, such as California, Colorado, Kentucky, New Hampshire, New Mexico, and Rhode Island, require health care providers to report suspected cases of partner abuse to authorities (Rodriguez, McLoughlin, Bauer, Paredes, & Grumbach, 1999). Although mandatory reporting of partner abuse is controversial (Rodriguez et al., 1999), it is necessary for anyone working with battered victims in health care settings, especially mental health professionals, to know the local and state laws regarding mandatory reporting of partner abuse.

Whether or not the woman has been assaulted, it is important to continue safety planning. If the therapist has previously worked with the woman to develop a safety plan, the task is to help her implement appropriate aspects of the plan. This may include finding a safe place to stay for a while, calling the police, or, if the batterer is on probation, calling his probation officer. If the woman has not previously developed a safety plan, many of the steps discussed earlier will need to be covered.

In addition to assessing the battered woman's safety, it is important to assess her potential for violence against either herself (i.e., suicide) or her partner. Suicidal ideation reveals the desperation, hopelessness, and degradation many battered women feel. Sometimes, these extreme feelings lead to plans for retaliatory violence and even homicide. Dealing with such thoughts and feelings, if they are reported, is extremely important. Although there is no formula for managing such intense feelings, we have found a number of efforts to be helpful. Fundamentally, a suicidal or assaultive individual needs to hear expressions of support and concern from the therapist. We assume that the individual would not have called had he/she not wanted support and assurance. Therefore, simply telling a client that you do not want them to commit suicide or assault/kill their partner is a good start.

It is also important to assess the seriousness of suicidal or violent ideation. The therapist should differentiate idea from intent, plans, and the availability of means to implement plans. Many people in crisis wish they or their partner were dead but "would never do it" or "have not considered any plan." If a plan is in place, the caller's ability to carry it out must be assessed. For example, if she wants to shoot her partner, it is important to know whether there is a gun at her immediate disposal, whether the gun is loaded or ammunition is easily accessible, and her own subjective assessment of the likelihood that she will attempt to carry out her plan.

If it is judged that the risk of harm to herself or someone else is not imminent, it is still important to discuss the costs and benefits of any such violence. Such discussion could focus, for example, on the well-being of the children if she kills herself, on whether it is worth getting arrested and punished for assaulting or killing her partner, and on whether nonviolent alternatives such as shelter safety or restraining orders are preferable.

If the risk of imminent harm is judged to be high, steps must be taken to protect and warn potential victims. For purposes of this discussion, "protection" could mean helping the woman get to a shelter where she can cool down and rethink her situation. In extreme cases, temporary hospitalization may be necessary.

Once a plan of action has been mutually agreed on, it is important to have the caller review what she will do to implement and execute the plan. At this point, a follow-up contact should be arranged. Depending on safety considerations, it may be necessary to leave the specific time of contact open and allow the woman to call in when she feels safe. If the therapist commits to initiating the follow-up contact, an exact time should be specified and then rigidly adhered to. Follow-ups for acute crises should not exceed 24 hours if possible. It is important to stabilize and resolve matters of safety and lethality quickly so that other related therapy can proceed. Finally, crisis contacts must be documented.

The Male Offender

In general, male offenders are reluctant to seek help and are therefore less likely than battered women to call someone when they are in a crisis. On the other hand, if a therapist has established a trusting, collaborative relationship with a violent man and has permitted crisis calls as part of his safety/control plan, the man may call.

When a therapist takes a call from a violent man, the therapist must acknowledge the internal barriers the man overcame to make the call. This can be accomplished by a simple statement such as, "I'm really glad you called. I know it was hard to do. But you've taken an important step in helping yourself." After establishing a willingness to collaborate with the man to resolve his crisis, it is important to ascertain whether an assault has occurred and whether his partner is with him at his location.

If she is present, steps outlined in the previous section can be followed in talking with her. It should be noted, however, that speaking with the therapist is the woman's option, not the perpetrator's. This expectation can be communicated by simply stating, in a matter of fact way, "I want to speak with your partner just to reassure myself that she's okay." This communicates to the man that his actions have consequences for his partner's well-being and that her safety is the therapist's overriding concern.

Further discussion with the offender centers around the necessity of avoiding violence or, if violence has occurred, not repeating it. If no violence has occurred, it should be neither moralistically condemned nor "understood." Violence must be responded to as being wrong and as providing evidence that the man must continue (or begin) treatment to stop his violence. If no violence has occurred, the man can be told that the crisis call is a sign of strength as he is responsibly taking steps toward nonviolence.

If the therapist is familiar with the caller and has previously conducted safety/control planning, much of the call will center around reviewing appropriate options from that plan. Examples of such options include spending the night with a friend or relative, avoiding alcohol and drugs, and taking extended time-outs. If the woman has left the residence for the night, the batterer should be encouraged to respect her decision and to view her absence as a time-out rather than an abandonment. The emotional pain he may feel in her absence can be interpreted as a cue for him to continue working on changing his abusive behavior, which led to her leaving in the first place.

As with female callers, dangerousness must be assessed and judgments of high risk for imminent violence must be addressed. For example, one of the authors (L. K. H.) received a call from a highly intoxicated client who was distraught over the recent breakup of his relationship; he was talking on the telephone with his shotgun on his lap and threatened suicide after finishing the conversation. While talking to the client, L. K. H. notified a clinic associate of the situation and asked the associate to call the police. The police arrived while the client was still on the telephone. He surrendered and was taken to a local hospital for emergency psychiatric hospitalization. Following stabilization and release from the hospital, he resumed batterer's treatment and alcohol rehabilitation.

In less severe cases, no-suicide and no-violence "contracts" can be developed and agreed to as part of the overall control plan. Follow-up contacts should be part of the control plan and should be explicit. To further enhance the concept of self-responsibility, the offender should be assigned the task of making the follow-up call. Thorough documentation of the crisis contact should be completed.

THERAPIST SAFETY ISSUES IN CRISIS MANAGEMENT

Perhaps the most typical questions we are asked is, "Aren't you afraid for your safety?" and "What do you do when a batterer comes after you?" These questions betray a common underlying fear that working with victims and perpetrators of partner violence is a dangerous occupation for the therapist. Collectively, we have worked in the field of partner violence for 39 years. One of us (L. K. H.) has worked full time for more than 16 years, treating and studying domestically violent men. During that time, neither of us has been the object of physical attack or even a direct threat to our safety. There are currently no published data to determine the uniqueness of our experience. However, informal conversations with colleagues suggest that physical assault of the therapist is rare, and direct threats are infrequent. This is not to suggest that those who work with battered women need not be concerned about attack; even experienced therapists take various precautions when working with an offender in crisis.

Acceptance and Listening

Perhaps the most important skill for working with an offender who is in crisis is to understand and accept his feelings and his struggle for control while remaining clear that his abusive, manipulative, and aggressive behaviors are not acceptable. This is best accomplished through careful listening and engaging him in dialogue rather than preaching, moralizing, and asserting professional authority in an attempt to control him. The latter strategies will be ineffective and could place the therapist at risk. Because batterers are very power oriented and acutely aware when others try to control them, efforts to dominate a batterer can result in an escalating power struggle that could result in injury. Hence, it is better to help the offender to control his actions by demonstrating to him an acceptance of his negative feelings and a willingness to help him resolve his crisis, even if he does not "get his way."

The following is an example of a response to an angry offender.

An offender was notified by a receptionist that he would not be seen for an intake interview because he was 30 minutes late for the appointment. He became irate and verbally abusive in the presence of people in the waiting room. The therapist invited him into an office to discuss the matter. As he approached, the client angrily pointed at the therapist's face and demanded to be seen "or else!" Once in the office, with the door left slightly ajar, the client was invited to sit down. The client refused, so both men stood. The client was encouraged to explain the reasons for the anger. He adamantly demanded to be seen because he "showed up" and had not known that he would not be seen just because he was late. The therapist acknowledged the client's anger and the fact that the client might not have known of the program policy that arrivals later than 15 minutes were not seen. Therefore, the therapist offered to allow the client to reschedule his appointment rather than return to court for having missed this session. The client, while still angry, accepted the offer and indicated that he would be on time for future sessions.

In analyzing this case, the therapist avoided a loud, hostile, and potentially violent confrontation. This was done by removing the client from a public area, collaborating with him to determine the cause of his upset, yet remaining firm about not seeing him for a therapy session that day. The client's anger was viewed as acceptable (even if based on faulty and naive assumptions), as demonstrated by a willingness to talk about it and to find a solution. However, the hostile, aggressive behavior was not reinforced in that the therapist did not counter-aggress and steadfastly refused to see the client for that session. Nevertheless, because the client did show up and may not have known of the tardiness policy, he was offered an alternative to being terminated from the program. Assertion of power, moralizing that the client should have been on time, and referral back to court could have escalated the tensions and resulted in aggression. Although still unhappy, the client left the situation having accepted the alternative and resolving to be on time in the future.

Other principles for safety management can also be noted in this case. First, the therapist did not completely close the door—only enough to provide basic privacy without becoming isolated from the clinic. Because the client had blown up in front of other clinic staff, they were aware of his location and could monitor the situation for any disturbances. Further, the slightly open door provided the therapist and the client with a quick exit if necessity. Hence, the environment was structured to minimize feelings of being trapped.

In addition, when the client refused to sit, the therapist also chose to stand. Maintaining a parallel physical posture, while also maintaining a reasonable distance (about one arm's length), equalized the power distribution. As the goal of crisis management is to reduce threat through collaboration, sharing power in the interaction is essential.

If You Are Assaulted

There is no easy answer to the question of what to do in the case of an actual attack. The domestic violence literature generally does not address the management of aggressive patients, although other readings may be appropriate. Many procedures developed for use in inpatient settings may not be appropriate in the outpatient context. For example, a therapist could learn various restraint holds and blocking techniques but must also learn the limitations of such self-defensive maneuvers, both in terms of practicality (i.e., how effective they are in any given situation) and in terms of liability (i.e., how much, if any, force a health care provider can apply to a client). Certainly prevention is the preferable approach to managing safety in working with violent offenders. If attacked, however, the therapist is generally encouraged to prosecute to the full extent of the criminal code. An attorney should be consulted for guidance.

Preventive Actions

As demonstrated in the previous case, there are a number of steps that can be taken to prevent an assault. These include listening and collaborating with the client, avoiding isolation, and maintaining a safe distance. Some offices can easily be equipped with an electronic "panic button" to notify security of a serious situation. Clients in crisis should be seen only in a professional setting, where other staff and assistance are available if needed.

If a therapist feels uneasy or threatened in a situation, he/she should be concerned about safety outside the clinic setting. The following simple measures can be taken to avoid hazards outside the clinic:

1. If driving, park in an open, well-lit area and take the least obstructed route to and from the car; avoid shortcuts past bushes or recessed doorways. If possible, have security or another staff person accompany you to the car.
2. When driving, take different routes to and from work; change your routine frequently.
3. If possible, enlist neighbors to monitor and notify you of any unusual activities around your residence.
4. If necessary, secure an unlisted or unpublished telephone number. Install a caller-identification system to identify and document the source of phone calls. If telephone harassment occurs, times and dates should be documented. Arrangements can be made with the telephone company to install telephone traps, which can determine the source of harassing calls. Such documentation can provide additional corroborating evidence in the event of prosecution.

CONCLUSION

In summary, there is no one thing a therapist should do to prevent an assault against him/herself or against the client's partner. In some cases, an assault may occur regardless of steps taken. This is because the perpetrator alone is responsible for choosing to be violent. Nevertheless, there are a number of things that can be done to reduce the probability of an assault.

A primary goal is to develop safety/control plans. The key ingredients of such interventions are based on a number of assumptions. First, safety of potential victims is of primary concern. Second, the offender, alone, is responsible for his violence and for taking appropriate steps to stop it. Third, the potential victim, while not responsible for the offender's violence, is responsible for taking steps to secure safety, either through prevention and avoidance strategies or through escape from attack.

Working with cases of partner violence is difficult. It often requires multiple meetings to develop appropriate problem solutions and resolve crises. Sometimes, despite the hard work, violence still occurs. Therefore, such work can be frustrating and stressful. But when a battered woman finds safety for herself and her children, and when an offender actively stops his offending, the rewards can be profound and the healing can begin.

REFERENCES

Adams, D. (1988). Counseling men who batter: A profeminist analysis of five treatment models. In M. Bograd & K. Yllo (Eds.), *Feminist perspectives on wife abuse* (pp. 176–199). Beverly Hills, CA: Sage.

Aldarondo, E. (1992, August). *Cessation and persistence of wife assault: A longitudinal analysis of 772 couples.* Paper presented at the meeting of the American Psychological Association, Washington, DC.

Ambuel, B., Hamberger, L. K., & Lahti, J. (1997). The Family Peace Project: A model for training health care professionals to identify, treat, and prevent partner violence. In L. K. Hamberger, S. Burge, A. Graham, & A. Costa (Eds.), *Violence issues for health care educators and providers* (pp. 55–82). Binghamton, NY: Haworth Press.

American College of Emergency Physicians. (1995). Emergency medicine and domestic violence. *Annals of Emergency Medicine, 25,* 442–443.

American Medical Association. (1992). American Medical Association diagnostic and treatment guidelines on domestic violence. *Archives of Family Medicine, 1,* 39–47.

Avni, N. (1991). Battered wives: The home as a total institution. *Violence and Victims, 2,* 137–149.

Browne, A. (1987). *When battered women kill.* New York: Free Press.

Cascardi, M., Langhinrischen, J., & Vivian, D. (1992). Marital aggression: Impact, injury, and health correlates for husbands and wives. *Archives of Internal Medicine, 152,* 1178–1194.

Cantos, A. L., Neidig, P. H., & O'Leary, K. D. (1994). Injuries of women and men in a treatment program for domestic violence. *Journal of Family Violence, 9,* 113–124.

Dutton, M. A. (1992). *Empowering and healing the battered woman.* New York: Springer.

Douglas, M. A., & Strom, J. (1988). Cognitive therapy with battered women. *Journal of Rational-Emotive and Cognitive-Behavior Therapy, 6,* 33–49.

Feld, S. L., & Straus, M. A. (1989). Escalation and desistance of wife assault in marriage. *Criminology, 27,* 141–159.

Feldbau-Kohn, S., Heyman, R. E., & O'Leary, K. D. (1998). Major depressive disorder and depressive symptomatology as predictors of husband to wife physical aggression. *Violence and Victims, 13,* 347–360.

Feldhaus, K. M., Koziol-McClain, J., Amsbury, H. L., Norton, I. M., Lowenstein, S. R., & Abbott, J. T. (1997). Accuracy of 3 brief screening questions for detecting partner violence in the emergency department. *Journal of the American Medical Association, 277,* 1357–1361.

Fleury, R. E., Sullivan, C. M., Bybee, D. I., & Davidson II, W. S. (1998). "Why don't they just call the cops?" Reasons for differential contact among women with abusive partners. *Violence and Victims, 13,* 333–346.

Ganley, A. (1987). Perpetrators of domestic violence: An overview of counseling the court-mandated client. In D. J. Sonkin (Ed.), *Domestic violence on trial: Psychological and legal dimensions of family violence* (pp. 155–173). New York: Springer.

Gleason, W. J. (1997). Psychological and social dysfunctions in battering men: A review. *Aggression and Violent Behavior, 2,* 43–52.

Goldberg, W. C., & Tomlanovich, M. C. (1984). Domestic violence victims in the emergency departments: New findings. *Journal of the American Medical Association, 251,* 3259–3264.

Gondolf, E. W. (1994). Lethality and dangerousness assessments. *Violence Update, 4,* 8, 10.

Gondolf, E. W., & Foster, R. (1991). Pre-treatment attrition in batterer programs. *Journal of Family Violence, 6,* 337–350.

Hamberger, L. K. (1992). Identifying and intervening with men who batter. In M. Hendricks-Matthews (Ed.), *Violence education: Toward a solution* (pp. 55–66). Kansas City, MO: Society of Teachers of Family Medicine.

Hamberger, L. K. (1997). Female offenders in domestic violence: A look at actions in context. *Aggression, Assault and Abuse, 1,* 117–129.

Hamberger, L. K., & Ambuel, B. (1997). Training psychology students and professionals to recognize and intervene into partner violence: Borrowing a page from medicine. *Psychotherapy: Theory, Research, Practice and Training, 34,* 375–385.

Hamberger, L. K., Ambuel, B., Marbella, A., & Donze, J. (1998). Physician interaction with battered women: The women's perspective. *Archives of Family Medicine, 7,* 575–582.

Hamberger, L. K., & Hastings, J. E. (1986). Characteristics of spouse abusers: Predictors of treatment acceptance. *Journal of Interpersonal Violence, 1,* 363–373.

Hamberger, L. K., & Lohr, J. M. (1989). Proximal causes of spouse abuse: Cognitive and behavioral factors. In P. L. Caesar & L. K. Hamberger (Eds.), *Treating men who batter: Theory, practice and progams* (pp. 53–76). New York: Springer.

Hamberger, L. K., Lohr, J. M., Bonge, D., & Tolin, D. F. (1996). A large sample empirical typology of male spouse abusers and its relationship to dimensions of abuse. *Violence and Victims, 11,* 277–292.

Hamberger, L. K., Lohr, J. M., Bonge, D., & Tolin, D. F. (1997). An empirical classification of motivations for domestic violence. *Violence Against Women, 3,* 401–423.

Hamberger, L. K., & Potente, T. (1996). Counseling heterosexual women arrested for domestic violence: Implications for theory and practice. In L. K. Hamberger & C. Renzetti (Eds.), *Domestic partner abuse* (pp. 53–75). New York: Springer.

Hart, B. (1991, August). *Duties to warn and protect.* Paper presented at the meeting of the American Psychological Association, San Francisco.

Hart, B. (1994). Lethality and dangerousness assessments. *Violence Update, 4,* 7–8.

Hart, B., & Stuehling, J. (1992). *Personalized safety plan.* Unpublished manuscript, Pennsylvania Coalition against Domestic Violence, Redding, PA.

Harway, M., & Hansen, M. (1990). Therapists' recognition of wife battering: Some empirical evidence. *Family Violence Bulletin, 6,* 16–18.

Harway, M., Hansen, M., & Cervantes, N. N. (1997). Therapist awareness of appropriate intervention in treatment of domestic abuse: A review. *Journal of Aggression, Maltreatment, and Trauma, 1,* 27–40.

Holtzworth-Munroe, A., Bates, L., Smutzler, N., & Sandin, E. (1997). A brief review of the research on husband violence: Part I. Maritally violent versus nonviolent men. *Aggression and Violent Behavior, 2,* 65–99.

Holtzworth-Munroe, A., Beatty, S. B., & Anglin, K. (1995). The assessment and treatment of marital violence: An introduction for the marital therapist. In N. S. Jacobson & A. S. Gurman (Eds.), *Clinical handbook of couple therapy* (pp. 317–339). New York: Guilford Press.

Holtzworth-Munroe, A., & Hutchinson, G. (1993). Attributing negative intent to wife behavior: The attributions of maritally violent versus nonviolent men. *Journal of Abnormal Psychology, 102,* 206–211.

Holtzworth-Munroe, A., Smutzler, N., & Bates, L. (1997). A brief review of the research on husband violence: Part III. Sociodemographic factors, relationship factors, and differing consequences of husband and wife violence. *Aggression and Violent Behavior, 2,* 285–307.

Holtzworth-Munroe, A., Smutzler, N., & Sandin, B. (1997). A brief review of the research on husband violence: Part II. The psychological effects of husband violence on battered women and their children. *Aggression and Violent Behavior, 2,* 179–213.

Hotaling, C. T., & Sugarman, D. B. (1986). An analysis of risk markers in husband to wife violence: The current state of knowledge. *Violence and Victims, 1,* 101–124.

Kuhl, A. F. (1984). Personality traits of abused women: Masochism myth refuted. *Victimology, 9,* 450–462.

Langhinrischen-Rohling, J., Schlee, K. A., Monson, C. M., Ehrensaft, M., & Heyman, R. (1998). What's love got to do with it?: Perceptions of marital positivity in H-to-W aggressive, distressed, and happy marriages. *Journal of Family Violence, 13,* 197–212.

Miles, A. (1999). How to care for both victim and victimizer in an emotionally abusive marriage. *Leadership, 20,* 97–100.

National Medical Association. (1995). National Medical Association surgical section position paper on violence prevention. *Journal of the American Medical Association, 273,* 1788–1789.

O'Leary, K. D., Barling, J., Arias, I., Rosenbaum, A., Malone, J., & Tyree, A. (1989). Prevalence and stability of physical aggression between spouses: A longitudinal analysis. *Journal of Consulting and Clinical Psychology, 57,* 263–268.

O'Leary, K. D., Vivian, D., & Malone, J. (1992). Assessment of physical aggression against women in marriage: The need for multimodal assessment. *Behavioral Assessment, 14,* 5–14.

Pagelow, M. D. (1984). *Family violence.* New York: Praeger.

Pence, E. (1989). Batterer programs: Shifting from community collusion to community confrontation. In P. L. Caesar & L. K. Hamberger (Eds.), *Treating men who batter: Theory, practice and programs* (pp. 24–50). New York: Springer.

Quigley, B. M., & Leonard, K. E. (1996). Desistance of husband aggression in the early years of marriage. *Violence and Victims, 11,* 355–370.

Rasche, C. (1988, November). *Domestic murder-suicide: Characteristics and comparisons to nonsuicidal mate killings.* Paper presented at the meeting of the American Society of Criminology, Chicago.

Rodriguez, M. A., McLoughlin, E., Bauer, H. M., Paredes, V., & Grumbach, K. (1999). Mandatory reporting of intimate partner violence to police: Views of physicians in California. *American Journal of Public Health, 89,* 575–578.

Rogge, R. D., & Bradbury, T. N. (1999). Till violence does us part: The differing roles of communication and aggression in predicting adverse marital outcomes. *Journal of Consulting and Clinical Psychology, 67,* 340–351.

Saunders, D. G. (1989a). Family violence. *Emergency Care Quarterly, 7*(1), 51–61.

Saunders, D. G. (1989b, November). *Who hits first and who hits most? Evidence for the greater victimization of women in intimate relationships.* Paper presented at the meeting of the American Society of Criminology, Reno, NV.

Sonkin, D. J., Martin, D., & Walker, L. E. (1985). *The male batterer: A treatment approach.* New York: Springer.

Stets, J. E., & Straus, M. A. (1990). Gender differences in reporting marital violence and its medical and psychological consequences. In M. A. Straus & R. J. Gelles (Eds.), *Physical violence in American families* (pp. 151–165). New Brunswick, NJ: Transactions.

Straus, M. A. (1979). Measuring intrafamily conflict and violence: The Conflict Tactics (CT) Scales. *Journal of Marriage and the Family, 4,* 75–88.

Straus, M. A., & Gelles, R. J. (1986). Societal change and change in family violence from 1975 to 1985 as revealed by two national surveys. *Journal of Marriage and the Family, 48,* 465–479.

Straus, M. A., Hamby, S. L., Boney-McCoy, S., Sugarman, D. B. (1996). The revised Conflict Tactics Scales (CTS2): Development and preliminary psychometric data. *Journal of Family Issues, 17,* 283–316.

Sugarman, D. B., & Hotaling, G. T. (1997). Intimate violence and social desirability: A meta-analytic review. *Journal of Interpersonal Violence, 12,* 275–290.

Strube, M. J. (1988). The decision to leave an abusive relationship: Empirical evidence and theoretical issues. *Psychological Bulletin, 104,* 236–250.

Vivian, D., & Heyman, R. E. (1996). Is there a place for conjoint treatment of couple violence? *In Session, 2,* 25–48.

Vivian, D., & Langhinrichsen-Rohling, J. (1994). Are bi-directionally violent couples mutually victimized? A gender-sensitive comparison. *Violence and Victims, 9,* 107–124.

Walker, L. E. A. (1979). *The battered woman.* New York: Harper & Row.

Waltz, J., Babcock, C., Jacobson, N. S., & Gottman, J. (1991, November). *Husband and wife reports of interspousal violence: Sex differences in minimization.* Paper presented at the meeting of the Association for the Advancement of Behavior Therapy, New York.

Warshaw, C. (1993). Domestic violence: Challenges to medical practice. *Journal of Women's Health, 2,* 73–79.

SUGGESTED READINGS

Hamberger, L. K., (1997). Cognitive behavioral treatment of men who batter their partners. *Cognitive and Behavioral Practice, 4,* 147–169.

Hamberger, L. K. (1996). Group treatment of men who batter their female partners. *In Session, 2,* 49–62.

Hamberger, L. K., & Barnett, O. W. (1995). Assessment and treatment of men who batter. *Innovations in clinical practice: A sourcebook, 14,* 31–54.

Holtzworth-Munroe, A., Beatty, S. B., & Anglin, K. (1995). The assessment and treatment of marital violence: An introduction for the marital therapist. In N. S. Jacobson & A. S. Gurman (Eds.), *Clinical handbook of couple therapy* (pp. 317–339). New York: Guilford Press.

15

Divorce

Donald K. Granvold

Many articles have been written about divorce. Few, however, have been focused specifically on how to treat it. This chapter is devoted to the treatment of divorce crises. Divorce is a process of cumulative loss and adaptation demands punctuated by discrete, repetitive crises. The experience of divorce is highly stressful for most who experience it and people's responses to the stress of divorce are variable including depression, anxiety and panic, hostility and anger, substance abuse, and in extreme cases, suicide and homicide. Although loss is a universal human experience, it is apparent that people are ill prepared for the intensity of the loss of love. Humans strongly attach to one another in committed relationships and, for many, letting go of that intimate connection is extremely difficult and emotionally taxing, whether or not they still feel "in love" with the mate. Furthermore, because intimate relationships so often produce children, couples who divorce are highly likely to continue some relationship well after the divorce is final. The ongoing postdivorce relationship between ex-spouses affords many crisis opportunities.

It should be noted that the research findings presented below are exclusive of gay and lesbian couples and nonmarried committed relationship couples. These couples obviously experience crises of the same nature as their married counterparts. Furthermore, gay and lesbian couples have a variety of additional challenges that have high crisis potential (Granvold & Martin, 1999). The information on stress and the clinical content presented in this chapter are highly applicable to these populations.

DIVORCE RATES

Divorce is a relatively common phenomenon in the United States and in countries across the world. As noted in Table 15.1, divorce in the United States is approximately twice that of divorce in much of continental Europe, Sweden, and Japan. The rates in all these countries, however, represent a significant

TABLE 15.1. International Comparison of Divorce Rates

Country	Year	Divorce rate per 1,000
Japan[a]	1997	1.78
United States[b]	1995	4.44
Germany[b]	1995	2.07
France[b]	1996	1.90
Italy[b]	1994	0.48
United Kingdom[b]	1994	2.97
Sweden[b]	1996	2.40

[a]Data from Minister's Secretariat (1999).
[b]Data from United Nations Secretariat (1998).

number of people enduring the emotional upheaval and resulting adaptation demands of relationship dissolution.

In the United States, the divorce rate reached a record high in 1981 when 1.21 million people (600,000 couples) divorced (5.3 per 1,000 population), affecting some 3 million men, women, and children (National Center for Health Statistics, 1986). There were 1.182 million divorces in the United States in 1990, 4.7 per 1,000 population, and 20.9 per 100 married women ages 15 and over (Monthly Vital Statistics Report, 1990). According to 1997 provisional data, there were 1.163 million divorces annually, 4.3 per 1,000 population. Data released by the United States Census Bureau in early 1999 show the United States divorce rate at around 50%, up from 43% in 1988. Despite the moderate decline since the 1981 high, divorces continue to occur at a remarkable rate in the United States and to a lesser but significant rate abroad.

DIVORCE AND WELL-BEING

Holmes and Rahe (1967) found divorce to be the second most severe form of distress one can undergo (death of a loved one being the most severe). This finding continues to be regarded as an accurate reflection of the accommodation demands of divorce. Research findings from a variety of sources support the association of stress demand and psychological and emotional maladjustment (Beck, 1993; Meichenbaum, 1994; Seaward, 1999). It is also well documented that couple relationship problems are highly associated with psychological disorders (Beach, Sandeen, & O'Leary, 1990; Epstein & Schlesinger, 1994; Michelson, 1987). Furthermore, divorce among men and women is one of the most highly rated risk factors associated with major depression (Anthony & Petronis, 1991; Gallo, Royall, & Anthony, 1993; Weissman, Bruce,

Leaf, Florio, & Holzer, 1991). Conversely, the presence of a satisfying, committed couple relationship has been found to be associated with low rates of depression (Costello, 1982).

The significantly higher suicide rate of separated and divorced individuals compared to their married counterparts is yet another indicator of the instability of those experiencing relationship dissolution (Cantor & Slater, 1995; Trovato, 1986). A recent study by the National Institute for Healthcare Research in Rockville, Maryland, found that divorced people in the United States are *three times* as likely to commit suicide as are married people. Divorce currently ranks as the number one factor linked with suicide rates in major cities. In a recent Australian study, separated males were found to commit suicide at 6.2 times the rate of married males, and separated females were found to commit suicide at 1.7 times the rate of married females (Cantor & Slater, 1995). It can be concluded that marital separation and divorce pose significant mental health risks. The consequences are meaningful not only to the divorcing couple, but also to their children, extended family, friends, and to society at large.

DEFINITION OF CRISIS

A number of definitions of the term *crisis* have been posited (Bard & Ellison, 1974; Burgess & Holstrom, 1974; Freeman & Dattilio, 1994, and Chapter 1, this volume; Goldenberg, 1983; McCubbin & Patterson, 1983; Olson, 1997; Roberts, 1990; Slaiku, 1990). As I have stated elsewhere, drawing from various authors, a crisis comprises three elements: (1) the presence of a precipitating stressful, life-changing or life-threatening event/circumstance; (2) the individual's perception of the event/circumstance as a significant threat; and (3) the individual's current inability to cope with the threat or to mobilize the psychological and/or physical resources to facilitate resolution (Granvold, 2000). To consider an event to be crisis precipitating, the individual must cognitively appraise the event as a significant threat to the self-system. Consistent with Lazarus (1989), the degree of threat is the consequence of primary and secondary appraisals. Primary appraisals establish the relevance of an event to one's well-being or steady state (dynamic homeostasis), whereas secondary appraisals reflect the individual's coping capacities and available resources to meet the demand. Hence, to consider an individual in crisis involves a precipitating circumstance that is perceived by the individual as posing a psychosocial accommodation significantly beyond the individual's belief in his/her capacity to cope, adjust, or integrate. The personal consequences of a crisis may take the form of emotional and psychological unrest as well as physical trauma and detrimental somatic outcomes. Furthermore, many times personal crises have a detrimental impact on social relationships.

To clarify, a crisis state may be avoided when an individual appraises the stressors to be manageable challenges (McCubbin & McCubbin, 1989). A stressor becomes a crisis state when the resources the individual has mobilized and his/her expectations of exercising mastery in the situation fail to result in reduction of the pressure from the stressor or stressors (Epstein & Schlesinger, 1994, and Chapter 12, this volume). Given individual differences and differential availability of resources, one person's crisis is another's triumph over adversity. Therapists are likely to encounter clients who exhibit mastery over stressors that for most people typically would result in a crisis state, whereas others experience a crisis when confronted with "seemingly manageable" stressors. Inasmuch as positive coping and effective resource mobilization contribute to successful stress management, Bandura's (1977a) contention that performance accomplishments raise self-efficacy should be emphasized. In effect, the client who successfully meets crisis-level challenges may learn resiliency and greater mastery expectations for the future (enhanced self-efficacy). There is mounting evidence that many people who experience seriously adverse events realize positive change (McMillen, 1999). Among the potential positive changes is the stress inoculation effect that results from overcoming adversity. Through successful crisis resolution, stressors that previously would have produced disorganization and destabilization are overcome and equilibrium restored without reaching a crisis state. It is also noteworthy that a crisis may occur in the context of constructive change. Positive events that stimulate remarkable change and adaptation may have both positive and negative outcomes (Freeman & Dattilio, 1994, and Chapter 1, this volume; Slaiku, 1990). Although positive consequences of life-changing events may be predominant (e.g., greater self-sufficiency; rejuvenation), some negative outcomes may reach crisis proportions (e.g., uncertainty, demand for undeveloped skills). Occasionally, individuals seek a divorce with a collaborative sense of well-being in their decision to dissolve the marriage. The "healthy divorce" is one in which the couple plans and achieves a constructive rather than a destructive transition to life apart (Everett & Everett, 1994). Although the transition to single life may be relatively smooth, the pervasive change demands may thrust the individual into disequilibrium given the demands of new roles, novel or greatly altered relationships with significant others, or unfamiliar and challenging responsibilities. For example, an individual who considers her divorce to have been a positive action and has experienced both an amicable parting and a successful transition to singlehood, may nevertheless experience a crisis in the role of single parent. The crisis she encounters is a secondary consequence of her "healthy divorce."

To summarize, based on the tripartite definition of crisis delineated above, a stressor becomes a psychological crisis only when the individual experiences a threat to self so intense that his/her characteristic capacities to cope and resolve distress are surpassed, or alternatively, the individual's characteristic capacities to cope and resolve distress are so markedly compromised that an otherwise manageable challenge becomes a crisis. In either circumstance, the individual's cognitive functioning and the availability of social and instrumental resources play critical roles in distinguishing a manageable stressor from a crisis.

THE CRISIS OF DIVORCE

As noted above, an event may become a crisis for an individual based on the intensity of the demand or, alternatively, when an otherwise manageable stressor is experienced while coping abilities and capacities to effectively accommodate change demands are markedly impaired. An individual going through divorce will likely experience *discrete events* of crisis intensity at various points during the process of coming apart and, for many, long after the divorce is final. Furthermore, the divorce process characteristically involves repetitive "waves" of emotionally challenging interchanges and deliberations that have a cumulative wearing effect on the individual. Dealing with loss has the effect of reduced coping ability (Freeman & Dattilio, 1994, and Chapter 1, this volume). The *cumulative effects* of loss and adaptation coupled with prolonged and repetitive trauma may render the separated/divorced person vulnerable to stress responses in stimulus conditions that otherwise would be taken in stride. The magnitude of relationship loss and the protracted nature of the divorce process contribute to both discrete event and cumulative effect crisis responses.

To further clarify the crisis potential of the divorce process, consider the following stages of divorce and their concomitant challenges: (1) decision making, (2) physical separation and the transition to being single, and (3) postdivorce recovery (Granvold, 1994; 2000). Each of these stages poses unique challenges to the individual and each is replete with crisis potential.

Divorce *decision making* is the culmination of heightened relationship dissatisfaction, interpersonal tension, and protracted ambivalence and indecision. Privately held internal dialogues, emotionally charged couple deliberations, disclosures and discoveries, painful conclusions, and future "coming apart" planning characterize this stage. Often a singular event will produce the final decision to divorce. Should the event, itself, be a crisis (e.g., physical abuse, substance abuse, financial irresponsibility, sexual impropriety), the individual may respond with thoughts, emotions, and behaviors that are otherwise uncharacteristic of them (Granvold, 2000). For example, upon discovering that her husband was sexually involved with another woman, a client whom I had been seeing with her husband during their divorce decision making, burned all his clothing in the middle of the front yard of their home. The action was uncharacteristic of her, albeit highly effective in communicating her disapproval to her "soon-to-be-ex-husband." The *separation and transition* phase is a period of negotiation in which extremely difficult decisions must be made. Decisions about child custody, visitation, child support, alimony, and the division of property are typically highly emotionally charged. Values regarding marriage, parenting, and property ownership become compromised, thrusting individuals into emotional upheaval. Legal deliberations are biased toward adversarial interchanges and positioning. Even in those divorces in which there is high amicability, the legal process may be emotionally upsetting. Physical separation and autonomous functioning give rise to the stark awareness that the marriage is over. The availability of the ex-mate as a "best friend," coparent, domestic coworker, and decision-making collaborator is past. For some this is a relief; for others these changes represent profound loss.

During *postdivorce recovery,* the individual seeks closure on the marriage (acceptance of the end of the marriage), adjusts to single parenting, and assumes the identity and social functioning of a single person. Acceptance of the divorce involves "object loss trauma" (Rice & Rice, 1986), accommodation of rejection for those rejected by the ex-mate, and the revisioning, restructuring, and reordering of oneself (Granvold, 1989, 2000). Even though there may be an erosion in feelings of love, attachment to the love object may persist (Weiss, 1975). The mere sight of the ex-mate during recovery, particularly if the ex-mate appears romantically involved with another, may produce a crisis state.

The experience of divorce is highly idiosyncratic. Some experience a relatively smooth transition from married to single. Others, however, encounter intense and repetitive crises. It is these individuals for whom crisis intervention procedures are so important. Consider the individuals who continue to experience frequent and extreme conflict throughout the divorce process and thereafter. Meichenbaum (1994) refers to such prolonged trauma as "Type II" trauma, the result of repeated and sustained ordeal stressors. Also noteworthy in its relevance to divorce, Meichenbaum (1994) notes evidence that traumas caused by human intention are even worse than natural disaster trauma. Inasmuch as prolonged, repetitive, and intentional stressors are more likely to produce posttraumatic stress disorder (Tomb, 1994), the individual who is continuously traumatized by another human being is vulnerable to remarkable psychological, emotional, and physical ill effects. This is the plight of the divorcing individual who experiences intense, repetitive, and/or abusive interactions with the marital partner during any phase of the divorce process or after the divorce is final.

THE CONSTRUCTIVIST MOVEMENT
WITHIN COGNITIVE THERAPY

Traditional or orthodox cognitive therapy developed out of a realist philosophical tradition (Beck, 1976; Beck, Rush, Shaw, & Emery, 1979; Ellis, 1958, 1962). Albert Ellis, Aaron T. Beck, and George Kelly (1955) were the three most influential theorists in shaping the cognitive revolution in psychotherapy. Ellis's rational-emotive therapy (RET) and Beck's cognitive therapy (CT) prompted clients to perform a "rational analysis" of their cognitions, seek evidence to validate or invalidate them, and restructure them on the basis of logic or evidence. Their consistent incorporation of behavioral change objectives along with cognitive change had obvious appeal to those trained in social learning theory. Today, most cognitive intervention approaches include a behavioral activation or skills development component and are consequently more accurately described as *cognitive-behavioral* methods.

The application of behavioral, cognitive, and constructivist methods to divorce crises will be detailed in the crisis intervention section of this chapter. In the remainder of this section I will address the constructivism movement within contemporary psychology and ultimately identify some practice commonalities between CT and constructivism.

Constructivism

The influence of postmodernism is evident in contemporary psychology. Although there is no coherent school of postmodern psychology, the predominant collectivity of postmodernists espouse a constructivist philosophy. Constructivism has been described as more of a philosophical context within which practice is done than a technique (Anderson, 1990), but many salient practice implications may be drawn from constructivism.

Constructivism stands in contrast to realism ontologically. According to realism, a singular, fixed, knowable, external reality exists. Constructivism asserts that "humans actively create and construe their personal and social realities" (Mahoney, 1988, p. 364). The meaning of any stimulus whether discrete or elaborate; physical, psychological, or metaphysical; an event, circumstance, or condition is the creation of the individual. It is really more consistent with constructivism to say that the *meanings* of any stimulus are the unique creations of the individual because multiple possibilities exist. The notion that a universally definable reality exists (realism or logical positivism) against which individual constructs are appraised as *rational* or *irrational* is abandoned in favor of the view that "reality" as a cocreation of the individual and the environment is to be discovered, defined, and its consequences elaborated. The implications of realism are that it is possible to achieve a "reality check" and that "truth" exists objectively. R. A. Neimeyer (1993) notes that, according to this correspondence theory of truth, "the validity of one's belief systems is determined by their degree of 'match' with the real world, or at least with the 'facts' as provided by one's senses" (p. 222). Constructivism rejects validity in favor of *viability*. The viability of any construct (conceptualized personal reality) "is a function of the consequences for the individual or group that provisionally adopts it (cf. von Glasersfeld, 1984) as well as its overall coherence with the larger system of personally or socially held beliefs into which it is incorporated" (R. A. Neimeyer, 1993, p. 222). The constructivist, then, rather than seeking a "reality check" is likely to focus on the various ways of construing a situation, event, or circumstance and their corresponding consequences. The issue is one of determining the pragmatic and adaptive consequences of the client's constructions (Rosen,

1993), taking into account such socially embedded values as social responsibility and humane functioning (Bandura, 1986, 1996a, 1996b; Granvold, 1996a).

The focus on viability is central to the meaning-making process therapeutically. "When a given construct renders the client significantly vulnerable, disempowered, disenfranchised, or otherwise personally, interpersonally, or socially disadvantaged, the onus is on the therapist to collaborate with the client in the elaboration of new meanings less encumbered with negative consequences for self and others" (Granvold, in press). Together the client and therapist collaboratively generate alternative constructs and evaluate the current and projected consequences (viability) of the alternative constructions.

For clients who retain rather inexorable views of their divorce, or are highly confused, ambivalent, and unclear about what to think (often clouded by their emotions), the therapist challenges the client with the expansion of their current constructs and the generation of possible alternative meanings. The client learns that there are variable meanings possible and, through Socratic questioning by the therapist, develops skills in making personal appraisals of the projected consequences associated with each construct. In this manner, clients process possibilities and determine the thoughts, beliefs, actions, and emotions that best produce the realization of their short- and long-term goals.

Constructivist Metatheory

No singular succinct theory can be delineated to describe constructivism. Several theories, however, undergird the practice of constructivist psychotherapy. Among the most broadly embraced are systems theory, life span development theory, and attachment theory (Granvold, 1996b, in press; Guidano, 1988, 1991; Mahoney, 1991, in press; R. A. Neimeyer, 1993, 1995). Constructivist psychotherapists conceptualize human functioning and human change from an evolutionary, systems perspective in which early experiences with attachment figures shape self-schemata that remain change-resistant and powerful in their ongoing influence on human functioning. The concept of early-forming self-schemata has been a central theme in Beck's CT model and, as such, represents a historic point of theoretical correspondence between constructivism and CT. In their human systems and life span development views, constructivists tend to examine relational connections among constructs and to put situational discomfort, distress, and challenge in a context of ongoing self-development, evolving self-identity, and increasing complexity. Rather than instructing clients in the disputation of circumscribed thought units, as early cognitivists tended to do, assessment and intervention are oriented to broader, more developmentally focused meaning-making processes (R. A. Neimeyer, 1993). (For additional information on constructivism, see Franklin & Nurius, 1998; Mahoney, 1995; Martin, 1994; Maturana & Varela, 1987; G. J. Neimeyer, 1993; Neimeyer & Mahoney, 1995; Sexton & Griffin, 1997.)

Orthodox Cognitivism and Constructivism

The question has been asked, "Are Ellis and Beck rationalists or constructivists?" (Rosen, 1993). Although admitting a rationalist perspective in his early
work, Ellis (1990) contends that RET is highly constructivist. Beck's CT
model reflects elements of both perspectives. Beck has consistently acknowledged that individuals attach unique meanings to life situations and that these
cognitive representations are products of both cognitive processing bias and
schematic functioning. His professed departure from constructivism is his contention that "there is an independent reality that does not originate in the
knower (although it is the basis of the cognitive constructions that determine
affect and behavior), and that general laws and meanings can be attained
through reason, science, and technology (Held, 1995, 1996)" (Clark, Beck, &
Alford, 1999, p. 62).

On a practical level, Beck often Socratically guides clients in the *elaboration*
of their meanings with questions such as, "Are there other ways of viewing
that?" and he prompts consideration of the personal and social *consequences* of
clients' thoughts and beliefs. Furthermore, Beck teaches CT therapists to guide
clients not only in determining consequences but also in making judgments
about those consequences with questions such as, "What are the advantages
and disadvantages to you in maintaining this view?" (Rosen, 1993). It is
through questions such as these that Beck's CT model focuses on the *viability* of
constructs and prompts clients to generate alternative meanings that hold
greater promise. Some therapists may find essential tensions between cognitive
and constructive approaches in the ways human distress is conceptualized and
treatment strategies formulated; others may selectively embrace components of
each in matching treatment methodology to the unique personal qualities and
life challenges clients bring to therapy.

CRISIS INTERVENTION: INTEGRATION OF COGNITIVE-BEHAVIORAL AND CONSTRUCTIVIST METHODS

The model of treatment that I practice with those in the crisis of divorce (and
other clients as well) incorporates behavioral methods, orthodox cognitive
methods, and constructivist conceptualizations and methods (Granvold, 1989,
1994, 1996b, 2000). The unifying factor is the view that cognitive functioning
(structure, process, and products) plays a central role in the human condition
and in human change.

Engaging the Client and Processing Emotions

Consistent with the definition of crisis specified earlier, the therapist should
gain an in-depth understanding of the current crisis event, access the client's

unique meaning-making perspective on the stressor, and assess the responses to the stressor that reflect the client's current impaired ability to adequately cope. The initial effort is one of *understanding* and *empathizing* with the client in his/her crisis. Inasmuch as people's responses to crises are highly emotional, the potential exists that the processing of information may be "clouded" by emotional reactivity. Feelings such as hurt, anger, guilt, resentment, shame, and fear may be predominant and render clients incapable of clearly perceiving the situation and its short- and long-term consequences, and further, limit their efficacy expectations in relation to the crisis. The therapist can expect a stream of cognitive distortions, faulty attributions, and expressed intentions to exhibit extreme behavioral responses when the client is in an emotionally agitated state. *This is not the time to challenge these expressions.* Here is an example:

> Recently, a divorced client whom I have been seeing regarding her forthcoming remarriage arrived at the appointment a couple hours after learning that her ex-husband violated a standing court order by moving out of state with their daughter. The session began with a diatribe of emotionally driven expressions, uncontrollable crying, and expressions of intense anger, grief, and loss. I responded with expressions of empathy, sympathy, supportiveness, statements of agreement with her that her ex-husband was responsible for wrongdoing, and expressions of disgust regarding her ex-husband's behavior. Retaliatory threats, venomous and profane castigations, and cognitive distortions such as personalization were ignored. Approximately half-way into the session, the intensity of her emotional responsivity had abated and a problem-solving process was initiated, the most immediate outcome of which was the conclusion that she call her divorce attorney immediately. The last few minutes of the session were devoted to her strengths, resiliency, efficacy expectations, and the possibility, but uncertainty, that her daughter would be returned to the community.

Although it is not uncommon for emotions to distort reasoning during intense reactions to a crisis, emotions also may serve important adaptive functions. Watson and Greenberg (1996) note that "emotions give individuals important information about the significance and meaning of events; reveal individuals' needs, desires, and values; and organize individuals to prioritize goals and to act" (pp. 256–257). During the course of crisis intervention, it is the therapist's responsibility to facilitate the expression of emotions and to guide the meaning-making process in a way that promotes the adaptive functions of emotions.

Risk Assessment

Early in the first session with the divorcing client in crisis, it is extremely important that a risk assessment be completed. The vulnerabilities of individuals experiencing marital disruption and divorce include low self-esteem, depression, hopelessness, anxiety and fear of the unknown, loneliness, isolation, and sexually transmitted disease. As I have stated elsewhere, this combination of vulnerabilities coupled with a depletion in coping ability leaves this population highly at risk of depression, suicide, and substance abuse (Granvold, 2000). In very rare instances clients pose homicidal risk. Given the potential, dire consequences of homicidal ideation, risk assessment should also address aggressive thoughts and actions against the (ex)mate, death wishes, and desires to see the (ex)mate in physical pain. (The reader is directed to the following sources for information on suicidal risk assessment and prevention: Beck, 1987; Beck, Resnik, & Lettieri, 1986; Beck, Rush, Shaw, & Emery, 1979; Bongar, 1991; Freeman & Reinecke, 1993; Freeman & White, 1989; Meichenbaum, 1994; Reinecke, 1994, and Chapter 4, this volume).

Assets and Strengths Assessment

Just as it is important to conduct a risk assessment, it is also important to gather information on the client's personal strengths, coping abilities, available resources, and efficacy expectations regarding the current crisis. People are highly resilient and many have endured remarkable crises in their lives. It is assumed that people possess strengths in terms of resiliency under adversity, regenerative potential, viable human resources (e.g., intelligence, creativity, perseverance), ability to learn, healing power, and life energy (Saleebey, 1992). The strengths assessment shifts the focus away from pathology, dysfunction, and distress, thereby drawing the client's attention to compensatory qualities of potential use in the current crisis. By becoming informed of these competencies the therapist can prompt their greater activation and collaborate with the client in building on existing skills and resources.

Intervention

It is a challenge to write about specific ways to treat people in crisis because of the broad range of ways people define, experience, and ultimately respond to crisis. Divorce crises are highly personal inasmuch as divorce challenges our most basic views about how we are to live life. Divorce crises have been described as products of discrete events or the culmination of cumulative stress, and opportunities for onset range from well before the estrangement is a divorce to long after it has been realized. Given this variability, the following intervention content is intended to promote general understanding with the expectation that clinically unique, innovative, and creative applications will be made of the ideas presented.

Social Learning Theory and Behavior Change

From a learning theory perspective, attention is given to the determination and understanding of various behaviors, cognitions (beliefs, expectations, information processing), emotional responses, and physiological factors the client has learned and received reinforcement for exhibiting. Consistent with Bandura's social learning theory formulation, it should be emphasized that cognitive mediation plays a crucial role in the development and regulation of behavior (Bandura, 1977b). Consequently, although specific behavior change interventions are formulated, they are often coupled with cognitive change. Behavioral strategies developed with the client include components such as counterconditioning, flooding (implosion), stimulus-control methods, reinforcement, shaping, modeling, stress management procedures (e.g. deep muscle relaxation), behavior rehearsal, and skills training (Granvold, 1989, 1994). Behavioral activation objectives and homework are utilized to promote *in vivo* change in behavioral, cognitive, emotive, and physiological functioning.

Behavioral change methods are highly appropriate for the client in divorce crisis. Behavioral inclinations of clients under stress may be to approach, attack, avoid, or flee (Beck, 1993). Aggressive divorcing clients who have been rejected by the mate often go on the attack. They actively seek contact with the estranged spouse to convince the mate to reconsider, or alternatively, to exact punishment for the rejection. They stalk, accost, verbally and physically attack, and seek retaliation through creating problems for the (ex)mate at his/her place of employment, at church, and with family and friends. The behavioral component of the treatment with these individuals involves the use of behavioral contracting focused on withholding aggressive and confrontational behavior and exercising impulse control. The more common response among both those choosing to terminate the relationship and those rejected is avoidance and withdrawal. In response to crisis, these individuals tend to activate "safety behaviors" in the form of social withdrawal, physical inactivity, and substance use/abuse (insulation against pain). Withdrawal may have short-term benefits, but it becomes counterproductive if it is sustained. With clients who are inactive, behavioral objectives are focused on the reactivation of social, recreational, personal development, and mastery-oriented activities as important components in the recovery process.

Cognitive Therapy

The contemporary model of cognitive theory and therapy is a schema-based information processing paradigm comprising *structures, processes,* and *products* (Clark, Beck, & Alford, 1999). Cognitive *structures* comprise symbolic meaning networks and associative linkages, the meaning matrix into which stimuli are processed (Ingram & Kendall, 1986). Schemata are the basic elements of this meaning matrix and function as relatively enduring, inflexible, and largely tac-itly held rules, beliefs, and assumptions. Constructivists and traditional cogni-tivists are in agreement that schematic functioning has a profound impact on human functioning and human change. These deep cognitive structures (Gui-dano, 1988) or core ordering processes (Mahoney, 1991) operate largely at an abstract or unconscious level and are considered to govern the individual's con-scious processes. Furthermore, schemata are considered to be difficult to ac-cess, and once accessed they are difficult to change. Their change resistance is considered to be highly important in the preservation of the integrity of the self-system.

Cognitive *process* is the dynamic operation of the information processing system. It is hypothesized that schemata function with variable thresholds of activation. Activation of many self-schemata depends on the environmental de-mands (internal and external) placed on the individual (Clark, Beck, & Alford, 1999). This activation feature is highly relevant to clients in divorce crisis. *Maladaptive or dysfunctional self-schemata that have remained dormant may become acti-vated as a consequence of the stress demands of the crisis.* For example, the latent belief "I am unlovable unless I stay married" becomes activated with the onset of the divorce crisis. Should this specific schema have a low activation threshold, the mere threat of divorce may result in schematic activation and set in motion cor-responding emotional and behavioral responses. It is important to note that cognitive processing may be done with awareness or at a nonconscious level, and not all schema activation is under voluntary control.

Processing involves functions such as perception, selection, concentration, recall, coding, reasoning, decision making, and impulse control. These process-ing functions become disrupted when the individual is under extreme stress (Beck, 1993). The consequences are that the individual is highly vulnerable to cognitive distortions, the activation thresholds of dysfunctional schemata be-come lowered significantly, voluntary control processes become impaired, and the individual becomes hypervigilant and hypersensitive to "threatening" stim-uli. This erosion in cognitive functioning leaves the individual vulnerable to ex-treme emotional responses and the activation of uncharacteristic or dysfunc-tional behavior.

For example, a divorcing woman who is experiencing extreme emotional pain of rejection construes her husband's quest to be awarded joint custody of their children as an act of aggression toward her. The intensity of her feelings of rejection and the pervasive consequences of the impending divorce have pro-duced a state of crisis. She intensely agonizes over the visitation rights the court has temporarily awarded her husband (although they are minimal) and finds it difficult to enjoy her children when they are with her due to her preoccupation with the upcoming weekend that they will spend with their father. With family and friends, she repeatedly focuses conversations on the custody petition. Comments from her family that perhaps she should consider the potential positives in a joint custody arrangement are viewed as expressions of disloyalty to her. This exemplar reflects extreme, one-sided judgments, preoccupation with perceived "threatening" behavior (weekend visitations), and questionable interpretations.

Products of the information processing model are the thoughts, beliefs (accessed), attributions, expectations, standards, decisions, images, emotions, and behavior considered to be largely determined by the activation of meaning-assigning structures (Clark, Beck, & Alford, 1999). Keep in mind that there is a reciprocal relationship among structure, process, and outcomes: Each influences and is influenced by the other. People continually evaluate, interpret, and appraise internally generated information and externally derived stimuli. This appraisal process inherently involves bias and inconsistency and consequently the *products* of these deliberations are biased and distorted to some extent. Through his research, Beck has concluded that people routinely and "automatically" apply their beliefs to life events (Beck, 1967, 1976). These automatic thoughts (ATs) are surface-held beliefs considered to be highly influential in both human distress and discomfort, as well as in human comfort, satisfaction, and states of emotional well-being. When questioned, the individual can espouse the beliefs, standards, rules, and expectations that he/she maintains as guiding principles of life. These caveats are termed automatic thoughts because the individual does not consciously consider them during information processing.

ATs are important intervention points with those in divorce crisis. Examples of typical ATs include: "When you get married, you are supposed to stay married." "If I divorce, I am a loser (failure)"; "I must save my marriage"; "We must remain married for the sake of the children"; "I cannot be a father (mother) if I am divorced"; "I can't stand life without the love of my mate"; "People won't respect me if I divorce"; "I'll never love (marry) again." Cognitive intervention involves accessing ATs and targeting them for elaboration.

In the following example, a client who has been separated from her husband for 7 months is approaching the legal finalization of the divorce. For most people, peak stress events in the divorce process are physical separation, date of filing (or being served the petition), and final court hearing (Chiraboga & Cutler, 1977). For this client, the impending finalization produced a state of crisis. Although she did not initiate the divorce, she has felt "empty" in the relationship for several years. She was reared to believe the "intrinsic permanence" view of marriage: Marriage has inherent value and one is morally obligated to sustain it despite one's satisfaction level (Scanzoni, 1972). The predominant AT she has in relation to the divorce becoming legally final is, "I'm a loser," a thought that is highly compatible with the philosophy about marital commitment that she has integrated. She presented for therapy in a state of severe depression regarding the impending final court hearing (BDI-II score: 44). In the following excerpt, the objectives are: (1) to demonstrate the unappealing consequences of the predominant AT, (2) to introduce the idea that there may be other ways of viewing the situation (that her "reality" of the divorce may take on several meanings), and (3) to determine the consequences of one of the alternative meanings. Connecting her ATs with other beliefs such as the intrinsic permanence of marriage ethic and other self-schemata followed this early cognitive elaboration effort.

THERAPIST: What crosses your mind when you think of the divorce being final?

CLIENT: What a loser I am.

THERAPIST: I see. What are the consequences of thinking of yourself as a loser?

CLIENT: Well, I don't feel very good about it. . . . I feel down . . . depressed. And I don't want to see anyone.

THERAPIST: So the thought, "I am a loser because I'm divorced" results in feeling down, depressed and you want to withdraw from people.

CLIENT: That's right.

THERAPIST: Do you like these results—depression and withdrawal?

CLIENT: Not really, but I don't see myself changing any time soon.

THERAPIST: Since you really don't like these consequences, suppose we explore your situation and see if there are any other ways of looking at it. Think back once again to the divorce being final, what other thoughts do you have about it, besides "I'm a loser"?

CLIENT: I guess that I am somewhat relieved because we really hadn't been getting along for years.

THERAPIST: Okay, so one other thought is, "I'm relieved." What other thoughts do you have? Perhaps you can come up with several more.

CLIENT: Let me see [pauses to think]. Well, I got married when I was 19 years old so I have never been on my own as an adult. This will give me an opportunity to sort of find out who I am. I've been Joe's wife for 10 years. Also, I will be free of Joe's criticism. I could never seem to do things right in his eyes.

THERAPIST: Let's go over these thoughts now. In addition to "I'm a loser," you have added "I'm relieved," "I'll have an opportunity to find out who I am as a single adult," and "I'll be free of Joe's criticism." Have I missed anything, or stated anything incorrectly?

CLIENT: No, I think those are the other thoughts that I mentioned.

THERAPIST: Something important has happened here, Sue. You've established that there is more than one way of looking at the divorce. And perhaps you've only begun to scratch the surface of the many, many thoughts you may actually have about the divorce. Earlier I asked you for the consequences of the thought, "I'm a loser." Now, take one of the other thoughts and let's see what the consequences are of that thought. For a moment, contemplate the thought, "I'll be free of Joe's criticism." [pause] What kinds of feelings do you have now?

CLIENT: I feel somewhat relieved. I can't say that I feel good, but I don't feel worthless like I sometimes did when Joe would start in on me.

THERAPIST: So, rather than feeling down, you feel relieved, and not bad about yourself.

CLIENT: That's right.

THERAPIST: Again keeping the thought, "I'll be free of Joe's criticism," do you feel as inclined to stay away from people, to withdraw?

CLIENT: No, not really. I'm not ready to party or anything, but I have a few girl friends that I wouldn't mind seeing.

This example demonstrates the following:

- Exposure of a negative AT, "I'm a loser."
- Determination and analysis of the *consequences* of the thought (both feelings and behavior).
- Personal appraisal of the consequences ("Do you like these consequences?").
- Generation of alternative constructs as a means of challenging the active AT.
- Selection of one of the alternative constructs to demonstrate the benefits of cognitive elaboration.
- Determination and analysis of the *consequences* of the new construct (feelings and behavior).

Constructivist Therapy

One of the major influences of constructivist philosophy on crisis intervention is the way in which the divorce crisis is conceptualized. It is imperative to address the client's immediate, extreme stress responses, but the crisis is regarded as a potentially positive self-system *perturbation*. States of extreme disequilibrium, although discomforting, may produce remarkable adaptive change in the individual's ongoing evolution. Divorce is viewed in the context of the life span. The crisis of divorce is conceptualized as a tremendous opportunity for constructive change and rejuvenation. Its positive potential is emphasized. Crises may optimally result in increased knowledge of self and, if capitalized on, they may stimulate the proactive establishment and movement toward achievement of creative change objectives in the client's course of life.

Therapy is focused on the personal meanings of clients' explicit statements with the objective to gain insight into broader systems of personal constructs

(R. A. Neimeyer, 1993). As noted above, the developmental dimensions of the client's crisis and its context are examined with attention given to primary attachment relationships, significant intimate relationships, and remarkable life events that may have strongly influenced self-schemata. Emotions, rather than being considered "negative" are treated as highly informative. Intervention tends to be "reflective, elaborative, and intensely personal, rather than persuasive, analytical, and technically instructive" (R. A. Neimeyer, 1993, p. 224).

Although there is no narrowly defined model, the following enumeration is reflective of constructivist psychotherapy:

1. Conceptualize divorce as a self-system perturbation.
2. Seek to access self-schemata activated by the divorce process with the objective of modifying core ordering processes through construct elaboration.
3. Explore primary attachment relationships as they relate to views of self and the world including the attachment relationship with the ex-spouse.
4. Promote a view of self as a multifaceted and ever-changing "system" of identity meanings, rather than a singular, fixed self.
5. Promote emotional expressiveness through guided discovery, imagery, imaginary dialogues (empty chair technique), and therapeutic rituals.
6. Utilize personal narratives and journaling as change mediums.
7. Accentuate client strengths, personal and social resources, creativity, coping capacities, and resiliency.
8. Collaborate with the client in constructing change mediums, models, and techniques with which the therapist has an expertise and that "fit" the client.

CASE STUDY

Dave presented for therapy shortly after his wife, Amy, told him that she wanted a divorce. Dave and Amy, married 10 years, had two children ages 4 and 6. Dave was devastated by Amy's intention to file for divorce. He reported being extremely tearful and was experiencing depressive symptomatology including poor concentration, sleep disturbance, loss of appetite, dysphoria, and fleeting thoughts of suicide. (Suicidal risk assessment revealed no planning, a strong commitment to life, and confidence that he would never bring harm to himself.) Dave was preoccupied with thoughts of Amy, her total unwillingness to try to salvage the marriage, and the impending divorce. He felt anxious and was fearful about his unknown future. Dave could not believe that Amy no longer loved him and that she was ready to "break up our family." During the next several weeks, it became clear that the divorce was to become a reality.

Dave expressed feelings of tremendous loss. Not only was he upset over losing Amy, he felt that he was losing out on "rightful" parenthood.

The intervention with Dave included several constructivist elements, along with cognitive-behavioral intervention. The stress associated with losing Amy as his wife and the reduced access to his children (traditional visitation rights by temporary court order) was conceptualized as an opportunity to demonstrate his resiliency and creative problem solving. Although initially he responded passively to the legal proceedings, he fairly quickly took a proactive stance in seeking joint custody of the children. This was done through discussions with Amy, rather than through attorneys. The empty chair technique was utilized to rehearse these discussions. This technique was effective in limiting the angry expressions of his feelings of hurt. The imaginary enactments began with expressions of hurt, anger, betrayal, emotional expressions of incredulity, and acrid verbal attacks of Amy, and evolved to focused, emotionally controlled, caring expressions of a parenting plan of foremost benefit to the children and to both Amy and Dave. When Dave felt adequately prepared, he discussed with Amy his desire for joint custody of the children. Amy ultimately agreed to amend her divorce petition to reflect joint child custody.

As Dave became increasingly certain of the divorce, he maintained the view that he should never have married Amy. Dave was guided in putting the marriage into a broader perspective in which he might value this marriage and contemplate the positive meanings the relationship held as part of his evolving development. Further, Dave sought answers to why the divorce was happening. Although Amy maintained that she "merely fell out of love" with Dave, she had expressed concerns to Dave through the years about certain behaviors, attitudes, and relationship skill "deficiencies" (emotionally unavailable, poor communicator, unromantic). Dave initiated journaling in these two areas: valuing the marriage even though it is ending; determining answers to why it is ending. It was emphasized that one can never arrive at definitive answers as to why divorce happens, but some insights may be gained (potentially useful in future relationships). Dave journaled approximately daily and brought journal content into therapy for discussion. Through his journaling, Dave began to construe the marriage as more positively meaningful. In his quest for answers, Dave identified and recorded key family of origin factors in his development as a person and related some of this information to his relationship with Amy. He began to forge a different perspective on the marriage and its dissolution, and he came to understand himself better as he reviewed his family history and his life with Amy. He took that information and set goals and aspirations for his future with a greater sense of conviction in his capacity to influence the course of his life. Although he remained unhappy about the divorce and continued to feel the pain of his losses, he maintained confidence in his abilities to cope and felt positive about his future as a single parent.

CONCLUSION

There is much yet to be learned about how to help people conceptualize, experience, accommodate, and personally gain from divorce crises, and all forms of crises for that matter. This, however, is one of the challenges that helping professionals have assumed. In this chapter, the goal has been to bring attention and give form to the crises of divorce, and to promote the application of cognitive-behavioral and constructivist approaches to divorce crisis intervention. These approaches hold much promise in ameliorating human distress and in promoting creatively adaptive and subjectively successful evolving selfhood.

REFERENCES

Anderson, W. T. (1990). *Reality isn't what it used to be*. San Francisco: Harper & Row.

Anthony, J. C., & Petronis, K. R. (1991). Suspected risk factors for depression among adults 18–44 years old. *Epidemiology, 2*, 123–132.

Bandura, A. (1977a). Self-efficacy: Toward a unifying theory of behavioral change. *Psychological Review, 84*, 191–215.

Bandura, A. (1977b). *Social learning theory*. Englewood Cliffs, NJ: Prentice Hall.

Bandura, A. (1986). *Social foundations of thought and action: A social cognitive theory*. Englewood Cliffs, NJ: Prentice Hall.

Bandura, A. (1996a). Reflections on human agency: Part I. *Constructive Change, 1*(2), 3–12.

Bandura, A. (1996b). Reflections on human agency: Part II. *Constructivism in the Human Sciences, 1*(3–4), 5–15.

Bard, M., & Ellison, K. (1974). Crisis intervention and evidence of forcible rape. *The Police Chief, 41*, 68–73.

Beach, S. R. H., Sandeen, E. E., & O'Leary, K. D. (1990). *Depression in marriage*. New York: Guilford Press.

Beck, A. T. (1967). *Depression: Causes and treatment*. Philadelphia: University of Pennsylvania Press.

Beck, A. T. (1976). *Cognitive therapy and the emotional disorders*. New York: International Universities Press.

Beck, A. T. (1987). Hopelessness as a predictor of eventual suicide. *Annals of the New York Academy of Sciences: Psychobiology of Suicidal Behavior, 487*, 90–96.

Beck, A. T. (1993). Cognitive approaches to stress. In P. M. Lehrer & R. L. Woolfolk (Eds.), *Principles and practice of stress management* (2nd ed., pp. 333–372). New York: Guilford Press.

Beck, A. T., Resnik, H. L. P., & Lettieri, D. J. (1986). *The prediction of suicide*. Philadelphia: Charles Press.

Beck, A. T., Rush, A. J., Shaw, B. F., & Emery, G. (1979). *Cognitive therapy of depression*. New York: Guilford Press.

Bongar, B. (1991). *The suicidal patient: Clinical and legal standards of care*. Washington, DC: American Psychological Association.

Burgess, A., & Holstrom, L. (1974). *Rape: Victims of crisis*. Bowie, MD: Robert J. Brady.

Cantor, C. H., & Slater, P. J. (1995). Marital breakdown, parenthood, and suicide. *Journal of Family Studies, 1*(2), 91–104.

Chiriboga, D. A., & Cutler, L. (1977). Stress responses among divorcing men and women. *Journal of Divorce, 1,* 95–106.

Clark, D. A., Beck, A. T., & Alford, B. A. (1999). *Scientific foundations of cognitive theory and therapy of depression.* New York: Wiley.

Costello, C. G. (1982). Social factors associated with depression: A retrospective community study. *Psychological Medicine, 12,* 329–339.

Ellis, A. (1958). Rational psychotherapy. *Journal of General Psychology, 59,* 35–49.

Ellis, A. (1962). *Reason and emotion in psychotherapy.* New York: Lyle Stuart.

Ellis, A. (1990). Is rational emotive therapy (RET) "rationalist" or "constructivist"? In A. Ellis & W. Dryden (Eds.), *The essential Albert Ellis* (pp. 114–141). New York: Springer.

Epstein, N., & Schlesinger, S. E. (1994). Couples problems. In F. M. Dattilio & A. Freeman (Eds.), *Cognitive-behavioral strategies in crisis intervention* (pp. 258–277). New York: Guilford Press.

Everett, C., & Everett, S. V. (1994). *Healthy divorce.* San Francisco: Jossey-Bass.

Franklin, C., & Nurius, P. S. (Eds.). (1998). *Constructivism in practice: Methods and challenges.* Milwaukee, WI: Families International.

Freeman, A., & Dattilio, F. M. (1994). Introduction. In F. M. Dattilio & A. Freeman (Eds.), *Cognitive-behavioral strategies in crisis intervention* (pp. 1–22). New York: Guilford Press.

Freeman, A., & Reinecke, M. (1993). *Cognitive therapy of suicidal behavior.* New York: Springer.

Freeman, A., & White, D. M. (1989). The treatment of suicidal behavior. In A. Freeman, K. M. Simon, L. E. Beutler, & H. Arkowitz (Eds.), *Comprehensive handbook of cognitive therapy* (pp. 321–346). New York: Plenum.

Gallo, J. J., Royall, D. R., & Anthony, J. C. (1993). Risk factors for the onset of depression in middle age and later life. *Social Psychiatry and Psychiatric Epidemiology, 28,* 101–108.

Goldenberg, H. (1983). *Contemporary clinical psychology* (2nd ed.). Monterey, CA: Brooks/Cole.

Granvold, D. K. (1989). Postdivorce treatment. In M. Textor (Ed.), *The divorce and divorce therapy handbook* (pp. 197–219). Northvale, NJ: Jason Aronson.

Granvold, D. K. (1994). Cognitive-behavioral divorce therapy. In D. K. Granvold (Ed.), *Cognitive and behavioral treatment: Methods and applications* (pp. 222–246). Pacific Grove, CA: Brooks/Cole.

Granvold, D. K. (1996a). Challenging roles of the constructive therapist: Expert and agent of social responsibility. *Constructivism in the Human Sciences, 1,* 16–21.

Granvold, D. K. (1996b). Constructivist psychotherapy. *Families in Society: The Journal of Contemporary Human Services, 77*(6), 345–359.

Granvold, D. K. (in press). Constructivist theory and practice. In P. Lehmann & N. Coady (Eds.), *Theoretical perspectives in direct social work practice: An eclectic-generalist approach.* New York: Springer.

Granvold, D. K. (2000). The crisis of divorce: Cognitive-behavioral and constructivist assessment and treatment. In A. R. Roberts (Ed.), *Crisis intervention handbook: Assessment, treatment, and research* (2nd ed.). Oxford, UK: Oxford University Press.

Granvold, D. K., & Martin, J. I. (1999). Family therapy with gay and lesbian clients. In C. Franklin & C. Jordan (Eds.), *Family practice: Brief systems methods for social work* (pp. 299–320). Pacific Grove, CA: Brooks/Cole.

Guidano, V. F. (1988). A systems, process-oriented approach to cognitive therapy. In K. S. Dobson (Ed.), *Handbook of cognitive-behavioral therapies* (pp. 307–354). New York: Guilford Press.

Guidano, V. F. (1991). *The self in process.* New York: Guilford Press.

Held, B. S. (1995). *Back to reality: A critique of postmodern theory in psychotherapy.* New York: Norton.

Held, B. S. (1996). Constructivism in psychotherapy: Truth and consequences. *Annals of the New York Academy of Sciences, 775,* 198–206.

Holmes, T. H., & Rahe, R. H. (1967). Social adjustment rating scale. *Journal of Psychosomatic Research, 11,* 213–218.

Ingram, R. E., & Kendall, P. C. (1986). Cognitive clinical psychology: Implications of an information processing perspective. In R. E. Ingram (Ed.), *Information processing approaches to clinical psychology* (pp. 3–21). New York: Academic Press.

Kelly, G. A. (1955). *The psychology of personal constructs.* New York: Norton.

Lazarus, R. S. (1989). Constructs of the mind in mental health and psychotherapy. In A. Freeman, K. M. Simon, L. E. Beutler, & H. Arkowitz (Eds.), *Comprehensive handbook of cognitive therapy* (pp. 99–121). New York: Plenum.

Mahoney, M. J. (1988). The cognitive sciences and psychotherapy: Patterns in a developing relationship. In K. S. Dobson (Ed.), *Handbook of cognitive therapies* (pp. 357–386). New York: Guilford Press.

Mahoney, M. J. (1991). *Human change processes: The scientific foundations of psychotherapy.* New York: Basic Books.

Mahoney, M. J. (Ed.). (1995). *Cognitive and constructive psychotherapies: Theory, research, and practice.* New York: Springer.

Mahoney, M. J. (in press). *Constructive psychotherapy: Exploring principles and practical exercises.* New York: Guilford Press.

Martin, J. (1994). *The construction and understanding of psychotherapeutic change: Conversations, memories, and theories.* New York: Teachers College Press.

Maturana, H., & Varela, F. (1987). *The tree of knowledge.* Boston: New Science Library.

McCubbin, H. I., & Patterson, J. M. (1983). The family stress process: The double ABCX model of adjustment and adaptation. In H. I. McCubbin, M. B. Sussman, & J. M. Patterson (Eds.), *Social stress and the family: Advances and developments in family stress theory and research* (pp. 7–37). New York: Haworth Press.

McCubbin, M. A., & McCubbin, H. I. (1989). Theoretical orientations to family stress and coping. In C. R. Figley (Ed.), *Treating stress in families* (pp. 3–43). New York: Brunner/Mazel.

McMillen, J. C. (1999). Better for it: How people benefit from adversity. *Social Work, 44*(5), 455–468.

Meichenbaum, D. (1994). *A clinical handbook/practical therapist manual for assessing and treating adults with post-traumatic stress disorder (PTSD).* Waterloo, Ontario: Institute Press.

Michelson, L. (1987). Cognitive-behavioral assessment and treatment of agoraphobia. In L. Michelson & L. M. Ascher (Eds.), *Anxiety and stress disorders: Cognitive-behavioral assessment and treatment* (pp. 213–279). New York: Guilford Press.

Minister's Secretariat, Statistics and Information Department. (1999, February 5). *Vital statistics of Japan.* Tokyo: Minister of Health and Welfare.

Monthly Vital Statistics Report. (1990). Vol. 43, No. 9, Supplement.

National Center for Health Statistics. (1986, September 25). Advance report of final divorce statistics. In *1984 Monthly Vital Statistics Report, 35*(6) (Supp. DHS Pub. No. PHS 86–1120). Hyattsville, MD: U.S. Public Health Service.

Neimeyer, G. J. (Ed.). (1993). *Constructivist assessment: A casebook.* Newbury Park, CA: Sage.

Neimeyer, R. A. (1993). An appraisal of constuctivist psychotherapies. *Journal of Consulting and Clinical Psychology, 61,* 221–234.

Neimeyer, R. A. (1995). Constructivist psychotherapies: Features, foundations, and future directions. In R. A. Neimeyer & M. J. Mahoney (Eds.), *Constructivism in psychotherapy* (pp. 11–38). Washington, DC: American Psychological Association.

Neimeyer, R. A., & Mahoney, M. J. (Eds.). (1995). *Constructivism in psychotherapy.* Washington, DC: American Psychological Association.

Olson, D. (1997). Family stress and coping: A multi-system perspective. In S. Dreman (Ed.), *The family on the threshold of the 21st century: Trends and implications.* New York: Erlbaum.

Reinecke, M. A. (1994). Suicide and depresion. In F. M. Dattilio & A. Freeman (Eds.), *Cognitive-behavioral strategies in crisis intervention* (pp. 67–103). New York: Guilford Press.

Rice, J. K., & Rice, D. G. (1986). *Living through divorce: A developmental approach to divorce therapy.* New York: Guilford Press.

Roberts, A. R. (1990). An overview of crisis theory and crisis intervention. In A. R. Roberts (Ed.), *Crisis intervention handbook* (pp. 3–16). Belmont, CA: Wadsworth.

Rosen, H. (1993). Developing themes in the field of cognitive psychology. In K. T. Kuehlwein & H. Rosen (Eds.), *Cognitive therapies in action: Evolving innovative practice* (pp. 403–434). San Francisco: Jossey-Bass.

Saleebey, D. (1992). Introduction: Power in the people. In D. Saleebey (Ed.), *The strengths perspective in social work practice* (pp. 3–26). White Plains, NY: Longman.

Scanzoni, J. (1972). *Sexual bargaining.* Englewood Cliffs, NJ: Prentice Hall.

Seaward, B. L. (1999). *Managing stress: Principles and strategies for health and wellbeing.* Sudbury, MA: Jones & Bartlett.

Sexton, T. L., & Griffin, B. L. (Eds.). (1997). *Constructivist thinking in counseling practice, research, and training.* New York: Teachers College Press.

Slaiku, K. A. (1990). *Crisis intervention* (2nd ed.). Boston: Allyn & Bacon.

Tomb, D. A. (1994). The phenomenology of post-traumatic stress disorder. In D. A. Tomb (Ed.), *The psychiatric clinics of North America* (Vol. 8). Philadelphia: Saunders.

Trovato, F. (1986). The relationship between marital dissolution and suicide: The Canadian case. *Journal of Marriage and the Family, 48,* 341–348.

United Nations Secretariat. (1998). *Demographic yearbook* (1996 ed.). New York: Department for Economic and Social Information and Policy Analysis, United Nations Secretariat.

von Glasersfeld, E. (1984). An introduction to radical constructivism. In P. Waltzlawick (Ed.), *The invented reality* (pp. 17–40). New York: Norton.

Watson, J. C., & Greenberg, L. S. (1996). Emotion and cognition in experiential therapy: A dialectical constructivist perspective. In H. Rosen & K. T. Kuehlwein (Eds.), *Constructing realities: Meaning-making perspectives for psychotherapists* (pp. 253–274). San Francisco: Jossey-Bass.

Weiss, R. S. (1975). *Marital separation.* New York: Basic Books.

Weissman, M. M., Bruce, M., Leaf, P., Florio, L., & Holzer, C. (1991). Affective disorders. In L. Robins & E. Regier (Eds.), *Psychiatric disorders in America* (pp. 53–80). New York: Free Press.

SUGGESTED READINGS

Beck, A. T. (1993). Cognitive approaches to stress. In P. M. Lehrer & R. L. Woolfolk (Eds.), *Principles and practice of stress management* (2nd ed., pp. 333–372). New York: Guilford Press.

Clark, D. A., Beck, A. T., & Alford, B. A. (1999). *Scientific foundations of cognitive theory and therapy of depression.* New York: Wiley.

Franklin, C. & Nurius, P. S. (Eds.). (1998). *Constructivism in practice: Methods and challenges.* Milwaukee, WI: Families International.

Granvold, D. K. (in press). The crisis of divorce: Cognitive-behavioral and constructivist assessment and treatment. In A. R. Roberts (Ed.), *Crisis intervention handbook: Assessment, treatment, and research* (2nd ed.). Oxford, UK: Oxford University Press.

Meichenbaum, D. (1994). *A clinical handbook/practical therapist manual for assessing and treating adults with post-traumatic stress disorder (PTSD).* Waterloo, Ontario: Institute Press.

Roberts, A. R. (Ed.). (in press). *Crisis intervention handbook: Assessment, treatment, and research* (2nd ed.). Oxford, UK: Oxford University Press.

Textor, M. (Ed.). (1989). *The divorce and divorce therapy handbook.* Northvale, NJ: Aronson.

16

Critical Incident
Stress Debriefing

Kenneth R. Harbert

This chapter describes a comprehensive, systemic, and multicomponent approach to traumatic stress. This integrative, comprehensive approach offers prevention and mitigation of critical incident (traumatic) stress.

CRISIS

Crisis has many meanings. These meanings change depending on an individual's past experience and his/her understanding of stresses in everyday living. For some individuals critical life events or a sudden turning point in life may present itself as a crisis. For others, this same life event may offer both opportunity and threat. Life, as we know it today, operates in the nanosecond of the computer, via the Internet, or through the handy cellular phone. The world is full of situations that are often unpleasant, embarrassing, and even life threatening. Companies that offer online stock trading have in-house psychologists to support their stockbrokers. Financial survival and everyday lives are affected by the hyperspeed information age that exists today. Crisis brings a new meaning to the terms eustress and distress that Selye (1956) defined more than 40 years ago.

Often events occur that we cannot control: Our cars break down, the kids get sick the day of an important meeting, the computer crashes in the middle of an essential report. These events are often referred to as "crises." Sometimes these crises occur as a combination of events that make instant decisions necessary.

Hoff (1995) defined *crisis* in the clinical sense as an acute emotional upset arising from situational, developmental, or sociocultural sources and resulting in a temporary inability to cope by means of one's usual problem-solving ability. Trauma may or may not be associated with a crisis. The way that each individual deals with a crisis is unique to his/her coping ability, values, life experiences, fears, expectations, and beliefs. A group of history teachers may see an accidental electrocution as a dramatic traumatic event, but health care workers in an emergency room might see the same event as nothing out of the ordinary. Crisis does not occur in isolation, there is often a dynamic interplay between stress, event, and perhaps trauma. Yet trauma is neither general everyday stress nor simply a life crisis. Traumatic stress is an extreme event far out of the normal range of daily life.

TRAUMA

Janet (1889) wrote that intense emotional reactions make events traumatic by interfering with the integration of the experience into existing schemes. He believed that intense emotions cause memories of particular events to be dissociated from consciousness and instead stored as visceral sensations or visual images. van der Hart, Brown, and van der Kolk (1989) described how Janet thought that the physiological response to trauma accounted for the continued emergency responses to subsequent stresses. Janet claimed that fear needs to be tamed for proper cognitive appraisal and for appropriate action. He felt that experiences that overwhelm people's coping mechanisms set the stage for automatic and excessive reactions to subsequent stressors. Further, van der Hart, Brown, and van der Kolk (1989) described how trauma victims seemed to react to memories of the original trauma and that many were unable to put the event aside into the past. Clinicians, researchers, and educators have devoted a great deal of study to psychological trauma in the last 50 years (most notably Horowitz, 1976; Green, 1985; Wilson, 1989; van der Kolk, 1994; Terr, 1990; Pennebaker & Susman, 1988; Figley, 1995a; Mitchell, 1983; Williams, 1987; Wilson & Raphael, 1993; Erickson, 1976; Danieli, 1988; Mitchell & Bray, 1990; Cobb & Lindemann, 1943; and Mitchell & Everly, 1996). Freud's (1954) work with war neuroses lead him to believe that trauma was biologically based.

Mitchell and Bray (1990) defined traumatic stress as the stress response produced when a person is exposed to a disturbing traumatic event. This reaction to a traumatic event may be immediate or delayed.

In 1985 Figley described traumatic stress reaction as the natural and consequent behaviors and emotions that have a set of conscious and unconscious actions and behaviors associated with dealing with the stressors or memories of the experience. He described experiences that are so traumatically stressful and place such high demands on the person for change that the person's psychosocial resources are challenged sufficiently to create pathology. The resulting pathologies are labeled as traumatic stress disorders.

In 1995 he identified different specific types of trauma. These include *simultaneous trauma,* which takes place when all members of a group are directly affected at the same time. An example of this is when a hurricane hits a small community. Another type of trauma he described is *vicarious trauma,* which occurs when a single member is affected but is out of contact from other members of a community or group. An example of this type of trauma would be the trauma experienced following a plane crash by the family members or home communities of victims of the crash. This type of trauma occurs because of imagined or perceived concerns or fears, not direct experience, and the intensity of the trauma will vary depending on the closeness of family or community ties. Vicarious trauma can also apply to the therapist that listens to stories of pain and suffering day after day. Families and communities suffer more, however, because of their empathic personal connections to victims. *Intrafamilial trauma* is trauma and/or abuse that takes place when one member causes emotional injury to another member. Finally, he identified *secondary trauma* as something that occurs when the traumatic stress seems to cause effects in other members of a group, not involved directly with the event. Figley (1995a) refers to this phenomenon both as *secondary traumatic stress* (STS) and *secondary traumatic stress disorder* (STSD).

Horowitz (1991) described how trauma presents an assault on fundamental beliefs necessary for survival in the world. A traumatic event presents a clear threat to the existing conceptual framework by which the world is understood. In order to protect this framework, the mind automatically inhibits its own perception of the event and reduces the information being processed. Traumatic stress occurs when interpretation of traumatic events, coping ability, and the limitations of individual or group resources lead to stress so severe that relief is not found in usual ways.

Traumatic stress has had many names over the last 100 years. These include medical terms such physioneurosis or military terms such as *shell shock, traumatic neurosis,* or *combat fatigue.* Occupational nomenclature such as *operational exhaustion* and *compensation neurosis* are also used. Currently, researchers and clinicians are still trying to define how traumatic stress differs from other stressors.

Traumatic stress is elusive because as our society changes, so will the societal view of trauma. An example of historical trauma are the heroic stories of World War II soldiers involved in the D-Day operation, recalled by veterans years later, in part as a result of current retellings such as the movie *Saving Private Ryan.*

Traumatic stress differs from general stress, cumulative stress, or even distress. Traumatic events affect the psychological functioning and coping ability of victims. These are not events of simple distress but rather traumatic events outside the realm of normal, everyday life experience that have had lifetime effects on the survivors, caregivers, and families.

Although there is some historical documentation of how traumatic stress affects individuals, researchers still try to understand the interactions of individuals and the stressor event, including variables such as the individual or group personalities, coping processes involved, and the psychological and biological mechanisms affected by trauma.

There are significant differences between disasters of natural origin and traumatic events of human origin. Natural events are uncontrolled, violent forces of nature (fire, water, wind), which can pale in comparison to disasters or events brought about by human agents. A child is killed in a drive-by shooting. This random act of violence is not inevitable, yet a child dies suddenly, and without reason. Natural catastrophes have "causes"; deaths by drive-by just "happen."

Although the term *traumatology* has been used in medical nomenclature to describe the team of specialists that deal with multisystem traumatic wounds or injuries, the psychological definition is much more recent. Donovan (1991) defined "traumatology as the study of natural and man-made trauma, and the geophysical response to the horrors of human inadvertent or volitional cruelty, the social and psychobiological effects thereof, and the predictive–preventive–interventionist pragmatics which evolve from that study" (pp. 433–436). Further traumatology recognizes that human experience is mediated physiologically and thus has physiological consequences. The physiological response to trauma is entirely interpretative, which is one reason different individuals respond differently to potentially traumatic events. If traumatic experience can be formative and deformative, it can also be reformative. Figley (1993) used the term *traumatology* to describe the investigation and applications of knowledge about the immediate and long-term psychosocial consequences of highly stressful events and the factors that affect those consequences.

The reaction to a traumatic stressor begins with the response to the event and continues as long as symptoms are present. Symptoms may be swift in onset, as in an acute reaction, within minutes after an event. This response might be a normal grief response, as would be expected after a tragedy.

If intense symptoms persist, or if the symptoms appear days or weeks after the event and then continue, a cumulative or delayed stress reaction may be present. A posttraumatic syndrome of symptoms may last months or decades. Avoidance behavior may be present in all of these, and the emotional response may impair the person's ability to function and relate to other people. There are many variables that determine how someone might be affected by traumatic stress, including age, experience, expectations, interpretations, understanding, and perceptions of the traumatic event. Recovery from a traumatic event can be affected by personality, nature of the stressors experienced, coping resources, support resources, and the nature of the adaptation, which may involve a positive change in character.

DIMENSIONS OF TRAUMATIC STRESS

Janet (1889) contended that when people react to experiences with "vehement emotions," it interferes with information processing and appropriate actions. The hyperarousal is responsible for the memory disturbances that accompany traumatization and interferes with the way that information is processed on a verbal, symbolic level. This hyperarousal causes memories to be split off from consciousness and to be experienced only somatically. Fragments of these "visceral" memories return later as physiological reactions, emotional states, visual images, or behavioral reenactments.

Pavlov (1926) investigated the trauma response as the result of physiological changes in behavior. He defined the term *defensive reaction* for a cluster of innate reflexive responses to environmental threats.

Selye (1956) described the pituitary–adrenocortical response to experimental stressors. He described a general adaptation syndrome, which detailed the characteristic responses to major personal threats—alarm, resistance, and, ultimately, exhaustion. Stress, he said, was the rate of all the wear and tear caused by life. These were separated into "eustress," or good stress, such as that caused by marriage, and "distress," such as that caused by divorce.

The term *gross stress reaction* was included in the first edition of the *Diagnostic and Statistical Manual of Mental Disorders* in 1952. Gross stress reaction was defined as the reversible and transient response to stress. This diagnosis was removed in the second edition, only to return after significant modification in the third and fourth editions. DSM-IV (American Psychiatric Association, 1994) states that posttraumatic stress disorder (PTSD) can be acute, chronic, or delayed.

A new category, which is described as *acute stress disorder,* differs from PTSD in terms of time, onset, and duration of symptoms. Symptoms typically occur within four weeks of the incident and last minimum of two days to a maximum of four weeks.

The new interpretation states that acute stress disorders are human responses to a traumatic event in which the person experienced, witnessed, or was confronted with an event that involved actual or threatened death or serious injury or even a threat to the physical integrity of self or others. Johnson (1998) asserted that the DSM-IV definition does not adequately cover the acute stress responses of children. Horowitz (1991) and van der Kolk (1987) explained the process of posttraumatic reactions as largely based in cognitive psychology and learning theory. These theories are important because they account for four common phenomena associated with posttraumatic stress: denial, psychic numbing, reexperiencing, and affective disorder symptoms.

Wilson (1989), Pynoos (1990), Green (1985), Erickson (1976), and Haley (1974) have all described the process, but in different terms and with different focuses. Wilson described traumatic events as variables that include eleven dimensions: degree of life threat; degree of bereavement or loss of significant others; rate of onset and offset of the stressors; duration and severity of the stressors; level of the displacement and dislodging of persons from their community; exposure to death, dying, injury, destruction, and social chaos; degree of moral conflict inherent in the situation; role in the trauma (agent versus victim); location of trauma; complexity of the stressor; impact of the trauma in the community. He demonstrated that the more these dimensions are present in any particular trauma, the greater the potential for producing a pathological outcome.

Other variables such as social support, personality and situational variables will interact with those dimensions in determining posttrauma adaptation.

Traumatic events can be experienced alone, with others, or in the context of a community experience. Several examples in the 1990s were the school shooting incidents across the United States. Although most studies on traumatic stress disorders have focused on adults, a number of studies have emerged which focus on the effects of trauma at various age levels.

Pynoos (1990) described anxiety disorders, chronic hyperarousal, cognitive distortion, and cognitive denial in acutely traumatized children. He pointed out nonverbal signs of posttraumatic stress that are of special note in assessment among younger children. Harber and Pennebaker (1993) discussed overcoming traumatic memories.

Green described applying eye movement desensitization and reprocessing (EMDR) to the treatment of traumatized children. Herman (1992) talked about trauma and recovery during the aftermath of violence from domestic abuse to political terror. Ornitz and Pynoos (1989) discuss startle modulation in children with PTSD. Pynoos (1990) listed a range of behaviors manifested by children who have undergone acute posttraumatic stress. Terr (1981, 1990) discussed psychic trauma in children and the fact that children do not experience intrusive imagery or flashbacks.

Erikson described the term *loss of community* in relationship to the massive social and individual trauma that occurred during the Buffalo Creek Dam disaster (a devastating flood that killed over 125 people and displaced thousands in West Virginia in 1972). This event not only exposed the survivors to high degrees of death, dying, and destruction; it eliminated many of the normal social support systems necessary for recovery. Haley described the impact of traumatic stress on the psychotherapists that care for this diverse populations of victims.

Traumatic Stress Psychobiology

The limbic system plays an important role in guiding the emotions that stimulate the behavior necessary for self-preservation and survival of the species. MacLean (1985) pointed out that it is responsible for complex behaviors such as feeding, fighting, fleeing, and reproduction. The limbic system also assigns free-floating feelings of significance, truth, and meaning to experience (Bremner & Narayan, 1998). The limbic system is also the primary area of the central nervous system (CNS) in which memories are processed and is most likely the location of explanations for the memory disturbancesthat follow trauma. The hippocampus, which records in memory the spatial and temporal dimensions of experiences, does not fully mature until the third or fourth year of life. Sudden and overwhelming stress is accompanied by the release of many endogenous neurohormones, such as cortisol, epinephrine and norepinephrine, vasopressin, oxytocin, and endogenous opioids.

Squire (1987) reported that the hippocampal localization system remains vulnerable to ongoing disruption and severe or prolonged stress can suppress hippocampal functioning. Post, Pickar, Ballenger, and Naber (1984) discussed how the limbic system involves *kindling,* which is repeated stimulation, and oversees sensitization of limbic neuronal circuits. These lower firing neuronal thresholds can cause long-term alterations in excitability after a traumatic event. Trauma might then lead to lasting neurobiological and behavioral changes mediated by alteration in the temporal lobe.

van der Kolk (1996) described the shrinking of the hippocampus after severe trauma, due to the increased levels of cortisol, which can be toxic to the hippocampus. Lowered serotonin activity in traumatic stress is at the core of a diminished efficacy of the behavioral inhibition system, which in turn is responsible for the continuation of emergency responses to minor stresses long after the actual trauma has ended.

Squire (1987) described the body's responses to these increased physical or psychological demands by releasing norepinephrine from the locus coeruleus and adrenocorticotropin (ACTH) from the anterior pituitary. Peripherally the body's stress response consists of the secretion of norepinephrine by the sympathetic nerves and of epinephrine by the adrenal medulla. These hormones help mobilize the energy necessary to deal with the stressors ranging from increased glucose release to enhanced immune function. In a well-functioning organism, stress produces rapid and pronounced hormonal responses.

Post, Pickar, Pallenger, and Naber (1984) described how chronic persistent stress blunts this affective stress response and induces sensitization. They state that after prolonged stress secretion of corticotropin releasing factor (CRF) results in less cyclic AMP formation and ACTH release because of down regulation of CRF receptors. Therefore, the release of the stress hormone ACTH is controlled by complex regulatory mechanisms. They describe that multiple factors such as CRF, vasopressin, catecholamines, and other hormones stimulate ACTH release by acting on the anterior pituitary.

van der Kolk (1994) described how the impact of traumatic memories interferes with declarative memory but does not inhibit implicit memory that controls conditioned emotional responses, skills and habit, and sensations related to experience. He described two types of abnormalities following trauma. The first consists of heightened responsiveness to trauma-specific stimulus. The second consists of overarousal to intense stimuli that are not trauma related, as other arousal symptoms to loud noises or other abrupt but trauma-neutral experiences. He pointed out that the over-activation of the autonomic nervous system results from a lack of integration of highly emotionally charged memories with the cognitive structuring of experience.

The rapidly expanding knowledge of the effects of traumatic stress on the central nervous system provides the awareness that memory and ongoing functions of memory are at the core of the psychological disruptions seen with chronic traumatic stress disorders and posttraumatic stress disorders.

Those who experience traumatic stress may benefit from a variety of medications including, but not limited to, benzodiazepines and tricyclic antidepressants, which decrease the long-term effects of inescapable shock and seem to have some use in the pharmacotherapy of treating severe traumatic stress. Davidson and Nemeroff (1989) proposed that the selection of the right medication is dependent on understanding the basic neurobiology of the type of arousal.

EFFECT OF TRAUMA ON PROFESSIONAL HELPERS

Helpers and caregivers are expected, by society and by peers, to provide treatment to the victims of traumatic events. Their role during and after the traumatic event can be both physically and emotionally demanding. Lamberg (1999) reported that they also are expected to cope with these events without having serious emotional problems themselves. She reported that physicians are reluctant to seek psychological help, due to issues of trust and role delineation. She revealed that peers, patients, family members, and society expect outcomes that leave health care workers feeling being a good practitioner means leading a masochistic life. Vicarious traumatization can occur in a health care professional or helper who is exposed secondhand to trauma. This has been seen with therapists, counselors, and community workers who provide crisis intervention and psychological assistance to victims. Myers (1995) found that the more the helper connects with those helped, the greater the helper's vulnerability to what Figley (1995b) termed secondary traumatic stress disorder. Caregivers and helpers who deliver lifesaving skills for seriously ill or dying patients often find it difficult, if not impossible, to share their feelings and fears with family and friends who did not share in the experience. Therapists may find it difficult to deal with the graphic accounts of the traumatic event of their clients. It is safe to watch these traumatic events on television shows such as *ER*, but the real traumatic events may leave the victim and/or helper with significant problems with decision making and concentration, detachment, guilt, numbness, and problems with sleeping.

The issue of work-related secondary traumatic stress has brought about many different terms including *compassion fatigue* (Figley, 1991, 1995b); *countertransference* (Haley, 1974); secondary traumatic stress and vicarious traumatization is often displayed by mental health workers supporting clients with posttraumatic stress disorders, which have been combined and described as secondary traumatic stress disorders. Trauma affects many individuals involved either directly or indirectly with the event. The impact of trauma on physicians, nurses, emergency personnel (Mitchell, 1983); police officers (Williams, 1987); and firefighters (Robinson & Mitchell, 1995) have been well documented.

Fitzpatrick and Wilson (1999) found a link to the violence that abortion workers face and the risk of developing posttraumatic stress disorder. They felt that health care workers and mental health workers in high-risk environments experiencing chronic exposure to violence might experience more mental health problems.

McCann and Pearlman (1990) found that the cumulative nature of vicarious trauma emphasizes the profound effects on the helper's sense of meaning, identity, worldview, and beliefs about self and others. Pearlman and Saakvitne (1995) found that work with trauma forces caregivers/helpers to acknowledge daily the reality of trauma in the world; become aware of the potential for traumatic hurt and loss in their own lives; confront reminders of personal past traumas; deal with those who manifest powerful needs and mistrust; and those who are reenacting painful, abusive, and denigrating relationships within the patient/client situation; and understand those who often cast them in dangerous or exploitative roles that may assault their sense of self-worth. The traumatic event may create difficult images and information for the caregiver/helper to understand, especially if symptoms in the caregiver/helper develop and interfere with his/her daily lives or family interaction.

Trauma and exposure to trauma in others can cause concerns of self-worth and identity in the caregiver/helper. Arvay and Uhlemann (1996) found in a study of stress in counselors dealing with traumatic stress clients that 14% of counselors working with trauma victims reported traumatic stress levels similar to those experienced by clients with PTSD. This is quite significant as they cite other studies that report rates of only 7% to 11% of PTSD among victims exposed to violent crime, deaths, and accidents, and 5% to 8% rates of PTSD among victims of environmental trauma. They found that 16% of counselors working with trauma victims reported emotional exhaustion and burnout. Compare this with studies cited showing 2% to 6% rates of burnout among psychotherapists not specializing in trauma.

HELPING THE HELPERS

The response to trauma varies with each individual, from the person on the street to the clinic mental health worker providing crisis intervention. Harbert and Hunsinger (1991) described how health care workers can fully recover within days or weeks of a traumatic event; yet a few may be so overwhelmed that their ability to function at work and in relationships with family members and/or friends is jeopardized.

Historically one of the first health care centers to offer assistance to health care workers facing traumatic stress was the Shock Trauma Center in Baltimore, Maryland. Epperson-Sebour (1977) was concerned with the turnover of experienced staff nurses. As a social worker in the family support services department, she developed a series of educational stress management programs in the mid-1970s.

Flanagan (1954) proposed a method of job analysis having workers keep a daily diary cataloguing specific successful and unsuccessful behaviors on the job. These "critical incidents" were believed to be powerful predictors of success or failure on the job. Later Mitchell (1983) borrowed this term from the field of organizational behavior, to describe the issues of traumatic stress among emergency medical personnel, which he termed "critical incident stress."

Everly and Mitchell (1997) discuss the use of this comprehensive management concept by other professional groups that have benefited from its use as a crisis intervention modality. These groups include mental health care systems, health care systems, psychiatric hospitals, rescue and disaster personnel, nursing personnel, jurors, military personnel, and educational systems.

Robinson and Murdoch (1991) strongly recommend using peer support groups working closely with mental health professionals to overcome traumatic stressors. They point out that the two groups should train together, work together, and undergo cross-field education (e.g., the mental health personnel should ride on emergency vehicles; the emergency technicians should learn basic counseling skills.) They feel the alliance between mental health professionals and peer support personnel will offer alternative and mutually supportive services. They go on to support the use of the critical incident stress management (CISM) model that is used by the International Critical Incident Stress Foundation.

Harbert (1992) describes a hospital-based CISM team at Geisinger Medical Center a 500-bed multispecialty tertiary care center in central Pennsylvania. They established one of the first interdisciplinary CISM teams within a rural tertiary medical center to react to critical incident stress. The overall purpose of the CISM team was to provide rapid first response to issues that required primary, secondary, or tertiary crisis intervention. Primary intervention was provided for those most directly affected. Secondary intervention was provided for those who were observers of the event. Tertiary intervention was provided for those indirectly affected, such as family members or caregivers. The CISM team at Geisinger Medical Center conducted critical incident stress management when requested by any hospital staff member or supervisor through the hospital operator. The team was available any time incidents might occur on a 24-hour, 7-day-a-week basis.

The Geisinger team included physicians, physician assistants, nurses, social workers, emergency medical personnel, life flight personnel, mental health specialists, pastoral counselors, and an assigned administrator. All team members received basic and advanced training from the International Critical Incident Stress Foundation. The nursing, physician, and physician assistant members of the team were all active members of a regional CISM team and had participated in a number of CISM interventions. After three years of functioning, the CISM team found that early and appropriate intervention did significantly reduce the psychological impact of critical incidents (Harbert, 1992).

Wilson and Lindy (1995) describe the role of therapists as creating a protective context of sustained empathic inquiry, within which the trauma victim can integrate his/her traumatic experiences. The idea is that listening to the client's pain, suffering, and traumatic circumstances elicits stressful reactions in the therapist. They go on to describe two different types of countertransference reactions that occur when dealing with traumatic stress patients. The first is a general underresponsiveness to the person. During this encounter the therapist may dissociate themselves from the speaker and may experience a numbing response, deny or discount the validity of the clients experience, minimize the seriousness, avoid thinking about the clients needs, detach themselves from the client, or become overly clinical with the client. They describe this as therapist shutdown, becoming underresponsive after a long period of overresponsiveness. The second type of countertransference is overresponsiveness to the client. This occurs when the therapist has an overly responsive countertransference reaction.

Education programs preparing helping professionals (therapist, physicians, nurses, teachers, and social workers) often spend very little time focusing on the effects of countertransference.

Harbert (1999) described a mutilevel, comprehensive, "best practice" approach to developing undergraduate and graduate traumatic stress management programs for health care professionals. He describes the use of this "best practice" program in providing self-care, understanding traumatic stress, and the conceptual framing of critical incident stress management. He has used this approach for medical students, nurse practitioners, physician assistants, and postgraduate physicians in family practice.

Yassen (1993) has suggested an approach to self-care and prevention that includes physical, social, and professional approaches. Munroe et al. (1995) suggested that individual approaches are not enough, because the problem is generated in part by the workplace environment. They recommended incorporating the awareness of the depleting aspects of the work into the organization's attitudes toward and procedures for conducting business. In a similar vein, Pines and Aronson (1986) pointed out that people always have a need for appreciation, support, respect, and approval from their coworkers, not only at the time of crisis.

CRITICAL INCIDENT STRESS MANAGEMENT

Everly and Mitchell (1997) pointed out that the comprehensive nature of the CISM formulation finds its historical roots in the work of Caplan (1964), who proposed the idea of primary, secondary, and tertiary prevention of crisis.

Mitchell and Everly (1993) developed an integrated, multicomponent intervention system that focuses on reducing the frequency, duration, severity, and impairment from psychological crises. This system focuses on the value of mitigating the impact of the traumatic event on the people involved and assists in restoring understanding and healing after the event.

The effectiveness of their CISM system has been evaluated using qualitative analyses, as well as through controlled investigations and meta-analyses (Everly & Mitchell, 1998). Avery, King, Bretherton, and Orner (1999) raised questions for the need for further evidence-based rationales for advocating early therapeutic or nontherapeutic intervention when using the CISM model.

CISM is not a model of psychotherapy, but rather a supportive and preventive system using a comprehensive approach to critical incident stressors. Everly & Mitchell (1997) describe CISM as a subset of the "crisis intervention" model. They relate that the success and/or failure of CISM services depend on the knowledge, training, and skill of those providing the traumatic stress services. Cudmore (1996) discusses how nurses perceive the need for and the use of two types of CISM interventions when critical incidents occur. It is essential that the CISM worker have the ability and knowledge to choose the right intervention and then apply that intervention at the right time for the right reason as factors that can enhance or inhibit the success of a CISM program. They feel that their comprehensive, integrative, multicomponent crisis intervention system offers a powerful and cost-effective approach to crisis response using a supportive approach.

The CISM system is used by over 300 trauma response teams that operate in 19 nations. These teams have assisted with worldwide disasters and critical incidents all over the globe since the late 1980s.

CISM interventions are grounded in the dynamics of good communication. The seven core CISM interventions are

1. Preincident preparedness training
2. Individual one-on-one psychological support
3. Demobilizations
4. Critical incident stress debriefing (CISD)
5. Defusing
6. Family support
7. Referral mechanisms

These interventions are discussed in more detail further on.

The overall goals of CISM intervention (Everly & Mitchell, 1997) are (1) reducing the incidence, duration, and severity of or impairment from traumatic stress arising from crisis and disaster situations; (2) facilitating the access to formal mental health assessment and treatment if it is needed; and (3) helping others help themselves.

CISM provides a safe, supportive opportunity for individuals to express, self-disclose, and understand their emotions and reactions to something out of the ordinary. It focuses on separating what is perceived as real by an individual from what others at the incident or event recall as their perceptions, allowing for confirmation of the incident and the role of the individuals or group during the event CISM is grounded in communication protocols and provides calm communication, in a nonthreatening environment, which aligns and does not contradict communication between group members. CISM offers the opportunity for members of a group to express fears, concerns, and regrets within a group of peers while also having a CISM team of trained peers and mental health professionals provide them with support.

CISM should only be used by individuals who have been specifically trained in its uses. Having a background in medicine, psychiatric, psychology, nursing, or any other professional discipline does not automatically ensure that individuals understand or can use this technique. Everly and Mitchell (1997) point out that CISM training is focused on communication skills, understanding traumatic stress, and explores the signs and symptoms of traumatic stress. CISM training focuses on recovery and offering hope to individuals and groups. The key to successful use of this technique is that the team leader and team members have been trained and certified in this technique through the International Critical Incident Stress Foundation (ICISF).

CISM INTERVENTIONS FOR TRAUMATIC STRESS

Trauma occurs so rapidly that often many victims are left without understanding exactly what happened. Without communication we cannot understand another's interpretation of an event or issue, and we may hinder constructive crisis resolution. Crisis intervention and especially CISM offers the uniqueness of others' perceptions and the satisfaction of people helping others and helping themselves. As CISM groups are brought together to discuss the event during each of the interventions, they discover that their own capacities for interpretations of these events are as diverse as are the group members themselves.

Communication helps the person recall their traumatic experiences through emotional display, behavior, and verbal communication. Trust is an important and vital point of self-disclosure, which is why CISM encourages only those involved in the event to be present and to keep the entire process confidential. Victims find that friends or counselors may not listen because the event or incident is so overwhelming. Those involved in the incident are willing to discuss it in hopes of putting closure to the event along with their negative feeling, thoughts, and memories of the event.

Everly and Mitchell (1998) described CISM as an integrated, multicomponent system that offers a full range of services spanning the full crisis spectrum from precrisis preparation and on-scene support through postcrisis intervention and referral for formal mental health assessment and treatment.

The right type of intervention is essential, as is the proper timing in choosing the people who need assistance—not everyone needs help. Different interventions exist to fit the circumstances of the event. At times individual support is needed; at other times team or group support is needed.

Adaptation and accommodation of specific interventions to fit the circumstances are essential to deliver the best help to those who need it. Standardized training and CISM team experience (especially using peer team members) are crucial elements in using the right group of response personnel.

McGee (1974) found that individuals and groups in crisis need an opportunity to talk out the experience and express their feelings of fear, panic, and loss within a safe environment. He also described their need to become fully aware and accept what has happened to them. He points out that they need to resume activity and begin reconstructing their lives with the social, physical, and emotional resources available. He feels that people need to be listened to with concern and sympathy and understand the reality of what has happened a bit at a time.

McGee (1974) discussed the need for traumatic stress victims to make contact with friends, coworkers, and relatives and to find other resources to begin the process of social and physical reconstruction. Many of these opportunities are provided for with the interventions offered by CISM (Everly & Mitchell, 1997).

Emotional recovery requires that traumatized individuals be able to incorporate events into their everyday lives and to maintain at least some perception of control. Individuals have different perceptions of traumatic events and having the ability to understand these perceptions is central to understanding and resolving crisis. If a situation seems beyond one's control self-blame may be used as a way to cope with the event. It is important that victims attribute responsibility to the true source of traumatic stress rather than to themselves. Traumatized people should be linked to self-help and advocacy groups through which they might channel their anger into constructive action for necessary change (Wilson, 1989).

Preincident Preparedness Training

The first intervention in the CISM system of interventions is labeled *preincident preparation: psychological preparedness training* and occurs in the precrisis phase. This intervention is designed to set the appropriate expectation for the event while enhancing the behavioral response to the event. It is appropriate for personnel at risk from operational traumatic stress, such as helpers or health care workers in at-risk areas or health care students who will face real trauma situations. The goals of preincident preparation include setting appropriate expectations for actual experiences, increasing cognitive resources relevant to a crisis, and/or teaching behavioral stress management and personal coping techniques with the goal of preventing psychological dysfunction and disorder.

Education before traumatic stress is one of the most important components of a systematic, comprehensive, and multicomponent approach to the management of traumatic stress. Professional programs at the graduate level should assess the importance of providing this type of training prior to having students enter their clinical phase and evaluate the need for this type of training within their region for practicing professionals. Harbert's (1999) "best practice" model proposes providing health care professionals traumatic stress education at the undergraduate, graduate, and postgraduate level. One of his best practice models incorporates traumatic stress education throughout a system-directed approach to clinical medicine within a graduate physician assistant program. Harbert (1998) described how this best practice model of CISM could be used as a preventive educational model for use with medical students, nurse practitioners, and physician assistants.

One-on-One Psychological Support

The second intervention is individual psychological support, which can be applied on-scene during a crisis event or at any time after an event. A key factor here is that this intervention is done one-on-one by a mental health professional. Everly and Mitchell (1997) have described one specific protocol entitled the SAFER model, which peer counselors or mental health professionals can use for conducting individual crisis response interventions. The SAFER model includes stabilization of the situation, acknowledgement of crisis, facilitation of understanding, encouragement of adaptive coping, restoration of independent functioning, or referral for continued care. It may be used on-site or on-scene or anywhere at any time after the initial crisis or event occurs. This intervention should only be provided by a mental health professional.

Demobilization

The intervention that is best used at mass disaster sites to assist disaster response personnel to decompress and transition from the disaster site to home or work. This transitional intervention with large groups of 50 or more is termed a "demobilization," and involves offering refreshments and comfort within a safe environment and informal briefing about stress, trauma, and coping techniques. This usually takes about 20 to 30 minutes and is provided by a person trained in CISM techniques. This type of intervention provides a psychological and temporal transition from the traumatic event to some form of normalization (Everly & Mitchell, 1997)

Demobilization also provides an opportunity for psychological and psychophysiological decompression. This intervention sets realistic expectations for the psychological consequences of the crisis event and facilitates access to psychological and physical support systems.

Defusing

Defusing, primarily discussion or a short process for small groups, may be provided at the site of the incident or event after disengagement from the activity itself or in the immediate postevent phase within 12 hours after an incident or event. Defusing involves assessing individuals at the site of the incident and spending about 25 to 45 minutes focusing on group discussions of the incident. Defusings are be shortened versions of the debriefing and affirm the value of the personnel involved in the trauma, restore cognitive processing of the event, establish a safe place for group communication, and equalize the amount and fact-versus-fantasy of the information between members of a group involved in the event. Defusings are designed to reduce acute stress and tension levels among teams or groups involved in a traumatic event (Everly & Mitchell,1997).

Critical Incident Stress Debriefing

The critical incident stress debriefing (CISD) is the most complex of all the CISM interventions. This intervention was originally designed to reduce stress in emergency personnel but since the early 1990s it has been applied to a diverse group including college students, educational systems, law enforcement, health care systems, nursing personnel, military personnel, physician assistants, and physicians.

CISD is a specific model of psychological debriefing, developed by Mitchell (1983). It is a group process, employing both crisis intervention and educational processes, focusing on mitigating or resolving the psychological distress associated with a critical incident or traumatic event. Everly and Mitchell (1997) described it as an intervention designed to facilitate psychological closure to a traumatic event. They also point out that it is structured to move from nonthreatening information cognitive phases to affective phases.

The CISD team consists of a mental health professional and one or more peer support personnel. Both of these team members have received standardized training in CISM. This is a peer-managed and peer-driven process that uses mental health professionals for supervision and guidance.

This technique is utilized with a homogenous group of individuals who have experienced a traumatic event or crisis. The technique should be used at least 24 hours after the traumatic event has ended, or at least 24 hours after individuals have been operationally disengaged from the event with the clear expectation of not having to return to the event. This point of timing is essential if CISD is to be effective in mitigating the adverse psychological impact of a traumatic event. CISD's overriding goal is to facilitate psychological closure to a traumatic event.

CISD consists of a seven-phase protocol. The overall strategy for a CISD team is to start at the beginning, which is usually the easiest to discuss, and then move gradually into more emotionally intense discussions. Then the group is gradually brought back out of the intense discussions to the less intense discussions. The intervention includes: the introduction phase, the fact phase, the thought phase, the reaction phase, the symptom phase, the teaching phase, and the reentry phase.

CISD provides a finite behavioral structure. The process is initiated engaging the cognitive domain and is ideal for those persons engaged in the cognitive domain using cognitive analysis or denial mechanisms. It aligns with their psychological posture rather than contradicting or opposing it, avoiding the risk of initiating group conflict. As the CISD process continues affective ventilation or self-disclosure may be achieved.

Introduction Phase

The introduction sets the stage for all of the other phases of the debriefing. Objectives include introducing the CISD team members and the team leader (establishing the leadership of the team), and explaining the purpose of the meeting, the process, and the rules and guidelines of CISD. The latter include the following:

1. No one in the group has rank over another.
2. Everyone speaks for him/herself only.
3. No recorders or note taking are allowed.
4. Because CISD is neither a critique nor an investigation, participants are instructed not to disclose any information that would jeopardize an official investigation or would constitute an admission of criminal activity or deliberate violations of any usual policies and/or procedures.
5. No one is allowed to leave the room and not return.
6. Everyone is important to the complete process and is there to help him/herself and each other.
7. Whatever is stated in the room is confidential and it stays in the room (this applies to the team and the participants).
8. Participants are asked to turn off pagers, radios, and distracting devices.

Other objectives include gaining the cooperation of the participants, answering any questions or concerns from the group, and last, but not least, encouraging mutual help.

Fact Phase

The fact phase encourages participants to describe the traumatic event from their own perspective. Facts are a collection of items outside of oneself. Facts are impersonal. Discussions of facts are not as distressing as attempting to talk about how one feels, which is a very personal discussion. The team leader will start by stating:

> "We were not present during the event. We only know bits and pieces of the incident. It would be very helpful to hear from each of you, what your role was during the incident, and what you saw and heard happen. If you choose not to speak, that is Okay. Just shake your head and we will pass right over you."

This should be repeated by saying, "What we need to know is who are you, what was your job or role during the incident, what happened from your point of view." Often during the answers to these questions participants will spontaneously begin to show emotions. When participants in a debriefing are asked to describe the facts of the situation and they begin to express their emotions, it is a sign of how badly they have been affected by the event.

Thought Phase

This phase begins with the team leader asking the participants to state what their first thought or most prominent thought was once they got off an "autopilot" mode of operating or functioning. This phase allows the participants to describe their cognitive reactions to the event and to begin to transition to the affective domain.

The thought phase is the transitional phase between the factual world and the world that is close and personal. Facts are often outside of a person, but thoughts are internal and are part of the inner person. This is the phase in which participants may express anger at team members or at others regarding the event. The CISD team must be very alert to all participants' reactions during this phase.

Reaction Phase

The most emotional phase of CISD is the reaction phase. This phase identifies the most traumatic aspect of the event for participants who wish to speak and to allow for cathartic ventilation. This phase is entirely in the affective domain.

The question raised by the team leader is, "What was the worst thing about this incident, event or situation for you personally?" Other questions that follow for the group may include, "What bothered you the most?"; "If you could erase one part of this event what would it be?"; and "What aspect caused you the most pain?"

The discussion at this point is free ranging. Up until this phase the team leader has directed each of the questions to each member of the group in a round robin fashion usually starting from her/his right to left, or from left to right. But during the reaction phase anyone that wants to speak may do so.

This is the toughest point for the participants—now they are wrestling with the emotions they have begun to connect with the event. Some comments will trigger strong verbal group responses. Emotions will often pour out; sometimes they will be held back but the body language of the participant is screaming in anger or grief. This phase may last anywhere up to 40 minutes. When the discussion drops off or questions asked by the team members end with little or no response, it is a signal to move on to the next phase, the symptom phase.

Symptom Phase

The symptom phase is another transition phase. Everly and Mitchell (1997) described the objective as beginning to move the group back from the emotionally laden content of the reaction phase toward a more cognitively oriented area of discussion. The symptom phase is a natural part of the overall process from the cognitive domain to the emotional and then back to the cognitive domain. The debriefing is always continued to the end to complete the process and to restore people to the cognitive level so that they can resume the normal responsibilities of their lives, armed with their customary set of psychological defenses intact.

The symptom phase is initiated when the team asks the participants to describe any cognitive, physical, emotional, or behavioral experiences they may have encountered while they were working or since the event occurred. Everly and Mitchell (1997) stated that on occasion "the participants are reluctant to bring up their symptoms because they fear that they are the only ones and that their symptoms may be abnormal" (p. 55).

This phase identifies any symptoms of distress that individuals wish to share and to potentiate the initial transition from the affective domain back to the cognitive domain. This phase typically lasts up to 20 minutes. Once the number of responses decreases dramatically, the team makes a decision to move into the next phase of the debriefing, the teaching phase.

Teaching Phase

The teaching phase facilitates a return to the cognitive domain by normalizing and demystifying the event and the reactions of the participants. This phase of the debriefing offers the participants stress management and coping techniques and education that can be used to reduce current and possible future stress. A natural transition is to affirm that the symptoms mentioned in the symptoms phase are normal reactions to a traumatic event. Team members describe typical symptoms of distress and caution the group about other symptoms that they might encounter.

Instructions are given regarding diet, exercise, rest, talking to significant others, talking to each other, supporting each other, avoiding alcohol and caffeine. This phase allows team members to focus specific information to specific participants who have described particular concerns or issues of discomfort. The whole group gets the message, but the individual picks up on the importance to self. This is also the time to ask if there was anything that happened during the event that made it a little less painful or chaotic? This is also a good time to point to simple successes and the fact that the helpers did what was expected and what they were trained for and they did it well. With this closing comes the final phase, the reentry phase.

Reentry Phase

The last phase of the debriefing is the time to clarify issues, answer questions, make summary statements to the group and return the group to their normal functions. This phase puts closure on the discussions that have just occurred in the debriefing.

A good way to end is for the team leader to say, "Let me try to summarize what we have covered here during this process together." The entire CISD team should offer thoughts from their hearts and minds. This is the time for respect, encouragement, appreciation, support, and final direction. Team members may wish to end this session with contact with each participant thanking them shaking their hands, offering positive eye contact, and thanking them for participating.

Traumatic stress intervention begins with the establishment of trust and communication. Group therapy is useful for caregivers because there is peer support and understanding of the professional issues. The opportunity to help oneself while helping others also appeals to many caregivers.

As noted previously, traumatic events may be experienced alone, with other persons, or by a community. When trauma is experienced alone, the individual may feel helpless, vulnerable, terrorized, fearful, and at the mercy of fate. In groups, processes such as contagion, rumors, myths, social pressures, and expected norms of regulation also exert social and psychological group effects.

RECOVERY FROM TRAUMATIC STRESS

The first step to recovery from traumatic stress, whether the response is acute, delayed, or chronic, is awareness. Awareness involves recognition of the signs and symptoms that may or may not be related by the person to the experience or event. This is often not an easy task.

Recognition may be masked because of chemical impairment, time, denial, and "macho" defensive mechanisms. Often caregivers wear their lack of sleep and experience of horrible traumas and dramatic deaths like badges of courage.

Caregivers are told in their training, by society and by their experienced peers that they should be able to handle whatever traumatic situations come along. The cost of being "superhuman" is to suffer human stress disorders.

Recovery from trauma may be a lifelong process. The residue of the trauma may be a lifelong process. The residue of the trauma may be triggered by normal life crises, stages of ego development, the aging process, or incidents similar to the initial traumatic event. Methods of intervention and treatment are growing and becoming more refined as traumatic stress responses are better understood. No one intervention modality is better than another. Consideration must be given to individual and group differences and preferences. The goals are to restore healing, human dignity, and self-worth, and to improve the quality of life, promote emotional stability and expressiveness and offer peace with oneself, present and past.

REFERENCES

American Psychiatric Association. (1994). *Diagnostic and statistical manual of mental disorders* (4th ed.). Washington, DC: Author.

Arvay, M., & Uhlemannn, M. (1996). Counsellor stress in the field of traumas: A preliminary study. *Canadian Journal of Counseling/Revue Canadienne de Counseling, 2,* 96–98.

Avery, A., King, S., Bretherton, R., & Orner, R. (1999, Spring). Deconstructing psychological debriefing and the emergence of calls for evidence-based practice. *Traumatic Stress Points,* 7–8.

Bremner, J., & Narayan, M. (1998). The effects of stress on memory and the hippocampus throughout the life cycle. *Developmental Psychopathology, 10,* 871–886.

Caplan, G. (1964). *Principles of preventive psychiatry.* New York: Basic Books.

Cobb, S., & Lindemann, E. (1943). Neuropsychiatric observations after the Coconut Grove fire. *Annals of Surgery, 117,* 814–824.

Cudmore, J. (1996). Do nurses perceive the need for defusing and debriefing in the emergency department? *Nursing in Critical Care, 1*(4), 188–193.

Davidson, J. R. T., & Nemeroff, C. B. (1989). Pharmacotherapy in PTSD: Historical and clinical considerations and future directions. *Psychopharmacology Bulletin, 25,* 422–425.

Danieli, Y. (1988). Treating survivors and children of survivors of the Nazi holocaust. In F. Ochberg (Ed.), *Post-traumatic therapy and victims of violence* (pp. 278–295). New York: Brunner/Mazel.

Donovan, D. (1991). Traumatology: A field whose time has come. *Journal of Traumatic Stress, 4*(3), 433–436.

Epperson-Sebour, M. (1977). Families in sudden crisis. *Social Work Health Care, 2,* 3.

Erickson, K. (1976). *Everything in its path: Destruction of community in the Buffalo Creek flood.* New York: Simon & Schuster.

Everly, G. S., & Mitchell, J. (1997). *Critical incident stress management, CISM, a new era and standard of care in crisis intervention* (pp. 7–10). Ellicott City, MD: Chevron.

Everly, G. S., & Mitchell, J. (1998, Fall). Primer on critical incident stress management: A new era in crisis intervention. *Trauma Stress Points,* 6–11.

Figley, C. R. (1985). *Introduction. Trauma and its wake. The study and treatment of PTSD.* New York: Brunner/Mazel.

Figley, C. (1993). Foreword. In J. Wilson & B. Raphael (Eds.), *International handbook of traumatic stress syndromes* (pp. 2–4). New York: Plenum.

Figley, C. R. (Ed.). (1995a). *Compassion fatigue: Coping with secondary traumatic stress in those who treat the traumatized.* New York: Brunner/Mazel.

Figley, C. R. (1995b). Compassion fatique: Toward a new understanding of the costs of caring. In B. H. Stamm (Ed.), *Secondary traumatic stress* (pp. 23–25). Lutherville, MD: Sidran Press.

Fitzpatrick, K., & Wilson, M. (1999). Exposure to violence and posttraumatic stress symptomatology among abortion clinic workers. *Journal of Traumatic Stress, 12,* 239–241.

Flanagan, J. C. (1954). The critical incident technique. *Psychological Bulletin, 51,* 327–330.

Freud S. (1954). *A general introduction to psychoanalysis.* New York: Perma Giants.

Green, A. (1985). Post-traumatic symptoms of incest victims. In S. Eth & R. S. Pynoos (Eds.), *Post traumatic stress disorder in children* (pp. 145–149). Washington, DC.: American Psychiatric Press.

Haley, S. A. (1974). When the patient reports atrocities: Specific treatment considerations of the Vietnam veteran. *Archives of General Psychiatry, 30,* 191–196.

Harber, K., & Pennebaker, J. (1993). Overcoming traumatic memories. In S. Christianson (Ed.), *The handbook of emotion and memory: Research and theory* (pp. 199–221). Hillsdale, NJ: Erlbaum.

Harbert, K. (1992). *The development and use of CISM teams within a rural teritary hospital.* Poster and paper presented at the meeting of the Agency for Health Policy and Research, Atlanta, GA.

Harbert, K. (1998). *Traumatic stress and CISM: Caring for the providers.* Paper resented at the 26th annual American Academy of Physician Assistant conference, Salt Lake City, UT.

Harbert, K. (1999). *Traumatic stress and CISM: Best practice approach to curriculum development.* Paper presented at the Association of Physician Assistant Programs Northeast consortium, Philadelphia, PA.

Harbert, K., & Hunsinger, M. (1991). Impact of traumatic stress disorders on caregivers. *Journal of the American Academy of Physician Assistants, 4,* 384–394.

Herman, J. L. (1992). *Trauma and recovery: The aftermath of violence—from domestic abuse to political terror.* New York: Basic Books.

Hoff, L. A. (1995). *People in crisis: Understanding and helping* (4th ed.). San Francisco: Jossey-Bass.

Horowitz, M. (1976). *Stress response syndrome.* New York: Jason Aronson.

Horowitz, M. (1991). *Person schemas and maladaptive interpersonal patterns.* Chicago: University of Chicago Press.

Janet, P. (1889). *L'automatisme psychologique.* Paris: Alcan.

Johnson, K. (1993). *School crisis management: A hands-on guide to training crisis response teams.* Alameda, CA: Hunter House.

Johnson, K. (1998). *Trauma in the lives of children.* Alameda, CA: Hunter House.

Lamberg, L. (1999). Roots of physician stress explored. *Journal of the American Medical Association, 282*(1), 13–14.

MacLean, P. D. (1985). Brain evolution relating to family, play and the separation call. *Archives of General Psychiatry, 42,* 405–417.

McCann, I. L., & Pearlman, L. A. (1990). Vicarious traumatization: A framework for understanding the psychological effects of working with victims. *Journal of Traumatic Stress, 3*(1) 131–149.

McGee, R. K. (1974). *Crisis intervention in the community.* Baltimore, MD: University Park Press.

Mitchell, J. T. (1983). When disaster strikes. . . The critical incident stress debriefing process. *Journal of Emergency Medical Services, 8*(1), 36–39.

Mitchell, J. T., & Bray, G. (1990). *Emergency services stress, guidelines for preserving the health and careers of emergency services personnel.* Englewood Cliffs, NJ: Brady Publishing.

Mitchell, J. T., & Everly, G. S. (1993). *Human elements training for emergency services, public safety and disaster personnel.* Ellicott City, MD: Chevron.

Munroe, J. F., et al. (1995). Preventing compassion fatigue: A team treatment model. In C. R. Figley (Ed.), *Compassion fatigue: Coping with secondary traumatic stress disorder in those who treat the traumatized* (pp. 319–328). New York: Brunner/Mazel.

Myers. D. (1995). Worker stress during long-term disaster recovery efforts. *Innovations in disaster and trauma psychology: I. Applications in emergency services and disaster response.* Baltimore, MD: Chevron.

Ornitz, E., & Pynoos, R. (1989). Startle modulation in children with post-traumatic stress disorder. *American Journal of Psychiatry, 147,* 866–870.

Pavlov, I. V. (1926). *Conditioned reflexes: An investigation of the physiological activity of the cerebral cortex.* New York: Dover.

Pearlman, L., & Saakvitne, K. (1995). *Trauma and the therapist.* New York: Norton.

Pennebaker, J. W. (1985). Traumatic experience and psychosomatic disease. *Canadian Psychologist, 26,* 82–95.

Pennebaker, J. W., & Susman, J. (1988). Disclosure of traumas and psychosomatic processes. *Social Science, and Medicine,* 26,327–332.

Pines A., & Aronson, E. (1986). *Career burnout.* New York: Free Press.

Post, R. M., Pickar, D., Ballenger, J. C., & Naber, D. (1984). Endogenous opioids in cerebrospinal fluid: Relationship to mood and anxiety. In R. M. Post & J. C. Ballenger (Eds.), *Neurobiology of mood disorders* (pp. 226–229). Baltimore, MD: Williams & Wilkins.

Pynoos, R. (1990). Posttraumatic stress disorder in children and adolescents. In B. Garfinkel, G. Carlson, & E. Weller (Eds.), *Psychiatric disorders in children and adolescents* (pp. 14–21). Philadelphia: Saunders.

Robinson, R. C., & Mitchell, J. T. (1995). Getting some balance back into the debriefing debate. *The Bulletin of the Australian Psychological Society, 17*(10), 5–10.

Robinson R., & Murdoch, P. (1991). *Guidelines for establishing peer support programs in emergency services.* Melbourne, Australia: Waterwheel Press.

Selye, H. (1956). *The stress of life.* New York: McGraw-Hill.

Squire, L. R. (1987). *Memory and the brain,* New York: Oxford University Press.

Terr, L. (1981). Psychic trauma in children. *American Journal of Psychiatry, 138,* 14–19.

Terr, L. (1990). *Too scared to cry: Psychic trauma in childhood.* New York: Basic Books.

Williams, T. (Ed.). (1987). *Post traumatic stress disorders: A handbook for clinicians.* Cleveland, OH: Disabled American Veterans National Headquarters.

Wilson, J. P. (1989). *Trauma, transformation, and healing: An integrative approach to theory, research, and post-traumatic therapy.* New York: Brunner/Mazel.

Wilson J. P., & Raphael, B. (Eds.). (1993). *International handbook of traumatic stress syndromes.* New York: Plenum.

Wilson, J., & Lindy, J. (1995). Empathic strain and countertransference. In J. Wilson, & J. Lindy (Eds.), *Countertransference in the treatment of PTSD* (pp. 227–254). New York: Guilford Press.

van der Hart, O., Brown, P., & van der Kolk, B. A. (1989). Pierre Janet's treatment of posttraumatic stress. *Journal of Traumatic Stress, 2,* 379–396.

van der Kolk, B. A. (1987). *Psychological trauma.* Washington, DC: American Psychiatric Press.

van der Kolk, B. A. (1994). The body keeps score: memory and the evolving psychobiology of posttraumatic stress. *Harvard Review Psychiatry, 1,* 253–265.

van der Kolk, B. A., MacFarlane, A. C., & Weisaeth, L. (Eds.). (1996). *Traumatic stress: The effects of overwhelming experiences on mind, body, and society.* New York: Guilford Press.

Yassen, J. (1993, Spring). Groupwork with clinicians who have a history of trauma. *NCP Clinical Newsletter, 3*(2), 10–11.

SUGGESTED READINGS

Everly, G., & Mitchell, J. (1997). *Innovations in disaster and trauma psychology: Critical incident stress management, a new era and standard of care in crisis intervention.* Ellicott City, MD: Chevron.

Johnson, K. (1998). *School crisis management: A team training guide.* Alameda, CA: Hunter House.

Mitchell, J., & Everly, G. (1996). *Critical incident stress debriefing: An operations manual for the prevention of traumatic stress among emergency services and disaster workers* (2nd ed.). Ellicott City, MD: Chevron.

Wilson, J. (1989). *Trauma, transformation, and healing: An integrative approach to theory, research, and posttraumatic therapy.* New York: Brunner/Mazel.

Wilson, J., & Raphael, B. (Eds.). (1993). *International handbook of traumatic stress syndromes.* New York: Plenum.

17

Medical Patients in Crisis

Robert A. DiTomasso
Donna M. Martin
Karel D. Kovnat

Patients in crisis frequently present to primary care physicians in the ambulatory care setting. In a now classic study that examined the content of family practice (Marsland, Wood, & Mayo, 1976), 4% of the patient visits were classified as psychiatric or social crises. A quarter of a century later, these findings still appear to be accurate. Primary care physicians actually spend about one-fourth of their time treating psychiatric conditions and, in so doing, deliver mental health services to about one-half of the patients seeking care for depression (Robinson, 1998). For those cognitive-behavioral clinicians practicing in medical settings, the implications are clear. The need for effective and efficient crisis intervention methods is critical.

As direct service providers, cognitive-behavioral psychologists are often called on to intervene with patients in crisis. As consultants, these clinicians may be asked to provide services to physicians and other health care practitioners to assist them in dealing more effectively with crisis patients in the future. Finally, as teachers, clinicians are expected to educate physicians about useful models and strategies designed to facilitate interactions with patients in crisis. In this chapter, we delineate a cognitive-behavioral model of crisis intervention for the practicing clinician in the medical setting. We achieve this goal by discussing the crisis patient, the nature of crises, the most common precipitants of crises in the medical patient, cognitive-behavioral techniques of crisis intervention, and a case study to illustrate these principles.

CRISIS IN THE MEDICAL PATIENT

Definitions of crisis abound in the literature (Gilliland & James, 1997). We define a *crisis* as an experience during which an individual confronts a stressor that is perceived as insurmountable despite the use of typical approaches to problem solving and coping. By this definition, the individual in crisis perceives the stressor as a threat to his/her physical, psychological, or emotional well-being. During a period of crisis, the behavioral, emotional, motivational, and cognitive systems of the individual react in ways that are consistent with themes of threat and loss. We propose that the cognitive system plays a central role in organizing the responses of the individual (Freeman & DiTomasso, 1994; Freeman & DiTomasso, in press). In this sense, the occurrence of a medical problem in one's life is by itself not enough to precipitate a crisis. Rather, it is the perception of the problem or obstacle as a serious threat that essentially defines its potential for inducing crisis. The individual's appraisal that an event is threatening is crucial for setting the crisis state in motion. However, even more critical is the appraisal that the individual's coping resources are overwhelmed and ineffective.

Crises are those life events that attack or threaten a person's sense of security and control (Eppersen-Sebour, 1990; Parad & Parad, 1990). In medical settings, crises exist on a continuum ranging from life events that are biological certainties, such as menopause, to random events, such as car accidents (Parad & Parad, 1990). In medical patients, the so-called *reality stressors* include health problems, death, divorce, separation, loss of job, and financial problems (Feinstein & Carey, 1999). All individuals may be presumed to have developed some methods for coping with life events. Most individuals, however, typically do not prepare themselves for traumas resulting from the fact that the human body is a living organism. For instance, most people are simply not prepared for the sudden or insidious onset of chronic diseases, such as multiple sclerosis, or the personal grief of infertility or other childbearing dilemmas (Elkin, 1990). Similarly, one can hardly be expected to prepare for a tragic car accident or a child born with severe birth defects. These very personal threats to one's sense of control can be quite disruptive to daily functioning by fostering a sense of emotional turmoil and difficulty adapting (Dohrenwend & Dohrenwend, 1982; Feinstein & Carey, 1999). By virtue of being human, everyone is susceptible to such threatening traumas. At some point during the course of the life cycle, all individuals may be expected to assume the role of the medical patient. However, when there is no simple or quick medical solution, the person's ability to cope may be overtaxed (Taylor, 1986).

The role of dysfunctional beliefs, attitudes, assumptions, and behavior in ultimately contributing to crises is quite clear. Individuals too often approach life denying the real possibilities associated with lifestyle risk habits. We all know cigarette smokers who continue to smoke despite the attendant health problems and fatality rate associated with this behavior (Klesges et al., 1988), diabetics who do not adhere to proper self-care behaviors, and cardiac patients who continue to eat high-cholesterol diets. Individuals too often do not engage in health-promoting behaviors, the consequence of which can be a major disease that presents a crisis to the patient (Baum & Posluszny, 1999). Despite the fact that early detection is significantly related to a positive prognosis for a number of medical problems, simple patient education, self-examination, and medical tests are underutilized by patients (McKee, Lurio, Marantz, Burton, & Mulvihill, 1999; Myers, 1999; Sarrel, 1999). In sum, the *presence of dysfunctional beliefs about health* is the key that turns a medical problem into a medical crisis.

The failure to perform health-promoting behaviors can be associated with crises in medical patients in a number of ways. First, the lack of perceived threat, the denial of the usefulness of behavior change in reducing threat, and the perceived cost of behavior change significantly contribute to the development of serious illness. Second, an individual's intention to change may be mediated by a decisional balance between the perceived costs and benefits of a particular behavior (Campbell et al., 1998; Rakowski et al., 1992). In other words, an individual might not see changes as likely to be "worth it." Unfortunately, many people do not perceive themselves as vulnerable to real medical threats and, as a result, do not engage in preventive behaviors. Third, failure to perform such behaviors may be due to lack of information or economic resources. Avoidance of health screening is one example. Failure to seek follow-up after diagnosis of disease and noncompliance with treatment recommendations are other important factors ultimately contributing to crisis in medical patients (DiTomasso & Mills, 1990; McKee et al., 1999; Myers, 1999). Medical conditions, ignored or left unattended, can develop into serious pathology and precipitate crises that might, in many instances, have been averted. Perhaps the most compelling aspect of a medical crisis is the threat it poses to the individual's physical and mental well-being. All the self-defining constructs and coping skills an individual has developed over a lifetime will be seriously challenged and possibly overwhelmed in the face of crisis (Kahana, Kahana, Harel, & Rosner, 1988). The medical system is assumed to be a necessary component of healing, but it is often not sufficient. A strong relationship between thoughts, feelings, and behaviors, on the one hand, and how well people weather illness and health problems, on the other hand, is receiving considerable support in the health psychology literature (Baum & Posluszny, 1999). These findings suggest an interesting reciprocal relationship: The perception of a medical problem may precipitate a crisis that, in turn, may exacerbate the original medical condition. As a consequence of a medical problem, a crisis may complicate and undermine recovery by creating a vicious cycle for the patient.

We liken this crisis state to that observed in response to other traumatic life events whereby a patient's method of coping is threatened and overwhelmed. The situation in which patients find themselves has been aptly described by Hyer, Woods, and Boudewyns (1991) who noted,

> Until a traumatic life event can be successfully integrated into the existing self-structure, the psychological components of the event remain in memory as determinants of internal stimuli, where they foster stress symptoms. These stressor elements seek to be examined and battle for some kind of "fit" with the already existing schema. Both schema and memory contents wage a psychic war on the information processing battlefield. (p. 133)

The challenge to a medical patient in this situation may be so intense that the individual's sense of cognitive equilibrium is disturbed. This sense of disequilibrium is usually so uncomfortable that the individual is motivated to find a resolution to the dilemma (Ditto, Jermott, & Darley, 1988; Parad & Parad, 1990). As noted above, intense levels of stress may further exacerbate an existing physical illness, which may further compromise the patient's ability to cope.

Only recently have we begun to address the psychological components of these dilemmas (Rose, 1991). Because there appears to be a short window of opportunity when coping mechanisms are in flux, it is beneficial to receive treatment early in this process (Gilliland & James, 1997). Early intervention with the medical patient in crisis may offer some distinct advantages. The patient may be more physically and psychologically healthy and, thereby, more able to collaborate in constructing and implementing new coping mechanisms. Early treatment may also help to preclude the formation of a negative cognitive set for treatment outcome. This cognitive set, formed by repeated failure experiences on the part of the patient in attempting to cope, may undermine the patient's belief about the realistic likelihood of a positive outcome. Successful early intervention may offer some prophylaxis and offset this potential problem. Some authors report that short-term (about 12 weeks) interventions are as effective or even more effective in helping individuals deal with crisis (Parad & Parad, 1990). Cognitive-behavioral approaches may, then, be particularly advantageous in treating the crisis patient. The following addresses the possible causes of crises in the medical patient.

CAUSES OF CRISIS

The question of what may reasonably be expected to precipitate a crisis in a medical patient is intriguing. Although there may be consensus about the types of events most people would find stressful, the mere presence of a problem or obstacle does not necessarily signal that the onset of a crisis state is imminent. From a cognitive-behavioral perspective, a crucial question concerns what differentiates those instances when an event precipitates a crisis versus those when it does not. The answer, in part, lies in the basic assumptions held about a particular event and their inherent relationship to the person's thoughts, behaviors, and feelings. The special meaning an event holds for a particular patient is crucial in driving the patient's reaction to that event (Feinstein & Carey, 1999). The more extreme and negative an individual's interpretation of an event, the more intense the emotional response to that event. Based on our clinical experience, we would further hypothesize that there are a variety of factors that would be more likely to be associated with the onset of a crisis. We divide these factors into the following areas: triggering events, cognitive factors, behavioral factors, and physical factors.

Triggering Events

The *type, number, timing,* and specific *nature* of events appear to be important factors. Most of the work on the nature of situations that can precipitate a crisis has centered around life events. Certain events appear to be inherently more stressful than others and, as a result, events, such as death of a spouse, are more likely to be associated with illness and distress. The combined effect of a number of life events is also important. However, it is the meaning that the event has for this person, rather than its occurrence per se, that determines the emotional reaction. In other words, similar triggering events may be perceived and responded to in an idiosyncratic manner. The underlying schemata activated by an event play a significant determining role in guiding the individual's responses. Such schemata are likely to be activated in situations that are similar to situations in which they were learned and that are, by definition, similar to the triggering event. What is implied here is a vulnerability to certain triggering events to account for individual differences in onset of crisis across people (Freeman & DiTomasso, in press). Theoretically, there are any variety of life events that alone or in combination could conceivably precipitate a crisis. Not surprisingly, these types of stressors in the general medical patient are in many ways not unlike those found in other populations. In the general medical setting, patients frequently seek help during times of crisis. Because psychological distress may manifest itself in the form of physical symptoms, medical patients are likely to turn to their primary care physician for help. Given the subjective experience of anxiety and turmoil that is characteristic of crises, patients may naturally seek out their family physician for medication or emotional support. Many of the most stressful events a person can experience fall within the realm of problems first dealt with by primary care physicians by the very nature of their role.

Cognitive Factors

A variety of cognitive factors play a role in increasing the likelihood that a crisis might ensue in response to a particularly stressful event. These include unrealistic beliefs, attitudes, and assumptions; cognitive distortions; biased recall and perception; negative view of self, world, or future; decreased self-efficacy; and lack of accurate information. These factors alone or in combination with other factors including behavioral deficits, emotional state, and physical state, may be sufficient to precipitate a crisis.

1. *Unrealistic beliefs, attitudes, and assumptions.* In the cognitive realm, unrealistic schemata play a more central role than other cognitive factors. The onset of a triggering event is presumed to activate an underlying schema previously learned in the context of a highly charged emotional situation similar to the triggering event. This schema is likely to have a determining influence on thoughts,

behaviors, and emotional reactions of the patient (Beck, 1976; Needleman, 1999; Persons, 1989). The entrenched meaning of the event can be found in schemata and corollary schemata where themes of loss and threat are likely to be present and evidenced in the automatic thoughts of the patient. These schemata will influence a person's reaction to the news of a medical problem and adjustment to the medical problem itself.

2. *Cognitive distortions.* Distorted styles of processing information may make it more likely for a person to enter a crisis state. It is easy to understand how cognitive distortions (e.g., arbitrary inference) about an event concerning one's health may color an accurately perceived event or worsen the implications of a misperceived event. Likewise, the patient who catastrophizes about the meaning of a diagnosed medical problem would be expected to react in a more extreme manner.

3. *Biased recall and perceptions.* Patients are more likely to recall negative memories when in negative moods. In this sense the patient may experience negative memories that further distort perceptions. The patient may also become attentionally primed to assimilate more negative information about the current medical event.

4. *Cognitive triad.* The negative view of self, world, and future (Beck, 1976) may undermine the patient facing a major stressful event. Those patients with low self-esteem may be more prone to become guilt-ridden and unnecessarily blame themselves for the illness. Likewise, a negative view of the world may reinforce this guilt-ridden position. Finally, a negative view of the future may further demoralize the patient by reinforcing hopeless feelings and helpless ideas about the current medical situation.

5. *Self-efficacy.* The patient's belief in his/her ability to cope with the situation is another important variable. Those with low self-efficacy would not be expected to fare as well and this attitude may further serve to undermine necessary coping efforts. Positive health outcomes can be associated with a patient's sense of control and efficacy.

6. *Lack of information.* The patient's misinformation or lack of information about a particular medical condition could significantly contribute to distress. We suspect that this situation may occur by allowing negative fantasies and cognitive distortions to flourish, which may, in turn, lower the threshold for crisis onset.

Behavioral Factors

A number of factors related to the behavior of the patient may increase the likelihood of a crisis or worsen an already existing crisis.

1. *Lack of coping strategies.* A previous history of unsuccessful coping marked by the absence of effective cognitive and behavioral strategies facilitates a crisis state. Previous experience in handling stressors and a repertoire of

useful strategies from which to choose are likely to enhance one's ability to effectively confront major stressors.

2. *Negative means of coping.* The absence of positive coping strategies and reliance on negative means to cope are likely to intensify the crisis situation. Here, we are referring to the use of alcohol, drugs, and suicide attempts, which is likely to undermine the patient even further.

3. *Lack of available social support.* The presence of a social support network is likely to buffer the patient against the effects of a crisis. A patient without such support may be isolated and left to deal with the physical and psychological aftermath of a problem alone.

4. *Inability to request support.* The inability to access support that could be available is another important factor detrimental to successfully coping with a medical crisis.

Physical Factors

The physical well-being of the individual is another particularly important variable. The presence of a physically taxing disorder may lower the patient's threshold to respond negatively to a stressor. Objectively less intense stressors may now be enough to precipitate a reaction. In effect, illness may lower one's tolerance for dealing with events.

Overall, a comprehensive approach to assessment and intervention that addresses the various possible factors related to crisis is sorely needed. We propose that a cognitive behavioral assessment and treatment package is an effective and efficient alternative in this regard.

COGNITIVE-BEHAVIORAL TECHNIQUES OF CRISIS INTERVENTION

The basic tenets of cognitive-behavioral therapy make it well suited to the needs of the patient in crisis. Before discussing specific techniques, however, a brief review of our rationale is warranted. The cognitive-behavioral approach has been characterized by the following adjectives: active, directive, goal-oriented, collaborative–empirical, psychoeducational, and problem-focused (Freeman & DiTomasso, in press). Each of these characteristics plays a vital role in helping the crisis patient. The crisis patient typically experiences a significant level of emotional tension coupled with exhaustion of coping attempts, which have not succeeded in facilitating adjustment to a new level. For these reasons, the cognitive approach to assessment and intervention, where the role of the therapist is active, is important. Actively working with the patient to confront the stressor and the associated cognitive, behavioral, and emotional sequelae is essential in helping the patient. The collaborative–empirical perspective communicates to the patient a joint, evidence-based effort to overcome this problem, where the sole efforts of the patient have been fruitless. The directive stance of cognitive therapy is likely to be well tolerated by an overwrought patient whose major problems center around disorganization and lack of ability to self-direct. The problem-focused approach is likely to further motivate the patient to deal specifically with the problem in a systematic fashion. Likewise, this goal-oriented approach is likely to focus resources in a proactive direction by guiding the patient toward crisis resolution. Finally, the psychoeducational aspects of cognitive therapy may foster self-understanding and knowledge and help to reduce the likelihood of future crisis episodes. In sum, the cognitive-behavioral approach has specific characteristics that make it particularly useful in working with patients in crisis.

In the medical setting, the crisis patient may present in a variety of ways. Sometimes the patient's "ticket of admission" to the office is in reality quite different from the actual reason for which the patient presents. This situation may cause some practical and logistical problems in the medical setting. The length of time slots for visits are typically allotted beforehand at the time the appointment is made, according to the stated reason for the visit. In such instances medical personnel must be particularly attuned to the psychosocial arena, especially subtle cues of distress in the patient, even to begin to recognize the need to address an issue. The patient may present with some benign physical complaint or perhaps some physical symptom that is a somatic manifestation of the stress he/she is undergoing. On the other hand, an exacerbation of an existing medical condition may signal that the patient is in a state of crisis. Dangerously high blood pressure in a hypertensive, angina in a cardiac patient, and uncontrollable blood sugars in a diabetic are just a few examples. Other patients may complain of acute symptoms of anxiety or depression or some combination of medical and psychological symptoms. The mind–body linkage is never more apparent than in the medical setting. The patient with a potentially life-threatening condition who is also in a state of psychological crisis presents a clinical dilemma. Careful consideration must be given to both aspects of the situation. However, psychological intervention should be delayed until the patient is medically stable. To do otherwise may risk a catastrophic medical event.

The cognitive-behavioral approach to the crisis patient is useful for assessment and intervention. In our experience a variety of techniques have been important in assisting the patient in overcoming the crisis and achieving a higher level of adjustment. These techniques are discussed in detail in subsequent sections.

1. *Form a working alliance.* The formation of a working alliance must begin immediately when providing psychological services to the crisis patient. In view of the significance of a sound working alliance in traditional non-crisis-oriented treatment, forming a working alliance with the patient in crisis is equally, if not even more, important. The construct of the working alliance has been positively correlated with treatment outcome across a wide variety of

therapies and outcome measures. According to Bordin (1979) and Gelso and Carter (1985), the working alliance comprises three components: (a) agreement about the goals of treatment, (b) agreement about the tasks in and outside of session to achieve the goals, and (c) the emotional bond that develops between the participants. In the absence of a working alliance, there is no foundation on which interventions can rest. Likewise, absent or ill-defined agreement about goals and tasks in the absence of a therapeutic relationship robs the patient of the opportunity for growth and may contribute to the further disorganization and emotional upheaval in the crisis patient.

2. *Provide a collaborative focus to the sessions.* One hallmark of the cognitive-behavioral approach is that therapy is a collaborative enterprise. This approach may be at odds with what patients typically experience in a medical setting where the patient may be placed in a more passive, recipient role. Obviously, this collaboration depends on the orientation and philosophy of the medical setting and its physicians, so some reorientation of the patient may be required. The establishment of a collaborative focus offers many advantages in working with the crisis patient who probably has already tried to confront the situation alone with little to no success. First, fostering collaboration actively engages the patient in the process of resolving the crisis through problem solving and the development of coping strategies. Second, the patient is more likely to experience some sense of relief in "joining forces" with an expert in tackling a difficult problem. Third, collaboration provides the expectation that the patient has a contribution to make to problem resolution that is as important, if not more so, than that of the therapist. Finally, collaborative empiricism coupled with the therapist's attitude may help tip the scale for the patient in favor of the belief that the problem can be solved and that adjusting to a major problem is possible.

3. *Emphasize relationship factors of empathy, respect, and genuineness.* Relationship factors play a rather significant role in the treatment of medical patients. Patients whose physicians, for example, are perceived as more empathic, understanding, approachable, warm, and caring, are more likely to adhere to treatment, remain under the care of the physician, seek out care in times of serious illness, and be more satisfied with the services they receive (DiTomasso & Willard, 1991). A relatively frequent complaint of medical patients is the dehumanizing experience in medical settings.

The importance of relationship factors to the outcome of the therapeutic process is also well documented. Although more recent research suggests that the Rogerian relationship factors (empathy, unconditional positive regard, and genuineness) account for only a minor portion of the variance in outcome, few would argue that they are not important. For example, some authors (Gelso & Carter, 1985) suggest that these factors exert their influence through the fostering of the working alliance. Cognitive therapists view the therapeutic relationship as necessary but not sufficient for change to occur. Note, however, that Burns and Nolen-Hoeksema (1992) report that therapist empathy makes an independent, substantial, and positive contribution to the outcome of cognitive therapy with depressives. Suffice it to say that psychological contact in a time of crisis with a warm, empathic, and genuine human being who respects the patient helps to form a solid foundation for the assessment and intervention process. Given the seemingly limitless availability of cognitive-behavioral interventions, there may be a temptation to overlook the value of relationship variables.

4. *Explore the patient's distress.* In assessing the crisis patient, the clinician must thoroughly explore and analyze the precise nature of the symptoms experienced by the patient. The time of onset, nature, intensity, frequency, and duration of the patient's symptoms should be clearly specified to determine the exact nature of the problem. The profoundly depressed suicidal patient experiencing an acute psychotic break obviously needs a different set of interventions than the patient with a recent onset of panic attacks. Specific questions aimed at clarifying the precise nature of the patient's symptom complex and likely diagnosis are essential in treatment planning. Relatively brief, standardized, reliable, valid measures such as the Beck Depression Inventory (Beck, Steer, & Garbin 1988), the Beck Anxiety Inventory (Beck, Epstein, Brown, & Steer, 1988) and the Beck Hopelessness Scale (Beck, Weissman, Lester, & Trexler, 1974) will be particularly useful in expediting this process. Moreover, these instruments may alert the clinician to issues such as hopelessness or suicidality that require the clinician's immediate attention. Failure to deal with such issues may unnecessarily expose the patient to a life-threatening risk. In addition, ignoring a factor such as the hopelessness of the patient may sabotage the efforts of the clinician in mobilizing the patient to actively apply cognitive and behavioral strategies that foster problem solving and coping.

5. *Identify and discuss and analyze the event that precipitated the crisis.* Another important task for the clinician is to elicit information about the triggering event. The nature of the event could provide useful clues about potential vulnerabilities of the patient by allowing the clinician to formulate some clinically useful hypotheses about underlying schemata. The clinician must consider why a particular event or series of events precipitated the reaction in this particular patient at this particular time. By discussing the event, the clinician is likely to develop a sense of the patient's perception of the event. If a series of events has occurred, their sequence, timing, and nature may prove quite useful in facilitating an understanding of the patients' reactions.

6. *Elicit the patient's perception of the event.* The clinician should identify the idiosyncratic meaning that the crisis event has for the patient. Information gathering is one of the key tasks for the clinician. There are a variety of standardized techniques for identifying such information. One direct method is to ask the patient in a straightforward manner what the triggering event means for him, his life, and his future. The clinician can also keep a running list of the automatic thoughts of the patient and look for a common theme or themes. In addition, the downward arrow technique (see Burns, 1980) may also be useful

here. Finally, much in the spirit of Persons (1989) and Needleman (1999), the clinician can examine the thoughts, feelings, and behaviors of the patient and postulate what hypothetical core schemata most parsimoniously account for the reactions of the patient.

7. *Identify the most disturbing aspects of the problem situation.* By identifying what makes a situation so distressing for the patient, the therapist is able to direct therapy toward achieving more significant change. When these disturbing aspects become targets for intervention, the patient is also more likely to view the therapy experience as more meaningful.

8. *Examine the patient's history.* Other important tasks are to explore the patient's history for possible prior episodes of crisis, similar previous events that may have precipitated a crisis, how well the patient handled these crises, and what strategies helped most in the past. This information can provide the clinician with potentially useful clues. Generalizing successes can help to bolster the patient's belief in being able to cope with the medical crisis.

9. *Screen the patient for suicidality.* Medical patients in crisis may become completely demoralized and hopeless. Beware of patients with suicidal ideation who have one or more of the following characteristics: a rigid thinking style; poor problem-solving skills; a history of suicide attempts; alcohol or drug abuse; impulsivity; psychotic symptoms (command hallucinations); absence of deterrents; hopelessness; a well-conceived, specified plan; and a method that is lethal and available. Such patients may be at imminent risk for suicide, viewing it as a means of escaping or avoiding some dreaded consequence perceived to be associated with their medical diagnosis. Patients, who are HIV-positive or who are suffering from AIDS, are at greatly increased risk for suicide. The clinician must also be on the alert for homocidality, especially in those patients with a prior history of violent acting out behavior. Some patients may accurately or mistakenly attribute the disease acquisition to a particular person and may seek to retaliate.

10. *Emphasize patient's strengths.* The clinician should actively search for strengths the patient possesses and utilize these in the service of helping the patient help him/herself to adjust. This approach will sharply contrast with the typical focus on pathology and the disease model in the medical setting.

11. *Set realistic goals mutually.* The development of mutually agreed upon goals provides numerous advantages for the patient. First, it helps to focus the sessions by delivering specific outcomes to be achieved. Second, it provides the patient with the view that there is a demarcation for the end of crisis therapy. Third, it reinforces what types of outcome can realistically be achieved in therapy and therefore may help to increase the patient's motivation.

12. *Foster the patient's understanding from a cognitive-behavioral perspective.* In many instances, the patient may not have a means of assimilating the experience he/she is undergoing. Using the experiences of the patient to help him/her understand reasons that he/she is reacting in this manner is essential. This

framework allows the patient to place the crisis situation and associated thoughts, feelings, and behaviors in perspective and to begin to assume some objectivity in this situation.

13. *Help the patient examine dysfunctional cognitions.* The cognitive-behavioral therapist must assist the crisis patient in examining his/her cognitions to determine their validity and adaptivity. Helping the patient examine these thoughts in an objective manner and as hypotheses to be tested is crucial. The therapist must be especially careful to avoid talking the patient out of his/her reaction, which might be perceived as insensitivity to the patient's plight. Actively teaching the patient to identify, evaluate, and restructure faulty cognitions is crucial.

14. *Assess available coping strategies.* The clinician should make a concerted effort to determine what coping strategies the patient has tried with the explicit goal of developing more effective ones. By exploring these strategies, the therapist seeks to understand the extent to which the strategies have been successful, as well as what may have contributed to failure. Thus, the therapist gets a sense of what types of strategies may have a greater likelihood of success. Such an assessment also provides an opportunity for collaboration.

15. *Assist the patient in understanding the problem realistically.* A central tenet of the cognitive approach is an emphasis on the power of realistic thinking as opposed to the power of positive thinking. The therapist should at all costs avoid attempts to talk patients out of their problems. The patient must learn to realistically appraise the negative aspects and consequences of the problem and develop a plan that resolves the problem. Medical problems often present very clear negative consequences (e.g., permanent loss of function) for the patient that require adjustment (Nezu, Nezu, Friedman, Faddis, & Houts, 1998). To avoid or deny these consequences may set up the patient for further stress.

16. *Identify obstacles to implementing problem-solving strategies.* Prior to implementing a strategy, the therapist should use questioning and imagery to identify any issues (e.g., a negative expectation about the potential success of a strategy) that could undermine the effective implementation of the strategy. Addressing these issues beforehand allows the clinician to help the patient deal with problems that could interfere with the successful application of strategies.

17. *Use a graduated approach to task assignment.* Given the likely state of the patient, breaking down an assignment into manageable steps is important. In most instances the patient's crisis reaction is evidence that the problem as a whole is overwhelming. Using a step-by-step approach provides necessary practice that is likely to increase success. More importantly, it breaks seemingly overwhelming tasks into manageable components.

18. *Use behavior rehearsal.* Once agreement has been obtained about a problem solving strategy, the therapist should rehearse the plan with the patient. This rehearsal might entail imaginal rehearsal or role playing to ensure that the behavior is performed in a way that maximizes the likelihood of a positive outcome. It may also provide opportunities for therapist modeling, reinforcement, and shaping.

19. *Inoculate the patient against negative factors.* The therapist should work with the patient specifically to inoculate him or her against factors that are likely to interfere with success. These may involve dealing with cognitive or interpersonal barriers in the environment that undermine the patient's efforts at coping.

20. *Use homework assignments.* Mutually and carefully designed homework assignments that address important facets of the problem are essential, but they must be developed in such a way as to have a great likelihood of being completed successfully. These assignments serve several important functions. First, they are a means of keeping the patient active in working toward the goal of eventual adjustment as opposed to wallowing passively in a sea of emotion. Second, homework assignments provide a bridge between the intra- and extrasession experiences of the patient. Third, they also provide an opportunity for the patient to try new and alternative ways of thinking, feeling, and acting.

21. *Alleviate patient uncertainty.* Perhaps one of the most stressful aspects of dealing with a medical crisis is the uncertainty. The patient is likely to focus on the worst possible scenario. By educating the patient about the problem, there is opportunity to plan how to deal with the various facets of the medical condition, which may serve to reduce anxiety.

22. *Help the patient manage negative affect.* Specific cognitive-behavioral techniques that help the patient manage negative affect are useful. Strategies such as relaxation training help to reduce debilitating levels of tension and increase the patient's confidence that he/she can exert some control over symptoms (DiTomasso, in press).

23. *Consider utilizing peer support.* A considerable amount of relief can be provided by another patient who has gone through a similar experience and resolved it successfully. There are individual differences in the willingness of patients to agree to such arrangements. Also, careful consideration must be given to selecting a support person who is interpersonally skilled. At the least, such an arrangement may help the patient feel validated regarding his/her experience and not as alone. There is some comfort in knowing others have experienced a similar problem.

24. *Provide reinforcement for achievements.* The therapist should also provide ample social reinforcement for achievements, however minor. This type of recognition from an authority figure can help motivate the patient further. It may also increase the likelihood of continued efforts on the part of the patient toward resolving the problem.

25. *Monitor symptoms throughout.* The therapist should encourage ongoing patient self-monitoring of symptoms and provide the patient with a means of charting this information in written format. Weekly administration of standardized psychological inventories such as the Beck Depression Inventory (Beck, Steer, & Garbin, 1988) will prove useful. These data provide an ongoing record of the success of the intervention and as such positively reinforce the patient's efforts in resolving the crisis (DiTomasso & Colameco, 1982).

CASE STUDY

A 35-year-old lesbian woman sought crisis treatment with one of us (R. A. D.) following urgent referral from her family physician. Approximately 4 weeks prior to seeking treatment, the patient required a surgical removal of her right eye following the discovery of a malignant melanoma behind her retina. The patient reported that she had experienced some visual changes in the months preceding the surgery and had sought consultation with an ophthalmologist who "could find nothing wrong at that time." She had been encouraged, however, to monitor any visual changes and to seek a follow-up appointment. The patient described her "style" as typically one of denial and avoidance, "I put things aside and move ahead." Consequently, it was not until the visual changes finally reached the point of being intolerable that she again sought treatment with her ophthalmologist. Following an examination he immediately referred her to a nearby major tertiary eye care center. A tumor in her eye was discovered, and it had progressed to such a point that radiation therapy would have resulted in blindness.

Following further consultation, the patient was informed of the seriousness of her condition and scheduled for surgery within the next 2 days. The suddenness, urgency, and immediacy of the situation clearly prevented her from mobilizing her resources to effectively cope with the situation. While on the operating room table prior to anesthesia, the patient vividly recounted her stark realization that the ceiling lights would be "the very last thing that I would see with both of my eyes." After surgery the patient was discharged in 1 day and experienced a moderately severe depression that became progressively worse over the several weeks preceding psychological treatment. She was also guilt-ridden over whether she might have handled the situation differently and thus saved her eye.

By the time she sought therapy, she already had a prosthetic eye in place and was complaining of extreme difficulty adjusting to this situation. She reported that her perception of herself had changed so dramatically, "it's like the right side of my face is not there anymore." There were also changes in her depth perception that created several practical problems for her in conducting activities of daily living. Although she attempted to reinforce the idea that she would be able to get through this crisis, she found herself becoming progressively more and more depressed. These depressed feelings were accompanied by a sense of estrangement from herself. She noted, "I don't feel like I'm the same person" as well as "I see things in my life differently now."

Her only reprieve from the extreme level of self-preoccupation and stress was when she was sitting in a dark room, "because it doesn't matter then," as she could not notice the blindness. At the time of treatment she was experiencing a moderately severe depressed mood nearly every day, most of the day accompanied by a variety of other symptoms including weight loss, loss of interest, decreased energy, crying spells, guilt, difficulty concentrating, and loss of pleasure. Her depressed mood was accompanied by a moderately severe level of anxiety that also was significantly interfering with the quality of her life. To complicate her situation, about a week prior to the surgery, she had lost her job. Her family physician instituted a trial of antidepressant medication.

A review of her family history and development provided some interesting insights into her difficulties in dealing with her situation. The patient reported that she grew up in a household with an overbearing mother and as a result had an unhappy childhood. Apparently for years her mother resisted the patient's attempts at independence and the patient always felt a great deal of unrealistic expectations from her mother. Her father, with whom she reported getting along well, was someone who didn't express emotions or affection very much. She also had two older brothers who were living out of state but with whom she got along well. They were usually a source of support for her.

She had a 12-year relationship with a woman who was not handling the fact that she had surgery very well at all. Despite having been intimately involved with this individual for a rather long period of time, at the point when she needed a great deal of support, her lover was unable to provide it for her. She quite naturally was feeling she was a low priority in her lover's life. Also, as a result of her surgery, her mother attempted to make her more dependent, which created a great deal of resentment. Moreover, the patient's family members were apparently extremely uncomfortable discussing the surgery itself or the impact it was having on the patient.

Perhaps the most distressing aspect of the situation surrounded the patient's beliefs that "the right side of my head is no good to me anymore" and the view that "the right side of my face is dead." She also believed that she would never be able to adjust to the situation as these feelings and problems were likely "to go on for ever and ever." She had considerable fear that "the problem would travel to my left eye" and that she would "die of cancer." She also had perfectionistic tendencies, which significantly contributed to difficulty adjusting to this situation. The patient reported, "I don't want to be known as the person who lost her eye." As a result, she felt compelled to make the prosthetic eye look as normal as possible and actually at one point sought plastic reconstructive surgery to achieve that goal. Not unexpectedly this increased her depression as it reactivated numerous thoughts, images, and concerns from her first surgery.

In subsequent weeks there were periods in which she had what she described as "very low times," typically precipitated by difficulties she was experiencing with her prosthetic eye. For example, in two different situations with strangers, when her prosthetic eye dislodged, people had visible, negative, emotional reactions. In exploring these situations, the patient realized that she did not "want to face how it looked and [didn't] want other people to have to see this." She viewed her prosthetic eye "as gruesome to look at." Although she seemed to be progressing, it was clear that she was in many ways actively avoiding thinking about the experience of having had her "eye ripped out of

[her] head." She also reported difficulties in reconciling how "strange it was to see two eyes looking at [her] but seeing back with only one."

There were also experiences of feeling significantly overwhelmed at least several times a week when she came face-to-face with the reality of her situation. Likewise, there was marked anger and resentment about the manner in which she was treated by her surgeon. She sensed that she was just another case and was viewed as the "choroidal melanoma." She was also grappling with many memories of her original experience immediately following surgery, when, for example, one surgeon "took my prosthesis and threw it on the table." Such incidents made her feel further dehumanized.

Other upsetting aspects of her experience surrounded the manner in which her physician communicated with her. For example, she vividly recalled being told that the removal of her eye was a "relatively minor procedure" and she was discharged from the hospital in one day. Her interpretation was that if this were true she should have improved quickly. When she did not, it created more stress and depression. It was apparent that the patient was misinformed about some aspects of her recovery, which created unrealistic expectations. When these were unmet, she was further demoralized.

Treatment Plan

The crisis treatment of this patient utilized a cognitive-behavioral focus. Significant emphasis was placed on the development of a working alliance with this patient whose style of needing to feel independent prevented support forthcoming from her environment. The goal was explicitly discussed: to help her adjust to this extremely traumatic situation. The patient and therapist further agreed about what needed to occur in therapy in order to achieve this particular goal. From the outset, the collaborative nature of the sessions was emphasized. This was particularly important in view of the patient's resistance to her mother's attempts to place her in a dependent role now that she was going through this crisis. It was absolutely essential to handle this issue in a delicate fashion. While providing the patient the opportunity to obtain support, the therapist also emphasized that she was an individual with many resources—there was much that she could contribute to the resolution of her problem. In addition, considerable efforts were made to create a therapeutic climate in which the patient could feel understood by a warm, empathic, caring, genuine individual. This was particularly important in a patient who had difficulty seeking support from her environment and opening up in her extra-therapy relationships about what was distressing her.

The patient and therapist also explored the particular aspects of the patient's symptoms to help her develop some meaning from what she was experiencing at this time. Although the Beck Depression Inventory revealed a moderately severe level of depression, she was not totally hopeless or suicidal. We discussed the particular circumstances leading to the event that precipitated the crisis. This was important in understanding the particular insults that the patient had experienced as well as what aspects of the situation made it so distressing for her. Obviously, the patient's perception of this event and the impact that it would have on her future were particularly important. The therapist's understanding of both her situation and the practical consequences of blindness in one eye helped the patient feel more understood and able to examine her situation a bit more objectively.

There were no previous crises of this sort in the patient's history. However, her style, which she described as "denying and just moving on" when she confronted problems, was useful in understanding her reaction in this instance. She was now in a situation that was extremely difficult for her to deny, as it had so many observable consequences for her daily life. The patient was clear about the goals of the therapeutic encounter being her goals and she learned to understand what she was experiencing from a cognitive-behavioral perspective. She found Socratic questioning and the essential types of questions to ask herself (e.g., "What evidence is there that I will never adjust to this?") to be particularly helpful in changing her mood.

Considerable emphasis was placed on the development of coping strategies for dealing with everyday problems in her environment. These problems included adjusting to being blind in one eye, asserting herself to her mother, and seeking and requesting support from another close relative. The therapist emphasized the realistic consequences of her medical problem and helped her to learn as much as she could about adjusting to these problems.

Between sessions, emphasis was given to task assignments that were designed to help her gain more control over her life. For example, homework assignments included how to ask for support from her lover and her brothers, asserting herself to her overly intrusive mother, discussing the impact of her medical condition on her life with friends, and seeking information from her physicians to help clarify her uncertainties and concerns.

Time in sessions was allotted to rehearsing how to accomplish these tasks and dealing with issues that could potentially undermine her implementing the plan, for instance, thoughts such as, "It won't make a difference anyway." She was also referred to a support program for patients with prosthetic eyes. Subsequent to her formal crisis therapy, bimonthly booster sessions were conducted.

Follow-up revealed that she had acquired a new perspective regarding the practical problems of being sighted in one eye. She remarked, "I realize now that things which are inconveniences for everyone are a bit more difficult for me—this doesn't make it seem so terrible." She also indicated that, "Things that used to be devastating to me [referring to her blindness] are no longer so—that's the way things are—I'm living with it [having one eye]." Finally, perhaps even more reflective of her new level of adaptation, she noted that in life "problems do occur and I have to expect them and be prepared to handle them." Her Beck Depression Inventory score was now in the normal range.

Over the next several months, the patient started an Internet business with one of her brothers and began travelling around the country for business-related matters. At 10-year follow-up, the patient continued to be successfully self-employed and is reportedly "doing great." She continues prescribed medical follow-up on a periodic basis with her family physician to rule out metastasis. There has been no recurrence of crisis. At this time, she remains cancer free and is enjoying life.

REFERENCES

Baum, A., & Posluszny, D. M. (1999). Health psychology: Mapping biobehavioral contributions to health and illness. *Annual Review of Psychology, 50,* 137–163.

Beck, A. T. (1976). *Cognitive therapy and the emotional disorders.* New York: International Universities Press.

Beck, A. T., Epstein, N., Brown, G., & Steer, R. A. (1988). An inventory for measuring clinical anxiety. *Journal of Consulting and Clinical Psychology, 56,* 893–897.

Beck, A. T., Steer, R. A., & Garbin, M. D. (1988). Psychometric properties of the Beck Depression Inventory: Twenty-five years later. *Clinical Psychology Review, 8,* 77–100.

Beck, A. T., Weismann, A., Lester, D., & Trexler, L. (1974). The measurement of pessimism: The Hopelessness Scale. *Journal of Consulting and Clinical Psychology, 42,* 861–865.

Bordin, E. S. (1979). The generalizability of the psychoanalytic concept of the working alliance. *Psychotherapy: Theory, Research and Practice, 16,* 252–260.

Burns, D. D., (1980). *Feeling good.* New York: Signet

Burns, D. D., & Nolen-Hoeksema, S. (1992). Therapeutic empathy and recovery from depression in cognitive-behavioral therapy. *Journal of Consulting and Clinical Psychology, 60,* 445–449.

Campbell, N. C., Ritchie, L. D., Thain, J., Deans, H. G., Rawles, J. M., & Squair, J. L. (1998). Secondary prevention of coronary heart disease: A randomized trial of nurse led clinics in primary care. *Heart, 80*(5), 447–452.

DiTomasso, R. A. (in press). Deep muscle relaxation exercises. In R. E. Rakel (Ed.), *Saunders manual of medical practice* (2nd ed.). Philadelphia: Saunders.

DiTomasso, R. A., & Colameco, S. (1982). Patient self-monitoing of behavior. *Journal of Family Practice, 15*(1), 79–88.

DiTomasso, R. A., & Mills, O. (1990). The behavioral treatment of essential hypertension: Implications for medical psychotherapy. *Medical Psychotherapy, 3,* 125–134.

DiTomasso, R. A., & Willard, M. (1991). Development of a patient satisfaction questionnaire in an ambulatory setting. *Family Medicine, 23*(2), 127–131.

Ditto, P. H., Jermott III, J. B., & Darley, J. M. (1988). Assessing the threat of illness: A mental representational approach. *Health Psychology, 7*(2), 183–201.

Dohrenwend, B. S., & Dohrenwend, B. P. (1982). Some issues in research on stressful life events. In T. Millon, C. Green, & R. Meagher (Eds.), *Handbook of clinical health psychology* (pp. 91–101). New York: Plenum.

Elkin, E. F. (1990). When a patient miscarries: Implications for treatment. *Psychotherapy, 27*(4), 600–606.

Epperson-SeBour, M. (1990). Psychosocial crisis services in the Maryland emergency services system. In H. J. Parad & L. G. Parad (Eds.), *Crisis intervention book 2: The practitioner's sourcebook for brief therapy* (pp. 209–226). Milwaukee: Family Service America.

Feinstein, R. E., & Carey, L. (1999). Crisis intervention in office practice. In R. E. Feinstein & A. A. Brewer (Eds.), *Primary care psychiatry and behavioral medicine: Brief office treatment and management pathways* (pp. 430–447) . New York: Springer.

Freeman, A., & DiTomasso, R. A. (1994). The cognitive model of anxiety. In B. B. Wolman & G. Stricker (Eds.), *Anxiety and related disorders: A handbook* (pp. 74–90). New York: Wiley.

Freeman, A. & DiTomasso, R. A. (in press). Cognitive therapy of anxiety. In D. J. Stein & E. Hollander (Eds.), *Textbook of anxiety disorders.* Washington, DC: Amercian Psychiatric Press.

Gelso, C. J., & Carter, J. A. (1985). The relationship in counseling and psychotherapy: Components, consequences, and theoretical antecedents. *The Counseling Psychologist, 13,* 155–243.

Gilliland, B. E., & James, R. K. (1997). *Crisis interventions strategies* (3rd ed.). Pacific Grove, CA: Brooks/Cole.

Hyer, L., Woods, M. G., & Boudewyns, P. A. (1991). PTSD and alexithymia: Importance of emotional clarification in treatment. *Psychotherapy, 28*(1), 129–139.

Kahana, E., Kahana, B., Harel, Z., & Rosner, T. (1988). Coping with extreme trauma. In J. P. Wilson, Z. Harel, & B. Kahana (Eds.), *Human adaptation to extreme stress: From the Holocaust to Vietnam* (pp. 55–80). New York: Plenum.

Klesges, R. C., Somes, G., Pascale, R. W., Klesges, L. M., Murphy, M., Brown, K., & Williams, E. (1988). Knowledge and beliefs regarding the consequences of cigarette smoking and their relationships to smoking status in a bi-racial sample. *Health Psychology, 1*(5), 387–401.

Marsland, D. W., Wood, M., & Mayo, F. (1976). A data bank for patient care, curriculum, and research in family practice: 526, 196 patient problems. *Journal of Family Practice, 3,* 25.

McKee, M. D., Lurio, J., Marantz, P., Burton, W., & Mulvihill, M. (1999). Barriers to follow-up of abnormal Papanicolaou smears in an urban community health center. *Archives of Family Medicine, 8*(2), 129–134.

Myers, M. G. (1999). Compliance in hypertension: Why don't patients take their pills? *Canadian Medical Association Journal, 160*(1), 64–65.

Nezu, A. M., Nezu, C. M., Friedman, S. H., Faddis, S., & Houts, P. S. (1998). *A problem solving approach: Helping cancer patients cope.* Washington, DC: American Psychological Association.

Needleman, L. (1999). *Cognitive case conceptualization: A guidebook for practioners.* Mahwah, NJ: Erlbaum.

Parad, H. J., & Parad, L. G. (1990). Crisis intervention: An introductory overview. In H. S. Parad & L. G. Parad (Eds.), *Crisis intervention book 2: The practitioner's sourcebook for brief therapy* (pp. 3–66). Milwaukee, MN: Family Service America.

Persons, J. (1989). *Cognitive therapy in practice: A case formulation approach.* New York: Norton.

Rakowski, W., Dube, C. E., Marcus, B. H., Prochaska, J. O., Velicer, W. F., & Abrams, D. B. (1992). Assessing elements of women's decisions about mammography. *Health Psychology, 11*(2), 111–118.

Robinson, P. (1988). Behavioral health services in primary care: A new perspective for treating depression. *Clinical Psychology: Science and Practice, 5*(1), 77–93.

Rose, D. S. (1991). A model for psychodrama psychotherapy with the rape victim. *Psychotherapy, 828*(1), 85–95.

Sarrel, P. M. (1999). Improving adherence to hormone replacement therapy with effective patient-physician communication. *American Journal of Obstetrics and Gynecology, 180*(3–11), supplement, 337s-340s.

Taylor, S. E. (1986). *Health psychology.* New York: Random House.

SUGGESTED READINGS

Dohrenwend, B. S., & Dohrenwend, B. P. (1982). Some issues in research on stressful life events. In T. Millon, C. Green, & R. Meagher (Eds.), *Handbook of clinical health psychology* (pp. 91–101). New York: Plenum.

Tulkin, S. R. (1987). Health care services. In G. C. Stone, S. M. Weiss, J. D. Matarazzo, N. E. Miller, J. Rodin, C. D. Belar, M. J. Follick, & J. E. Singer (Eds.), *Health psychology: A discipline and a profession* (pp. 121–136). Chicago: University of Chicago Press.

18

Traumatized Psychotherapists

Laurence Miller

The noblest service comes from nameless hands.
And the best servant does his work unseen.

—OLIVER WENDELL HOLMES

All interest in disease and death,
Is only another expression of interest in life.

—THOMAS MANN

So you think helping people is easy? Rewarding? Professionally satisfying? Actually, it's one hell of a way to make a living. Those in the crisis intervention and trauma therapy field know that our clientele often do not welcome our interventions, nor do they always follow our advice. In fact, they blame us when things go wrong. Alternatively, they sometimes seem so desperate and needy that it feels like nothing we can do will take a meaningful bite out of their plateful of despair. Just in case we have still retained some shred of motivation, society ceaselessly reminds us how it increasingly devalues those in the "helping professions" as surplus service providers, undeserving of respect or adequate recompense, until some headline tragedy forces the helpers' roles into the spotlight. And when the spectacle fades, so does the importance of what we do—until next time.

Doing crisis intervention and trauma therapy is not for wimps; it is tough, demanding work that can take an exhausting toll on practitioners. If that were not enough, crisis therapy can be a dangerous profession, especially when caseloads include severely disturbed, potentially violent patients, usually seen in institutional psychiatric and forensic settings, but increasingly turning up in routine clinical practice. Therapists and mental health care professionals are sometimes assaulted, some are seriously injured, and a few of our colleagues have been killed (Miller, 1998a, 1998c).

429

Is it any wonder that many of our colleagues stress out, burn out, or are driven out of the crisis response field? Before this happens, though, we ought to offer (or take) a dose of our own medicine and apply the skills and techniques we use for others to our own wounded ranks. We do what we do, after all, because crisis intervention and trauma work involve a unique combination of sharply honed, action-oriented skills with compassionate concern for the human community. Stressful work with stressed people is going to produce stress effects (Miller, 1994, 1998b, 1999a, 1999b, 1999c). Effectively helping the helpers is perhaps the greatest form of collegial and interdisciplinary respect (Miller, 1995, 1998a; Miller & Schlesinger, in press). Although diverse groups of helpers may seem worlds apart in terms of intervention orientation, philosophy, and practical implementation, I have been impressed with how similar—indeed, universal—are the issues and challenges that confront police officers, firefighters, paramedics, emergency room nurses, disaster rescuers, and mental health clinicians, just to name a few (Miller, 1995, 1998a, 1998c, 1999a, 2000). This chapter describes the particular stresses and intervention strategies for those helpers that are often on the front lines of crisis intervention: emergency mental health clinicians and trauma therapists.

STRESS AND COPING
IN MENTAL HEALTH PROFESSIONALS

Therapists who work on a regular basis with traumatized patients and people in crisis may be subject to special stresses. Trauma workers are surrounded by the extreme intensity of trauma-inducing events and their aftermaths. Figley (1995) identifies several reasons that trauma therapists are especially vulnerable to what he terms *compassion fatigue*. First, empathy is a major resource for trauma workers in helping the traumatized. Although empathizing with the trauma victim and family members helps to understand and relate to their experience, in the process, therapists may be traumatized themselves. Second, many trauma therapists have experienced some traumatic event in their lives and this unresolved trauma may be activated by reports of similar traumas in patients (McCann & Pearlman, 1990). There is thus a danger of the crisis worker's overgeneralizing from his/her own experiences and methods of coping, and overpromoting those methods with patients. Finally, special stresses are attendant to working with traumatized children (James, 1989; Johnson, 1989; Miller, 1999a, 1999b).

As the therapist begins to lose objectivity and overidentify with patients, depression may develop. The therapist may start to "not give a damn" about patients—or anyone else. Therapists may be relieved when "difficult" patients cancel sessions (Moon, 1999). Crisis clinicians may walk around dreading their beepers and cell phones going off, announcing the next emergency they must respond to (Talbot, Dutton, & Dunn, 1995). The stress effects may spill over into the therapist's family life as he/she becomes more withdrawn and emotionally unavailable (Cerney, 1995). Other therapists may become "trauma junkies," increasingly reinforced by the lurid thrill of working with such dramatic cases, but in the process sacrificing their clinical objectivity and effectiveness (Yassen, 1995).

McCann and Pearlman (1990) coined the term *vicarious traumatization* to describe the transformation that occurs within the trauma therapist as a consequence of empathic engagement with patients' trauma experiences and their sequelae. These effects do not arise solely from one therapy relationship but are cumulative across time and number of helping relationships. The *burnout* literature (Ackerly, Burnell, Holder, & Kurdek, 1988; Deutsch, 1984; Gilliland & James, 1993; Pearlman & MacIan, 1995; Rodolfa, Kraft, & Reiley, 1988) suggests that being younger or newer to trauma work is associated with the highest levels of burnout. As in any field, a certain selection process seems to operate, so that there emerges a delicate balance, in terms of clinical effectiveness, between being too fresh and callow versus being too encrusted and emotionally shriveled.

Talbot, Dutton, and Dunn (1995) described some of the distinctive features that make trauma and crisis work stressful for psychotherapists. First, there is the urgency and immediacy of the response. The crisis response is usually of an outreach or in-the-field nature, which means that the therapist has little or no control over many aspects of the situation: when it happens, where it happens, who will be there, and what services will be required. Typically, there is no advance notice, little time to prepare, limited time for individual interventions, lack of space, and unfamiliar, even dangerous surroundings.

In a crisis, therapists need to be able to work speedily and effectively to stabilize the situation. The cumulative volume of the work, both in terms of the number of people requiring attention in any one crisis and numerous successive crises, can exert a debilitating effect. In addition, emotional intensity is high and victims are often in a regressed and decompensated state. Victims themselves may perceive therapeutic interventions as intrusive and become resistant or hostile. Clinicians accustomed to structured therapeutic interactions may find themselves feeling overwhelmed when confronted by trauma victims whose needs are largely for basic empathy and containment. Often there is nothing to do but listen, and even this may be an extremely difficult task under chaotic circumstances. Also, there is typically little or no history regarding the precrisis or premorbid functioning of the victims. The crisis often occurs within an organizational context—for instance, the criminal justice system—that makes particular demands on first responders, which may be at odds with the needs and wishes of the victim or the clinician (Spungen, 1998; Talbot, Dutton, & Dunn, 1995).

The stresses of crisis intervention can affect mental health clinicians in a number of ways. In the aftermath of their interventions with victims of armed bank holdups, Talbot and colleagues (1995) reported often finding themselves feeling isolated, angry, tense, confused, powerless, hopeless, anxious, emotionally exhausted, and overwhelmed with responsibility. Patients' problems seem alternately insignificant or insurmountable, and the clinicians may begin to lose perspective and to overidentify with their patients. Clinicians may intellectualize, becoming overly rigid and inflexible in their thinking. Using denial as a protective strategy, clinicians are often unaware of the way in which the work has affected them, and the recollection among different emergency callouts becomes blurred.

These clinicians often feel exhausted; increase their alcohol use; suffer somatic symptoms such as headaches, gastrointestinal complaints, and sleep disturbances with nightmares; experience increased sensitivity to violence in general; and become emotionally demanding of family and friends. They become increasingly tense and distractible, expecting the phone to ring at any moment announcing yet another crisis or emergency (Talbot, Dutton, & Dunn, 1995). Clearly, in these situations, some sort of appropriate intervention is needed.

INTERVENTIONS WITH MENTAL HEALTH CRISIS PERSONNEL

General Considerations

In general, incident-specific, one-time interventions will be most appropriate for handling the effects of overwhelming trauma on otherwise normal, well-functioning personnel. Where posttraumatic sequelae persist, or where the psychological problems relate to a longer-term pattern of maladaptive functioning under relatively routine stresses, more extensive individual psychotherapeutic approaches are called for (Miller, 1998c).

Critical Incident Stress Debriefing

The stress debriefing approach has grown out of the general field of crisis intervention and is an important element of all therapeutic work with traumatized patients. *Critical incident stress debriefing,* or CISD, has been organizationally formalized for law enforcement and emergency services primarily by Mitchell and his colleagues (Mitchell, 1983, 1988; Mitchell & Bray, 1990; Mitchell & Everly, 1996). CISD is now implemented in public safety departments throughout the United States, Britain, Europe, Australia, and other parts of the world (Dyregrov, 1989). CISD is often subsumed under the broader umbrella category of *critical incident stress management* (CISM), which includes a range of preventive and crisis intervention strategies, such as one-on-one defusings, large-scale demobilizations, and other approaches (see Mitchell & Everly, 1996; Harbert, Chapter 16, this volume). In many respects, CISD epitomizes the cognitive-behavioral approach to crisis intervention. It is a structured technique designed to promote the emotional processing of traumatic events through the ventilation and normalization of reactions, as well as preparation for possible future experiences (Mitchell & Everly, 1996). Flexible adaptations of CISD have included applications to individual, family, child, and group therapy (Miller, 1998c).

A CISD debriefing typically is a peer-led, clinician-guided process, although the individual roles of clinicians and peers may vary from setting to setting. The staffing of a debriefing usually consists of one or more mental health professionals and one or more peer debriefers—that is, fellow police officers, firefighters, paramedics, or crisis clinicians who have been trained in the CISD process and who may have been through critical incidents and debriefings in their own careers.

A typical debriefing takes place within 24 to 72 hours after the critical incident and consists of a single group meeting that lasts 2 to 3 hours, although shorter or longer meetings may be dictated by circumstances. Group size may range from a handful to a roomful, the deciding factor usually being how many people will have time to fully express themselves in the number of hours allotted for the debriefing. Where large numbers of crisis workers are involved, such as in large-scale disaster rescues, several debriefings may be held successively over the course of days to accommodate all the personnel involved (Mitchell & Bray, 1990; Mitchell & Everly, 1996).

The formal CISD process consists of seven key phases:

1. *Introduction.* The introduction phase of a debriefing is the time in which the team leader—either a mental health professional or peer debriefer, depending on the composition of the group—gradually introduces the CISD process, encourages participation by the group, and sets the ground rules by which the debriefing will operate. Generally, these involve confidentiality, attendence for the full session, nonforced participation in discussions, and the establishment of a noncritical atmosphere.

2. *Fact phase.* During this phase, the group members are asked to briefly describe their job or role during the incident and, from their own perspective, provide some facts regarding what happened. The basic question is, "What did you do?"

3. *Thought phase.* The CISD leader asks the group members to discuss their first and subsequent thoughts during the critical incident: "What went through your mind?"

4. *Reaction phase.* This phase is designed to move the group participants from a predominantly cognitive and intellectual level of processing to a more emotionally expressive and cathartic mode: "What was the worst part of the incident for you?" It is usually at this point that the meeting gets intense, as members take their cue from one another and begin to vent their distress. Clinicians and peer-debriefers keep a keen eye out for any adverse reactions among the personnel.

5. *Symptom phase.* This begins the movement back from the predominantly emotional processing level to the cognitive mode. Participants are asked to describe cognitive, physical, emotional, and behavioral signs and symptoms of distress that appeared at the scene or within 24 hours of the incident; a few days after the incident; and continually, persisting even at the time of the debriefing. This allows for sharing and universalizing of potentially disorienting stress symptoms and reactions in a constructively intellectualized, problem-solving discussion. The question here is, "What have you been experiencing since the incident?"

6. *Education phase.* Continuing the move back toward cognitive processing, information is exchanged about the nature of the stress response and the expected physiological and psychological reactions to critical incidents. The clearest role for the mental health professional in this phase is as teacher and expert in traumatic stress effects. This serves to normalize the stress and coping responses and provides a basis for questions and answers.

7. *Reentry phase.* This is a wrap-up, during which any additional questions or statements are addressed, referral for individual follow-ups are made, and general group bonding is reinforced: "What have you learned?"; "Is there anything positive that can come out of this experience that can help you grow personally or professionally?"; "How can you help one another in the future?"

This is not to suggest that these phases always follow one another in unvarying, mechanical sequence. On the contrary, in practice I have found that once group participants feel comfortable with the debriefing process and start talking, the fact, thought, and reaction phases often blend together. Indeed, as Mitchell and Everly (1996) recognize, it would seem artificial and forced to abruptly interrupt someone expressing emotion just because it's not the "right phase." Initially, debriefings should adhere to the stepwise sequence, but as long as the basic rationale and structure of the debriefing are maintained, the therapeutic effect will usually result. In most cases, clincian team leaders have to assertively step in only when emotional reactions become particularly intense, or where one or more group members begin to blame or criticize others.

Special Applications of CISD to Mental Health Clinicians

Since the mid-1970s, the standard "Mitchell model" of CISD has been used with wide success all over the world, with diverse groups of emergency service, military, and civilian personnel (Miller, 1995, 1998c; Mitchell & Bray, 1990; Mitchell & Everly, 1996). In an effort to expand and refine its clinical applicability, in the 1990s some innovative adaptations of the basic CISD technique began to be applied in different settings and for diverse groups of crisis respond-ers. This section will describe some recent applications of the CISD approach to mental health professionals.

Psychological Debriefing

Concepts such as *vicarious traumatization* (McCann & Pearlman, 1990) and *com-passion fatigue* (Figley, 1995) remind us of the cumulatively stressful effect on trauma therapists of working with successive cases of wounded and shattered patients. The very empathy we rely on to connect with our traumatized pa-tients and establish a healing relationship also carries the risk of emotional con-tagion that may lead to therapeutic burnout or depression (Moon, 1999). Could applying a CISD approach to therapist critical incident stress provide a salubrious taste of our own medicine (Miller, 1998a)?

Talbot, Dutton, and Dunn (1995) argue that psychotherapists, more so than other crisis workers, require specifically "psychological" understanding and integration to be able to function and intervene effectively. These authors' own program (Manton & Talbot, 1990; Talbot, Dutton, & Dunn, 1995) has evolved largely through their work with bank employee victims of armed hold-ups and the mental health clinicians who debrief them. In this model, the aim of psychological debriefing for mental health clinicians is to help them deal with the stresses of trauma work via ventilation, catharsis, and sharing of expe-riences, in order to achieve psychological mastery of the situation and prevent the development of more serious delayed stress syndromes. Particularly impor-tant for psychotherapists is the careful exploration of their identification with the victim's experience, which enables them to properly assimilate the burden of empathy. Finally, the therapists are helped to integrate the traumatic experi-ence and make a transition back to everyday life.

In this model, the debriefing of the debriefers is attended by two or more psychologists who were not part of the original civilian debriefing; for clarity, I have referred to them as *secondary debriefers* (Miller, 1998a, 1998c). The therapist debriefing is held away from the crisis scene as soon as is practicable for all in-volved therapists to attend.

In Talbot and colleagues' (1995) psychological debriefing model, the de-briefing procedure incorporates the crisis event, the responses to that event by the psychologists, and the processes occurring in the debriefing itself. Its aim is to tie in and make sense of the crisis and the subsequent counseling so that a clear, total picture is formed. The secondary debriefer is consequently dealing with a number of different levels of the crisis: the event itself, the victims' re-sponses to the event, the psychotherapists' responses to the event, the psycho-therapists' responses to the victims, and each psychotherapist's personal and professional response to the events. In essence, the secondary debriefer as-sumes a form of clinical supervisor role to help each therapist reach an understanding of the interventions that were made, assess those that were useful, explore possible alternatives, and decide on future actions.

The secondary debriefer needs to normalize the experiences of fearfulness and sadness that follow the traumatic event. Part of his or her responses may also involve what Talbot and colleagues call a *parallel process,* in which the psychotherapist is experiencing what the victims have experienced. Past unresolved issues may also come up, particularly if there have been violence or abuse experiences in the therapists' histories. Fully dealing with countertransference issues is usually beyond the scope of a single debriefing, but these should be followed up by further treatment if necessary (Maier & Van Ryboeck, 1995; Miller, 1998c).

In Talbot and colleagues' (1995) system, to help make sense of the therapists' experiences in the original crisis and in the present debriefing, the secondary debriefer brings together his/her knowledge of the original crisis victims as individuals and as a group, and his/her understanding of the operative psychological processes. Because more psychological knowledge is often associated with more intellectualized and sophisticated defenses, the secondary debriefer, consistent with the supervisor role, may need to be somewhat more confrontive with the debriefed therapists than clinicians typically are with civilian victims or, for that matter, than debriefers might be with other crisis responders, such as police officers, firefighters, or paramedics. The ultimate goal is to tie in themes and personal issues, draw parallels, and put the incident into perspective.

Finally, as in a therapeutic session, the secondary debriefer needs to summarize, to contain, and to make sense of what occurred. Talbot and colleagues (1995) asserted that it can be useful for the individual therapists to verbalize what they have gained and learned from working in the crisis and from the victim debriefings. To continue personally and professionally, psychotherapists need to have a sense of mastery of the experience, as well as the assurance of feeling valued, worthwhile, and positive about themselves and their work. Cognitive understanding and adaptive self-insight give psychotherapists mastery of the situation, objectivity, and a theoretical base from which to make interventions. This is essential in order for them to continue to function as effective trauma psychotherapists. The same recommendations apply to therapists in all specialties (Miller, 1992, 1993).

The Assaulted Staff Action Program

Building on a combination of the CISD model and individual cognitive-behavioral therapeutic approaches, Flannery and colleagues (Flannery, 1995; Flannery, Fulton, Tausch, & DeLoffi, 1991; Flannery, Penk, Hanson, & Flannery, 1996; Flannery et al., 1998) have developed a comprehensive, voluntary, peer-help, systems approach, called the Assaulted Staff Action Program

(ASAP), for health care staff who have been attacked by patients at work. ASAP provides a range of services including individual critical incident debriefings of assaulted staff, debriefings of entire wards, a staff victims' support group, employee–victim–family debriefing and counseling, and referrals for follow-up psychotherapy as indicated. The ASAP team structure comprises 15 direct-care staff volunteers. The ASAP team director is responsible for administering the entire program and for ensuring the quality of the services.

When combined with preincident training and stress management, this approach has proven helpful in the aftermath of patient assaults on employee victims and in significantly reducing the overall level of violence itself. In facilities where it has been applied, the ASAP program is reported to have reduced staff turnover, sick leave, industrial accident claims, and medical expenses as the overall assault rates have declined. The developers of the ASAP model point out that the costs associated with the entire program are less than that of one successful lawsuit.

Flannery (1995) recommends the following basic steps in implementing an organization's own ASAP: (1) develop administrative support for the program; (2) tailor the model for the individual facility; (3) recruit the team members; (4) train the team; (5) field the completed service. Each step generally takes about 1 month, so teams can be online within about 6 months.

Process Debriefing

As psychotherapists become more involved in the critical incident stress field, it is inevitable that we will see more psychologically sophisticated analyses of the cognitive-behavioral and psychodynamic processes involved in debriefing methods, along with more complex and nuanced intervention approaches. Hopefully, this will not sacrifice the basic on-the-street adaptability and clinical "user-friendliness" of the stress debriefing model; indeed, it would be ironic if greater depth of understanding led to a more narrow range of practical applicability.

Dyregrov (1997) described a CISD-type model of intervention termed *process debriefing*, incorporating the same basic structure as the Mitchell model, but placing more emphasis on analyzing and addressing the group dynamics that actually take place in a debriefing. Characteristics of process debriefing include (1) strong mobilization of group support; (2) primary use of other group members to normalize reactions to stress; (3) active use of the group as a resource; (4) limiting the number of participants to 15 members per group; and (5) emphasis on the role of the group leader and coleader in providing a model of communication by the way they interact with one another.

In this sense, process debriefing seems to represent a species of cognitive-behavioral group therapy more than being a strict CISD approach. Indeed, although pointing out that formal mental health credentials are no guarantee of therapeutic effectiveness, Dyregrov (1997) emphasizes the need for group leaders to have the necessary knowledge, training, and experience to positively influence the group experience. Accordingly, he cites several criteria for effective therapists, including genuineness in the helping relationship, provision of a safe and trusting atmosphere of nonpossessive warmth, and accurate, empathic, moment-by-moment understanding of the patient. Much of this will be familiar to practitioners of group therapy approaches (Courchaine & Dowd, 1994), and of course, much of the same criteria for clinical effectiveness apply to therapists in all areas of practice (Miller, 1993).

A more intensive concern for group dynamics characterizes the content of process debriefing, but the structure of the session itself stays fairly close to the Mitchell model, with some modifications. Dyregrov (1997) conceptualizes the nature and purpose of the introduction and fact phases of the debriefing in terms of an inclusive *relationship phase,* in which the trust, authority, and structure of the group is established. Other modifications include (1) the importance of debriefing preparation by the leader and coleader, in terms of learning about the nature of the critical incident and the composition of the group; (2) an emphasis on the relationship between the leader and coleader during the debriefing in providing a model of healthy interaction; (3) the importance of microcommunication, such as voice inflection, eye contact, and nonverbal signals; (4) the importance of sensitively varying the intervention style for different groups—for example, police officers, paramedics, nurses, or psychotherapists; and (5) the role of the physical environment or setting of the debriefing in influencing the group process.

As highly trained clinical practitioners, we can well empathize with therapists who feel that their rich and varied clinical skills are often underutilized in the structured setting of an emergency service debriefing. However, we must remember that the CISD model was developed precisely for its utility as a first-line, first-aid approach to mental health crisis intervention and trauma care. The melding of more sophisticated psychodynamic group therapy approaches with the CISD model is certainly to be welcomed, and may in fact be an indispensible component for certain groups, such as traumatized psychotherapists (Miller, 1998a; Talbot, Dutton, & Dunn, 1995).

But, *as* therapists, we need to take responsibility for knowing our patients, and for tailoring our interventions accordingly. With certain groups, cognitively and psychodynamically rich and sophisticated clinical interventions may be piercingly effective in drawing out inhibited feelings and leading to shared expression and resolution of shock and trauma. For other groups, however, the therapist's knowledge and skills must remain more under the surface, the debriefing appearing to occur smoothly and naturally, while the unseen influence of the clinician's knowledge, talent, and training produces no brilliant therapeutic fireworks but is effective precisely because it makes the whole process "look easy."

PSYCHOTHERAPY WITH TRAUMA THERAPISTS AND MENTAL HEALTH CRISIS INTERVENTION PERSONNEL

Sometimes the psychic cuts go deeper, and the psychological field dressing of the CISD approach must be supplemented by more intensive and extensive individual psychotherapeutic modalities. As with CISD approaches, the particular intervention strategy must be tailored to the clinical species of crisis intervention specialist we treat.

Ironic but true: Many therapists don't like therapy—for themselves, that is. In order to reach this group of helpers, special adaptations to the therapeutic model and process are necessary.

General Decompression and Self-Help Measures

It sounds deceptively obvious that all therapists should establish and maintain a balance between their professional and personal lives, but for trauma therapists this is especially important (Cerney, 1995). Some authorities recommend that a sense of civic responsibility expressed in social activism can be an outlet for frustration and serve to productively bind anxiety and focus energies (Comas-Diaz & Padilla, 1990; Yassen, 1995)—as long as such activism does not become an obsessional, self-destructive "crusade." Letting the public know your views, beliefs, and ideals can be a potent antidote to the secretive and silencing nature of the trauma. What may seem like small acts of activism can also combat powerlessness, the feeling that "with all I do, I don't make a dent." Self-help also occurs in the shape of formal or informal support groups or incorporating stress-reduction activities and exercises into the therapist's daily life (Saakvitne & Pearlman, 1996).

Therapeutic Support for Traumatized Therapists

In cases where therapists have been directly traumatized, as when assaulted in mental health or criminal detention facilities, institutional leaders can take the following steps to ensure that traumatized workers are not stigmatized and ostracized by their colleagues (Catherall, 1995). First, leaders must recognize that other employees may have an emotional reaction to the traumatized worker. Second, leaders must create regular opportunities for the group to meet and talk about their exposure to traumatic stress. It is most effective if someone in a position of authority takes responsibility for normalizing the experience. Finally, leaders must actively encourage the group to see the individual traumatized worker's reaction as a common group problem and deal with it on that basis.

In dealing with countertransferential reactions to aggressive and violent patients, Maier and Van Ryboek (1995) described the following institutional policy and procedure. In this model, staff are expected to identify and share feelings with their peers and supervisors in forums provided by the clinical administration. Should these feelings interfere with the ability to provide effective and humane treatment to a patient, staff are expected to address the relevant issues. The formal personnel process may be utilized to shape the required change, including referral to the employee assistance program (EAP). If, over time, the staff member is unable to keep feelings of fear and anger from affecting his/her work performance, a change in work area or assignment may be in order.

Typically, nursing and mental health staff victims of workplace violence such as assaults by patients, experience intense emotional reactions (Lanza, 1995, 1996; Miller, 1997). They may want to talk about their reactions but feel it is "unprofessional" to do so. Victims typically do not expect to receive support from hospital administrators, despite their history of loyal service to the institution, and this may produce further anger and demoralization.

Blaming oneself is often a way to impute at least some kind of meaning and controllability to an otherwise incomprehensible catastrophic event. Self-blame can be functional, if it involves attributions to one's specific behavior in a specific situation, rather than to enduring personality characteristics, the often-cited difference between *behavioral self-blame* and *characterological self-blame*. But even behavioral self-blame is not helpful if victims feel that they used appropriate precautions, followed all the safety rules, and bad things happened anyway; this may produce a sense of helplessness and failure. Both administrators and clinicians can help assaulted staff sort out the realities of safe conduct from runaway catastrophic fears and fantasies.

Obviously, all of these supportive measures depend on a certain degree of trust and cooperation within an organization. This may not always be forthcoming, however, or it may not go far enough. In more complex cases, or those involving more disabling traumatization, therapists may need more focused, individualized therapy.

Psychotherapy with Traumatized Therapists

Perhaps not surprisingly, the literature is sparse on therapeutic modalities for therapists themselves. Traumatized therapists who enter treatment require their own therapists to be accepting, nonjudgmental, and empathic, without becoming enmeshed or overawed—in other words, similar to the kind of therapist most effective in treating other traumatized patients. One of the most difficult issues traumatized therapists face is the assault on their perceptions of the world and its inhabitants (Cerney, 1995; Figley, 1995).

Cerney (1995) has treated a number of therapists suffering from secondary trauma, or vicarious traumatization, using a suggestive imagery technique (Grove & Panzer, 1991). Although there is no hypnotic induction per se, when patients are asked to form an image, they often spontaneously go into a suggestible trance state. When patients present a nightmare, flashback, or other type of intrusive thought or imagery, they are asked to redream the dream or go over the experience again. At the point at which the traumatic event is about to begin, the therapist suggests they freeze the scene so that they can program how the scenario is to proceed. They are then asked if they would like to enter the scene—be it dream, memory, or flashback—from the distance of a mature, safe perspective. Or they may bring anyone they wish into the scene with them and thereby restructure it in a less threatening and more empowering way.

Specific techniques aside, when working with traumatized clinicians, I have found the biggest challenge to be that of maintaining flexibility of the therapist's role. At one moment, these clinician–patients will want you to be a colleague with whom they can share "war stories;" the next moment, they may become helpless and dependent, expecting you to offer them some brilliant insight into restoring their motivation and revivifying their career. Complicating the process is the general sense of underlying stress and burnout we all feel in confronting the social and economic changes in mental health care.

In workshops and individual approaches, probably the most effective approach I've utilized is similar to that used with "burnout cases" from other professions: Find a new way to use your talents and abilities. As simplistic as this may sound, part of this approach comes from the field of rehabilitation, which emphasizes the concept of *transferable skills*. If therapists can forge new niches for themselves, such as teaching, writing, consulting, or social activism, and if they can learn not to put all their technical eggs in one professional basket, a creative diversification of practice may be an antidote to demoralization and burnout. Alternatively, passionate devotion to a single burning cause may be as effective, or more effective, in jumpstarting the commitment process to renewed professional and personal growth. As we tell our patients, the proper solution depends on the nature of the problem and the nature of the person. This is true for ourselves as well.

CASE STUDY

Therapist Smith was a 55-year-old married, male psychologist who began work at an inpatient psychiatric and substance abuse rehab facility to supplement his private practice income, which was beginning to dwindle under the onslaught of HMO regulation. Therapist Jones was a 29-year-old, single female clinical social worker who had been a therapist and case manager at a shelter for abused women and children before beginning work as a clinician on the same unit as Smith at nearly the same time. Smith, after an almost 30-year career as an independent, outpatient clinical psychologist, resented the hospital job as an unwanted but necessary compromise to maintain his family's lifestyle. Jones, a 5-year veteran of domestic violence shelter work and suicide hotlines, saw the relatively "normal" psychiatric cases of the hospital as a professional respite from her prior steady clinical diet of acute crisis intervention work.

One afternoon, a cocaine and alcohol-dependent bipolar patient, who had been discharged a week earlier when his insurance ran out, appeared abruptly at Smith and Jones's unit to visit a former roommate who was still hospitalized. Once on the unit, he produced a handgun and announced that he was there to "rescue" the former roommate. Smith emerged from his office cubicle and immediately had the gun shoved in his face. A few tense moments ensued, when Jones came around a corner and confronted the scene of Smith held at bay while the rest of the staff and patients stood around, unable to intervene for fear of Smith being killed. Jones attempted to defuse the situation and talk down the disturbed intruder, but apparently moved threateningly close and was stuck twice, on the head and cheek, by the barrel of the gun. Fortunately, the second blow resulted in the assailant losing his grip on the weapon, which fell to the floor, and he was immediately subdued by hospital staff using standard takedown procedures.

"I've had it with this crap," later exclaimed the uninjured but clearly traumatized Smith during a mandated EAP counseling session. Rather than deal with the potential violence of the hospital unit, he opted to go back to private practice on whatever terms were financially realistic, because "I sure as hell don't get paid enough to get shot." Still, for months, he experienced nightmares, anxiety, and depression, had trouble concentrating during his therapy sessions, became irritable and detached with friends and family, and eventually retired from practice about a year after the incident. Through it all, he refused any kind of therapeutic help himself, because, "What good is all this therapy bullshit anyhow?"

Jones spent a day at a local medical hospital being treated for a fractured cheekbone. Less than a week later, she was back at work. She attended the mandated EAP counseling session, but did not like the counselor, so sought her own therapist through her company insurance plan. She attended this therapy for about 3 months, then felt she had worked through the traumatic event sufficiently to continue her career and life. She noticed a tendency to become overinvolved in her work, which she half-jokingly described to a coworker as "my intellectualized counterphobic defense," but was eager to move on in her career as a therapist and case manager.

Individual psychodynamics aside, it is clear that Smith, already tired and demoralized from having to make a second-choice career move just to stay ahead financially, needed very little in the way of a traumatic event to propel him into full-scale burnout. Jones, on the other hand, although hardly happy about being pistol-whipped in the first few weeks of a new job, was able to assimilate this traumatic event by virtue of her prior experience with "hard-case" clientele, her ability to utilize adaptive defenses such as humor and sublimation, her willingness to seek help as necessary, and her goal-oriented ambition to advance in her career.

SUMMARY AND CONCLUSIONS

Trauma therapists and other crisis personnel need to be mindful of their own needs as clinicians and as helping human beings who regularly deal with dark aspects of human nature and sometimes refractory types of psychotherapy patients. Continued education and training, interaction and cross-fertilization with peers, interdisciplinary collaboration, periodic diversion into pleasant activities, development of a sense of mission and purpose, and willingness to access help for ourselves when necessary can protect against premature burnout and contribute to our effectiveness as helpers and healers. The same recommendations apply equally to crisis responders in all fields (Miller, 1998c). We serve others best when we take care of ourselves.

REFERENCES

Ackerly, G. D., Burnell, J., Holder, D. C., & Kurdek, L. A. (1988). Burnout among licensed psychologists. *Professional Psychology: Research and Practice, 19,* 624–631.

Catherall, D. R. (1995). Preventing institutional secondary traumatic stress disorder. In C. R. Figley (Ed.), *Compassion fatigue: Coping with secondary traumatic stress disorder in those who treat the traumatized* (pp. 232–247). New York: Brunner/Mazel.

Cerney, M. S. (1995). Treating the "heroic treaters." An overview. In C. R. Figley (Ed.), *Compassion fatigue: Coping with secondary traumatic stress disorder in those who treat the traumatized* (pp. 131–149). New York: Brunner/Mazel.

Comas-Diaz, L., & Padilla, A. (1990). Countertransference in working with victims of political repression. *American Journal of Orthopsychiatry, 60,* 125–134.

Courchaine, K. E., & Dowd, E. T. (1994). Groups. In F. M. Dattilio & A. Freeman (Eds.), *Cognitive-behavioral strategies in crisis intervention* (pp. 221–237). New York: Guilford Press.

Deutsch, C. J. (1984). Self-reported sources of stress among psychotherapists. *Professional Psychology: Research and Practice, 15,* 833–845.

Dyregrov, A. (1989). Caring for helpers in disaster situations: Psychological debriefing. *Disaster Management, 2,* 25–30.

Dyregrov, A. (1997). The process in psychological debriefing. *Journal of Traumatic Stress, 10,* 589–605.

Figley, C. R. (1995). Compassion fatigue as secondary traumatic stress disorder: An overview. In C. R. Figley (Ed.), *Compassion fatigue: Coping with secondary traumatic stress disorder in those who treat the traumatized* (pp. 1–20). New York: Brunner/Mazel.

Flannery, R. B. (1995). *Violence in the workplace.* New York: Crossroad.

Flannery, R. B., Fulton, P., Tausch, J., & DeLoffi, A. (1991). A program to help staff cope with psychological sequelae of assaults by patients. *Hospital and Community Psychiatry, 42,* 935–942.

Flannery, R. B., Hanson, M. A., Penk, W. E., Goldfinger, S., Pastva, G. J., & Navon, M. A. (1998). Replicated declines in assault rates after implementation of the Assaulted Staff Action Program. *Psychiatric Services, 49,* 241–243.

Flannery, R. B., Penk, W. E., Hanson, M. A., & Flannery, G. J. (1996). The Assaulted Staff Action Program: Guidelines for fielding a team. In G. R. VandenBos & E. Q. Bulatao

(Eds.), *Violence on the job: Identifying risks and developing solutions* (pp. 327–341). Washington, DC: American Psychological Association.

Gilliland, B. E., & James, R. K. (1993). *Crisis intervention strategies* (2nd ed.). Pacific Grove, CA: Brooks/Cole.

Grove, D. J., & Panzer, B. I. (1991). *Resolving traumatic memories: Metaphors and symbols in psychotherapy.* New York: Irvington.

James, B. (1989). *Treating traumatized children: New insights and creative interventions.* New York: Free Press.

Johnson, K. (1989). *Trauma in the lives of children: Crisis and stress management techniques for counselors and other professionals.* Alameda, CA: Hunter House.

Lanza, M. L. (1995). Nursing staff as victims of patient assault. In C. R. Figley (Ed.), *Compassion fatigue: Coping with secondary traumatic stress disorder in those who treat the traumatized* (pp. 131–149). New York: Brunner/Mazel.

Lanza, M. L. (1996). Violence against nurses in hospitals. In G. R. VandenBos & E. Q. Bulatao (Eds.), *Violence on the job: Identifying risks and developing solutions* (pp. 189–198). Washington, DC: American Psychological Association.

Maier, G. J., & Van Ryboek, G. J. (1995). Managing countertransference reactions to aggressive patients. In B. S. Eichelman & A. C. Hartwig (Eds.), *Patient violence and the clinician* (pp. 73–104). Washington, DC: American Psychiatric Press.

Manton, M., & Talbot, A. (1990). Crisis intervention after an armed hold-up: Guidelines for counselors. *Journal of Traumatic Stress, 3,* 507–522.

McCann, I. L., & Pearlman, L. A. (1990). *Psychological trauma and the adult survivor: Theory, therapy, and transformation.* New York: Brunner/Mazel.

Miller, L. (1992). Cognitive rehabilitation, cognitive therapy, and cognitive style: Toward an integrative model of personality and psychotherapy. *Journal of Cognitive Rehabilitation, 10*(1), 18–29.

Miller, L. (1993). Who are the best psychotherapists? Qualities of the effective practitioner. *Psychotherapy in Private Practice, 12*(1), 1–18.

Miller, L. (1994). Civilian posttraumatic stress disorder: Clinical syndromes and psychotherapeutic strategies. *Psychotherapy, 31,* 665–664.

Miller, L. (1995). Tough guys: Psychotherapeutic strategies with law enforcement and emergency services personnel. *Psychotherapy, 32,* 592–600.

Miller, L. (1997). Workplace violence in the rehabilitation setting: How to prepare, respond, and survive. *Florida State Association of Rehabilitation Nurses Newsletter, 7,* 4–6.

Miller, L. (1998a). Our own medicine: Traumatized psychotherapists and the stresses of doing therapy. *Psychotherapy, 35,* 137–146.

Miller, L. (1998b). Psychotherapy of crime victims: Treating the aftermath of interpersonal violence. *Psychotherapy, 35,* 336–345.

Miller, L. (1998c). *Shocks to the system: Psychotherapy of traumatic disability syndromes.* New York: Norton.

Miller, L. (1999a). Treating posttraumatic stress disorder in children and families: Basic principle and clinical applications. *American Journal of Family Therapy, 27,* 21–34.

Miller, L. (1999b). Posttraumatic stress disorder in child victims of violent crime: Making the case for psychological injury. *Victim Advocate, 1,* 6–10.

Miller, L. (1999c). Workplace violence: Prevention, response, and recovery. *Psychotherapy, 36,* 160–169.

Miller, L. (2000). Law enforcement traumatic stress: Clinical syndromes and intervention strategies. *Trauma Response, 6*(1), 15–20.

Miller, L., & Schlesinger, L. B. (in press). Those they left behind: Victims and survivors of serial killers. In L. B. Schlesinger (Ed.), *Serial offenders: Current thought, recent findings, unusual syndromes.* Boca Raton, FL: CRC Press.

Mitchell, J. T. (1983). When disaster strikes: The critical incident stress process. *Journal of the Emergency Medical Services, 8,* 36–39.

Mitchell, J. T. (1988). The history, status, and future of critical incident stress debriefing. *Journal of the Emergency Medical Services, 13,* 47–52.

Mitchell, J. T., & Bray, G. P. (1990). *Emergency services stress: Guidelines for preserving the health and careers of emergency services personnel.* Englewood Cliffs, NJ: Prentice Hall.

Mitchell, J. T., & Everly, G. S. (1996). *Critical incident stress debriefing: An operations manual for the preservation of traumatic stress among emergency services and disaster workers* (2nd ed.). Ellicott City, MD: Chevron.

Moon, E. (1999, February). How to handle the high cost of caring. *Professional Counselor,* 18–22.

Pearlman, L. A., & MacIan, P. S. (1995). Vicarious traumatization: An empirical study of the effects of trauma work on trauma therapists. *Professional Psychology: Research and Practice, 26,* 558–565.

Rodolfa, E. R., Kraft, W. A., & Reiley, R. R. (1988). Stressors of professionals and trainees at APA-approved counseling and VA medical center internship sites. *Professional Psychology: Research and Practice, 19,* 43–49.

Saakvitne, K. W., & Pearlman, L. A. (1996). *Transforming the pain: A workbook on vicarious traumatization.* New York: Norton.

Spungen, D. (1998). *Homicide: The hidden victims. A guide for professionals.* Thousand Oaks, CA: Sage.

Talbot, A., Dutton, M., & Dunn, P. (1995). Debriefing the debriefers: An intervention strategy to assist psychologists after a crisis. In G. S. Everly & J. M. Lating (Eds.), *Psychotraumatology: Key papers and core concepts in posttraumatic stress* (pp. 281–298). New York: Plenum.

Yassen, J. (1995). Preventing secondary traumatic stress disorder. In C. R. Figley (Ed.), *Compassion fatigue: Coping with secondary traumatic stress disorder in those who treat the traumatized* (pp. 178–208). New York: Brunner/Mazel.

SUGGESTED READINGS

Figley, C. R. (Ed.). (1995). *Compassion fatigue: Coping with secondary traumatic stress disorder in those who treat the traumatized.* New York: Brunner/Mazel.

Gilliland, B. E., & James, R. K. (1993). *Crisis intervention strategies* (2nd ed.). Pacific Grove, CA: Brooks/Cole.

McCann, I. L., & Pearlman, L. A. (1990). *Psychological trauma and the adult survivor: Theory, therapy, and transformation.* New York: Brunner/Mazel.

Miller, L. (1998). *Shocks to the system: Psychotherapy of traumatic disability syndromes.* New York: Norton.

Mitchell, J. T., & Everly, G. S. (1996). *Critical incident stress debriefing: An operations manual for the preservation of traumatic stress among emergency services and disaster workers* (2nd ed.). Ellicott City, MD: Chevron.

19

Legal and Ethical Issues

Leon VandeCreek
Samuel Knapp

Crisis intervention is an important service that mental health professionals perform. As with any other professional service, the practitioner is required to adhere to certain legal and ethical standards of behavior. Failure to do so could place the professional at risk for a malpractice suit, charges of ethical misconduct, investigation by a licensure board, and other forms of civil liability.

Crisis intervention work is often arduous. The requests for services may come at inopportune times or from persons who walk into the office without an appointment. Sometimes such patients are accompanied by police or relatives who have been under stress and present themselves in a demanding or rude manner. The mental health professional may not have the time or opportunity to seek consultation or to give much thought to the case.

In one sense, the most severely disturbed patients may be the easiest to evaluate. The dangerousness of their behaviors and the intensity of their distress may leave no doubt that hospitalization or referral is the proper course of action. When the dangerousness is more remote or when the distress is less severe, however, the decisions become more difficult. At what point does a person's refusal to eat constitute neglect of self? When is a suicidal gesture severe enough to be considered a suicidal act? When does a person's behavior cross the line to posing imminent danger to self or others? And what is the prevailing standard of care that must be followed in crisis situations?

No mental health professional can make these decisions with complete accuracy. Despite our extensive study of human behavior, we are limited in our ability to predict dangerousness or to anticipate the course of a disorder. Furthermore, the stakes are often high in crisis situations. Recommending patients for involuntary hospitalization may lead to a deprivation of their civil liberties and may make some patients more resistant to seeking treatment voluntarily in the future. On the other hand, failure to hospitalize a person may mean that a life is endangered.

This chapter reviews several of the areas in which professionals may face ethical and legal challenges in managing patients in crisis situations. Suggestions for conducting a risk-managed practice are offered.

LEGAL AND ETHICAL REGULATION OF PRACTICE

Crisis intervention, like other forms of professional practice, is regulated by a variety of mechanisms, such as malpractice law, other tort remedies, and the codes of ethics of professional associations and licensing boards. Four criteria must be met to sustain a malpractice charge.

First, the practitioner must have a professional relationship with the patient. This criterion is usually met when the practitioner accepts the patient's request for care. If a crisis occurs in the midst of ongoing therapy, then this criterion clearly has already been met. There is some ambiguity with this criterion, however, when practitioners receive contacts from potentially new patients who are in crisis. Does a crisis telephone call establish a therapist–patient relationship? Courts have suggested that it does if the practitioner offers advice or agrees to see the patient for treatment.

Second, it must be proven that the practitioner's behavior deviated from the accepted standard of care used by other practitioners of similar orientation and in similar circumstances. Typically courts rely on expert testimony to determine the appropriate standard of care. Practitioners who claim to be specialists are expected to adhere to the standards of their specialty. The trend in health care litigation is also to rely on a national standard of care rather than on a local standard of care.

Third, it must be shown that the practitioner's negligent care was the proximate cause of an injury to the patient. Traditionally, proximate cause is defined as a cause that produces an injury in a natural and continuous sequence, unbroken by any other intervening causes. The breach must be the sole cause of the injury. Today, a more liberal definition of proximate cause has become increasingly common. Now, the "but-for" and the "substantial-factor" tests have been allowed by some courts. The but-for test requires that the patient establish that it was more probably true that the injury would not have happened but for the practitioner's acts; the substantial-factor test requires that the acts of the defendant be just that, a substantial factor.

Finally, the patient must prove that an injury resulted from the proximate cause. Claims of injury in mental health have taken many forms, including emotional distress, divorce, harm to self and others, and appearance of new symptoms or an exacerbated state of an already existing condition. Patients may claim any form of injury, although the patient must prove that the injury exists and was caused by the practitioner's conduct.

The courts recognize that mental health treatment is not an exact science and that bad outcomes may occur even when appropriate care has been provided. An unwelcomed outcome in treatment, therefore, is not necessarily evidence of negligence. The question is whether the practitioner followed accepted procedures in assessing and treating the patient.

In addition to charges of malpractice, crisis intervention workers may also be liable for other torts (or wrongdoings) such as malicious prosecution, abuse of process, or false imprisonment. Each of these torts has its own specific criteria and is usually invoked in the context of involuntary civil commitments and will be discussed below.

ACCEPTING AND REFERRING PATIENTS

Depending on the setting, practitioners may or may not have the right to refuse to accept particular patients who require crisis intervention care. In private settings practitioners may decline to accept patients who appear to require crisis intervention care. Public settings and managed care settings often do not allow such refusals. Regardless of the setting, once a patient has been accepted into care, the practitioner must provide the necessary care or refer the patient. Practitioners may not refuse to provide crisis care to their ongoing patients just because they do not prefer to work under crisis conditions or because their busy schedules do not lend themselves to crisis care.

Practitioners or settings that advertise crisis intervention services and telephone crisis centers may be held to higher standards of care (a standard of specialists) for crisis contacts than are general practitioners. It is good practice when referring crisis patients to assure that they have in fact availed themselves of alternative services.

Practitioners have a responsibility to convey relevant information when making a referral. For example, in *Greenburg v. Barbour* (1971), a physician had allegedly failed to inform the admitting physician at a hospital of the dangerousness of a man seeking treatment at the hospital. The patient was not admitted and subsequently became assaultive. The court held that the failure to transmit this important information concerning violent behavior was contrary to acceptable medical practice.

Practitioners must also be alert to the potential for charges of abandonment if patients are not provided adequate care when in crisis. De facto abandonment could occur if practitioners, while on vaction, do not provide adequate coverage for patients, if the practitioners' schedules are so overloaded that they cannot accommodate the needs of their existing patients, or they fail to provide 24-hour crisis services to patients in need of immediate care.

DANGEROUS PATIENTS

Although patient homicides and suicides are rare, they do occur. The rate of suicide has been increasing rapidly in the last decade, and all mental health practitioners can expect to treat a suicidal patient sometime in their careers. Few things concern a practitioner as much as managing a patient who poses a danger to self or others.

Danger to Others

The California court case of *Tarasoff v. University of California et al.* (1976) established a duty to protect identifiable victims from physical harm at the hands of patients. Courts in several other states have drawn similar conclusions; every state court that has faced situations similar to *Tarasoff* has ruled that it would adopt a duty to protect. Consequently, it is probably prudent for mental health practitioners to follow the guidelines laid out in *Tarasoff* or in similar court decisions in their own states. As noted further on, several states have enacted statutes that may provide direction to practitioners who manage dangerous patients (see details on *Tarasoff* and related cases in Knapp & VandeCreek, 1982; Knapp, VandeCreek, & Shapiro, 1990; VandeCreek & Knapp, 1993).

Three general principles can be gleaned from *Tarasoff* and subsequent cases that can guide psychotherapists in considering potential liability. These principles are (1) foreseeability of harm, (2) identifiability of the victim, and (3) the ability of the psychotherapist to protect a potential victim. Generally, courts have concluded that the duty to protect is activated only by threats of serious bodily harm to identifiable victims. Unless state law requires it, the duty does not usually mandate warning a potential victim; rather a warning is one possible way to discharge the duty. The *Tarasoff* court stated, "the psychotherapist can take one or more of various steps, depending on the nature of the case, including warning the intended victim or others likely to apprise the victim of the danger, notifying the police, or taking whatever steps are reasonably necessary under the circumstances" (p. 334). Contrary to popular misconception, the *Tarasoff* court did not create a "duty to warn." The court concluded that "a therapist should not be encouraged routinely to reveal such threats; such disclosures could seriously disrupt the patient's relationship with his therapist and with the person threatened" (p. 347). The necessity for issuing a warning against the wishes of the patient appears to be rare. Often psychotherapists can mobilize the healthy aspects of the patient and gain permission to advise an identifiable victim (Beck, 1987). In addition, changes within psychotherapy, even having the potential victim participate in therapy, may be clinically indicated (Roth & Meisel, 1977; VandeCreek & Knapp, 1993; Wexler, 1980). Psychotherapists can sometimes rely on involuntary or voluntary hospitalizations to diffuse the danger. If warning the victim appears to be essential, it is preferable to do so with the consent or at least the awareness of the patient. Although courts in several states have followed *Tarasoff* closely, a few have expanded the duty to protect when there is no identifiable victim, but rather when the victim falls within a "zone of danger." In *Lipari v. Sears* (1980), a court found liability to the public at large. A former Veterans Administration inpatient discontinued day treatment, purchased a shotgun, and shot several people at a nightclub. The federal court ruled that the psychotherapists had a responsibility to protect the public even though no specific victim was identifiable. It is not necessary that the psychotherapist "knew the identity of the injured party, but only that therapist could have reasonably foreseen unreasonable risk of harm to injured party or a class of persons of which injured party was a member" (p. 186). The case was settled out of court for $200,000 (Beck, 1987).

However, courts in at least two states have ruled that the "duty to protect" does not apply to them. In *Boynton v. Burglass* (1991) the Third District Court of Appeals of Florida declined to adopt the *Tarasoff* standard for Florida. In *Nasser v. Parker* (1995), the Virginia Supreme Court ruled that psychotherapists have no duty to control the behavior of outpatients. This is an area of law that is continually evolving and psychotherapists should be aware of the standard their state has adopted.

Statutory Remedies

Several states have enacted legislation to guide and protect mental health practitioners who face *Tarasoff*-like situations. Although the wordings of these laws vary from state to state, they have several common ingredients. They specify how psychotherapists may fulfill their duty to protect, and they provide immunity from suit for breaking confidentiality, if this occurs in the process. Most such statutes permit therapists to discharge the duty through warning the potential victim or notifying the police. Most laws define *foreseeability* as when the patient makes a threat against an identifiable victim.

The intent of these laws is laudable, and they will protect psychotherapists from lawsuits based on a global duty to protect the public when no specific victims can be identified or when the patient has not made an explicit threat. But, despite these positive features, these laws do not remedy all the legal and clinical problems that may arise in duty-to-protect situations. First, the laws do not encourage thorough assessments of dangerous patients because the laws permit a psychotherapist to avoid liability when the patient has not made a direct threat of violence. Consequently, psychotherapists can minimize liability by overlooking or avoiding issues of violence even though exploration of violence might be clinically indicated. Second, these laws provide no immunity for most reasonable professional activities that may avert danger. These statutes provide immunity when psychotherapists warn the intended victim, notify the police, or seek involuntary commitment, but these actions are not necessarily the optimal response to violent threats. Instead, psychotherapists may alter the nature of psychotherapy to include more frequent contacts with the patient, include the intended victim in psychotherapy, teach anger control techniques to the patient, request that the patient lock up weapons in a bank vault or other secure place, or other changes in therapy that will mobilize the patients' inhibitions against dangerous acts (Roth & Meisel, 1977; VandeCreek & Knapp, 1993).

Only Colorado's law suggests protection from liability for these therapeutic options under the vague phrase "other appropriate action." The net result of current duty-to-protect laws may be to encourage warnings or civil commitments that have statutory protection and discourage other more therapeutically indicated actions that do not have protection (Appelbaum, 1988).

Duty to Protect and HIV/AIDS

In recent years psychotherapists have faced a unique twist to the duty to protect as some patients may pose a risk to infect others with HIV/AIDS. The question arises of whether the duty to protect applies to persons who threaten others by their sexual behavior or through sharing intravenous needles. Practitioners need to consult their state laws for guidance.

In those states that do have a confidentiality statute for HIV-positive patients, the case law on a "duty to warn" is just beginning to emerge. For example, physicians have been held liable for failing to notify identifiable victims of the HIV status of their patients (see review by Wavle, 1997). No case law could be found holding psychotherapists liable for failing to warn an identifiable third party about the danger of HIV infection from a patient. However, in *N.O.L. v. District of Columbia* (1995), health care providers were prohibited by the District's law from disclosing the HIV status of the patient to his wife. Despite this lack of existing case law, a case finding liability for a mental health professional for failure to disclose to a readily identifiable third party is conceivable in some jurisdictions. Long-standing precedents have required physicians to notify identifiable third parties of contagious diseases (see review by Bateman, 1992) and in at least one case (*Reisner v. Regents of the University of California*, 1995), a physician was found liable for failure to notify a patient of her HIV status and was liable to her future sexual partner, who also contracted the infection from her. Fortunately, a body of literature has demonstrated effective programs that can lead to a substantial reduction in high-risk behavior (see e.g., Kelly, 1995; National Institute of Mental Health, 1998). Mental health practitioners who are treating HIV-positive patients should not force themselves into dichotomous thinking of either warning or not warning. Instead they should focus on effective interventions that have some likelihood of reducing high-risk behavior. Even when permitted by law, warning should only be considered as an absolute last resort after attempts at voluntary disclosure or habit change have failed.

Suicide

Most practitioners will become involved in at least some suicide crises. A recent review of risk assessment for suicidal patients estimated that 10% to 15% of patients with major psychiatric disorders will die by suicide (Brent, Kupfer, Bromet, & Dew, 1988).

Courts have typically followed three criteria for assessing professional liability in cases of suicide (Knapp & VandeCreek, 1983). The first criterion involves *foreseeability* of a suicide attempt. Liability has not been found when patients have unexpectedly attempted suicide (*Dalton v. State,* 1970; *Paradies v. Benedictine Hospital,* 1980). However, when the treatment plan overlooks, ignores, or neglects evidence of suicidal tendencies, then courts have found liability (*Dinnerstein v. U.S.,* 1973; *Eady v. Salter,* 1976).

The second criterion is *reasonableness of professional judgment in treatment.* Severely depressed patients require more precautionary care than do less severely depressed patients. The failure to take reasonable precautions when suicidal intent is recognized would be grounds for liability. For example, in *Texarkana Memorial Hospital, Inc. v. Firth* (1988) a woman was admitted for suicidal risk and psychosis. When she was admitted, the locked ward of the hospital had no open beds. Consequently, she was sedated and placed in an open ward with no special suicide precautions. When she wakened, she jumped to her death. Her estate was awarded $950,000 for gross negligence by the hospital.

The third criterion addresses the *thoroughness with which the treatment plans are implemented.* In *Abille v. U.S.* (1980), the government was judged to be liable when a nurse ignored the physician's instructions and allowed a depressed patient (who later committed suicide) to leave the ward without an escort. In *Cominsky v. State of New York* (1979), a hospital was found at fault for failure to observe closely a patient as the physician had ordered; however, the physician was not found at fault. In contrast, the failure of a psychotherapist to inform other staff members about an increase in suicidal potential might leave the therapist liable but absolve the uninformed staff. Practitioners may also be found liable for failure to exercise proper judgment when releasing hospitalized suicidal patients. For example, in *Bell v. New York City Health & Hospitals Corporation* (1982), the court imposed liability when the psychiatrist released a patient but failed to request prior treatment records, failed to consider entries in the patient's chart documenting assaultive tendencies on the ward the previous day, and failed to inquire into the nature of his auditory hallucinations even though a nurse had made entries into his chart about them on three consecutive days.

There is no duty to warn relatives of potential suicides. In *Bellah v. Greenson* (1978), a California court refused to extend the duty to protect to suicidal patients. In this instance, a psychiatrist was treating a young woman who subsequently committed suicide. Although she had revealed the suicidal ideation to her psychiatrist, he did not reveal that to her parents. The parents brought suit, charging that the psychiatrist had a *Tarasoff* duty to notify them of her suicidal tendencies. The court disagreed, stating that "*Tarasoff* requires only that a therapist disclose the contents of a confidential communication where the risk to be prevented thereby is the danger of violent assault, and not where the risk of harm is self-inflicted harm or property damage" (pp. 539–540). Of course, practitioners have the responsibility to take reasonable steps to prevent suicides and may, if their discretion leads them, take unusual steps, including notifying friends or relatives.

A serious threat of suicide also may suspend confidentiality rules. This is, when practitioners conclude that a threat of suicide is imminent, they may breach confidentiality in order to save the patient's life. To our knowledge, no court has found liability when practitioners have enlisted the aid of others to protect a patient from suicide. Likewise, ethics codes of mental health professions permit disclosure of confidential information in order to protect patients from harm.

CHILD ABUSE

Child abuse is a generic term that refers to *nonaccidental physical injury, neglect, sexual abuse, and emotional abuse of a child.* Different states may have different specific definitions and inclusions, but all states include at least nonaccidental injury and neglect within their definition of child abuse. All states require professionals who are treating abused children to make reports when appropriate, but the criteria of "appropriateness" differ. Some states require professionals to report child abuse whenever they come across it in the course of their professional activities. This would mean, for example, reporting patients who admit in therapy to child abuse even if it occurred several years before. Other states do not require the reporting of abusers unless the abused child was also seen in therapy. Child abuse reporting laws typically apply to a wide range of professionals, including mental health providers. According to these laws, the professional is required to report suspicion of abuse. The threshold for reporting is low to insure the reporting of all potential cases and to leave the final determination in the hands of the child welfare agency.

Child abuse reporting laws include incentives to report in the form of immunity for reports made in good faith and penalties for mandated reporters who fail to make appropriate reports. In order for bad faith to be proven, it must be determined that the reporter knew that no abuse had occurred but made the report anyway.

Critics contend that mandatory reporting laws create more problems than they solve. For example, adults who seek treatment to improve their child-rearing skills and who admit to abuse may find that their family structure is threatened when a report is made. Such patients may be penalized for being candid with their therapists. The process of reporting and the subsequent investigation may create a crisis within the family, and if the therapist reported the suspected abuse, the parents may feel betrayed and refuse to continue in treatment even though treatment was the best way to strengthen the family.

Practitioners are placed in a precarious position with regard to abuse reporting. On the one hand, therapists encourage patients to be candid and to share even their best-kept secrets, and patients expect these communications to be held confidential. When practitioners must then report a suspicion of abuse, both parties rightfully feel violated. Practitioners may take some precautions to prevent or minimize the impact of these conflicts. Practitioners can inform patients at the outset of treatment, or at later appropriate times, about the limits to confidentiality. Practitioners who work with children and with families with whom issues of abuse are to be expected can make special efforts to develop collegial relationships with staff members of child welfare agencies. Thus, when abuse reports must be made, the practitioner can accurately inform the patients about what to expect. Further, if a cooperative relationship is in place, child welfare agencies may also be willing to let the practitioner play a primary role in addressing an abuse problem.

CIVIL COMMITMENTS

The grounds for liability in cases of involuntary civil commitments have broadened in recent years. Mental health professionals have been found liable for infringement of civil rights under Section 1983 of the Civil Rights Act of 1871 and for failure to commit an individual who is subsequently an actor in a tragedy (Knapp & VandeCreek, 1987). Practitioners who are involved in involuntary hospitalizations are often given broad immunity by state laws for their role in the commitment process. The purpose of these immunity statutes is to free practitioners from the fear of lawsuits when making difficult decisions under trying circumstances. For example, immunity is provided for the exceptions to confidentiality that usually occur when practitioners share clinical information within the inpatient setting. Nevertheless, these immunity laws are seldom blanket immunities; practitioners are still obligated to follow appropriate standards of care. For example, practitioners are not immune from lawsuits for negligent assessment or treatment prior to or following a civil commitment.

In addition to being liable for malpractice, practitioners could face tort damages for malicious prosecution, false imprisonment, or abuse of process. A finding of malicious prosecution requires a commitment proceeding to have lacked probable cause and to have been initiated with malice, not justice, as its motive. For example, in *Pellegrini v. Winter* (1985), the patient alleged that the civil commitment examination had been procured by the malicious filing of a petition that was based on testimony that the petitioner knew to be false.

False imprisonment refers to confinement in a hospital by force or threat of force without following lawful procedures. In *Eilers v. Coy* (1984) the parents of a member of a religious cult held their adult son for deprogramming for more than 5 days. Although the court was sympathetic to the interests of the parents, it noted that the verdict of false imprisonment was appropriate because the son was held against his will without following prescribed commitment procedures. A court also found false imprisonment in *Dick v. Watonwan*

County (1983) in which two alcohol counselors detained the parents of a teenager who claimed her parents were alcoholic. The counselors never attempted to contact the girl's psychotherapist to verify her reports nor did they obtain a physician's examination of the parents as required by law. Abuse of process involves using the legal process to accomplish a purpose for which it was not designed by employing threats. An example would be initiating a civil commitment for reasons other than treatment of mental illness. For example, in *Maniaci v. Marquette* (1971) a university physician initiated an involuntary commitment of a college student who had made plans with her parents to leave school and had withdrawn money from her account at the school bank. When questioned by the university officials about her plans, however, she refused to cooperate. The officials then committed her until they could reach her parents, without any intention of providing her with psychiatric care.

A malpractice claim could also be raised if a tragedy could be linked to a practitioner's failure to initiate a commitment for a patient. Liability will not occur automatically if a commitment is not pursued and a tragedy occurs; commitment laws are permissive, not mandatory. That is, mental health professionals may, but are not required to, seek a commitment for patients who satisfy the criteria. Commitment is not the only treatment option for dangerous outpatients. Instead, practitioners, following acceptable standards of treatment, may seek other treatment avenues such as a voluntary commitment, a day treatment program, modification of medications, or closely monitored outpatient psychotherapy.

If mental health professionals elect not to pursue commitment of a patient who meets the criteria, they should carefully document the reasons for the decision, and when appropriate, obtain consultation from colleagues with expertise in working with such patients. Of course, practitioners cannot be held liable for the failure to commit when they did not have statutory authority to do so. For example, in *Richards v. Douglas County* (1983), an employee of a mental health department was found not liable for failing to commit a patient who later stabbed an innocent bystander. The patient had not met commitment criteria at the time the request had been made.

SUMMARY

Many scholars agree that the mental health field will face increasing claims of malpractice, particularly as the laws become more complex. As mental health practices become more sophisticated and effective and thereby more standardized, it will become easier to establish standards of care. This precision will reduce the difficulty in defining what is inadequate care and ironically may make it easier for patients to demonstrate malpractice.

Institutions and practitioners can take several steps to minimize the risks of malpractice. They should (1) maintain accurate records of patient care,

(2) obtain informed consent of treatment plans, (3) ensure that all practitioners remain current in knowledge and skills in their areas of practice, (4) strive to honor patient's rights to confidentiality, (5) accept only as many patients as can be carefully treated, and (6) exercise caution with new modalities of health care.

REFERENCES

Appelbaum, P. (1988). The new preventive detention: Psychiatry's problematic responsibility for the control of violence. *American Journal of Psychiatry, 145,* 789–795.

Abille v. United States, 482 F. Supp. 703 (N.D. Cal. 1980).

Bateman, Y. (1992). Liability of doctor or other health practitioner to third party contracting contagious disease from doctor's patient. *American Law Reports, 5,* 370–393.

Beck, J. (1987). The psychotherapists' duty to protect third parties from harm. *Mental Disability Law Reporter, 11,* 141–148.

Bellah v. Greenson, 146 Cal. Rptr. 535 (1978).

Bell v. New York City Health & Hospitals Corporation, 90 A.D.2d 270, 456 N.Y.S.2d 787 (1982).

Boynton v. Burglass, 590 So.2d 446 (Fla. 3 dist. 1991).

Brent, D. A., Kupfer, D. J., Bromet, E. J., & Dew, M. A. (1988). The assessment and treatment of patients at risk for suicide. In A. J. Frances & R. E. Hales (Eds.), *American Psychiatric Press review of psychiatry* (Vol. 7, pp. 353–385). Washington, DC: American Psychiatric Press.

Cominskey v. State of New York, 71 A.D.2d 699, 418 N.Y.S.2d 233 (1979).

Dalton v. State, 308 N.Y.S.2d 441 (1970).

Dick v. Watonwan County, 562 F. Supp. 1083 (1983).

Dinnerstein v. United States, 486 F.2d 34 (2nd Cir. 1973).

Eady v. Salter, 380 N.Y.S.2d 737 (A.D. 1976).

Eilers v. Coy, 582 F. Supp 1093 (D. Minn. 1984).

Greenberg v. Barbour, 322 F. Supp 745 (1971).

Kelly, J. (1995). *Changing HIV risk behavior: Practical strategies.* New York: Guilford Press.

Knapp, S., & VandeCreek, L. (1982). *Tarasoff:* An update. *Professional Psychology, 13,* 511–516.

Knapp, S., & VandeCreek, L. (1983). Malpractice risks with suicidal patients. *Psychotherapy: Theory, Research and Practice, 20,* 274–280.

Knapp, S., & VandeCreek, L. (1987). A review of tort liability in involuntary civil commitment. *Hospital and Community Psychiatry, 38,* 648–651.

Knapp, S., VandeCreek, L., & Shapiro, D. (1990). Statutory remedies to the duty to protect: A reconsideration. *Psychotherapy, 27,* 291–296.

Lipari v. Sears, 497 F. Supp. 185 (D. Neb. 1985).

Maniaci v. Marquette, 184 N.W.2d 168 (1971).

Nasser v. Parker, 455 S.E.2d 502 (Va. Sup. Ct.).

National Institute of Mental Health Multisite HIV Prevention Trial Group. (1998). The NIMH Multisite HIV Prevention Trial: Reducing HIV sexual risk behavior. *Science, 280,* 1889–1894.

N.O.L. v. District of Columbia, 674 A.2d 498 (D.C. 1995).

Paradies v. Benedictine Hospital, 431 N.Y.S.2d 175 (App. Div. 1980).

Pellegrini v. Winter, 476 So.2d 1363 (Fla. Dist. Ct. App. 1985).

Reisner v. Regents of the University of California, 31 Cal. App. 4th 1195 (Cal. Ct. App. 1995).

Richards v. Douglas County, 328 N.W.2d 783 (Neb. 1983).

Roth, L., & Meisel, A. (1977). Dangerousness, confidentiality, and the duty to warn. *American Journal of Psychiatry, 134,* 508–511.

Tarasoff v. Regents of the University of California, 551 P.2d 334 (1976).

Texarkana Memorial Hospital, Inc. v. Firth, 746 S.W.2d 494 (1988).

VandeCreek, L., & Knapp, S. (1993). *Tarasoff and beyond* (2nd ed.). Sarasota, FL: Professional Resource Press.

Wavle, T. (1997). HIV and AIDS test results and the duty to warn third parties: A proposal for uniform guidelines for Texas professionals. *St. Mary's Law Journal, 28,* 783–831.

Wexler, D. (1980). Victimology and mental health law: An agenda. *Virginia Law Review, 66,* 681–711.

SUGGESTED READINGS

Borum, R. (1996). Improving the clinical practice of violence risk assessment: Technology, guidelines, and training. *American Psychologist, 51,* 945–956.

Kelly, J. (1995). *Changing HIV risk behavior: Practical strategies.* New York: Guilford Press.

Monahan, J. (1993). Limiting therapist exposure to *Tarasoff* liability. *American Psychologist, 48,* 242–250.

Truscott, D., Evans, J., & Mansell, S. (1995). Outpatient psychotherapy with dangerous clients: A model for clinical decision making. *Professional Psychology: Research and Practice, 26,* 484–490.

VandeCreek, L., & Knapp, S. (1993). *Tarasoff and beyond* (2nd ed.). Sarasota, FL: Professional Resource Press.

Index

459